The Bible and Radiocarbon Dating

Archaeology, Text and Science

The Bible and Radiocarbon Dating

Archaeology, Text and Science

edited by

Thomas E. Levy
&
Thomas Higham

Equinox Publishing Ltd

e**q**uinox

Sheffield   Oakville

Published by

UK: Equinox Publishing Ltd., Unit S3, Kelham House, 3 Lancaster Street, Sheffield, S3 8AF
USA: DBBC, 28 Main Street, Oakville, CT 06779

www.equinoxpub.com

First published 2005

Library of Congress Cataloguing-in-Publication Data
A catalogue record for this book is available from the Library of Congress

ISBN   184553056X   9781845530563   (hardback)
        1845530578   9781845530570   (paperback)

Typeset by Forthcoming Publications Ltd
www.forthcomingpublications.com

Printed and bound by Lightning Source

Contents

VI. HISTORICAL CONSIDERATIONS

VII. CONCLUSION

Preface

The idea for this book germinated when one of us (TL) was on sabbatical in 2003 at the Oxford Centre for Hebrew and Jewish Studies located in the magnificent Jacobean manor house in the Oxfordshire village of Yarnton. During that period, we had the good fortune of meeting during TLs visit to the Oxford Radiocarbon Accelerator Unit (ORAU). Together, we spearheaded a radiocarbon dating project of samples from the Iron Age site of Khirbat en-Nahas in southern Jordan. As work progressed, emails began to fly between ORAU, Yarnton, and many of the key players in Israel, Jordan, and around the world who have been trying to date Iron Age sites that are linked to problems associated with Biblical history. By the end of the sabbatical, we decided to mount an international conference or workshop at Yarnton Manor that would bring together many of the leading archaeologists, Biblical historians, Egyptologists, and radiocarbon dating specialists working on these problems. To tackle the chronological issues linked with working in the 'Biblical' periods, especially the Iron Age (ca. 1200–586 BCE), we felt it imperative to take an interdisciplinary perspective on the problem.

We are especially fortunate to have had laboratory representatives from the four main institutions who have carried out radiocarbon analyses of Iron Age materials from Israel and Jordan attending the meeting. These included the Oxford Radiocarbon Accelerator Unit (University of Oxford), Centre for Isotope Research (University of Groningen), NSF Arizona AMS Facility (University of Arizona), and the Radiocarbon Laboratory (Weizmann Institute of Science, Rehovot).

Oxford was selected as the best location for this conference because it is roughly midway between the Middle East and the United States, making it the most economic option for such an international gathering of researchers.

We are grateful to His Royal Highness Prince Hassan bin Talal of the Hashemite Kingdom of Jordan for opening the conference with warm and insightful remarks concerning the importance of radiocarbon dating and objectivity in the archaeology of the southern Levant. We especially appreciate the participation of Ghazi Bisheh, former Director General of the Department of Antiquities of Jordan, for delivering HRH Prince Hassan's speech and participating in the conference discussions.

Tom Levy would like to thank his colleagues and friends in the UCSD Judaic Studies Program for their long-term support of his research in Israel and Jordan. These individuals include David Noel Freedman, Richard Elliott Friedman, David Goodblatt, Deborah Hertz, and William H.C. Propp.

We would like to sincerely thank our publisher, Janet Joyce and Equinox Publishing Ltd in London for supporting this conference in association with the Judaic Studies Program at the University of California, San Diego. We also appreciate the help of Equinox staff members Valerie Hall and Heidi Robbins for their assistance. Thanks also to Duncan Burns of Forthcoming Publications for copy-editing and typesetting this book.

We are grateful to the Oxford Centre for Hebrew and Jewish Studies (OCHJS) and in particular, its president, Peter Oppenheimer, for their support and hosting the conference. We also would like to thank Annabelle Young of the OCHJS for helping with the on-site planning of the conference, Brian the OCHJS driver, and other staff members for making the conference run so smoothly. Finally, a special warm thank you to Alina Levy for organizing all the logistics of the conference, keeping all the speakers to time, and being the best travel companion (for one of the Toms).

Thomas E. Levy
Thomas Higham
Oxford and San Diego, April 2005

Top row (from left to right): Bill Schniedewind, David Wengrow, John Camp, Ami Mazar, Paul-James Cowie, Baruch Halpern, Ilan Sharon, Hendrik Bruins, Maryanne Newton, Hershel Shanks, Hans van der Plicht, Christopher Bronk Ramsey, Baruch Brandl, Eli Piasetzky, guest.

Middle row (from right to left): Alina Levy, Bill Dever, Andrew Sherratt, Elisabetta Boaretto, Stephan Munger, Ayelet Gilboa, Anabel Zarzecki-Peleg, Nava Panitz-Cohen, Sue Sherratt.

Bottom row (from left to right): Israel Finkelstein, Tom Higham, Magen Broshi, Tom Levy, David Ilan, Ghazi Bisheh, Norma Franklin.

Primary Iron Age (ca. 1200–500 BCE) sites from the southern Levant mentioned in this volume (image courtesy of Stephen Batiuk and Timothy Harrison).

Abbreviations

ABD	David Noel Freedman (ed.), *The Anchor Bible Dictionary* (New York: Doubleday, 1992)
ADAJ	*Annual of the Department of Antiquities of Jordan*
AASOR	Annual of the American Schools of Oriental Research
BA	*Biblical Archaeologist*
BAR	*Biblical Archaeology Review*
BASOR	*Bulletin of the American Schools of Oriental Research*
HSS	Harvard Semitic Studies
IEJ	*Israel Exploration Journal*
JNES	*Journal of Near Eastern Studies*
JSOT	*Journal for the Study of the Old Testament*
JSOTSup	*Journal for the Study of the Old Testament*, Supplement Series
NEA	*Near Eastern Archaeology*
OIP	Oriental Institute Publications
PEQ	*Palestine Exploration Quarterly*
RB	*Revue biblique*
RSV	Revised Standard Version
VT	*Vetus Testamentum*
VTSup	*Vetus Testamentum*, Supplements

I.
INTRODUCTION TO THE PROBLEMS

1 Introduction: Radiocarbon Dating and the Iron Age of the Southern Levant

Problems and potentials for the Oxford conference

Thomas E. Levy and Thomas Higham

Abstract

According to historical sources, the Iron Age in the southern Levant spans approximately 1200 to 586 BCE. To non-archaeologists, the 'Iron Age' sounds rather boring. However, this roughly 600 year period of time encompasses the history of ancient Israel and her neighbors as depicted in the Old Testament or Hebrew Bible, which is the purview of what used to be called Biblical Archaeology. The archaeology of the Holy Land (Israel, Jordan, Palestinian territories, southern Lebanon/Syria, and the Sinai Peninsula), the geographic setting where most of the events and characters described in the Hebrew Bible took place, is of intrinsic importance to both believers and those interested in three of the world's great religions—Judaism, Christianity, and Islam. These religions represent more than 3.2 billion people or 52.8% of the world population today. While theology and historical fact fall between belief and the empirical world, issues concerning the historicity of the Hebrew Bible mean something to at least half the world's population. Until recently, the only extra-biblical sources for critically examining the Hebrew Bible were the limited number of contemporary Mesopotamian, Egyptian and local Levantine inscriptions (Pritchard 1969). The paucity of ancient textual data, the increase in forgeries, the problems of the relative dating of Iron Age archaeological materials and deposits from the Levant, and the lack of objective chronological tools made testing the historicity of the Hebrew Bible speculative at best. However, the recent application of high precision radiocarbon dating methods to key Biblical sites such as Tel Dor, Megiddo, Tel Reḥov, and other locales have infused new hope and scholarly excitement in the quest to test the historicity of aspects of the Hebrew Bible (Bruins, van der Plicht, and Mazar 2003a). To help answer these questions with the scientific tools of the 21st century, the papers in this book take an interdisciplinary approach to the problems of chronology and historicity of the Hebrew Bible by bringing together field archaeologists currently excavating key Iron Age sites in Israel and Jordan, specialists using and developing the most current radiocarbon dating and calibration methods, Biblical scholars and ancient historians, Egyptologists, and other specialists. While the 10th-century BCE debate concerning the historicity of the Biblical figures David (Daoud) and Solomon (Suleiman) are one of the most hotly debated topics in Levantine Iron Age archaeology today and are examined closely in this book, many other issues concerning a variety of historical problems from the 12th to the 9th centuries BCE are discussed here. One of the results of this book is the demonstration that traditional Biblical archaeology has been transformed into the 'New Biblical Archaeology'.

Introduction

The southern Levant (modern Israel, Jordan, and the Palestinian territories, southern Lebanon/ Syria and the Sinai Peninsula) is holy land to *three* world religions—Judaism, Christianity and Islam. Believers and affiliates of these great religions make up more than 3 billion people—over half the world's population. They all have a vested interest—religious, intellectual, and/or political—in this small land bridge that joins Southwest Asia and the African continent. From the highlands of Judea and Samaria and the West Bank, to the coastal areas of Israel; from the plateau and lowlands of Jordan to the Negev and Sinai deserts—this land provides the geographical setting where the stories of the patriarchs and prophets revealed to us in sacred Scriptures took place. This is the land where the material culture of these ancient societies lay buried. From its 19th–century beginnings until today, the primary force that still drives the major excavation projects in this area is the ancient scriptures—first the Hebrew Bible or Old Testament, then the New Testament and finally, the Koran. This can be documented by the amount of money invested in archaeological projects in the region by period. Say the words 'Levantine Archaeology' and most people around the world will have no idea what we are speaking about. This book is about exploring the historicity of aspects of the Hebrew Bible through archaeological research using the most objective scientific dating methods currently available. It is based on an international conference of Levantine archaeologists, Biblical scholars, Egyptologists and radiocarbon dating specialists that took place in September 2004, at Yarnton Manor—home of the Oxford Centre for Hebrew and Jewish Studies.

From a methodological perspective, this book will speak to all scholars interested in the relationship between archaeology and history. Both of these fields of inquiry about the past have had a kind of love–hate relationship based on the perceived reliability of one being able to glean more 'truth' about the past than the other. Representing one of the most negative views of archaeology is Philip Grierson (1959: 129) who wrote that

> 'the archaeological evidence…in its very nature substitutes inference for explanation. It has been said that the spade cannot lie, but it owes this merit to the fact that it cannot even speak'.

On the positive side is John Moreland (2001), who in his recent summary of the relationship of archaeology and textual evidence entitled *Archaeology and Text*, argues that we have now gone beyond the 'servant and master' relationship where the word always took precedence over artifacts. Due to the robust methodological underpinnings of archaeology, it can no longer be viewed as the 'handmaiden' of history, where history provided the historical framework based on written texts and archaeology simply supplied the matter to illustrate history. For Moreland (2001: 31) the relationship between history and archaeology can now be renegotiated due to the realization that both artifacts and ancient texts played active roles in the production, negotiation, and transformation of social relations in past societies. Thus, structurally similar critical methodologies can be applied to both archaeological and textual data to objectively understand the social context in which these data are interwoven in our quest to understand ancient societies. However, when researchers study historical ancient societies within the time span of ca. 3000 BCE to 500 CE, the paucity of written texts and inscribed evidence inevitably means that alternative sources of objective chronometric data are needed for establishing crucial chronological sequences so that historical and anthropological modeling can take place. This is the case for historical archaeologists working in regions as disparate as south India (Abraham 2003), Mesoamerica (Hodell *et al.* 2001; Pohl 2002; Pope *et al.* 2001), Mesopotamia (Guilderson, Reimer, and Brown 2005; Hasel 2004; Weiss *et al.* 1993), the Aegean (Manning *et al.* 2001, and Chapter 7, this volume), or the Levant discussed in this volume. Until fairly recently, amongst archaeologists, the application of radiocarbon dating in Near Eastern archaeological contexts has been characterised by a great deal of scepticism over its usefulness, particularly in terms of its precision. The prevailing notion has been that in light of ceramic typologies, textual and historical information, and cross-correlated material culture from the wider eastern Mediterranean, there really is little need for absolute scientific dating (see Bruins 2001; van der Plicht and Bruins 2001). This situation is now beginning to change, but researchers wanting to take advantage of the available on-line calibration curves to establish sub-century chronological resolution, must overcome, as Guilderson, Reimer, and Brown (2005: 364) point out, 'the calibration curve and its inherent limitations'. Bronk Ramsey (Chapter 5, this volume) discusses these problems in detail with special attention to the southern Levant. The chapters presented in this book demonstrate that Levantine archaeologists working with the historical, especially Biblical periods, have stepped up to the plate to apply the new advances in radiocarbon calibration and chronological modeling that can serve as touchstone for historical archaeologists working around the globe.

Use the words 'Biblical Archaeology' and it is fair to say that most people will understand we are dealing with the archaeology of the Hebrew Bible and New Testament. Given our scholarly obligation to transmit the knowledge we discover to the public, it seems appropriate to maintain the concept—Biblical Archaeology—for those periods that have direct relevance to these scriptures. This is especially true for the Iron Age, the main theme of this book, which is the primary time-slice in which the main events of the Hebrew Bible take place: the Exodus, the settlement of the Tribes of Israel in the land, the histories of the United Monarchy, the Divided Kingdoms of Judah and Israel, and neighboring polities such as Edom, Moab, Philistia, and others. Testing theories concerning the historicity of the processes, events and individuals associated with the Iron Age are contingent on our use of objective tools for dating. This is as true today as it was over hundred years ago when Sir Flinders Petrie first developed the principle of relative dating or seriation in Egypt.

Over the past two decades, the term 'Biblical Archaeology' has taken on a pejorative con-notation precisely because of the intimate relationship bound up in this term's allusion to the mutual relationship between text and artifact—in this case the emotionally charged views of the Hebrew Bible or Old Testament and the tangible material past. A number of scholars have summarized the nature and history of this debate including P.R.S. Moorey (1991), J. Laughlin (2000), I. Finkelstein and N. Silberman (2001), B. Halpern (1995, 1997), W.G. Dever (2001), and others. The public shift away from using the term 'Biblical Archaeology' is perhaps marked best by the American Schools of Oriental Research (ASOR) decision to change the name of their flagship public outreach journal, *Biblical Archaeologist*, to *Near Eastern Archaeology* in 1998. In the early 1980s, Dever (1981), under the influence of the 'New Archaeology' emanating out of the University of Arizona (cf. Schiffer 1976), argued strongly for the independence of historical Levantine archaeology (traditional Biblical archaeology) from it's perceived inferior role as 'handmaiden' to ancient Near Eastern textual scholarship (especially Biblical scholarship) by advo-cating the use of the term 'Syro-Palestinian Archaeology' to separate it from its role as 'servant' to the Biblical 'master'. This effectively 'killed' Biblical archaeology as a separate field of inquiry within academic discourse, particularly in the United States. It is ironic that by the early 1990s, Dever (1990) was calling for a 'New Biblical Archaeology' in light of the development of 'Post-Processual Archaeology' (cf. Hodder 1986) and its critique of the New Archaeology that showed how it failed to integrate the role of history in explanations of culture change. Post Processual archaeology invigorated Dever, Lawrence Stager (1990) and others with rediscovered confidence that text (the Hebrew Bible) and artifact could be studied together in systematic and objective ways through rigorous methodologies advanced not only by anthropological archaeologists (Levy [ed.] 1995), but historians using the Annales historiography approach (cf. Bintliff 1991; Knapp 1992; Stager 1988, 1990). But it was premature to call for a New Biblical Archaeology, in the early 1990s because historical (Biblical) archaeologists working in the southern Levant had not fully embraced the science-based methodologies to control time (chronometric methods) and space (e.g. Geographic Information Systems [GIS] and other digital processing technologies [Levy *et al.* 2001]) that underlie mainstream science-based/anthropological archaeology today. As seen in this volume, archaeologists working on the problem of text and archaeology for the Iron Age history of the Levant have now taken the 'methodological ball'—and run with it. They have redefined the domain of Biblical Archaeology into something new—the New Biblical Archaeology for the beginning of the 21st century.

The Quest for Controlling Time in Biblical Archaeology

Scientific excavations have taken place in the southern Levant since the late 19th century with Petrie's pioneering excavations at Tell el-Hesi, where early on, he applied his revolutionary relative dating system known as 'sequence dating' to date archaeological deposits found on this Palestinian tel. It was Petrie's revolutionary development of seriation dating that earned him the reputation of a genius because, for the first time, archaeologists had an objective method of dating archaeological assemblages and deposits (Moorey 1991). From a global perspective as well as its beginning in the Holy Land, archaeology's most precious commodities have been the control of 'time' and 'space'. *Time*—to clarify historical events and processes; and *Space*—to isolate the material remains associated with history in meaningful social and temporal contexts (Levy *et al.* 2001).

   As shown in the papers presented in this volume, the embrace of science-based methods in the archaeology of the Levant, whether we are talking about radiocarbon dating of Iron Age deposits, provenance studies of the Late Bronze Age Amarna tablets (Goren, Finkelstein, and Na'aman 2004), or Neutron activation studies of *l'melch* jars, it seems fair to suggest that a radically different paradigm now exists for the Bronze and Iron Age archaeology of the southern Levant from the traditional Biblical archaeology that was attacked in the 1980s and 1990s (Dever 1982, 1990). Perhaps we can now speak of a New Biblical Archaeology that fundamentally integrates Biblical and extra-Biblical texts, rigorously recorded and analyzed archaeological data to control time and space, and anthropological models to help flesh out new understandings of how and when historical processes occurred in the Holy Land. There will be much controversy in how we interpret high precision radiocarbon dates and other science-based data; however, we have passed the point of no return—absolute dating techniques are now an integral part of our tool box and must be applied in 21st-century Iron Age archaeological research (see Fig. 1.1).

   How do the seemingly irreconcilable schools of current Biblical scholarship affect the 'New Biblical Archaeology'? Not as much as some pundits would have us believe. Cultural relativism has practically destroyed cultural anthropology, history, and other disciplines in the humanities and social sciences, mostly because there is no consensus on methodology—that is how to record and analyze data. However, the situation for archaeology is markedly different and there is no need to panic (as Finkelstein alludes to in Chapter 3, this volume). Biblical textual scholarship has mostly fallen victim to relativism because of a lack of concern with methodology. It is difficult to learn a minimum of 9 ancient and modern languages to work with the Hebrew Bible. The result has been the emergence of the so-called 'Biblical minimalist' approach that is based on pure 'literary criticism' and is embodied in the Sheffield and Copenhagen 'schools' (cf. Davies 1992; Thompson 1999). The so-called 'maximalist' or traditional approach is rooted in historical analysis and command of the ancient languages, history, and archaeology and is characteristic of programs at Harvard University, Penn State University, UCLA, Jerusalem University, and UCSD (Dever 2003; Zevit 2001). Rather than 'maximalist', this group should probably be referred to as 'Historicist' or something similar. The tools traditional Biblical scholars use to investigate the historicity of the Hebrew Bible are outlined in Figure 1.2.

The New Biblical Archaeology Tool Box

| Hebrew Bible (Old Testament) Extra-Biblical texts (contemporary) | Archaeological Data *Space*: GIS *Time*: Science-Based Applications: For Dating and Provenance | Anthropological and Historical Models |

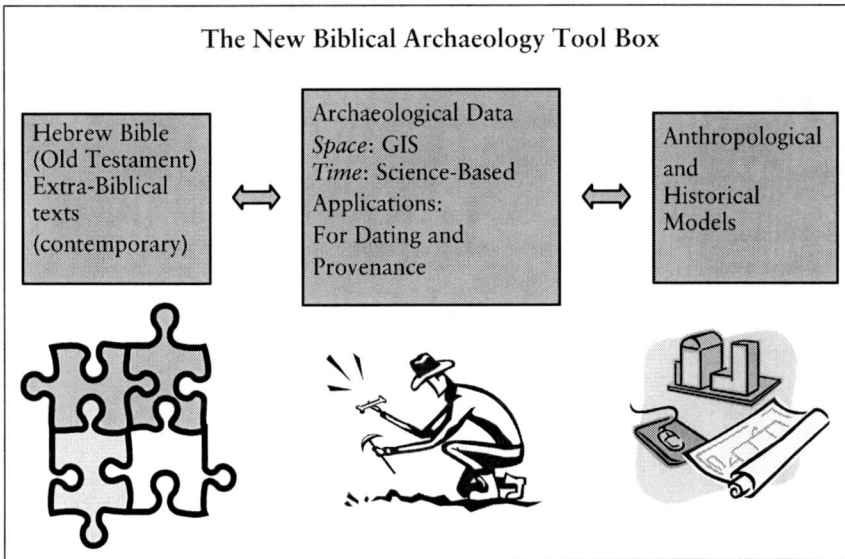

Figure 1.1. The 'New Biblical Archaeology' and the interrelationship between text (Hebrew Bible and other ancient Near Eastern documents), archaeology in the 21st century, and anthropology.

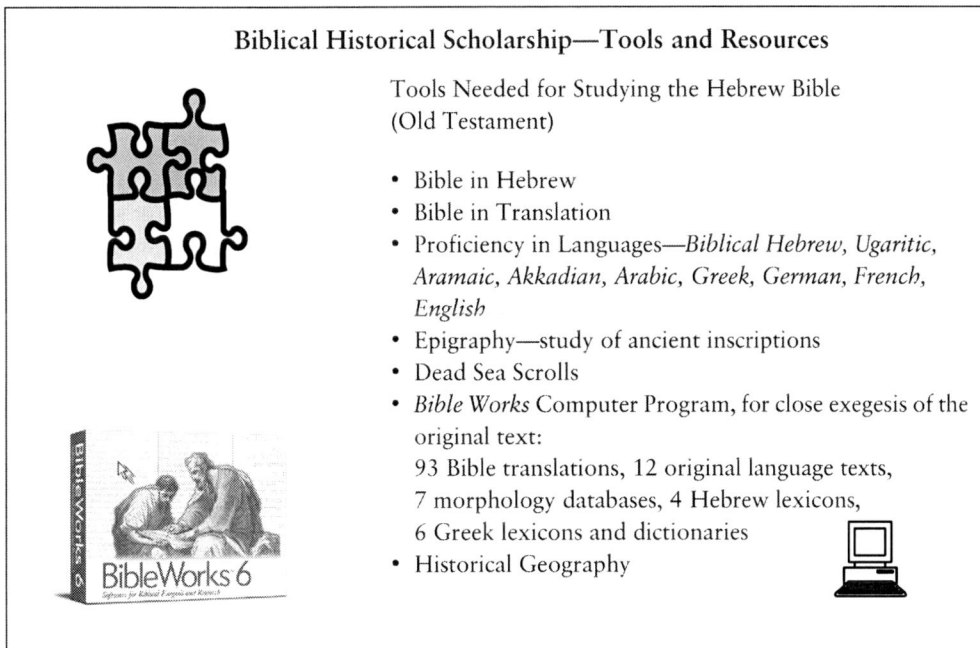

Biblical Historical Scholarship—Tools and Resources

Tools Needed for Studying the Hebrew Bible (Old Testament)

- Bible in Hebrew
- Bible in Translation
- Proficiency in Languages—*Biblical Hebrew, Ugaritic, Aramaic, Akkadian, Arabic, Greek, German, French, English*
- Epigraphy—study of ancient inscriptions
- Dead Sea Scrolls
- *Bible Works* Computer Program, for close exegesis of the original text:
  93 Bible translations, 12 original language texts, 7 morphology databases, 4 Hebrew lexicons, 6 Greek lexicons and dictionaries
- Historical Geography

BibleWorks 6

Figure 1.2. Tools used by traditional Biblical scholars to investigate the historicity of the Hebrew Bible.

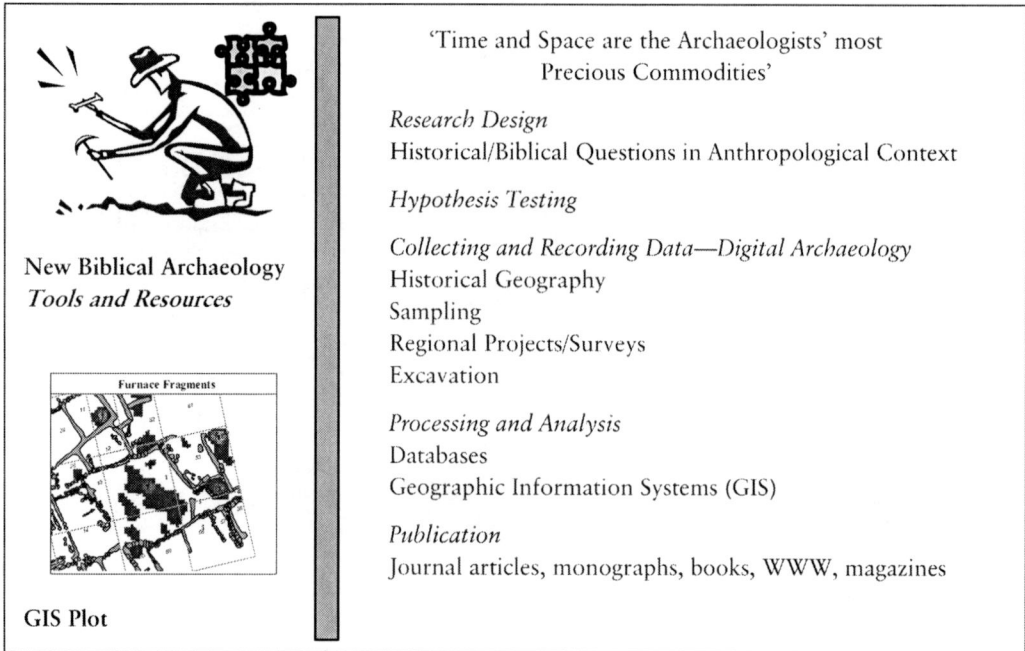

'Time and Space are the Archaeologists' most
Precious Commodities'

Research Design
Historical/Biblical Questions in Anthropological Context

Hypothesis Testing

Collecting and Recording Data—Digital Archaeology
Historical Geography
Sampling
Regional Projects/Surveys
Excavation

Processing and Analysis
Databases
Geographic Information Systems (GIS)

Publication
Journal articles, monographs, books, WWW, magazines

New Biblical Archaeology
Tools and Resources

Furnace Fragments

GIS Plot

Figure 1.3. The Process of Historical (New Biblical) Archaeology Research
in the Levant in the 21st century.

While we have many problems in our field, archaeology does not have the major methodological issues of cultural relativism because, regardless of our theoretical school of thought, we all strive to adhere to an accepted scientific methodology based on the idea that our results should be replicable (Renfrew and Bahn 2004). Acknowledging that archaeology is the 'science of destruction', we all hold fast to the primacy of excavating in the most precise way and surveying using the most accurate techniques so that the archaeological data we collect can be reconstructed in 3-dimensions back in the laboratory with as much precision as possible. By this we mean that any archaeologist should be able to take our records and reconstruct the stratigraphy and contextual information from an excavation and/or survey in the same manner. How successful each excavation and survey project is in achieving this goal is another issue. The point is that all archaeologists strive for this given the resources and equipment at their disposal. Thus, the degree to which we believe in the veracity of the ancient texts or Scriptures is completely separate from archaeology's embrace of the scientific method.

With the adoption of radiocarbon dating as a key element in the new Biblical archaeologist's tool box as evidenced by the teams of archaeologists represented here from important Iron Age sites, the field has joined the mainstream of science-based archaeological research. The 2003 *Science* journal article summarizing high precision radiocarbon dates for Iron Age destruction levels at Tel Reḥov (Bruins, van der Plicht, and Mazar 2003a), and the competing views it has generated for the traditional 'high' and alternative 'low' chronologies for the Iron II period, has brought the discussion of Iron Age archaeology in the Holy Land to the attention of scientists and the educated elite around the world. The debate in *Science* and subsequent publications was one of the catalysts for convening the conference/workshop in Oxford (Bruins, van der Plicht, and Mazar 2003b; Finkelstein and Piasetzky 2003). This Oxford conference was interdisciplinary and made up of archaeologists, Biblical scholars, dating experts in radiocarbon and dendrochronology methods, and Egyptologists. Each of these fields is a scientific and intellectual world unto themselves and this highlights why 21st-century archaeology can only be an interdisciplinary endeavor (see Fig. 1.3). Without the close collaboration of these disciplines, it would be impossible to tackle the issues that are central to Iron Age or Biblical Archaeology today. This is why each of the main archaeology teams represented at the conference, whether they worked in Israel or Jordan, brought along their own physicist! In Figure 1.2, above, some of the main historical, anthropological, and radiocarbon dating issues that are tackled in this volume are summarized.

Biblical Archaeology Issues Tackled with Radiocarbon Dating

From a processual and historical perspective, the contributors to this volume explore a wide range of issues from the settlement of the Tribes of Israel, the history of the United Monarchy and Divided Kingdoms of Judah and Israel, the history of neighboring polities such as Edom, Moab and Philistia, and the recognition of historical events in the archaeological record such as the Egyptian king Shishak and his campaign into the southern Levant. From the perspective of an Egyptologist, Andrew Shortland (Chapter 4) presents one of the most rigorous analyses to date of the calendrical chronology associated with Shishak's south Levantine campaign. As one of the key issues concerning the historicity of Solomon (1 Kings 14.25-26), this chapter has important implications for many of the papers in this volume. The stakes are considerable as the competing High and Low chronologies, summarized by Ami Mazar and Israel Finkelstein, respectively, will show (Chapters 2, 3, 13–18, 21, this volume; see also Fig. 1.4 [next page]). Was Solomon ruler over a developed state capable of organizing public works at Megiddo, Hazor and Gezer, as depicted in the Hebrew Bible, or was he in reality a petty chief whose persona and exploits were inflated by the later Deuteronomistic history? For both believers and non-believers in the historicity of Solomon (Suleiman) as well as other Biblical figures, the deliberations in this book will be of importance and great interest.

One of the key developments in enabling us to extract greater levels of chronometric precision in archaeological dating is the application of Bayesian statistical methods and 'wiggle-match dating'. Beginning in the early 1990s, a series of papers by Caitlin Buck and colleagues at Nottingham, and now Sheffield University, outlined the basis of the method, an ingenious amalgamation of Thomas Bayes' original paradigm—archaeological prior knowledge and relative dating—and radiocarbon dates obtained from organic remains from within archaeological sequences. Since this time, the method, made possible for general users only through powerful computer software programmes, has heavily impacted our ability to date the past more precisely. Bayesian calibration modeling enables an archaeologist to build a chronology for a site, in many cases using archaeological phases or contexts that themselves are not directly radiocarbon dated. This represents a quantum difference over what has gone before, and means that further thought is required when considering which samples, and how many, ought to be selected for radiocarbon dating. Bayliss and Bronk Ramsey (2004), in a general review of the first few years of the use of Bayesian models in radiocarbon dating write that, *on average*, when considering the 2000 radiocarbon dates analysed for English Heritage since the introduction of formal model building, a 35% reduction in calibrated uncertainties in dates has been achieved. In Chapter 5, C. Bronk Ramsey describes the methodological approach in straightforward terms, with specific examples of relevance to the Near East. In particular, he addresses chronological problems where sub-century precision is required. I. Sharon, A. Gilboa, E. Boaretto, and T. Jull (Chapter 6) utilise Bayesian methods in their discussion of results from the largest dating project for this period. The Iron Age Dating Project has processed some 400 radiocarbon dates. In their chapter, Sharon *et al.* discuss the archaeological and statistical rationale for why their work supports the low chronology.

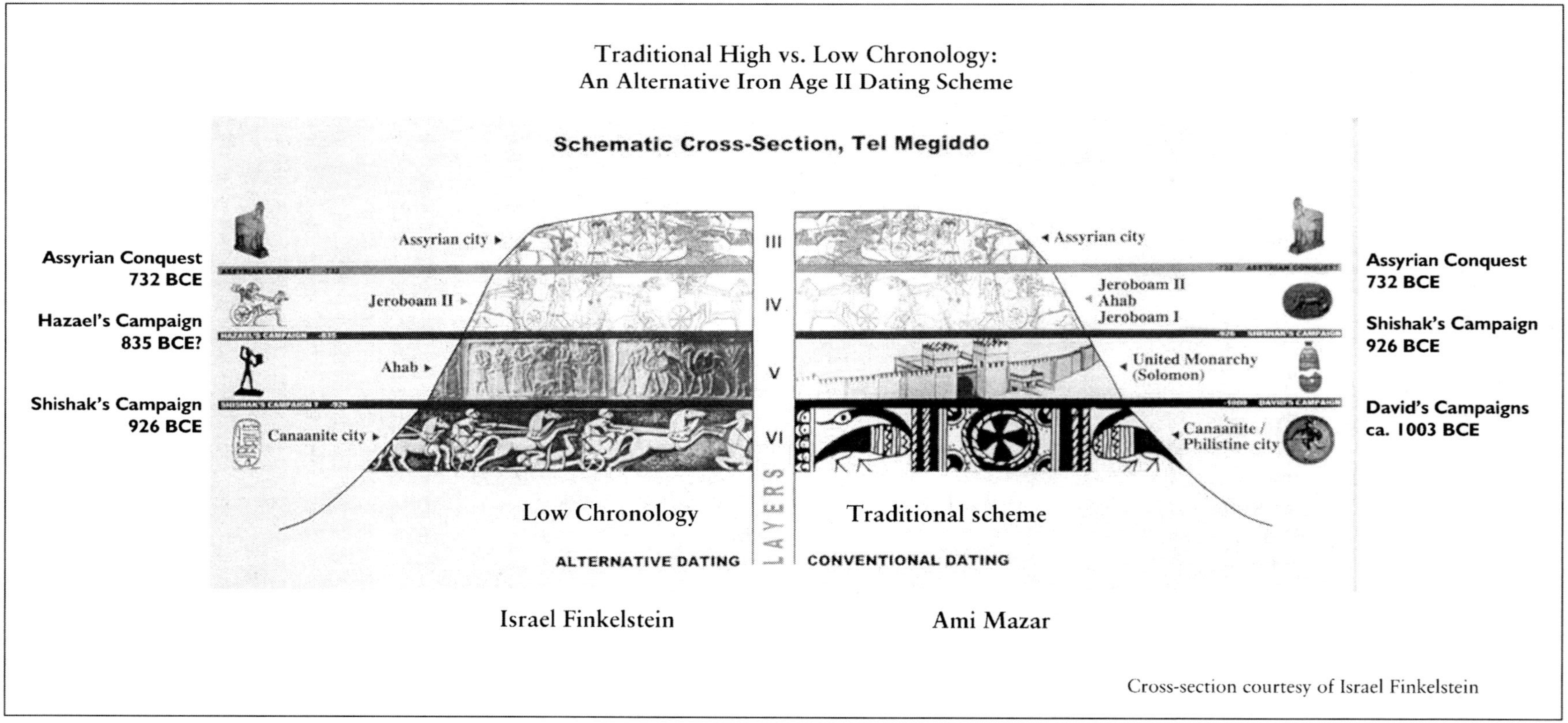

Figure 1.4. Traditional High vs. Low Chronology: An Alternative Iron Age II Dating Scheme reflected in the Iron Age Stratigraphy at Megiddo.

The bulk of the papers in this book focus on the application of radiocarbon dating to some of the Iron Age problems outlined above. Working in Jordan, two major Iron Age projects are summarized—the first concerning the Jabal Hamrat Fidan excavations at the Iron Age metal production center at Khirbat en-Nahas (KEN) in the paper by T. Levy *et al.* (Chapter 10), and the second concerning the Iron Age at Tall Mādabā by T.P. Harrison and C. Barlow (Chapter 12). Levy *et al.*'s paper presents over 25 new dates for KEN, a GIS-based study of the contextual data concerning the dates and their implications for the history of metal production at the site. This work builds on a preliminary study of ^{14}C dating for KEN which effectively pushes back the Iron Age history, with all the Biblical associations, 100 to 500 years earlier than previous researchers assumed (cf. Levy *et al.* 2004). This archaeological and spatial analysis is complemented by Higham *et al.* (Chapter 11), who deal once more with the Bayesian modeling of the radiocarbon results. The results point to the centrality of the 9th century BCE for building, metal working, and other activities at the site. Harrison and Barlow's study in Moab dove-tails with the Iron Age work in Edom as it highlights just how difficult it is for archaeologists to identify and study culturally and territorially defined polities referred to in ancient Near Eastern sources such as extra-Biblical and Biblical sources. Moab is blessed by the 19th-century discovery of the Mesha inscription dating to the mid-9th century BCE. Harrison and Barlow summarize the Tall Mādabā Archaeological Project's ongoing investigations of the Iron Age levels at Mādabā, which is consistently identified in the documentary record as a major settlement in the central highland region of Moab during the Iron Age. They also present the results of recently analyzed radiocarbon evidence that contribute toward the continuing effort to gain a better understanding of the historical social evolution of this part of Jordan, and its broader role in the cultural and political history of the southern Levant.

Aegean imports found at Iron Age sites in the southern Levant have long been a critical source of chronological data for Biblical archaeology. Thus, it is important that new developments concerning radiocarbon dating in the eastern Mediterranean (outside the southern Levant) contexts are examined (Chapters 7–9). Dendrochronology assumes particular importance, due mainly to its potential age resolution: it enables the highest dating precision of all methods, at best to annual or sometimes even subannual resolution in rare cases. In Europe and North America, the tree ring research that underpinned the radiocarbon calibration helped to expand the dendro technique much more widely. In this volume, M.W. Newton, K.A. Wardle, and P.I. Kuniholm describe recent work in the Mediterranean and its wider relevance for the periods under examination (Chapter 8). This is a major area of importance for Near Eastern chronologies because of the potential of its dating precision. S. Manning, B. Kromer, and colleagues (Chapter 7) present findings from their East Mediterranean Radiocarbon Intercomparison Project (EMRCP). Questions have sometimes arisen regarding the applicability of using averaged calibration curves produced from trees in North America and Europe in other areas because there are small latitudinal changes in the ^{14}C concentration (McCormac, Baillie, and Pilcher 1995). The most notable of these is between the hemispheres, which averages about 30–40 years. Manning and colleagues show that, on the whole, Aegean and East Mediterranean dates can be corrected using the mid-latitude northern hemisphere calibration curves of INTCAL98 (now superceded by INTCAL04 [Reimer *et al.* 2004]). They warn, however, that there are some small offsets between dated dendrochronological wood samples of local Mediterranean origin and INTCAL, which are centred in particular on times of solar minima. These offsets may assume significance only for calibration at particularly high levels of precision. At other times they are of geophysical interest only. In Chapter 9, S. Sherratt's provocative observations on the problems of linking the eastern Mediterranean archaeological chronologies with high precision radiocarbon dates suggest that in some cases, as archaeologists, we must accept the limitations that accompany dates.

For Iron Age archaeologists working in Israel the major battleground concerns the dating of Shishak's campaign (ca. 923 BCE) and its implications for the historicity of King Solomon. Perhaps the major testing ground for identifying destruction levels linked to Shishak has been the work carried out by Ami Mazar at Tel Reḥov (Chapters 13–15). In a synthetic chapter concerning the archaeology, stratigraphy, ceramics, and high precision radiocarbon dates from Tel Reḥov, Mazar, H. Bruins, N. Panitz-Cohen, and J. van der Plicht carefully build their case for making this historical identification. This is supplemented by van der Plicht and Bruins' discussion of the quality control of the Tel Reḥov dates processed in the Groningen laboratory (see Chapters 13 and 14). To establish a case against Mazar *et al.*'s more traditional high chronology, I. Piasetzky and I. Finkelstein present a different kind of statistical analysis of radiocarbon dates from Megiddo, Tel Dor, Tel Reḥov, and Tel Hadar in support of the low chronology (Chapter 16). In an alternative view to Mazar's team, Finkelstein (Chapter 17) argues against the idea that Tel Reḥov can serve as a principal anchor for Iron Age II chronology by suggesting there are problems with the most recent series of radiocarbon dates from Tel Reḥov as well as in the interpretation of the stratigraphy of the site. Finkelstein goes on to offer an alternative, low chronology view, that support his dating of ashlar palaces at Megiddo to the first half of the 9th century BCE, rather than the 10th century BCE. In an archaeological architectural analysis of the Iron II depostis from Samaria and Megiddo (Chapter 18), N. Franklin offers an additional case in support of the low chronology.

The study of Iron Age sites in Israel is completed by two papers in support of the high chronology. Examining radiocarbon dates from the early Iron Age strata at Tel Dan (Chapter 19) in the north of the country, Bruins, van der Plicht, D. Ilan and E. Werker argue in favor of the high Chronology. Moving south, Bruins and van der Plicht present some of the first radiocarbon determinations for the Iron Age desert fortresses of Israel and the Sinai (Chapter 21) which they argue lend support to the high chronology. In D. Master's (Chapter 20) summary of the Iron I chronology of Ashkelon, the major Philistine city on the coast of Palestine, the problems and potential for using radiocarbon dating at the site are discussed.

The book concludes with a series of chapters that consider the problems and pitfalls of using epigraphic (ancient writing sources) and the Biblical texts for what they say about aspects of history embedded in the Hebrew Bible and extra-Biblical sources. S. Münger (Chapter 23) discusses one of the most important epigraphic sources for cross-dating Iron Age deposits in the southern Levant— Egyptian stamp-seal amulets (most often referred to as scarabs)—found at various sites in the region. This is followed by W. Schniedewind (Chapter 24) who focuses on some of the problems of paleographic dating of Iron Age materials. William Dever (Chapter 25), the most senior conference participant and most long-term field worker concerning problems relating to archaeology and the Hebrew Bible, reflects on the problems of Iron Age chronology and history writing in Levantine/Biblical archaeology. The radiocarbon dating and the Iron Age of the southern Levant project is completed by B. Halpern's (Chapter 26) in depth discussion of the intricacies of historiography and the Hebrew Bible—especially the books of 1 and 2 Samuel and their implications for writing a history of ancient Israel. Taken together, the chapters in this book present the most recent data and analyses of issues concerning radiocarbon dating and the Old Testament/Hebrew Bible. This project has been carried out by many of the leading scholars in the fields needed to tackle this 21st-centruy endeavor including archaeologists, anthropologists, Egyptologists, Biblical historians, and specialists in radiocarbon dating. As the conference on which this book is based took place in Oxford, it is fitting that it concludes with the erudite remarks of one of the University of Oxford's most wide-ranging scholars and archaeologists—A. Sherratt. As he points out (Chapter 27), by the end of the meeting at Yarnton Manor, after much deliberation over radiocarbon dating, archaeology, and history, there was a point when the two sides seemed on the brink of agreement. The two sides he refers to are those scholars who argue their data support a more historic David and Solomon based on the Hebrew Bible and those who argue their data indicate that these figures were more mythical than real. We leave it to the reader, after reading and weighing up the evidence presented here, to decide which scholarly camp has prevailed.

References

Abraham, S.A. (2003) Chera, Chola, Pandya: Using Archaeological Evidence to Identify the Tamil Kingdoms of Early Historic South India. *Asian Perspectives* 42: 20-23.

Bayliss, A., and Bronk Ramsey, C. (2004) Pragmatic Bayesians: A Decade of Integrating Radiocarbon Dates in Chronological Models. In *Tools for Constructing Chronologies*, edited by C.E Buck and A.R. Millard (Lecture Notes in Statistics 177; London: Springer): 25-41.

Bintliff, J.L. (1991) *The Annales School and Archaeology* (Leicester: Leicester University Press).

Bruins, H. (2001) Near-Eastern Chronology: Towards an Integrated ^{14}C Time Foundation. *Radiocarbon* 43: 1147-54.

Bruins, H.J., J. van der Plicht, and A. Mazar (2003a) ^{14}C Dates from Tel Rehov: Iron-age Chronology, Pharaohs, and Hebrew Kings. *Science* 300: 315-18.

—(2003b) Response to Comment on '^{14}C Dates from Tel Rehov: Iron-Age Chronology, Pharoahs, and Hebrew Kings'. *Science* 302: 568c.

Davies, P.R. (1992) *In Search of 'Ancient Israel'* (JSOTSup 148; Sheffield: JSOT Press).

Dever, W.G. (1981) The Impact of the 'New Archaeology' on Syro-Palestinian Archaeology. *BASOR* 242: 15-29.

—(1982) Retrospects and Prospects in Biblical and Syro-Palestinian Archaeology. *BA* 45: 103-107.

—(1990) Biblical Archaeology: Death and Rebirth?. In *Biblical Archaeology Today: The II International Congress on Biblical Archaeology*, edited by A. Biran and J. Aviram (Jerusalem: Israel Exploration Society): 706-22.

—(2001) *What Did the Biblical Writers Know and When Did They Know It?* (Grand Rapids: Eerdmans).

—(2003) *Who were the Israelites, and Where Did They Come From?* (Grand Rapids: Eerdmans).

Finkelstein, I., and E. Piasetzky (2003) Comment on '^{14}C Dates from Tel Rehov: Iron Age Chronology, Pharoahs, and Hebrew Kings'. *Science* 302: 568.

Finkelstein, I., and N.A. Silberman (2001) *The Bible Unearthed—Archaeology's New Vision of Ancient Israel and the Origin of its Sacred Texts* (New York: The Free Press).

Goren, Y., I. Finkelstein, and N. Na'aman (2004) *Inscribed in Clay—Provenance Study of the Amarna Letters and other Ancient Near Eastern Texts* (Tel Aviv University Monograph Series 31; Tel Aviv: Tel Aviv University).

Grierson, P. (1959) Commerce in the Dark Ages: A Critique of the Evidence. *Transactions of the Royal Historical Society* 9: 123-40.

Guilderson, T.P., P.J. Reimer, and T.A. Brown (2005) The Boon and Bane of Radiocarbon Dating. *Science* 307: 363-64.

Halpern, B. (1995) Erasing History: The Minimalist Assault on Ancient Israel. *BR* 11: 26-35, 47.

—(1997) Text and Artifact: Two Monologues? In *Constructing the Past, Interpreting the Present*, edited by N.A. Silberman and D. Small (JSOTSup 237; Sheffield: Sheffield Academic Press): 311-41.

Hasel, M.G. (2004) Recent Developments in Near Eastern Chronology and Radiocarbon Dating. *Origins* 56: 6-31.

Hodder, I. (1986) *Reading the Past: Contextual Approaches to Interpretation in Archaeology* (Cambridge: Cambridge University Press).

Hodell, D.A., *et al.* (2001) Solar Forcing of Drought Frequency in the Maya Lowlands. *Science* 292: 1367-70.

Knapp, A.B. (1992) Archaeology and Annales: Time, Space, and Change. In *Archaeology, Annales, and Ethnohistory*, edited by A.B. Knapp (Cambridge: Cambridge University Press): 1-21.

Laughlin, J.C.H. (2000) *Archaeology and the Bible* (London: Routledge).

Levy, T.E. (ed.) (1995) *The Archaeology of Society in the Holy Land* (London: Leicester University Press).

Levy, T.E., *et al.* (2001) Interface: Archaeology and Technology—Digital Archaeology 2001: GIS-Based Excavation Recording in Jordan. *The SAA Archaeological Record* 1: 23-29.

—(2004) Reassessing the Chronology of Biblical Edom: New Excavations and ^{14}C dates from Khirbat en-Nahas (Jordan). *Antiquity* 78: 863-76.

Manning, S.W., *et al.* (2001) Anatolian Tree Rings and a New Chronology for the East Mediterranean Bronze–Iron Ages. *Science* 294: 2532-35.

McCormac, F.G., M.G.L. Baillie, and J.R. Pilcher (1995) Location-Dependent Differences in the ^{14}C Content of Wood. *Radiocarbon* 37: 395-407.

Moreland, J. (2001) *Archaeology and Text: Duckworth Debates in Archaeology* (London: Gerald Duckworth).

Moorey, P.R.S. (1991) *A Century of Biblical Archaeology* (Louisville, KY: Westminster/John Knox Press, 1st edn).

Pritchard, J.B. (1969) *Ancient Near Eastern Texts Relating to the Old Testament* (Princeton, NJ: Princeton University Press, 3rd edn).

Reimer, P.J., *et al.* (2004) INTCAL04 Terrestrial Radiocarbon Age Calibration, 0-26 kyr BP. *Radiocarbon* 46(3): 1029-58.

Pohl, M.E.D. (2002) Olmec Origins of Mesoamerican Writing. *Science* 298: 1984-87.

Pope, K.O., *et al.* (2001) Origin and Environmental Setting of Ancient Agriculture in the Lowlands of Mesoamerica. *Science* 292: 1370-73.

Renfrew, C., and P. Bahn (2004) *Archaeology—Theories, Methods and Practice* (London: Thames & Hudson).

Schiffer, M.B. (1976) *Behavioral Archeology* (New York: Academic Press).

Stager, L.E. (1988) Archaeology, Ecology, and Social History: Background Themes to the Song of Deborah. In *Congress Volume: Jerusalem 1986*, edited by J.A. Emerton (VTSup 40; Leiden: Brill): 221-34.

—(1990) Toward the Future: It's Just a Matter of Time. In *The II International Congress on Biblical Archaeology*, edited by A. Biran and J. Aviram (Jerusalem: Israel Exploration Society): 746-55.

Thompson, T.L. (1999) *The Mythic Past: Biblical Archaeology and the Myth of Israel* (New York: Basic Books).

Van der Plicht, J., and H. Bruins (2001) Radiocarbon Dating in Near-Eastern Contexts: Confusion and Quality Control. *Radiocarbon* 43: 1155-66.

Weiss, H. *et al.* (1993) The Genesis and Collapse of Third Millennium North Mesopotamian Civilization. *Science* 261: 995-1004.

Zevit, Z. (2001) *The Religions of Ancient Israel—A Synthesis of Parallactic Approaches* (London/New York: Continuum).

2 The Debate over the Chronology of the Iron Age in the Southern Levant

Its history, the current situation, and a suggested resolution

Amihai Mazar

Abstract

The subject of the Oxford conference—the chronology of the Iron Age of the southern Levant in the 12th–9th centuries BCE in light of current debates and ^{14}C dating—is of great interest among a wide circle of scholars from various disciplines, since it has a variety of implications for related fields of research. The subject is important for the archaeology of the Levant, Cyprus, and Greece; it has far-reaching implications for the utilization of archaeology in the study of the emergence of various ethnic and geo-political units of the period, such as ancient Israel, the Philistines, the Phoenician city-states, the Aramean states and the Transjordanian states of Ammon, Moab, and Edom. The subject is essential for proper evaluation of correlations and contradictions between archaeology and the biblical text.

The focus of this volume should be on the dating of the transition from the Iron Age I to the Iron Age II and the duration of the sub-period widely known today as the Iron Age IIA. To estimate the latter, we need solid relative chronology and as precise as possible absolute dates for certain occupation strata, regional pottery assemblages, and architectural complexes. More than thirty excavated sites in Israel and Jordan are available for comparative study. They differ in the quantity of data recovered and published, the quality of the excavation, and the state of publication, but together they represent a huge puzzle, the pieces of which have to be correlated and integrated into a comprehensive picture. Accepted dates for the various strata and contexts are essential for interpretation, but alas, no such consensus exists today. Here I will attempt to diagnose the reasons for the disagreements and to examine whether current advances in scientific dating methods may help us to reach some agreement or at least to minimize the gap between the various views.

Short History of Iron Age subdivisions

Typical of biblical archaeology, the debate over Iron Age chronology was always based on a mixture of pure archaeological analysis on the one hand and attempted correlations with biblical and extra-biblical sources on the other. It started with the University of Chicago Oriental Institute excavations at Megiddo during the 1930s, when the excavators identified the 'chariot city' of Stratum IV as Solomonic. In 1940, John Crowfoot, in light of his excavations at Samaria, called for a lowering of the date of Megiddo Stratum IV to the Omride period, due to the architectural similarity between Samaria and Megiddo (Crowfoot 1940; see Franklin [Chapter 18, this volume] for a similar view).

Table 2.1. Divisions of the Iron Age in Israel.

Wright 1961	
Iron IA:	1200–1150 BCE
Iron IB:	1150–1000 BCE
Iron IC:	1000–918 BCE
Iron IIA:	900–800 BCE
Iron IIB:	800–587 BCE
Aharoni and Amiran 1958	
Israelite I:	1200–1000 BCE
Israelite II:	1000–840 BCE
Israelite III:	840–587 BCE
Aharoni 1982; *EAEHL* 1978; Herr 1997; Herzog 1997; Mazar 1990; *NEAEHL* 1993	
Iron IA:	1200–1150 BCE
Iron IB:	1150–1000 BCE
Iron IIA:	1000–925 BCE
Iron IIB:	925–720 BCE
Iron IIC:	720–586 BCE
Barkay 1992 and Ben-Tor [ed.] 1992	
Iron I:	1200/1150–1000 BCE
Iron IIa:	1000–800 BCE
Iron IIb:	800–700 BCE
Iron IIIa:	700–586 BCE
Iron IIIc:	586–520 BCE
Current Suggestion (A. Mazar)	
Iron IA:	1200–1140/1130
Iron IB:	1150/40–ca. 980 BCE
Iron IIa:	ca. 980–ca. 840/830 BCE
Iron IIb:	ca. 840/830–732/701 BCE
Iron IIIa:	732/701 BCE–605/586 BCE
Iron IIIc:	605/586–520 BCE

In the early 1950s, Benjamin Maisler (Mazar) (1951) and Gus van Beek (1951, 1955) debated over the dates of Tell Abu Hawam Stratum III and of Cypro-Phoenician Black-on-Red pottery. While Van Beek claimed that both should be dated to the 10th century BCE, Maisler (Mazar) advocated that Tell Abu Hawam III dated to the 9th century BCE, claiming that it was destroyed by Hazael, King of Damascus. This debate recalls our current one.

William. F. Albright, Ernest Wright, and their followers, including most Israeli scholars until the present day, defined the 10th century until Shoshenq I (hereafter: Shishak) invasion (traditionally dated to 925 or 918 BCE; 917 BCE according to A. Shortland [Chapter 4, this volume]) as an independent archaeological sub-period, designated as 'Iron IC' by Wright (1961: 97 Chart 8) and 'Iron IIA' by the *EAEHL* (IV, 1226; *NEAEHL*: IV, 1529). This approach isolated the time of the United Monarchy as a defined archaeological sub-period. Some considered the 9th century BCE as a separate sub-period, while others combined it with the 8th century as a single sub-period (thus the *EAEHL*). An alternative approach was suggested by Aharoni and Amiran following the excavations at Hazor (Aharoni and Amiran 1958). In their view, Hazor Strata Xb, Xa, IXb, IXa, and VIII indicate a single archaeological sub-period of long duration that included both the 10th and the 9th centuries BCE. They denoted this period 'Iron II' and dated it to 1000–800 BCE. Their approach was subsequently rejected by most scholars (including Aharoni himself in later publications), but was retained by Gabriel Barkay and Amnon Ben-Tor, in a general account of the archaeology of Israel (Barkay 1992: 302-307; Ben-Tor [ed.] 1992: 2). They used the term Iron Age IIA for the time period of 1000–800 BCE. From a biblical history point of view, this sub-period included both the time of the United Monarchy and that of the Omride Dynasty and its aftermath. In my general book (Mazar 1990: 30) I followed the Albright/Wright/*EAEHL* approach; however, I am now convinced that the division suggested by Aharoni and Amiran and maintained by Barkay is preferable, although it needs some modification (see further below).

Yadin's Paradigm and its Aftermath

Since 1958 Yigael Yadin developed the earlier ideas of Albright and Wright into a well-defined paradigm for the 'archaeology of the United Monarchy', based on the excavations at Hazor, Megiddo, and Gezer (for his final view and earlier references see Yadin 1972: 135-64). He was followed by most archaeologists working in Israel, and his main points were accepted even by those who rejected some of his conclusions and suggested revisions to his scheme. The following is a short summary account.

Megiddo is the key site for this subject. Stratum VIA was the last Canaanite city at that site. It was destroyed by an intense conflagration ca. 1000 BCE or somewhat later, perhaps when conquered by David. It was replaced by the poorly built town of Stratum VB, which was attributed to the time of David. The later Stratum VA–IVB was considered to be the Solomonic city *par excellence*; it included, according to Yadin, two monumental palaces, a six-chambered gate, and a casemate wall. This city was conquered by Shishak and was replaced during the Omride period in the 9th century by the city of Stratum IVA, with its stables, massive city wall, and reuse of the Solomonic six-chambered gate. This city survived until the Assyrian conquest of 732 BCE. Aharoni (1972), followed by Zeev Herzog (1997: 211-14),[1] and David Ussishkin (1980, 1990; Ussishkin in Finkelstein and Ussishkin 2000: 600), pointed out the stratigraphic difficulties in Yadin's scheme, in particular regarding the six-chambered gate and the suggested casemate wall, but they all accepted Yadin's idea of a Solomonic city with monumental buildings at Megiddo. At Hazor, the dense stratigraphy enabled Yadin to date Stratum X with its six-chambered gate to the time of Solomon; Stratum IXa–b to the time between Solomon and Ahab; Stratum VIII to the Omride Dynasty; and Stratum VII to the post-Omride period. This scheme has been retained and substantiated by the current expedition headed by Amnon Ben-Tor (Ben-Tor and Ben-Ami 1998). The six-chambered gate and a short segment of a casemate wall at Gezer were dated to the 10th century by Yadin, and this date was later accepted by the Hebrew Union College excavators, who uncovered also a large public building next to the gate (Dever 1986).

Kathleen Kenyon, who accepted Yadin's Solomonic paradigm regarding Solomon's buildings, nevertheless suggested a later date in the 9th century for the pottery found in these buildings, based on parallels from Samaria, thereby suggesting a separation between 'Building Period' and 'Pottery Period' at Samaria and Megiddo (Kenyon 1964). Her opinion was most influential on scholars like Nicolas Coldstream, who, in the 1960s, used it to establish the chronology of the Greek Proto-Geometric and Geometric periods (Coldstream 1968: 302-305). As we shall see, it seems to me today that Kenyon was close to the correct solution for our problem.

---

1.   Herzog 1992: 250-53 accepted Aharoni's view and dated Megiddo IVB–VA (which he denotes VA) to the time of David; yet a few years later he dated the same 'palaces city' to the time of Solomon (Herzog 1997: 212-14). He accepts Aharoni's view that the six-chambered gate belongs to Stratum IV, which in his later view should be dated to the Omride period.

During the 1970s and 1980s, there was almost a consensus concerning the dating of two main pottery assemblages that are of interest to us here:

a. The late Iron Age I assemblage, represented by the pottery from the destruction layers of Megiddo VIA, Tell Qasile X, Tel Masos II, and parallel strata at other sites, was dated to the late 11th or early 10th century BCE.

b. The Iron IIA assemblage, with northern and southern variants, represented by the destruction layers of Megiddo VA–IVB, Taanach Period IIB, Yokneam XIV, Beth Shean S-1 (in the Hebrew University excavations), Lachish V, Arad XII, and parallel strata at other sites, was dated by most scholars to the 10th century, until Shishak's raid.

The deconstruction of the Albright/Yadin 'Solomonic paradigm' began during the 1970s with Benno Rothenberg's and later by Gary Pratico's demolition of Nelson Glueck's concept of 'Solomon's copper mines' in the Timnah Valley in the Arabah and of his identification of Ezion Geber with Tell el-Kheleifeh. Twenty years later, in the late 1990s, questions were raised concerning the core of the paradigm by J. Wightman (1990) and especially by David Jamieson-Drake (1991) whose influential book included a frontal attack from an archaeological standpoint on the very concept of the United Monarchy of ancient Israel. This work fell like a ripe apple into the hands of historians and biblical scholars of the European 'revisionist school' who were inclined to minimize or reject altogether the historicity of the entire or parts of the biblical narrative. This book also inspired the work of Israel Finkelstein.

Finkelstein's Low Chronology (LC)

Since 1996, Finkelstein (1995, 1996) went one step further by suggesting the wholesale lowering by 50–80 years of archaeological assemblages traditionally attributed to the 12th–10th centuries BCE. His first point was the date of the appearance of the local Mycenaean IIIC or 'Philistine Monochrome' pottery. Following Ussishkin (1985), he suggested lowering the appearance of this pottery by 50 years until after the end of the Egyptian presence in Canaan. This subject is beyond the scope of the present discussion, but it should be mentioned that several recent studies and discoveries, such as those at Ashkelon, negate this approach; in fact, none of the excavators of Philistia find this suggestion acceptable. It also creates unsolvable problems in correlating the archaeology of Philistia with that of Cyprus (Dothan and Zukerman 2003; Mazar 1985 and forthcoming; Sherratt and Master [Chapters 9 and 20, this volume;). ^{14}C dates for this period are not of much help, due to the many wiggles and complicated shape of the calibration curve for the 11th and 12th centuries BCE. Consequently, Finkelstein suggested lowering the dates of late Iron Age I assemblages from the late 11th century to the 10th century BCE and the lowering of traditional 10th century BCE assemblages to the 9th century BCE. His view became known as the 'Low Chronology' for the Iron Age of Israel. This suggestion empties the 10th century BCE of its traditional contents. Sites and strata that were traditionally dated to the late 11th century BCE, such as Megiddo VIA, are dated to the 10th century BCE, until Shishak's campaign (Finkelstein 1998a, 1998b, 1999b, 2002a, 2002b, 2004, and Chapters 3 and 17, this volume).

In a separate study based on ^{14}C dates from Tel Dor, Ayelet Gilboa and Ilan Sharon suggest an even lower chronology from that suggested by Finkelstein (see below).

Review of Finkelstein's Low Chronology

Since it was initially suggested in 1996, the LC and the historical perspectives that followed it have become the subject of continued controversy. I started the debate with a comprehensive review of this theory from an archaeological perspective (Mazar 1997) and others followed (Ben-Shlomo,

Shai, and Maeir 2004: 2; Ben-Tor 2000; Ben-Tor and Ben-Ami 1998; Bunimovitz and Faust 2001; Byrne 2002; Dever 2001: 131-38; Harrison 2003; Herzog and Singer-Avitz 2004; Kletter 2004 [the most comprehensive review of many aspects of the LC and its historical implications]; Singer-Avitz 2002;[2] Zarzecki-Peleg 1997). Today, most archaeologists in Israel still hold with the conventional chronology, while a few support the LC (Gilboa and Sharon 2001, 2003; Gilboa, Sharon, and Zorn 2004; Herzog 2002 but no more in Franklin [Chapter 18, this volume]; Herzog and Singer-Avitz 2004 [see footnote 2]; Knauf 2002).

The period under debate is framed by upper and lower anchors. The upper anchor is in the 12th century BCE, represented by the well-established correlations between the Egyptian Twentieth Dynasty and several sites in the Levant, in particular Beth-Shean (Level VI of the University of Pennsylvania excavations and Strata S-4 and S-3 of the Hebrew University excavations), Megiddo (Stratum VIIA), Lachish (Level VI), Tel Sera' (Stratum IX), and the Timnah Valley copper mines (Mazar 1990: 295-300; 1993; 2002: 264-72). The end of these strata, in several cases as a result of violent destruction, occurred towards the end of the Egyptian presence in Canaan, during the reigns of Ramesses IV to VI, until ca. 1140/1130 BCE. The lower anchor is related to the Assyrian conquests between 732 and 701 BCE. Destruction layers related to these conquests were identified at many sites such as at Dan, Hazor, Tel Kinneret, En-Gev, Beth-Shean, Tel Reḥov, Megiddo, Yoqneʿam, Samaria, Tell el-Farʿah, Khirbet Marjameh, Timnah (Tel Batash Stratum III), Lachish (Stratum III), Beth Shemesh and Tell Beit Mirsim. Related destructions occurred also at Tel Beer-Sheba (Stratum II) and Arad (Stratum VIII). There is a consensus concerning the dates of these destructions and thus they can be taken as a datum line for further discussion. Between these two secure anchors is a period of about 400 years, which leaves us with enough room for a continuous debate.

A major point in this debate is the question of whether we are able to establish secondary chronological anchors between the two main ones mentioned above.

There are two such minor anchors on which all the sides in this debate agree. The first is represented by the site of Jezreel excavated by Ussishkin and John Woodhead (1997). The history of Jezreel is known only from the Hebrew Bible, yet all scholars agree that Jezreel was indeed the second residence of the Omride Dynasty and that it was destroyed soon after the end of that dynasty, ca. 840–830 BCE. Pottery assemblages from the destruction of Jezreel can thus safely be dated to this time. Orna Zimhoni, who published the pottery from Jezreel, pointed out its similarity to the pottery from the 'Solomonic' Stratum VA–IVB at Megiddo, and this was one of Finkelstein's main arguments for lowering Megiddo Stratum VA–IVB to the time of the Omride Dynasty in the 9th century BCE. However, Zimhoni has also shown that similar pottery was found in the construction fills below the royal enclosure of Jezreel, probably originating from a dismantled earlier village that could date to the 10th century BCE (Zimhoni 1997: 29-56). This suggests that the same pottery assemblage continued throughout much of the 10th and 9th centuries. Such a long duration of the same assemblage was also observed at Hazor, Tel Reḥov, and other sites, and this, in my view, is the key to the resolution of our debate.

Another secondary chronological anchor is related to Arad and the Negev Highlands sites. All agree that at Arad, either Stratum XII or Stratum XI must be identified as the 10th-century settlement mentioned in Shishak's inscription (Aharoni 1981: 182-91). Many of us agree that it should be the Stratum XII village rather than the Stratum XI citadel (thus Finkelstein 2002b;

---

2.   I included Singe-Avitz in this category since her conclusions concerning Arad and Lachish in the cited paper fit the conventional chronology. In Herzog and Singer-Avitz (2004) both authors accept the long duration for the Iron Age IIA (most of both the 10th and 9th centuries BCE) as suggested by me since 1997.

Herzog and Singer-Avitz 2004; Mazar 1990: 373; Singer-Avitz 2002).[3] Arad thus provides an agreed reference point for the pottery of the Northern Negev in the second half of the 10th century. Yet this agreement works against Finkelstein's LC, since the pottery assemblage from Arad XII is identical to that found at other sites that have been dated to the 10th century BCE according to the conventional chronology, like Lachish Stratum V and various parallel levels (Mazar and Panitz-Cohen 2001: 277-79; Singer-Avitz 2002: 114). Concerning the Negev Highland settlements, Finkelstein (1984) dated them to the 11th century BCE, forcing an historical interpretation which would fit this period; more recently he lowered this date to the 10th century BCE, in accord with his LC (Finkelstein 2002b) and thus he now agrees to the mainstream conventional dating of these sites (Cohen 1980; Cohen and Cohen-Amin 2004; Haiman 2003; Herzog and Singer-Avitz 2004: 225-26; Mazar 1990: 390-96). He also accepts the view, long ago suggested by Cohen, Meshel, and others, that these sites should be identified with the dozens of Negev sites mentioned by Shishak. The interpretation of these sites as related to the United Monarchy as suggested by Cohen and others remains in my view the most feasible one. The pottery from the Negev Highland sites is typical Iron IIA pottery. If Arad XII and the Negev Highland sites can be dated to the 10th century BCE according to both the conventional and the LCs, so can be Lachish V, Beer Sheba VI–V, Tell Beit Mirsim B3, Tel Batash IV, Tell Qasile IX–VII, Gezer VIII, Beth-Shemesh IIa, and so on, all with the same pottery. This conclusion (based, as mentioned above, on agreements between all sides in this debate) makes the LC impossible, at least in Judah, Northern Negev, and the southern coastal plain. Consequently, the picture emerging concerning the status of Judah in the 10th century BCE must differ from that described by Finkelstein (1999a).

Shishak's raid has been considered by many as a benchmark for the late 10th century BCE, yet there are diverse views concerning the question of whether Shishak indeed destroyed cities, and if so, which archaeological levels can be identified as having been destroyed by him. Our suggestion that a vast destruction layer at Tel Reḥov should be attributed to Shishak since the place is mentioned in his inscription and since this destruction can be dated to the second half of the 10th century (Bruins, van der Plicht, and Mazar 2003; Mazar 1998) was severely attacked by Finkelstein and Piasetzky (2003). Yet at the same time Finkelstein (2002b) suggested that a series of other destructions should be attributed to Shishak, even at sites not mentioned in his list, such as Tel Miqne-Ekron Stratum IV. This dual approach remains mysterious to me. We should either believe that Shishak simply moved through the country without causing destructions (thus Na'aman 1998) or leave open the possibility that indeed he destroyed cities and settlements (perhaps only partly), and in such a case the search for such destruction layers remains a legitimate one, particularly in a place like Reḥov which is mentioned in his list. This latter approach is more feasible in my view. Lawrence Stager brought up the case of Taanach as an example of a city mentioned in Shishak's list where only one destruction level—that of Period IIB—can be identified as the city destroyed by him. The pottery from this level is identical to that of Megiddo VA–IVB, and thus another benchmark for the 10th century BCE may be suggested. Finkelstein tried to resolve the Taanach case by lowering Period II to the 9th century BCE and Periods IA and IB to the 10th century BCE, yet this claim must be rejected on the basis of pottery analysis: as shown by Rast (1978) the pottery from Period IA–B is close to that of the Late Bronze Age and fits the 12th century BCE (Mazar 2002: 278-79).[4]

---

3.   A variation is Herzog's view (2002: 92-93) that Arad XII was constructed during the 10th century BCE, but continued to survive well into the 9th century. This suggestion is not repeated in Herzog and Singer-Avitz (2004), where Arad XII is dated to the 10th century alone, before Shishak's raid.

4.   Finkelstein's discussion of Taanach (1998b) is based on dismissing the pottery from Period I as irrelevant due to the fact that most of it included only sherds. Yet such a dismissal stands against the principles of archaeological investigation. Rast's conclusions were carefully crafted and should not be rejected.

Thus, Jezreel, Arad, the Negev Highlands, and Taanach may be taken as 'mini-anchors' in the problematic 400-year time-span described above. Evaluation of these points of reference negates Finkelstein's LC.

The Modified Conventional Chronology and Iron IIA Material Culture

The results of the archaeological work of the 1990s and renewed analysis of various sites led me to change my previous view and accept Aharoni and Amiran's scheme from 1958 with some modifications. Recognizing the long duration of the Iron IIA pottery period, I suggested that the boundary between Iron I and Iron II be placed somewhere in the first quarter of the 10th century BCE (an estimated date is ca. 980 BCE) and that the end of the Iron IIA period should be some 150 years later, after the end of the Omride Dynasty and the destruction of Jezreel, ca. 840/830 BCE (Mazar in Coldstream and Mazar 2003: 40-44; Mazar 1997: 164; Mazar in Mazar and Carmi 2001: 1340). This scheme enables the definition of three major pottery periods in the 450 years between ca. 1150 and 700 BCE: Iron IB, Iron IIA, and Iron IIB, each with regional variations and each lasting about 150 years (Table 2.1). These scheme is supported by ^{14}C dates from Tel Rehov (Mazar *et al.* [Chapter 13, this volume]). Such a scheme may be defined as 'Modified Conventional Chronology' (MCC) for the Iron Age in Israel. It was recently accepted by several scholars as the best resolution for Iron Age chronology (Ben-Shlomo, Shai, and Maeir 2004: 2; Herzog and Singer-Avitz 2004).

In contrast to Finkelstein's view, I suggest that during the first half of the 10th century BCE a major change took place in the material culture throughout the country; this change brought to an end the Canaanite Second Millennium culture as is best demonstrated by Stratum VIA at Megiddo and related strata in the northern valleys, such as Yoqne'am, Dor and Tell Keisan. The new material culture is characterized by various aspects—from new modes of pottery production (dominance of red slip and hand burnish, disappearance of the Canaanite painted pottery tradition) to settlement patterns, architecture and religious art.

It should though be acknowledged that a definition of the material culture of the United Monarchy is strewn with difficulties. Since archaeology supplies the only first-hand evidence for this period, apart from Shishak's inscription at Karnak, it is essential to define properly which archaeological remains can be dated to the time of this kingdom. The MCC with its long duration of the Iron Age IIA suggested above makes this goal hard to achieve, since we cannot say categorically whether a certain Iron IIA archaeological context belonged to either the 10th or the 9th centuries BCE. In my view both options are open in many cases, while Finkelstein's view does not leave such an option and according to him all Iron Age IIA contexts should be dated to the 9th century BCE alone (2004: 185). I claim that the archaeological picture is far from being 'crystal clear', and that the traditional paradigm of 'the archaeology of the United Monarchy' remains a legitimate possibility, though not mandatory (for summaries see Dever 1990; Mazar 1990: 368-402). Thus, I see no difficulty in retaining the 'Solomonic' date of the monumental palaces 6000 and 1723 at Megiddo. Their dating to the 9th century BCE (a main point in Finklestein's theory; see also Franklin [Chapter 18, this volume]) would leave for the entire 100 years between ca. 980 and 880–860 BCE, a poor ephemeral occupation level at Megiddo (Stratum VB). This is not impossible, but not very feasible, especially when taking into consideration the tight stratigraphy and pottery developments at sites like Hazor and Tel Rehov, and the clear 10th-century BCE date of two Iron IIA levels at Tel Rehov. The strongest point in favor of a 9th-century BCE date of the Megiddo palaces is their building technique and masons marks which resemble those at Samaria (Finkelstein 2004:185; Franklin [Chapter 18, this volume]). Yet this resemblance can be explained if we assume that both kings—Solomon and Ahab—used Phoenician masons. Builders families or builders guilds might have retained similar building techniques and masons marks during a time period of less than one hundred years. Thus, this argument should not be taken as decisive.

Herzog and Singer-Avitz (2004: 227-36) proposed to divide the Iron IIA in Judah into two sub-phases—Early Iron IIA and Late Iron IIA—with the border between them ca. 900 BCE. In their view, the occupation strata of the earlier phase represent unfortified villages which cannot reflect the existence of a state in the 10th century BCE, while urbanism and monumental architecture started only with the second phase and reflect the emergence of Judah as an independent state from ca. 900 BCE. Thus, in their view even according to the MCC there is no place to a strong United Monarchy in the 10th century BCE. This may be correct to some extent, though I am not convinced that we can be so precise in dating certain Iron IIA strata to either before or after the critical line of ca. 900 BCE.

A Few Words on ^{14}C Dating

Since the mid-1990s, the potential of radiometric dating in helping to resolve the Iron Age chronological debate has been realized. The first studies on this subject were carried out in the laboratory of the Weizmann Institute of Science at Rehovot under the supervision of Israel Carmi. The samples measured in those years came from Dor (Gilboa and Sharon 2001, 2003; Sharon 2001), Tel Beth-Shean and Tel Rehov (Mazar and Carmi 2001; some measured at Tucson), Tel Hadar, and Megiddo. Since 2002 about 60 dates from Tel Rehov were measured at the Groningen University laboratories in the framework of a joint research directed by Hendrik Bruins, Hans van der Plicht, and myself (Mazar *et al.* [Chapter 13, this volume]). A large scale project on this subject is currently being conducted by I. Sharon, E. Boaretto, A. Gilboa, and T. Jull (Chapter 6, this volume). Since this is the main subject of the present volume, I will limit myself here to a few comments as a consumer of ^{14}C dating over the past seven years.

In the Beth Shean Valley Archaeological Project (Tel Beth-Shean and Tel Rehov excavations) we obtained about 100 ^{14}C dates from the Early Bronze I through the Iron IIA periods, measured in four different laboratories. The results enable appreciation of both the capabilities of the method as well as its limitations and possible flaws. The many stages of selecting the samples, the pre-treatment, the method and process of dating, and the wide standard deviation of Accelerator Mass Spectrometry dates may create a consistent bias, outliers, or an incoherent series of dates. The calibration process adds further problems, related to the nature of the calibration curve in each period. In our case, there are two difficulties: one is the many wiggles and the shape of the curve for the 12th–11th centuries BCE. This leads to a wide variety of possible calibrated dates within the 12–11th centuries BCE. The other problem is the plateau between 880 and 830 BCE, and the curve relating to the last third of the 10th century BCE, which in certain parts is at the same height as the 9th century BCE plateau. In many cases the calibrated dates of a single radiocarbon date is in both the 10th and the 9th centuries BCE, and in the 9th century BCE more precise dates between 880 and 830 BCE are impossible. These limitations are frustrating, and make close dating during this time frame a difficult task. It seems that in a debate like ours, over a time-span of about 80 years, we push the radiometric method to the edges of its capability, and perhaps even beyond that limit. In spite of these difficulties, our series of dates from Tel Rehov measured at Groningen provided a coherent sequence that fits the MCC as suggested above (see papers on Tel Rehov in this volume).

Gilboa and Sharon (2002, 2003; Sharon *et al.* [Chapter 6, this volume]) suggested, albeit hesitantly, an ultra-LC based on 22 dates prepared by Israel Carmi at Rehovot during the 1990s. Similarly, Finkelstein and Eli Piasetzky (2003) base their arguments for a LC on dates measured at Rehovot during the same years, of samples from Tel Hadar, Tel Rehov, and Dor. However, Bruins, van der Plicht, and myself have shown that dates of samples from Tel Rehov measured at Rehovot during the mid- to late 1990s were consistently lower by about 100 years than the dates of samples from the same loci or very close loci from identical stratigraphic horizon measured at Groningen using two different methods (for details see Mazar *et al.* [Chapter 13, this volume]). Yet even in the series of coherent dates from Groningen, we have some outliers. We await results of the project directed by Boaretto, Gilboa, Jull, and Sharon, in which samples from many sites have been dated, but for the time being, we have to rely on the published evidence, and this comes from a few sites that have yielded contradicting results. Some of the Iron IIA samples from Strata VI and V at Tel Reḥov were definitely dated to the 10th century BCE alone, and Bayesian statistics made on samples from Tel Reḥov indicate a transition date between the Iron Age I and Iron Age II somewhere around 980–970 BCE (Bruins *et al.* [Chapter 19, this volume]). Even Finkelstein and Piasetzky (2003: 288-92) admitted, based on these dates, that the Iron IIA probably started around 920 BCE, higher than the general 9th-century BCE date given to this period previously by Finkelstein. The difference between us now is merely 60 years for the beginning of the Iron IIA and zero for its end. This difference corresponds to the time-frame traditionally assigned to David and Solomon. Is it a coincidence? I doubt it.

The Low Chronology and Biblical History: Some Problems in Interpretation

A major difficulty in dealing with our subject is the biases relating to biblical and extra-biblical texts. Traditional 'biblical archaeology' always dealt with the question to what extent certain archaeological assemblages could be related to certain historical events, phenomena, and personalities described in the Bible or mentioned in written sources outside the Bible. The historicity of the biblical narrative concerning the period of the Judges, the United Monarchy, and the emergence of Israel and Judah as states have come under scrutinizing, critical, and skeptical review in the past two decades. Many authors have pointed out the biased positions of traditional biblical archaeology in these matters. Scholars belonging to the 'Albright school' tradition and the much-related 'Israeli school' represented by Benjamin Mazar, Yohanan Aharoni, Avraham Malamat, Yigael Yadin, among others, and their followers, were accused of a naive reading of the Bible and a simplistic, straightforward interpretation of the archaeological data, perceived as no more than an illumination of the biblical account (see Dever 2001: 23-52 for a survey of the various views and references). On reading the vast literature of the past two decades, one cannot avoid asking whether scholars who are trying to deconstruct the traditional 'conservative bias' are not biased themselves by their own historical concepts. In other words, it seems to me that the same charges used against conservative traditional biblical archaeologists can be made against a broad spectrum of minimalists, revisionists, post-modernists, or whatever term we use for a variety of current writers. All too often, archaeological issues are mistreated by scholars of all various schools of thought when it is used for historical interpretation. Lack of first-hand knowledge of the data, false methodologies, and pre-conceptions often result in biased, sometimes unacceptable, interpretations.

Some authors have claimed that archaeology should be used in a more sophisticated manner, and indeed that it, and not the text, can and should serve as the major source for objective interpretation of what actually occurred during those hundreds of silent years, for which we have almost no textual sources other than the biblical narrative itself. This approach gave archaeology additional weight as a supposedly objective source for evaluating questions like those regarding the origins of Israel and the rise of the Israelite state. But can archaeology indeed respond to such a challenge?

Table 2.2. Synchronic table of main Iron Age sites in Israel.

(Note that in this table no attempt was made to illustrate the possible subdivision of the Iron IIA period to 'pre-Shoshenq' and 'post-Shoshenq' sub-phases—for such an attempt see Herzog and Singer-Avitz 2004: 227-36)

Site	Iron IA 1200–1140/30 BCE	Iron IB 1140/30–1000/980 BCE	Iron IIA 1000/980–840/830 BCE	Iron IIB 840/830–732/701 BCE	Iron IIC 732/701–605/586 BCE
Dan	VI Vb Va		IV	III	II
Hazor	XII/XI		Xb Xa IXb IXa VIII	VII VI Vb Va	IV III
Tel Kinneret		V	IV III	II	I
Beth Shean (Pennsylvania)	Level Lower VI	Part of level Upper VI and part of Lower V	Part of Lower V	Upper V IV	
Beth Shean (Hebrew University)	S-4 S-3 N-4 Q-1	S-2	S-1 P-10 P-9	P-8 P-7	(P-6)
Tel Rehov	D-7 D-6	D-5 D-4 D-3 VII	VI V IV	III	II
Megiddo	VIIA	VIB VIA	VB IVB–VA ———→	IVA	III
Taanach	IA	IB	IIA IIB	III IV	V
Yoqne'am	XVIII	XVII	XVI XV XIV XIII	XII	XI
Tel Qiri		IX VIII	VIIA	VIIB–VIIC	VI V
Tell Keisan	13	12 11 10 9c-9a	8c–8a	7 6	5 4b 4a
Tell Abu Hawam		IV–1–IV4	IV5 III	0	
Dor*	B/4? G/11a?	B/13–B/9 G/10–G6b D2/12–D2/8c	B/8 D2/8c G/6a	Various remains	Various remains
Tel Mevorakh		VIII	VII		
Tell el Far'ah		VIIa	VIIb VIIc	VIId	VIIe
Samaria (pottery periods)		I	I–II	III IV V VI	VII
Jerusalem (Y. Shiloh)	15		14 13	12	11 10
Aphek	X10	X9	X8	X7 X6	
Tell Qasile		XII XI X	IX VIII		'VII'
Gezer	XIV	XIII XII XI X	IX VIII	VII VI	V
Beth Shemesh**		III / 6 5 4	IIa–IIb / 3 ———→	IIc / 2	1
Timnah (Tel Batash) Mirsim		V	IV	III	II
Ekron (Tel Miqne)	VII	VI V IV	III	II	1b 1a
Ashdod	XIIIb	XIIIa XII XI	X IX	VIII	VII VI
Gath (Tel Safit) (temporary)			5 4	3	
Lachish	VI	Gap	V IV	III	II
Tel Sera'	IX	VIII	VII	Gap?	VI
Tel Beer Sheba		IX VIII VII	VI V	IV III II	
Arad			XII XI	X IX VIII	VII VI
Tel Masos and Negev Highland	III II ———→		I Negev Highland sites		

* after Gilboa and Sharon 2003. ** Upper line after E. Grant and G.E. Wright; Lower line Tel Aviv University excavations directed by S. Bunimovitz and Z. Lederman, information accepted May 2005.

Finkelstein's works provide ample examples of the methodological problems related to this type of research. The historical implications of his LC relate to both the period of settlement and that of the United Monarchy of David and Solomon. Regarding the former, the LC should have caused him to reshape his previous views concerning the Israelite settlement in the hill country, including the interpretation of his excavations at Shiloh and 'Izbet Sartah as well as his views concerning the settlements in the Northern Negev (Tel Masos) and the Negev Highlands (Finkelstein 1984). For example, the LC creates a possible time span of some 300 years for the hill country 'settlement' material culture assemblage, represented in sites like Giloh, Ai, Shiloh, Mount Ebal, and so on, and characterized by Collared Rim jars.[5] This is an unfeasible conclusion in light of the thin accumulation and short lifetime of almost all the 'settlement' sites in the highlands. Alternatively, Finkelstein's numerous suggestions concerning many sites attempt to fit the results to his LC despite much evidence to the contrary. Numerous examples were surveyed by me in previous studies and will not be repeated here (Mazar 1997, 2002, 2004). It will suffice to restate a few points such as the abrupt emergence of a sophisticated Israelite state in the 9th century BCE; the condensing of too many archaeological strata (at Hazor, Tel Reḥov, and elsewhere) into a short period of less than 70 years in the 9th century BCE; the distorted and incorrect conclusions relating to certain sites like Taanach (see above), Beth Shean, and others; the description of Megiddo as un unfortified city in the 9th century BCE, when most other Iron Age cities were well fortified; the unfeasible lowering of the date of the Stepped Structure in Jerusalem to the 9th or 8th centuries BCE. The inner contradiction of the LC relating to Arad was mentioned above (for these and additional points see Kletter 2004).

Finkelstein's LC fits the historical perspective suggested by several authors over the past decade, namely, that the kingdom of David and Solomon did not exist in reality, and that the first Israelite state was the Northern Kingdom of Israel in the 9th century BCE (see Finkelstein 1999a, 2004; Finkelstein and Silberman 2001: 123-45; several papers in Handy [ed.] 1997). Yet one is obliged to ask the chicken-and-egg question: Was the LC born as result of an independent archaeological endeavor or was it made to fit a certain historical paradigm? In each of Finkelstein's articles since 1996, the archaeological discussion and the historical evaluation of the United Monarchy are intermingled. He and Ussishkin have strongly attacked the approach of the traditional 'Albrightian' biblical archaeology, which, in their view, attempted to fit the archaeological evidence into a conservative interpretation of the biblical narrative (for example Ussishkin 2003: 532). Do we now see the same method in reverse? If the answer to this question is positive, the new paradigm is no better than the traditional way of thinking in biblical archaeology.

Conclusions

The suggested MCC appears to be the most reasonable and acceptable chronology for the 10th–9th centuries BCE in the Southern Levant. It indicates a long duration of the same material culture throughout most of these centuries, and also results in an even and logical subdivision of the period from ca. 1130 to ca. 732/700 BCE into three more or less even time units, each with its own material culture traits. This view appears to have become the dominant among many archaeologists currently working in Israel. This MCC fits the archaeological data from many sites, and the radiometric dates from Tel Reḥov. One problem with this chronology is the difficulty in separating

---

5.   Collared Rim jars are known to appear during the 13th century BCE in well dated contexts such as Aphek and Beth Shean. According to the LC they were still abundant in what supposed to be 10th century BCE contexts such as Megiddo VIA (for their appearance in this level, see Harrison 2003). The result, according to the LC, is a 300 years duration for the Collared Rim jars; the hill country settlement sites are 'floating' in this wide chronological span.

the 10th century from the 9th century BCE. Current and future research in well stratified sites might enable more refined separation between early and late Iron IIA assemblages, as indeed was already suggested in several cases (the Northern Negev, Dor, Tel Rehov and other sites; see papers in this volume by Mazar *et al.* [Chapter 13], Sharon *et al.* [Chapter 6], Zarzecki-Peleg [Chapter 22], as well as Gilboa and Sharon 2003; Herzog and Singer-Avitz 2004).[6]

In historical terms, the MCC utilized here enables to retain most of the traditional archaeological picture relating to the 10th century BCE and the United Monarchy, though skepticism may arise even according to this system. Yet even if we accept the traditional 10th century BCE dates of strata like Megiddo VA–IVB, Hazor X, and so on, and buildings like the Stepped Stone structure in Jerusalem, the emerging archaeological picture would not necessarily point to a United Monarchy of an excessive size or magnitude. It rather indicates a shift in the material culture during the 10th century BCE, revival of urban life in a slow process (including the erection of fortifications in certain selected sites), limited monumental architecture which indicates central administration (at places like Megiddo, Gezer, and Jerusalem), evidence for revival of trade with Phoenicia and Cyprus, and limited (probably indirect) connections with Greece (Coldstream and Mazar 2003). The network of settlements in the Northern Negev and the Negev Highlands may be related to copper production at Feinan which flourished during this time and perhaps was related to the emergence of Edom (Levy *et al.* [Chapter 10, this volume]).

The kingdom of David and Solomon has to be evaluated as a modest yet vivid beginning of the Israelite monarchic period; elsewhere I summarized the data suggesting that the United Monarchy has to be evaluated as an exceptional and temporary achievement resulting from the abilities, charisma, and achievements of the two successive rulers—David and Solomon—in a time of a political vacuum and in a limited geographic scope (Mazar 2004: 19-22). The name of the kingdom of Judah as *bytdwd* ('The House of David') as documented on the 9th century BCE Aramean stele from Tel Dan, is an exceptional extra-biblical evidence for the impact of David as a historical figure. Archaeology is very limited in its ability to evaluate the historicity of the biblical narrative relating to the half-century or so of David and Solomon. It can provide us only a general framework into which we may fit some of the finds related to this period. It is our primary duty, before any further interpretation, to date correctly the finds, and this is the goal of the present Symposium.

Postscript

In a paper dedicated to the intercomparison of ^{14}C dating at Weizmann Institute, Tucson, and Groningen laboratories (with positive results relating to the correlation between currently measured dates in all three laboratories), Boaretto *et al.* (2005: 46) bring results of 32 dates from 10 sites, including from Tel Aviv University excavations at Megiddo. No calibrated dates are presented in the paper, since the interest of the authors was in comparing the BP dates. Yet a calibration of these dates with OxCal 3.9 software fits with my MCC and contradicts the LC.

Most revealing are the results from Megiddo. Two dates from Stratum K4 which correlate with Stratum VIA are presented in Table 2.3.

---

6.   Gilboa and Sharon (2003), based on a study of the pottery sequence at Tel Dor, suggested to subdivide the Iron I and IIA (as appear in Table 2.1, *EAEHL* and my usage) into seven phases, four of them corresponding to the Iron Age IB (denoted by them Ir1a(e); Ir1a(l), Ir1a/b and Ir1b). This division of the Iron Age IB (as used by me here), is unjustified in my view in light of the continuity in pottery traditions throughout this period. The complex terminology used by these authors is not of great help. Their phase Ir1/Ir2 appears to correspond to the end of the Iron IB (parallel to Megiddo VIA). Herzog and Singer-Avitz (2004) suggested subdividing the Iron IIA into two subphases: early and late. This approach may be justified in light of their study of southern sites and our results at Tel Rehov, as presented in Chapter 13, this volume.

Table 2.3. ^{14}C of seeds from Megiddo Stratum K-4 (=VIA).

Sample No.	BP	1 sigma	2 sigma
RT3944	2957±31	1260–1230 (14.7%) 1220–1120 (53.5%)	1300–1040 (95.4%)
T18163a	2864±40	1130–970 (61.2%) 960–940 (7%)	1190–1170 (2.2%) 1160–1140 (1.9%) 1130–910 (91.3%)

The first is too high by at least one hundreds year even for the conventional chronology which dates the destruction of Stratum VIA ca. 1000 BCE. The second fits the conventional chronology. Both dates contradict Finkelstein's attribution of the destruction of Stratum VIA by Shishak.

Two dates from Megiddo Stratum H-5 (=VB–IVA) (Table 2.4) are of special interest since this is the 'Solomonic' city according to Yadin, while Finkelstein suggested lowering this stratum to the 9th century BCE. The two dates are clearly in the 10th century BCE; the second one is even too high according to the conventional chronology.

Table 2.4. ^{14}C of seeds from Megiddo Stratum H-5 (IVB-VA).

Sample No.	BP	1 sigma	2 sigma
T18167	2796±28	1000–985 (7%) 975–900 (61.2%)	1010–890 (86.2%) 880–830 (9.2%)
RTT3949	2859±34	1110–1100 (3.3%) 1080–970 (55.1%) 960–930 (95.4%)	1190–1180 (1%) 1130–910 (94.4%)

The main results of the additional dates published in this paper mostly fit the MCC. The following is a superficial survey.

Iron I

The dates from Iron I pits at Hazor are mostly too early for the Iron I date of this stratum; the latest are in the mid-11th century BCE; dates from Tel Reḥov D-4, Tel Miqne VB and Tel Keisan 9a fit the conventional dating in the 11th century BCE; the 7 dates from Yoqne'am XVII fit the conventional late 11th-century BCE date for the destruction, except one that is too high (yet made on charcoal) and one that is somewhat too low. Of the four dates from Tell Qasile X, three fit the conventional date in the late 11th century BCE, and only one is an outlier (9th century BCE). One date from Tel Reḥov D-3 fits, or at least don't contradict, our results as presented in Chapter 13 of this volume.

Iron IIA

Dates from Tel Reḥov, Rosh Zayit, Hazor IX, and Bethsaida are all in the 10th or late 10th–early 9th centuries BCE and are in line with the conventional dates as suggested by the excavators (two of the Tel Reḥov dates are somewhat too low). Yoqne'am XIV which was dated by the excavators to the second half of the 10th century BCE is dated by three samples to the 9th century; Hazor X provided one date in the 10th century BCE and three at the second half of the 9th century—two of these being too low even according to the LC, and appearing to be outliers. Two dates from Hazor IX fit the excavators date in the early 9th century BCE.

Thus, these rich new data from Megiddo support in my view the MCC as presented in this study.

References

Aharoni, M. (1981) The Pottery of Strata 12–11 of the Iron Age Citadel at Arad. *Eretz Israel* 15: 181-204.

—(1982) *The Archaeology of the Land of Israel* (Philadelphia: Westminster Press).

Aharoni, Y. (1972) The Stratification of Israelite Megiddo. *JNES* 31: 302-11.

Aharoni, Y., and R. Amiran (1958) A New Scheme for the Subdivision of the Iron Age in Palestine. *IEJ* 8: 171-84.

Barkay, G. (1992) The Iron Age II–III. In *The Archaeology of Ancient Israel*, edited by A. Ben–Tor (New Haven: Yale University Press): 302-73.

Ben-Shlomo, D., I. Shai, and A. Maeir (2004) Late Philistine Decorated Ware ('Ashdod Ware'): Typology, Chronology, and Production Centers. *BASOR* 335: 1-34.

Ben-Tor, A. (2000) Hazor and the Chronology of Northern Israel: A Reply to Israel Finkelstein. *BASOR* 317: 9-16.

Ben-Tor, A. (ed.) (1992) *The Archaeology of Ancient Israel* (New Haven: Yale University Press).

Ben-Tor, A., and D. Ben-Ami (1998) Hazor and the Archaeology of the Tenth Century. *IEJ* 48: 1-37.

Boaretto, E., *et al.* (2005) Dating the Iron Age I/II Transition in Israel: First Intercomparison Results. *Radiocarbon* 46(1): 39-55.

Bruins, H., J. van der Plicht, and A. Mazar (2003) ^{14}C Dates from Tel Reḥov: Iron Age Chronology, Pharaohs, and Hebrew Kings. *Science* 300: 315-18.

Bunimovitz, S., and A. Faust (2001) Chronological Separation, Geographical Segregation, or Ethnic Demarcation? Ethnography and the Iron Age Low Chronology. *BASOR* 322: 1-10.

Byrne, R. (2002) Statecraft in Early Israel (PhD dissertation, The Johns Hopkins University, Baltimore).

Cohen, R. (1980) The Iron Age Fortresses in the Central Negev. *BASOR* 236: 61-79.

Cohen, R., and R. Cohen-Amin (2004) *Ancient settlement of the Negev Highlands*, II (Jerusalem: The Israel Antiquity Authority).

Coldstream, N. (1968) *Greek Geometric Pottery* (London: Methuen).

Coldstream, N., and A. Mazar (2003) Greek Pottery from Tel Rehov and Iron Age Chronology. *IEJ* 53: 29-48.

Crowfoot, J.W. (1940) Megiddo—A Review. *PEQ*: 132-47.

Dever, W.G. (1986) Late Bronze Age and Solomonic Defences at Gezer: New Evidence. *BASOR* 262: 9-34.

—(1990) Monumental Architecture in Ancient Israel in the Period of the United Monarchy. In *Recent Archaeological Discoveries and Biblical Research*, edited by W.G. Dever (Seattle: University of Washington Press): 85-118.

—(2001) *What Did the Biblical Writers Know and When Did They Know it?* (Grand Rapids and Cambridge: Eerdmans).

Dothan, T., and A. Zukerman (2003) A Preliminary Study of the Mycenaean IIIC:1 Pottery Assemblages from Tel Miqne-Ekron and Ashdod. *BASOR* 333: 1-54.

EAEHL—Stern, E. (ed.) (1972) *The Encyclopedia of Archaeological Excavations in the Holy Land* (Jerusalem: Israel Exploration Society).

Finkelstein, I. (1984) The Iron Age 'Fortresses' of the Negev Highland: Sedentarization of the Nomads. *Tel Aviv* 11: 82-84

—(1995) The Date of the Settlement of the Philistines in Canaan. *Tel Aviv* 22: 213-39.

—(1996) The Archaeology of the United Monarchy: An Alternative View. *Levant* 28: 177-87.

—(1998a) Bible Archaeology or Archaeology of Palestine in the Iron Age? A Rejoinder. *Levant* 30: 167-73.

—(1998b) Notes on the Stratigraphy and Chronology of Iron Age Ta'anach. *Tel Aviv* 25: 208-18.

—(1999a) State Formation in Israel and Judah. *NEA* 62: 35-52.

—(1999b) Hazor and the North in the Iron Age: A Low Chronology Perspective. *BASOR* 314: 55-70.

—(2002a) Chronology Rejoinder. *PEQ* 134: 118-29.

—(2002b) The Campaign of Shoshenq I to Palestine. *ZDPV* 118: 109-35.

—(2004) Tel Rehov and Iron Age Chronology. *Levant* 36: 181-88.

Finkelstein, I., and E. Piasetzky (2003) Wrong and Right; High and Low: ^{14}C dates from Tel Rehov and Iron Age Chronology. *Tel Aviv* 30: 283-95.

Finkelstein, I., and N. Silberman (2001) *The Bible Unearthed* (New York: The Free Press).

Finkelstein, I., and D. Ussishkin (2000) Archaeological and Historical Conclusions. In *Megiddo III: The 1992–1996 Seasons*, edited by I. Finkelstein, D. Ussishkin, and B. Halpern (Tel Aviv: Tel Aviv University): 576-605.

Gilboa, A., and I. Sharon (2001) Early Iron Age Radiometric Dates from Tel Dor: Preliminary Implications for Phoenicia and Beyond. *Radiocarbon* 43(3): 1343-52.

—(2003) An Archaeological Contribution to the Early Iron Age Chronological Debate: Alternative Chronologies for Phoenicia and Their Effects on the Levant, Cyprus and Greece. *BASOR* 332: 7-80.

Gilboa, A., I. Sharon, and J. Zorn (2004) Dor and Iron Age Chronology: Scarabs, Ceramics Sequence and ^{14}C. *Tel Aviv* 31: 32-59.

Haiman, M. (2003) The 10th century B.C. Settlement of the Negev Highlands and Iron Age Rural Palestine. In *The Rural Landscape of Ancient Israel*, edited by A.M. Maeir, S. Dar, and Z. Safrai (BAR International Series 1121; Oxford: Archaeopress): 71-90.

Handy, L.K. (ed.) (1997) *The Age of Solomon* (Leiden: Brill).

Harrison, T. (2003) The Battleground: Who Destroyed Megiddo? *BAR* 29.4: 28-35.

Herr, L.G. (1997) The Iron Age II Period: Emerging Nations. *BA* 60(2): 114-83.

Herzog, Z. (1997) *Archaeology of the City* (Tel Aviv: Tel Aviv University).

—(2002) The Fortress Mound at Tel Arad: An Interim Report. *Tel Aviv* 29: 3-109.

Herzog, Z., and L. Singer-Avitz (2004) Redefining the Centre: The Emergence of State in Judah. *Tel Aviv* 31: 209-44.

Jamieson-Drake, D.W. (1991) *Scribes and Schools in Monarchic Judah* (JSOTSup 109; Sheffield: Sheffield University Press).

Kenyon, K.M. (1964) Megiddo, Hazor, Samaria and Chronology. *Bulletin of the Institute of Archaeology, University of London* 4: 143-56.

Kletter, R. (2004) Chronology and United Monarchy. *ZDPV* 120: 13-54.

Knauf, E.A. (2002) Low and Lower? New Data on Early Iron Age Chronology from Beth Shean, Tel Reḥov and Dor. *Biblische Notizen* 112: 21-27.

Maisler, B. (1951) The Stratification of Tell Abu Hawam on the Bay of Acre. *BASOR* 124: 21-25.

Mazar, A. (1985) The Emergence of the Philistine Culture. *IEJ* 35: 95-107.

—(1990) *The Archaeology of the Land of the Bible (ca. 10000–586 B.C.E.)* (New York: Doubleday).

—(1993) Beth Shean in the Iron Age: Preliminary Report and Conclusions of the 1990–1991 Excavations. *IEJ* 43: 201-29.

—(1997) Iron Age Chronology: A Reply to I. Finkelstein. *Levant* 29: 157-67.

—(1998) The 1997–1998 Excavations at Tel Reḥov: Preliminary Report. *IEJ* 49: 1-42.

—(2002) Megiddo in the Thirteenth–Eleventh Centuries B.C.E.: A Review of Some Recent Studies. In *Studies in Archaeology and Related Disciplines*, edited by E.D. Oren and S. Ahituv (Aharon Kempinski Memorial Volume, Beer Sheba XV; Beer Sheba: Beer Sheba University): 264-82.

—(2004) Jerusalem in the 10th Century BCE: The Half Full Glass. In *New Studies on Jerusalem*, Vol. 10, edited by E. Baruch and A. Faust (Ramat-Gan: Ingberg Rennertt Center for Jerusalem Studies [Hebrew]).

—(forthcoming) Myc IIIC in the Land of Israel: Its Distribution, Date and Significance. In *The Synchronisation of Civilization in the Eastern Mediterranean in the Second Millennium B.C. II: Proceedings of the SCIEM 2003 EuroConference*, edited by M. Bietak (Vienna).

Mazar, A., and I. Carmi (2001) Radiocarbon Dates from Iron Age Strata at Tel Beth Shean and Tel Reḥov. *Radiocarbon* 43: 1333-42.

Mazar, A., and N. Panitz-Cohen (2001) *Timnah (Tel Batash) II: The Pottery and Other Finds from the Iron Age II and Persian Periods. Second Final Report on the Excavations between 1977–1989* (Qedem 41; Jerusalem: The Hebrew University).

Na'aman, N. (1998) Shishak's Campaign to Palestine as Reflected by the Epigraphic, Biblical and Archaeological Evidence. *Zion* 63: 247-76 (Hebrew).

NEAEHL—Stern, E. (ed.) (1993) *The New Encyclopedia of Archaeological Excavations in the Holy Land* (Jerusalem: Israel Exploration Society).

Sharon, I. (2001) 'Transition Dating'—A Heuristic Mathematical Approach to the Collation of Radiocarbon Dates from Stratified Sequences. *Radiocarbon* 43: 345-54.

Singer-Avitz, L. (2002) Arad: The Iron Age Pottery Assemblages. *Tel Aviv* 29: 110-214.

Rast, W. (1978) *Taanach I. Studies in the Iron Age Pottery* (Cambridge, MA: American Schools of Oriental Research).

Ussishkin, D. (1980) Was the 'Solomonic' City Gate at Megiddo Built by King Solomon? *BASOR* 239: 1-18.

—(1985) Levels VII and VI at Tel Lachish and the End of the Late Bronze Age in Canaan. In *Palestine in the Bronze and Iron Ages*, edited by J.N. Tubb (Papers in Honor of Olga Tufnell; London: The Institute of Archaeology): 13-230.

—(1990) Notes on Megiddo, Gezer, Ashdod and Tel Batash in the Tenth to Ninth Centuries B.C. *BASOR* 277/278: 71-91.

—(2003) Jerusalem as a Royal and Cultic Center in the 10th–8th Centuries B.C.E. In *Symbiosis, Symbolism and the Power of the Past: Canaan*, edited by W.G. Dever and S. Gitin (Winona Lake, IN: Eisenbrauns): 529-38.

Ussishkin, D., and J. Woodhead (1997) Excavations at Tel Jezreel 1994–1996: Third Preliminary Report. *Tel Aviv* 24: 6-72.

Van Beek, G.W. (1951) Cypriote Chronology and Dating of Iron I Sites in Palestine. *BASOR* 124: 26-29.

—(1955) The Date of Tell Abu-Hawam Stratum 3. *BASOR* 138: 34-38.

Wightman, G.J. (1990) The Myth of Solomon. *BASOR* 277/278: 5-22.

Wright, G.E. (1961) Archaeology of Palestine. In *The Bible and the Ancient Near East: Essays in Honor of W.F. Albright*, edited by G.E. Wright (The Biblical Colloquium, 1961; repr. Winona Lake, IN: Eisenbrauns, 1979): 73-112.

Yadin, Y. (1972) *Hazor* (London: The British Academy).

Zarzecki-Peleg, A. (1997) Hazor, Jokneam and Megiddo in the Tenth Century B.C.E. *Tel Aviv* 24: 258-88.

Zimhoni, O. (1997) *Studies in the Iron Age Pottery of Israel* (Tel Aviv: Tel Aviv University).

3 A Low Chronology Update

Archaeology, history and bible

Israel Finkelstein

Abstract

The aim of this chapter is to present an up-to-date overview of the Low Chronology system for the late Iron I and early Iron II strata in the Levant, a system I first proposed in two articles which were published about a decade ago (Finkelstein 1995, 1996a). These articles have generated a fierce debate (e.g. Ben-Tor 2000; Ben-Tor and Ben-Ami 1998; Mazar 1997), which was a major stimulant behind the introduction of large-scale radiocarbon projects into Iron Age archaeology. And though the gap between my system and the reasonable voice in the traditional camp is narrowing (the 'extended conventional chronology'—Mazar in the Radiocarbon Dating conference, Oxford 2004; see also Mazar 2004: 31), the dispute is far from being resolved.

The Foundations of the Traditional Chronology

The traditional system for the chronology of the late Iron I and early Iron II strata in the Levant is based on two pillars: (1) The date of Philistine pottery and its implications to the end of the Iron I; (2) The date of the Iron IIA strata in the north. These two pillars are certainly related, but they are not necessarily dependent on each other (*contra* Bunimovitz and Faust 2001: abstract; Mazar 1997). In other words, the acceptance or rejection of one does not call for a similar attitude to the other. And I should say from the outset, these two pillars have very little to do with archaeology. Rather, they are based mainly—the second pillar solely—on the biblical account of the early history of Israel. In other words, this is a unique (and annoying) case in which archaeologists compromised the evidence provided by their own discipline in favor of the one-sided interpretation of the textual material provided by another discipline, material which has been the focus of a fierce dispute since the early 19th century.

The *first pillar* is the Albright/Alt Philistine paradigm (1932: 58; 1944, respectively), according to which:

1. The Philistines were settled by Ramesses III in his strongholds in Canaan immediately after his battles with the Sea Peoples in his eighth year, that is, in 1175 BCE.
2. The biblical Philistines can be equated with the archaeological Philistines of the Iron I.
3. The power of the Iron I Philistines was broken by the expansion of the Israelite empire under King David. And since the accession of King David has been dated—according to the biblical numbers—to ca. 1000 BCE, this datum has been taken to represent the end of the independent chapter of Philistine material culture and the transition from the Iron I to the Iron II (e.g. Dothan 1982: 296).

Results of excavations in three of the major mounds in Philistia—Ashdod, Tel Miqne and Ashkelon—have been presented as perfectly fitting this paradigm. The first phase of the Philistine presence, characterized by locally made Myc IIIC:1b pottery (also known as Monochrome), was dated to a period starting in ca. 1175 BCE and lasting until the withdrawal of the Egyptians from Canaan a few decades later (e.g. Mazar 1985; Stager 1995). The second phase, characterized by bichrome ware, has been dated thereafter, in the late 12th and 11th centuries BCE. Destruction layers at the end of the Bichrome phase have been dated to ca. 1000 BCE and associated with King David's conquests (e.g. Dothan 1982: 296; B. Mazar 1951).

The *second pillar* which supports the traditional chronology is the reconstruction—according to the biblical testimony—of a great United Monarchy of Israel, established in the course of the military exploits of King David and stabilized in the days of his son Solomon, who ruled over a glamorous, rich and prosperous state. According to this paradigm Solomon engaged in monumental building activities in several administrative centers of his state and hence his empire can be traced archaeologically (e.g. Dever 1997; Stager 2003; Yadin 1970). These ideas—that archaeology can render the biblical descriptions of the United Monarchy historical—go back to the Albright school of thought in the 1930s. Nelson Glueck, for example, virtually 'invented' the smelting plant of King Solomon at Tell el-Khuleifeh ('Pittsburg of Palestine', he called it [1940: 5])—a site which has not produced pre-ca. 700 BCE remains (Pratico 1993).

But it was Yigael Yadin, following his excavations at Hazor and Megiddo in the late 1950s and early 1960s, who 'canonized' this historical reconstruction—and with it the traditional chronology system. Yadin's historical and chronological construct was based on:

1. The dating of the six-chambered gates at Hazor, Magiddo and Gezer to the days of King Solomon, following the biblical text in 1 Kings 9.15 (Yadin 1958).
2. The dating of the two ashlar palaces at Megiddo to the 10th century BCE based on the biblical idea of a glamorous Solomonic empire which was ruled from an elaborate capital in Jerusalem (Yadin 1970).

Two more finds at Megiddo seemed to support Yadin's interpretation: the major city *before* the city of the palaces (Stratum VIA) was destroyed by a terrible fire, and the next city, built on top of the palaces (Stratum IVA), featured the famous stables. Yadin's interpretation (1970) seemed to fit the biblical testimony perfectly: Canaanite Megiddo was devastated by David; the palaces represent the Golden Age of Solomon; their destruction by fire could be attributed to the campaign of Pharaoh Shoshenq I (biblical Shishak) to Palestine (Megiddo is mentioned in Shoshenq I's Karnak list and an unstratified fragment of a Shoshenq I stele was found at the site in the 1920s); and the stables were constructed in the early 9th century BCE, in the days of King Ahab who is reported to have faced Shalmaneser III at Qarqar with a huge force of 2000 chariots.

What's Wrong with the Traditional Chronology

As far as I can judge, not one of the arguments of the traditional chronology can withstand a thorough scrutiny, free of theological or simply romantic bias.

The Iron I
There can be no doubt that the Egypto-Canaanite system of the Late Bronze Age continued to function at least until the days of Ramesses IV (Finkelstein forthcoming). Scarabs of this Pharaoh were found in several clear late Late Bronze contexts, such as Lachish (Lalkin 2004), Cemetery 900 at Tell el-Farah and Beth-shemesh. Stratum IX at Tel Sera produced a hieratic inscription from

year 22 + X of an Egyptian Pharaoh—doubtless Ramses III (Goldwasser 1984). And different finds. from Deir el-Balah which found their way to the antiquity market hint that the site continued to function in the time of the 20th Dynasty, possibly until the days of Ramses VI (Giveon 1977). In the north of Canaan Megiddo was not destroyed before the days of Ramesses III; in fact, it was probably still occupied in the days of Ramesses VI (Singer 1988–89; Ussishkin 1995). And a group of finds from Beth-shean testify that the Egyptian stronghold there still functioned in the days of Ramesses IV (Finkelstein 1996b: 173).

According to the Philistine paradigm, this is the period of time when the Philistines were settled in Egyptian forts—exactly the kind of sites that are listed above. One could have expected that at least the major sites in Philistia would yield a stratum with a mixed Philisto-Egyptian material culture. This is not the case. Not a single locally made Myc IIIC:1b ('Monochrome') sherd has ever been found in any of these strata, even at sites located only a few kilometers away from the main Philistine centers. And no less important—not a single Egyptian 20th-Dynasty vessel (to differ from residual sherds) has been found in any of the Monochrome strata. These phenomena are too widespread to be explained as co-existence between the two cultures—that is, the Philistines took over part of Philistia while Egypt continued to control some sort of a nearby enclave, without any connection between the two parties over a period of several decades (Bietak 1993; Dothan 1992: 97; Redford 1985: 217-18; Singer 1985: 114; Stager 1995).

Bunimovitz and Faust (2001) have traveled far, to seek ethnographic case studies from the Baringo district in Kenya, to show that two distinct cultures can coexist without mixing much of their material traits. But the quantity and variety of contemporary human cultures enable the archaeologist to find a parallel to every historical phenomenon. In fact, ethnography can supply examples to conflicting situations; the task of the archaeologist is to set the rules of comparison. And comparing 20th-century AD African tribes to the 12th-century BCE Egyptian Empire in the Levant, or to the 12th-century BCE migrants from the Aegean basin, is a farce.

In any event, Tel Miqne and Ashdod seem to have supplied evidence that the Monochrome phase postdated the Egyptian rule. In both sites the remains of the two cultures seem to have been found one on top of the other (Finkelstein 1995: 223; Finkelstein and Singer-Avitz 2001), meaning that the two parties—Egyptians and Philistines—are separated stratigraphically, that is, chronologically and not geographically. There is no clue for the settlement of the Sea People, Philistines included, before the 1140s or 1130s BCE. The early phase of Philistine settlement started approximately at that time and lasted until the end of the 12th century BCE. The Bichrome phase should be dated, accordingly, to the 11th and much of the 10th centuries BCE. The Iron I/Iron IIA transition could not have taken place before the late 10th century BCE.

There is a somewhat humoristic side to all this. One can hardly assume that Tel Miqne and Ashdod were the only cities that had been destroyed earlier than the late Ramesside period. So the only explanation to what *really* happened, according to the traditional view, is the following: One night the Philistines who had already lived in these cities for a few decades (without any distinctive feature in their material culture), engaged in some sort of a wild beer or wine party, got drunk, and put their own cities—their own houses—to the torch. After all, they were Philistines, weren't they? In any event, the morning after, horrified by what they saw, they rebuilt their devastated cities and continued to live in them. But all this got them a bit homesick, so they decided to start producing monochrome pottery—the kind of pottery that they still remembered from their hometowns, which they had left several decades earlier... The beauty of this theory is that it provides a clue for the Aegean origin of the Philistines: their behavior resembles that of the boorish centaurs, who got drunk and violent in the wedding of Pirithous...

The Early Iron II

Yadin's 'Solomonic' theory was haunted by severe problems from the outset. First, the gate at Megiddo was built *later* than the gates of Hazor and Gezer, as it connects to the Stratum IVA city wall (Ussishkin 1980). Second, similar gates have been discovered at other places in the country, among them sites that date to the late 9th or 8th centuries BCE (Lachish and Tel Ira) and sites built outside the borders of the great United Monarchy *even* according to the maximalist view, for example, the 8th-century gate at Ashdod and the 9th- or 8th-century gate at Kh. Mudeineh eth-Themed in Moab (for the former see Finkelstein and Singer-Avitz 2001: 243-44; Ussishkin 1990: 77-82; for the latter see Daviau 1997: 225).

Yadin argued that his theory is based on three pillars: stratigraphy, chronology and the biblical text:

> Our decision to attribute that layer to Solomon was based primarily on the 1 Kings passage, the stratigraphy and the pottery. But when in addition we found in that stratum a six-chambered, two-towered gate connected to a casemate wall identical in plan and measurement with the gate at Megiddo, we felt sure we had successfully identified Solomon's city. (1970: 67)

Yet, it is clear that Yadin's dating rests only on the biblical text and that in any event, all three pillars cannot withstand a thorough scrutiny. Stratigraphy provides us only with relative chronology and old pots do not carry a date label. Still, some of my opponents argue that the Solomonic strata at Megiddo, Hazor and Gezer were dated according to a well-defined family of vessels—the red-slip and burnished pottery—which dates to the 10th century BCE:

> The pottery from this destruction layer included distinctive forms of red-slipped and slipped and hand burnished pottery, which have always been dated to the late 10th century... Thus, on commonly accepted ceramic grounds—not on naive acceptance of the Bible's stories—we dated the Gezer walls and gates to the mid-to-late 10th century. (Dever 2001a: 132)

In fact, the opposite is true; Dever dates this pottery type to the 10th century because it was found in the so called 'Solomonic strata':

> The key stratum seems to be Gezer Field III Phase UG3A, which is both very short and historically exceptionally well positioned. It comes after the Solomonic building period, richly documented by biblical and historical data and secured by comparative regional archaeological and architectural criteria combined with comparative pottery criteria. (Holladay 1990: 62-63)

In simpler words, the key stratum is dated by the pottery. The pottery is dated by its relationship to the six-chambered gate, which is, in turn, dated according to the biblical testimony to the days of Solomon; a classical circular reasoning.

This leaves us with the biblical passage of 1 King 9.15—the *only* true pillar in Yadin's theory and the only basis for the entire structure of the archaeology of the 10th century in the entire Levant (and beyond, since the chronology of the Iron Age strata in the Levant reflects on the dating of Iron Age Greek pottery; see, e.g., Coldstream 2003). So this is the moment to take a close look at this crucial verse and its background.

The idea that the book of Kings, which was put in writing not earlier than the late 7th century BCE, includes historic information about the days of King Solomon, who ruled centuries earlier, comes from a broader perception—that the author had access to archival material in Jerusalem, which included documents from the time of Solomon or immediately after his days. This perception, in turn, was based on a still broader theory, advocated by great German biblical scholars such as Leonard Rost (1982 [1926]) and Gerhard von Rad (1966 [1944]: 176-204), that the reign of Solomon should be seen as a period of exceptional enlightenment, during which (or immediately thereafter) great historical works—such as the Succession History—had been written in Jerusalem (see also Halpern 2001). And this theory was founded on the biblical testimony—another perfect circular reasoning.

Regardless of the chronology debate, archaeology has produced a totally different picture. In the 10th century Jerusalem was a small, poor, unfortified village (Finkelstein 2001; Ussishkin 2003); meticulous surveys show that the highlands of Judah—the backbone of the supposed great United Monarchy—was sparsely inhabited in the 10th century by a dozen of small villages, with a population of no more than a few thousand people (Lehmann 2003). There is no sign of monu-mental building activity in 10th-century Judah; there is no sign of industrialization of agricultural output; there is no evidence for mass production of pottery; there is no mark of settlement hierarchy. And most important of all, over a century of excavations in every sector of Jerusalem and in every significant site in Judah failed to reveal any evidence for a meaningful scribal activity and literacy in the 10th century (Finkelstein 1999; Jamieson-Drake 1991). *All* these characteristics —of an advanced state and a literal society—appeared much later, in the late 8th and 7th centuries BCE, when Judah grew to become a fully developed bureaucratic state (for the pottery see Zimhoni 1997: 170-72; for the industrialization of the agricultural output see Eitan-Katz 1994; for the weights see Kletter 1991; for ostraca see Sass 1993; Renz 1995: 38-39; for seals and seal impres-sions see Avigad and Sass 1997: 50-51). To sum up this point, modern archaeology has proven that the idea of an archive in Jerusalem, which kept genuine 10th-century records, is an absurd notion which is founded on the biblical testimony rather than on any actual evidence. Needless to say, this is the demise of the 10th-century anchor of 1 Kings 9.15.

But what *is* the reality behind this verse? There is no question that the biblical description of the United Monarchy draws a picture of an idyllic golden age; and that it is wrapped in the theological and ideological goals of the time of the authors (e.g. Finkelstein and Silberman 2001: 123-45; Knauf 1991; Miller 1997; Niemann 1997; Van Seters 1983: 307-12). The entire description of the reign of King Solomon in the book of Kings is based on two foundations: realities of the time of the compilation of the text, or a bit earlier, and the ideology of late-monarchic Judah (Knauf 1991; Finkelstein and Silberman forthcoming). The mention of the three great *Northern* cities in 1 Kings 9.15 could have been taken from 8th-century BCE realities, before the fall of the North, still remembered in Judah and projected into its semi-mythical early history, with the goal of looking at a promising future based on that mythical, glamorous past (for somewhat similar views see Knauf 1997: 91-95; Niemann 2000). Roaming Megiddo, Hazor and Gezer with this verse at hand to look for 10th-century monuments, is therefore a terribly naive endeavor.

The same holds true for assigning destruction layers in the north to King David in ca. 1000 BCE. There is no clue for great Davidic wars of conquests (which could have hardly been undertaken with a population of maybe 500 adult males in 10th-century Judah); the biblical account of David's wars is influenced by 9th- and possibly 8th-century realities (Na'aman 2002); and putting aside the forty-year reign formula for David and Solomon, we do not know when exactly in the 10th cen-tury David ruled.

The conventional theory raises other severe historical and archaeological problems, beyond the interpretation of the biblical narrative and the archaeological record according to the biblical narrative:

1. The rise of territorial states in the Levant was an outcome of the westward expansion of the Assyrian empire in the early 9th century BCE. Ancient Near Eastern records leave little doubt that all major states in the region—Aram Damascus, Moab, Ammon and northern Israel—developed in the 9th century BCE (Finkelstein 1999; for the Aramaeans further to the north see, e.g. Sader 2000). It is extremely difficult to envision a great empire ruled from the almost empty, marginal region of the southern highlands (and from a small village) a century before this process.

2. The northern part of Israel yielded evidence for two major destruction horizons between the end of the Late Bronze Age and the Assyrian conquest: Megiddo VIA and Megiddo VA–IVB and their contemporary strata. Most supporters of the traditional chronology have dated the first to ca. 1000 BCE and assigned it to King David and the second to the late 10th century BCE and assigned it to the campaign of Pharaoh Shoshenq I (e.g. Dever 1997: 239-43; Harrison 2003; Yadin 1970; and Stager 2003 for Shoshenq I). This has caused a major historical problem: the well documented assault of Aram Damascus on the Northern Kingdom in the 830s BCE, mentioned in reliable biblical prophetic stories and backed by the Tel Dan stele, is left with no destruction layer, not even at Tel Dan, which must have been conquered by Hazael.

3. A tomb at Kefar Veradim in the north yielded an Assyrian-shaped gadrooned bronze bowl (Alexandre 2002a) with Iron IIA pottery assemblage (Alexandre 2002b). The former does not appear before the 9th century BCE. Applying the traditional chronology brings about an absurd situation in which the inscription is dated to the 11th century BCE, the pottery to the 10th century BCE and the bowl probably to the 9th century BCE (Sass forthcoming).

4. Most problematic: Over a century of archaeological explorations in Jerusalem—the capital of the glamorous *biblical* United Monarchy—failed to reveal evidence for any meaningful 10th-century building activity. The famous stepped stone structure, which has been presented as the most important United Monarchy remain (e.g. Cahill 2003; Mazar 1997: 164), was probably built *earlier* and renovated during the centuries (Finkelstein 2001). Pottery which dates to the 9th if not the 8th century BCE was found between its surface courses (Steiner 1994: 19). The common pretext, that the 10th-century BCE remains were eradicated by later activity, is misleading, as monumental fortifications from the Middle Bronze and from the late Iron II did survive later occupations (Reich and Shukron 2000).

Beyond all this there is the problem of the synchronization with the neighboring lands. Regarding the correlation between Levantine and Greek pottery sequences, 'the "low chronology" recently advanced in Israel offers the more credible pace of development in the Aegean' (Coldstream 2003: 256). And concerning Syria, 'considerations of historical and archaeological nature point to the beginning of the 9th century as a reliable turning point from the Iron I to Iron II' (Mazzoni 2000: 121).

An Alternative Chronology

So much for the negative evidence; more straightforward clues come from two sites related to the Omride Dynasty—Samaria in the highlands and Jezreel in the Valley.

Ashlar blocks uncovered in the foundations of Palace 1723 at Megiddo which dates to Stratum VA–IVB—the layer which Yadin associated with the time of King Solomon—carry unique masons' marks (Lamon and Shipton 1939: 25). These are found in one other site, in fact mainly—possibly only—in one other building in Israel—the palace of the Omride Dynasty at Samaria (Reisner, Fisher and Lyon 1924: I, 119-20; II, Pl. 90: e-f). These masons' marks are so distinctive that they must have been executed by the same group of masons. The similarity in the construction techniques between the two edifices was first noticed by Clarence Fisher (1929: 58), the excavator of both Megiddo and Samaria, and John Crowfoot (1940: 146), the second excavator of Samaria; was forgotten with the beginning of the Solomonic frenzy (Guy 1931) and has recently been revived by Norma Franklin (Chapter 18, this volume). However, one palace was dated to the 10th century and the other to the 9th century BCE. There are only two alternatives here: either to push the Megiddo building ahead to the 9th century BCE, or to pull the Samaria palace back to the 10th century BCE. Needless to say, the former alternative, which is supported by historical sources, is the only possibility. The biblical testimony, that Samaria was built by the Omrides, is backed by Assyrian texts that relate to the Northern Kingdom as *bit omri*, that is, 'the House of Omri'—the typical genre of calling a state after the founder of its capital.

Excavations at Jezreel, located less than ten miles to the east of Megiddo, revealed equally surprising results. The destruction layer of the Omride compound, dated to the mid-9th century BCE, yielded a pottery assemblage identical to the Megiddo VA–IVB assemblage, which has traditionally been dated to the late 10th century BCE (Zimhoni 1997: 38-39). In a desperate attempt to save the idea of a great United Monarchy, Ben-Tor (2000) suggested that the Jezreel pottery belongs to an earlier phase at the site. This means that the large-scale leveling operations, transportation of fills, deposition of the earth in its place, and the construction of the casemate compound did not damage the old vessels—which were still standing there intact... Miracles do happen in the Holy Land, but this is a bit too much. So in this case too we need either to push the Megiddo assemblage ahead or to pull the Jezreel assemblage back. Once again the former is the only option, as the prophetic biblical story on the killing of Joram King of Israel and Ahaziah King of Judah by Jehu is supported by the Tel Dan Stele (Schniedewind 1996). Let me repeat this: in both cases—of the mason's marks and the pottery assemblages—the only alternative is to down-date the Megiddo palaces to the first half of the 9th century BCE.

So far I have dealt with traditional archaeology and biblical exegesis. Can we add to these circumstantial considerations more accurate pieces of evidence?

The first clue *may* come from Egypt. Münger (2003) has dealt with a group of 'mass produced' Egyptian amulets found in large numbers in the Levant. They seem to have been mass made in the Delta in the time of Pharaohs Siamun and Sheshonq I, who both ruled in the 10th century BCE. (Needless to say, the ostensibly Egyptian-based dating of Sheshonq's campaign to 926 BCE is based solely on the biblical testimony.) Yet, in Israel these amulets appear for the first time in the Megiddo VIA horizon, which was previously dated to the 11th century BCE. At Dor five such amulets were found in one room with a late Iron I (Megiddo VIA horizon) pottery assemblage (Gilboa, Sharon and Zorn 2004). Many of the objections to this idea may be sound, but Münger's theory is still a valid (if not preferable) possibility.

The second and main independent clue is radiocarbon measurements. In order not to repeat arguments that have recently been published, I just wish to note that:

1. Eliezer Piasetzky and I have shown that much of the data published so far—from Tel Dor, Tel Rehov, Tel Hadar and Megiddo—fit better the Low Chronology system (Finkelstein and Piasetzky 2003a).

2. Bruins, van der Plicht and Mazar (2003) have published a second series of radiocarbon readings from Tel Rehov, which they interpret as supporting the traditional chronology. Yet, Piasetzky and I have shown that there is a lower alternative to the interpretation of these measurements, which better fits the general picture provided by both radiocarbon and stratigraphy (Finkelstein and Piasetzky 2003b, 2003c). In fact, when the ceramic and stratigraphic arguments are added to the interpretation of the calibration curve, even the new Tel Rehov results support the Low Chronology (Finkelstein 2004 and Chapter 17, this volume). Stager's festive statement that the Tel Rehov readings put 'the last nail in the coffin of Finkelstein's theory' (Holden 2003: 229, 231) has therefore turned into a boomerang before the ink dried.

Arguments Raised Against the Low Chronology

Some have tried to gain a moment of fame by attempting to participate in the hot chronology debate, with quite amusing results, which demonstrate a complete misunderstanding of the whole issue. Harrison's long discussion of the Megiddo evidence (2003) is meaningless, as it is based on the traditional arguments: King David destroyed Megiddo VIA; Solomon built Megiddo VA–IVB, and so on. And Gal's statement (2003: 149) that 'the identification of Horvat Rosh Zayit with biblical Cabul…and its association with the "Land of Cabul" relate it to both King Solomon and Hiram of Tyre…thus providing it with an appropriate historical–geographical basis' (he means chronological basis) is the ultimate manifestation of the circular reasoning syndrome.

But there have been serious challenges, which needed to be addressed. Following are three examples which I have not treated in this article so far:

1. The *Taanach* argument of Lawrence Stager (in a lecture in San Francisco, 1998; 2003: 66). Pharaoh Sheshonq I, who campaigned in Palestine in the second half of the 10th century BCE, mentions Taanach in his Karnak list. According to Stager Taanach features only one destruction layer—the one corresponding to a Megiddo stratum which is traditionally dated to the 10th century BCE. Yet, a re-evaluation of the Taanach finds (Finkelstein 1998) clearly points to an earlier stratum which was also destroyed in a fierce fire. This provides a conflagration layer at Taanach for whoever is seeking a Sheshonq destruction.

2. The *density of strata* argument, raised by Mazar (1997: 163) and Ben-Tor (2000). If the date of 10th-century BCE strata is lowered to the early 9th century, too many strata are left in northern Israel for the relatively short period of time until the Assyrian takeover in 732 BCE. There are several answers to this argument: first, the traditional dating does the same to earlier strata; second, the number of strata depends on the quality of excavations; third, the history of border sites (such as Hazor—the subject of Ben-Tor's complaint) was more turbulent then that of inland sites (such as Megiddo).

3. The *how can you accept one biblical testimony and reject another* argument (e.g. Ben-Tor 2000: 12, 14; Mazar 1999: 40 note 38). Put simply, the question is: How can one reject the historicity of the biblical testimony on the building activities of Solomon and at the same time accept the historicity of the verses on the construction of Samaria by Omri? The answer is surprisingly simple: accepting the historicity of one verse and rejecting another is *exactly* the meaning of two centuries of biblical scholarship. As I have mentioned above, the biblical description of the Solomonic state is idealized, with many references to realities of much later times in Israelite history (e.g. the story of the visit of the Queen of Sheba in Jerusalem and the trade expeditions from Ezion-geber, which must reflect the participation of Judah, under Assyrian domination, in the intensive Arabian trade). In fact, there is not a single major item in that description, which cannot be explained on late-Monarchic background (Knauf 1991; Finkelstein and Silberman forthcoming). The description of the Omride state is minimal, negative, but far more accurate historically. It is enough to mention again the role of the Elisha cycle in the events involving the fall of the Omride Dynasty, including the role of Hazael King of Damascus, which is backed by the Tel Dan stele.

4. Finally, the *Finkelstein stands alone* argument of William Dever (2001b: 68) is just too tempting to be ignored. The number of supporters of each camp in this debate depends on who and how one counts. If researchers directly involved in the debate are counted, the majority, I suspect, is not on Dever's side. The reader should also pay attention to the most illuminating fact, that all desertions are from the traditional to the low chronology.

Dever has now prepared the ground for his own desertion: 'Caution is indicated at the moment; but one should allow the possibility of slightly lower 10th–9th centuries BCE dates' (in the abstract of his lecture in the Radiocarbon Dating conference at Oxford, 2004). In any event, looking at the high-quality scholars on my side (see the temporary and far from complete list in Finkelstein and Silberman 2002: 66-67), I can only hope to be always able to stand similarly alone.

Conclusion

Lowering the date of 11th-century BCE assemblages to the early-to-mid 10th century, and 10th-century BCE assemblages to the early 9th century, with the late Iron I/early Iron IIA transition fixed in the late 10th century BCE, cures all the maladies of the traditional Levantine chronology. It means:

1. Placing the Greek Protogeometric pottery from Dor, Tel Hadar and Tel Rehov in its more proper place (from the Aegean perspective, see, e.g., Coldstream 2003).
2. Harmonizing the evidence for dating the pottery sequences in Israel and Syria.
3. Dating state formation in Israel together with other areas of the Levant and western Asia, in the early 9th century BCE.
4. Providing the 'missing' destruction layer in the north for the Aramaean assault on the Northern Kingdom in the mid-9th century BCE.
5. Dating the identical mason marks at Megiddo and Samaria to the same period.
6. Dating the identical pottery assemblages of Megiddo VA–IVB and Jezreel in the same time zone.
7. Avoiding an absurd reconstruction of a great empire ruled from an empty highlands and a tiny village.
8. Reconstructing a logical history of the Levant in the 10th and 9th centuries BCE which is compatible with the general picture of the history of the ancient Near East.
9. And no less important, putting the strata in their proper place according to recent radiometric results.

The only disadvantage of the Low Chronology—at least for some—is that it pulls the carpet from under the biblical image of a great Solomonic United Monarchy and puts the spotlight on Northern Kingdom of the Omride Dynasty as the real first prosperous state of early Israel. Here is the dilemma: How can one diminish the stature of the 'good guys' and let the 'bad guys' prevail?

References

Albright, W.F. (1932) *The Excavation of Tell Beit Mirsim*. I. *The Pottery of the First Three Campaigns* (AASOR 12: New Haven: American Schools of Oriental Research).

Alexandre, Y. (2002a) A Fluted Bronze Bowl with a Canaanite–Early Phoenician Inscription from Kefar Veradim. In *Eretz Zafon: Studies in Galilean Archaeology*, edited by Z. Gal (Jerusalem: Israel Antiquities Authority): 65-74.

—(2002b) The Iron Age Assemblage from Cave 3 at Kefar Veradimin. In *Eretz Zafon: Studies in Galilean Archaeology*, edited by Z. Gal (Jerusalem: Israel Antiquities Authority): 53-63

Alt, A. (1944) Ägyptische Tempel in Palästina und die Landnahme der Philister. *ZDPV* 67: 1-20.

Avigad, N., and B. Sass (1997) *Corpus of West Semitic Stamp Seals* (Jerusalem: The Israel Academy of Sciences and Humanities).

Ben-Tor, A. (2000) Hazor and Chronology of Northern Israel: A Reply to Israel Finkelstein. *BASOR* 317: 9-15.

Ben-Tor, A., and D. Ben-Ami (1998) Hazor and the Archaeology of the Tenth Century B.C.E. *IEJ* 48: 1-37.

Bietak, M. (1993) The Sea Peoples and the End of the Egyptian Administration in Canaan. In *Biblical Archaeology Today, Proceedings of the Second Intermantional Congress on Biblical Archaeology, Jerusalem 1990*, edited by A. Biran and J. Aviram (Jerusalem: Israel Exploration Society): 292-306.

Bruins, H.J., J. van der Plicht and A. Mazar (2003) ^{14}C Dates from Tel Reḥov: Iron Age Chronology, Pharaohs, and Hebrew Kings. *Science* 300: 315-18.

Bunimovitz, S., and A. Faust (2001) Chronological Separation, Geographical Segregation, or Ethnic Demarcation? Ethnography and the Iron Age Low Chronology. *BASOR* 322: 1-10.

Cahill, J.M. (2003) Jerusalem at the Time of the United Monarchy: The Archaeological Evidence. In *Jerusalem in the Bible and Archaeology: The First Temple Period*, edited by A.G. Vaughn and A.E. Killebrew (Atlanta: Society of Biblical Literature): 13-80.

Coldstream, N. (2003) Some Aegean Reactions to the Chronology Debate in the Southern Levant. *Tel Aviv* 30: 247-58.

Crowfoot, J.W. (1940) Megiddo—A Review. *PEQ*: 132-47.

Daviau, P.P.M. (1997) Moab's Northern Border, Khirbet al-Mudayana on the Wadi ath-Thamad. *BA* 60: 222-28.

Dever, W.G. (1997) Archaeology and the 'Age of Solomon': A Case Study in Archaeology and Historiography. In *The Age of Solomon: Scholarship at the Turn of the Millennium*, edited by L.K. Handy (Leiden: Brill): 217-51.

—(2001a) *What did the Biblical Writers Know and When did they Know it?* (Grand Rapids: Eerdmans).

—(2001b) Excavating the Hebrew Bible, or Burying It Again? *BASOR* 322: 67-77.

Dothan, T. (1982) *The Philistines and their Material Culture* (Jerusalem: Israel Exploration Society).

—(1992) Social Dislocation and Cultural Change in the 12th Century B.C.E. In*The Crisis Years: The 12th Century B.C. From Beyond the Danube to the Tigris*, edited by W.A. Ward and M. Sharp Joukowsky (Dubuque, IA: Kendall/Hunt): 93-98

Eitan-Katz, H. (1994) Specialized Economy of Judah in the 8th–7th Centuries BCE (MA thesis, Tel Aviv University [Hebrew]).

Finkelstein, I. (1995) The Date of the Philistine Settlement in Canaan. *Tel Aviv* 22: 213-39.

—(1996a) The Archaeology of the United Monarchy: An Alternative View. *Levant* 28: 177-87.

—(1996b) The Stratigraphy and Chronology of Megiddo and Beth-shan in the 12th–11th Centuries B.C.E. *Tel Aviv* 23: 170-84.

—(1998) Notes on the Stratigraphy and Chronology of Iron Age Taanach. *Tel Aviv* 25: 208-18.

—(1999) State Formation in Israel and Judah, A Contrast in Context, A Contrast in Trajectory. *NEA* 62(1): 35-52

—(2001) The Rise of Jerusalem and Judah: The Missing Link. *Levant* 33: 105-15.

—(2004) Tel Reḥov and Iron Age Chronology. *Levant* 36: 181-88.

—(forthcoming) Is the Philistine Paradigm Still Viable? *Proceedings of the 2nd EuroConference of 'SCIEM 2000'* (Vienna).

Finkelstein, I., and E. Piasetzky (2003a) Recent Radiocarbon Results and King Solomon. *Antiquity* 77: 771-79.

—(2003b) Wrong and Right; High and Low—^{14}C Dates from Tel Reḥov and Iron Age Chronology. *Tel Aviv* 30: 283-95.

—(2003c) Comment on '^{14}C Dates from Tel Reḥov: Iron-Age Chronology, Pharaohs, and Hebrew Kings'. *Science* 302: 568b.

Finkelstein, I., and N. Silberman (2001) *The Bible Unearthed: Archaeology's New Vision of Ancient Israel and the Origin of its Sacred Texts* (New York: The Free Press).

(2002) The Bible Unearthed: A Rejoinder. *BASOR* 327: 63-73.

—(forthcoming) *In Search of David and Solomon* (New York: The Free Press).

Finkelstein, I., and L. Singer-Avitz (2001) Ashdod Revisited. *Tel Aviv* 28: 231-59.

Fisher, C.S. (1929) *The Excavation of Armageddon* (OIP 4; Chicago: The University of Chicago Press).

Gal, Z. (2003) The Iron Age 'Low Chronology' in Light of the Excavations at Horvat Rosh Zayit. *IEJ* 53: 147-50.

Gilboa, A., I. Sharon and J. Zorn (2004) Dor and Iron Age Chronology: Scarabs, Ceramic Sequence and [14]C. *Tel Aviv* 31: 32-59.

Giveon, R. (1977) Egyptian Finger Rings and Seals from South of Gaza. *Tel Aviv* 4: 66-70.

Glueck, N. (1940) The Third Season of Excavations at Tell el-Kheleifeh. *BASOR* 79: 2-18.

Goldwasser, O. (1984) Hieratic Inscriptions from Tel Sera in Southern Canaan. *Tel Aviv* 11: 77-93.

Guy, P.L.O. (1931) *New Light from Armageddon* (OIP 9; Chicago: The University of Chicago Press).

Halpern, B. (2001) *David's Secret Demons: Messiah, Murderer, Traitor, King* (Grand Rapids: Eerdmans).

Harrison, T.P. (2003) The Battleground: Who Destroyed Megiddo? Was it David or Shishak? *BAR* 29(6): 28-35, 60, 62.

Holden, C. (2003) Dates Boost Conventional Wisdom about Solomon's Splendor. *Science* 300: 229-31.

Holladay, J.S. (1990) Red Slip, Burnish, and the Solomonic Gate-way at Gezer. *BASOR* 277/278: 23-70.

Jamieson-Drake, D.W. (1991) *Scribes and Schools in Monarchic Judah* (JSOTSup 109; Sheffield: Almond Press).

Kletter, R. (1991) The Inscribed Weights of the Kingdom of Judah. *Tel Aviv* 18: 121-63.

Knauf, E.A. (1991) King Solomon's Copper Supply. In *Phoenicia and the Bible*, edited by E. Lipinski (Leuven: Peeters): 167-86.

—(1997) Le roi est mort, vive le roi! A Biblical Argument for the Historicity of Solomon. In *The Age of Solomon: Scholarship at the Turn of the Millennium*, edited by L.K. Handy (Leiden: Brill): 81-95.

Lalkin, N. (2004) A Ramesses IV Scarab from Lachish. *Tel Aviv* 31: 17-21.

Lamon, R.S., and G.M. Shipton (1939) *Megiddo I* (OIP 42; Chicago: University of Chicago Press).

Lehmann, G. (2003) The United Monarchy in the Countryside: Jerusalem, Judah, and the Shephelah during the Tenth Century B.C.E. In *Jerusalem in the Bible and Archaeology: The First Temple Period*, edited by A.G. Vaughn and A.E. Killebrew (Atlanta: Society of Biblical Literature): 117-62

Mazar, A. (1985) The Emergence of the Philistine Material Culture. *IEJ* 35: 95-107.

—(1997) Iron Age Chronology: A Reply to I. Finkelstein. *Levant* 29: 155-65.

—(1999) The 1997–1998 Excavations at Tel Rehov: Preliminary Report. *IEJ* 49: 1-42.

—(2004) Greek and Levantine Iron Age Chronology: A Rejoinder. *IEJ* 54: 24-36.

Mazar, B. (1951) The Stratification of Tell Abu Huwam on the Bay of Acre. *BASOR* 124: 21-25.

Mazzoni, S. (2000) Syria and the Chronology of the Iron Age. *Revista sobre Oriente Próximo y Egipto en la antigüedad* 3: 121-38.

Miller, M.J. (1997) Separating the Solomon of History from the Solomon of Legend. In *The Age of Solomon: Scholarship at the Turn of the Millennium*, edited by L.K. Handy (Leiden: Brill): 1-24

Münger, S. (2003) Egyptian Stamp-Seal Amulets and their Implications for the Chronology of the Early Iron Age. *Tel Aviv* 30: 66-82.

Na'aman, N. (2002) In Search of Reality Behind the Account of David's Wars with Israel's Neighbours. *IEJ* 52: 200-24.

Niemann, H.M. (1997) The Socio-Political Shadow Cast by the Biblical Solomon. In *The Age of Solomon: Scholarship at the Turn of the Millennium*, edited by L.K. Handy (Leiden: Brill): 252-99

—(2000) Megiddo and Solomon: A Biblical Investigation in Relation to Archaeology. *Tel Aviv* 27: 61-74.

Pratico, G.D. (1993) *Nelson Glueck's 1938–1940 Excavations at Tell el-Kheleifeh: A Reappraisal* (Atlanta: Scholars Press).

Redford, D.B. (1985) The Relations Between Egypt and Israel from El-Amarna to the Babylonian Conquest. In *Biblical Archaeology Today: Proceedings of the International Congress on Biblical Archaeology Jerusalem, April 1984*, edited by J. Amitai (Jerusalem: Israel Exploration Society): 192-205.

Reich, R., and E. Shukron (2000) The Excavations at the Gihon Spring and Warren's Shaft System in the City of David. In *Ancient Jerusalem Revealed*, edited by H. Geva (Jerusalem: Israel Exploration Society): 327-39.

Reisner, G.A., C.S. Fisher and D.G. Lyon. *Harvard Excavations at Samaria* (Cambridge, MA: Harvard University Press).

Renz, J. (1995) *Die Althebräischen Inschriften, Teil 1: Text und Kommentar* (Darmstadt: Wissenschaflische Buchgesellschaft).

Rost, L. (1982) *The Succession to the Throne of David* (Historic texts and interpreters in biblical scholarship 1; Sheffield: The Almond Press [originally published 1926]).

Sader, H. (2000) The Aramaean Kingdoms of Syria Origin and Formation Processes. In *Essays on Syria in the Iron Age*, edited by G. Bunnens (Louvain: Peeters): 61-76.

Sass, B. (1993) The Pre-Exilic Hebrew Seals: Iconism vs. Aniconism. In *Studies in the Iconography of Northwest Semitic Inscribed Seals*, edited by B. Sass and C. Uehlinger (Fribourg: Fribourg University Press): 194-256.

—(forthcoming) *The Alphabet at the Turn of the Millennium* (Tel Aviv: Institute of Archaeology).

Schniedewind, W.M. (1996) Tel Dan Stela: New Light on Aramaic and Jehu's Revolt. *BASOR* 302: 75-90.

Singer, I. (1985) The Beginning of Philistine Settlement in Canaan and the Northern Boundary of Philistia. *Tel Aviv* 12: 109-22.

—(1988–89) The Political Status of Megiddo VIIA. *Tel Aviv* 15–16: 101-12.

Stager, L.E. (1995) The Impact of the Sea Peoples in Canaan (1185–1050 BCE). In *The Archaeology of Society in the Holy Land*, edited by T.E. Levy (London: Leicester University Press): 332-48.

—(2003) The Patrimonial Kingdom of Solomon. In *Symbiosis, Symbolism, and the Power of the Past: Canaan, Ancient Israel, and their Neighbors from the Late Bronze Age through Roman Palestine*, edited by W.G. Dever and S. Gitin (eds.) (Winona Lake, IN: Eisenbrauns): 63-74.

Steiner, M. (1994) Re-dating the Terraces of Jerusalem. *IEJ* 44: 13-20.

Ussishkin, D. (1980) Was the 'Solomonic' City Gate at Megiddo Built by King Solomon? *BASOR* 239: 1-18.

—(1990) Notes on Megiddo, Gezer, Ashdod, and Tel Batash in the Tenth to Ninth Centuries B.C. *BASOR* 277/278: 71-91.

—(1995) The Destruction of Megiddo at the End of the Late Bronze Age and its Historical Significance. *Tel Aviv* 22: 240-67.

—(2003) Solomon's Jerusalem: The Text and the Facts on the Ground. In *Jerusalem in the Bible and Archaeology, the First Temple Period*, edited by A.G. Vaughn and A.E. Killebrew (Atlanta: Society of Biblical Literature): 103-16.

Van Seters, J. (1983) *In Search of History* (New Haven: Yale University Press).

Von Rad, G. (1966) *The Problem of the Hexateuch and Other Essays* (Edinburgh: Oliver & Boyd [originally published 1944).

Yadin, Y. (1958) Solomon's City Wall and Gate at Gezer. *IEJ* 8: 80-86.

—(1970) Megiddo of the Kings of Israel. *BA* 33: 66-96.

Zimhoni, O. (1997) *Studies in the Iron Age Pottery of Israel: Typological, Archaeological and Chronological Aspects* (Tel Aviv: Institute of Archaeology).

4 Shishak, King of Egypt

The challenges of Egyptian calendrical chronology

A.J. Shortland

Abstract

In reconstructing ancient historical chronologies, much use has been made of chronological pins between neighbouring states, linking their chronologies together. This chapter examines one such pin, the attack of Shishak, King of Egypt on the Levant in the early first millennium BCE. Due to the danger of circular arguments, it works entirely from Egyptian records, rather than combining these with biblical or Assyrian dates as is normal. It assesses the way the Egyptian chronology is put together and its strengths and weaknesses and goes on to examine in detail the Third Intermediate Period, specifically the 22nd and 25th Dynasties. In doing this it draws extensively on Kitchen (1986), a standard reference work for this period, but one that may not be totally accessible to those not specializing in Egyptian archaeology. The chapter concludes that the most likely *minimum* reconstruction of the date of the accession of Shishak/Sheshonq I is 941 BCE, with dates in the mid-940s BCE being the most likely overall. This supports biblical dates for the attack well, which would conventionally place the accession of Shishak/Sheshonq I in 945 BCE. It emphasizes that, while not perfect, the Egyptian chronology is very robust and internally consistent, even without reference to external events.

Introduction

The reconstruction of ancient chronologies is always a difficult issue, and often a contentious one. This is especially so when, as is usually the case, the chronology is constructed from many different types of evidence: textural, archaeological, astronomical, scientific, and so on, each bringing with it its attendant specialist who may have little or no appreciation of the complexities, strengths and weaknesses of the contributions to the subject of the other disciplines. Add to this the interconnectedness of ancient nations and therefore the necessity to take into account the histories of several neighbouring states when considering one, and the situation is ripe for confusion and dispute.

The aim of this chapter is to look again at one incident where two of these ancient nations are apparently interconnected. The textural reference is shown below:

'In the fifth year of King Rehoboam, Shishak king of Egypt attacked Jerusalem. He carried off the treasures of the Temple of the Lord and the treasures of the royal palace. He took everything, including all the gold shields Solomon had made'. (1 Kings 14.25-26)

Here there is apparently a clear reference to an Egyptian king appearing in the history of Israel. This is important since Egypt has one of the best calendrical chronologies of all the ancient states and if the attack on Jerusalem left a destruction layer that could be identified, then it would provide a valuable chronological 'pin' for the reconstruction of the history of Jerusalem and beyond. The event can be dated to 925 BCE using internal evidence from the Bible (Kitchen 1986, 1991; Redford 1992; Rohl 1995). This has been used as a calendrical pin to reconstruct *Egyptian* chronology in the past, Egyptian chronology being manipulated, consciously or unconsciously, to fit this date. Obviously, using Egyptian chronology to then support the biblical date for the attack of Shishak forms a very tight circular argument to the benefit of neither Egyptian or Israelite chronologies. Therefore the question this chapter addresses is: What can and cannot be said about the date of this attack?

In the first instance, it is absolutely vital to define which lines of evidence will be used and which will not. It will be assumed that the biblical text describing the attack of Shishak on Jerusalem represents a real, historical event and that the facts given in the text are broadly accurate. Taking this real historical event, it is beyond the author's expertise to criticize the 925 BCE biblical date, *so this date will be ignored completely*. This removes the problem of circularity that could potentially be an issue as described above. Instead, the date of the attack will be reconstructed *entirely from the use of Egyptian records*. Such is the complexity of the Egyptian chronology that to disassemble it all and reconstruct it would be a research project lasting years and requiring many specialists. This has not been possible before the preparation of this study. The scope is therefore limited to the most obvious lines of evidence and has drawn extensively on the masterly work of Professor Kenneth Kitchen, *The Third Intermediate Period in Egypt* (Kitchen 1986), for the majority of its primary evidence. This is a highly technical account and not immediately accessible to the non-specialist. The salient facts are therefore drawn out of it and presented in a more general way. The study is also limited to the assessment of just one date—the date of the attack—not the reconstruction of the whole Third Intermediate Period (TIP), let alone the whole dynastic chronology. The date will not have the certainty that a larger study would have the potential to give it, but, within the error bars given, it should provide reasonable accuracy. It will especially address the question as to whether it is possible to shorten the chronology, in other words, move the attack of Shishak into the 9th century BCE, which might fit better with a proposed 'low chronology' of the Levant.

Who was 'Shishak'?

Determining the identity of Egyptian kings from a single name transliterated into another language has potential problems. However, the identity of 'Shishak' is reasonably secure since it is very close to the Egyptian name 'Sheshonq' (also transliterated Shoshenq, Shoshenk, and several other variations). Five kings of the 22nd and 23rd Dynasties carried the name Sheshonq as their birth name or *nomen* (Shaw and Nicholson 1995). The name is Libyan in origin and carries no Egyptian meaning, unlike most truly Egyptian kings names (Schott 1989). It is therefore probable that at least the first Sheshonq and maybe others after him were actually known by this name as opposed to one of the other names that an Egyptian king possessed. Of the five kings, *Sheshonq I Hedjkheperra Setepenra* (conventionally 945–924 BCE) seems the most likely contender (see Fig. 4.1). Sometimes his nomen is shortened, the 'n' being left out (Schott 1989) giving 'Sheshoq', or to use the standard transliteration *š3–š3–k* (see Fig. 4.1, line 3), which seems very close to the biblical name. More importantly, Sheshonq I inscribed a relief known as the 'Bubastite Portal' on the walls of the Temple of Karnak at Thebes (Epigraphic Survey 1936–86), in which he claimed to have campaigned in Judah and Israel during his reign, capturing many cities. The exact route and nature of the campaign has been much debated (Kitchen 1986: 293-300), but it remains highly probable that this relief represents an account of a real historical event. It seems most likely that Sheshonq I was therefore the 'Shishak' of the Bible and the attacker of Jerusalem.

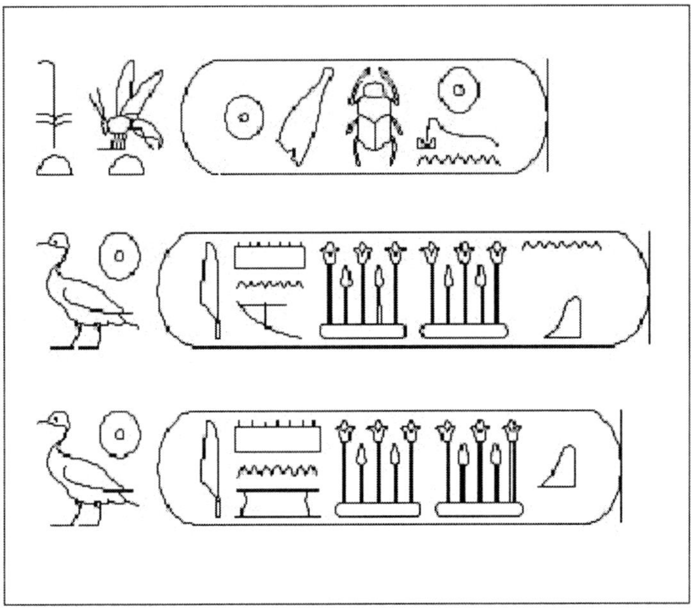

Figure 4.1. Three of the names of Sheshonq I: Line 1, *Hedjkheperra Setepenra*; Line 2 *Shashank Merimen*; Line 3, a rare alternative to Line 2 lacking an 'n', *Shashak Merimen*.

Egyptian Chronology

> Historical and archaeological chronologies of Egypt…have long provided a backbone for establishing timescales…in world history and archaeology… However, they do not provide that backbone easily or with uniform exactitude. (Kitchen 1991)

The question therefore becomes: When did Sheshonq I reign, and for how long? Ideally what is needed is a complete record of events from Sheshonq I's reign through to a known and widely agreed point in history. Such a point is the sacking of Thebes by Ashurbanipal in 664 BCE, quelling the rebellion of the Egyptian king Taharqa. This is attested by many later ancient authors, in contemporary Assyrian texts and in stelae connected with the Apis bulls and agreed even by those who reconstruct the earlier chronologies in radically different ways (Kitchen 1986; Rohl 1995; Roux 1992). It represents a fixed point and if Sheshonq I's reign can be determined relative to it, a certain number of years before, then an absolute date can be placed on the reign.

In order to attempt to do this it is necessary to look in a little detail at how the Egyptian calendrical chronology is constructed. Briefly, the chronology is based on various different lines of evidence, specifically:
1. Archaeology
2. Synchronisms
   - Astronomy
   - Lunar sightings
   - Eclipses
3. Heliacal rising of Sirius
4. King lists and other genealogical lists

Archaeology

Applying simple stratigraphic laws like superposition can generate an order of reigns of the kings. These can be as simple as New Kingdom buildings being built on Middle Kingdom predecessors, or later kings usurping earlier monuments replacing earlier cartouches with their own. Sufficient evidence can be built up from these relatively simple techniques to put most kings of the three main Kingdoms into an approximate order. To this order can be added textual information drawn from stelae, relief and tomb. Often a date is given at the beginning of such texts—'In the Xth year of King Y...'—from which it can be deduced that, providing the text is accurate, King Y must have reigned for at least X years. Once again, in many periods of Egyptian history such references are not uncommon. Thus, using purely archaeological evidence, plus the evidence of monumental inscriptions and other epigraphic data, the kings can be ordered and a *minimum* number of years given.

Synchronisms

The second way of constructing the chronology is closely related to the stratigraphic techniques applied in archaeology. It is possible to link the chronologies of adjacent states by finding either an historical reference to one state in the records of another or, more commonly, a stylistically dateable object from a foreign state in a sealed stratigraphic context in another. One of the most important of such synchronisms for this study is the sacking of Thebes by Ashurbanipal in 664 BCE discussed above, a 'fixed point' mentioned in many texts and the starting point for search for the dates for Shoshenq I.

Astronomy

Much has been written on the application of astronomy to Egyptian chronology (Parker 1974). Several lines of astronomical evidence can be used, specifically lunar, solar and astral. Lunar sightings concern the rising of the new moon, which was sometimes recorded as occurring on a certain day of the year. The Egyptian year was divided into three seasons: *akhet* ('inundation'), *peret* ('emergence') and *shemu* ('harvest'). Each season had four months, each of 30 days. To the end of this year of 360 days were added five epagomenal days to make an Egyptian year of 365 days (Parker 1950). Papyrus Leiden 350 lists that in the 52nd year of the reign of Ramesses II the new moon rose on the 27th day of the second month of *peret* (II *prt* 27)(Casperson 1988; Dodson 2000; Parker 1957). This precise information can be used to give a date, because only in certain years will the new moon rise on this day. Unfortunately, while this does not happen every year, it does happen quite frequently, giving us possible dates for the accession of Ramesses II of 1304, 1290, 1279 (the commonly accepted one), 1253, 1228, 1214 or 1203 BCE and many more outside the 13th century BCE, which is usually considered on other grounds as appropriate for the reign of Ramesses II (Dodson 2000; Parker 1957). This frequent periodicity of the lunar observations is, along with their rareness, their major weakness.

Solar observations—specifically eclipses—are somewhat different. These are very rare and can be dated very precisely. For example, there is a record that immediately following the death of Psammetichus I there was a major eclipse. The only eclipse visible in Egypt around the correct time occurred on 30 September 610 BCE, giving a date of 610 BCE for the end of the reign of this king (Hornung 1965; Kitchen 1991). Unfortunately, that is the only relevant eclipse date in the Egyptian record and is not useful for the dating of Shoshenq I, since it is after the well recognised date of 664 BCE.

Finally and most debatable of all, are the astral observations. These concern the star Sirius (*Alpha Canis* Major), known to the Egyptian as *Sopdet* and the Greeks as *Sothis*, the brightest star in the sky (after the sun) and extremely significant in Egyptian religion (Parker 1976). While stars close to the north pole are visible throughout the year in the northern hemisphere, those that lie closer to the ecliptic are not visible all the year since for part of it they lie close to the suns disc and are therefore invisible. This happens to Sirius during the early summer, and the first day that Sirius is again visible in the early morning just before the sun rises is known as the heliacal rising of Sirius. Coincidentally, this rising happens to correspond with the flooding of the Nile (the inundation), which was supposed to be the first season of the Egyptian year (Parker 1950, 1976). Presumably, when the calendar was first set up this was indeed the case and I *akhet* 1, New Year's day, did correspond with the heliacal rising of Sirius and the start of the inundation. Unfortunately, or perhaps fortunately from a chronological point of view, owing to an unforeseen complication in the Egyptian calendar, this synchronicity of events did not last very long. The problem was that the Egyptian calendar year was 365 days long, whereas a solar year is actually 365.24224 days long (Kitchen 1991), nearly a quarter of a day longer (hence modern leap years). Hence four years from the setting-up of the calendar, the calendar was one day early (Sirius rose on I *akhet* 2) and it continued to get earlier and earlier. After 120 years it was a full month early and after 480 years Sirius rose and the inundation began on the first day of the season of *peret*. This slow creep continued until 1460 years after the setting-up of the calendar, when everything was back to where it started and the whole cycle could begin again (Kitchen 1991). Therefore an observation of Sirius rising on a particular day in Egyptian history would only happen once in 1460 years—a potentially very powerful tool for the assessment of chronologies.

Unfortunately, there are several complications to this simple pattern. First, the observation of the heliacal rising of Sirius is latitude dependent (Kitchen 1991; Parker 1976). The further north you are, the earlier you see it. The variation is about 1 day per degree of latitude, which would make four years difference to a chronology. Second, there are potential problems with altitude and weather, which could also affect the date and visibility of the rising. However, even given these complications, it remains potentially a very valuable tool.

There are three observations of the heliacal rising of Sirius that are of importance (Kitchen 1991; Parker 1976). The most recent was by the Roman author Censorinus, in his work *De Die Natali Liber ad Q. Caerellium* (Censorinus, 1983 edn). He recorded that Sirius rose on the first day of the Egyptian year exactly 100 years before the day about which he was writing, namely, on 20 July 139 AD. This record is supported by a second reference to the event by Claudius Ptolemy in his book *Almagest*, and a more debatable one by Theon of Alexandria (Mackey 1993). Hence the calendar can be fixed with the Egyptian New Year (1 *akhet* 1) corresponding with the heliacal rising of Sirius in 139 AD, then 1460 years before that in 1321 BCE and before that in 2781 BCE. This is the framework in which other observations of Sirius need to be fitted. However, there are only two of them: Papyrus Berlin 10012 and Papyrus Ebers.

The Berlin papyrus was found in the 12th-Dynasty Funeral complex near Memphis. It is dated to the 7th year of the reign of a king who is not mentioned, but was most likely Senuseret III (Parker 1976). It states 'the going forth of Sopdet will happen on IV *peret* 16'. The 'going forth of Sopdet' is usually translated as the heliacal rising of Sirius. Calculating from the Censorinus New Year observation, this puts the 7th year of Senuseret III as 1871 BCE. However, the rising of Sirius is latitude dependent, and it is unknown where the observation was made. The 1871 BCE applies if the observation was made in the then capital of Memphis, near to where the papyrus was found. This is the most accepted interpretation. However, if the observation was made in Thebes, then the date could be twenty years earlier. Whatever the date, it represents the earliest known calendrical 'pin' in human history.

The second reference to Sopdet/Sirius in Papyrus Ebers (Parker 1976) is more debatable. This is dated to the 9th year of Amenhotep I, and seems to suggest that the heliacal rising of Sirius took place on III *shemu* 9, giving a date for the observation of 1517 BCE (Kitchen 1991). However, the interpretation of the text has been questioned, and this date is now no longer thought to be as reliable as it once was. As can be seen from this very brief résumé, the two Sothic dates have an element of flexibility to them and one can reasonably be discounted altogether. They are also too early to be of great use in the interpretation of the date of Shoshenq I.

King Lists

Fundamental to the study of Egyptian chronology are the king lists. These are lists of rulers, usually the purported ancestors of the current king, which are rarely displayed on temple walls, tomb reliefs or stelae. The most important of these king lists are:
1.   Hall of the Records, Temple of Amun, Karnak (Tuthmosis III, ca. 1450 BCE)
2.   Temple of Abydos (Seti I, ca. 1250 BCE)
3.   Temple of Ramesses II at Abydos (ca. 1250 BCE)
4.   Tomb chapel of Tjunuroy (official of Ramesses II) at Saqqara (ca. 1250 BCE)
5.   Palermo stone, 5th Dynasty (ca. 2400 BCE)(Kitchen 1991)

However, all these lists are dated before Sheshonq I, so do not include him or his descendents. They are therefore of no direct use in this case. Much more interesting is the most important of all the regnal lists, those produced by a priest named Manetho, who lived and worked in the 4th and/or 3rd centuries BCE (Kitchen 1991). He seems to have access to the archive of the Egyptian temples, and from these produced a list of Egyptian kings from the earliest times, which he divided into 30 dynasties, divisions which are still used to this day (Manetho, 1940 edn). He dedicated his study to Ptolemy II (285–246 BCE), which places the completion of this work either in, or soon after, this reign. Why he put this list together is unknown, as is whether this was a common occupation for an Egyptian priest. It must be assumed that it was not, since Manetho's king list, written in Greek and known as the *Aegyptiaca*, is a unique (if indirect) survivor (Manetho, 1940 edn).

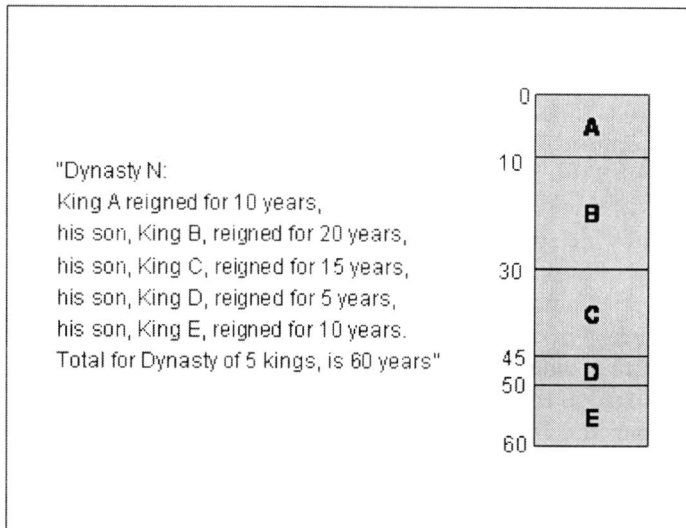

"Dynasty N:
King A reigned for 10 years,
his son, King B, reigned for 20 years,
his son, King C, reigned for 15 years,
his son, King D, reigned for 5 years,
his son, King E, reigned for 10 years.
Total for Dynasty of 5 kings, is 60 years"

Figure 4.2. The idealized reconstruction of a chronology following a Manetho-type king list with regnal lengths.

Unfortunately, Manetho's original manuscript copy has been lost. Instead, we have a series of sometimes contradictory fragments in the writings of later authors, specifically Josephus, Julius Africanus, Eusebius and George called Syncellus (Manetho, 1940 edn). All had there own political agenda in writing their works and this should be borne in mind when their accounts are assessed. An idealised form of Manetho's king lists is shown in Figure 4.2.

Creating the timeline shown on the left assumes that Manetho is accurate in his list in that he has neither missed out any kings or added additional ones. It assumes that the order Manetho lists is correct, and that the reign lengths are accurate with no co-regencies. Table 4.1 shows Manetho's 21st Dynasty (Manetho, 1940 edn), which stands up quite well to modern archaeological discoveries that have a bearing on the chronology. As can be seen, all the kings are present and almost all in the right order. Many of the reign lengths also appear to be accurate. Unfortunately, this level of precision does not always seem to be the case. Table 4.2 shows Manetho's 22nd Dynasty (Manetho, 1940 edn), one that is directly relevant to the question of the dates of Sheshonq I.

Table **4.1.** Manetho's 21st Dynasty (Manetho, 1940 edn) compared to the currently accepted version (Shaw and Nicholson 1995).

Accepted				Manetho (via Africanus)		Manetho (via Eusebius)	
7 Kings	from (BCE)	to (BCE)	length of reign	7 kings of Tanis = 130		7 kings of Tanis = 130	
Smendes	1069	1043	26	Smendes	26	Smendis	26
Amenemnisu	1043	1039	4				
Psusennes I	1039	991	48	Psusen(n)es	46	Psusennes	41
				Nephercheres	4	Nephercheres	4
Amenomope	991	984	7	Amenophthis	9	Amenophthis	9
Osorkon the Elder	984	978	6	Osochor	6	Osochor	6
Siamun	978	959	19	Psinaches	9	Psinaches	9
Psusennes II	959	945	14	Psusennes II	14	Psusennes	35
Total			124		114		130

Table **4.2.** Manetho's 22nd Dynasty (Manetho, 1940 edn) compared to the currently accepted version (Shaw and Nicholson 1995).

Accepted				Manetho (via Africanus)		Manetho (via Eusebius)	
Bubastite - 10 Kings	from (BCE)	to (BCE)	length of reign	9 kings of Bubastis 120		3 kings of Bubastis 49	
Shoshenk I	945	924	21	Sesonchis	21	Sesonchosis	21
Osorkon I	924	889	35	Osorthon	15	Osorthon	15
Shoshenk II	890	890	1	3 other kings	25		
Takelot I	889	874	15				
Osorkon II	874	850	24				
Takelot II	850	825	25	Takelothis	13	Takelothis	13
Shoshenk III	825	773	52	3 other kings	42		
Pimay	773	767	6				
Shoshenk V	767	730	37				
Osorkon IV	730	715	15				
Total			231		95		49

Sheshonq I features as the first king, which agrees with archaeological and other textual sources and with a reign length that agrees with the highest archaeologically attested one. His son Osorkon I is correctly listed as second, but with a reign length that is shorter than that seen in the archaeology by probably 20 years. After that, other than two vague mentions of '3 other kings' and

Takelot I (or II), the list is virtually useless, the Dynasty length being given either as 120 years in Africanus (although the total of the reign lengths is only 95, i.e., it is internally inconsistent) or 49 years (Eusebius), well short of the modern accepted length of 231 years.

This leads to an obvious question—why was Manetho apparently accurate for some periods and not for others? Part of the answer may be related to the quality of the primary material Manetho had to draw upon. It is not known what records he had, but it seems reasonable to expect that in some periods these may have been less abundant or accurate. This is perhaps especially so for periods where Egypt was ruled by more that one king, reigning from different and competing capitals. Unfortunately for this study, the 22nd to 25th Dynasties of Egypt represent one of the most complex periods, where at one stage no fewer than four dynasties ruled simultaneously (see Fig. 4.3). First, this may have been as difficult for Manetho to sort out as it is for us now, but secondly, there is a political issue involved too. Egypt always wanted to depict itself as a united land, bound together by the king. The imagery of this is all over temples and tombs, the king often being depicted as physically tying together the papyrus symbolising Lower Egypt with the lotus of Upper Egypt, using one of many dualistic symbologies. Dissent and schism were unacceptable, and often 'airbrushed' out of Egyptian history altogether (cf. Hatschepsut, the Amarna period, etc.). Whether Manetho simply did not have the information, or whether he deliberately manipulated it to present the 'politically correct' view of a single, unified Egypt throughout its history, or a combination of both, is uncertain. Either way, reading Manetho one is left with the impression that Egyptian history was neatly linear—king following king, dynasty following dynasty.

Manetho's king list must therefore be treated with great caution. It is only one of a series of tools that can be applied to the question of when Shoshenq I reigned. As with all the tools, it is not perfect and its application is open to debate and conjecture.

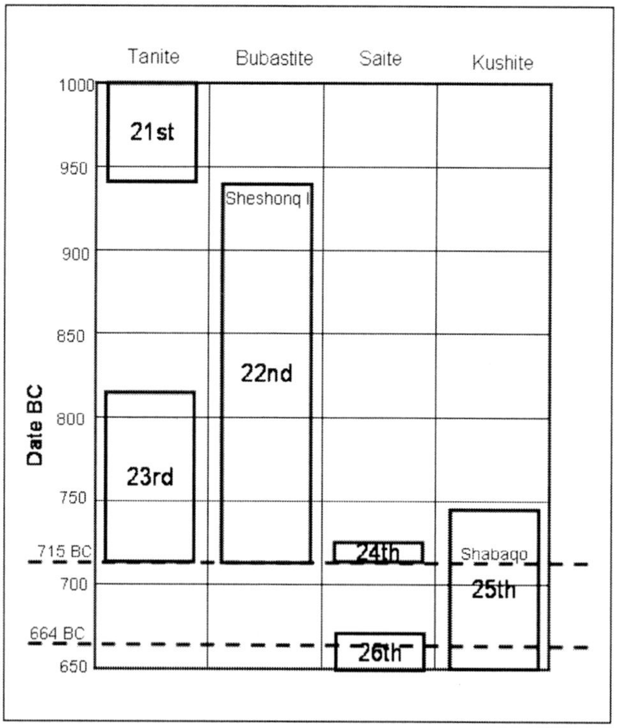

Figure 4.3. Conventional reconstruction of the simultaneous dynasties of the Third Intermediate Period (after Shaw and Nicholson 1995).

In addition to Manetho and the other king lists, there are other genealogies that are important and provide evidence for the chronology. These include lists of High Priests of Amun, Prophets of Amun, Viziers and other officials and chiefs. Two of these are of relevance to this study, although in a wider study all could and should be taken into account. The first of these is the Pasenhor genealogy (Kitchen 1986: 105-108), written on a dedicatory stelae in the Serapeum, near Memphis, and stretching for 15 generations of this family. The second is the genealogy of the Apis bulls, the main purpose of the Serapeum, which was their burial place (Kitchen 1986; Mariette 1882). The cult of the bulls was closely linked to the king, and only one animal was selected as the Apis bull at a time. On the death of this animal it was embalmed and buried in the underground vaults of the Serapeum, with the regnal year and king of its birth and death usually being recorded, along with its age (Kitchen 1986: Table 20). As such this also gives valuable chronological information.

Dating Sheshonq I

The complexity of the Egyptian TIP means that dating Sheshonq I is not a simple, straightforward matter. However, this complexity can be simplified given that the date of Sheshonq is the only thing of interest and the reconstruction of the TIP need only be carried out with respect to this aim. Figure 4.3 shows why this is so.

Table 4.3. Relationships between successive kings and highest regnal lengths (Kitchen 1986).

22nd Dynasty	Relationship	Accepted	Highest regnal length
Sheshonq I		21	21
Osorkon I	S	35	33
[Sheshonq II]			
Takelot I	S	15	14
Osorkon II	S	24	23
Takelot II	GS	25	25
Sheshonq III	?S	52	49
Pimay	S	6	6
Sheshonq V	S	37	38
Osorkon IV	S	15	—
25th Dynasty			
[Piankhy]			
Shabaqo	B	14	15
Shabitqo	N	12	3
Taharqa	HB	26	26
	total	282	253
Sheshonq I, yr1		945 BCE	917 BCE

S = Son; GS = Grandson; B = Brother; HB = Half-brother; N = Nephew

Due to the fact that several dynasties were ruling at once, the direct line from Sheshonq to the 'fixed' date of the sacking of Thebes at 664 BCE need only pass through the 22nd and 25th Dynasties. As long as the organization of the dynasties in Table 4.2 is correct and the knowledge of these two dynasties precise, then there is no need to worry about what is happening in the other four (21st, 23rd, 24th and 26th). Table 4.3 shows the succession of the kings in the 22nd and 25th Dynasties following Kitchen (1986: 450 and 453). As can be seen, the succession through the 22nd Dynasty is fairly smooth and attested, sons succeeding fathers. The only possible break is the accession of Sheshonq III, who usurped the throne from Osorkon, the son of Takelot II, but may have been another son of this king, so the succession here is indirect, but not really in any doubt.

Table 4.3 also shows the highest attested regnal length for the different kings. This can be regarded as a minimum reign length, since there is the possibility of longer reigns with the relevant evidence for it missing. However, in the top half of the table, within a year or so, there is not much dispute, with the highest regnal length being accepted as the length of the reign. The total length from the accession of Sheshonq I to the death of Sheshonq V is therefore 209 years minimum by highest regnal year, or 215 years in the accepted version where other factors are taken into account. The general length of this period can be supported by the use of a second genealogy, that of Pasenhor, a Memphite priest. The source is a dedicatory stelae in the Serapeum, set up by Pasenhor in the 37th year of Sheshonq V. In it he records his ancestry, which enters the royal line at Osorkon II and nine generations back reaches Sheshonq I. If one assumes that on average each generation is 18–20 years, then adds the 37 years that he states for Sheshonq V, this ends up as somewhere between 200 and 220 years approximately, supporting the general length of the royal chronology presented in Table 4.3 at least up to the death of Sheshonq V.

The first major problem is the reign of Osorkon IV, a 'powerless shadow-pharaoh' (Kitchen 1986: 372), where there are no regnal dates known (Kitchen 1986: 372 and 453). It is known that he and his predecessor Sheshonq V ruled simultaneously with Piankhy of the 25th Dynasty and the length of his reign can be calculated from two significant pins that occur in his reign. First, as Kitchen (1986: 372-76) and others have persuasively argued, he is probably the pharaoh 'So' of another biblical reference:

> Shalmaneser king of Assyria came up to attack Hoshea, who had been Shalmaneser's vassal and had paid him tribute. But the king of Assyria discovered that Hoshea was a traitor, for he had sent envoys to So king of Egypt, and he no longer paid tribute to the king of Assyria, as he had done year by year. Therefore Shalmaneser seized him and put him in prison. (2 Kings 17.3-4)

This is dated to 726/725 BCE on biblical grounds (Kitchen 1986: 372). The second reference is to 'Shilkanni', identified as Osorkon IV (p. 376), buying off the attacking Sargon II (722–705 BCE) with the gift of twelve horses. This is dated to 716 BCE by attaching it the Assyrian eponym chronology. Both of these pins will, for the sake of this exercise, be ignored, in favour of dealing solely with Egyptian internal dates.

Using Egyptian records the problem of how long Osorkon IV reigned can be overcome using the Apis bull genealogy. One bull (*Apis 24, 1*) is known to have been installed in the 37th year of Sheshonq V and died, probably after 16 years, in the 6th year of the 24th-Dynasty pharaoh Bakenranef (Kitchen 1986: Table 20). Before the burial vault was sealed, an epigraph of the 2nd year of the 25th-Dynasty pharaoh Shabaqo was written on the walls (pp. 378-79). Therefore, year 2 Shabaqo is also 16 years after the death of Sheshonq V. Shabaqo was the sole ruler of all of Egypt, so Osorkon IV, the last ruler of the 22nd Dynasty and the divided Egypt, must have reigned for about 15 years (p. 376).

The second significant problem is seen when examining the later 25th Dynasty. Once again there is one king, Shabitqo, for whom the highest regnal length is only 3 years, but he is thought to have reigned for more like 12 years (Kitchen 1986: 453). The best evidence for this comes again from pins to the Assyrian chronology, but since only internal evidence is being considered here, then again the Apis bull chronology can be used. *Apis 25, 2* was installed in 14th, and probably last, year of the reign of Shabaqo and died aged 16 years, probably in the 4th year of Taharqa (Kitchen 1986: Table 20). This would give the intervening Shabitqo a reign of 12 years, exactly what would be predicted from the external Assyrian pins. Thus Shabitqo, whilst only being attested for 3 years, must have reigned longer than this. His successor Taharqa came to an end in his rebellion against Ashurbanipal in 664 BCE, the 'fixed point' agreed by many associated chronologies.

Conclusion

Dating the accession to the throne of Sheshonq I is therefore a matter of adding up the reigns of the intervening kings and then applying this to the fixed point of 664 BCE. The order of the kings is fairly well established, and proceeds mostly in a sensible father-to-son pattern. The gap between the two dynasties can be bridged by reference to the extremely useful *Apis 24, 1*, which also gives a sensible reign length for the shadowy Osorkon IV. In the simplest form, the date of the accession of Sheshonq I can be taken as the total of the highest regnal dates of all the kings of the 22nd and 25th Dynasties. This would be 253 years, giving a date of 917 BCE. However, this is not the best fit to all the data, and ignores hard evidence from the Apis and Pasenhor genealogies. Using these, Osorkon IV's reign must be extended from the nonsensical zero to 15 years and Shabitqo from 3 to about 12 years. This lengthens the chronology by 24 years, and takes it back to 941 BCE. Thus from entirely internal Egyptian evidence, a minimum date of 941 BCE and a probable date in the mid-940s BCE must be postulated as the most likely date for the accession of Sheshonq I. This is remarkably close to the date derived from the use of external evidence (945 BCE), strengthening the assessment that the chronologies here are coherent and reasonable.

The actual date of the campaign of Sheshonq is based on the fact that the reliefs in the Bubastite Portal are unfinished and therefore the campaign and the reliefs are interpreted as falling late in his reign. Since he reigned for 21 years, year 20 is usually cited as the year of the campaigns, a date of 925 BCE. Speculation has been made that the campaigns represented in the Bubastite Portal may be just one of several campaigns made by Sheshonq I in the Levant, and attacks may have been made earlier in his campaign, leaving destruction layers in the Levantine cities perhaps dating to the 940s and 930s BCE. This is possible, but no evidence exists from Egyptian records for such attacks. While there are inconsistencies with tying the Bubastite Portal campaign in with the damage on the ground seen in archaeological excavation, from an entirely Egyptian point of view, it still remains the best fit.

As can be seen, the Egyptian chronology, like that of all other ancient chronologies, requires contradictory evidence to be weighed and assessed before a most likely chronology can be drawn up. It is not perfect, not free of error and not 'set in stone', but is subject to new findings and new interpretations. It does, however, stand up remarkably well to such findings, and the arguments now usually revolve around one or two years on the end of reigns and the affiliations of individual kings rather than wholesale changes in the length or nature of the chronology. As such we can be very confident of ascribing the accession of Sheshonq I to the middle of the 940s BCE.

References

Casperson, L.W. (1988) The Lunar Dates of Ramesses II. *JNES* 47: 181-84.

Censorinus (1983 edn) *Censorini De die natali liber ad Q. Caerellium : accedit anonymi cuiusdam epitoma disciplinarum (fragmentum Censorini)* (ed. N. Sallmann; Leipzig: Teubner).

Dodson, A. (2000) Towards a Minimum Chronology for the Third Intermediate Period. *Bulletin of the Egyptological Seminar* 14: 7-18.

Epigraphic Survey (1936–86) *Reliefs and Inscriptions at Karnak* (Chicago: Oriental Institute).

Hornung, E. (1965) Die Sonnenfinsternis nach dem Tode Psammetichs I. *Zeitschrift für Aegyptische Sprache* 92: 38-39.

Kitchen, K.A. (1986) *The Third Intermediate Period in Egypt* (Warminster: Aris & Phillips, 2nd edn).

—(1991) The Chronology of Ancient Egypt. *World Archaeology* 23: 201-208.

Mackey, D.F. (1993) The Sothic Star Theory of the Egyptian Calendar (unpublished thesis, University of Sydney).

Manetho (1940 edn) *Aegyptiaca* (trans. W.G. Waddell; London: Loeb Classical Library).

Mariette, A. (1882) *Le Sérapéum de Memphis* (Paris: F. Vieweg).

Parker, R.A. (1950) *The Calendars of Ancient Egypt* (Chicago: The University of Chicago Press).

—(1957) The Lunar Dates of Thutmose III and Ramesses II. *JNES* 16: 39-43.

—(1974) Ancient Egyptian Astronomy. *Philosophical Transactions of the Royal Society of London* 274: 51-65.

—(1976) The Sothic Dating of the 12th and 18th Dynasties. In *Studies in honour of George R Hughes: Studies in Ancient Oriental Civilisations 39*, edited by J.H. Johnson and E.F. Wente (Chicago: The University of Chicago Press): 177-89.

Redford, D. (1992) *Egypt, Canaan, and Israel in Ancient Times* (Princeton, NJ: Princeton University Press).

Rohl, D. (1995) *Test of Time* (London: Century).

Roux, G. (1992) *Ancient Iraq* (London: Penguin, 3rd edn).

Schott, E. (1989) *Die Namen der Pharaonen* (Göttingen: Weender Druckerei).

Shaw, I., and P.T. Nicholson (1995) *British Museum Dictionary of Ancient Egypt* (London: British Museum Press).

II.
SOME METHODOLOGICAL ISSUES

5 Improving the Resolution of Radiocarbon Dating by Statistical Analysis

Christopher Bronk Ramsey

Abstract

Radiocarbon dating of individual samples only yields limited chronological precision (typically of the order of 150–200 years for 95% confidence). This is in large part due to the complex nature of the calibration curve. Only by using large numbers of radiocarbon determinations together can we hope to resolve chronological issues at the sub-century level. Interpretation of such datasets is very difficult to do accurately by eye and for this reason statistical methods are needed. The methods most often employed are those of Bayesian analysis. Such methods do indeed allow us to improve our precision beyond that which is possible for single age determinations by radiocarbon but, critically, they also allow us to see the limitations in our data. In cases where statistical analysis shows that the radiocarbon measurements cannot resolve the chronological issues we need to accept that we must rely on other forms of archaeological information and interpretation.

Introduction

The conference at Yarnton was very closely focussed on specific chronological issues in the Iron Age of the Levant. These issues are of critical importance to the understanding of the interrelationship of the polities of the region and would be of academic interest in any other region under archaeological investigation. However, in this case the arguments are given even more prominence because of the implications for our interpretation of the nature of King Solomon's political impact. The main debate is most clearly seen in the differing interpretations put forward for Tel Rehov (Chapters 13–17, this volume) but also bring in almost all of the other research presented in this volume. From the exchanges published in the journal *Science* on this topic (Bruins, van der Plicht, and Mazar 2003; Finkelstein and Piasetzky 2003; Bruins and van der Plicht 2003), it can be seen that the chronological arguments amount to about a hundred years at most. From the historical point of view such a period of time is very significant, being of the order of three generations, but from the point of view of radiocarbon dating, where a single calibrated date rarely gives a range (95% probability) of less than 100–200 years, this is too short a time interval to resolve easily. Largely for this reason, radiocarbon has often been ignored when confronting issues of this kind. However, where other forms of scholarship fail to produce a consensus it clearly makes sense to try to use scientific dating techniques to inform the argument. We do, however, still have the problem that we are at the limit of what the method can achieve and so we have to use all of the tools at our disposal to pool the information from various sources.

The Problem

Given that any single measurement is usually unable to resolve issues at the level of one hundred years or less it is necessary to use many measurements made on samples from different periods to try to uncover the underlying chronology. In doing so we are essentially using two main datasets: the radiocarbon measurements on known-age, dendro-chronologically dated wood which make up the radiocarbon calibration curve (Reimer *et al.* 2004; Stuiver *et al.* 1998), and the measurements on the material from the contexts of interest. We are then using these datasets to try to determine both the true dates of the samples we have measured and also the dates of key changes in a particular site, or region, which we assume to be related in some way to the samples measured. Thus we typically have tens to hundreds of measurements on our samples being used to estimate a slightly larger number of unknown dates with some prior information about their relationship—a multivariate statistical problem of a very high order.

In order to cope with this problem, it is normally broken down into two stages. The first stage is calibration of each of the individual dates onto the calendar timescale—this is a relatively simple operation and gives a probability density function (PDF) for the true age of each sample $L_i(t_i)$. In the nomenclature generally used in such analyses, this PDF is referred to as the 'likelihood' that a particular calendar date is associated with the radiocarbon measurement or 'observation' made on the sample. An example calibration is shown in Figure 5.1. This process is common to almost all radiocarbon calibration programs and is almost universally applied. From this 'likelihood' distribution it is possible to derive a range of most likely dates that encompass 95% of the area of the PDF. These are the ranges normally calculated as part of the calibration.

It should be emphasised that in converting a radiocarbon date to a calendar date we often end up with multimodal distributions that are very far from being Normal. It is also the case that radiocarbon dates from a representative selection of dated material (e.g. a whole sequence of tree rings) are not evenly distributed in radiocarbon age. It is therefore very difficult to interpret distributions of raw uncalibrated dates in a robust way since doing so essentially ignores the complexity of the calibration dataset.

After this calibration stage we then have many individual probability distributions and we have to use these to infer information about the chronology of a site or region, and this is where the difficulties often arise. Up to this stage we can treat each of the age determinations as being essentially independent. At some level this is an approximation since they are all based on the same calibration dataset and they may share some measurement uncertainty from the radiocarbon laboratory. However, such effects are usually of minor significance since the uncertainties in the measurements on unknown samples are usually much larger than those of the calibration curve, the numbers of measurements are usually lower. Also important is the fact that within the laboratory the uncertainty quoted on the unknown sample usually only has a very small systematic component from shared measurements on standards. This is not to say that samples cannot have systematic biases due to environmental effects and/or chemical pre-treatment deficiencies. This is an important issue to which we will return later.

The problem we have, then, is how to synthesise the observations made on the individual dated samples with our understanding of the chronology we wish to study.

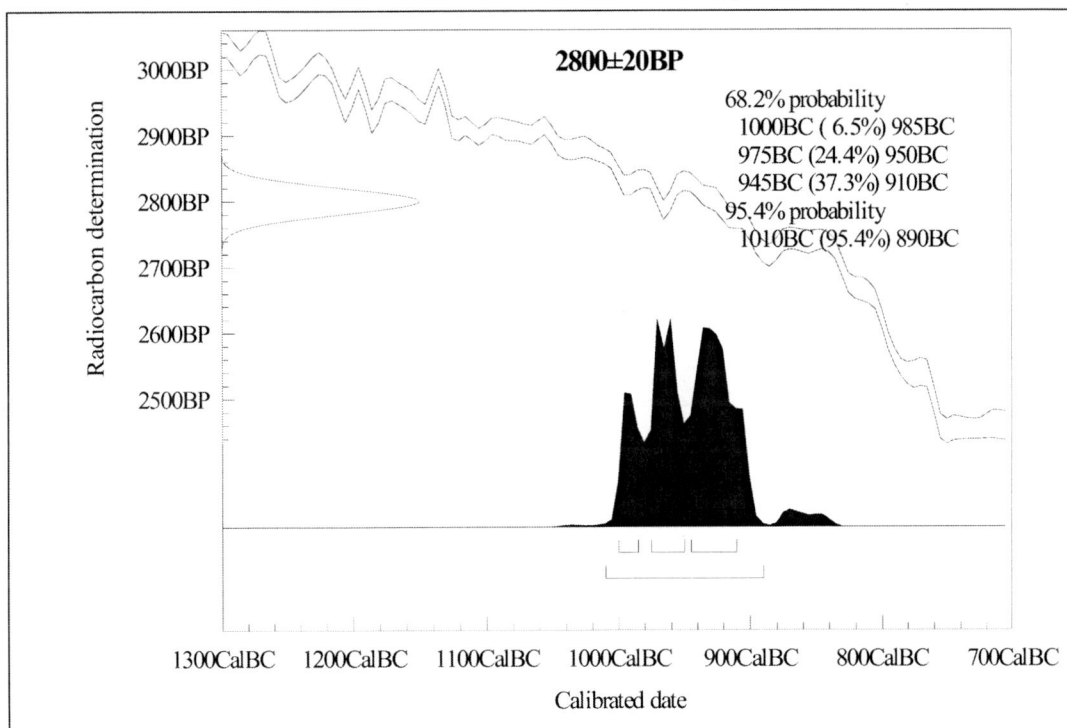

Figure 5.1. This shows a typical radiocarbon calibration plot showing the probability density function (PDF) associated with the date and the ranges calculated from it. The Gaussian curve on the left shows the likelihood of particular radiocarbon concentrations, and the calibration curve can be seen going from top left to bottom right.

Introducing Statistical Methods

To progress from single observations to general chronological conclusions we need to have some model of the underlying events. This is true whether we use a statistical methodology or try to use our instincts to interpret the results by eye. There are three main reasons for using statistical methods rather than relying on interpretation by eye:

- Evaluating multivariate data with >10 degrees of freedom is very difficult to do by eye.
- Statistical analysis requires us to make explicit our underlying model of the chronological processes rather than taking it for granted and leaving it implicit.
- Such analysis is able to determine the uncertainty in any conclusions drawn from the data.

Most people are familiar with model-based statistical methods, even if they are not often described in this way. An obvious example is the Normal distribution and it is worth considering how we might use such a model in a chronological context. Our chronological model would be the events of interest clustered around a mean date μ with a standard deviation of σ. Given the measurements of the dates of events for which we have measurements $t_1, t_2 \dots t_n$ we can use classical statistics to estimate μ and σ. This sort of model is so useful that the statistics for it are in almost every textbook on statistics. However, it is not a very useful model in the chronological context since events are rarely distributed in this way.

The model that is most often used in archaeological chronology is based on the notion of uniform phases of activity. In this, if we have a series of related events $t_1, t_2 \ldots t_n$, we assume that these are all drawn from a phase that had a particular start and end date, which we will term b_{start} and b_{end}. So we can write down that:

$$b_{start} < t_1, t_2 \ldots t_n < b_{end}$$

(1)

We also assume that within the phase the probability of any of the events occurring is uniform and that we have no other information about b_{start} and b_{end}. From these two postulates we can see that the probability per unit time of any particular value of t_i is equal to:

$$1/(b_{end} - b_{start}) \quad \text{for } b_{start} < t_i < b_{end}$$

$$0 \qquad\qquad \text{for } t_i < b_{start} \text{ or } b_{end} < t_i$$

(2)

This part of the description of the events within a phase is independent of the actual measurements of sample age. In Bayesian statistics this model is referred to as the 'prior'. In addition to this we do also have the information ('likelihoods') from the measurements made on $t_1, t_2 \ldots t_n$, and so we need to combine these with 'priors' of the model to draw our conclusions. Bayes theorem essentially says that we do this by multiplication. If we consider all possible combinations of $b_{start}, t_1, t_2 \ldots t_n, b_{end}$ which are consistent with the above constraints (1) the overall probability of any particular combination is proportional to:

$$1/(b_{end} - b_{start})^n \times \prod_{i=1,n} L_i(t_i)$$

(3)

Since the number of possible combinations scales as $(b_{end} - b_{start})^n$, this actually gives us an equal likelihood of any particular span (without the information from the actual measurements) and therefore the model is suitably neutral.

As with the Normal distribution model, we are estimating two parameters, b_{end} and b_{start}, for which we have no direct measurements and we are also refining our estimates for each of the unknown sample ages t_i. This model was first devised by Buck, Litton, and Smith (1992) and is implemented in OxCal (Bronk Ramsey 1995, 2001; Bronk Ramsey, van der Plicht, and Weninger 2001), BCal (Buck, Christen, and James 1999) and Datelab (Nicholls and Jones 2001) in essentially the same form. There are some minor additional components to consider as the models are scaled up to multiple phases (see, e.g., Bronk Ramsey 2001) but the model essentially remains rather simple.

For more mathematical detail see the references above and also Buck and Millard (2004).

Application of Statistical Methods

Of course, in reality, as with classical statistical methods, the problem in applying a chronological model to a real situation is one of trying to relate the parameters of the model to the underlying events. It must be stressed from the outset that any application of such a model is in itself an interpretation of the data. No two practitioners are likely to apply the model in the same way to the same data. This is not a weakness in the methodology it is simply that in order to go from multiple individual observations to a summary of the data it is necessary to specify the way in which the events are related. As stated above, one of the important reasons for using such methods is that it forces one to make these relationships clear.

One weakness that is present in the model presented above, however, is that many archaeological samples do not necessarily fit into the uniform phase model described above. It is instructive to take the example of Tel Reḥov discussed in several papers in this volume (see Chapters 13–15). If a simple phase model is used that assumes that all of the material from each phase is uniformly distributed throughout that phase, then it turns out that a Bayesian analysis (see later in this paper) clearly shows up a bimodal distribution permitting either of the two interpretations of the data originally put forward by Bruins, van der Plicht, and Mazar (2003) and Finkelstein and Piasetzki (2003). However, since the material dated in fact comes largely from destruction layers it makes sense to treat the material as coming from later in each phase—and if this is allowed for it tends to favour an earlier chronology (see Bruins *et al.* [Chapter 15, this volume]). It is likely that were datable material available from a more continuous record this would help to resolve the chronology. You can see from these arguments that the statistical analysis does get us further forward because:

- It allows us to see that the data are probably insufficient to resolve the issues with any degree of certainty.
- We are made aware that the understanding of the site taphonomy is critical. We ask: How did the material in the destruction layers get there?
- A possible sampling strategy is suggested in that if material from occupation layers were available, it would be likely to yield less ambiguous results.

The latter point is particularly important. It is possible to simulate the effects of having samples at particular points in a stratigraphic sequence with an assumed chronology to see how the precision of any analysis would be affected by such further information.

To illustrate this we can perform a simple simulation with the Tel Reḥov data in mind. We will take just three phases:

- Phase VI (stratum VI in the Bruins, van der Plicht, and Mazar 2003 paper)
- Phase V occupation
- Phase V destruction (accumulation of material deposited during this destruction—perhaps up to 10 years for grains)

We then have four phase boundaries:

- Start of VI
- VI to V
- Start of collection of destruction layer material
- End of V

For the purposes of this simulation we will make the following assumptions: a) there is only datable material from Phase VI and from the Phase V destruction level (but not from the Phase V occupation); b) the date of the material from the Phase V destruction level is 910-900 BCE; c) Phase VI is dated by material from a decade about either 975 BCE or 925 BCE. These assumptions broadly reflect the nature of the evidence and discussion in Bruins, van der Plicht, and Mazar (2003) and Finkelstein and Piasetski (2003). In the analysis, we assume that for the levels of stratum VI and the destruction layer of V we have 10 normal precision Accelerator Mass Spectrometry (AMS) dates (with an uncertainty of ± 30 ^{14}C BP) and in this case the IntCal98 (Stuiver *et al.* 1998) calibration curve has been used as it was for the original calibrations. You can see the results of the analysis for the data of the end of stratum VI (the start of the occupation of level V) in Figure 5.2. What is clear from this analysis is that the controversy in the results of the Tel Reḥov dating is predictable from the simulation—radiocarbon evidence for this part of the chronology does not readily distinguish between the two postulated dates.

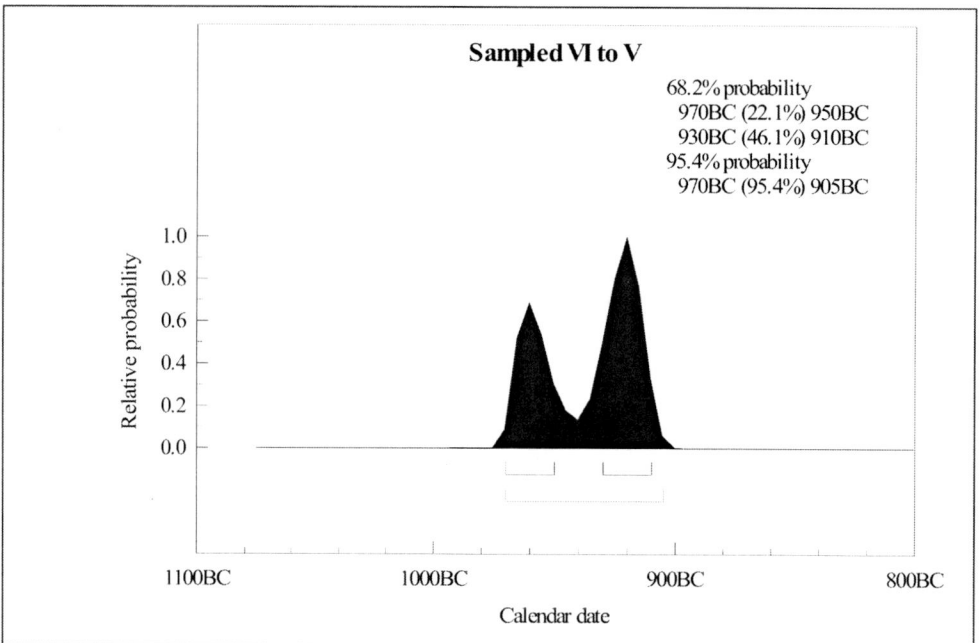

Figure 5.2. These figures show the result of simulating the dating of the level VI and the destruction level of phase V for Tel Reḥov in the case (a) where the true date of stratum VI is about 975 BCE and (b) in the case where the true date is about 925 BCE.

Since the presentation of the original radiocarbon data from Tel Rehov (Bruins, van der Plicht, and Mazar 2003), more work has been done on the material from the site. In particular this has given very high precision measurements on some of the key contexts and also allows us to put together a much more comprehensive model than the simple three phase one outlined above. This has produced a more robust dataset which does indeed indicate an early chronology as originally postulated (Bruins *et al.* [Chapter 15, this volume]), and although there is still some bimodality in the results, it is hard to argue from this data that the date for the transition from Iron Age IB to IIA at this site is 920 BCE or later (although the possibility does remain at a low probability).

Limitations of Statistical Methods

The most obvious limitation is that the models available are often not perfectly matched to our understanding of the underlying data (see above). However, this is probably not the most significant limitation. More important is that any statistical methods are only as strong as the underlying data and this is where the most valid criticism can be found for their use. There are methods available for testing the internal consistency of the data (see, e.g., Bronk Ramsey 1995, 2001; Christen 1994) but this is not the only issue. Indeed, in many of the cases presented in this volume, the internal consistency of the results is excellent. More important is the possible presence of some systematic effects in the radiocarbon concentration, which are either not taken into account in the expression of the errors, or are in some way systematic, making the assumption of independence of the individual dates invalid. Fortunately it turns out that in the case of calibrated radiocarbon dates entered in a model of this kind, most of the precision comes from the steepest parts of the calibration curve. The net effect of this is that the chronological results are usually relatively insensitive to small biases in the radiocarbon concentration (assuming these are less than the scale of the wiggles in the radiocarbon calibration curve—ca. 30 ^{14}C years; see Bronk Ramsey, van der Plicht, and Weninger 2001).

We can use an analogy here—the fact that the radiocarbon concentration is only imperfectly known and has non-monotonic variations means that we have a blurred image of the chronologies we study with radiocarbon. The statistical methods used in their analysis (largely similar to those used by High Energy Physicists in analysing the results of particle physics experiments) are potentially very powerful in refocusing and removing the distortion from this image. However, such analysis is also capable of magnifying any imperfections in our data, and in our understanding of our data. For this reason any such analysis should always be treated as an interpretation open to later re-evaluation and re-interpretation as better evidence comes to light.

An important guard against any such shortcomings is to test how sensitive the results are to small changes in the model or in the data included in the analysis. This sort of sensitivity analysis can tell you, for example, whether a particular result is critically dependent on a very small number of high precision measurements or whether it stands up if only the samples from the most secure contexts are included in the analysis (see, e.g., Bronk Ramsey, Manning, and Galimberti 2004, and some examples in Bruins *et al.* [Chapter 15, this volume]).

Conclusions

Statistical analysis becomes essential when trying to resolve high resolution chronological issues with radiocarbon dating. The complex nature of the calibration curve means that intuitive fitting is extremely difficult to achieve.

The strength of such mathematical analysis lies not only in the conclusions that it allows us to draw from complex data but also in the demonstration of what we cannot resolve given the available information. In the case of Tel Reḥov, for example, mathematical analysis shows that the data was indeed ambiguous in terms of calibration as the debates between various contributors to this volume suggest. Bayesian modelling, however, based on detailed stratigraphic information with many coherent radiocarbon results, is capable of improving the resolution of some of the inherent difficulties.

References

Bronk Ramsey, C. (1995) Radiocarbon Calibration and Analysis of Stratigraphy: The OxCal Program. *Radiocarbon* 37(2): 425-30.

—(2001) Development of the Radiocarbon Program OxCal. *Radiocarbon* 43(2A): 355-63.

Bronk Ramsey, C., S.W. Manning, and M. Galimberti (2004) Dating the Volcanic Eruption at Thera. *Radiocarbon* 46(1): 325-44.

Bronk Ramsey, C., J. van der Plicht, and B. Weninger (2001) 'Wiggle Matching' Radiocarbon Dates. *Radiocarbon* 43(2A): 381-89.

Bruins, H.J., and J. van der Plicht (2003) Response to Comment on '[14]C Dates from Tel Reḥov: Iron-Age Chronology, Pharaohs, and Hebrew Kings'. *Science* 302: 568c.

Bruins, H.J., J. van der Plicht, and A. Mazar (2003) [14]C Dates from Tel Reḥov: Iron-Age Chronology, Pharaohs, and Hebrew Kings. *Science* 300: 315-18.

Buck, C.E., J. Andres Christen, and G.N. James (1999) An online Bayesian Radiocarbon Calibration Tool. *Internet Archaeology* 7: <http://intarch.ac.uk/journal/issue7/buck/index.html>.

Buck, C.E., C.D. Litton, and A.F.M. Smith (1992) Calibration of Radiocarbon Results Pertaining to Related Archaeological Events. *Journal of Archaeological Science* 19: 497-512.

Buck, C.E., and A.R. Millard (eds.) (2004) *Tools for Constructing Chronologies* (London: Springer Verlag).

Christen, J. (1994) Summarizing a set of Radiocarbon Determinations: a Robust Approach. *Applied Statistics* 43: 489-503.

Finkelstein, I., and E. Piasetzki (2003) Comment on '[14]C Dates from Tel Reḥov: Iron-Age Chronology, Pharaohs, and Hebrew Kings'. *Science* 302: 568b.

Nicholls, G.K., and M. Jones (2001) Radiocarbon Dating with Temporal Order Constraints. *Journal of the Royal Statistical Society, Series C* 50(4): 503-21.

Reimer, P.J., *et al.* IntCal04 Terrestrial Radiocarbon Age Calibration, 0-26 cal kyr BP (2004) *Radiocarbon* 46: 1029-58.

Stuiver M., *et al.* (1998) INTCAL98 Radiocarbon Age Calibration, 24000-0 cal BP. *Radiocarbon* 40(3): 1041-83.

6 The Early Iron Age Dating Project

Introduction, methodology, progress report and an update on the Tel Dor radiometric dates*

Ilan Sharon, Ayelet Gilboa, Elisabetta Boaretto, and A.J. Timothy Jull

Abstract

The Iron Age Dating Project was initiated four years ago in order to suggest a radiometric way out of the apparent stalemate reached in the debate over early Iron Age chronology in Israel. It is based on the conviction that a question of such a tight resolution requires an extensive database, carefully selected from many sites and dated by different methods and different laboratories. This is the only means by which inevitable archaeological and analytical errors may be identified and eliminated. The data set, about 100 samples from 21 sites in Israel, producing more than 400 individual measurements, requires explicit and versatile methods for the statistical modeling of the dates. This paper introduces the archaeological, analytical and statistical rationale of the project, alongside partial results. In addition, we present new dates from Tel Dor, the site that produced the first radiometric sequence empirically supporting the low chronology. These new dates, measured by different laboratories, corroborate the previous conclusions regarding Tel Dor. They again support the low chronology, as do the preliminary results of the Iron Age Dating Project.

Introduction

In 1996, two of us (A.G. and I.S.) sent ten samples from the early Iron Age sequence at Tel Dor to be dated by the Radiocarbon Dating Laboratory, Weizmann Institute of Science, Rehovot, then headed by Israel Carmi. Shortly afterwards Israel Finkelstein's first paper advocating a 'low chronology' for the Iron Age in Israel (1996) was published. The Dor dates turned out to be low, even somewhat lower than Finkelstein's suggested chronology. This was totally unexpected and in fact somewhat startling, but we decided not to trouble our minds, and sent eleven more samples to the Radiocarbon Dating Laboratory at Rehovot and one to Beta Analytic inc., Miami, FL. The results were the same. These dates (Gilboa and Sharon 2001; Sharon 2001; the stratigraphy and ceramic composition of the Dor sequence is presented in Gilboa and Sharon 2003) were the first empirical evidence demonstrating that the low chronology cannot be simply brushed away.

Still, we were skeptical. Such a chronological shift, with its tremendous implications, cannot be based on 22 dates from a single site. Rather than publish these results and be done, three of us (I.S., A.G., E.B.) proposed a much wider study. It was our conviction that in order to construct a

---

*   RT = conventional radiocarbon date; RTT = AMS date.

statistically viable data-base we would have to consider *hundreds* of dates from meaningful contexts in many sites, measured by different labs and methods. A general solution to the chronological problem meant that rather than dating individual contexts, or (supposed) historical events, what we needed was to date the (beginning and end of) chronological *horizons*. Such horizons would first need to be defined, chiefly by ceramic considerations. Furthermore, to overcome the menacing *chaine* of pitfalls—problems of archaeological contexts, ceramic seriation, sample preservation, laboratory procedures and statistical modeling—a concerted effort by a multidisciplinary team would be needed.

We approached all the excavators who, to our knowledge, possessed organics from such contexts as are described above. With the remarkably unstinting collaboration of all of them we collected more than 100 samples from 21 sites in Israel, from which more than 400 measurements have been produced, most of them already available. Other aspects, mainly bearing on characterization of the raw material for analysis, still await their completion. All the samples were dated at the Radiocarbon Dating Laboratory at Rehovot, and 22 were double-checked at the Arizona Accelerator Mass Spectrometry (AMS) Laboratory, Tucson. Calibration of dates employs the INTCAL98 radiocarbon calibration curve (Stuiver *et al.*, 1998).

The initially projected length of the project was four years, and the cost of some 400 radiocarbon determinations considerable. The initial Israel Science Foundation grant we were awarded for this purpose covered, however, only two years and half of the costs. It is only recently that additional funding has been obtained that will enable us to complete the project as planned.

A laboratory intercomparison based on 22 of the samples (Boaretto *et al.* 2005) has shown that there are no systematic differences between the participating laboratories and methods. This intercomparison assures the accuracy of the 400 radiocarbon dates produced.

Meanwhile, there have been several developments in ^{14}C dating on the Levantine Iron Age scene. Chiefly, the publication of another substantial database—32 dates from Tel Reḥov, measured at the Centre for Isotope Research, University of Groningen—purported to support the 'high' chronology, and refute the 'low' one (Bruins, van der Plicht, and Mazar 2003). The discrepancy between the Dor data set and that of Reḥov was explained by the Reḥov team by claiming that in the 1990s the Rehovot lab was experiencing difficulties, which caused its dates to be consistently too low (Mazar 2004: 31-34). Although these allegations were not supported by any explicit reasoning, we re-measured the 'suspect' Dor sequence, by extended replication and intercomparison.

The results of these investigations are presented here, together with the methodologies used to analyze the partial data sets we have examined so far and by which we propose to investigate the full data set once all the dates are measured, and once the checks that are still pending are completed. The focus of this paper is on methodology. But while the case studies presented here are shown mainly for the purpose of illustrating the methods used, and the results should be considered provisional, the direction in which they are all pointing is clear.

Archaeological Considerations

As a result of his own set of radiocarbon dates, A. Mazar recently proposed what he terms the 'extended conventional chronology' (e.g. Bruins, van der Plicht, and Mazar 2003: 318; Mazar 2004: 30-31). This 'extension' incorporates most of the 10th and 9th centuries BCE within Iron IIA. This, in itself, is quite a generous concession towards the low chronology, which has somehow passed practically unnoticed. Thus, at least one consensus (or near consensus) seems to have formed in the last two years: that the ceramic culture termed in Israel Iron Age IIA encompasses at least the first 70 years or so of the 9th century BCE. The debate, therefore, centers on the *beginning* of the sequence and may be narrowed down to two questions:

1. How do we *define*, stratigraphically and artifactually, the transition between the cultural entities we term Iron Age I and II in many different sites covering a large geographical area? What transition are we actually after? Do we seek to date the late Iron I destructions (such as Megiddo VIA)? Or the transition between the Iron Age I and the Iron Age II *ceramic* assemblages? (Does this latter transition bear any meaning at all for issues of state formation, emerging identities, etc.?) Or do we aim at dating the transition from non-monumental to monumental stages at sites attributable to Israelite entities? All these are not necessarily co-terminus nor contemporaneous.
2. How do we date those transitions?

Let us start where we in fact did—at Tel Dor, in E. Stern's excavations. The phases of interest in the very detailed early Iron Age typo-stratigraphic sequence we defined there (Gilboa and Sharon 2003) are the last three horizons, termed by us 'Ir1b', transitional 'Ir1|2' and 'Ir2a'.

The Ir1b horizon at Dor can easily be correlated by its 'local' ceramic components to the latest Iron I contexts in sites along the northern coast, in the 'Akko plain, in the western Jezreel valley and in Galilee. These are, for example, Sarepta E2 (in Trench Y), Tyre XIII, Tell Keisan (9a and part of b), Megiddo VIA, Yoqne'am XVII, 'En Hagit, and Kinneret V. As in other regions of the Levant at this period, most of the ceramic inventories in these regions are very localized. Correlation to regions farther afield may be offered based on two components which transcend regional boundaries: decorated Phoenician wares and Cypro-Geometric imports (henceforward CG). This is the horizon in which Phoenician Bichrome ware appears, gradually evolving from earlier decorated types, and in which the first CG wares are attested, of early to mid-CG I types. Thus, a correlation is established with contexts such as Tell Qasile X, and, of course, with the first-to-middle part of CG I in Cyprus (the common terminology for this horizon, as in Mazar 1990: Table 6, is Iron Age IB).

The next horizon is what we termed the transitional Ir1|2 horizon. In terms of the local pottery it does indeed differ from the previous horizon, but not drastically. Some types disappear, some are newly introduced and some changes are traceable only quantitatively. Phoenician Bichrome pottery is still present, but its repertoire has changed. Likewise, the local assemblage, including decorated Phoenician wares, differs—but again only slightly—from that of the following Ir2a horizon.

So why, one may ask, introduce here a new terminology? Why not cluster these contexts with either the preceding Ir1b or the subsequent Ir2a? The first reason was explicated above. They are not *really* like either previous or subsequent horizons—and neither are they 'more like Iron Age I' or vice versa. At a deeper theoretical level the question is how ceramic assemblages (and material culture in general) change and how such changes are modeled in the periodization schemes we use (granted that for didactic and heuristic reasons it is often expedient to agglomerate assemblages at different sites into coarse categories). But does such a 'punctuative' view of material culture faithfully reflect material culture change? The theory that Mazar *et al.* espouse is that ca. 980 BCE 'Israelite' material culture (or at least ceramic tradition) undergoes a sudden revolutionary change (between the hardly excavated Stratum VII and Stratum VI at Reḥov)—and thereafter the Iron Age IIA tradition stays virtually unchanged for about 150 years (represented by Strata VI–V–IV at Reḥov) before undergoing another abrupt change into Iron Age IIB. The alternative view is the 'durative' one, which assumes that, except in rare 'traumatic' cases, material change is continuous and gradual, which is specifically true for ceramics. A seriative periodization scheme like the one introduced for Dor and Phoenicia enhances such a view of material change. Zarzecki-Peleg (Chapter 22, this volume) introduces a similar scheme (and similar terminology) for the Iron Age IIA–B sequence. Under such a view, a radical difference between the assemblage of one stratum and the next implies either a gap or a long-lived stratum only the end of which is represented in the ceramic assemblage. Thus, three successive strata which are nearly identical ceramically, as at Reḥov, are better explained as occupying a short rather than extended range of time.

That the period we designate 'Ir1|2' is not an insubstantial temporal entity is evident from its Cypriot component. At Dor, Cypriot pottery of this horizon is typologically later than that of the previous levels, but still earlier than that of the next. It corresponds to types occurring in the second part of CG I in Cyprus (CG IB), and to types often attributed to CG II (see Gilboa 1999: Figs. 4–6). These two typological groups cannot really be differentiated temporally even in Cyprus (e.g. Coldstream 1999). They are clustered here into one entity, termed CG IB/II. There are no CG III types in the Ir1|2 horizon and no Black-on-Red (BoR). How long a time-span must be allowed for the CG IB–II development is at the moment unclear. The Cypriot vista of this horizon means that the Ir1|2 horizon is earlier than assemblages termed elsewhere in Israel 'early Iron IIA', since these are usually accompanied by CG III imports, most commonly BoR. Indeed, at Dor too, the next horizon, that of Ir2a (equaling Iron IIA), is the one which bears the first CG III ceramics. Recently, A. Mazar (2004: 30) suggested that the Ir1|2 horizon at Dor parallels Stratum VI at Tel Reḥov, which he designated Iron IIA. To evaluate this suggestion it is crucial to know when the first CG III imports are attested at Reḥov. If they already occur in Stratum VI then this stratum must be later than our transitional horizon.

When searching for this horizon at other Phoenician sites the clearest comparable horizon may be identified at Tyre. There, Stratum XIII belongs to Ir1b, signifying the beginning of the Phoenician Bichrome group, containing early CG I imports, and other ceramic components comparable to this horizon at Dor. Then come Strata XII–X (for which the designation strata is somewhat of an overstatement). They comprise a succession of fills, usually not segregated by floors, relating, in many cases, to the same sets of walls. The ceramic repertoire evolves slowly, but changes are evident in the Phoenician Bichrome assemblage, and chiefly in the vista of Cypriot ceramics. These are typologically later than the early CG I horizon attested in Stratum XIII, but still earlier than CG III. Like at Dor, they find parallels in CG IB/II contexts in Cyprus. The CG III horizon at Tyre is first clearly attested in Stratum IX. Other comparable contexts in Phoenicia are those at Sarepta (Strata E1 and possibly D2 in Trench Y), Tell Keisan (Stratum 8c and possibly 8b), and Tel Mevorakh (Stratum VIII) (see discussions in Gilboa and Sharon 2003).

Three sites outside Phoenicia are pertinent to this discussion. At Yoqne'am, in the western Jezreel valley, the last Iron I entity (our Ir1b) is Stratum XVII, terminating in a destruction. Subsequently, the first occupation to have produced some evidence of monumental constructions is Stratum XIV, an Iron IIA horizon, including BoR. But in between the two, two intermediate levels were recognized stratigraphically: the first, Stratum XVI, is termed by Zarzecki-Peleg 'early Iron IIA'. The ceramic assemblage in it is not quite like those preceding or succeeding it. On the one hand, the pottery reveals marked continuity with Stratum XVII, but on the other, the first traces of Iron IIA phenomena, including red slip, are in evidence. Stratum XVI is comparable to our 'Ir1|2', namely, a 'post-Megiddo VIA' horizon occupation, but pre-BoR. This level, in turn, is followed by Stratum XV, whose ceramic horizon is very similar to that of the subsequent XIV, including, *inter alia*, red-slipped vessels and BoR. This stratum equals the Phoenician Ir2a as defined by us. It represents an unfortified village, preceding the Stratum XIV monumental constructions (for Yoqne'am, see Zarzecki-Peleg 2005a, 2005b; Chapter 22, this volume). The Yoqne'am sequence is an excellent case study for the questions we presented above: Where does the transition between the Iron Age I and Iron Age II occur there? After the destruction of the last 'clear Iron Age I' stratum (XVII)? After Stratum XVI, when the ceramic assemblage is finally of 'real' Iron II character? Or after Stratum XV, when the fortifications are built?

At Tell el-Hamma in the Beth She'an valley, within the detailed Iron Age sequence, the three best-defined strata are those which were violently destroyed, and thus preserved extensive ceramic assemblages. Two of these are relevant here. The earliest one is best defined as a late Iron I assemblage, comparable to our Ir1b horizon—to contexts such as Yoqne'am XVII and the like; it terminates in a severe conflagration. The second destroyed stratum already boasts a typical Iron IIA assemblage, with, for example, abundant red slip and BoR. In between these two, however, is a clearly defined architectural phase. As this intermediate phase did not suffer destruction, its ceramic assemblage is more difficult to define, but according to the excavators (J. Cahill, personal communication) it probably fits our transitional horizon. (The third destruction at Tell el-Hamma is later than our scope here; for the sequence and its ceramics, see Cahill, in press.)

At Megiddo, the Stratum VIA destruction bears all the hallmarks of our Ir1b (see Gilboa and Sharon 2003: 55-57). According to the Oriental Institute stratigraphic sequence, the next stratum is VB. This phase is unfortified and non-monumental, but apparently quite long-lived. The ceramic assemblage, unfortunately, is not yet really defined. In the Tel Aviv Megiddo III volume (Finkelstein, Zimhoni, and Kafri 2000) an effort was made to extract from the American reports those loci that best represent this stratum, mainly those sealed under the Palace 1723 courtyard. The pottery from these loci can be defined as Iron Age IIA. It is very similar to the subsequent VA–IVB assemblage, including few BoR pieces and at least one Cypriot Bichrome III bowl, and is drastically different from the VIA assemblage. However, as recently suggested by Zarzecki-Peleg (personal communication, to be presented in her PhD dissertation), it is not at all certain that the courtyard surfaces recorded by the Chicago excavators are the earliest surfaces associated with Palace 1723. They may actually be a later addition to it, and thus the pottery sealed under them may well belong to VA–IVB and not to VB. The subsequent, monumental VA–IVB Stratum is a clear Iron IIA horizon, with abundant BoR.

Based both on stratigraphic and typological considerations some of the Megiddo excavators postulated a hiatus in occupation after the destruction of Stratum VIA (see references in Gilboa and Sharon 2003: 57). This suggestion is difficult to assess. If indeed the VB assemblage turns out to be an Iron IIA one, then certainly this suggestion is warranted, and then this gap probably parallels the horizon we term transitional Iron I|II. Another possibility (Zarzecki-Peleg, personal communication, to be presented in her PhD dissertation) is that—at least in Yadin's excavation areas—a third sub-phase, VC, exists, and covers this transitional horizon.

Additional information regarding this transitional period may be extracted from Area K of the Tel Aviv expedition (Finkelstein, Zimhoni, and Kafri 2000; Lehmann, Killebrew, and Gadot 2000). After the destruction of level K-4, which equals VIA, a meager resettlement is attested, K-3, subdivided into three stages. The first, K-3b, is represented mainly by floors and is devoid of walls, at least in the excavated area. The second, K-3a2, exhibits some modest constructions and the third, K-3a1, comprises some alterations of the latter. Stratum K-3 was correlated with the American VB and is followed by Stratum K-2, which equals the American VA–IVB. These equations, however, are based mainly on stratigraphic considerations, as the pottery from these phases is very meager. The scant pottery published from this sequence would seem to suggest that the last two phases are well within the Iron IIA ceramic horizon, but not the early one, which is much more akin to VIA. Here again then, like at Yoqne'am, at least one horizon, K-3b, might belong to the period we would define as 'Ir1|2'. The amount of pottery published from these three sub-phases is insufficient for any conclusion, though. Whether there is an 'Iron Age I|II' horizon at Megiddo, or a gap, or indeed an abrupt changeover from Iron Age I to Iron Age II as is being suggested by the Rehov excavators, is a question that remains to be answered.

So where does one posit the Iron I|II transition at Megiddo? After the VIA destruction? After K-3b, with the formation of the Iron II ceramic assemblage? Or after K-3a, when the first public architecture is in evidence?

Thus, the need to define a transitional period is definitely warranted on stratigraphical grounds (in the southern part of the country, the horizon recently defined by Z. Herzog and L. Singer-Avitz [2004] early Iron Age IIA may parallel this period, but this needs a more careful investigation). But is it, chronologically speaking, meaningful at all? Do we have any means to assess its length? Here is where ceramic considerations come into play. The fact that at sites like Megiddo the Iron I and IIA ceramic assemblages are drastically different needs no demonstration. Practically the whole assemblage has changed. In Cyprus too, the difference between CG IA and CG III is typologically significant, but the length of this evolution is likewise difficult to assess. Such overall transformations do not occur overnight, whatever social or political phenomena one may choose to invoke. A significant stretch of time must be postulated here, a generation—more probably two—it is difficult to tell.

Contexts and Samples

The date-producing assemblages of the Iron Age Dating Project were segregated into the following horizons:

- A group of seven samples comprising Late Bronze (LB) and transitional LB|Ir1 contexts. They include Aphek X-12, Tel Miqne-Ekron VIIb, Tell Keisan 13 and Megiddo K-6 (probably to be equated with the Chicago excavators' Stratum VIIA). The Late Bronze and the Late Bronze | Iron Age transition is not part of this project, and no attempt was made to systematically collect samples from these horizons. These few samples represent opportunistic samples from sites in which other horizons were sampled more extensively. Thus, no conclusions should be drawn from this arbitrary collection and these dates were included in the analyses only to provide *termini post quem* to the region of interest.

- An early Iron I group (our Ir1a and Ir1a|b; for this terminology see Gilboa and Sharon 2003) with 14 samples. These include Bet Shemesh 6 and 5, Tel Miqne-Ekron VI and V and Dor D2/13-12.

- A Late Iron I group (our Ir1b) of 26 samples, including Megiddo K-4 (= VIA in Chicago terminology), Tell Keisan 9a-b, Yoqne'am XVII, Dor D2/9-10, Reḥov D3, the first destroyed stratum at Tell el-Hamma, Tell Qasile X and Tel Hadar IV. Ceramically, the Ir1b group is the best-defined horizon in our sequence. These samples represent the temporal horizon variously referred to as 'late Iron Age I', 'terminal Iron I', 'Iron IB' or simply 'the Megiddo VIA–Qasile X horizon'. The two latter destructions may engender a punctual view of the 'termination of the Iron I' by some catastrophe (e.g. 'Davidic conquests'). But let us not be misled—this apparently is a long period, represented at sites like Dor, Tell Keisan and Kinneret by several architectural phases. The attribution of two sites to this horizon is not entirely secure: it is unclear if Tel Hadar IV, whose ceramic composition is more akin to regions east of the Jordan river, belongs here, and at the moment it is likewise unknown whether Tel Reḥov D3 could qualify as 'Ir1b'.

In addition to these, there are 14 samples from Iron Age I contexts for which no finer determination can be made at this stage. These include Reḥov D4, Hazor XII-XI, Shiloh V, el Akhwat and Tell el-Rumeidah (Hebron) VII. These samples are included in the 'agglomerative' model, setting out the midpoint between all 'Iron Age I' and 'Iron Age II' dates, but are not used in the finely-seriated model (for the models, see below). Altogether there are at present 56 samples from Iron Age I.

The only dates relating to the Iron I|II transitional period are three samples from Dor D2/8c and one sample from Aphek X-8. This should be considered the main archaeological lacuna in our sequence. As mentioned, it is yet unclear whether Tel Hadar IV belongs here and its dates, for the time being, are considered late Iron I.

Early Iron IIA contexts include at present 19 samples from Hazor X (a and b), Megiddo H-5 (coeval with VA–IVB), Dor D2/8b, Yoqne'am XIVb and the second destruction at Tell el-Hamma. Only one sample (from Hazor IX) was classified as 'Late Iron IIA', but 7 were grouped as 'General Iron Age IIA' with no attempt at further refinement at this stage—see comments about the 'general Iron Age I' designation above. These include samples from Rehov E1b (= Stratum V?), H. Rosh Zayit, Sulem and Moza. Bethsaidah is also included here, although we have yet to see the ceramic assemblage associated with the samples.

Finally, 9 samples are from contexts of very late Iron IIA characteristics (described by their excavators and in the literature variously as 'terminal Iron Age IIA', 'transitional Iron Age IIA|B' or 'early Iron Age IIB'). These include samples from late Beth Shemesh 3, Tell es-Safi 4 (the main destroyed stratum), the upper Iron Age destruction level at Tell el-Hamma and Tel Zayit. As in the case of the group at the very beginning of the series, we made no attempt to exhaustively sample these late horizons—nor do we claim that all of them are contemporaneous. We use this group merely to provide a *terminus ante quem* for the earlier groups.

Altogether, there are at present 36 Iron Age II samples, of which 19 are defined as early.

The distribution of the dates on both sides of the transition we are seeking is thus not symmetric. On the Iron I side of the transition we possess 56 samples, including 26 from major late Iron I destructions, which may very well be close to the transition. On the other hand—not only do we have very few dates from the transitional horizon, but Iron IIA dates, especially those designated early Iron IIA, are more problematic. First, they are fewer (19). Second, ceramically speaking, some of the contexts designated early Iron IIA are not the very first Iron IIA horizons at their respective sites: this is the case regarding at least Hazor Xa, Yoqne'am XIVb, Rehov V and probably Megiddo H-5. Third, even in cases where the dates originate from very first Iron IIA contexts, it is possible that they belong to the end of these occupations, and thus may be somewhat distant from the transition.

Still, the Iron IIA dates do represent fairly well those contexts, especially in the north, which traditionally were considered the hallmark of Solomonic times, like Hazor X, Meggido VA–IVB and their contemporaries—Yoqne'am XIV and the second destruction phase at Hamma (for example in Mazar 1990: Chapter 9).

Statistical Modeling

Replication

All the radiocarbon measurements in this study were replicated in one form or another. We therefore need to think about how to deal with multiple measurements. The first issue is: should we combine them at all?

There are well-established statistical rules for combining repetitive measurements of the same phenomenon (Bevington and Robinson 1992). As with any other statistical method, one needs to be aware of the assumptions behind the mathematical model and to assess whether the real-life situation fits these assumptions, fully or partially. In the case of replicated radiocarbon measurements the assumption is that one replicates *the same measurement* several times *under the same conditions*, and that the only reason for variation is the stochastic nature of the individual measurements, as represented by the individual error-estimates.

The question is whether several dates of (what is taken to be) the same archaeological or historical event (e.g. burnt deposits of the same typological horizon at one site, or several destruction layers attributed to the same military campaign) constitute an independent replication of the same measurement. It is obvious, however, that radiocarbon dating does not measure historical events, but the ^{14}C concentration in a material linked via a fairly long chain of inference to an event one wants to interpret. In our case, even assuming that two or more samples are indeed a product of the same historical event (i.e. that no archaeological contamination or error has occurred), they may have been deposited in different micro-environments, undergone different chemical treatments and then have been measured using different methods in different laboratories and/or different machines, and compared to different standards. Can one, in good faith, say that this constitutes a 'repetition of the same measurement under the same conditions'?

The χ^2 test is designed to test just this—but like all other statistical tests it is a negative check, in other words, given a set of data which is widely divergent (relative to the quoted measurement error) it will indicate that such divergence *is not likely* to be caused merely by stochastic fluctuation. The usual procedure is to combine radiocarbon dates as a weighted average of the individual measurements:

$$\left(M = \sum_j \frac{Measurement_j}{\sigma_j^2} \middle/ \sum_j \frac{1}{\sigma_j^2}\right) \text{ and the combined error as } \overline{\sigma} = \left(\sum_j \sigma_j^{-2}\right)^{-\frac{1}{2}}$$

Note that the last formula has a mathematical property: the combined error is always smaller than the smallest individual error in the series and hence always decreases with each added replication, meaning that given enough measurements of an event, one can asymptotically reduce the error-estimate to zero, no matter how noisy the replicated set is. Obviously, when the demand that the set be a replication of the same measurement is not satisfied, such precision would be spurious.

Identification of Outliers

To analyze our large set of dates (acquired during a period of three years) we need a consistent strategy to identify and treat outlying measurements. Obviously, simply ignoring ones which do not fit our preconceptions would not do. Even limiting the 'massaging' of the database only to cases of apparent discrepancy (for example, consistently removing the low or the high dates from a replicated set in order to get a better fit) would inevitably skew the results. We experimented with several different strategies, as described below.

The *standardized residual* $d_i = (m_i - M)/\sigma_i$ denotes the divergence of one measurement m_i of a replicated series from an estimate M of the central moment of that series (average, weighted average, median or some other 'consensus' value) with the measurement error σ_i as a unit. Assuming the series comprises independent repetitions of the same measurement M (see above for the precise meaning of 'independent repetitions of the same measurement'), the distribution of the d_i's should be standard normal ($d_i^2 \sim N[0,1]$, i.e. 68% of them should be between +1 and –1; 95% between +2 and –2 etc.) and their sum-of-squares should have a χ^2 distribution with [# of repetitions minus 1] degrees freedom ($\Sigma_i d_i^2 \sim \chi_{i-1}^2$). Note that these two demands are not synonymous. If replication is extensive enough it is probable that one or even several measurements in it would diverge by more than 2 error-terms from the norm. On the other hand it is possible that a distribution *without* any obvious outliers would not pass the χ^2 test—for instance, if more than one third of the d_i's are located in the –2 to –1; +1 to +2 ranges. In our study we regard any measurement with a standardized residual of more than ±2 as a potential outlier, and any replication which does not pass a χ^2 test (at 5%) as suspect. Note that the FIRI definition for outliers (Scott 2003: 170) is less stringent.

Once outliers have been identified, there remains a problem of how to treat them. The dilemma here is that, on the one hand, basing conclusions on data known to be partially faulty would not be prudent. On the other hand, the greatest danger in this sort of study is selectivity—explicitly or implicitly removing data that are not consistent with one's preconceived interpretation. The experimental design we devised allows us to distinguish several types of outliers:

1. A divergent result within a series of measurements made under identical conditions in one laboratory. The probable source of error is the measurement itself.
2. Divergent results between measurement methods or laboratories. The probable source of error here are laboratory procedures.
3. Results which replicate well, but radically deviate from their supposed archaeological placement, in other words, diverge significantly from other measurements of the same typo-stratigraphic horizon, or unequivocally do not fit the typo-stratigraphic sequence. The probable source of the error is archaeological.

Treatment of Outliers

Different strategies of dealing with divergent data are found in the literature. The ones used in the current study are given below.

First, suspect measurements were rechecked to see if some independent cause (procedural or archaeological) for the aberrant reading could be located. If so, *all* the measurements in which the same anomaly was found were eliminated—whether or not they agreed with other results. Excluded in this way were the following cases:

1. Visual and microscopic examination of some of the graphite targets that were used in the accelerator and gave divergent results had indeed shown an anomalous behavior of the graphite in the cathode during the sputtering process (Fig. 6.1). The possible reason for this phenomenon is improper pressing of the graphite. All these targets were excluded from the study.

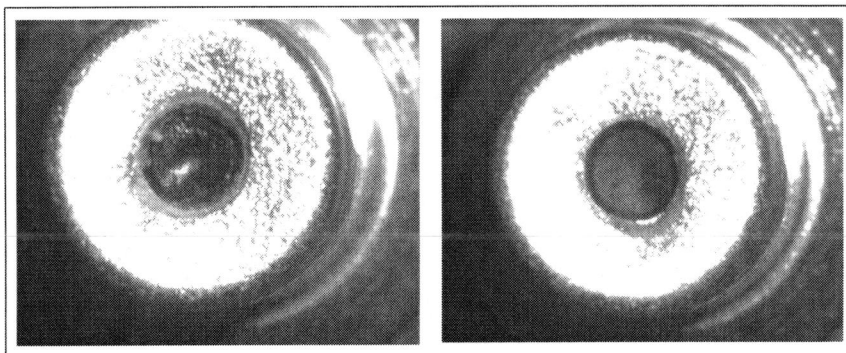

Figure 6.1. Image of the cathodes of two of the replicates of sample RTT 3809.
On the left side is the 'bad' cathode with visible crust; on the right side is the
'good' cathode where the graphite is still visible as a flat homogeneous layer.

2. One method evaluated in the Weizmann laboratory to cross-check the samples prepared for liquid scintillation was to extract a small amount of CO_2 during sample preparation and measure it with Accelerator Mass Spectrometry (AMS). It turned out that these samples fluctuated widely. We do not yet know the exact reason for this. As this exercise is not part of the normal operational run in the laboratory it was decided to defer investigation of this phenomenon and simply not use results obtained this way.
3. A fairly consistent offset was noted on intercomparison samples prepared and dated in the Arizona laboratory and labeled 'b'. These samples were run differently than the rest of the

Arizona targets (labeled 'a' and 'aa'). CO_2 from these samples was run through a mass-spectrometer before graphitization to measure the $\delta^{13}C$. We suspect a contamination effect due to this procedure.

4. The samples excluded on archaeological grounds were: (4.1) Hazor XII/XI samples RTT 3700, 3701, 3702, 3703, 3704. These were charcoal samples taken from pits dug into the burnt Late Bronze Age palace. Some of these proved to date to (non-terminal) Late Bronze and even Middle Bronze Age. Such dates are obviously residual, and fit the dates obtained on constructional wood from the palace. The entire set was not used. However, these dates are still useful for the purpose of intercomparison, residuality notwithstanding. (4.2) Tel Zayit. This sample (RT 4287) produced a late Byzantine/Early Islamic date. (4.3) Tel Miqne (RTT 4288). This sample was excluded after the archaeological context was rechecked because of the much too low radiocarbon age obtained. The excavator confirmed that the sample's locus was disturbed. (4.4) The whole Moza set (RT 4583, 4584, 4586, 4587) was excluded, although dates were acceptable, because the pottery in the sampled contexts included redeposited Bronze Age artifacts together with the Iron Age ceramics, which indicated that other materials in this context may also be residual.

In a few cases, we noted that a single AMS batch had several outliers. In these cases we prepared and ran again several of the samples used in these batches (from the material left at Weizmann). Such re-runs account for samples with many replications (typically three Arizona measurements and six Weizmann ones).

After these checks, we ran each model in three different modes:

1. *Uncombined.* In this mode each replication is treated as an independent measurement, thereby avoiding the complication of combining measurements altogether. All measurements, potential outliers included, are considered. This has the effect of delaying the decision of what to do with them to the next step of the analysis (modeling, see below). At that time, outliers will appear as misfits, and may either be thrown out, or left in (at the possible price of a low general fit for the model).

   Two deficiencies of this method need be considered. First, measurements replicated many times will count more than ones replicated a few times or not at all—but then combining replicated dates (and hence reducing the error-estimation) has a very similar effect. With Bayesian intuition, this can be justified by the argument that we are more certain about dates for which we have more information. A second problem may arise at the modeling stage. An implicit assumption made by the Bayesian modeling of phases is that the prior distribution of measurements across the phase is uniform, namely, that it is equally likely that our samples represent any point in time within the phase. This is a hard demand to meet even at the best of times. We have *a priori* knowledge that some episodes within the phase (e.g. destruction) are more likely to produce organic samples. When we run uncombined replications, we definitely know this assumption to be untrue—as distinct sampling points are measured several times. In our case the phases to be dated are quite short (probably not much longer than the measurement uncertainties) and therefore the violation of the uniformity assumption may not distort the results much. The choice boils down to which violated assumption does more damage—combining measurements known to be different, or treating non-uniformly distributed dates as if they were uniform. Testing *both* models can provide us with information on the robustness of the data set. If neither assumption is violated in any serious way, the results of both should be quite similar.

2. *Removing outliers*. As pointed out above, the problem is how to do this in an unbiased manner. The strategy used in this study is as follows: if a replicated set does not pass the χ^2 test, the measurement with the highest standardized residual (see definition above) is removed. Thus far, replicated sets have always passed χ^2 after the removal of a single outlier. No significant pattern relative to measurement methods or analytical procedures was found in the removed measurements, in other words, some were 'high' (relative to the other measurements in the set) and some were 'low'; This ensures that the removal of outliers in this manner does not introduce a bias, and incidentally validates the point that no systematic bias exists between laboratories or dating methods.

An additional consideration when removing outliers is how many should one remove. We defined potential outliers as measurements whose standardized residual has an absolute value of more than 2, that is, ones where the probability that the deviation from the group-norm is completely random is less than 5%. A data set of hundreds of individual measurements, however, will probably have several with an absolute residual exceeding 2—even if the deviations are completely random. We therefore defined an additional statistic—an overall χ^2—as the overall sum of squared residuals, across all samples and measurements. The distribution of this index (under the null assumption that the deviations from set-norms are random) should be χ^2 with [# of measurements minus # of replicated sets] degrees of freedom. The probability of this pooled χ^2 was checked at each individual removal, and the procedure ceased when this probability became sufficiently high.

3. *Widening the error-estimates*. For each replication, in addition to the weighted mean and combined error, we also calculated the arithmetic average and sampled standard deviation of the measurement—that is, we treated each measurement as a point estimate and disregarded the calculated measurement error altogether, using the spread between the measurements to assess the precision of the date. Of the two sets of central-moment and error-estimate one chooses in this mode the one which has a wider error-estimate (Bevington and Robinson 1992). This is a very conservative mode of operation. In some of the replications which contained outliers the error term becomes so wide that the date is rendered almost useless for our purpose, in other words, the effect is rather similar to that of simply discarding all the sets which contained outliers. A less severe *modus operandi* is to use the wider error-estimate only where the weighted average and combined error fail to pass the χ^2 test. This was the standard we used. As each of these modes has advantages and limitations, we checked each model and each dataset with all of them.

Modeling

The next step of analysis is to construct models for the collation of all of the dates together with the order of the contexts from which they were collected—as determined by stratigraphic and typological analyses. In the present study we employ the standard Bayesian inference approach (Bronk Ramsey 1994, 1995) in the OxCal 3.9 package. We experimented with several different models, each of which uses parts of the whole data set.

Agglomerated Model—Ir1 vs. Ir2: In this simplest model we group together *all* the dates from contexts that are archaeologically dated to the Iron Age I, and compare them to those that are attributable to the Iron Age IIA. Intermediary dates (e.g. the 'transitional Ir1|2' horizon at Dor) are excluded, as are the few dates we have for Late Bronze Age contexts or transitional LB|IrA, and dates bordering on, or already in, Iron Age IIB.

This model is the most robust (i.e. expected to have the least number of misfits [for a definition, see below]). It uses the widest subset of the data array. Lastly, at the present level of knowledge and consensus, there will be little or no disagreement in the archaeological community about the placement of contexts in it. In OxCal terminology, this model involves a sequence of two phases and three boundaries (of which only one—the Ir1|2 transition—is of interest), as follows:

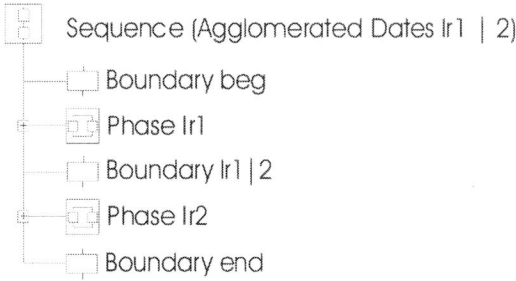

Sequence (Agglomerated Dates Ir1 | 2)

Boundary beg

Phase Ir1

Boundary Ir1 | 2

Phase Ir2

Boundary end

The first limitation of this model is that it does not make use of all the available information. But, more importantly—the whole idea of modeling the data is to limit the inherent uncertainty in radiocarbon measurement by constraining it to archaeological knowledge. Building a purposefully simplistic model defeats that purpose. Each of the agglomerated phases contains contexts known to be chronologically far, relatively speaking, from the transition of interest (for instance, ones from the very beginning of Iron Age I or relatively late within Iron Age IIA), and these might skew the result. Finally—as already discussed above—such a model excludes perhaps the most crucial data—those from contexts known to be transitional.

At the other end of the spectrum is the seriated model:

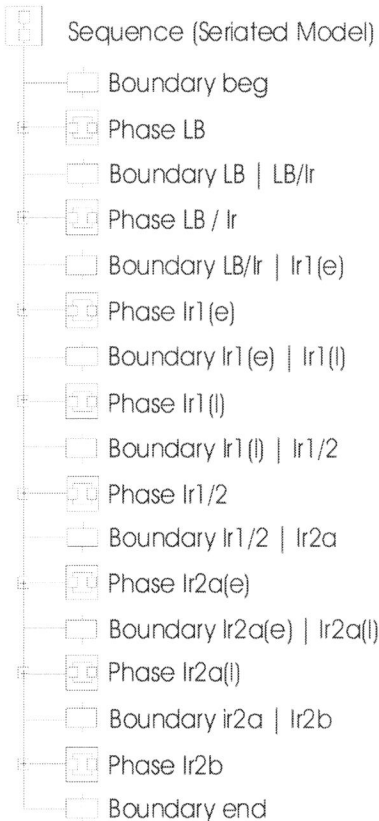

Sequence (Seriated Model)

Boundary beg

Phase LB

Boundary LB | LB/Ir

Phase LB / Ir

Boundary LB/Ir | Ir1(e)

Phase Ir1(e)

Boundary Ir1(e) | Ir1(l)

Phase Ir1(l)

Boundary Ir1(l) | Ir1/2

Phase Ir1/2

Boundary Ir1/2 | Ir2a

Phase Ir2a(e)

Boundary Ir2a(e) | Ir2a(l)

Phase Ir2a(l)

Boundary ir2a | Ir2b

Phase Ir2b

Boundary end

Here we tried to splice the relative chronological sequence as finely as is currently possible (the rationale and the contexts placed in each phase are explained above; see also Gilboa and Sharon 2003 for a detailed analysis of the relative sequence).

Several problems are associated with using a fine-grained model like this. First, quite a few assemblages *cannot* be classified with such exactitude and are therefore excluded from the analysis (for example, Rumeidah and Shiloh V); the database considered in this model is thus appreciatively smaller. Second, not all archaeologists will agree with our placement of each and every sample (though we contend that most will agree with *most* of them). Third, as this model is inherently more complex, it may suffer from more mis-fitted dates than the former one.

In between these two contrasting models, we considered an 'intermediate' one, in which we focused only on the more relevant data set. Namely, restricting the input only to dates from contexts that are late in the Iron Age I vs. early in the Iron Age II (phases 'Ir1[l]' and 'Ir2a[e]' in the terminology above) with or without modeling the 'Ir1|2' transitional phase as a separate entity. This will be referred to as the 'focused model'.

Sequence (Focused Model)

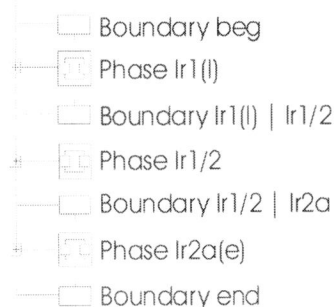

Boundary beg
Phase Ir1(l)
Boundary Ir1(l) | Ir1/2
Phase Ir1/2
Boundary Ir1/2 | Ir2a
Phase Ir2a(e)
Boundary end

Goodness of Fit

After the model is calculated and the optimal values are estimated for a given data set, not every datum will completely agree with them. Generally, the more elaborate the model, and the larger and/or more variegated the data set, the more deviations are to be expected. To differentiate between, on the one hand, 'outliers' in the sense used above and, on the other, measurements which significantly deviate from the optimal values estimated by the model, we will call the latter kind 'misfits'. Mis-fitted dates can be the result of measurement outliers, either purposely left in the model (as in the case where *all* [uncombined] measurements are left in for the model-run to sort out), or ones unrecognized by the previous set of statistics. They are more likely, though, to be the result of *archaeological* errors—either that the date of the organics does not fit the archaeological context (as in the case of old wood, or an intrusive organic specimen) or that the archaeological context is misplaced in the relative sequence for one reason or another. To give one (extreme) example—the charcoal samples taken from Iron Age I pits in Hazor, mentioned above, which turned out to be Middle Bronze Age wood, had given consistent dates under replication. Thus, they are not 'outliers' in the sense used above, but would nevertheless introduce noise into any model attempting to estimate the date of Iron Age I.

The degree to which the radiocarbon measurements actually agree with the contexts they are allocated to (i.e. to what extent the measured age actually falls within the range allocated to that context by the model) is measured in OxCal by *Agreement indices*. The agreement index for each individual measurement is the overlap integral between the prior and posterior distributions. In other words, this is the degree in which the measurement distribution (after calibration) overlaps with the same distribution after it has been 'clipped' by the archaeological (stratigraphical and typological) constraints imposed by the model. For each measurement i the agreement index A_i is defined as:

$$A_i = \frac{\int p(t)p'(t)dt}{\int p(t)p(t)dt}$$

where $p(t)$ is the prior (unconstrained) measurement distribution and $p'(t)$ is the posterior (constrained) distribution of t, which is a calibrated age range. A_i equals 1 if $p(t)$ and $p'(t)$ are identical. $A_i < 1$ if the bulk of the $p'(t)$ distribution does not overlap $p(t)$, and A_i will actually have values > 1 if $p'(t)$ forms a subset of the distribution $p(t)$. Whenever the agreement index for a date falls below 0.6 we regard that date as a potential misfit. The *overall agreement index* of the model is defined by multiplying all the individual agreement indices:

$$A_{overall} = \left[\prod_{i=1}^{n} A_i \right]^{1/\sqrt{n}}$$

Once the initial model is run and potential misfits are flagged, two courses of action exist: either do nothing—leave the poorly fitted observations in and say that the parameters of interest (in our case, the Iron Age I|II boundary) are the best that can be estimated given the data set and the contextual information we have; or to rerun the model step-wise, removing at each stage the measurement with the lowest agreement index until we reach a point at which the overall agreement index becomes acceptable.

In the research design thus outlined, each data set is combined in three different modes, and modeled in three different ways. This makes for a minimum of nine runs per data set. The stepwise removal of poorly fitted data produces many more. Results indicate—as might be expected for such a tight chronological dilemma—that wood-charcoal often gives significantly older results than short-lived samples from the same contexts. Thus, the entire modeling process needs to be duplicated—once for the entire data set and once for short-lived samples only. Furthermore, we can, and do, run various partial data sets—individual site models, regional models (e.g. only southern Phoenician sites, or only Philistine sites). Altogether this makes for many scores of different models that need to be evaluated. Naturally, no final verdict can be rendered until all the data are in and all these models are run. Several partial runs are presented below.

New Dor Dates and a Re-analysis of the Dor Sequence

As mentioned, A. Mazar has claimed, orally and in print, that the original Dor measurements that corroborate the 'low' chronology are flawed, and that in the 1990s, when these samples were measured, dates produced at Rehovot were biased (too low). Although we have shown already (Sharon *et al.* in press) that this discrepancy between the Dor and Rehov ('high') dates is much smaller than claimed, and that the Rehov sequence does not disprove the 'low chronology' hypothesis (see also Finkelstein and Piasetzky 2003), it became imperative to run another sequence of dates from Dor.

As the original 22 samples were no longer available, we chose different ones. In order to limit as far as possible any archaeological variability we chose only short-lived samples this time (olive pits), from a single area (D2). Wherever possible, we re-sampled the same contexts that produced the 1990s dates (though the earliest part of the D2 sequence, Phases 13 and 12, was not yet dug at the time that the previous data set was obtained). One sample was from phase D2/13, two from D2/12 (both of these fall within the early Iron Age I—but not its very beginning, Ir1a|b and earlier, cf. Gilboa and Sharon 2003: Table 1); two samples from Phases 10–9 (late Iron Age I [Ir1b in Dor terminology]); three from Phase 8c (Iron Age I|II transition [Ir1|2]) and one from 8b (beginning of Iron Age IIA [Ir2a]). Thirty-three measurements were made on these 9 samples—27 of them were prepared in Rehovot and run in Arizona (3 targets per sample) and 6 (3 measurement per sample) were prepared and run in Groningen (this is part of the intercomparison reported by Boaretto *et al.* 2005 and in Boaretto *et al.* in preparation).

There are no outliers among these 33 measurements (a situation that is more likely to be encountered in a well-stratified sequence from a single site/excavation area). It is thus possible to combine the different measurements of each sample, and running the sequence of nine samples produces no misfits. The transitions of interest are (Fig. 6.2):

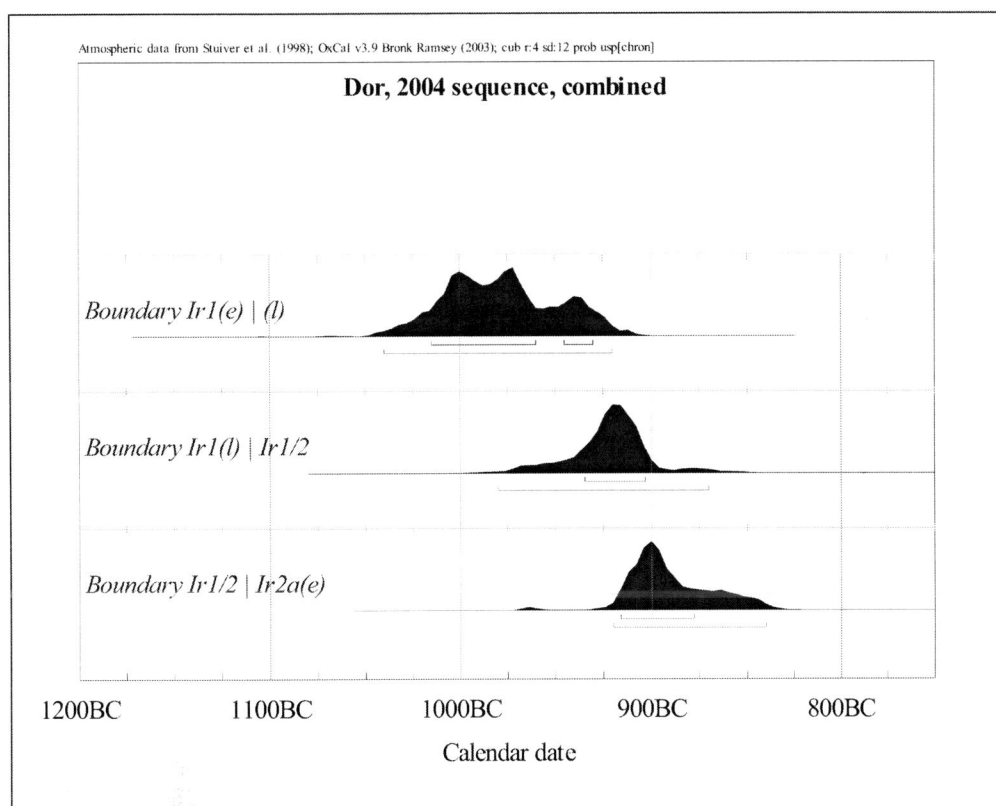

Figure 6.2. Ira1b|Ir1b; Ir1b|Ir1|2; Ir1|2|Ir2a boundaries in Area D2 at Dor based on 33 2004 measurements produced at Rehovot/Arizona, Arizona and Groningen (combined).

Running the model on the individual measurements detected no misfits and gave the following results (Fig. 6.3).

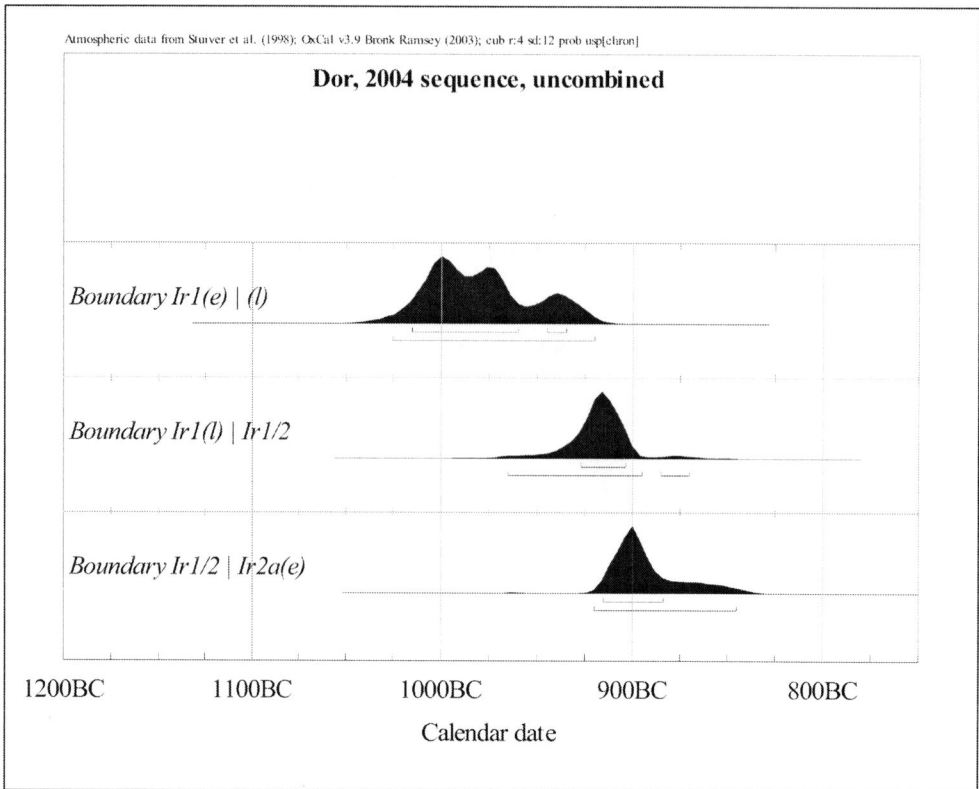

Figure 6.3. Ira1b|Ir1b; Ir1b|Ir1|2; Ir1|2|Ir2a boundaries in Area D2 at Dor based on 33 2004 measurements produced at Rehovot/Arizona, Arizona and Groningen (uncombined).

Compared with the previously published sequence (see Gilboa and Sharon 2003: Figs. 19–21) the transitions are slightly earlier, but they are very similar, and unequivocally support the 'low chronology'.

Another data set from Dor was produced early in the program (2003), as part of an attempt to compare Rehovot-prepared AMS samples with Liquid Scintillation Counting (LSC) dates measured at Rehovot. Six samples were taken from charcoal, all from the same locus in Phase D2/12 (Ir1a|b). Thirty-four dates were measured on these six samples: 24 AMS and 10 LSC. Two out of these 34 dates are outliers (RT 3623.1 and RT 3624.1) and one sample (RT 3625) is about 100 years (BP) older than the rest. By themselves, these dates cannot be used to calculate transitions. When added to the aforementioned data set, however, the transitions (Fig. 6.4) become:

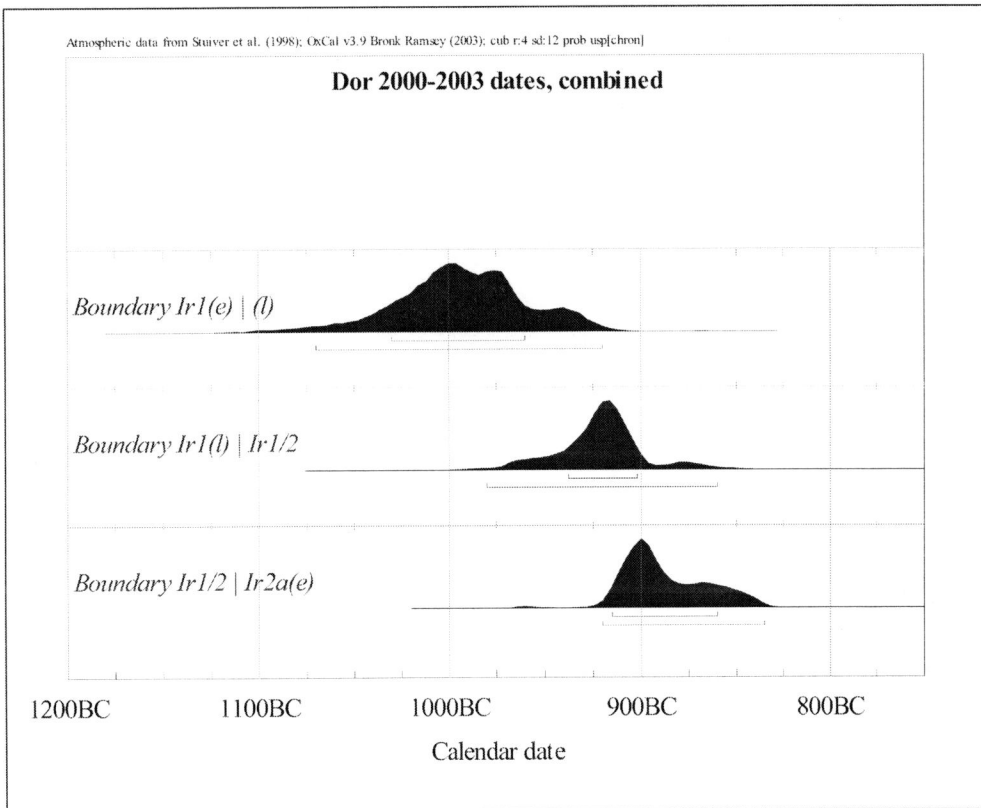

Figure 6.4. Ira1b|Ir1b; Ir1b|Ir1|2; Ir1|2|Ir2a boundaries in Area D2 at Dor
based on 75 measurements on 15 samples produced at Rehovot,
Rehovot/Arizona, Arizona and Groningen (combined).

In this analysis the samples were combined without the two outliers. It does include the one ill-fitted measurement (which does not sway the overall agreement index). Other permutations (uncombined measurements, stepwise exclusion of misfits) are almost identical.

The sequence of *all* Tel Dor dates (i.e. the above plus the previously published ones) now totals 37 samples and 99 individual measurements (of which two are discarded outliers). Running the model after discarding two misfits (RT 3625 already mentioned above, and RT 3106—one of the old LSC samples) gave the following result (Fig. 6.5):

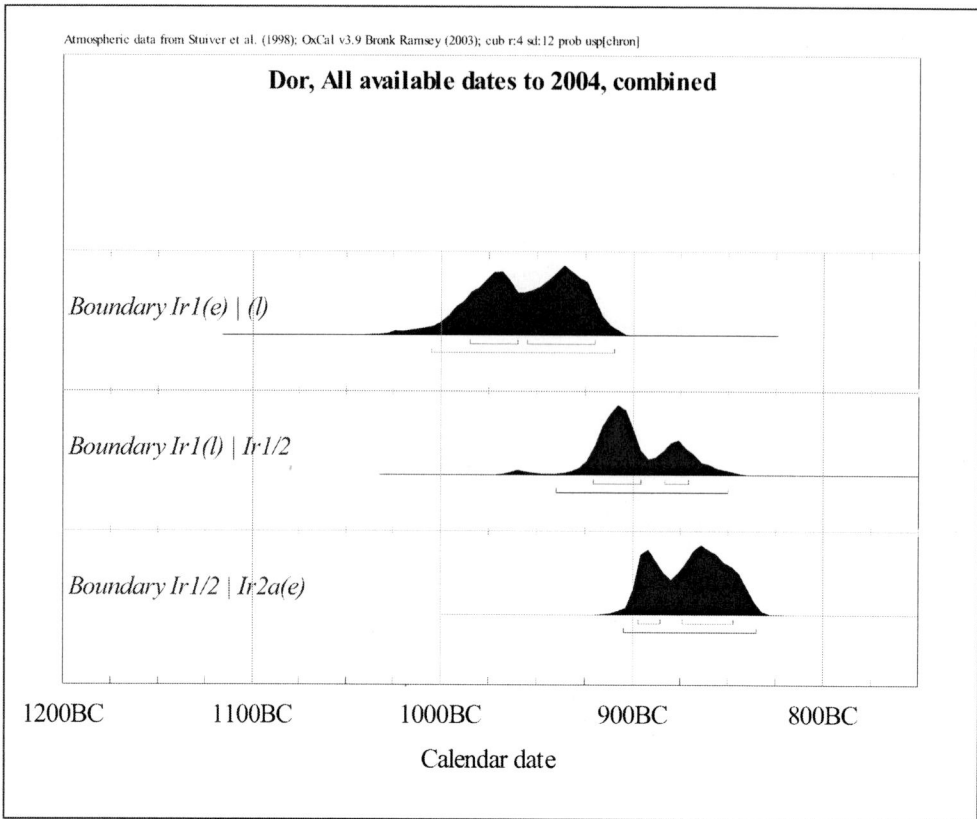

Figure 6.5. Ira1b|Ir1b; Ir1b|Ir1|2; Ir1|2|Ir2a boundaries at Dor based on all currently available (99) measurements produced at Beta Analytic, Rehovot, Rehovot/Arizona, Arizona and Groningen (1990s, 2003, 2004) (combined).

The differences between all these runs are minor—with peak points and edges of highest-density ranges differing within the range of a few decades. For the Ir1a|Ir1b transition there is a steady peak at ca. 975 BCE, though it shows some variability between runs and data sets, with a second peak about 25 years either before or after that peak (but, generally speaking, the determination of the Ir1a|Ir1b transition at Dor is not yet robust enough and requires more data). The transitions into the Ir1|2 'transitional phase' and between this transitional phase and 'real' Iron Age IIA (Ir2a) are steadier, the former varying between ca. 925 and ca. 875, the latter between ca. 900 or slightly earlier to ca. 850. In all, our previously published conclusions about Dor hold.

The Iron I|IIA Transition Date Using the Rehovot/Arizona Intercomparison Exercise Data

We have already introduced above the data set used for the Rehovot/Arizona intercomparison exercise (Boaretto *et al.* 2005). It is of interest to check the effect inter-laboratory/inter-method variability may have on the model. It is also instructive to compare the results obtained on this data set using different types of combination statistics.

Of the 22 samples on which intercomparison was performed, only 19 are usable for modeling (Fig. 6.6; the three charcoal samples from Hazor Stratum XII/XI, which produced dates definitely in the Middle and/or Late Bronze Age, were excluded, as they deviate so much as to create problems in the modeling run).

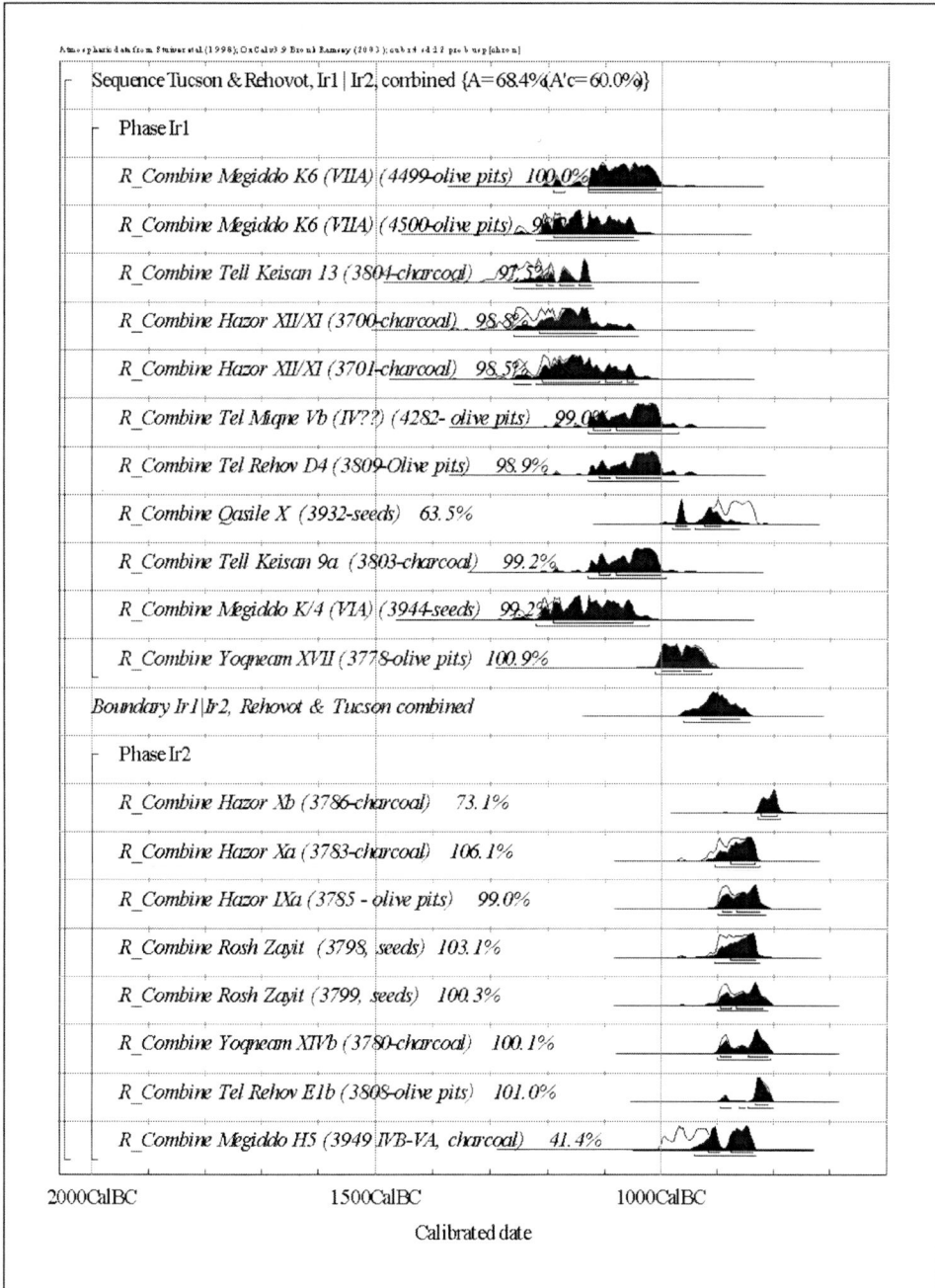

Figure 6.6. The 19 dates of the intercomparison samples used to calculate the Iron I | II transition (for individual measurements, see Boaretto *et al.* 2005).

We present here only the agglomerative model (all Iron I vs. all Iron II dates) and not the detailed sequence. The reason for this is that for at least four of the samples that participated in the intercomparison exercise a designation more precise than 'general Iron Age I' cannot be given at this point and excluding these would leave us with a rather small sample.

In the first run we inserted *all* the dates, without combining them in any way. Ninety-one individual measurements were thus entered—52 from Iron Age I contexts and 39 from Iron Age II. This run resulted in 9 measurements being identified as misfits (though several had agreement indices close to the 0.6 cutoff point) and produced the following distribution for the Iron Age I|II boundary (Fig. 6.7):

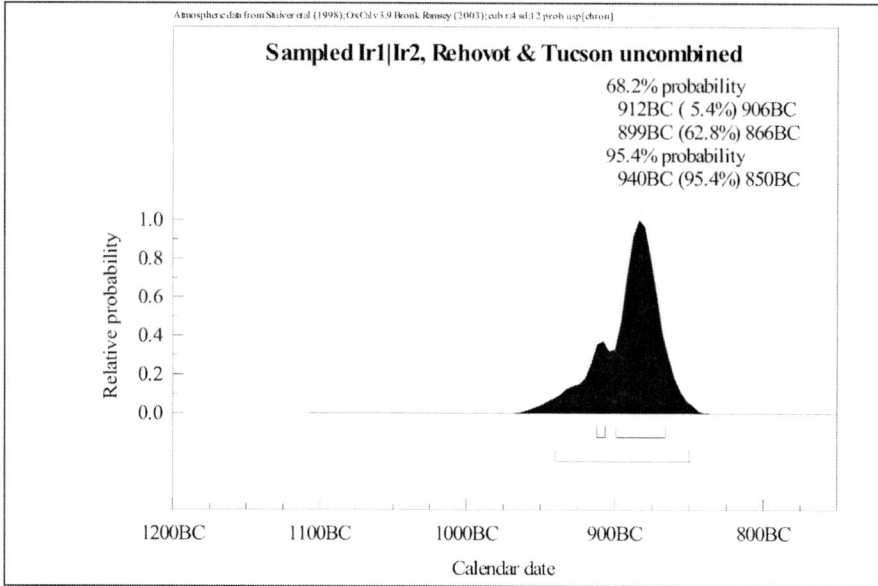

Figure 6.7. Iron Age I|II transition calculated based on 19 samples included in the intercomparison exercise (uncombined, including misfits).

Removal of the four most blatant misfits (RT 3932.6 from Qasile X [Ir1b], which gave a too-low date; RT 3786.4 from Hazor Xb [early Ir2a]—too low; RT 3785.3 from Hazor IX [late Ir2a]—too high; RT 3949.4 Megiddo H/5 [Ir2a]—too high) reduced the overall agreement index to an acceptable level (though there remain four mis-fitted measurements, we refrained from over-tampering with the data). The corrected boundary distribution becomes (Fig. 6.8):

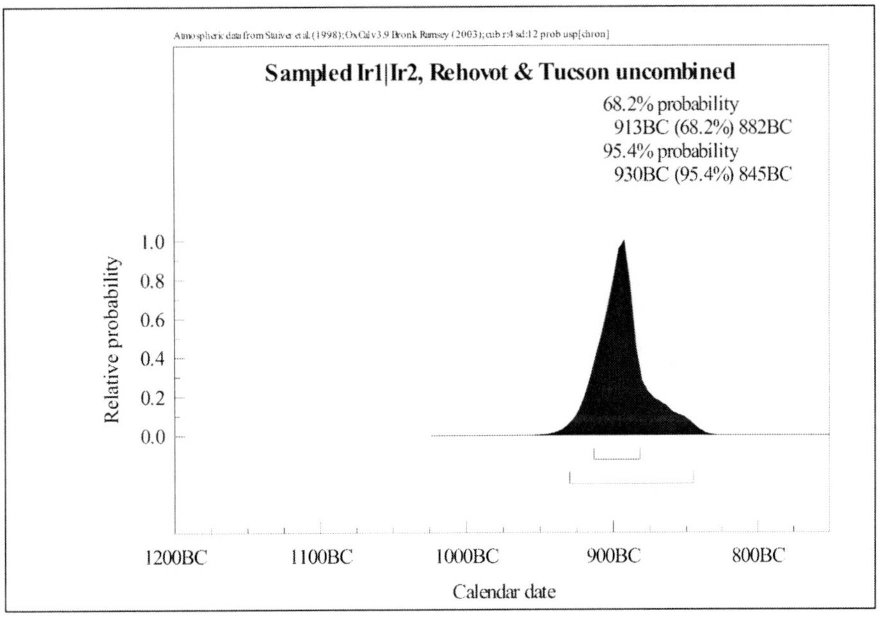

Figure 6.8. Iron Age I|II transition calculated based on samples included in the intercomparison exercise (uncombined, after removal of 4 misfits).

The next step is combining all the different measurements of each sample. χ^2 testing of all these combinations produced six outliers and if the results are modeled regardless, one misfit (RT 3949 Megiddo H/5 [Ir2a]—too high). The boundary distribution is (Fig. 6.9):

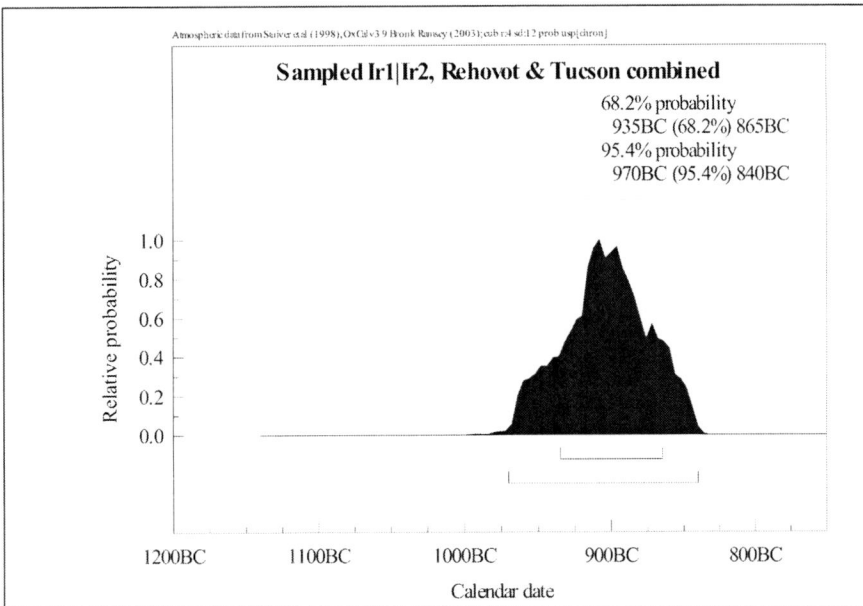

Figure 6.9. Iron Age I|II transition calculated based on samples included in the intercomparison exercise (combined, with 6 outliers and 1 misfit; for details see Boaretto *et al.* 2005).

Removing the six measurements with highest standardized residuals (7% of all measurements) we get an acceptable χ^2 and overall agreement values (though RT 3949 is still flagged as a misfit) and the distribution becomes (Fig. 6.10):

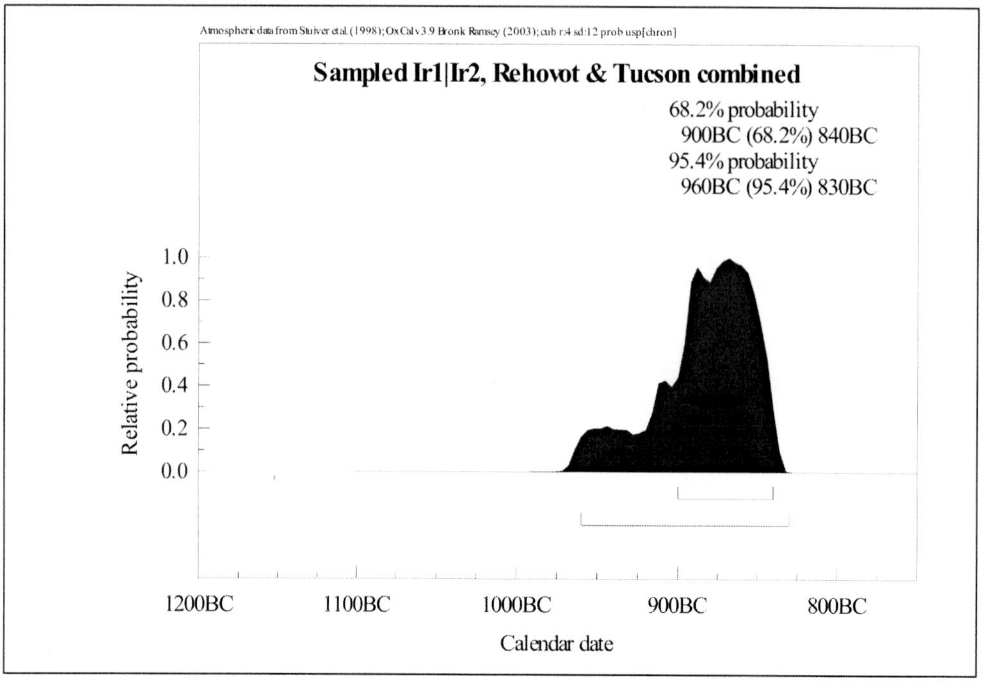

Figure 6.10. Iron Age I|II transition calculated based on samples included in the intercomparison exercise (combined, after removal of 6 outliers; 1 misfit left).

Note that the list of measurements with high standardized residuals (relative to other measurements of the same sample)—RTT 3932aa, RTT 3803.5, 3783.4, 3785.3, 3786.4 and 3949.5—by-and-large coincide with the list of misfits (relative to the final model results) in the former run. In fact, the only 'new entries' are RT 3803, charcoal from Tell Keisan 9a [Ir1b] in which one measurement (out of eleven) was markedly older than the rest (though not necessarily older than other Iron Age I dates) and RT 3932 from Tell Qasile X.

The latter sample introduces an interesting dilemma. The results of the individual measurements for RTT 3932 are (Table 6.1):

Table 6.1. Six measurements of sample RTT 3932 (Tell Qasile Stratum X).
For sample labels explanation see Boaretto *et al.* (2005).

Site and stratum	Age BP	σ	Residual		
Qasile X (RTT 3932.3)	2745	50	-0.143733		
Qasile X (RTT 3932.4)	2765	75	0.1708444		
Qasile X (RTT 3932.5)	2685	50	-1.343733		
Qasile X (RTT 3932.6)	2650	40	-2.554667		
Qasile X (RTT 3932a)	2780	35	0.7946665	χ^2	α
Qasile X (RTT 3932aa)	2862	40	2.7453332	16.6	1%

Note that these contain at least one measurement (RTT 3932.6), which is rather low, and one (RTT 3932aa), which is rather high. Removing *either* of these would make the rest of the set pass

χ^2 (though only barely so in the case of RT 3932aa). According to the exclusion rules expounded above, RT 3932aa (with a higher absolute residual) should be the one removed. If, however, we leave it in and remove 3932.6 instead, the model (as above, based on the intercomparison dates only) would produce dramatically different results (Fig. 6.11):

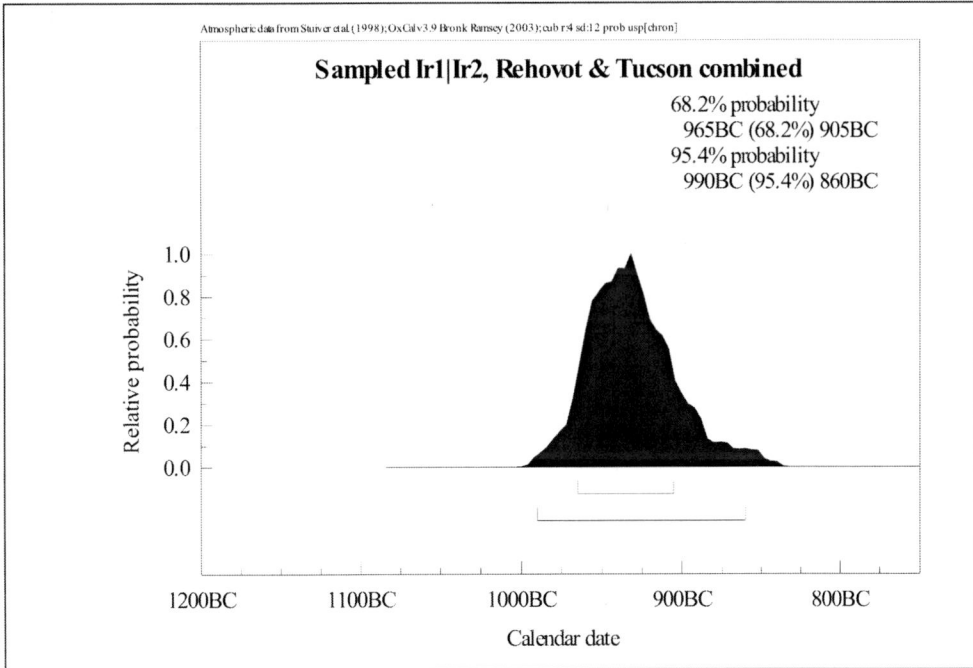

Atmospheric data from Stuiver et al. (1998);OxCal v3.9 Bronk Ramsey (2003);cub r:4 sd:12 prob usp[chron]

Sampled Ir1|Ir2, Rehovot & Tucson combined

68.2% probability
965BC (68.2%) 905BC
95.4% probability
990BC (95.4%) 860BC

Figure 6.11. Iron Age I|II transition calculated based on samples included in the intercomparison exercise (combined, after removal of 'low' outlier among the Qasile X RTT 3932 measurements instead of the 'high' one).

Although even in this model the weight of the distribution supports the low chronology hypothesis (in fact it peaks at exactly 925 BCE), this is the only model we have seen thus far in which the 'amended high chronology' hypothesis, that the Iron Age I|II boundary is at 980 BCE, is given more than a negligible credibility.

The fact that a single measurement out of ninety can shift the boundary distribution so dramatically gives one pause, and is further discussed below.

The third option for date-combination discussed above was using the simple average and standard-deviation-between-measurements rather than weighted average and combined error estimate whenever the latter fails the χ^2 test. Replacing the former with the combined dates for the six samples in which outliers were detected produces the following (Fig. 6.12):

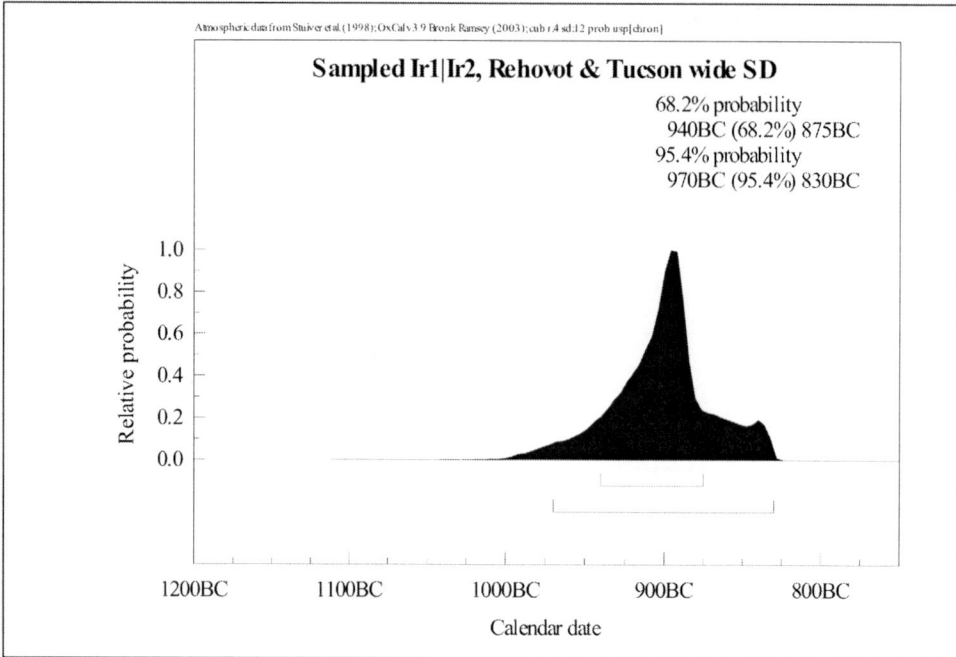

Figure 6.12. Iron Age I|II transition calculated based on samples included in the intercomparison exercise. For (13) samples passing χ^2 test, weighted average and combined error were used; and for (6) other samples simple averages and standard deviations between measurements were used.

Having thus investigated the effect of the combination algorithm—and having seen that it can make a substantial difference—although, in this case, not really substantial enough to change the preferred hypothesis, we turn to another question: What kind of an impact can different pre-treatment protocols have on the results? In the interest of brevity we shall test this on one model only—combined samples after exclusion of outliers (according to the procedure defined above).

Limiting our data set to the 22 samples pre-treated at Rehovot and measured by AMS at Arizona as part of the intercomparison exercise, we get four outliers (out of 55 measurements [see Boaretto *et al.* 2005] marked by the χ^2 test (RTT 3803.5, RTT 3786.4, RTT 3785.3 and RTT 3949.5—all of which were already encountered above). RT 3949 is, as before, a mis-fitted sample. After removal of the four outliers (but not of the misfit) the boundary is (Fig. 6.13):

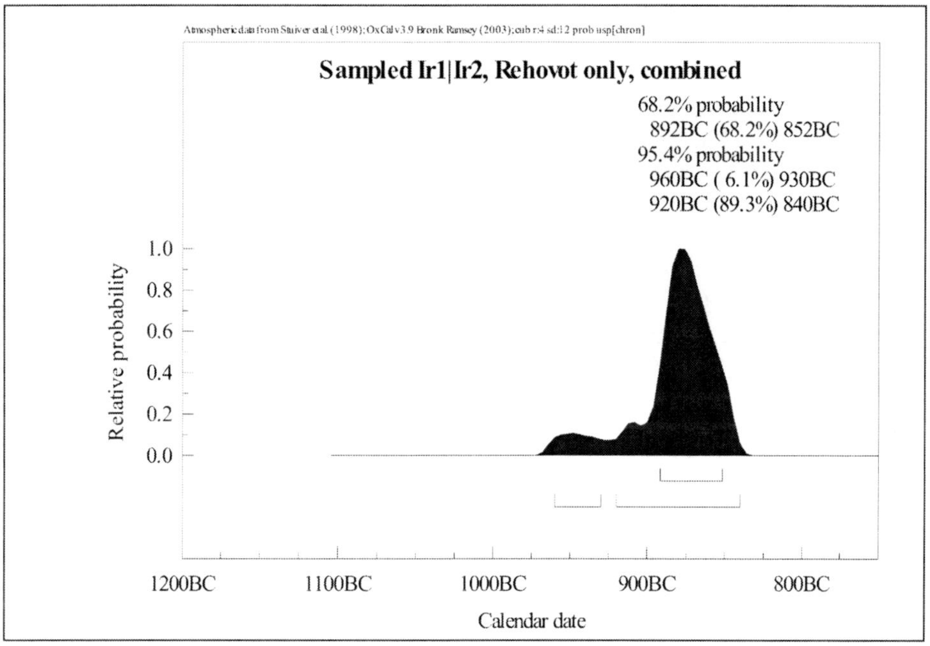

Figure 6.13. Iron Age I|II transition calculated based on samples included
in the intercomparison exercise, pre-treated at Rehovot and measured at Arizona.

We now consider *only* the Arizona part of the intercomparison. All the double-targets prepared and run at Arizona pass the χ^2 muster. Sample RT 3949 is still flagged as a too-old misfit. The Iron Age I|II boundary distribution is (Fig. 6.14):

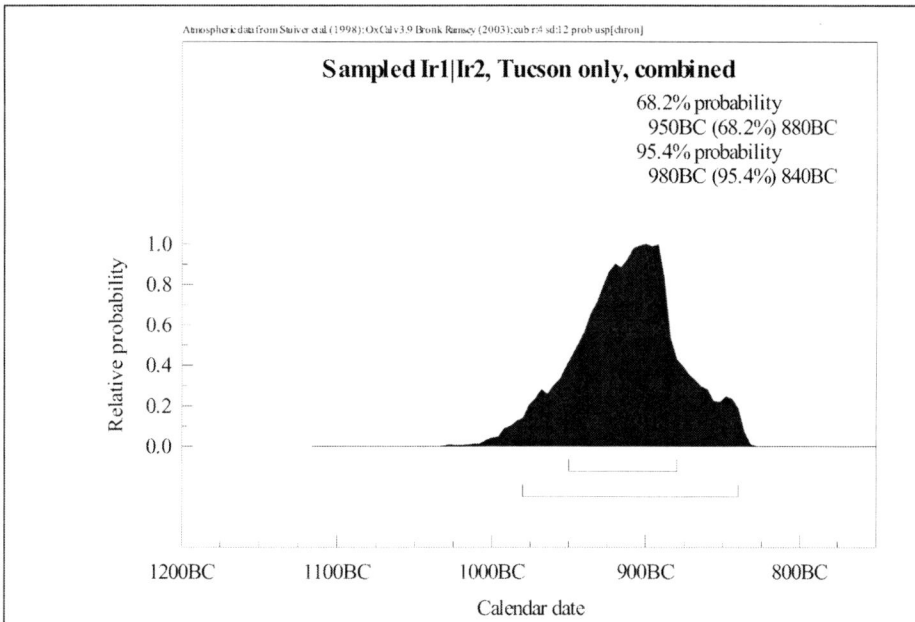

Figure 6.14. Iron Age I|II transition calculated based on samples included
in the intercomparison exercise, pre-treated and measured at Arizona.

The 95% highest density interval of both distributions is similar (980/960–840 BCE), and so are their peaks (ca. 875 vs. ca. 900) but the shape of the distribution, and consequently the 68% intervals, are quite different. Nevertheless, even under the 'older' distribution the likelihood of the 'conventional chronology' hypothesis is less than 2.5%.

A note of caution need be included here. In addition to obvious considerations like sufficient sample size, the data set for intercomparison was chosen so as to reflect the full range of sites and strata with which this study dealt. As such, it contains quite a few samples whose archaeological context is rather far away from the boundary of interest—e.g. Tell Keisan 13, or Megiddo K-6 which are manifestly early within the Iron Age I, or Hazor IX and Rosh Zayit IIa which are not the earliest Iron Age II strata in their respective stratigraphic sequences. As it happens, most of the late Iron Age I samples in this particular data set proved to be of the earlier variety within that period. Thus, a look at the actual calibrated distributions shows that while most of the Iron Age I samples cover the 12th–11th centuries BCE, and almost all Iron Age II samples fall within the 9th century BCE, only three out of the nineteen are actually squarely in the 10th century BCE. Two of these (RTT 3778—olive pits from Yoqne'am XVII and RTT 3932—lentils from Qasile X) are from Iron Age I contexts, while one (RTT 3949—from Megiddo H-5 = VA–IVB) is from an Iron Age IIA context. It is the inter-balance between these three samples which determines, almost exclusively, where the Iron Age I | II boundary (in this exercise) would fall within the 10th century BCE. Thus, a change in the range of 30 years occasioned by excluding the highest/lowest measurement within RTT 3932 can result in a shift of almost the same magnitude in the boundary distribution. Clearly, nineteen arbitrary Iron Age I vs. Iron Age IIA samples are not sufficient.

As repeatedly stated, only a small number of our dates have been presented here and not all the problems are resolved in our study at this time. Especially challenging will be the assessment of the effects of the dearth of the Iron I | II transitional period on the interpretation of our models. However, the trends which were manifest from the very beginning and which we alluded to in several partial presentations and publications have not diminished as more dates are compiled, and will probably not change materially as the final data set is being collated.

Acknowledgments

This research is being carried out with the support of the Israel Science Foundation (Grant No. 778/00), the Kimmel Center of Archaeological Sciences at the Weizmann Institute of Science, the Research Authority at Hebrew University, the Research Authority at the University of Haifa, and the US National Science Foundation (Grant EAR01–15488). It is now being continued with the aid of another Israel Science Foundation grant (No. 141/04). We acknowledge, with gratitude, the cooperation of the excavators and other scholars that contributed the samples, from the following sites: Tell el-Akhwat (A. Zertal), Aphek (M. Kochavi and Y. Gadot), Bethsaidah (R. Arav), Beth Shemesh (S. Bunimovitz and Z. Lederman), Dor (E. Stern), Tel Hadar (M. Kochavi and E. Yadin), Tell el-Hamma (J. Cahill), Hazor (A. Ben-Tor), Hebron (E. Eisenberg and the Israel Antiquities Authority), Tell Keisan (J.-B. Humbert), Megiddo (I. Finkelstein, D. Ussishkin and B. Halpern), Tell Miqne—Ekron (T. Dothan and S. Gitin), Moza (A. De Groot, Z. Greenhut and the Israel Antiquities Authority), Tell Qasile (A. Mazar), Tel Rehov (A. Mazar), Kh. Rosh Zayit (Z. Gal and the Israel Antiquities Authority), Tell es-Safi—Gath (A. Maeir), Shiloh (I. Finkelstein), Sulem (Y. Alexandre and the Israel Antiquities Authority), Yoqne'am (A. Ben-Tor) and Tel Zayit (R. Tappy). Talia Goldman of the Hebrew University was of invaluable assistance in sorting the Tel Dor organic samples.

References

Bevington P.R., and D.K. Robinson (1992) *Data Reduction and Error Analysis for the Physical Sciences* (Boston: WCB/McGraw-Hill).

Boaretto, E., *et al.* (2005) Dating the Iron Age I/II Transition in Israel: First Intercomparison Results. *Radiocarbon* 47(1): 39-55.

—(in preparation) New Iron Age Radiocarbon Dates from The Dor, Tell es-Safi, Yoqne'am and Tell Qasile: A Three-laboratories Cross-check.

Bronk Ramsey, C. (1994) Analysis of Chronological Information and Radiocarbon Calibration: The Program OxCal. *Archaeological Computing Newsletter* 41: 11-16.

—(1995) Radiocarbon Calibration and the Analysis of Stratigraphy: The OxCal Program. *Radiocarbon* 37(2): 425–30.

Bruins, H. J., J. van der Plicht, and A. Mazar (2003) ^{14}C Dates from Tel Rehov: Iron-Age Chronology, Pharaohs and Hebrew Kings. *Science* 300: 315-18.

Cahill, J. (in press) The Excavations at Tell el-Hammah: A Prelude to Amihai Mazar's Beth-Shean Valley Regional Project. In *'I will speak the riddles of ancient times' (Abiah chidot minei-kedem—Ps. 78.2b): Archaeological and Historical Studies in Honor of Amihai Mazar on the Occasion of his Sixtieth Birthday*, edited by P. de Miroschedji and A. Maeir (Winona Lake, IN: Eisenbrauns).

Coldstream, J.N (1999) On Chronology: The CG II Mystery and its Sequel. In *Cyprus: The Historicity of the Geometric Horizon*, edited by M. Iacovou and D. Michaelides (Nicosia: University of Cyprus): 109-18.

Finkelstein, I. (1996) The Archaeology of the United Monarchy: An Alternative View. *Levant* 27: 177-87.

Finkelstein I, and E. Piasetzky (2003) Wrong and Right; High and Low: ^{14}C Dates from Tel Rehov and Iron Age Chronology. *Tel Aviv* 30: 283-95.

Finkelstein, I., O. Zimhoni, and A. Kafri (2000) The Iron Age Pottery Assemblages from Areas F, K and H and their Stratigraphic and Chronological Implications. In *Megiddo III: The 1992–1996 Seasons*, II, edited by I. Finkelstein, D. Ussishkin, and B. Halpern (Tel Aviv Institute of Archaeology Monograph Series 18; Tel Aviv: Emery & Claire Yass Publications in Archaeology): 244–324.

Gilboa, A. (1999) The View from the East—Tel Dor and the Earliest Cypro-Geometric Exports to the Levant. In *Cyprus: The Historicity of the Geometric Horizon*, edited by M. Iacovou and D. Michaelides (Nicosia: University of Cyprus): 119-39.

Gilboa, A., and I. Sharon (2001) Early Iron Age Radiometric Dates from Tel Dor: Preliminary Implications for Phoenicia, and Beyond. *Radiocarbon* 43/3: 1343-51.

—(2003) An Archaeological Contribution to the Early Iron Age Chronological Debate: Alternative Chronologies for Phoenicia and their Effects on the Levant, Cyprus and Greece. *BASOR* 332: 7-80.

Herzog, Z., and L. Singer-Avitz (2004) Redefining the Centre: The Emergence of State in Judah. *Tel Aviv* 31: 209-44.

Lehmann, G., A. Killebrew, and Y. Gadot (2000) Area K. In *Megiddo III: The 1992–1996 Seasons*, I, edited by I. Finkelstein, D. Ussishkin and B. Halpern (Tel Aviv Institute of Archaeology Monograph Series 18; Tel Aviv: Emery & Claire Yass Publications in Archaeology): 123-39.

Mazar, A. (1990) *Archaeology of the Land of the Bible 10,000–586 B.C.E* (The Anchor Bible Reference Library; New York: Doubleday).

—(2004) Greek and Levantine Iron Age Chronology: A Rejoinder. *IEJ* 54: 24-36.

Scott, E.M. (2003) The Fourth International Radiocarbon Intercomparison (FIRI). *Radiocarbon* 45(2): 135-50.

Sharon, I. (2001) 'Transition Dating'—A Heuristic Mathematical Approach to the Collation of ^{14}C Dates from Stratified Sequences. *Radiocarbon* 43(3): 345-54.

Sharon, I., A. Gilboa, and E. Boaretto (in press) ^{14}C and the Early Iron Age of Israel—Where Are We Really At? A Commentary on the Tel Rehov Radiometric Dates. In *Proceedings of the 2nd EuroConference of 'SCIEM 2000'. Vienna, May 28 to June 1 2003* (Vienna: Austrian Academy).

Stuiver, M., *et al.* (1998) INTCAL98 Radiocarbon Age Calibration, 24 000—0 Cal AD. *Radiocarbon* 40: 1041-83.

Zarzecki-Peleg, A. (2005a) The Iron Age I (Strata XVIII–XVII). In *Yoqneam II: The Iron Age and the Persian Period*, edited by A. Ben-Tor, A. Zarzecki-Peleg, and S. Cohen-Anidjar (Qedem 6; Jerusalem: Israel Exploration Society and Institute of Archaeology): 10-89.

—(2005b) The Iron Age IIA (Strata XVI–XIV). In *Yoqneam II: The Iron Age and the Persian Period*, edited by A. Ben-Tor, A. Zarzecki-Peleg, and S. Cohen-Anidjar (Qedem 6; Jerusalem: Israel Exploration Society and Institute of Archaeology): 90-168.

III.
AROUND THE
EASTERN MEDITERRANEAN
IN THE IRON AGE

7 Radiocarbon Calibration in the East Mediterranean Region

The East Mediterranean Radiocarbon Comparison Project (EMRCP) and the current state of play

Sturt W. Manning, Bernd Kromer, Sahra Talamo, Michael Friedrich, Peter Ian Kuniholm, and Maryanne W. Newton

Abstract

This chapter offers a brief preliminary report on some aspects of the on-going EMRCP (as of AD 2004). The following findings are made: (1) generally Aegean and East Mediterranean samples can be used with the standard mid-latitude northern hemisphere calibration datasets (the IntCal curves); (2) that some small offsets exist particularly at times of significant solar minima including during the 8th century BCE.

Introduction

It is one of the fundamental tenets of radiocarbon dating that within each hemisphere the pre-industrial atmosphere was sufficiently well mixed to permit the use of a universal ^{14}C calibration dataset. Radiocarbon measurements available through to the early 1990s (e.g. Vogel *et al.* 1993; Stuiver and Becker 1993), as well as General Circulation Models (GCM) (Braziunas, Fung, and Stuiver 1995), supported this prerequisite. But then several studies reported significant location-dependent ^{14}C differences (see McCormac, Baillie, and Pilcher 1995, and references therein). Such issues could affect high-resolution radiocarbon dating. The EMRCP was therefore established to investigate this and related topics with specific reference to the accurate and precise employment of radiocarbon dating in the prehistoric Aegean and east Mediterranean region.

In a first stage of work we compared ^{14}C time series obtained from two key areas relevant for this issue—Central Europe and the Eastern Mediterranean—based on decadal wood samples from German Oak (from southern Germany) and Turkish pine (from Çatacık forest in western Anatolia) and juniper (from the archaeological site of Gordion and area dendrochronology). These first stage results have been reported previously (Kromer *et al.* 2001; Manning *et al.* 2001, 2003). In this chapter we illustrate the current extension of our work in the AD 1300–1800 and 900–600 BCE intervals, and comment on the state of play at present (as of AD 2004).

Samples

The samples described in this chapter come from the following locations:
1. *Central Europe*—the AD period samples come from timber found in historical buildings from several locations in southern Germany; and the BCE period sections come from finds of wood in gravel pits associated with the Main River. All samples are *Quercus robur*. They are labeled as GeO.
2. *Eastern Mediterranean*—the AD period samples come from the site of Çatacık forest in western Anatolia. These are *Pinus nigra*, labeled as CAT. The BCE period samples employ juniper wood from the long floating chronology established from the Gordion site materials from central Anatolia (Kuniholm 1977 and work since; samples used were GOR-2, *Juniperus foetidissima*, and GOR-3, *Juniperus excelsa*, both from the Midas Mound Tumulus, and GOR-161, *Juniperus excelsa* from the nearby Kizlarkaya Tumulus), and also pine samples from the Urartian archaeological site of Ayanis in northeast Anatolia (AYA 188B, 193, 193A, 201E, 315A: these wood and charcoal samples are likely *Pinus sylvestris* but cannot really be distinguished from *Pinus nigra* by wood anatomy alone), and juniper samples from the Middle Bronze Age archaeological site of Karahöyük-Konya in southwestern Anatolia (KBK 43, *Juniperus sp.*, probably *Juniperus foetidissima*). These samples are respectively labeled as GOR, AYA and KBK in the figures below.

Laboratory Procedures

Sampling
Dendrochronologically relatively dated wood samples were marked at annual increments and then dissected as precisely as possible into the requisite 10-year samples. For some extremely narrow-ring sections the potential for error is possible, but we believe that checking and care have prevented this. Coniferous samples split well between annual increments, and with care the respective samples are close to precise decades with little contamination. Oak can be more difficult to separate and lacks the same distinct physical cleavage property between rings. We believe we achieved close to precise decades but some very small amount of possible contamination from, or to, the previous ring cannot be entirely avoided. However, as a tiny fraction of the overall decade sample, this should be an insignificant issue.

Pre-treatment
Coniferous samples were pre-treated in a Soxhlet extraction. For all samples we used the modified AAA-procedure (80° 4% NaOH overnight, 30 minutes at 80° of 4% HCl, 1.5 hours at 80° of 4% NaOH, 30 minutes at 80° of 4% HCl). In our process a full-sized sample (15 to 20g of dry wood) delivers 4g of carbon.

Combustion
The samples were combusted in a 1.8 litre Parr bomb. We modified the original procedure (Dörr, Kromer, and Münnich 1989) by adding an additional precipitation step to guarantee highest possible gas purity for large (10 litre) CO_2 gas samples. In the new design 4–6 samples can be combusted and precipitated per day. CO_2 gas obtained by acidifying the precipitate is purified chromatographically over activated charcoal.

Measurement Precision

The samples are counted for 8 to 10 days in proportional counters in the Heidelberg Laboratory sub-basement counting room. Background and standard are corrected for minor fluctuations in atmospheric pressure and gas purity, respectively (Kromer and Münnich 1992). Typical precision is ca. 1.5‰, or about ±12–15 ^{14}C years at 1 Standard Deviation (σ) (68.2% confidence).

Findings

Interval AD 1300–1869 (see Fig. 7.1, Table 7.1)

We have compared same-age pairs of decadal samples of German oak with Turkish pine, as well as with the IntCal98 calibration set (Stuiver *et al.* 1998). In this time interval IntCal is mainly based on decadal samples of USA west coast Douglas fir and bi-decadal Irish oak, with therefore a significant bias to the decadal Pacific coast dataset. Overall, the mean difference of pairs of all three datasets is only a few years, and within available measurement precision (ca. 1.5‰) we cannot detect a measurable long-term ^{14}C gradient among the three datasets and regions.

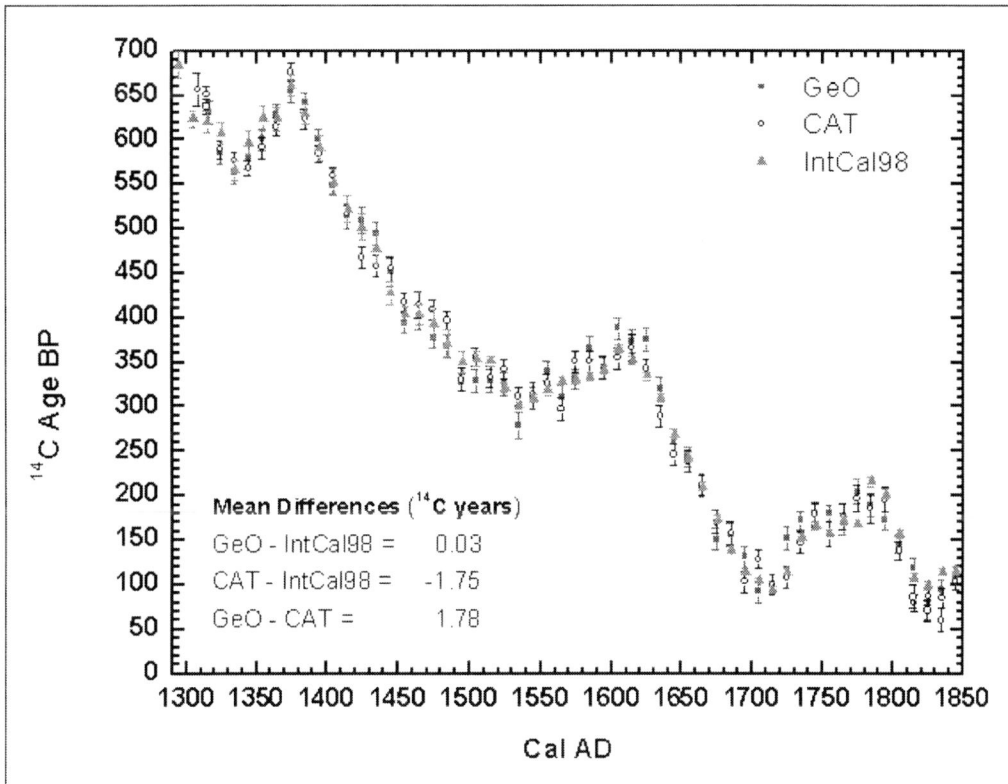

Figure 7.1. ^{14}C ages of EMRCP Anatolian pine (CAT) versus German oak (GeO) and IntCal98 over the period AD 1300–1850. The mean differences of the same-age pairs is very close to zero in each case.

Table 7.1. Comparison of AD period datasets.

	GeO–IntCal98 AD1300–1850	CAT–IntCal98 AD1300–1850	GeO–CAT AD1300–1850
Mean difference of pairs	0.03	–1.75	1.78
Observed Standard Deviation	21.24	18.16	18.4
Expected Standard Deviation	17.53	14.61	15.08
Ratio of Observed versus Expected Standard Deviation	1.21	1.24	1.2
Remaining Contribution	11.99	10.78	10.08

The ratio of observed versus expected standard deviation of the differences is ca. 1.2 to 1.24; some of the increase in variance may be caused by unknown laboratory errors. We note, however, that the increase seems stronger at times of strong variations in the atmospheric ^{14}C level, for example during the Spörer and Maunder solar minima, around AD 1490 and AD 1700, respectively. During high and rising atmospheric ^{14}C levels, the Anatolian samples seem depleted by around 1‰ compared to samples from Central Europe and (mainly) the Pacific coast, and vice versa outside these times. Thus there may be a small (± ca. 10 ^{14}C years) regional variation component within the overall dataset (Kromer *et al.* 2001).

The general conclusion we may draw, based on an extensive dataset of high-precision ^{14}C analyses, is that we have confirmed the assumption of a typically homogeneous ^{14}C level within available measurement precision at mid-latitudes within the Northern hemisphere (Manning *et al.* 2002). Only at intervals of considerably enhanced ^{14}C flux into the troposphere (solar activity minima) is there the potential for an enhanced seasonal ^{14}C cycle, which could be recorded in trees of differing growth seasons within this hemispheric zone (see below).

Interval 860–620 BCE (see Fig. 7.2)

Our measurements on decadal GeO samples agree well with the IntCal98 data, except for the interval 780–730 BCE, where our data are older than those measured by the Seattle laboratory on GeO, and by Belfast on Irish oak (these 780–730 BCE data contribute to the majority of the relatively large differences between datasets reported in Fig. 7.2). Part of the discrepancy seems to be an artefact caused by the extrapolation from original bi-decadal spacing of data in IntCal in this interval (this issue has been corrected in the new IntCal04 calibration dataset published since the present paper was submitted). Earlier, in the middle second millennium BCE, we have previously reported good agreement (apart from one decade—centered 1675 BCE) for EMRCP measurements on German oak samples 1705–1495 BCE when compared with Seattle laboratory data on similar wood (see Kromer *et al.* 2001: 2530; see Fig. 7.3).

The Anatolian chronologies are floating, but could be wiggle-matched to yield near-absolute ages within a narrow margin of a few calendar years (Manning *et al.* 2001, 2003) to IntCal98 (see Fig. 7.4 for state of affairs in 2004). As in the AD interval, we find a close agreement in ^{14}C age pattern between Anatolia and the trees grown in Central Europe (see also Fig. 7.3, where measurements on Anatolian juniper provide a good wiggle-match fit with both Seattle and EMRCP GeO datasets), but we again observe older ^{14}C ages (depletion in ^{14}C) at the strong ^{14}C rise between 800 and 750 BCE. With our new EMRCP data on GeO (the 'GeO' shown in Fig. 7.2) the difference is less prominent than when compared to IntCal98, but the trend remains.

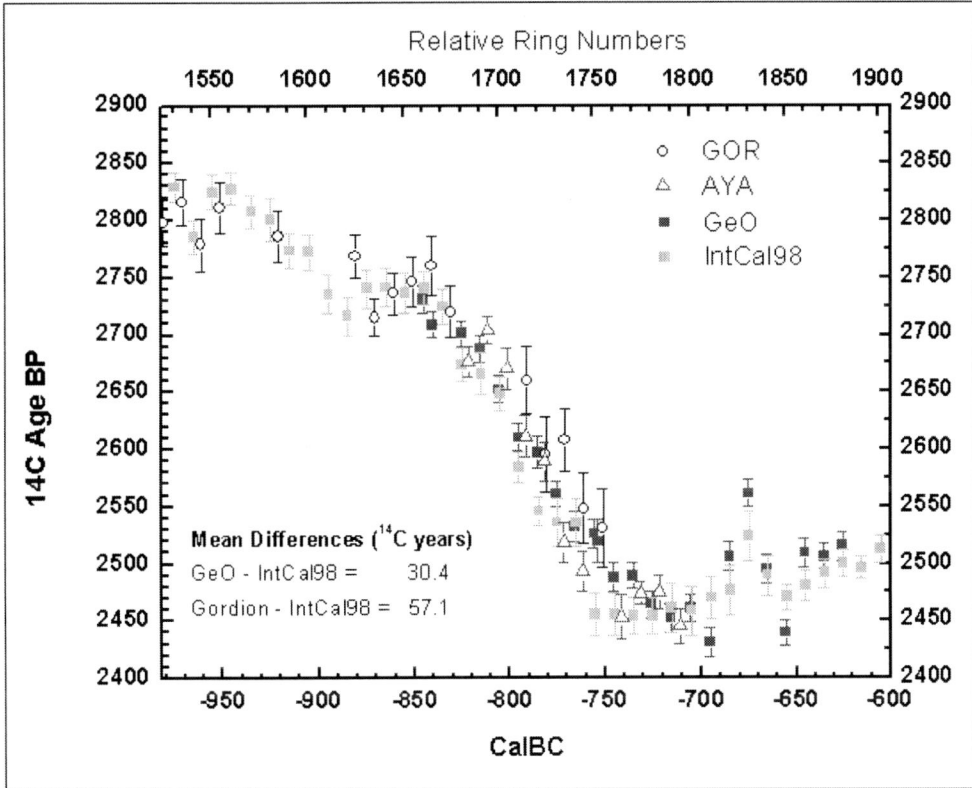

Figure 7.2. ^{14}C ages of Anatolian wood versus German oak and IntCal98 for the interval 860–620 BCE.

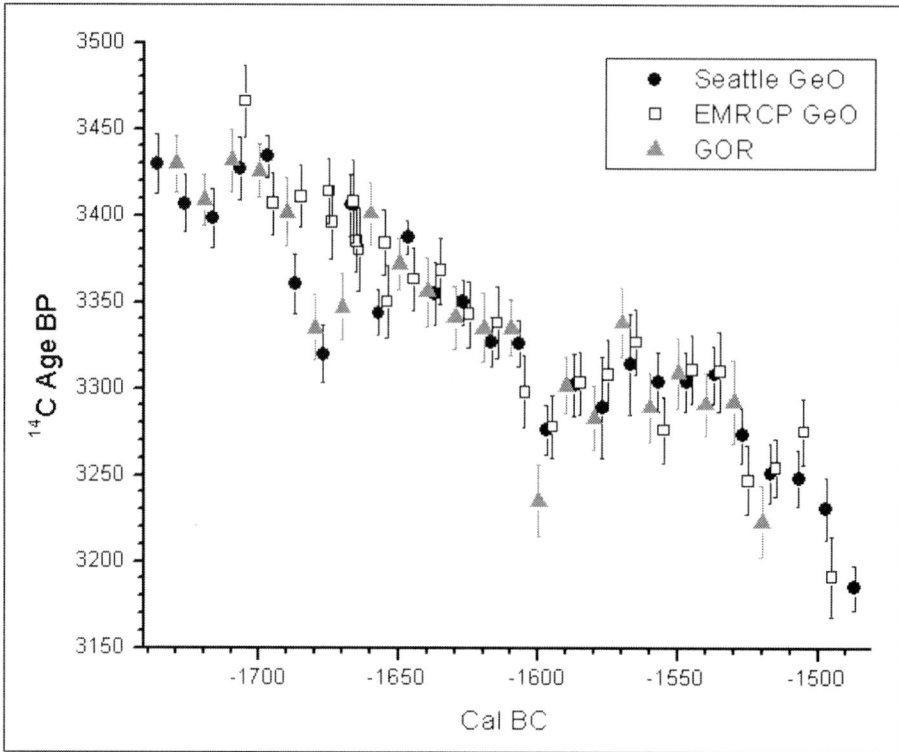

Figure 7.3. Comparison of EMRCP German oak (EMRCP GeO) with Seattle Laboratory measurements on similar German oak (Seattle GeO) (data from Stuiver, Reimer, and Braziunas 1998). The mean difference is approximately 2.3 ^{14}C years. The observed versus expected standard deviation is 29 against 22.5. The largest discrepancy occurs ca. 1675 BCE. Excluding this decade, the approximate mean difference becomes 1.4 ^{14}C years and the observed versus expected standard deviation 23.8 against 22.5 ^{14}C years. EMRCP data on juniper from Gordion (GOR) is shown also, according to its near-absolute wiggle-match placement (Manning *et al.* 2001, 2003). It agrees closely with the German oak data (including representation of the 'wiggle' comprising the 1685 BCE and 1675 BCE datapoints in the Seattle GeO set).

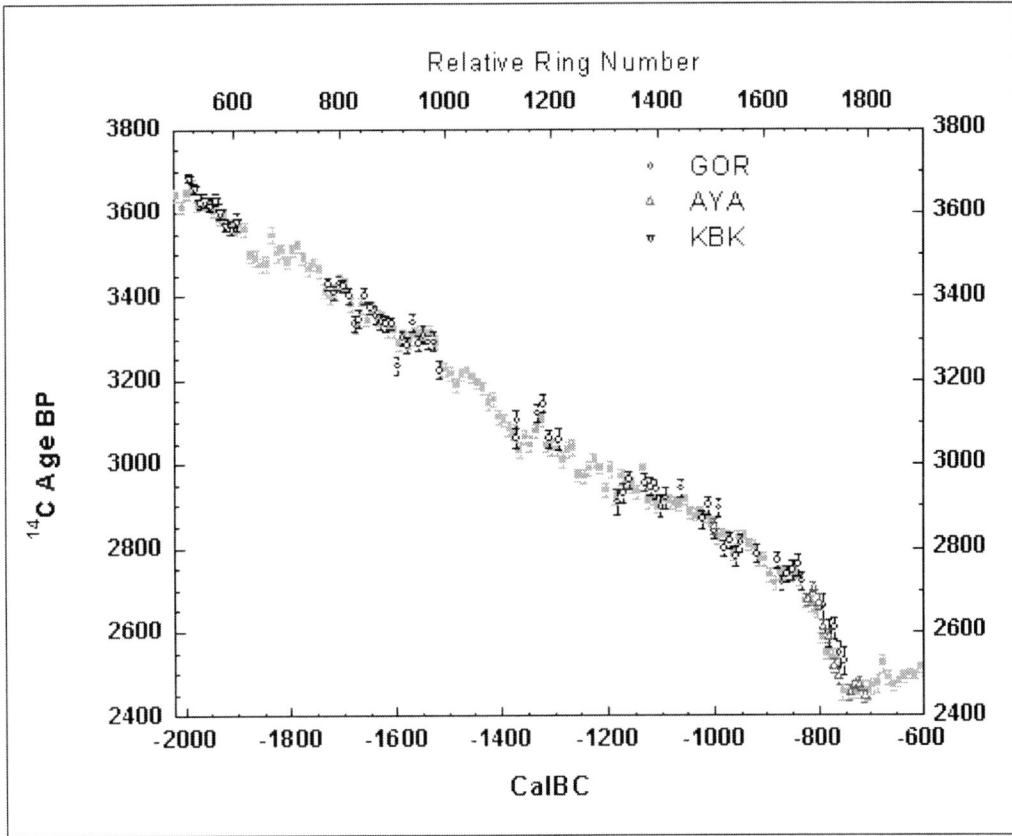

Figure 7.4. Wiggle-match placement of all (at time of writing) BCE period Anatolian dendrochronological samples (GOR, AYA, KBK) against IntCal98.

We interpret the ^{14}C depletion evident in ca. 800–750 BCE in central Anatolia as a manifestation of a natural seasonal cycle (Hesshaimer 1997) of tropospheric ^{14}C activity, and recorded by an earlier typical tree-growing season in central Anatolia compared to Central Europe and the Pacific coast (see Kromer *et al.* 2001). If we exclude modern fossil fuel and bomb components, this likely contributes a 1–2‰ variation in $\Delta^{14}CO_2$ (Levin and Hesshaimer 2000; Randerson *et al.* 2002). In pre-modern situations this typically will not really be detectable given available measurement precision, but, at times of deep solar minima such differences are exaggerated as ^{14}C production (and hence ^{14}C flux) is doubled when compared to the average of the 11-year solar cycle at high latitude, and so a detectable difference may just be apparent even within the mid-latitudes. We note the importance of the Ayanis samples in this regard. They are from a high altitude location (ca. 1866m) and from eastern Turkey. They do not exhibit the small offset ca. 800–750 BCE, and instead, more consistent with altitude and geographic context, mainly offer a growth season, and so radiocarbon measurements, close to the German oak.

Conclusions

Be not alarmed… In general, and over any long time interval, radiocarbon measurements on same age data agree well when comparing data from the Aegean and east Mediterranean with those from elsewhere in the mid-latitudes of the northern hemisphere—and in particular those measurements comprising the IntCal datasets. The standard pre-modern seasonal component, especially during times of an active sun (as recently) is broadly of the ca. 1‰ level, and so is not usually apparent. Laboratory and other error components are likely more significant sources of observed variability. However, during deep solar minima when ^{14}C production at mid- and high latitudes doubles, then a phase difference in growing seasons (and/or incomplete atmospheric mixing within the necessary timeframe) could account for apparent ca. 20–30 ^{14}C year differences between arid (and more southerly) and temperate (and more northerly) regions. This is a small offset (and one which applies only to special growing conditions as also shown further by ongoing work since submission of this paper). But it is of potential relevance at high-precision level in considerations of Aegean and east Mediterranean (including Levantine) chronology in, for example, the 8th century BCE (compare Reimer 2001: Figure).

Acknowledgments

We thank especially the Institute for Aegean Prehistory, and also the Heidelberg Academy of Sciences, the NSF, and the Natural Sciences and Engineering Research Council of Canada, for support towards this project.

References

Braziunas, T.F., I.Y. Fung, and M. Stuiver (1995) The Preindustrial Atmospheric $^{14}CO_2$ Latitudinal Gradient as Related to Exchanges among Atmospheric, Oceanic, and Terrestrial Reservoirs. *Global Biogeochemical Cycles* 9(4): 565-84.

Dörr, H., B. Kromer, and K.-O. Münnich (1989) Fast ^{14}C Sample Preparation of Organic Material. *Radiocarbon* 31: 264-68.

Hesshaimer, V. (1997) Tracing the Global Carbon Cycle Bomb Radiocarbon (PhD dissertation, Institute of Environmental Physics, University of Heidelberg).

Kromer, B., and K.-O. Münnich (1992) CO_2 Gas Proportional Counting in Radiocarbon Dating—Review and Perspective. In *Radiocarbon after Four Decades*, edited by R.E. Taylor, A. Long, and R.S. Kra (New York: Springer).

Kromer, B., *et al.* (2001) Regional $^{14}CO_2$ Offsets in the Troposphere: Magnitude, Mechanisms, and Consequences. *Science* 294: 2529-32.

Kuniholm, P.I. (1977) *Dendrochronology at Gordion and the Anatolian Plateau* (PhD dissertation, University of Pennsylvania; Ann Arbor: University Microfilms International).

Levin, I., and V. Hesshaimer (2000) Radiocarbon—A Unique Tracer of Global Carbon Cycle Dynamics. *Radiocarbon* 41: 69-80.

Manning, S.W., *et al.* (2001) Anatolian Tree-rings and a New Chronology for the East Mediterranean Bronze–Iron Ages. *Science* 294: 2532-35.

Manning, S.W., *et al.* (2002) No Systematic Early Bias to Mediterranean ^{14}C Ages: Radiocarbon Measurements from Tree-ring and Air Samples Provide tight Limits to Age Offsets. *Radiocarbon* 44: 739-54.

—(2003) Confirmation of Near-absolute Dating of East Mediterranean Bronze–Iron Dendrochronology. *Antiquity* 77 (295) <http://antiquity.ac.uk/ProjGall/Manning/manning.html>.

McCormac, F.G., M.G.L. Baillie, and J.R. Pilcher (1995) Location-dependent Differences in the ^{14}C Content of Wood. *Radiocarbon* 37: 395-407.

Randerson, J.T., *et al.* (2002) Seasonal and Latitudinal Variability of Tropospheric $\Delta^{14}CO_2$: Post Bomb Contributions from Fossil Fuels, Oceans, the Stratosphere, and the Terrestrial Biosphere. *Global Biogeochemical Cycles* 16(4) 1112 (doi: 10.1029/2002GB001876).

Reimer, P.J. (2001) A New Twist in the Radiocarbon Tale. *Science* 294: 2494-95.

Stuiver, M., and B. Becker (1993) High-Precision Decadal Calibration of the Radiocarbon Time Scale, AD 1950–6000 BC. *Radiocarbon* 35: 35-65.

Stuiver, M., P.J. Reimer, and T.F. Braziunas (1998) High-precision Radiocarbon Age Calibration for Terrestrial and Marine Samples. *Radiocarbon* 40: 1127-51.

Stuiver, M., P.J., *et al.* (1998) INTCAL98 Radiocarbon Age Calibration, 24,000-0 cal BP. *Radiocarbon* 40: 1041-83.

Vogel, J.C., *et al.* (1993) Pretoria Calibration Curve for Short-lived Samples, 1930–3350 BC. *Radiocarbon* 35: 73-85.

8 A Dendrochronological ^{14}C Wiggle-match for the Early Iron Age of North Greece

A contribution to the debate about this period in the Southern Levant

Maryanne W. Newton, Kenneth A. Wardle, and Peter Ian Kuniholm

Abstract

Decadal samples from a dendrochronology built from the tree-ring sequences of four trees in two stratigraphically defined phases at the site of Assiros in north Greece provide the first high precision wiggle-matched radiocarbon dates for a stratum containing a diagnostic ceramic artifact (a Protogeometric amphora).[1] The date points to a higher date than conventionally accepted for the appearance of this ceramic style in Greece and, by extension, any of the neighboring areas in the eastern Mediterranean to which this style of pot was exported. With respect to the focus of this volume, the study is a clear illustration of the difficulties involved in interpreting any ^{14}C date for this period. The wiggle-matched ^{14}C date, at 2σ, is 1091 ± 25 BCE, and this correlates with the dendrochronological date of 1078 + 4/–7 BCE. Dendrochronological crossdating can offer dates at annual resolution which, as with historical annals, is clearly the preferred resolution for understanding the complex archaeological footprints of multiple sites in a large area of the eastern Mediterranean in the early Iron Age.

...Why not have Protogeometric begin in 1100 BCE, instead of ca. 1050 BCE? The problem is in stretching the Geometric, as we would have to do, keeping the Thucydidean dates as fixed points (where are we if we don't?).

Years ago, Anthony Snodgrass hoped for a log, if possible one strategically placed, as in a magazine like the one at Tel Hadar, to answer our questions through dendrochronology. (Kopcke 2002)

We are appreciative of Professor Kopcke's comments, as we feel they get to the heart of the kinds of problems in early Iron Age chronology that prompted this volume. What follows is only a beginning.

Charred construction timbers collected during excavations at Assiros in north Greece provide the first direct near-absolute dates for the start of the Early Iron Age in Macedonia, and by

---

1.   Newton, Wardle, and Kuniholm (2005).

extension, in southern Greece.[2] The techniques of dendrochronological cross-dating and dendro-chronological ^{14}C wiggle-matching (DWM) are applied to archaeologically well-stratified charcoal samples, and provide two near-absolute dates that bracket the appearance of a diagnostic ceramic style (Fig. 8.1) that was exported and widely exchanged across the eastern Mediterranean, including to sites in the southern Levant.[3] Protogeometric sherds found at sites in the Levant so far are attributed to later stages in its development. However, raising the dates for the beginning of its appearance entails a reconsideration of recent proposals that Greek ceramics found in the East better 'fit' Finkelstein's proposed 'low' chronological scheme (Coldstream 2003; Fantalkin 2001). A discussion of the implications of the near-absolute dates at Assiros follows a review of the techniques used to arrive at them.

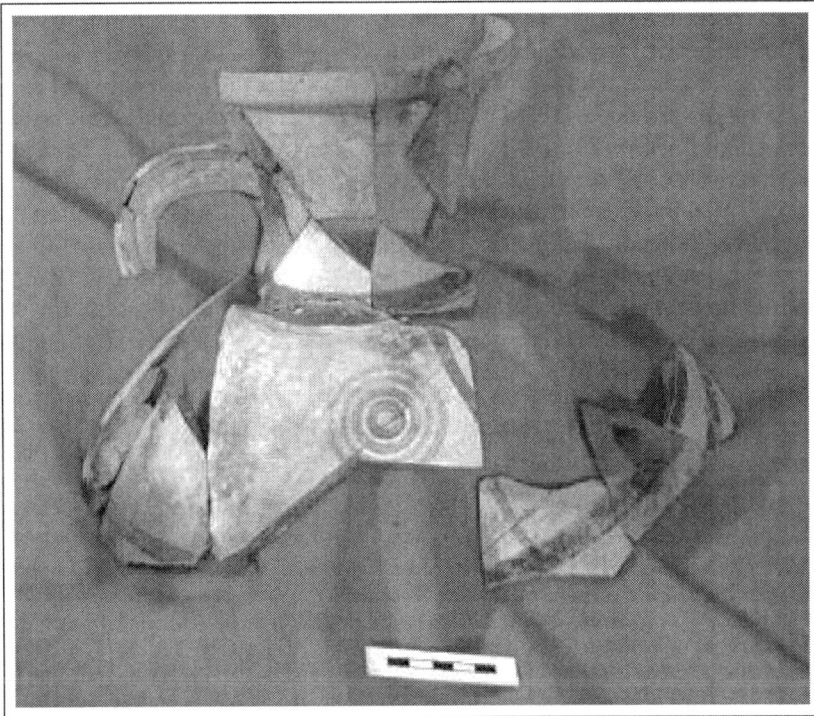

Figure 8.1. Assiros Phase 3 Protogeometric amphora.

2.   Scholars studying the early Iron Age in Greece have copious amounts of pottery, chiefly from funerary contexts, from which to develop a ceramics-based chronology, and for the earliest phases, most scholars have tended towards setting the beginnings of ceramic innovations in Greece to Attica, chiefly from finds of Protogeometric pots in graves in the Kerameikos in Athens. But the results of work at Lefkandi in Euboea have, for some scholars, prompted a re-evaluation of this thesis. With respect to 'hard' dates, the 'loose' historical dates for sites in the southern Levant at which have been found imports of Greek Protogeometric pots have contributed to the chronological problems. In what might be called a circular fashion, reconstructions of the chronology of the early Iron Age both in the Levant and in Greece have reached a standstill.

3.   There is some debate about where in the Early Protogeometric period this amphora falls, but Richard Catling in a recent study placed it early in the sequence (Catling 1998: esp. 161).

The DWM Model—The Radiocarbon

A 104-year sequence of tree rings based on the growth patterns of four trees that grew in the 12th and 11th centuries BCE can be matched with the Anatolian master dendrochronology sequence to give a probable cutting date of 1080[4] BCE +4/–7[5] for the trees used in the construction of the Phase 3 settlement of Assiros, and a date of 1070[6] BCE +4/–7[7] for the trees used in the buildings of the Phase 2 settlement which was constructed shortly after the Phase 3 buildings were destroyed by fire. It is the stratigraphic relationship between the floors of the Phases 3 and 2 settlements at Assiros which permits the fine dating of the appearance of the Protogeometric amphora which was found, broken, on the floor of Room 14 of the Phase 3 settlement. The excavators of this pot, given the total destruction by fire of both the Phase 3 and 2 settlements, do not believe that the wood used for either construction can be explained, or 'explained away',[6] as re-used.

Because of the necessarily qualified dendrochronological date,[7] a series of seven roughly bidecadal ^{14}C dates was run at the Institut für Umweltphysik at the University of Heidelberg (see BP dates in Table 8.1) to provide a DWM model to test the dendrochronological placement. Two of these decadal samples were run in 1999 in an earlier test of the suitability of the material for DWM analysis, and five more later selected to try to replicate the radiocarbon calibration curve in this difficult period. Against the internationally recommended INTCAL98 calibration curve (Bronk Ramsey 2001) the radiocarbon date of the last preserved ring of the 104-year Assiros dendrochronology falls, at 2σ, at 1091 ± 25 (95.4% probability) BCE (Figs. 8.2 and 8.3).[8] Even though the dating probabilities present alternative scenarios, the archaeologist must choose the one that best fits the stratigraphy and contextual understanding of the site. In our case, the stratigraphic relationship between the wood samples from Phases 3 and 2 at Assiros is certain, and the dendrochronological and radiocarbon results are consistent. Disregarding them will entail a string of examples all of which, from our perspective, amount to cases of special pleading.

---

4.   These dates include a conservative estimate (8 rings and 11 rings, respectively) for the number of rings missing at the end of the two sequences for which measurements made at the time of excavation were available (the two timbers from Phase 2). Since the measured dimensions of the reconstructed timbers are slightly smaller than those made by the excavator, and since no bark is preserved after the last measured ring, some rings may have been lost. In that case, the date for the cutting of the tree under analysis is given an estimate derived by dividing the estimate of the amount of radial wood missing by the average annual mature ring growth for each tree.

5.   Manning et al. 2001. The dates are qualified by +4/–7 years BCE. See also Manning et al. 2003.

6.   The stone footings of the Phase 4 walls built immediately above the mud brick walls of Phase 5 are an indication of the continuity of the settlement, and although there are but scant remains of the Phase 4 architecture, the alignment as fully indicated in the Phase 3 plan follows a new direction, one different from that laid out by the builders of the Late Bronze Age settlements in Phases 7, 6, and 5. The wood used in the Late Bronze Age buildings of Phases 6 and 5 had also burned, and the annual growth increments from four trees from these phases yields a 100-year dendrochronology against which the wood from Phases 3 and 2 does not crossdate. Furthermore, radiocarbon dates on all of the wood from these levels clearly distinguish two distinct periods of building activity, one in the early/mid 11th-century BCE, and the other in the mid-13th century BCE.

7.   The dendrochronology is neither long (it is only 104 years), nor robust (it is only four trees). This is in contrast to the long Bronze Age–Iron Age Master Dendrochronology against which it is compared (as of November 2004, it is 2009 years), which is robust over the years covered by Assiros Phases 3&2 dendrochronology (the number of samples varying between 35 and 91 per year).

8.   The calibrated dates as presented are calculated according to the first ring of the calibrated dendrochronological sequence, although the date we are interested in is that for the last ring of the sequence being wiggle-matched. Hence, all the calibrated dates presented in the text box next to the graph in Fig. 8.2 should have 98 years added, yielding lower (more recent) dates. The dates for the last preserved ring of the Phases 3&2 dendrochronology can be further quantified by adding the 3σ range which, at 99.7% probability, yields a calibrated date of 1102±38 BCE. But such fine parsing of statistical probabilities in radiocarbon dating misses the point here—that radiocarbon dates can be used to confirm a dendrochronological placement.

Table 8.1. ^{14}C determinations for Assiros Phases 3&2 DWM.

Heidelberg Sample #	Assiros Sample #	Dendrochronological relative years of selected decades	BP date
Hd-23249	ASR6&7 (2003)	991–1000, Midpoint 995.5	2935±14
Hd-23250	ASR6&7 (2003)	1010–1020, Midpoint 1015	2962±16
Hd-21076	ASR16 (2000)	1016–1028, Midpoint 1022	2925±29
Hd-23438	ASR16 (2004)	1026–1038, Midpoint 1032	3009±22
Hd-23254	ASR6&7 (2003)	1040–1050, Midpoint 1045	2927±16
Hd-23251	ASR6&7 (2003)	1060–1070, Midpoint 1065	2929±16
Hd-21077	ASR6&7 (2000)	1079–1091, Midpoint 1085	2906±23

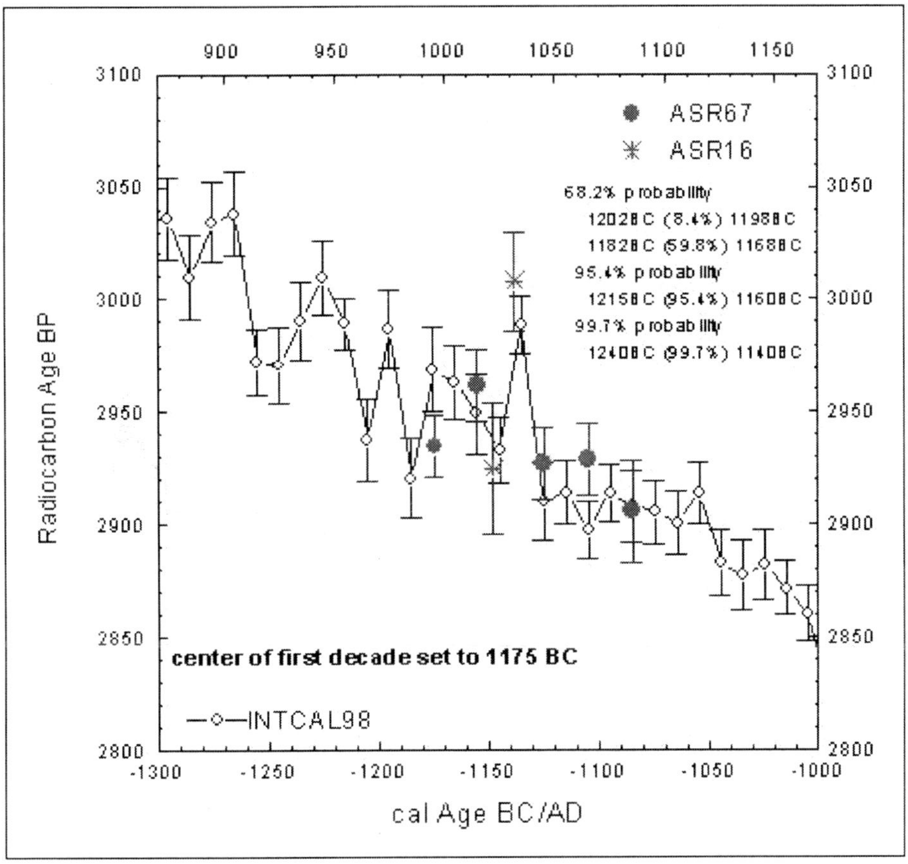

Figure 8.2. Assiros Phases 3&2 dendrochronological ^{14}C wiggle-match showing the fit of the seven determinations against the INTCAL98 calibration curve at the proposed dendrochronological date.

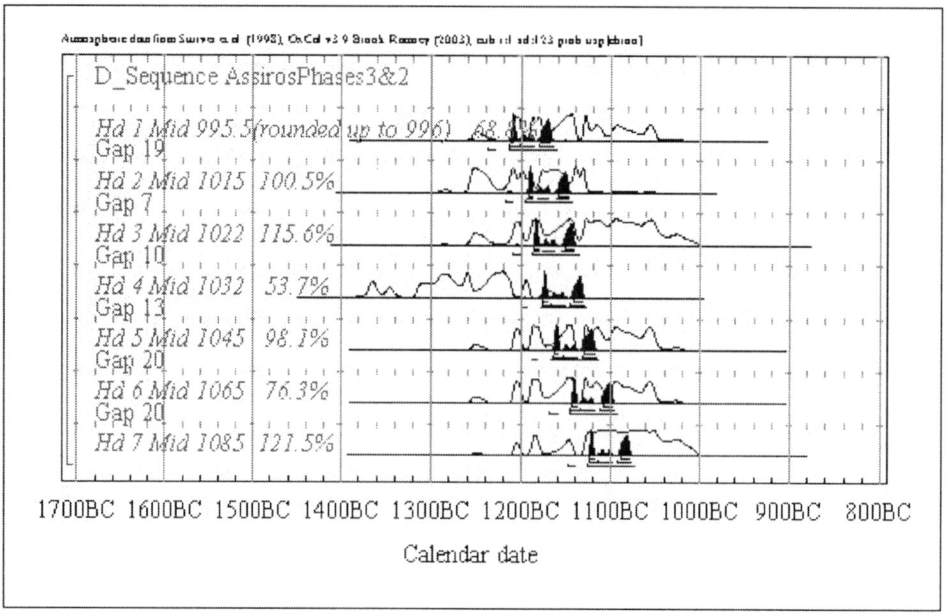

Figure 8.3. Composite probability plot of the calculated posterior distribution of the radiocarbon-dated decades according to the DWM model. The hollow background histograms show the total dating probability for each sample in isolation, whereas the much more tightly constrained solid black histograms show the total dating probability for each sample as part of the wiggle-match (note how this area is the same for every decade in the wiggle-match, essentially a graphic representation of the error associated with the wiggle-match). The upper and lower lines beneath the shaded histograms indicate the wiggle-match date ranges for each sample at respectively 1σ (68.4%), 2σ (95.4%), and 3σ confidence (99.7%).

Quo Vadis?

Figure 8.2 illustrates how the seven samples from Assiros are grouped together on the calibration curve. Since they are linked according to an absolute timescale, if one datum is moved within the limits of its error range, then the other six must move with it. No other 'fit' can be supported by this sequence of dates.[9] The calendar date for the last preserved ring of the Assiros Phases 3 & 2 dendrochronology must therefore, from radiocarbon data alone, be set at 1093 ± 22 BCE at 1σ (68.2% probability), or 1091 ± 24 BCE at 2σ (95.4 % probability), or 1102 ± 38 BCE at 3σ (99.7% probability).[10]

---

9. Analyses run in Heidelberg by Dr Sahra Talamo and Dr Bernd Kromer. The determination that is most important for the early placement is the fourth in series which, at 3009±22 BP, closely matches the peak in the INTCAL98 curve at 1135 cal BCE. We comment as a caveat that the radiocarbon dates for the dendrochronologically absolutely dated decade that is centered on 1135 BCE in the INTCAL98 calibration curve depends on an average of the available data, all from German oak, but measured at two different radiocarbon facilities, Seattle and Belfast. They do not statistically agree with one another, and work to replicate that decade is currently in progress. In preliminary versions we have seen of INTCAL 04, the formulas used will de-emphasize, but not remove, the 1135 BCE spike.

10. These estimated calendar ages are based on a DWM model of the final BP dates reported by the Heidelberg laboratory, and they differ slightly from dates presented at the conference in Thessaloniki in February 2004, and repeated in a press release by the University of Birmingham in May 2004. The differences are accounted for partly by slight changes in the final dates due to Heidelberg laboratory procedures for accounting for background radiation, and also by the use of

In reports already published, the dates assigned to each of the phases of the early Iron Age at Assiros were based on conventional archaeological dating (Coldstream 1977; Desborough 1952, 1964, 1972; Snodgrass 1971; Wardle 1989), and they allow a rough division of the time span between 1050 and 850 BCE to accommodate the four phases of construction at Assiros (4, 3, 2 and 1.5[11]) before abandonment of the site. These estimates were broadly compatible with the single ^{14}C sample from Phase 2 in the small group determined by the British Museum in 1982 (BM 1426: 2800±75BP, calibrated at 1σ between 1020 and 830 BCE, but, in consideration of the new evidence and noting the large error margin on this date, we note the 2σ range puts that date between 1190 and 800 BCE),[12] precisely in the period addressed in this volume.

Why might this be relevant? Because single ^{14}C determinations, or even groups of single determinations chosen to date a single event (or stratum), may be insufficient for negotiating the calibration curve over the years being examined. Hence, we employ the techniques of dendrochronology, based on the annual growth rings of trees, to do precisely what is needed—negotiate the calibration curve. In looking at charcoal from a site in Greece, we have the good fortune of having preserved wood charcoal that is both of a cross-datable species, and sufficiently long-lived. Figure 8.4 illustrates in bold the master tree-ring chronology for Phases 3 & 2 at Assiros, an average of the four measured ring series compiled from charcoal fragments from four oak timbers. It is this master dendrochronology that is compared to the master tree-ring chronology from Anatolia.

The fact that the Assiros dates apply to a widely distributed and recognizable ceramic artifact (a Protogeometric amphora) is a unique achievement for the study of Greek ceramics and the history of early Greece. Before proceeding to examine the significance of these dates for Macedonia, the Aegean and areas further afield, we address some of the objections which might be raised about them as they would, in raising the start date of Protogeometric, affect debate about interrelations in the eastern Mediterranean at the end of the Bronze Age, and about the pace and direction of change across the region in the early Iron Age.

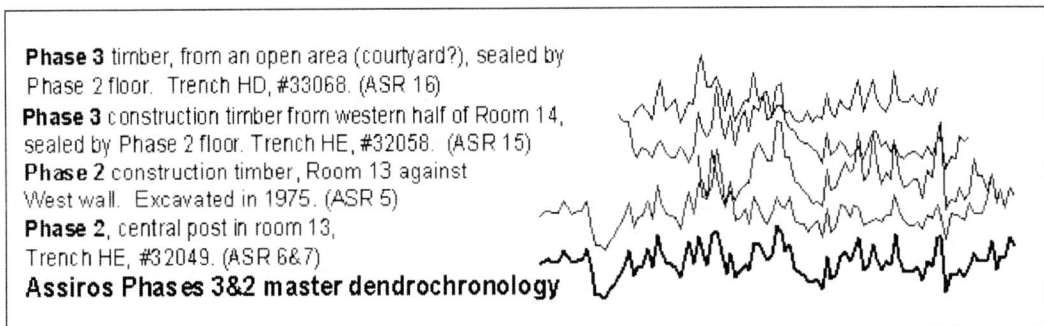

Phase 3 timber, from an open area (courtyard?), sealed by Phase 2 floor. Trench HD, #33068. (ASR 16)
Phase 3 construction timber from western half of Room 14, sealed by Phase 2 floor. Trench HE, #32058. (ASR 15)
Phase 2 construction timber, Room 13 against West wall. Excavated in 1975. (ASR 5)
Phase 2, central post in room 13, Trench HE, #32049. (ASR 6&7)
Assiros Phases 3&2 master dendrochronology

Figure 8.4. Assiros Phases 3&2 master dendrochronology (in bold) and its components.

---

different settings in OxCal to calculate the probabilities of the DWM. In February we used a wiggle-matching model in OxCal 3.9, with Resolution set to 4 (Bronk Ramsey's default setting), but here we set the Resolution to 1 based on consultations about the best method for high-precision wiggle-matching of near-decadal tree-ring sequences: this provides for a more direct correlation between the decadal samples of both data sets (the calibration curve and the Assiros Phases 3&2 data) without any additional smoothing. A resolution of 1 uses interpolations of the annual measurements of ^{14}C for each point on the calibration curve, and for each data point of the DWM. We use rounded annual outcomes in citing results. We thank Christopher Bronk Ramsey, Bernd Kromer, Sturt Manning, and Paula Reimer for their comments.

11.   This phase (1.5) was first observed at a late stage of the excavation after the other phases had been defined and numbered.

12.   Burleigh, Matthews, and Ambers (1982). The large range in the calibrated date, partly exacerbated by the large error on the ^{14}C date, is the residual effect of the shape of the calibration curve in these centuries.

First, the *cutting* date of the timber on the Phase 2 floor can be closely approximated, even though the bark is no longer present and the outer rings cannot clearly be demonstrated to be sapwood.[13] The timber on which the date is based was used as an unshaped post, and it is likely that the only processing of the wood before use was removal of the bark. Furthermore, the estimates for the slight ring loss from mechanical causes after burning suggest that both trees in the Phase 2 construction were cut in the same year, presumably for the same purpose, namely, to build the Phase 2 structure. The amphora has already been placed by Richard Catling in his 1998 study of Protogeometric pottery from the northern Aegean into his Group I. This group has a northern distribution from Macedonia to Troy and, more importantly, includes the central Aegean site of Lefkandi on the island of Euboea, the locus generally considered the source of Protogeometric in the Levant (Fig. 8.5).

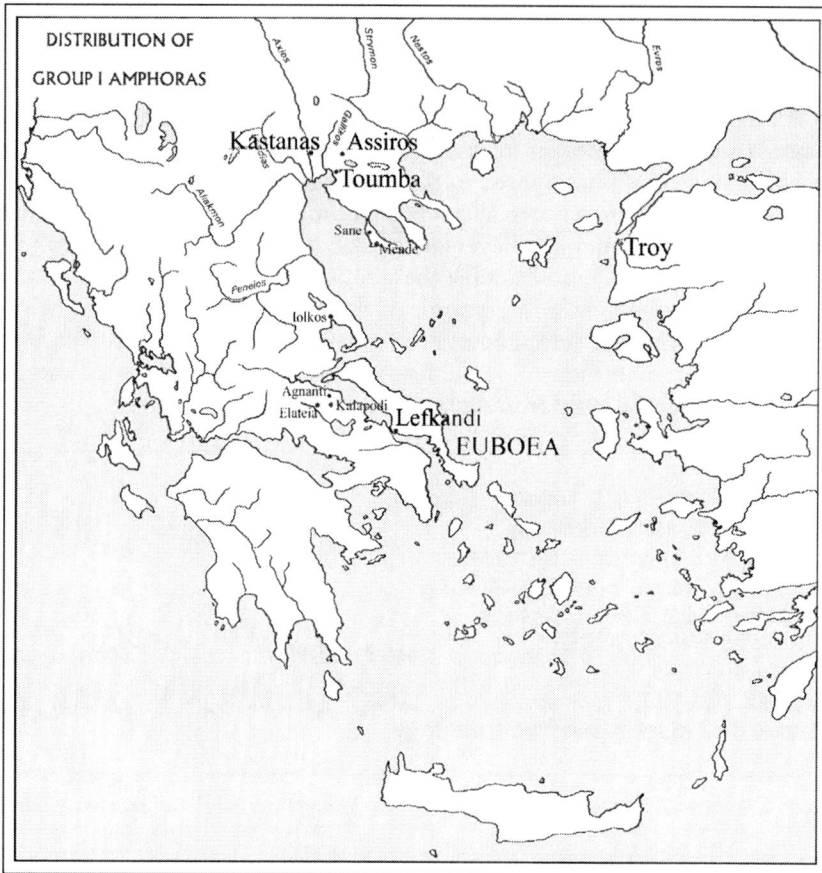

Figure 8.5. The Aegean distribution of Greek Protogeometric amphorae of a type classified by Richard Catling's work on material from Troy (map adapted from Catling 1998).

13.   The number of sapwood rings can, for oak, provide a valuable tool for dating the end of a tree's life. If any sapwood rings are present, an estimate for the total until bark can be added. Such an estimate for oak from north Greece and western Anatolia was presented in Kuniholm and Striker (1987). With charcoal, however, we are missing the most useful feature for identifying sapwood, that is, color change. The only anatomical feature that might be discernible in oak charcoal is the infilling of vessels with tyloses, but none of this could be observed in the carbonized Assiros samples.

If, as argued above, a date of 1070 BCE is accepted for the deposition of the Protogeometric amphora at Assiros, the inescapable corollary is that the date of the *start* of the Protogeometric period must be raised, perhaps by as many as 70 years (depending on which view is taken of the current start date), to allow time for the style to develop and be disseminated.

The appearance of Protogeometric pottery in the Levant must be traced via its appearance in Cyprus, as most reconstructions about the presence of Euboean Protogeometric in the East have identified Cyprus as the likely intermediary. In a recent article, Nicolas Coldstream presents two schemes for understanding the early Iron Age in Greece from Greek ceramics found outside of Greece from the perspective of an Aegeanist, and he prefers the 'low' chronological scheme offered by Finkelstein (Coldstream 2003; Finkelstein and Silberman 2001).

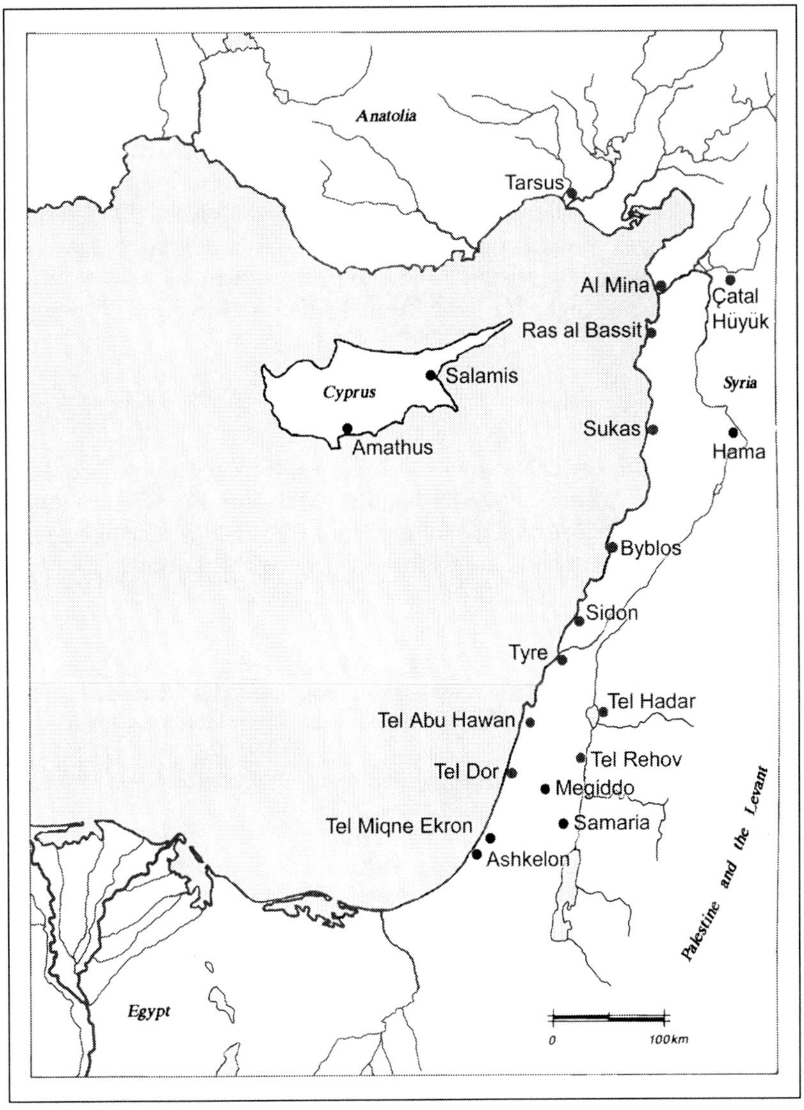

Figure 8.6. The distribution of Greek Protogeometric pottery in the Levant (map adapted from Lemos 2002).

The primary reason Coldstream offers is that the 'high' chronology would present 'an uncomfortable congestion' for the long development of LHIIIC and Sub-Mycenaean (Coldstream 2003; cf. also Coldstream and Mazar 2003). It may be time to reconsider the proposal that the LHIIIC period was a long one or at least one that, as Günter Kopcke suggested in his study of the crater from Tel Hadar (in the context of the Protogeometric in Greece), may have to be understood as a complicated pastiche of 'overlapping developments' (Kopcke 2002: 116). Amihai Mazar has reacted to Coldstream's hypothesis and concluded that it is not sustainable in the east (Mazar 2004). We agree; Coldstream's preferred chronological schema would not allow for the new evidence from Assiros.

Conclusion

This paper presents a new date for the start of the Protogeometric period in Greece. Although the ^{14}C wiggle-matched dendrochronological date provides, in its context, a *terminus ante quem* for the appearance of Protogeometric, it clearly needs to be understood in relation to the whole life history of the phases from which the trees used as construction timbers come. Radiocarbon dates for short-lived material from all phases at Assiros, and dendrochronological radiocarbon wiggle-matched dates on wood from earlier destruction levels should provide a fuller picture of the chronology of the later stages of the Bronze Age at Assiros. By integrating data into its broader context—internally, locally, and regionally[14]—we expect we will be able to provide a better context for understanding the high ^{14}C dates from Kastanas (Jung and Weninger 2002) and Toumba Thessalonikis,[15] too.

Acknowledgments

The Malcolm and Carolyn Wiener Laboratory for Aegean and Near Eastern Dendrochronology is supported by the National Science Foundation, the Malcolm H. Wiener Foundation, and individual Patrons of the Aegean Dendrochronology Project. For fundamental research permissions we thank the appropriate governmental authorities in Greece and Turkey.

References

Bronk Ramsey, C. (2001) Development of the Radiocarbon Program OxCal. *Radiocarbon* 43(2A): 355-63.

Burleigh, R., K. Matthews, and J. Ambers (1982) British Museum Natural Radiocarbon Measurements XIV. *Radiocarbon* 24: 243-44.

Catling, R.W.V. (1998) The Typology of the Protogeometric and Subprotogeometric Pottery from Troia and its Aegean Context. *Studia Troica* 8: 153-64.

Coldstream, J.N. (1977) *Geometric Greece* (London: E. Benn).

—(2003) Some Aegean Reactions to the Chronological Debate in the Southern Levant. *Tel Aviv* 30: 247-58.

Coldstream, J.N., and A. Mazar (2003) Greek Pottery from Tel Reḥov and Iron Age Chronology. *IEJ* 53.1: 29-48.

Desborough, V.R. D'a. (1952) *Protogeometric Pottery* (Oxford: Clarendon Press).

---

14. A point made clear by Gilboa and Sharon (2003), and briefly by Lemos (2002) and Coldstream (2003). A typological study of the local ceramics in north Greece is underway by Reinhard Jung in his work on the ceramics at Kastanas, a site with a much larger array of imported LHIIIC Mycenaean wares.

15. Two recent determinations for Phase 4 with LH IIIC pottery at Toumba Thessaloniki (DEM 1284 and 1285, S. Andreou, personal communication) are comparable to those for Phase 6 at Assiros, and we understand that additional samples are currently being processed.

—(1964) *The Last Mycenaeans and their Successors* (Oxford: Clarendon Press).

—(1972) *Greek Dark Ages* (London: Benn).

Fantalkin, A. (2001) Low Chronology and Greek Protogeometric Pottery in the Southern Levant. *Levant* 33: 117-25.

Finkelstein, I., and N.A. Silberman (2001) *The Bible Unearthed: Archaeology's New Vision of Ancient Israel and the Origin of its Sacred Texts* (New York: Free Press).

Gilboa, A., and I. Sharon (2003) An Archaeological Contribution to the Early Iron Age Chronological Debate: Alternative Chronologies for Phoenicia and their Effects on the Levant, Cyprus, and Greece. *BASOR* 332: 1-75.

Jung, R., and B. Weninger (2002) Appendix: Zur realität der Diskrepanz zwischen den kalibrierten ^{14}C-Daten und der historisch-archäologischen Datierung in Kastanas. In *Kastanas: die Drehscheibenkeramik der Schichten 19–11*, by R. Jung (PAS 18; Kiel: Oetker): 281-98.

—(2004) Kastanás and the Chronology of the Aegean Late Bronze and Early Iron Age. *In Radiocarbon and Archaeology: Proceedings of the Fourth Symposium, Oxford 2002* (Oxford: Oxbow Books): 209-28.

Kopcke, G. (2002) 1000 B.C.E.? 900 B.C.E.? A Greek Vase from Lake Galilee. In *Leaving No Stones Unturned: Essays on the Ancient Near East and Egypt in Honor of Donald P. Hansen*, edited by E. Ehrenberg (Winona Lake, IN: Eisenbrauns): 107-19.

Kuniholm, P.I., and C.L. Striker (1987) Dendrochronological Investigations in the Aegean and Neighboring Regions 1983–1986. *Journal of Field Archaeology* 14: 385-98.

Lemos, I.S. (2002) *The Protogeometric Aegean* (Oxford: Oxford University Press).

Manning, S.W., *et al.* (2001) Anatolian Tree Rings and a New Chronology for the East Mediterranean Bronze–Iron Ages. *Science* 294: 2532-35.

—(2003) Confirmation of Near-absolute Dating of East Mediterranean Bronze–Iron Dendrochronology. *Antiquity* 77, no. 295 <http://antiquity.ac.uk/ProjGall/Manningmanning.html>.

Mazar, A. (2004) Greek and Levantine Iron Age Chronology: A Rejoinder. *IEJ* 54: 24-36.

Newton, M.W., K.A. Wardle, and P.I. Kuniholm (2005). Dendrochronology and Radiocarbon Determinations from Assiros and the Beginning of the Greek Iron Age. *AEMΘ 17, 2003* (Thessaloniki): 173-90.

Snodgrass, A.M. (1971) *Dark Age of Greece: An Archaeological Survey of the Eleventh to the Eighth Centuries BC* (Edinburgh: Edinburgh University Press).

Wardle, K.A. (1989) Excavations at Assiros Toumba 1988: A Preliminary Report. *BSA* 84: 447-63ff.

9 High Precision Dating and Archaeological Chronologies

Revisiting an old problem

Sue Sherratt

Abstract

This study examines the varied types of data from which archaeologists seek to establish relative and absolute chronologies, particularly in the Late Bronze and Early Iron Ages of the Aegean and the Levant where there is a long tradition of writing 'history' from archaeology, and asks how far and in what ways we can best combine them. The conclusions are that, in general, they cannot be used to construct a single monolithic chronological structure characterised by ever finer resolution, and that perhaps we should accept the limitations of our chronologies more realistically than we sometimes do.

High Precision Dating and History

Chronology in general, and the chronology of the Early Iron Age southern Levant in particular, is one of those subjects which is almost always guaranteed to make one's head ache. This is not just because of the unusually contentious chronological problems, specific to the Early Iron Age Levant, which form the central subject of this volume, but also because when it comes to archaeological chronology generally we seem to spend much of our time trying to square circles, to combine chalk and cheese, by attempting to integrate into a single chronological scheme a number of different types of chronological frameworks that are based on quite different concepts of how the passage of time manifests itself in the archaeological record and, more importantly, how it can be measured. We find ourselves, in many ways, bashing our heads against a brick wall, much of the time attempting to do something that, viewed objectively from outside conventional archaeological ways of thinking, appears to run counter to common sense.

For the late second and early first millennia BCE, this is a problem which has perhaps been most acute in areas like the Aegean and the East Mediterranean, which lie on the fringes (either geographically or chronologically) of historical areas or periods like the Egyptian New Kingdom and Third Intermediate, Middle- and Neo-Assyria, and Archaic Greece. Their position in these respects has meant that the search for politico-military 'history', characteristic of Old World archaeology generally in the 19th and earlier 20th centuries, has been a particularly dominant and persistent part of archaeological tradition in these areas. Moreover, in both Greece and the Holy Land this has been further fuelled by the towering presence, looming over the archaeology, of the Homeric epics and the Hebrew Bible respectively, with their deep emotional significance to large sections of the population of a much wider European and transatlantic world. If the main aim of archaeology is to uncover ancient history (in the narrow sense of the word), or to prove the historicity of characters and events which figure in certain forms of ancient literature, then we need a truly historical chronology, like that of Classical Greece, based on archon lists and Olympic victors, or like that of ancient Egypt, based on royal reigns and conquests. This means that the archaeological record has to be calibrated in terms of single reliably recorded events—the sacking and destruction of a particular city, the death or accession of a particular ruler, the construction of a particular public building, the simultaneous re-location of a particular group of people—which require the ultimate in high precision dating.

It looks, at first glance, as though the potential for that ultimate in high precision dating is now finally with us, in the prospect of species- and regionally-consistent dendrochronological sequences which may eventually provide a continuous link with the present day, and which meanwhile (despite the problems presented by regional $^{14}CO_2$ offsets in the troposphere: Kromer *et al.* 2001; Manning *et al.* 2001a; Reimer 2001) will allow us to 'wiggle-match' floating sequences and calibrate with reliable precision the potentially much more plentiful supply of ^{14}C determinations. So all our problems will be solved. Or will they? Will we actually end up with something as useful as it seems? I think my answer is 'yes and no'. 'Yes', because if we want to put a precise date on the construction of a particular building, as long as we can be sure that we have the outer rings of the tree from which a particular beam was made, and as long as we can be sure that it was not re-used from an earlier building, then we shall be able to do it. 'No', partly because 'wiggle-matching' and calibration in itself will always be something of a creative art (Bronk Ramsey [Chapter 5, this volume]), but also because, more importantly, how far will this get us, unless we have a reliable and truly historical context in which to put it? The main use of such high chronological precision is in proving (or disproving) that we have found something we think we already know existed or happened. We may be able to show, for instance, that the tomb traditionally called Midas's tomb at Gordion (Young 1981) was constructed rather earlier (ca. 740 BCE) (Manning *et al.* 2001a: 2534) than the conventional date (696–95 BCE) for Midas's death provided by the late antique writer Eusebius (e.g. Helm 1956: 92). But, leaving aside the emotional thrill involved in gazing on the tomb of a famous historical or legendary character, does it really matter much whether the man buried in that tomb was someone called Midas (who may or may not have died in 696–95 BCE) or some other Phrygian bigwig with a different name? I am not sure that I, for one, care very much, since that tomb and its contents tell us much that is just as interesting as anything derived from literary history or legend, much of which seems improbable anyway. Similarly, if we believed that a Trojan War as described by Homer really took place at one of the wide range of dates later ascribed to it by various literary traditions, and if we were convinced that one of the successive cities of Troy was actually destroyed as a result of that war, high precision radiocarbon dating might be able to support or rule out the hypothesis that a particular building or habitation level of Troy was burnt within a particular narrow time span which was compatible with one of those dates. For many of us, however, this would contribute nothing to the problem of the historicity of the Homeric account of the Trojan War, and the question of the authenticity of the 'history' which we were trying to date precisely would remain entirely a matter of faith.

Absolute dating fixes, whether by conventional archaeological cross-referencing with historical chronologies, by high precision ^{14}C dating, by dendrochronology or any other scientific means either known or devisable, are not so much solutions to problems in themselves as contributory factors to much more complex methodological and theoretical problems concerning chronology and the way in which we use chronological information to interpret the archaeological record. These problems come down to the question of what we are actually dating—and why. By dendro-dating oak coffins or structural beams, or by taking ^{14}C measurements from short-life samples, such as a jarful of charred grain from a secure context, we may be able to put more or less precise dates (in some cases perhaps very precise dates) on single events—the burial of an individual (more precisely, the felling of the tree used for a coffin), or the construction or burning of a building—but it is not clear that this tells us much beyond the individual events to which these dates apply. It may give us a detailed and very precise chronology for the death of an individual person, or for the architectural history of a building or even a site, but it is not going to help provide a year-by-year chronology for the archaeological record in general, with a resolution comparable to a historical chronology, which we are sometimes encouraged to believe is an achievable and desirable goal (Manning 1998). Even if it did, what use is this without the detailed narrative history which can be firmly tied to it? The temptation is that, if we do not have the real history, we create a pseudo-event-centred history, by converting anonymous individuals into legendary characters or burnt buildings into invasions or conquests (Leonard 1988; Maier 1986). The interpretation of the Aegean prehistoric archaeological record for much of the 20th century depended on pretending that destructions which took place while similar pottery was in use happened, not just in the same archaeological time, but in the same real time, and converting these into major 'historical' events: a Dorian invasion which knocked out the Mycenaean palaces at the end of the Bronze Age, or an earlier conquest of Minoan Crete by Mycenaean Greeks. With the illusion of a historical chronology provided by dating methods of ever higher resolution, my fear is that the temptation will be to create more pseudo-history of this event-centred kind.

The Relativity of Ceramic Chronology

This brings me to another question: What does it mean to say, as has been stated recently, that the new dendro-dates from Assiros have provided an absolute date for the 'beginning of the Greek Iron Age' (or rather, its surrogate in the form of Protogeometric style pottery) of between 1080 and 1070 BCE (Kromer et al. 2004)? For a start, one has to understand that, from our current perspective, this has little or nothing directly to do with iron, but rather with a particular classification of ceramic styles which continue to be used, as a matter of convenience, to draw an arbitrary and entirely notional line between the Greek Bronze and Iron Ages. For this to seem even remotely comprehensible, it is necessary to appreciate the wider contexts of intellectual history in which the prehistoric archaeology of the Aegean and other areas of the Old World traditionally operated in the 19th and earlier 20th centuries AD, as a means of tracing, on the one hand, the technological progress of mankind, and, on the other hand, the 'prehistory' of particular 'peoples' (the conceptual entities on which modern nation states are built), whose essential and constant characteristics could conveniently be tracked through material cultural manifestations, such as the types and styles of pots they used or the way in which they disposed of their dead. As far as Greece is concerned, pottery labelled 'Geometric' (because of its style of decoration) was, from the late 19th century onwards, often associated with the arrival of northern ('Dorian') invaders who broke down the prehistoric ('Mycenaean') civilisation of Greece in the 12th and 11th centuries BCE and, in at least some versions, also introduced iron and cremation burial (Glotz 1925: 389; Skeat 1934; Tsountas and Manatt 1897: 131; cf. Hammond 1949). The appearance of both iron and 'Geometric' (or after ca. 1910 'Protogeometric') pottery was thus seen as evidence of a new group of people in southern Greece. Even after the gradual separation of the elements of this 'invader' package, beginning in the late 1920s, and the recognition that Protogeometric pottery continued to make use of shapes and decorations characteristic of late 'Mycenaean' pottery, the idea persisted that the emergence of the Protogeometric style marked an important watershed in early Greek history. Still in 1952, in the words of V.R.d'A. Desborough, 'it was the first example of a new creative spirit: the ideal of harmony and proportion, which is the distinguishing characteristic of Greek art and life' (1952: 298).

From a methodological point of view, however, we would recognise today that most of our current ceramic classifications, the demarcations between them, and their terminologies, are convenient constructs, and to a very large extent arbitrary. They are derived from 'snapshot' descriptions of pottery assemblages found in individual contexts, which are then increasingly 'normalised' outwards in space until we end with an artificial system of what we like to think of, for convenience, as stylistic 'phases' of more or less regional (or wider) application, each with its own label and occupying its own time-slot which is neatly distinguished from what precedes and follows it. However, it does not take much reflection to realise that, except perhaps in entirely exceptional circumstances, pottery is most unlikely to work like that. What the statement referred to above actually means in practice is that a pot showing a particular stylistic characteristic which we have been used to labelling 'Protogeometric' occurs at Assiros in a level which has been found to have a *terminus ante quem* of around 1070 BCE, based on a dendrochronological cross-date with the floating Anatolian Bronze Age to Iron Age dendrochronological sequence, itself dated by wiggle-matching (Manning *et al.* 2001a; Newton *et al.* [Chapter 8, this volume]). It does not mean that by around 1070 BCE we necessarily have the full range of shapes and decorative motifs which are usually lumped under a Protogeometric classification, or that these are by then found universally throughout a wide area, let alone that the Greek Iron Age has begun in anything other than a purely terminological sense.

The pot in question is a neck-handled amphora with at least two groups of compass-drawn concentric semicircles separated by a vertical stripe on the shoulder, classified, particularly on the grounds of this distinctive decoration, as Early Protogeometric (Wardle 1996: 455, Fig 3.2; Catling 1998: 161; Kromer *et al.* 2004: Fig. 1). Amphorae with similar decoration occur at a number of other places in northern and east-central Greece and at Troy, where they have been taken as evidence for a third phase of Troy VIIb (VIIb3) (Catling 1998: 154-64; Lenz *et al.* 1998: 194-97, Pls. 1, 2:1-2, 3-6). Catling suggests that they were products of some coastal region within this general area, possibly in north-central Greece, and comments that 'according to the prevailing current views on absolute chronology, [their] date...is likely to fall around the turn of the eleventh or in the early tenth century' (Catling 1998: 162-63, 155). These prevailing current views, it should be noted, which depend on an assumption that the characteristics which 'define' the Protogeometric style started in Athens, are actually derived from nothing more precise than the assignment of so many generations to each of the classificatory divisions of Late Helladic IIIC and Sub-Mycenaean pottery (Warren and Hankey 1989: 167-68). Particularly interesting (and perhaps relevant), however, in view of the new date from Assiros, are other suggestions, based on their association with pottery classified as late- or Sub-Mycenaean at sites in Macedonia, the Chalcidice and Phocis, that examples of this type of amphora decorated with compass-drawn concentric circles anticipate the Protogeometric style in southern Greece (Jacob-Felsch 1988; cf. Catling 1998: 163). Indeed, as early as the 1930s, both J.L. Myres and T.C. Skeat, for different reasons, suggested that the decoration of compass-drawn concentric circles, which distinguishes these amphorae, was first deployed in Macedonia (Myres 1930: 448-56; Skeat 1934). The point is not perhaps one of deciding which (if any) of these largely competing views is right or wrong, but that we simply do not know enough about the contexts and motivations underlying stylistic innovations and changes in pottery in general, or in individual shapes or decorative motifs in particular—the functional, aesthetic or practical impulses which constrain or otherwise affect them, the circumstances in which they may or may not spread from one place to another, the working lives of individual pots or types of pots and the differential circumstances in which they may be deposited —to be able to make such judgements with any confidence at all. All this must have an effect on the assurance with which we seek to square the circle by normalising ever narrower stylistic subdivisions of pottery into ever more refined general chronological frameworks in the hope that this will enable us to date the archaeological record as a whole more closely in absolute terms.

As it is, the quest for increasingly precise dates for our pottery classifications is, in my view, a wholly misguided one. The spuriously precise dates placed in some chronological schemes for the beginnings and ends of our arbitrary ceramic divisions merely encourage us to think subliminally of these pottery 'phases' in the same way as king-lists—which is, of course, nonsense. In this respect, there is much to be said for the strategy of the late Vincent Desborough who for the most part insisted on giving rounded dates to ceramic divisions and labels—that is, dates which were quite obviously notional, which did not pretend to know more than they did, and which included within them a give-or-take of several decades either side (Desborough 1964: 240-41). His date of around 1050 BCE for the notional start of the Greek (particularly Athenian) Protogeometric style seems to me perfectly compatible with the new dendrochronologically derived date associated with the amphora from Assiros, given the nationality of the former and the necessary standard deviation built into it, and given, too, the patchy and usually totally unguessable processes and impulses which lie behind ceramic changes, without any need for the latter to give rise to any great sensation. Taking a leaf out of Desborough's book, I would advocate a much more relaxed approach to ceramic-based chronologies which does not get too excited about the possibility of drawing sweeping chronological inferences from dating individual pots ever more precisely. The arch-typologiser of Mycenaean pottery, Arne Furumark, was himself at pains to point out that his typological divisions were intended to indicate the chronological relationships of the types, not of the specimens; and that the typological and chronological series should be regarded as quite separate entities which coincide only when the succession of types is dependent on factors which are themselves determined by chronological succession, with the result that the typological method is of value chiefly as a means of arranging and illuminating facts already established by other means of research (Furumark 1941: 5). We should forget precise dates: in the general scheme of ceramic-based chronological frameworks, these may often be meaningless. We should think of our pottery chronologies in terms of something like fuzzy elastic—both stretchable and compressible with no clear divisions between our snapshot-based classifications—or in terms of something like overlapping tectonic plates. And we should keep our ceramic sequences quite separate from our quest to date individual events (see also Zarzecki-Peleg [Chapter 22, this volume]). That way, when most of our everyday dating is still dependent on pottery, we will not be tempted to think we can have greater resolution than we can actually have, and to confuse ceramic changes with event-based history.

Iron Age Chronology in the Southern Levant: Disentangling Dates, Ceramics and Narrative History

This brings me at last to the question of the Early Iron Age chronology of the southern Levant. At the risk of upsetting everyone involved, I would also like to advocate a fairly relaxed attitude to this. One of the problems with it is that it, too, is a question of tangling up ceramics with history, and to that extent of bringing them into conflict with the kind of resolution demanded by a historical chronology (a question to which I will return below).

During the period at issue the southern Levant may perhaps best be described as 'proto-historic' or 'para-historic'. It has few or no contemporary historical documents of its own (barring the odd inscription mentioning the House of David [Biran and Naveh 1993, 1995]), and it has therefore traditionally been dependent on fitting its archaeology into the histories provided by Assyria and Egypt or into the narratives provided by later Biblical accounts, often according to what was once characterised by Leonard as the 'find-a-Pharaoh' system of dating (Leonard 1988: 330). The question of precise dating does, of course, play an important part in this. For instance, if one wants to identify sites or levels of sites caught up in the Assyrian campaign of 701 BCE, then it helps if one can obtain dates that are at least not incompatible with this. And indeed, there are excellent arguments, for its own sake, for obtaining much more comprehensive sequences of high precision ^{14}C dates from as many sites as possible in this general period, as Ayelet Gilboa, Elisabetta Boaretto, Ilan Sharon and their colleagues are now in the process of doing (Sharon *et al.* [Chapter 6, this volume]), as well as (if possible) for the construction of a dendrochronological sequence, as long as we do not abuse the results by over-interpreting them and by converting them too readily into known or imagined 'history'.

My own feeling is that the absolute parameters for either end of the chronology of the Iron Age are fairly firmly set more or less where they have traditionally been for a long time. At one end, we have convincing historical tie-ins with Assyria, as in the case of the siege of Lachish, which seems well enough documented historically, iconographically and archaeologically (Ussishkin 1982, 1990). At the other end, there seem to me to be sufficiently persuasive ceramic links between Ashdod Stratum XIIIb, Ugarit and tombs at Kition on Cyprus, which, when taken in conjunction with likely estimates for the end of Ugarit (Singer 1987, 1999; Yon 1992) and the plentiful series of ^{14}C dates for a range of Late Cypriot IIC sites on Cyprus (Manning *et al.* 2001b), suggest we should place the ceramic context of Ashdod XIIIb, under my fuzzy elastic way of thinking, at a notional date of around 1200 BCE, give or take a few decades on either side (cf. Dothan and Zukerman 2004: 4-6, Table 2). It does not seem to me, at any rate, that we can lower its date by 50 to 80 years, which is what the proposed low chronology seems to demand (Finkelstein [Chapter 3, this volume]), without doing violence both to the evidence from Ugarit and to the recent series of radiocarbon dates from Cyprus. What we could do with is a good series of high precision dates from the Ashdod sequence, and from the sequences at other sites such as Ashkelon and Tel Miqne, which may be able to demonstrate that we are roughly within the right half century. It will, however, be a long time (if ever) before any scientific method—including dendro-dating—will be able to give us both the precision and density of date series which will allow us unproblematically to link the archaeological record with the kinds of year-by-year events of recorded or literary 'history', even if this were desirable. In any case, in doing so, the risk is that we ignore the large amounts of other information that archaeology can give us that history never bothers about. I suspect, however, that if we do eventually achieve this kind of resolution, it might well have the entirely salutary effect of showing us that all those sites supposedly destroyed and rebuilt simultaneously by the invading Sea Peoples were actually destroyed and rebuilt over a more or less extended time span.

That is roughly where I stand at the moment. It seems to me that in between these two parameters at either end of the Iron Age there is still room for chronological flexibility, without this having any profound effect either on Biblical historicity or on such reliable information as may be provided (after appropriate source criticism) by Egyptian or Assyrian historical texts. Collective oral traditions, of the sort on which the historical books of the Old Testament are ultimately based, may well have a tendency to distort or exaggerate personalities or events, and even to shift them around in time and space, but they are rarely created out of nothing; and the only type of 'historicity' on which doubt might possibly be cast by chronological re-jigging is essentially a secondary, artificial one, formed by fundamentalist (or possibly naive) attempts to consistently match the archaeological record to specific episodes of Biblical history, by arguing, for instance, that a particular stratum at a particular site must be equated with the activities of a particular Biblical figure on the grounds of the scale or impressiveness of the extant remains. Partly, therefore, it is a question of how we relate the archaeological record to textual material. So far, the most copious, systematic and internally consistent ^{14}C sequence for this middle stretch (i.e. the end of Iron I to Iron IIB) comes from the site of Tel Reḥov, a site which appears among the list of cities conquered by Shishak I in his Palestinian campaign in the later 10th century BCE (Bruins, van der Plicht and

Mazar 2003; Mazar 2004; Mazar [Chapter 2, this volume]; cf. Mazar *et al.* [Chapter 13, this volume]; van der Plicht and Bruins [Chapter 14, this volume]). The dates for Stratum V suggest that *if* Shishak actually destroyed the places he is recorded as having conquered (Mazar [Chapter 2, this volume]), a destruction of this stratum is not incompatible with Shishak's campaign—but not much more than this. The dates for Stratum IV do not entirely rule this stratum out either, so that, as far as tying the archaeological record firmly in terms of its chronology to spot events of recorded history is concerned, we still have to be content with fuzzy approximation. No amount of manipulating the data by means of computer simulations to see what calibrated age range one would get from an actual date of 925 for the Shishak campaign actually changes this (Bruins, van der Plicht and Mazar 2003: 317, Fig. 2), since, not only is this calendrical date itself an approximation within a range of about 20 years (Finkelstein [Chapter 3, this volume]; Shortland [Chapter 4, this volume]), but the statistical averaging of its Stratum V comparanda is valid only if one can be sure that these all refer to the same event and is thus itself a product of the interpretation (Bronk Ramsey [Chapter 5, this volume]). Nevertheless, historical tie-ins apart, the Reḥov sequence of dates is an extremely useful sequence. It gives us approximate notional (fuzzy elastic) dates for Iron Age pottery assemblages, which seem to suggest that the conventional dating for these cannot be too far out—a suggestion supported both by recent dates from Khirbet en-Nahas in Jordan (Levy *et al.* 2004) and by the preliminary results of the recently initiated Iron Age dating project referred to above, which suggest a divergence of no more than about 20 years from the traditional notional date for the Iron IB/IIA transition (Sharon *et al.* [Chapter 6, this volume]), thus making the disagreement between the high and low chronologies for Iron IIA so small that, in terms at least of *archaeological* chronology, it ought to be regarded as insignificant. Interestingly, the sequence of ^{14}C determinations from Reḥov also suggests that, ceramically, there is little clear distinction over what is potentially a time span of up to a century and a half (covering possibly both Solomonic and Omride periods), further confounding the possibility of tight dating (or indeed historical identification) through the medium of pottery (Bruins, van der Plicht and Mazar 2003; Mazar [Chapter 2, this volume]).

I realise that anyone who is foolhardy enough to attempt to pour oil on troubled waters by suggesting that we can probably take a fairly relaxed attitude, at least over certain aspects of the chronological controversy, runs the risk of alienating both sides. So I might as well finish by annoying everyone further. One thing that I find immensely heartening about the low chronology advocated by Israel Finkelstein (1995, 1998) and others, at least at its upper end, is the effect it has had of forcing a break with the traditional chronology originally based on the arrival of the Philistines, along with their identifying pottery, immediately after the 8th year of Ramses III (that is, 1187 BCE on a highish Egyptian chronology, or 1177 on the lower chronology now generally in use [Kitchen 1987, 2000]). For the last one hundred years or more, this has been the cornerstone of the traditional chronology for the beginning of the southern Levantine Early Iron Age. The Peleset of the Egyptian records were identified with the Philistines of the Bible, and both were identified with a certain sort of pottery, with similarities to Aegean pottery, found at sites which lay in or around the territory of the Biblical Philistines. This arose from a kind of 19th-century archaeological literary-based mythology, at the root of which lay the unquestioned assumption that one could identify ethnic (or indeed national or racial) groups by the pottery they made and used. The appearance of 'Philistine' pottery marked the arrival of Philistines—and, indeed the beginning of the Iron Age (since they were thought to have brought iron technology with them). These were part of the hostile 'foreign countries...in their islands' (in the words of an inscription on Ramses III's mortuary temple at Medinet Habu) who encountered Ramses III's forces at the Delta in year 8 of his reign as the climax (by this Egyptian account) to the havoc and destruction they caused as they swept through other parts of the East Mediterranean. This was further elaborated into a neo-Classical mythology, based on a seamless blending of Classical legend and the archaeological interpretations of the time, which saw the Philistines and other 'Sea Peoples' as inhabitants of the Aegean driven eastward as migrant refugees by the incursion into the Greek mainland of blue-eyed, blonde-haired northerners, who destroyed the Mycenaean palaces 80 years after the Trojan War (Breasted 1935: 311-18; Myres 1930; Petrie 1890: 276; cf. Silberman 1998). These migrants destroyed various Levantine cities at the time of their massed attack on Ramses III in the 8th year of his reign, and thereafter settled in parts of the coastal Levant, or—according to some hypotheses —were deliberately settled by Ramses III to man his garrisons or in order otherwise to contain them. What this ultra-historical reconstruction meant was that what was called Philistine pottery could not be allowed to appear in the southern Levant before Ramses III's 8th year, which remains the orthodox view to this day. The discovery, at sites like Tel Miqne, Ashkelon and Ashdod, of what is sometimes called Philistine monochrome pottery, which pre-dates the bichrome pottery that was originally given the label 'Philistine', of itself necessitated a modification of the chronology, at least as far as the ceramic sequence was concerned. With the extension of the label 'Philistine' to the monochrome pottery, it too was given a *terminus post quem*—or indeed a starting date—of Ramses III's year 8, currently put at 1177 BCE (Dothan and Zukerman 2004: 43; Mazar 1985; Singer 1985; Stager 1995).

What Finkelstein, as the most vociferous advocate of the lower chronology, has done, is undermined the chronological (and therefore the historical) tie-in between Philistine monochrome pottery and year 8 of Ramses III, by arguing that the absence of Philistine monochrome pottery at sites close to the Philistine pentapolis, such as Lachish (Stratum VI) and Tel Sera' (Stratum IX), which have yielded 20th-Dynasty material, means that this pottery does not appear in the southern Levant until the end of, or after, the reign of Ramses VI (Finkelstein 1995: 224). This is a view with which I have a great deal of sympathy, not because of its chronological conclusions (which I think are unsustainable), but because it involves rejecting the idea of a simple one-to-one identification between people and pots, if merely in the extreme sense that certain pottery types can only and exclusively be used by those ethnic groups whose labels are attached to them (Finkelstein 1995: 220). Philistine monochrome is still identified with the Biblical Philistines, who are still regarded as incomers to the region (1995: 218, 220), but the arrival of those Philistines is postponed to sometime after the reign of Ramses VI in the late 12th century BCE (1995: 228). By converting what has traditionally been seen as an 'event' into a long, drawn-out process, Finkelstein has cast doubt on the possibility of using archaeology to write straightforward narrative history by implying that the elaborate historical superstructure we have constructed from archaeology on the basis of Classical legends, Egyptian propaganda and Biblical literature is decidedly precarious—as, indeed, by any objective standards it is likely to be. One perhaps wonders why, having deconstructed this superstructure and demolished Ramses III's year 8 as an anchor point by which to date the advent of Philistines and Philistine pottery, he and other advocates of the low chronology do not follow the logic of this to the extent of questioning whether we can really use what we call Philistine pottery as archaeological proof that Philistines 'arrived' (in the sense implied by the traditional narrative) in the southern Levant at all.

Indeed, both the textual and archaeological grounds for seeing a settlement of the southern Levant in the form of Philistines and other assorted Sea Peoples mass-migrating from the Aegean seem to me extremely shaky. There is virtually nothing in the Bible to suggest that Philistines were at any point regarded as newcomers to the region, apart from a couple of obscure remarks in Amos (9.7) and Jeremiah (47.4) which associate them with Caphtor, as rhetorical analogues in the one case of the deliverance of Israel from Egypt, and in the other of the external pollution represented by Sidon and Tyre. Elsewhere (e.g. Genesis 10.14; 1 Chronicles 1.12) Philistines and Caphtorites are clearly distinguished; and both, like Canaan, are assigned in the list of nations to the generations of Ham, rather than of Japheth whose genealogy produced the sons of Javan by whom the isles of the Gentiles were divided (Genesis 10.1-20). This seems strange, since one would expect that, if a genuine memory of Philistines as relatively recent immigrants from overseas had survived, it would have been in the political and ideological interests of early Israel, which cast Philistia very much in the role of the 'other', to have consistently preserved and emphasised this. Nor are the Egyptian texts, whether at Medinet Habu or in the Papyrus Harris, exactly crystal clear. Apart from the fact that the idea, as represented on the Ramses year 8 inscription, of a co-ordinated military confederation with the ability to mount simultaneously concerted attacks all over the Near East, from Hattusa to the Nile Delta, seems improbable—if not impossible—and is arguably better seen as an Egyptian political and ideological construct (Cifola 1988), they tell us nothing coherent or reliable about the settlement of any such people in Canaan (and are particularly reticent about the Peleset in this respect). Nor, for that matter, do they tell us where these people came from. The only real clue we get is that many of them were evidently at home on the sea, and that many of their activities were clearly hostile or threatening to the contemporary Egyptian state. As far as the archaeology, and particularly the pottery, is concerned, we certainly do not have to wait until after the events of Ramses III's year 8 to see what might loosely be regarded as pottery of Aegean type, but of East Mediterranean manufacture, appearing in the Levant. In Cyprus this happens well before the end of the 13th century BCE, long before any supposed wave of invasions at the beginning of Late Cypriot IIIA (Kling 1989); and for much at least of the latter part of the 13th-century Cyprus seems to have been exporting its own pottery of wheelmade painted Aegean type to the Levant, along with its more traditional handmade wares, as recent analyses of pottery from Tel Nami and 'Akko are beginning to make clear (Artzy 2005; cf. Leonard *et al.* 1993; Müller Celka 2004: 201; Yon, Karageorghis and Hirschfeld 2000: 64). In the Levant itself, it is becoming increasingly evident that, in various places as far apart as Ugarit and northern Sinai, shapes that we are fond of labelling 'Aegean', in painted wares similar to Aegean ware, and with decorations which reproduce or echo their Aegean counterparts, were already being produced locally or regionally before the end of LB IIB, including shapes which eventually form part of the Philistine repertoire (Leonard 1994: 9; Oren, in preparation; Sherratt, in preparation). Furthermore, there is nothing in this whole ceramic process, including the development and nature of Philistine monochrome pottery, which need have anything to do with the Aegean as such. If we are looking for outside models for what I would prefer to see as a form of import-substitution which spread progressively eastward, resulting in an increasingly limited repertoire as it did so (Dothan and Zukerman 2004: 44-45), particularly (in the Philistine case) by people with a very close interest in maritime trade and with a culture which reflected this, then we need look no further than Cyprus, which had a long history of selling pots of all types and wares to the Levant, and which certainly remained in close and unbroken contact with the Levantine coasts into the Early Iron Age.

I do not want to pursue this particular (and admittedly contentious) point of view further here. However, what I wish to suggest is that we critically re-examine the whole mythology surrounding the beginning of Iron IA, and with it the tight chronological constraints which are an integral part of this mythology by insisting that it be tied to Ramses III's year 8. This, it seems to me, has merely acted as an agent of distortion, as we manipulate the archaeological record—and the chronology— to fit a strait-jacket created by the need to hang the archaeology around supposed major events of a sudden nature for which pottery styles are seen as surrogate proof. In this respect, there is probably much to be said for the iconoclastic principles behind the proposed low chronology, which at least in part free us from this strait-jacket. This is not to say, however, that the low chronology itself seems to me sustainable, at least at this upper end of the problem, when its implementation plays havoc with what we can surmise, from different types of data, about the chronology of other regions or places in the East Mediterranean outside Israel. Paradoxically, by dropping the mythology and concentrating on the archaeology, it becomes easier to argue persuasively for the higher chronology on traditional *archaeological* grounds—that is, ceramic grounds and grounds of cross-links both with text-based dating for Ugarit and ^{14}C dating for Cyprus. My own view is that there is much to be said for seeing the onset of what we characterise archaeologically as Iron IA as a gradual process, which, on the ceramic evidence of Ashdod Stratum XIIIb, we might well argue is recognisably underway by the notional and unashamedly rounded date of around 1200 BCE. Someday we may have ^{14}C or even dendrochronological dates which we can at least say are not incompatible with this. We do not have to wait until Ramses III's 8th year; but, to those who still feel obliged to do so, I can offer the consolation that the fuzzy elastic of the only realistic sort of chronology applicable to the archaeological record in general can quite easily accommodate the 25 years or so that are required. Let us live and let live: narrative history is one thing, ceramics (and their approximate relative chronologies) another, high precision absolute dating yet another. They may touch each other from time to time, but we cannot weld them consistently and seamlessly together, let alone subordinate them to the privileged service of the first of these. They each represent different ways of measuring the passage of time, and together, but kept conceptually separate, they can greatly enrich our appreciation of the complexity of ancient life and society, from *temps recitatif* to *longue durée*.

References

Artzy, M. (2005) A Tale of Three Sites: LB II 'Mediterranean' Imports in Coastal Sites of the Carmel Ridge (Mycenaean Seminar, Institute of Classical Studies, University of London, 16 February 2005).

Biran, A., and J. Naveh (1993) An Aramaic Stele Fragment from Tel Dan. *IEJ* 43: 81-98.

—(1995) The Tel Dan Inscription: A New Fragment. *IEJ* 45: 1-18.

Breasted, J.H. (1935) *Ancient times: A History of the Early World* (Boston: Ginn, 2nd edn).

Bruins, H.J., J. van der Plicht and A. Mazar (2003) ^{14}C Dates from Tel Reḥov: Iron-Age Chronology, Pharaohs, and Hebrew Kings. *Science* 300: 315-18.

Catling, R.W.V. (1998) The Typology of the Protogeometric and Subprotogeometric Pottery from Troia and its Aegean Context. *Studia Troica* 8: 151-87.

Cifola, B. (1988) Ramses III and the Sea Peoples: A Structural Analysis of the Medinet Habu Inscriptions. *Orientalia* 57: 275-306.

Desborough, V.R. d'A. (1952) *Protogeometric Pottery* (Oxford: Clarendon Press).

—(1964) *The last Mycenaeans and their Successors* (Oxford: Clarendon Press).

Dothan, T., and A. Zukerman (2004) A Preliminary Study of the Mycenaean IIIC:1 Pottery Assemblages from Tel Miqne-Ekron and Ashdod. *BASOR* 333: 1-54.

Finkelstein, I. (1995) The Date of the Settlement of the Philistines in Canaan. *Tel Aviv* 22: 213-39.

—(1998) Philistine Chronology: High, Middle or Low? In *Mediterranean Peoples in Transition: Thirteenth to Early Tenth Centuries BCE*, edited by S. Gitin, A. Mazar and E. Stern (Jerusalem: Israel Exploration Society): 140-47.

Furumark, A. (1941) *Mycenaean Pottery: Analysis and Classification* (Stockholm: Kungl Vitterhets, historie och antikvitets akademien).

Glotz, G. (1925) *The Aegean Civilization* (trans. M.R. Dobie and E.M. Riley; New York: K. Paul/Trench/ Trubner).

Hammond, N.G.L. (1949) Dorians. In *The Oxford Classical Dictionary*, edited by M. Cary *et al.* (Oxford: Clarendon Press): 297.

Helm, R. (ed.) (1956) *Eusebius Werke. 7. Band. Die Chronik des Hieronymus* (Leipzig: J.C. Hinrichs).

Jacob-Felsch, M. (1988) Compass-drawn Concentric Circles in Vase Painting: A Problem of Relative Chronology at the End of the Bronze Age. In *Problems in Greek Prehistory*, edited by E.B. French and K.A. Wardle (Bristol: Bristol Classical Press): 193-99.

Kitchen, K.A. (1987) The Basics of Egyptian Chronology in Relation to the Bronze Age. In *High, Middle or Low? Acts of an International Colloquium on Absolute Chronology held at the University of Göteborg 20th-22nd August 1987, Part I*, edited by P. Åström (Göteborg: Åström): 37-55.

—(2000) The Historical Chronology of Ancient Egypt: A Current Assessment. In *The Synchronization of Civilizations in the Eastern Mediterranean in the Second Millennium B.C.*, edited by M. Bietak (Vienna: Verlag der österreichischen Akademie der Wissenschaften): 39-52.

Kling, B. (1989) *Mycenaean IIIC:1b and Related Pottery in Cyprus* (Göteborg: Åström).

Kromer, B., *et al.* (2001) Regional $^{14}CO_2$ Offsets in the Troposphere: Magnitude, Mechanisms, and Consequences. *Science* 294: 2529-32.

—(2004) Old Trees, New Dates and the End of Mycenaean Civilization. <http://artsweb.bham.ac.uk/aha/kaw/oldtreesnewdates.htm> (accessed 7 March 2005).

Lenz, D., *et al.* (1998) Protogeometric Pottery at Troia. *Studia Troica* 8: 189-222.

Leonard, A. (1988) Some Problems Inherent in Mycenaean Syro-Palestinian Synchronisms. In *Problems in Greek Prehistory*, edited by E.B. French and K.A. Wardle (Bristol: Bristol Classical Press): 319-31.

—(1994) *An Index to the LBA Aegean Pottery from Syria-Palestine* (Jonsered: Åström).

Leonard, A., *et al.* (1993) The Making of Aegean Stirrup Jars: Technique, Tradition, and Trade. *Annual of the British School at Athens* 88: 105-23.

Levy, T.E., *et al.* (2004) Reassessing the Chronology of Biblical Edom: New Excavations and ^{14}C Dates from Khirbat en-Nahas (Jordan). *Antiquity* 78: 865-79.

Maier, F.-G. (1986) Kinyras and Agapenor. In *Acts of the International Archaeological Symposium 'Cyprus between the Orient and the Occident'*, edited by V. Karageorghis (Nicosia: Department of Antiquities, Cyprus): 311-20.

Manning, S.W. (1998) From Process to People: *Longue durée* to History. In *The Aegean and the Orient in the Second Millennium. Proceedings of the 50th Anniversary Symposium, Cincinnati, 18–20 April 1997*, edited by E. Cline and D. Harris-Cline (Aegaeum 18; Liège, Belgium: University of Liège): 311-27.

Manning, S.W., *et al.* (2001a) Anatolian Tree Rings and a New Chronology for the East Mediterranean Bronze-Iron Ages. *Science* 294: 2532-35.

—(2001b) Absolute Age Range of the Late Cypriot IIC Period on Cyprus. *Antiquity* 75: 328-40.

Mazar, A. (1985) The Emergence of the Philistine Material Culture. *IEJ* 35: 95-107.

—(2004) Greek and Levantine Iron Age Chronology: A Rejoinder. *IEJ* 54: 24-36.

Müller Celka, S. (2004) La céramique mycénienne de l'Egée au Levant: 'mode d'emploi et précautions'. In *La céramique mycénienne de l'Egée au Levant. Hommage à Vronwy Hankey*, edited by J. Balensi, J.-Y. Monchambert and S. Müller Celka (Lyon: Maison de l'Orient): 183-207.

Myres, J.L. (1930) *Who Were the Greeks?* (Berkeley: University of California Press).

Oren, E. (in preparation) Aegean Trade in Canaan and Egypt at the End of LBA—Chronological and Typological Observations. In *The Philistines and Other 'Sea Peoples': Proceedings of an International Workshop in Memory of Prof. Moshe Dothan, May 1–3, 2001*, edited by M. Artzy, A. Killebrew and G. Lehmann.

Petrie, W.M.F. (1890) The Egyptian Bases of Greek History. *Journal of Hellenic Studies* 11: 271-77.

Reimer, P.J. (2001) A New Twist in the Radiocarbon Tale. *Science* 294: 2494-95.

Sherratt, S. (in preparation) The Ceramic Phenomenon of the Sea Peoples: An Overview. In *The Philistines and other 'Sea Peoples': Proceedings of an International Workshop in Memory of Prof. Moshe Dothan, May 1–3, 2001*, edited by M. Artzy, A. Killebrew and G. Lehmann.

Silberman, N.A. (1998) The Sea Peoples, the Victorians, and Us: Modern Social Ideology and Changing Archaeological Interpretations of the Late Bronze Age Collapse. In *Mediterranean Peoples in Transition, Thirteenth to Early Tenth Centuries BCE*, edited by S. Gitin, A. Mazar and E. Stern (Jerusalem: Israel Exploration Society): 268-75.

Singer, I. (1985) The Beginning of Philistine Settlement in Canaan and the Northern Boundary of Philistia. *Tel Aviv* 12: 109-22.

—(1987) Dating the End of the Hittite Empire. *Hethitica* 8: 413-21.

—(1999) A Political History of Ugarit. In *Handbook of Ugaritic studies*, edited by W.G.E. Watson and N. Wyatt (Leiden: Brill): 603-733.

Skeat, T.C. (1934) *The Dorians in Archaeology* (London: A. Moring).

Stager, L.E. (1995) The Impact of the Sea Peoples in Canaan (1185–1050 BCE). In *The Archaeology of Society in the Holy Land*, edited by T.E. Levy (London: Leicester University Press): 332-48.

Tsountas, C., and J.I. Manatt (1897) *The Mycenaean Age* (London: Macmillan).

Ussishkin, D. (1982) *The Conquest of Lachish by Sennacherib* (Tel Aviv: Tel Aviv University, Institute of Archaeology).

—(1990) The Assyrian Attack on Lachish: The Archaeological Evidence from the Southwest Corner of the Site. *Tel Aviv* 17: 53-86.

Wardle, K.A. (1996) Change or Continuity: Assiros Toumba at the Transition from Bronze to Iron Age. AEM ʾΑρχαιολογικὸ ῎Εργο στῆ Μακεδονία καὶ Θράκη 10: 443-60.

Warren, P., and V. Hankey (1989) *Aegean Bronze Age Chronology* (Bristol: Bristol Classical Press).

Yon, M. (1992) The End of the Kingdom of Ugarit. In *The Crisis Years: The 12th Century B.C. from beyond the Danube to the Tigris*, edited by W.A. Ward and M.S. Joukowsky (Dubuque: Kendall/Hunt): 111-22.

Yon, M., V. Karageorghis and N. Hirschfeld (2000) *Céramique mycénienne d'Ougarit* (Ras Shamra Ougarit 13; Paris: Editions Recherche sur les Civilisations/Association pour la Diffusion de la Pensée Française).

Young, R.S. (1981) *Three Great Early Tumuli* (Philadelphia: University Museum, University of Pennsylvania).

IV.
JORDAN IN THE IRON AGE

10 Lowland Edom and the High and Low Chronologies

Edomite state formation, the Bible and recent archaeological research in southern Jordan

Thomas E. Levy, Mohammad Najjar, Johannes van der Plicht, Neil Smith, Hendrik J. Bruins, and Thomas Higham

Abstract

This study explores the chronological assumptions that underlie the past 40 years of Iron Age archaeological investigations in southern Jordan and offers an alternative framework based on the application of high precision radiocarbon dating. The 2002 University of California, San Diego—Department of Antiquities of Jordan (UCSD—DOAJ) archaeological excavations at the copper production center of Khirbat en-Nahas (KEN) demonstrate monumental building and industrial scale copper production in two major phases dating to the 12th–11th and 10th–9th centuries BCE. Stratigraphic excavations, new high precision radiocarbon dating using short-life samples, and small finds such as ceramics, scarabs, and arrowheads from the site show the centrality of the Iron Age landscape in the copper ore-rich lowlands of Edom for the formation of complex societies in this part of the southern Levant. The new data presented here challenge previous assumptions about the Iron Age in Jordan, such as (a) the formation of the Iron Age kingdom of Edom only took place in the 7th and 6th centuries BCE and (b) no monumental building activities took place in Transjordan during the 10th century BCE. Bayesian statistical analyses of the radiocarbon dates from KEN are presented by Higham *et al.* (Chapter 11, this volume).

Introduction

This study discusses some of the archaeological and historical implications of the latest suite of high precision radiocarbon dates obtained from the Oxford and Groningen radiocarbon laboratories from the recent excavations at the Iron Age metal production center at Khirbat en-Nahas in Jordan. To appreciate the impact of these new radiometric dates on the Iron Age archaeology of southern Jordan, and radiometric dating on historical archaeology in general, some discussion of the role of text and archaeology must be discussed in order to attain some of the goals of a 'New Biblical Archaeology' outlined at the beginning of this volume (see Chapter 1). In the 19th century, systematic archaeological research in the southern Levant—the Holy Land—was born with the aim of exploring the relationship between text (the Hebrew Bible) and the newly understood field of archaeology. In 1865, the Palestine Exploration Fund—the first research organization devoted to the scientific investigation of the history of the land—was founded in London by a group of distinguished scholars and clergymen, with the express purpose of providing 'for the accurate and systematic investigation of the archaeology, topography, geology and physical geography, natural history, manner, and customs of the Holy Land, for biblical illustration' (cf. Moorey 1991). The unique historical relationship between the Hebrew Bible (Old Testament) and the landscape of Palestine created what might be called the 'tyranny of the text'. Accordingly, in approaching the archaeological record of the southern Levant, from its 19th-century beginnings until the mid-1970s, archaeologists consistently approached the archaeological record of the Holy Land by first examining biblical text and then searching for material culture proof to support the text as historical fact (Albright 1971; Glueck 1940a; Wright 1965). Following the discovery of inconsistencies between text and the archaeological record at key sites such as Jericho, which was supposed to have been destroyed by Joshua and the Israelite tribes at the end of the Late Bronze Age, cracks developed in the paradigm known as 'Biblical Archaeology'. By the 1970s, a growing number of researchers accepted that there were limitations on the role of archaeology in establishing the historicity of the Hebrew Bible along the lines that Albright (1932) and others had proposed. William Dever called for a more 'secular' archaeology in the Holy Land (Israel, Palestine, Jordan) that should redefine itself as secular 'Syro-Palestinian' Archaeology. This was an effort to shed the weight of the tyranny of the biblical text (Dever 1974, 1982) on the archaeological record of the southern Levant. Dever (1988) argued that freedom from the biblical text could be achieved by adopting the rapidly developing paradigm spearheaded by Louis Binford (1968) and known as the 'New Archaeology' with its emphasis on culture process—an approach that was specifically 'anti-historical.' While the achievements of the New Archaeology are many and include the adoption of the scientific method, quantification, investigative optimism, the importance of research design over simple data collection and other features that have become a mainstay of world archaeology today, by the early 1980s critics such as Ian Hodder (1982, 1987) showed many of the failings of the New or Processual Archaeology. Self-appointing themselves as the new 'Post-Processual' paradigm, Hodder, and others (Preucel and Hodder [eds.] 1996) pointed out that there was no single way to undertake archaeological inference as argued by the Processual archaeologists, that all interpretations were driven by the subjective views of the researchers, that even data is 'theory laden'—that is, many 'readings' are possible. The most significant Post-Processual critique, and most applicable to Levantine Archaeology, was the fact that Processual archaeology had an anti-historical bias that assumed a kind of 'universal humanism' making it possible to construct 'laws' of human behavior.

While Dever argued repeatedly for a 'secular' archaeology for the Holy Land that could be brought forth through the New/Processual Archaeology, this paradigm never really took off in Levantine Archaeology except in research embedded in the prehistoric and protohistoric periods (Levy 1996). Perhaps the notion that the Bible represents a kind of 'tyranny of the text' for archaeologists is simply inappropriate for the archaeology of the southern Levant where so much of the Hebrew Bible takes place. The leading historical archaeologists working in the southern Levant were primarily secular (Ben-Tor [ed.] 1992; Finkelstein 1988; Mazar 1990; Stager 1988); however, they could not ignore the centrality of the Hebrew Bible as a foundation—an ethno-historical source—for examining the archaeological record of the region. Historical archaeology (i.e. Middle Bronze–Iron Age) in the southern Levant did adopt many of the methodologies proposed by the New Archaeology, such as interdisciplinary research and a real interest in the application of new technologies for archaeological research. However, the question remained—how best to bring together text and archaeology. The emergence of the so-called Biblical Minimalist paradigm (cf. Davies 1992; Thompson 1999; Whitelam 1996) argued that the Hebrew Bible lacks any historical data whatsoever so it is a totally unreliable source. As discussed earlier (Levy and Higham [Chapter 1, this volume]), given the large number of interconnections between biblical and extra-biblical ancient sources (cf. Dever 2001, 2003), the Biblical Minimalist paradigm is untenable today. In some cases, adherents of this approach (Lemche 1998; Van Seters 1997) argue for the centrality of ancient texts for historical reconstruction—but give precedence to any written text outside of the Hebrew Bible. When researchers grasp on to any historical piece of data uncritically, whether it is the Hebrew Bible or extra-biblical textual data from media such as monumental inscriptions, ostraca (ink on pottery), engraved silver, inscribed stone seals or a seal impression, to interpret the archaeological record they run the risk of simplification and finding what their preconceived views want to find (Schniedewind 2004). For the past ca. 30 years, this is precisely what has characterized the Iron Age archaeology of southern Jordan, and in particular the region known from biblical and other sources (Bartlett 1989, 1992) as Edom. In what follows, we will illustrate how an over-reliance on extra-biblical textual data for ancient Edom has led to major chronological problems and consequently, problems with historical and anthropological interpretation. We argue that only with the enthusiastic adoption of radiocarbon dating for the Iron Age archaeology of the southern Levant will it be possible to objectively investigate the relationship between the historical texts and archaeology for this period.

Research Area: Highland–Lowland Dichotomy

The region of Edom in southern Jordan extends roughly from the Wadi al-Hasa in the north to the Wadi Hisma and Jabal Ram in the south, the Wadi Arabah on the west and Transjordanian desert plateau to the east (Bartlett 1992; Glueck 1940a). The two most important physiographic attributes of Edom include: (a) the presence of one of the richest copper ore deposits in the southern Levant (Hauptmann 2000) and (b) the marked geographic and environmental diversity between the 'lowlands' and 'highlands' of Edom. The differences between these two geomorphic zones are pronounced. For example, the edge of the highlands, overlooking the Wadi Arabah that separates modern Israel and Jordan, is characterized by elevations that reach over 1500 masl, a semi-arid landscape and pockets of Mediterranean rainfall zones with over 600 mm of average annual rainfall (Centre 2001). In contrast, the lowlands of Edom, with elevations reaching ca. −80 masl, is typical of the Saharo-Arabian desert phytogeographic zone with pockets of Sudanian flora (Danin 1983), with mean annual rainfall at less than 70 mm. This contrast in rainfall patterns between the highlands and the lowlands has made rainfed agriculture possible in the highlands and more limited agriculture (primarily with the aid of irrigation technologies) possible in the lowlands. More important, this environmental dichotomy had a profound effect on the need for herd animals such as sheep and goats and their annual movements in search of grazing land. For the most part, since at least the Early Bronze Age (Adams 2003; Levy *et al.* 2002) human occupation in Edom has been characterized by nomadic or semi-nomadic populations who have searched for ways to integrate the exploitation of seasonal resources available in both the highland and lowland regions. Thus, it is impossible to understand human settlement and the history of Edom without conceptualizing and integrating these two physiographic regions. However, over the past three decades, archaeologists interested in the Iron Age of Edom have overlooked the significance of the 'lowland'–'highland' dichotomy. Prior to the Jabal Hamrat Fidan Project (Levy 2002; Levy, Adams, and Najjar 1999, 2001), all the major Iron Age excavations in Edom took place in the highland zone (Bennett 1966b, 1977; Bennett and Bienkowski 1995a; Bienkowski 1990; Bienkowski and Adams 1999; Bienkowski and Bennett 2003). The lack of systematic archaeological exploration in the lowland zone also meant that the role of Iron Age copper production that took place in the lowlands was not fully investigated.

As part of the deep-time study of early metallurgy and ore procurement from the Neolithic to the Iron Age (Levy *et al.* 2001a), one of the goals of the Jabal Hamrat Fidan (JHF) Project, made up of a team of international researchers under the auspices of the UCSD—DOAJ, has been to help fill in the Iron Age research gaps that have developed due to the 'highland bias' in the Iron Age archaeology of Edom. The Jabal Hamrat Fidan is a narrow mountain range made up of Monzogranite (Rabb'a 1994) that stretches for ca. 8 km north/south along the eastern edge of the Wadi Araba and represents the 'gateway' to the copper ore rich district of Faynan. The research area includes some 280 km² and is west of the main Faynan valley where various archaeology teams from the Council for British Research in the Levant have carried out mostly surveys and some excavations (Barker *et al.* 1997, 1999, 2000). The main seasonal drainages in the JHF research area that have been intensively and systematically surveyed for archaeological sites include the Wadi Fidan (Levy *et al.* 2001a), Wadi al-Jariyeh, and Wadi al-Guwayb (Levy *et al.* 2003). In this study, we discuss the ramifications of the stratigraphic excavations and high precision radiocarbon dating for the largest Iron Age site in the Jabal Hamrat Fidan area, Khirbat en-Nahas. First, however, it is necessary to briefly review the chronological bias in the Iron Age archaeology of Edom and how that has affected interpretation of the evolution and history of the emergence of Edomite kingdom known primarily from the Hebrew Bible and some extra-biblical texts.

The Chronological Bias in the Iron Age Archaeology of Edom

Until quite recently, the Iron Age chronology of Edom rested on the discovery of a single clay seal impression discovered at the highland site of Umm el-Biyara during Crystal Bennett's excavations in the 1960s (Bennett 1966a, 1966b). The seal contains the name of Qos-Gabr and is known from the 7th-century BCE Assyrian annals of Esarhaddon (Prism B, ca. 673–672 BCE; Pritchard 1969: 291) and in the first campaign of Ashurbanipal (Cylinder C, ca. 667 BCE; Bienkowski 1992b; Pritchard 1969: 294). Using the concept of relative dating, scholars have taken the discovery of this extra-biblical text fragment to date the Iron Age pottery found in association with it at the Iron Age site of Umm el-Biyara. As Bienkowski (1992b: 99) pointed out some years ago, the seal impression of Qos-Gabr provides a *terminus post quem*[1] for dating the Iron Age pottery at Umm al-Biyara but did not indicate just how early the Iron Age pottery found in that assemblage dated back to in time. In fact, Bienkowski (1992b: 110) also alerted readers that unpublished radiocarbon dates from the German Mining Museum's soundings at Khirbat en-Nahas and radiocarbon dates that indicated much earlier dates for the Iron Age in Edom (ca. calibrated dates of ca. 1200–900 BCE with 'Midianite' pottery; see Levy *et al.* 2004). However, Bienkowski's caution and the later publication of the report of the soundings at Khirbat en-Nahas in German which included radiocarbon dates (Engel 1993; Fritz 1996) fell on deaf ears. Bennett's dating of the Iron Age in Edom to the 7th and 6th centuries BCE became the accepted standard for the Iron Age archaeology of this part of Jordan. A host of studies concerning Iron Age Edom were produced based on the assumptions established by the relative dating of Umm el-Biyara (Bennett and Bienkowski [eds.] 1995b; Bienkowski 1995; Hart 1989; Oakshott 1978, 1983; Pratico 1985, 1993b) and even more recent studies continue to work under the late 7th–6th-centuries BCE assumption for the emergence of the Edomite kingdom (Bienkowski and Bennett 2003; Crowell 2004; Porter 2004).

The enthusiasm that Bennett's late dating of Iron Age Edom received from scholars in the late 1970s to the 1990s, was in part against the views of the American archaeologist Nelson Glueck who pioneered archaeological surveys in Jordan and Iron Age excavations in Edom (Glueck 1938, 1939a, 1940a). Glueck took a more traditional view of Levantine archaeology and tended to accept extensive texts in the Hebrew Bible as historical fact in a way that many researchers believed to be biased (Dever 2000). Working in Edom, Glueck firmly believed that the majority of Iron Age mining activities in the Faynan district that he documented could be dated to the 10th century BCE

---

1.   *Terminus post quem*—refers to the notion that a datable object provides only the date on or after which the archaeological sediment layer that contains it was deposited.

(1940a: 69) and 9th century BCE (1940a: 86) and directly related to biblical texts such as 2 Samuel 8.13-15, 1 Kings 22.45, 48-50, 2 Chronicles 20.1ff., and many more. In the early 1990s, working with published Iron Age ceramic drawings, Israel Finkelstein (1992a, 1992b) suggested that indeed there was ceramic evidence (collared rim jars) of an early Iron Age occupation in Edom that pushed back this occupation considerably earlier than the view of Bienkowski (Bienkowski 1992a) and others. To help solve this chronological debate, which has profound implications for understanding the history and socio-economic processes that led to the rise of the Edomite kingdom—such as core-periphery relationships between Edom and the Assyrian empire on the one hand and Edom and neighboring small polities such as Israel and Judah—it was decided that as part of the JHF Project, large scale stratigraphic excavations would be carried out at the Iron Age copper production site of Khirbat en-Nahas.

Previous Fieldwork at Khirbat en-Nahas

Nelson Glueck's (1939a, 1940a) surveys in Edom were the first systematic investigation of the network of Iron Age metal production sites in the lowlands of Edom and recognized the centrality of the site of Khirbat en-Nahas (KEN) in that system.

Figure 10.1. Aerial view of Khirbat en-Nahas, Jordan
(courtesy of ROHR publications, Nicosia)

While the Czech Orientalist Alois Musil (1907) was the first to sketch the site in 1898, and the site was subsequently visited by Kirkbride, Horsfield, Head, and Fritz Frank (Frank 1934) before Glueck, it was Glueck who photographed and made detailed sketch maps of a full range of Iron Age metal production sites around KEN. Glueck assumed that the most important periods of metal production at Khirbat en-Nahas were during and after the reign of King Solomon (1940a: 60-61). The site was later cursorily surveyed by Burton MacDonald (1992). In the early 1990s, the German Mining Museum, under Andreas Hauptmann (2000), carried out technological studies at KEN (Engel 1993) and preliminary soundings at one of the buildings visible on the site surface (Fritz 1996). In addition to Building 200 (n = 1 radiocarbon sample), three slag mounds were sampled around the perimeter of the site providing a total of 8 Iron Age dates: East—near Fritz's Building 200 (n = 4 samples); North—HD 10991 (n = 1 sample); and West—near the fortress gate (n = 3 samples).

The dates from the German Mining Museum (GMM) work at KEN (Hauptmann 2000: 66) have been re-calibrated using Ox-Cal v3.6 in Figure 10.2 here. Published in the 1990s and 2000 (Hauptmann 2000) the dates clearly indicate two major phases of metal production at KEN during 12th–11th centuries BCE and 10th–9th centuries BCE and highlight a much earlier Iron Age occupation in Edom than suggested by many current researchers who focus on the highlands (Bienkowski 2001a, 2001b; Crowell 2004; Porter 2004). However, part of the problem with the GMM date sequence is that they are not tied to well-defined archaeological stratigraphy at KEN. Consequently, with the exception of the single date from Building 200 (HD 13978), all the dates come from industrial deposits that lack cultural material such as pottery, scarabs, ground stone, casting molds, and so on. This lack of association with cultural material may also have contributed to archaeologists paying little attention to the GMM KEN dates in constructing models of settlement and history for Iron Age Edom. The recent excavations at KEN by the JHF team (Levy *et al.* 2004) have resolved this problem by carrying out large-scale excavations in three different cultural contexts at the site: the fortress gate (Area A), a building devoted to metallurgical processing, and an industrial slag mound similar to those sampled by the GMM team.

The 2002 Field Work at Khirbat en-Nahas and New Radiocarbon Dates

Recently, the JHF team reported on a series of 10 high precision radiocarbon dates from the 2002 excavations at KEN and processed at the Oxford Radiocarbon Accelerator Unit (Levy *et al.* 2004). These included 4 dates from the Area A fortress, 4 dates from the Area S building complex and 2 dates from the Area M slag mound. These data and their analyses demonstrated how some of the chronological biases in the Iron Age archaeology of Edom could be surmounted with the aid of high precision radiocarbon dating. That study also showed that occupation began at KEN at least as early as the 11th century BCE and that the monumental fortress was built in the 10th century BCE. It also showed that complex societies existed in Edom that where heavily involved in the extraction of copper ore and production of copper long before the influence of Assyrian imperialism was felt in the region from the 8th–6th centuries BCE. To bolster the study of KEN and its chronological position in the Iron Age of Edom, an additional 27 carbon samples were processed from KEN for dating at the Centre for Isotope Research, Groningen, the Netherlands and are reported on here (Table 10.1).

Table 10.1. Radiocarbon Dates from Khirbat en–Nahas, Jordan.
Processed at the Groningen AMS Laboratory (see Higham *et al.* [Chapter 11, this volume] for 2 sigma values).

Stratum	Sample Details	Lab. No.r	AMS date BP	+/-	CalBC 1 sigma
	Area A				
A-2A	KEN L.21 - B.1069 Ash and slag layer	GrA-25311	2710	35	895–825
A-2A	KEN L.21 - B.1419	GrA-25312	2670	35	890–885, 835–800
A-2A	KEN L.21 - B.1458	GrA-25334	2910	50	1210–1010
A-2B	KEN L.74 - B.1659 Copper ind. Waste	GrA-25314	2705	35	895–825
A-2B	KEN L.74 - B.1655	GrA-25315	2705	40	895–825
A-2B	KEN L.74 - B.1642	GrA-25316	2815	40	1005–905
A-3	KEN L.89 - B.1840 Red sediment below indus.	GrA-25318	2920	35	1210–1045
A-3	KEN L.89 - B.1911	GrA-25354	2880	50	1185–1180, 1125–945
A-3	KEN L.53 - B.1332 Solid ash layer/ E probe	GrA-25321	2660	40	835–795
A-3	KEN L.94 - B.1944 Reddish-brown layer (surface?) NE cham	GrA-25322	2680	40	895–875, 835–800
A-4A	KEN L.58 - B.1409 Hard reddish surface/ S prb/u. L.57, 56	GrA-25320	2710	35	895–825
	Area S				
S-1	KEN L. 263 - B.5770 Ash Fill (AS) Large amounts of slag	GrA-25324	2720	35	895–830
S-1	KEN L.312 - B.6709 Silty Sed. (SD) bel. and w/ collapse RM 3	GrA-25325	2700	35	895–810
S-1	KEN L.317 - B.6389 Silty Sed. (SD) bel. and w/ collapse RM 2	GrA-25326	2735	35	900–835
S-1	KEN L.317 - B.6383	GrA-25328	2670	35	890–885, 835–800
S-1	KEN L.317 - B.6508	GrA-25342	2795	45	1000–895
S-2A	KEN L.301 - B.6041	GrA-25329	2705	40	895–825
S-2A	KEN L.301 - B.6103	(Levy *et al.* 2004)	2820	35	1005–920
S-2A	KEN L.322 - B.6943 Silty Sed. (SD) Outside Structure	GrA-25332	2715	40	895–830
S-2A	KEN L.340 - B.7594 Silty Sed. (SD) below and w/ collapse	GrA-25343	2720	45	900–825
S-2B	KEN L.336 - B.7524 Silty Sediment (SD) Outside Structure	GrA-25344	2770	45	970–835
S-2B	KEN L.338 - B.7418 Surface (SU) inside structure RM 2	GrA-25345	2780	45	995–840
S-3	KEN L.342 - B.7660 Slag Layer (SL) below RM 1	GrA-25353	2820	50	1040–900
S-3	KEN L.344 - B.7621 Slag Layer/Surface (SU) below RM 3	GrA-25347	2830	45	1045–915
S-4	KEN L.346 - B.7667 Silty Sed. (SD) above surface	GrA-25348	2770	45	970–835
S-4	KEN L.347 - B.7659 Fill above Surface (FS)	GrA-25349	2790	45	1000–865
S-4	KEN L.353 - B.7738 Surface (SU) below RM 1	GrA-25352	2800	45	1005–900

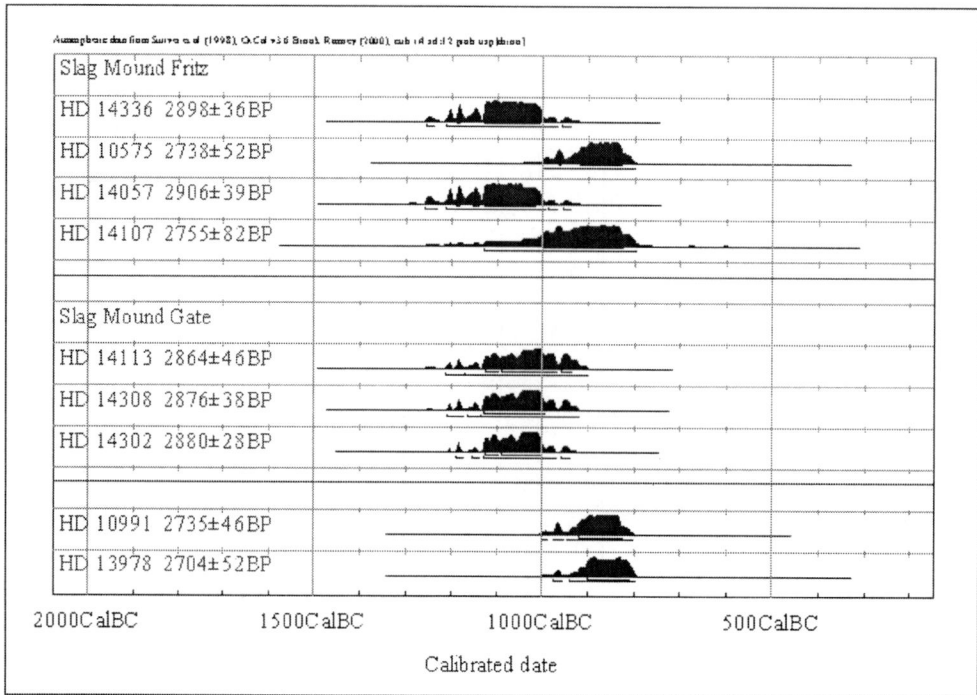

Figure 10.2. Calibrated radiocarbon dates from slag mounds and Room 200,
Khirbat en Nahas, Jordan (after Hauptmann 2000). HD 10991 = North slag mound, calibrated
910–820 BCE; HD 13978 = Building 200, calibrated 900–805 BCE.

In this section, we focus on presenting a snapshot of the archaeological deposits and the expanded number of radiocarbon samples processed at Groningen since the publication of our original suite of dates processed at the Oxford Radiocarbon Accelerator Unit (Levy *et al.* 2004). A detailed study of these dates is presented by Higham *et al.* (Chapter 11, this volume). Here we spotlight the cultural and historical implications of the dates.

The Iron Age Fortress at KEN (Area A)

The ca. 73 × 73 m² fortress at KEN had never been excavated before the 2002 field season and its dating was only speculative. To obtain an archaeological 'signature' of the fortress complex, we decided to focus our work on sampling what appeared to be the gate located on the western perimeter of the fortress. Although covered mostly in rough, possibly hewn, blocks of Burj Dolomite shale, the outlines of what appeared to be room cells or guard rooms could be detected protruding on the surface of rubble surrounding the gate (Figs. 10.3, 4). Broadly, 7 strata could be defined in Area A: A4, A3, A2b, A2a, A1b, and A1a. As A4 represents bedrock, we begin with the earliest construction phase—Stratum A3.

Figure 10.3. Gate at KEN before excavation, 2002.

Figure 10.4. Clearing the exterior of the gate at KEN, 2002.

Figure 10.5. The two northern guard rooms exposed in the KEN gate, 2002.

After clearing much of the collapse from the gate house, it was clear that we had found a typical Four-Chamber Iron Age Gate (Fig. 10.5). In the interests of preservation we left more than half of the gate house unexcavated for the future and focused our excavations on the two most northern rooms in the four-room gate house. As will be shown below, the passageway or street between the two sets of guard rooms had been intentionally sealed in antiquity, so it was decided to leave this blockage unexcavated. A summary of the different strata found in and around the gate house follows from the earliest building layer (Stratum A3) through the main occupations phases (Strata A2a and A2b). Some of the problems and potentials of these new dates are discussed below.

Stratum A3, Gate, Founding Phase

The Four-Chamber Gate was founded in Stratum A3 above the sterile bedrock stratum found in the earlier Stratum A4. One of the problems in excavating in and around the gate is that the different excavation areas inside and outside this structure were not connected stratigraphically but linked together based on the relative similarity of the depositional sequence in this single excavation area. Thus, on some occasions the possibility that later deposits infiltrated into lower stratum can not be ignored. Consequently, the date GrA-25320 (calBC 895–825) for Stratum A4 is too late for the basal layer at the site and comes from the main 9th-century BCE industrial activity that took place in this area when the gate was already abandoned. The four additional carbon samples selected for radiocarbon dating from Stratum A3 (Table 10.1: GrA-25318, GrA-25354, GrA-25321, GrA-25322) are also problematic but for the same and opposite reasons. GrA-25321 (calBC 835–795) and GrA-25322 (calBC 895–875, 835–800) seem to be from the basal portions of the 9th century BCE A2b industrial layer that were ascribed in the field to A3. Alternatively GrA-25318 (calBC 1210–1045) and GrA-25354 (calBC 1185–1180, 1125–945) are associated with 12th–11th-century BCE metalworking activities that took place in Area A before the construction of the gate (see Figs. 10.6, 8–9). When these dates are coupled with the Stratum A3 date from the Oxford lab (OxA-12366 [calBC 1000–985]), the main construction phase of the four chamber gate falls within the early 10th century BCE. Clearly more stratigraphic excavations are needed in and around the Area A gate to clarify the construction date of this structure on a more definitive basis.

Based on the radiocarbon determinations from the Oxford suite (Levy *et al.* 2004), those from Groningen published here, and the stylistic similarities of the gate at KEN with those from other Iron Age south Levantine fortresses, it seems safe at this point to date the KEN example to the Iron IIA period. As seen in Table 10.2, the KEN gate is most similar to the well-known examples of Megiddo IVA, Beersheva V and III, Tel Dan, Ashdod 10, and Tell en-Nasbeh (Early). The KEN gate has a façade of ca. 16.8 m and is smaller than the major Iron II settlement sites such as Megiddo IVA, Tel Dan, and Beersheva V, but on par with Beersheva III, Ashdod 10, and slightly larger than Tell en-Nasbeh (Early). The highly specialized nature of the KEN fortress which serviced the metal production activities of 10th–9th-century BCE Edom is thus enigmatic. The gate can be considered a mid-size example of the typical Iron IIA examples found in the southern Levant that was linked to a single role—helping to ensure the operation of copper production at KEN at the beginning of the Iron IIA period. If the perimeter of the KEN fortress is compared with other 10th–9th-century BCE fortresses in southern Israel, Jordan, and the Sinai Peninsula (Table 10.3), at ca. 73 × 73 m^2, the KEN fortress is one of the largest fortifications from this period in the southern Levant. The closest parallel to the KEN gate and fortress complex is the one excavated by Glueck (Glueck 1938, 1939b, 1940b) at Tell el-Kheleifeh near Aqaba on the Red Sea which he dated to the 10th (Period I), 9th (Period II), and 8th (Period III) centuries BCE (Glueck 1993). Although Pratico (1993a, 1993b) has gone to great lengths to re-date Tell el-Kheleifeh to mostly the 8th–6th centuries BCE, the similarities between the KEN gate and fortress and Tell el-Kheleifeh, as well as the ceramic assemblages, are so striking that we suggest that in light of the corpus of ^{14}C dates from KEN, the dating of Tell el-Kheleifeh needs to be reassessed once again in conjunction with future radiocarbon dates. Thus, a working hypothesis can be constructed that suggests that during the 10th and possibly the 9th centuries BCE, the KEN fortress played a pivotal role in the exploitation of copper ore and metal in the Faynan district and that it was part of an Iron IIA trade network that incorporated the early Hazevah fortress (Cohen and Yisrael 1995) on the western side of the Wadi Arabah with land trade routes leading to Israel and the Mediterranean and Tell El-Kheleifeh controlling seaborne trade to the south. As will be seen in the discussion of the following strata (A2b–A2a), considering the considerable energy that went into the construction of the KEN fortress, it is extremely puzzling that the KEN fortress seems to have had a relatively short-lived use. Additional excavations are needed in the gate to clarify the changing function of the gate and fortress.

Table 10.2. Characteristics of south Levantine Iron Age Four-Chamber Gates (Sources: Herzog 1992; Levy *et al.* 2004; A. Mazar [personal communication]).

Site	Façade (m)	Depth (m)	Passage width (m)	Depth of Chambers (m)	Width of Chambers (m)	Date of Construction
Megiddo IVA	25	15.5	4.2	3	8.2	Late 9th–8th century BCE
Beersheva V	20.8	12.6	4.2	3	6	End of 10th or 9th century BCE
Beersheva III	16.6	13.6	3.6	3	5	Early 8th century BCE
Tel Dan	29.5	17.8	3.7	4.5	9	9th century BCE foundation?
Ashdod 10	16.5	13.75	4.2	2.4	3.8	End of 11th or Early 10th century BCE
Tell en-Nasbeh (Early)	15	12	4	1.8	4.4	No hard data
Khirbat en-Nahas	16.8	10.6	3.63	2.9	3	10th century BCE

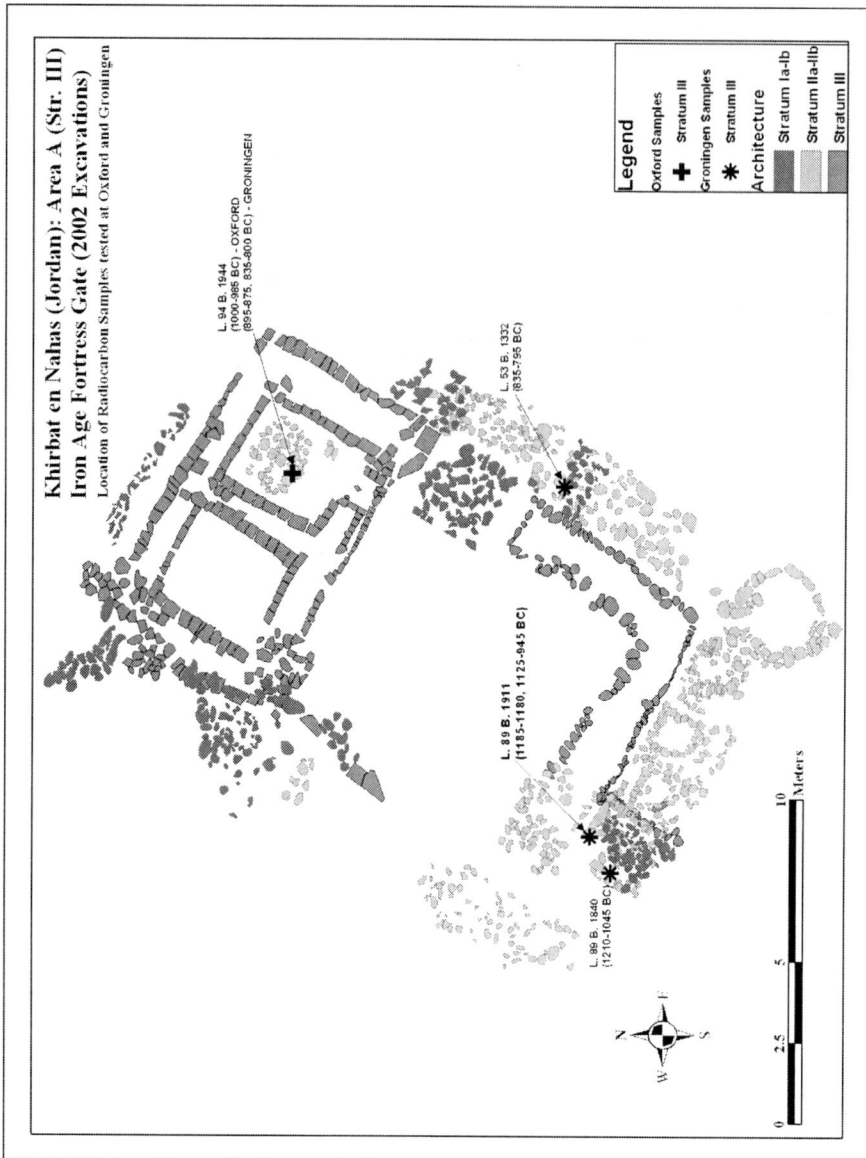

Figure 10.6. Area A, Stratum A3. KEN Gate with location of radiocarbon samples.

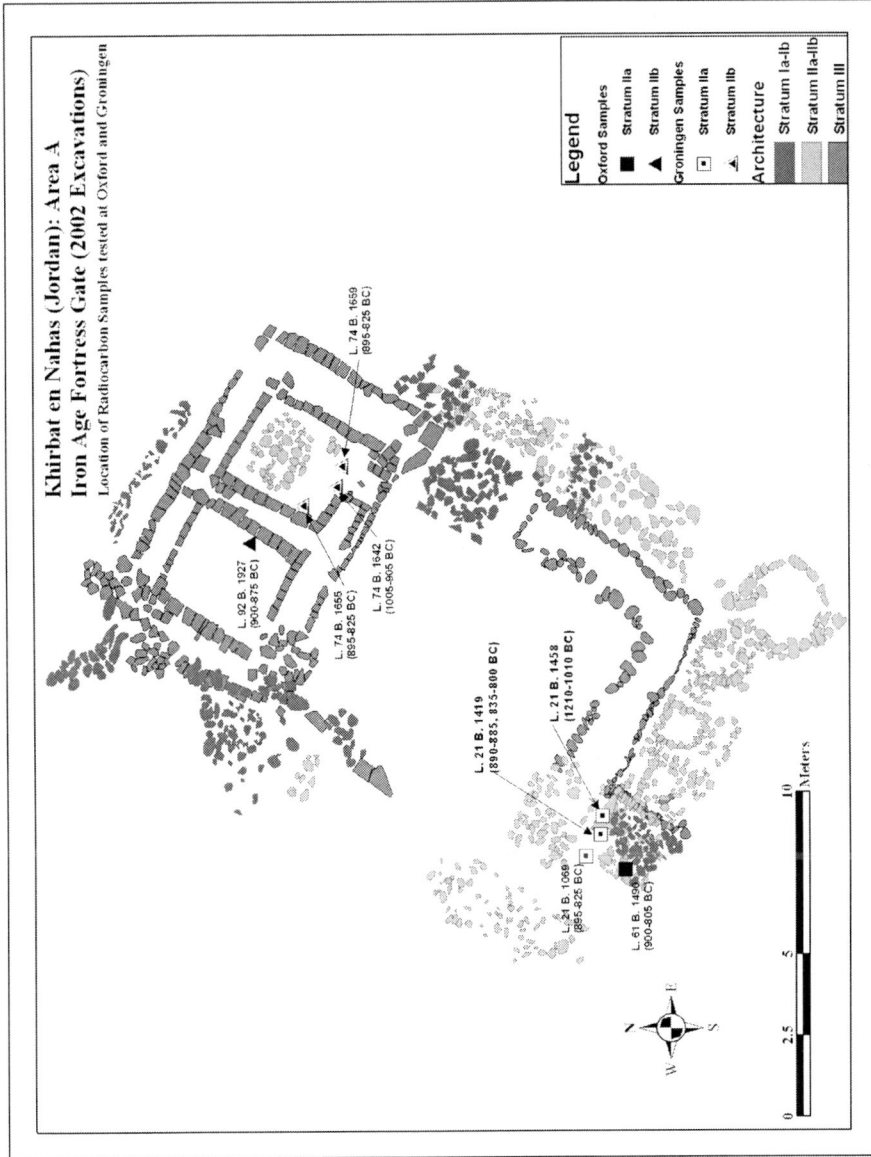

Figure 10.7. Area A, Stratum A2a and A2b.

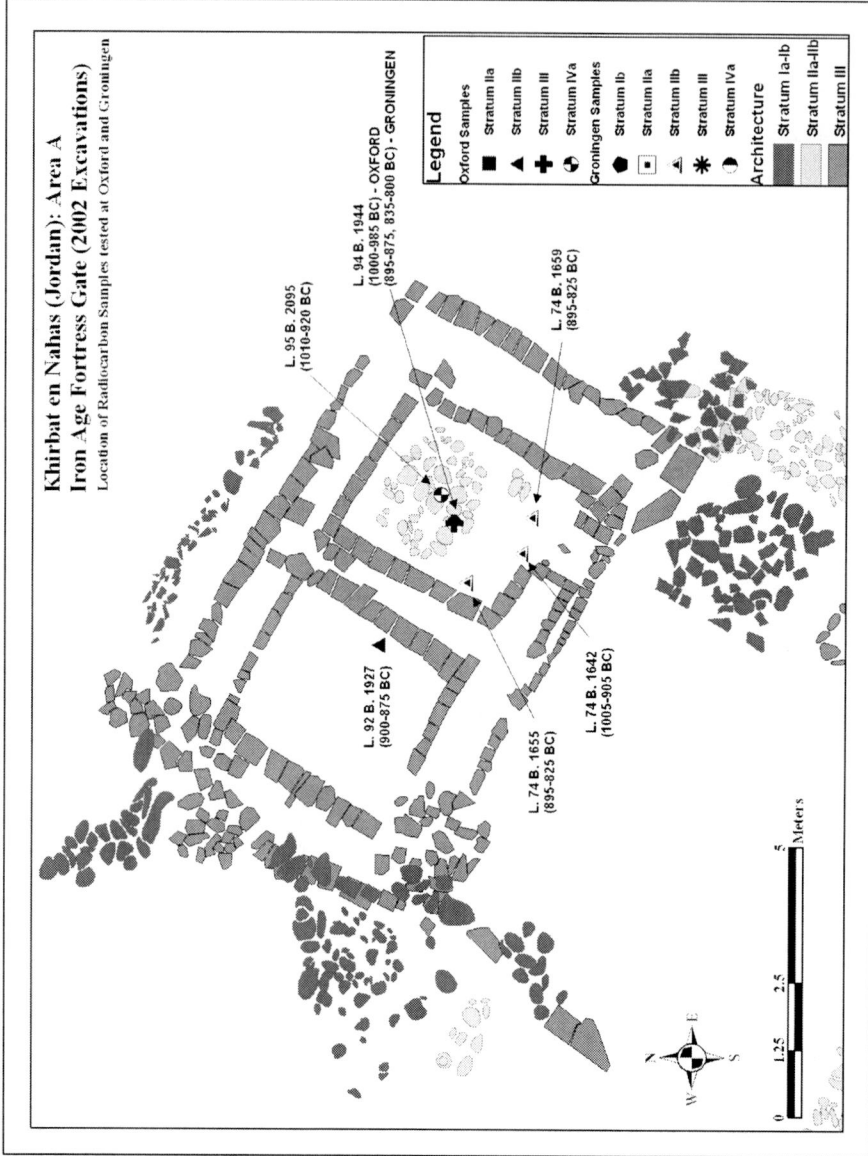

Figure 10.8. Area A, northern chambers with all radiocarbon samples.

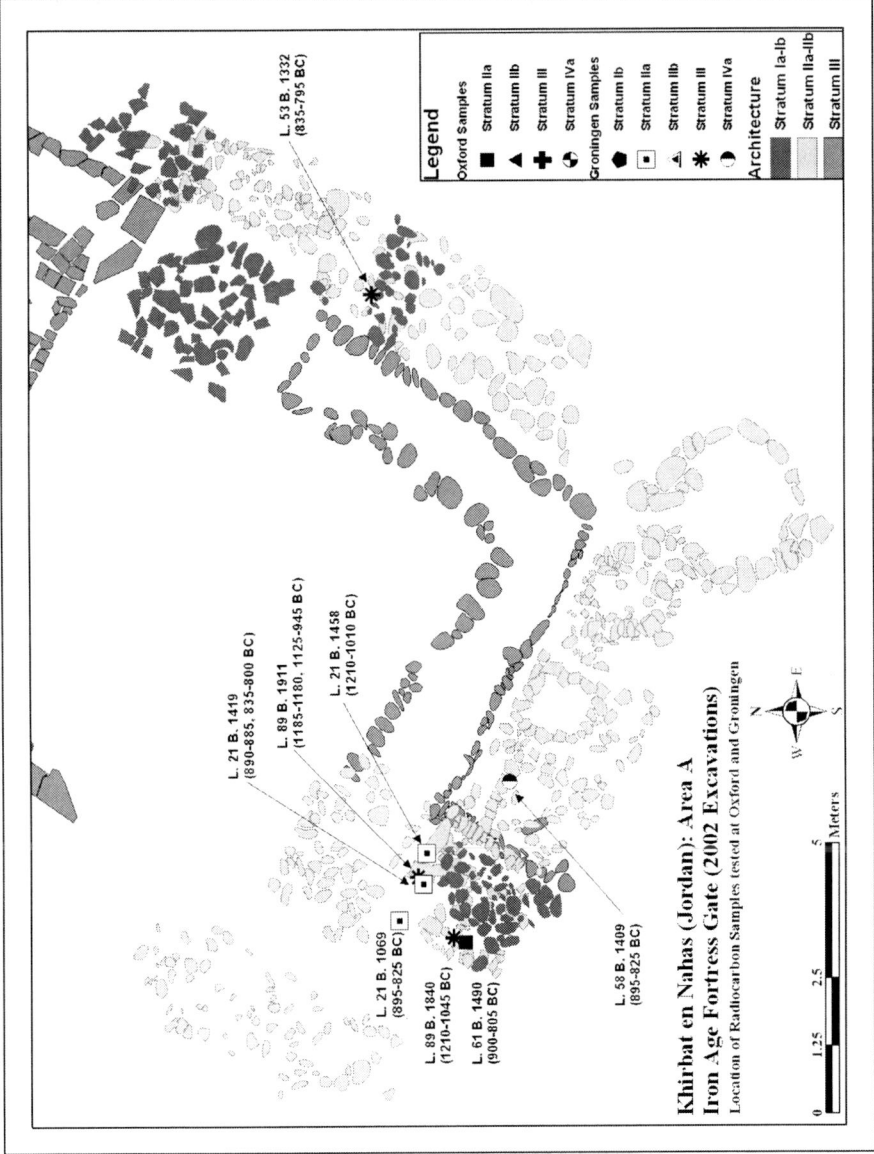

Figure 10.9. Area A, southern chambers with all radiocarbon samples.

Strata A2b and A2a, Gate

Stratum A2b. It is remarkable that shortly after the construction of the Khirbat en-Nahas gate, it seems to have gone out of use as defensive facility. There are two lines of evidence to suggest this. First, the passageway leading between the two sets of gate rooms was carefully filled with closing walls on each end of the passage, and a rock fill. As seen on the plan in Figure 10.7, both the western and eastern ends of the passage were closed in Stratum A2b with a stone wall. These closing walls, like the walls which indicate the location of the guard rooms of the gate house, were seen protruding out of the rubble fill covering the gate complex and easily mapped. Secondly, the eastern Stratum A2b closing wall was fully exposed during the excavations around this part of the gate revealing the careful work done to ensure the closure of the passage. As seen in Figures 10.11 and 10.12, this blockage was carefully constructed with tons of rock fill placed behind it to fill in the passage and render it useless. In addition to closing the passageway through the gate, the Stratum A2b activities included using the former guard rooms for smelting and other metal processing activities. Three new Groningen dates (GrA-25314 [calBC 895–825], GrA-25315 [calBC 895–825], and GrA-25316 [Table 10.1; calBC 1005–905), along with the Oxford date (OxA-12367 [calBC 900–875]) show that during the early 9th century BCE the gate and fortress ceased to have a military function.

Strata A2a. There may have been a brief abandonment phase in Area A (Fig. 10.7) at KEN following the heavy Stratum A2b metalworking activities at the site. The stratigraphic development of the site shows that a second metal processing layer is superimposed on Stratum A2b that has been labeled Stratum A2a. This stratum represents more scanty evidence of metal production with a series of rather ephemeral stone built installations attached around the perimeter of the gate including those areas directly in front of the passageway. Three new dates were processed at Groningen (Table 10.1): GrA-25311 (calBC 895–825), GrA-25312 (calBC 890–885, 835–800), and GrA-25334 (calBC 1210–1010). When these dates are considered along with the single date processed from this stratum in the Oxford lab (OxA-12368 [calBC 900–805]), it is clear that GrA-25334 is too old and represents an earlier piece of charcoal that was mixed in with material from this later stratum. As this stratum is characterized by many pit installations, the mixing hypothesis seems most accurate. Thus, Stratum A2a represents a late 9th-century BCE phase of metal production.

In summary, the expanded sample of radiocarbon dates for Area A at KEN indicates that in the 12th–11th centuries BCE, prior to the construction of the gate, Iron Age metal production activities had already begun at KEN. During the 10th century BCE, the Four-Chamber Gate was constructed in Stratum A3 and used for less than a century. In the following Stratum A2b, in the early 9th century BCE, the four-room gate ceased to function as a gate, was filled in and used for metal processing activities. By the end of the 9th century BCE, a second, more ephemeral phase (Stratum A2a) of metal production took place in and around the abandoned gate complex.

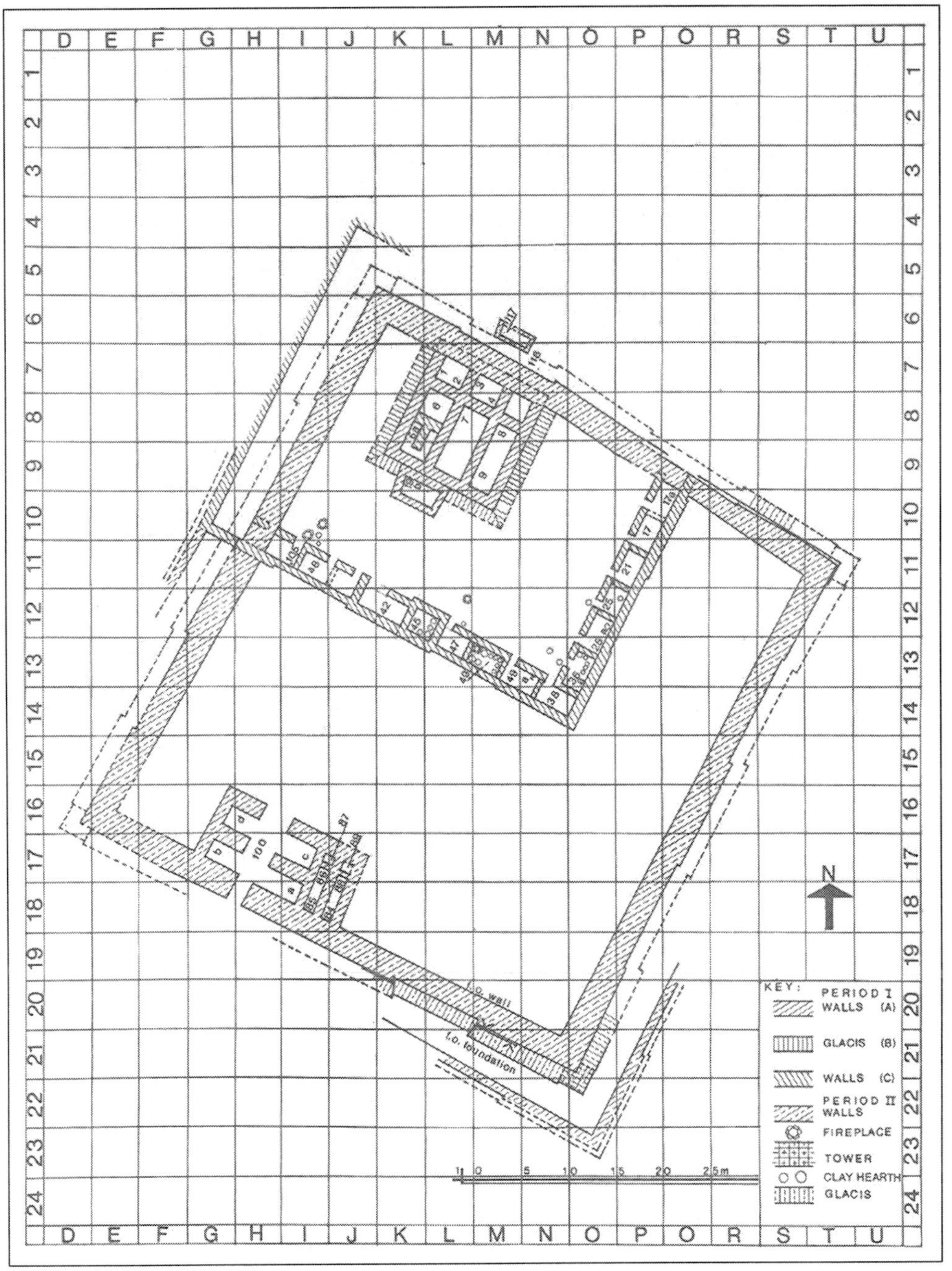

Figure 10.10. Glueck's (1940b) map of the fortress at Tell el-Kheleifeh, Jordan. Note similarity of this gate with the one at KEN.

Figure 10.11. Stratum A2b L. 42 blockage of passageway through Four-Chamber Gate.

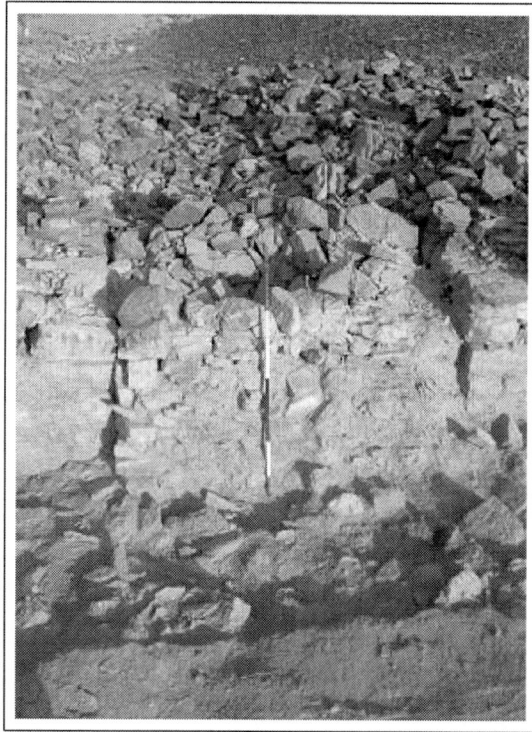

Figure 10.12. Detail of Stratum A2b L. 42 blockage of passageway
through Four-Chamber Gate.

Table 10.3. Desert Fortresses in the Negev, Sinai, and Wadi Arabah (Sources: Beit-Arieh [ed.] 1999; Cohen and Cohen-Amin 2004; Herzog 1992).

Fortress	Shape	Size (m)
Northern Negev		
Arad	Square	50 × 50
Uza	Rectangular	42 × 51
Horvat Tov	Square	30 × 40
Tel Ira VII	Irregular shape	100 × 320
Negev Highlands		
Horbat Rachava (Site 1)	Oval	60 × 70
Horbat Ha-Ru'ah (Site 8)	Oval	42 × 50
Qatef Shivta (Site 10)	Oval	25 × 36
Horbat Haluqim (Site 11)	Oval	21 × 23
Nahal Nitzana (Site 15)	Oval	Diameter = 20 m
Nahal Resisim (Site 20)	Oval	14 × 16
Nahal Horsha (Site 24)	Oval	22 × 38
Nahal L'ana (Site 26)	Oval	12 × 23
Sheluhat Qadesh Barne'a (Site 29)	Oval	25 × 48
Mesuda Nahal Sarfad (Site 31)	Oval	26 × 36
Nahal Elah (Site 34)	Oval	20 × 34
Mezudat Nahal 'Aqrav (Site 35)	Oval	40.25 × 45.5
Wadi al-Qedirat (Site 38)	Oval	22 × 33
Nahal Horesha (Site 39)	Oval	12 × 30
'Ein Qadeis (Site 44)	Oval	37.5 × 52.5
Nahal Alonim (Site 47)	Oval	13.5 × 20
Nahal Lutz (Site 48)	Oval	14.5 × 18.5
N.G. 266 (Site 49)	Oval	23 × 45
Tira (Site 4)	Irregular shape	32 × 78
Refed (Site 3)	Irregular shape	42 × 57
Har Boker (Site 12)	Rectangular	19 × 26
Har Reviv (Site 14)	Rectangular/Square	21 × 21
Har Eldad (Stie 18)	Rectangular	14 × 18
Nahal Tsana (Site 23)	Rectangular	15 × 17
Beer Hafir (Site 25)	Rectangular/Square	20 × 20
Nahal Zin (Site 27)	Rectangular	16 × 21
Rohovot (Site 33)	Rectangular	17 × 19
Nahal Boker (Site 5)	Fortlet with square towers	9.8 × 9.8
Ramat Boker (Site 7)	Fortlet with square towers	9 × 9
Nahal Avdat (Site 17)	Fortlet with square towers	9.2 × 9.9
Mezudat Nahal Yatir	Fortlet with square towers	10 × 10
N.G. 538 Ma'arav (Site 36)	Fortlet with square towers	8.84 × 9
Har Hamat (Site 43)	Fortlet with square towers	10 × 10
Horvat Meshora (Site 6)	Fortlet w/ mudbrick towers	10 × 16.87
Horvat Haro'ah (Site 8)	Fortlet w/ mudbrick towers	8 × 12
Beerotiyim (Site 19)	Fortlet w/ mudbrick towers	11.31 × 16.13
Har Gizron (Site 45)	Fortlet w/ mudbrick towers	3.76 × 4
Sinai		
Quseima 'Aharoni' fortress	Oval	26 × 28
Kadesh Barnea (earliest)	Oval	26 × 28
Kadesh Barnea	Rectangular	34 × 52
Wadi Arabah		
Yotvata	Trapezoid	40 × 64
Hatzevah	Square	100 × 100
Tell el-Kheleifeh	Square	45 × 45
Khirbat en-Nahas	Square	73 × 73

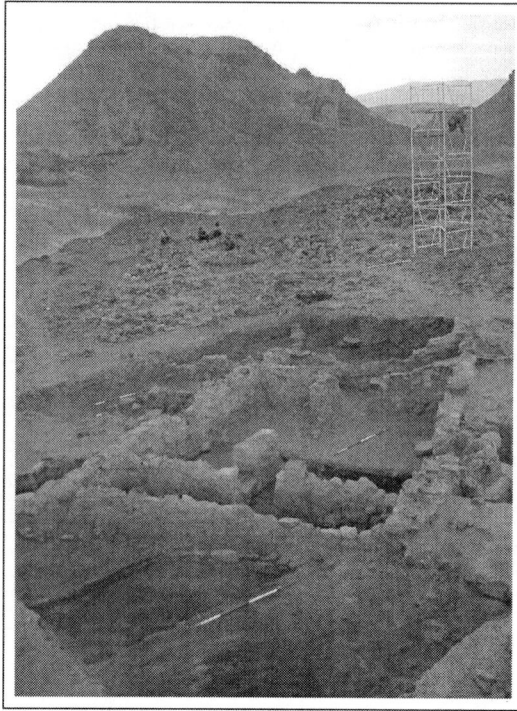

Figure 10.13. Overview of Area S. Building 200 (1133) from the German Mining Museum excavations is located to the right.

Figure 10.14. Overview of building in Area S, Khirbat en-Nahas.

Metallurgical Processing Building (Area S)

In our recent overview of the 2002 excavations and surveys in the Faynan district, we (Levy *et al.* 2003) described the Iron Age settlement along the Wadi Guwayb where Khirbat en-Nahas is located and one of its tributaries, the Wadi al-Jariyeh, as an 'Iron Age landscape' that reflected the organization and power of copper production in the Faynan district at this time. When examining the distribution of building remains across the site surface at KEN as seen in Figures 10.1 and 10.13–14, it can similarly be described as an Iron Age setting reflecting the power, organization, and fabrication of copper during the Iron I and Iron IIa–IIb periods writ large at a single locale. KEN is an extraordinary site in that virtually 100 per cent of the building remains visible on the site surface are associated with Iron Age ceramic remains. Based on the excavations by both the German Mining Museum (Fritz 1996) and those of the UCSD—DOAJ (Levy *et al.* 2004) teams, there seems little doubt that these buildings which extend over an area of ca. 10 ha all date to the Iron Age and almost reflect the very rare 'Pompeii principle' described by Michael Schiffer (1987) which relates to an archaeological site with an unusual degree of preservation, little evidence of post-depositional disturbance, and the documenting of 'frozen moments in time'. While KEN has certainly suffered from the vicissitudes of time, the later Iron Age strata at the site (ca. 9th century BCE) seem to represent abandonment where many artifacts were left *in situ*. Taken together, KEN represents a unique record of a Near Eastern Iron Age metal production factory town. The excavations in Area S represent the first systematic stratigraphic excavation of a building complex at KEN based on digital recording methods (Levy *et al.* 2001b) to ensure the utmost accuracy in data acquisition and analysis.

Stratum S4. This stratum represents the basal layer in Area S where several small (possible) cooking installations and isolated pockets of metal processing were found. Three new radiocarbon dates were processed from Stratum S4 (Table 10.1: GrA-25348 [calBC 970–835], GrA-25349 [calBC 1000–865], GrA-25352 [calBC 1005–900]). The first date processed from this stratum in the Oxford lab (OxA-12169 [calBC 1130–1015]) indicated a 12th–11th century BCE date. However, the new determinations point to the 10th–9th centuries BCE. Given the presence of Iron I scarabs from Area S (Levy *et al.* 2004), we suggest that the carbon samples collected from the small exposures in this area came from later contexts and that Stratum S4 should be dated to the Iron I period. This problem can only be resolved through more controlled excavations in other building complexes at KEN (see Figs. 10.13, 14).

Stratum S3. The most notable aspect of Stratum S3 at KEN is that it represents the first large scale evidence of metal smelting and processing in this part of the site. A thick layer of slag varying from 20–40 cm in thickness was found running under the entire S2b building structure in Area S (Fig. 10.16). This clearly shows that massive metal production occurred at KEN before the construction of many of the smaller 9th-century BCE buildings at the site such as the one in Area S and Building 200 (Fritz 1996). Two new radiocarbon dates were processed in Groningen from Stratum S3: GrA-25353 (calBC 1040–900) and GrA-25347 (calBC 1045–915) calibrated to the 11th and 10th centuries BCE. The Oxford date (OxA-12342 [calBC 1005–965]) is similar (see Higham *et al.* [Chapter 11, this volume]). The presence of a metal leaf-shaped arrowhead (Fig. 10.17) typical of the Iron I period (Mazar 1990) may add additional evidence to placing this industrial layer in the very late 11th–early 10th centuries BCE. Thus, it is possible that the widespread metal processing that occurred in Stratum S3 (Area S) was contemporary with the main occupation and use of the KEN fortress (Stratum A3) before it went out of use in Stratum A2b.

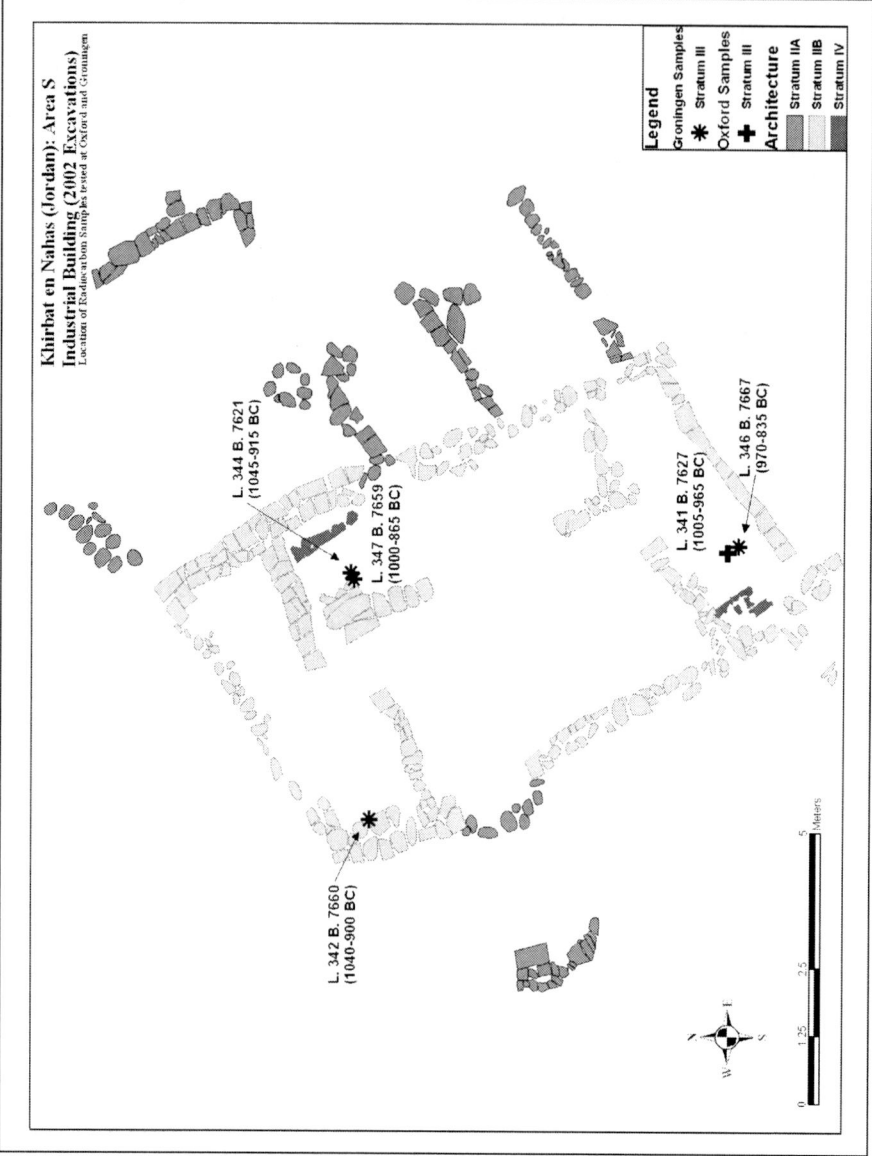

Figure 10.15. Map of Area S: Building with plot of radiocarbon date locations for Stratum S3 (note all these samples come from below the foundations of the Stratum S2 building).

Figure 10.16. Stratum S3 slag layer (L. 351) found below the building in Area S.

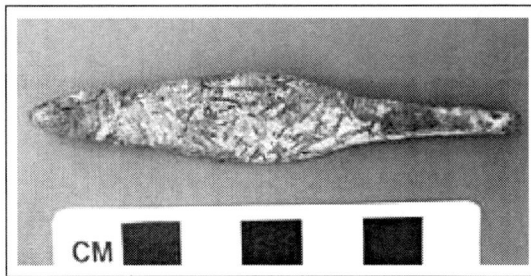

Figure 10.17. Leaf-shape metal arrowhead found in L. 344, Stratum S3.

Stratum S2b. Stratum S2b represents the main construction and use phase of the building in Area S. The building is a relatively small structure measuring ca. 6 × 10.20 m divided into four rooms (Fig. 10.18) and was primarily used to process slag from the nearby smelting operations. Based on over 350 ground stone artifacts including grinding slabs, mortars, pestles, and other objects found in association with thick deposits of crushed slag around the perimeter of this building, we assume slag was intensively crushed here to retrieve as much residual copper embedded in the slag as possible. The original Oxford date (OxA-12168 [calBC 905–830]) and two recently processed dates from Groningen (Table 10.1: GrA-25344 [calBC 970–835]; GrA-25345 [calBC 995–840]) suggest that the building was constructed and used primarily during the mid-9th century BCE. As seen in Figure 10.2, the single radiocarbon determination from Building 200 (HD 13978 [calBC 900–805]) also falls in the mid-9th century BCE. As a working hypothesis we suggest that after the fortress went out of use, there were widespread building activities at KEN when many of the structures visible on the site surface were constructed (see Figs. 10.1, 13).

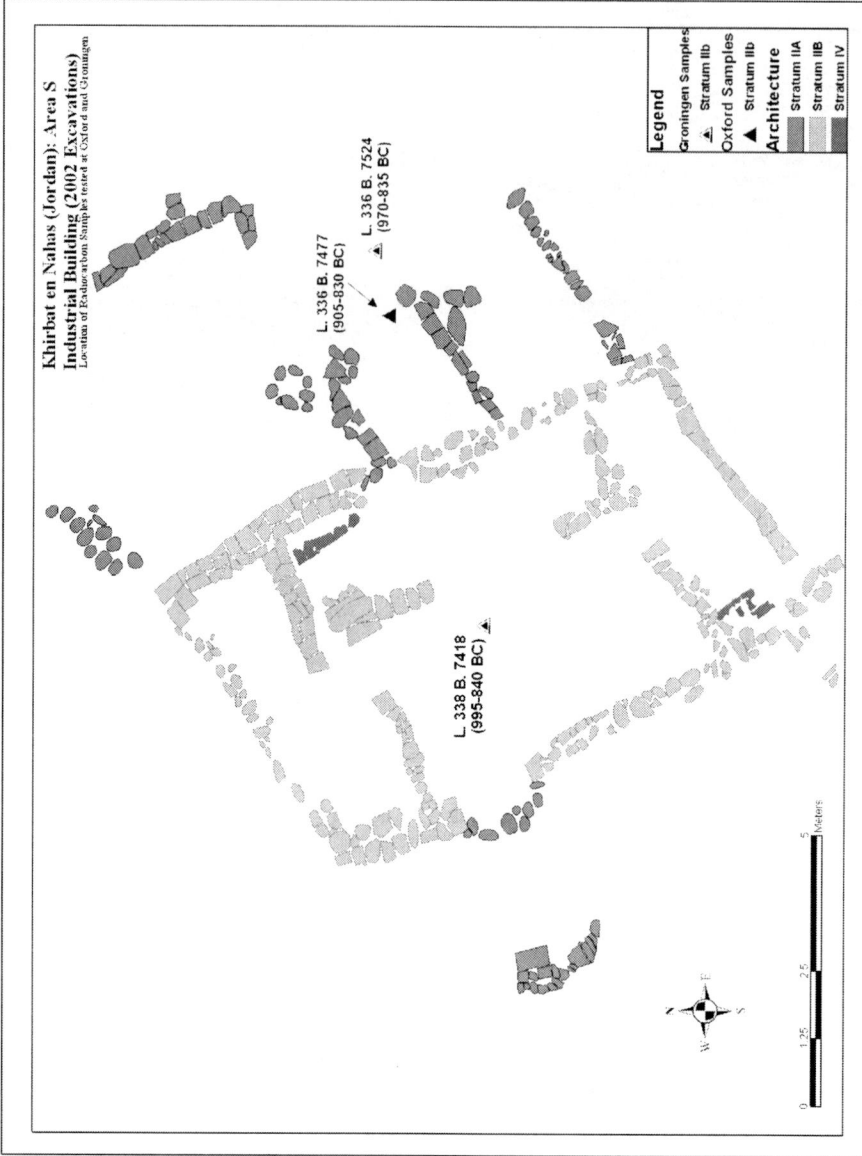

Figure 10.18. Building in Area S with Stratum S2b radiocarbon dates plotted. Samples come primarily from surfaces associated with these foundation walls.

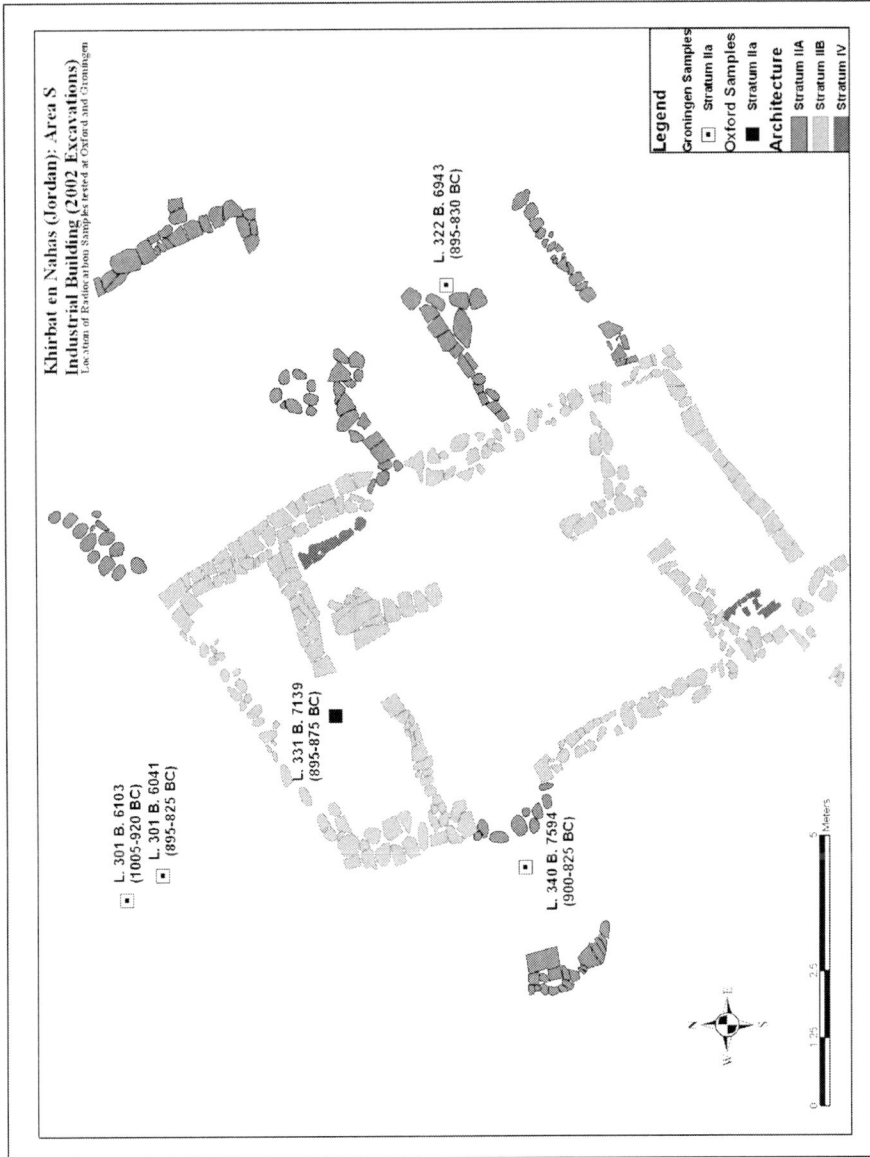

Figure 10.19. Building in Area S with Stratum S2a radiocarbon dates plotted. Samples come primarily from surfaces associated with these foundation walls.

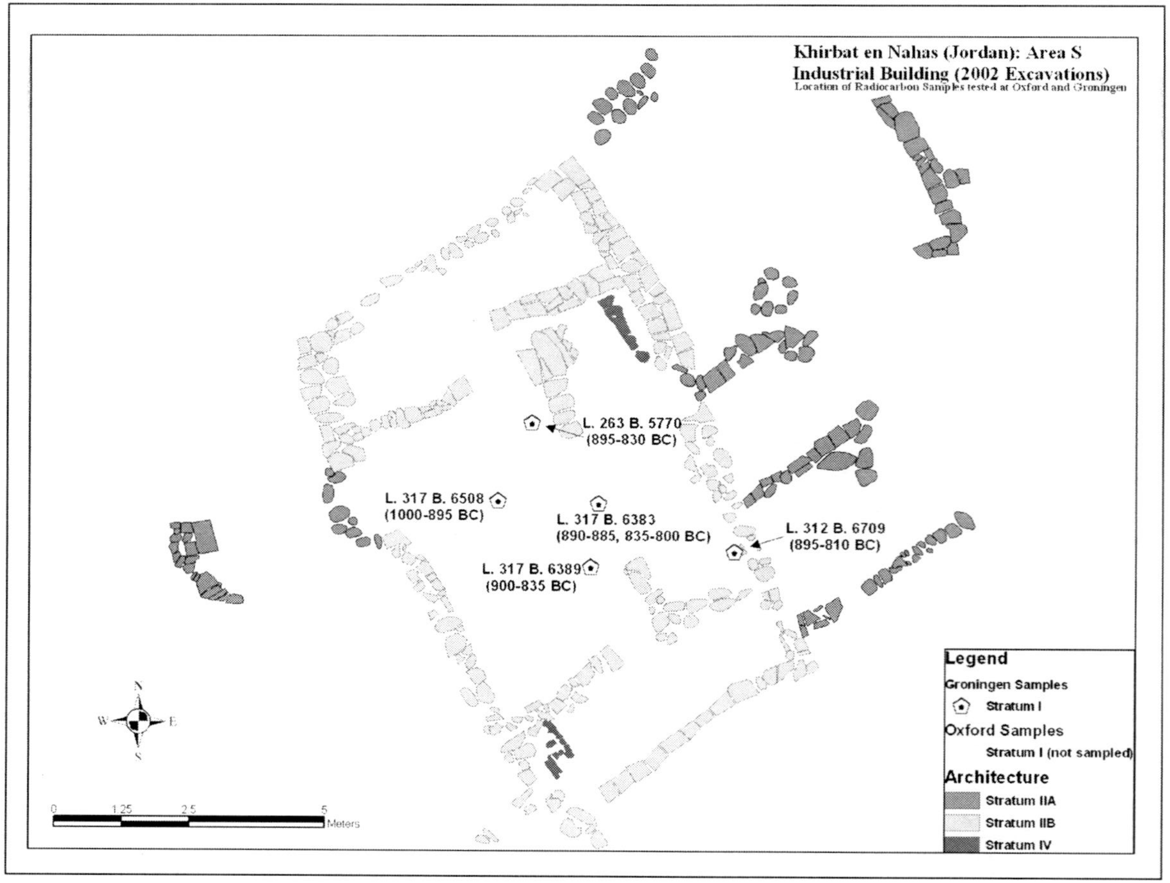

Figure 10.20. Building in Area S with Stratum S1 radiocarbon dates plotted.

Stratum S2a. This stratum represents a relatively short period of construction to enlarge the initial building plan of Stratum S2b. As seen in Figure 10.19, courtyards were added to the northeast of the four-room building in Area S and a second phase of surfaces was found inside the structure reflecting a re-use of the building. The original Oxford date (OxA-12274 [calBC 895–875]) has been augmented with four new Groningen dates (Fig. 10.19, Table 10.1; GrA-25343 [calBC 900–825], GrA-25332 [calBC 895–830], GrA-25331 [calBC 1005–920], GrA-25329 [calBC 895–825]). Given that one (GrA-25331) out of the five dates from this stratum is a somewhat earlier anomaly, we assume that it may represent an old wood problem. The Bayesian analysis of all these dates is presented by Higham *et al.* (Chapter 11, this volume). However, a general assessment of the suite of S2a dates suggests a mid-9th-century BCE occupation for this stratum very close in time to S2b.

Stratum S1. In this chapter, we present the first series of radiocarbon dates for Stratum S1 at KEN (Table 10.1). As this stratum was somewhat disturbed by post-depositional formation processes, we originally shied away from attempting to use radiocarbon to date this horizon (Levy *et al.* 2004). However, given the rich quantity of artifacts found in Stratum S1, we felt compelled to produce a relatively large sample of dates (GrA-25342 [calBC 1000–895]; GrA-25328 [calBC 890–885, 835–800]; GrA-25326 [calBC 900–835]; GrA-25325 [calBC 895–810]; GrA-25324 [calBC 895–830]). Stratum S1 activities occurred after an abandonment of the S2b–S2a occupation when there was an intentional in-filling of the four-room building to make a large enclosure. A scarab depicting a hunting scene was found in a fill from S1 (Basket: 6438, Locus 316; Levy *et al.* 2004: 875) and cannot be used to definitively date this specific stratum at KEN. Thus, at first glace these dates indicate a mid- to late 9th-century BCE date for Stratum S1. A clearer picture of this suite of dates is presented in the Bayesian analysis by Higham *et al.* (Chapter 11, this volume).

Area M—Slag Mound

Perhaps the most ubiquitous feature at KEN is the more than 30 extensive mounds of slag that mostly frame the perimeter of the site (Fig. 10.1; Levy *et al.* 2004: 869). The German Mining Museum team made soundings in three slag mounds at KEN and sampled examples on the west, north, and eastern boundaries of the site (Engel 1993; Hauptmann 2000). As noted above, these soundings produced an important series of dates (Fig. 10.2) that point to two major phases of metal production at KEN during the 12th–11th and 10th–9th centuries BCE. These soundings were made quickly by roughly sectioning the mounds so that carbon samples could be procured and an immediate picture of the phases of smelting revealed. While Engel (1993) suggested four major phases of smelting took place at KEN, our new data suggests more caution in making such an assessment. Using careful stratigraphic excavation methods, a ca. 5 m × 2.5 m sondage (Fig. 10.21) was dug through a slag mound located ca. 30 m south of Area S. This 6-week excavation was able to penetrate and accurately record only 1.2 m of the ca. 5 m deep slag mound. Within this exposure a minimum of 7 phases of smelting episodes was defined on the basis of identifying layers of large flat tap slag running across the section (Fig. 10.21). The radiocarbon dates from the top of this section (OxA-12436 [calBC 829–801]) and the base of this section (OxA-12437 [calBC 910–886]) suggest that in this relatively shallow sample of the slag mound there were two phases of smelting from the early 9th century BCE and early 10th–late 9th centuries BCE. This comes as no surprise given the findings of the Germans (Fig. 10.2). However, the excavations in Area M highlight the need carefully to excavate this (or another) slag mound to virgin soil so as to identify the full sequence of copper ore smelting activities during the Iron Age in Faynan.

    Perhaps the biggest surprise from the Area M excavation was the discovery of part of a large stone built building in close association with the slag mound (Figs. 10.21–22). As only a corner of the rectilinear building could be exposed (Fig. 10.22), it was impossible to trace a floor interior that might inform about the function of the structure and its relationship to the industrial activities at the site. However, a similar relationship has been documented for a later period site in the Faynan district, less than 2 km from KEN. Long ago, Glueck (1940: 66) described the nearby Medieval Islamic metal processing site of Khirbet Neqeib Aseimer as consisting of a large rectangular building with large deposits of slag abutting and surrounding it. Like Khirbet Neqeib Aseimer, the Area M rectilinear building and other similar occurrences at KEN were no doubt closely connected to the actual smelting process. This discovery adds another dimension to the high degree of Iron Age industrial specialization that took place at KEN.

Figure 10.21. Overview of excavations in the Area M slag mound at Khirbat en-Nahas, 2002. Note corner of building behind survey rod.

Figure 10.22. Detail of interior of the corner of large building found imbedded in and around the Area M slag mound. The foundations of the building are preserved to more than 2 m in depth.

Conclusions and Some Considerations of Iron Age History

For those of us working on the Iron Age archaeology of the southern Levant outside of Israel–Palestine, in neighboring regions such as Edom, the application of radiocarbon dating as an essential element in the tool box of archaeologists is now essential. As discussed here, the previous assumptions and dependence on the relative dating of ceramics linked to a paucity of extra-biblical textual discoveries is no longer tenable for Edom. Scholars working in other regions in Jordan, such as Moab (Harrison [Chapter 12, this volume) have also acknowledged that we have passed the point of no return and must employ high precision radiocarbon dating to critically test the relationship between history and archaeology in our region. In many respects, the bar has been raised for Iron Age archaeology by the recent publication by A. Mazar's team (Bruins, van der Plicht, and Mazar 2003a) of the radiocarbon dating project of Iron Age levels at Tel Rehov in the journal *Science*, which attempts to document evidence for the destruction of Iron Age towns in Palestine by the Egyptian pharaoh Shoshenq/Shishak I during the Iron IIA period. Whether Mazar's team is correct or not (Bruins, van der Plicht, and Mazar 2003b; Finkelstein and Piasetzky 2003; and in this volume, see Mazar *et al.* [Chapter 13], Sharon *et al.* [Chapter 6]; Bruins *et al.* [Chapter 19]) is immaterial—it is now impossible to carryout Iron Age historical archaeology without reliance on the object framework offered by ^{14}C dating methods.

The recent excavations at Khirbat en-Nahas show conclusively that Iron Age social complexity, and perhaps the emergence of the kingdom of Edom known from biblical texts began some 200–300 years earlier than previously assumed (Bennett 1992; Bennett and Bienkowski [eds.] 1995b; Bienkowski 2001a, 2001b). It is not necessary to look to a core civilization (Assyria or Egypt) to explain the rise of the Edomite kingdom (Porter 2004)—we should look for *local* processes of change, especially the relationship of the small neighboring polities such as Israel and Judah with Edom at the end of the Late Bronze Age, Iron I, and early Iron II periods. For ancient Edom, the key to the emergence of social complexity is in what happened in the lowlands—in the Faynan district, close to the rich copper ore resources. With the recent large scale excavations at KEN, there is now evidence that control of copper production and trade in copper was probably the main catalyst for the rise of social complexity in Iron Age Edom. While many researchers (Bienkowski 1992a; Bienkowski and van der Steen 2001; Finkelstein 1992a; Knauf-Belleri 1995) have argued that large scale trade in other goods, especially from Arabia, was the key factor in the rise of Edom as a state, this assertion has not been demonstrated with archaeological evidence—certainly not on the scale of the metallurgical evidence discussed here.

The architecture, *in situ* excavations of copper industrial remains and imports confirm two major phases of production in the 12–11th centuries BCE and 10–9th centuries BCE at Khirbat en-Nahas. We are now at the beginning of being able to engage the Hebrew Bible and extra-biblical sources for gleanings of historical fact and historical processes. However, the current suite of 37 radiocarbon dates from KEN are not without problems (see Higham *et al.* [Chapter 11, this volume]) and it is clear that many more samples must be tested from sealed archaeological deposits associated with 'cleaner' assemblages of ceramics, scarabs, seals and other archaeological evidence. While the current dates push the occupational history of Edom back to the 12th–9th centuries BCE, the sample size is too small to confront the arguments concerning the High and Low Chronologies for the Iron Age in Israel/Palestine. These dates do bring the Iron Age archaeology of Edom back, to a certain degree, to historical questions raised long ago by Nelson Glueck (1940) concerning the Iron I and Iron IIa. While lack of space prevents a detailed discussion here, the fact that Edom is mentioned no less than 99 times in the Hebrew Bible justifies a re-examination of some historical issues in relation to the new archaeological excavations in the lowland region to establish some working hypotheses for the Iron Age history of Edom. For example,

וְדִשׁוֹן וְאֵצֶר וְדִישָׁן אֵלֶּה אַלּוּפֵי הַחֹרִי בְּנֵי שֵׂעִיר בְּאֶרֶץ אֱדוֹם: ^{WTT} Genesis 36.21

These are the kings who reigned in the land of Edom, before any king reigned over the Israelites. (RSV)

Leaving aside the problem of the dating of the Hebrew Bible and the documentary hypothesis (Friedman 1988), Genesis 36.21 may be a minor footnote in the biblical text; however it does not exhibit an ideological stance, it is a neutral statement. While so-called Biblical minimalist scholars (Davies 1992; Thompson 1999; Van Seters 1997; Whitelam 1996) argue that the Hebrew Bible is pure myth lacking evidence of historicity, it is precisely in these 'footnotes' in the Hebrew Bible, which have no propaganda value or theological message, that some elements of history may be found. Baruch Halpern (Halpern 2001: 124-32) refers to the role of 'minimal text' in ancient historical documents for revealing historical events as 'the Tiglath-Pileser principle' and he presents a kind of historiographical method for how actual events can be gleaned from a critical reading of the ancient documents (in this case, both Assyrian and biblical sources). Thus, for the first time in biblical Edom, archaeological investigations at the lowland site of KEN provide radiometric data, scarab, arrowhead, Midianite ceramics, and other archaeological data to suggest a major industrial phase in the Iron I period. As this 12th–11th-centuries BCE metal production could only have been organized by a complex polity. While the RSV translation of the Hebrew אַלּוּפֵי is given as 'kings' it may better be translated as 'chieftains', perhaps along the lines of the complex chiefdoms referred to by Sahlins (1968: 24-25) as chiefdoms organized along conical clan lines such as among the nomads of Central Asia, the island societies of Polynesia and Micronesia, in Circum-Caribbean America societies and the Southwest African Bantu. Whether we call the early Iron Age society that inhabited the lowlands of Edom 'chiefs' or 'kings' is immaterial; the point is that Genesis 36.31

probably refers to the 'hereditary leaders who reigned in the land of Edom, before any hereditary leaders reigned over the Israelites'—a seemingly insignificant footnote in the biblical text that may help contextualize the socio-economic dynamics that existed in Edom during the 12th–11th centuries BCE. Another example is:

WTT 2 Samuel 8.14 וַיָּשֶׂם בֶּאֱדוֹם נְצִבִים בְּכָל־אֱדוֹם שָׂם נְצִבִים וַיְהִי כָל־אֱדוֹם
עֲבָדִים לְדָוִד וַיּוֹשַׁע יְהוָה אֶת־דָּוִד בְּכֹל אֲשֶׁר הָלָךְ׃

> And he put garrisons in Edom; throughout all Edom he put garrisons, and all the Edomites became David's servants. And the LORD gave victory to David wherever he went. (RSV)

As shown above, the earliest monumental building activity documented to date at KEN is the Iron IIa four chamber gate and fortress complex. Given the tapestry of different ethnic groups who occupied southern Canaan at the end of the Late Bronze–early Iron Age, which group may have been responsible for the construction of the KEN fortress? According to Halpern (2001: 4), the historical David appears in the books of 1 and 2 Samuel, and dies in 1 Kings 2. 2 Samuel 8.13-15 suggests that David's troops subjugated Edom and as illustrated above (2 Samuel 8.14), established garrisons all over Edom. Glueck (1940: 84-85) used these passages to suggest that David controlled the mines in the Faynan district and that this exploitation continued under Solomon. According to the biblical text (see below, 1 Kings 22.47) Israel ruled Edom through a deputy administrator (Na'aman 2004) whose place of residence is not known.

WTT 1 Kings 22.48 וּמֶלֶךְ אֵין בֶּאֱדוֹם נִצָּב מֶלֶךְ׃

> There was no king in Edom; a deputy was king. (RSV)

According to the traditional High Chronology (Rogerson 1999), the rule of these two kings would be from ca. 1000–931 BCE. According to these data, and the suite of radiocarbon dates now available from KEN, several working hypotheses may be suggested for the possible builders and controllers of the Stratum A3 gate and fortress complex: (a) David, (b) Solomon, (c) David and Solomon; or (d) the local Edomite population. Clearly, more data and analyses are needed to clarify this working hypothesis. According to the biblical text, following the death of Solomon and the emergence of the divided monarchy of Israel and Judah, it is inferred that the Edomites finally gained their independence from Judah during the reign of Jehoram which according to the traditional High Chronology dates to 848–841 BCE (Rogerson 1999) or the mid-9th century BCE.

WTT 2 Kings 8.20 בְּיָמָיו פָּשַׁע אֱדוֹם מִתַּחַת יַד־יְהוּדָה וַיַּמְלִכוּ עֲלֵיהֶם מֶלֶךְ׃

> In his days Edom revolted from the rule of Judah, and set up a king of their own. (RSV)

How to link the expansion in mid-9th century BCE metal production observed at KEN in the flurry of building activities seen in the Stratum S2b building (Fig. 10.18), the slag mounds (Fig. 10.10 and Building 200; Fritz 1996) to the biblical text? One working hypothesis is that following the Edomite revolt against Jehoram, the local Edomite population took over metal production at KEN, had no need for the garrison/fortress at the site and changed the organization of production at the site from one that was based on coercion (via the fortress) to an as yet undefined alternative form of organization.

While these are untested working hypotheses relating ancient Near Eastern texts to the archaeological record of Edom, they will 'only be tested adequately through larger scale excavations at Khirbat en-Nahas, in-depth studies of the full array of material culture represented at the site, and a much larger compendium of radiocarbon dates. How exactly does the copper ore-rich 12th–9th-centuries BCE metal producing region of Edom relate to the highland sites such as Busayra, Umm al-Biyara, Sela, and others?

The excavations at KEN and the radiocarbon dates originally published in the journal Antiquity (Levy *et al.* 2004) have sparked a great deal of welcome scholarly controversy on the Internet (<http://www.wadiarabahproject.man.ac.uk/>) and most recently in an article by Israel Finkelstein (2005) published in the journal *Tel Aviv*. However, as shown in this chapter with the publication of an additional 27 high precision radiocarbon dates accompanied by a more detailed discussion of the archaeology at the site, the data run contrary to Finkelstein's assertions. In short, we can close by concluding with a number of points that are contrary to Finkelstein. Our data indicate: a) the fortress at KEN is 'sandwiched' stratigraphically between two metal production horizons at the site, with the latest production layer dating to the mid-9th century BCE and do not indicate the suggested 8th century BCE domination of Edom; b) The fort was not cut into piles of copper industrial waste—these slag deposits, based on our excavations, accumulated around it; c) Copper production was especially active at KEN throughout the 10th to 9th centuries BCE—it did not shift to other neighboring sites. Radiocarbon dates from other secondary centers like Khirbat al-Jariyeh (Hauptmann 2000:66) show contemporaniety between KEN and its satellite sites. This is seen in the statistical analysis presented above, that is, if the Strata A3 and S3 are indicative of increased copper production, then this dates to after 900 BCE at A3 in the fortress area and after 950 BCE at S3 in the industrial building complex. In fact, the new KEN data, in conjunction with Hauptmann's work (2000) support the recent interpretations of the Iron Age settlement pattern data from the Wadi al-Guwayb and Wadi al-Jariyeh for a complex network of copper ore extraction and processing (Levy *et al.* 2003); d) the fortress at KEN did not exist during the 8th century BCE so it was not contemporary with the Assyrian palace compound at Busayra. Rather than trying to make KEN conform to preconceived models that posit Assyrian domination of Edom in the 8th and 7th centuries BCE, the new data show a much more complex situation between the lowlands and highlands of Edom and its relationship with neighboring regions throughout the Iron Age. Thus, more archaeological research is required before definitive historical interpretations can be made.

Acknowledgment

We are grateful to Dr Fawwaz al-Khraysheh, Director General of the Department of Antiquities of Jordan for his sage advice and support of the excavations at Khirbat en-Nahas. Thanks also to the Society for the Conservation of Nature in Jordan for permission to work in the Dana Nature Reserve where KEN is located. Thomas Levy is grateful to the C. Paul Johnson Family Charitable Foundation (Napa and Chicago) and the University of California, San Diego for providing him with the grants and other funding that made the excavations at KEN possible. We also appreciate the help of Dr Russ Adams (co-PI and ceramicist of the JHF project), Dr Jim Anderson (chief surveyor), supervisors Yoav Arbel, Lisa Soderbaum, Elizabeth Monroe, the entire JHF team and Sheik Abu Shushi and the Bedouin villagers at Qurayqira for all their support.

References

Adams, R.B. (2003) External Influences at Faynan During the Early Bronze Age: A Re-analysis of Building 1 at Barqa el-Hetiye, Jordan. *PEQ* 135: 6-21.

Albright, W.F. (1932) The Israelite Conquest of Canaan in the Light of Archaeology. *BASOR* 74:11-23.

—(1971) *The Archaeology of Palestine* (repr., Gloucester, MA: Peter Smith).

Barker, G.W., *et al.* (1997) The Wadi Faynan Project, Southern Jordan: A Preliminary Report on Geomorphology and Landscape Archaeology. *Levant* 29: 19-40.

—(1999) Environment and Land Use in the Wadi Faynan, Southern Jordan: The Third Season of Geoarchaeology and Landscape Archaeology (1998). *Levant* 31: 255-92.

—(2000) Archaeology and Desertification in Wadi Faynan. *Levant* 32: 27-52.

Bartlett, J.R. (1989) *Edom and the Edomites* (JSOTSup 77; Sheffield: Sheffield Academic Press).

—(1992) Edom. In *ABD*, II: 287-95.

Beit-Arieh, I. (ed.) (1999) *Tel 'Ira—A Stronghold in the Biblical Negev*, XV (Tel Aviv University Monograph Series; Tel Aviv: Tel Aviv University Institute of Archaeology).

Ben-Tor, A. (ed.) (1992) *The Archaeology of Ancient Israel* (New Haven: Yale University Press).

Bennett, C.M. (1966a) Fouilles d'Umm el-Biyara: Rapport Preliminaire. *RB* 73: 372-403.

—(1966b) Umm el-Biyara. *RB* 73: 400-401, pl. XXIIb.

—(1977) Excavations in Buseirah, Southern Jordan. *Levant* 9: 1-10.

—(1992) Neo-Assyrian Influence in Transjordan. In *Studies in the History and Archaeology of Jordan*, I, edited by A. Haddidi (Amman: Department of Antiquities of Jordan): 181-87.

Bennett, C.M., and P. Bienkowski (1995a) *Excavations at Tawilan in Southern Jordan* (Oxford: Published for the British Institute at Amman for Archaeology and History by Oxford University Press).

Bennett, C.M., and P. Bienkowski (eds.) (1995b) *Excavations at Tawilan in Southern Jordan* (Oxford: Published for the British Institute at Amman for Archaeology and History by Oxford University Press).

Bienkowski, P. (1990) Umm el-Biyara, Tawilan and Buseirah in Retrospect. *Levant* 22: 91-109.

—(1992a) The Beginning of the Iron Age in Edom: A Reply to Finkelstein. *Levant* 24: 167-69.

—(1992b) The Date of Sedentary Occupation in Edom: Evidence from Umm el-Biyara, Tawilan and Buseirah. In *Early Edom and Moab—The Beginning of the Iron Age in Southern Jordan*, edited by P. Bienkowski (Sheffield: J.R. Collis Publications): 99-112.

—(1995) The Edomites: The Archaeological Evidence from Transjordan. In *You Shall Not Abhor an Edomite for He is Your brother: Edom and Seir in History and Tradition*, edited by D.V. Edelman (Archaeological and Biblical Studies 3; Atlanta: Scholars Press): 41-92.

—(2001a) The Iron Age and Persian Periods in Jordan. In *Studies in the History and Archaeology of Jordan*, VII (Amman: Department of Antiquities): 265-74.

—(2001b) Iron Age Settlement in Edom: A Revised Framework. In *The World of the Aramaeans. II. Studies in History and Archaeology in Honour of Paul-Eugen Dion*, edited by P.M.M. Daviau, J.W. Wevers, and M. Weigl (JSOTSup 325; Sheffield: Sheffield Academic Press): 257-69.

Bienkowski, P., and R.B. Adams (1999) Soundings at Ash-Shorabat and Khirbat Dubab in the Wadi Hasa, Jordan: The Pottery. *Levant* 31: 149-72.

Bienkowski, P., and C.M. Bennett (2003) *Excavations at Busayrah* (Oxford: Oxford University Press).

Bienkowski, P., and E. van der Steen (2001) Tribes, Trade, and Towns: A New Framework for the Late Iron Age in Southern Jordan and the Negev. *BASOR* 323: 21-47.

Binford, L.R. (1968) Archaeological Perspectives. In *New Perspectives in Archaeology*, edited by S.R. Binford and L.R. Binford (Chicago: Aldine Publishing Company): 5-32.

Bruins, H.J., J. van der Plicht, and A. Mazar (2003a) ^{14}C Dates from Tel Rehov: Iron-age Chronology, Pharaohs, and Hebrew Kings. *Science* 300: 315-18.

—(2003b) Response to 'Comment on ^{14}C Dates from Tel Rehov: Iron-Age Chronology, Pharaohs, and Hebrew Kings'. *Science* 302: 568c-68d.

Centre, R.J.G. (2001) *Jordanian School Atlas* (Amman: Royal Jordanian Geographic Centre).

Cohen, R., and R. Cohen-Amin (2004) *Ancient Settlement of the Negev Highlands*, II (Jerusalem: The Israel Antiquity Authority).

Cohen, R., and Y. Yisrael (1995) The Iron Age Fortresses at En Haseva. *BA* 58: 223-35.

Crowell, B.L. (2004) On the Margins of History: Social Change and Political Development in Iron Age Edom (unpublished PhD thesis, University of Michigan).

Danin, A. (1983) *Desert Vegetation of Israel and Sinai* (Jerusalem: Cana).

Davies, P.R. (1992) *In Search of 'Ancient Israel'* (JSOTSup 148; Sheffield: JSOT Press).

Dever, W.G. (1974) *Archaeology and Biblical Studies: Retrospects and Prospects* (Evanston: Seabury-Western Theological Seminary).

—(1982) Retrospects and Prospects in Biblical and Syro-Palestinian Archaeology. *BA* 45: 103-107.

—(1988) Impact of the 'New Archaeology'. In *Benchmarks in Time & Culture: Essays in Honor of Joseph A. Callaway*, edited by J.F. Drinkard, G.L. Mattingly, and M. Miller (Atlanta: Scholars Press): 339.

—(2000) Nelson Glueck and the Other Half of the Holy Land. In *The Archaeology of Jordan and Beyond: Essays in Honor of James A. Sauer*, edited by L.E. Stager, J.A. Greene, and M.D. Coogan (Winona Lake, IN: Eisenbrauns): 114-21.

—(2001) *What Did the Biblical Writers Know and When Did They Know It?* (Grand Rapids: Eerdmans).

—(2003) *Who were the Israelites, and Where Did They Come From?* (Grand Rapids: Eerdmans).

Engel, T. (1993) Charcoal Remains from an Iron Age Copper Smelting Slag Heap at Feinan, Wadi Arabah (Jordan). *Vegetation History and Archaeobotany* 2: 205-11.

Finkelstein, I. (1988) *The Archaeology of the Israelite Settlement* (Jerusalem: Israel Exploration Society).

—(1992a) Edom in the Iron I. *Levant* 24: 159-66.

—(1992b) Stratigraphy, Pottery and Parallels: A Reply to Bienkowski. *Levant* 24: 171-72.

—(2005) Khirbet en-Nahas, Edom and Biblical History. *Tel Aviv* 32 (1): 119-25.

Finkelstein, I., and E. Piasetzky (2003) Comment on C-14 dates from Tel Rehov: Iron-Age chronology, Pharaohs, and Hebrew Kings. *Science* 302: 568.

Frank, F. (1934) Aus der Araba I: Reiseberichte. *ZDPV* 57: 191-280.

Friedman, R.E. (1988) *Who Wrote the Bible?* (London: Jonathan Cape).

Fritz, V. (1996) Ergebnisse einer Sondage in Hirbet en-Nahas, Wadi el-'Araba (Jordanien). *ZDPV* 112: 1-9.

Glueck, N. (1938) The First Campaign at Tell el-Kheleifeh (Ezion-Geber). *BASOR* 71: 3-17.

—(1939a) Explorations in Eastern Palestine, III (AASOR 18-19; New Haven: The American Schools of Oriental Research).

—(1939b) The Second Campaign at Tell el-Kheleifeh (Ezion-Geber: Elath). *BASOR* 75: 8-22.

—(1940a) *The Other Side of the Jordan* (New Haven: American Schools of Oriental Research).

—(1940b) The Third Season of Excavations at Tell el-Kheleifeh. *BASOR* 79: 2-18.

—(1993) Tell El-Kheleifeh. In *The New Encyclopedia of Archaeological Excavations in the Holy Land*, III, edited by E. Stern (Jerusalem: The Israel Exploration Society): 867-69.

Halpern, B. (2001) *David's Secret Demons—Messiah, Murderer, Traitor, King* (Grand Rapids: Eerdmans).

Hart, S. (1989) The Archaeology of the Land of Edom (unpublished PhD thesis, Macquarie University).

Hauptmann, A. (2000) *Zur frühen Metallurgie des Kupfers in Fenan* (Der Anschnitt: Zeitschrift für Kunst und Kultur im Bergbau 11; Bochum: Deutsches Bergbau-Museum).

Herzog, Z. (1992) Settlement and Fortification Planning in the Iron Age. In *The Architecture of Ancient Israel—From the Prehistoric to the Persian Periods*, edited by A. Kempinski and R. Reich (Jerusalem: Israel Exploration Society): 231-74.

Hodder, I. (ed.) (1982) *Symbolic and Structural Archaeology* (Cambridge: Cambridge University Press).

—(1987) The Contextual Analysis of Symbolic Meanings. In *The Archaeology of Contextual Meanings*, edited by I. Hodder (Cambridge: Cambridge University Press): 1-10.

Knauf-Belleri, E.A. (1995) Edom: The Social and Economic History. In *You shall not Abhor an Edomite for he is your Brother: Edom and Seir in History and Tradition*, edited by D.V. Edelman (Atlanta: Scholars Press): 93-117.

Lemche, N.P. (1998) *The Israelites in History and Tradition* (Louisville, KY: Westminster Press).

Levy, T.E. (1996) Anthropological Approaches to Protohistoric Palestine: A Case Study from the Negev Desert. In *Retrieving the Past—Essays on Archaeological Research and Methodology in Honor of Gus W. Van Beek*, edited by J.D. Seger (Winona Lake, IN: Eisenbrauns): 163-78.

—(2002) Tribes, Metallurgy, and Edom in Iron Age Jordan. *ACOR Newsletter* 14: 3-5.

Levy, T.E., R.B. Adams, and M. Najjar (1999) Early Metallurgy and Social Evolution: Jabal Hamrat Fidan. *ACOR Newsletter* 11: 1-3.

—(2001) Jabal Hamrat Fidan. *American Journal of Archaeology* 105: 442-45.

Levy, T.E., *et al.* (2001a) Early Metallurgy, Interaction, and Social Change: The Jabal Hamrat Fidan (Jordan) Research Design and 1998 Archaeological Survey: Preliminary Report. *Annual of the Department of Antiquities of Jordan* 45: 1-31.

—(2001b) Interface: Archaeology and Technology—Digital Archaeology 2001: GIS-Based Excavation Recording in Jordan. *The SAA Archaeological Record* 1: 23-29.

—(2002) Early Bronze Age Metallurgy: A Newly Discovered Copper Manufactory in Southern Jordan. *Antiquity* 76: 425-37.

—(2003) An Iron Age Landscape in the Edomite Lowlands: Archaeological Surveys along the Wadi al-Guwayb and Wadi al-Jariyeh, Jabal Hamrat Fidan, Jordan, 2002. *Annual of the Department of Antiquities Jordan* 47: 247-77.

—(2004) Reassessing the Chronology of Biblical Edom: New Excavations and [14]C Dates from Khirbat en-Nahas (Jordan). *Antiquity* 78: 863-76.

MacDonald, B. (1992) *The Southern Ghors and Northeast 'Arabah Archaeological Survey* (Sheffield Archaeological Monographs 5; Sheffield: J.R. Collis Publications).

Mazar, A. (1990) *Archaeology of the Land of the Bible* (New York: Doubleday).

Moorey, P.R.S. (1991) *A Century of Biblical Archaeology* (Louisville, KY: Westminster/John Knox Press, 1st edn).

Musil, A. (1907) *Arabia Petraea. I. Moab. II. Edom: Topograhischere Reisebericht* (Wien: Alfred Holder).

Na'aman, N. (2004) Sources and Composition in the Biblical History of Edom. In *Sefer Moshe: The Moshe Weinfeld Jubilee Volume—Studies in the Bible and the Ancient Near East, Qumran, and Post-Biblical Judaism*, edited by C. Cohen, A. Hurvitz, and S.M. Paul (Winona Lake, IN: Eisenbrauns): 313-20.

Oakshott, M.F. (1978) A Study of the Iron Age II Pottery of East Jordan with Special Reference to Unpublished Material from Edom (unpublished PhD thesis, University of London).

—(1983) The Edomite Pottery. In *Midian, Moab and Edom: The History and Archaeology of Late Bronze and Iron Age Jordan and North-West Arabia*, edited by J.F.A. Sawyer and D.J.A. Clines (JSOTSup 24; Sheffield: JSOT Press).

Porter, B.W. (2004) Authority, Polity, and Tenuous Elites in Iron Age Edom (Jordan). *Oxford Journal of Archaeology* 23: 373-95.

Pratico, G.D. (1985) Nelson Glueck's 1938–1940 Excavations at Tell el-Kheleifeh: A Reappraisal. *BASOR* 159: 1-32.

—(1993a) Kheleifeh, Tell-El. In *The Encyclopedia of Archaeological Excavations in the Holy Land*, III, edited by E. Stern (Jerusalem: Israel Exploration Society): 869-70.

—(1993b) *Nelson Glueck's 1938–1940 Excavations at Tell el-Kheleifeh—A Reappraisal* (AASOR 3: Atlanta: Scholars Press).

Preucel, R.W., and I. Hodder (eds.) (1996) *Contemporary Archaeology in Theory—A Reader* (Cambridge, MA: Blackwell).

Pritchard, J.B. (1969) *Ancient Near Eastern Texts Relating to the Old Testament* (Princeton, NJ: Princeton University Press, 3rd edn).

Rabb'a, I. (1994) *The Geology of the Al Qurayqira (Jabal Hamra Faddan) Map Sheet No. 3051 II* (Geology Directorate Geological Mapping Division Bulletin 28; Amman: Geology Directorate Geological Mapping Division).

Rogerson, J. (1999) *Chronicle of the Old Testament Kings* (London: Thames & Hudson).

Sahlins, M. (1968) *Tribesmen* (New Jersey: Prentice–Hall).

Schiffer, M.B. (1987) *Formation Processes of the Archaeological Record* (Albuquerque: University of New Mexico Press).

Schniedewind, W.M. (2004) *How the Bible Became a Book* (Cambridge: Cambridge University Press).

Stager, L.E. (1988) Archaeology, Ecology, and Social History: Background Themes to the Song of Deborah. In *Congress Volume: Jerusalem*, edited by J.A. Emerton (VTSup 40; Leiden: Brill): 221-34.

Thompson, T.L. (1999) *The Mythic Past: Biblical Archaeology and the Myth of Israel* (New York: Basic Books).

Van Seters, J. (1997) *In Search of History: Historiography in the Ancient World and the Origins of Biblical History* (Winona Lake, IN: Eisenbrauns).

Whitelam, K.W. (1996) *The Invention of Ancient Israel: The Silencing of Palestinian History* (New York: Routledge).

Wright, G.E. (1965) *Shechem, the Biography of a Biblical City* (New York: Mc-Graw Hill).

11 Radiocarbon Dating of the Khirbat en-Nahas Site (Jordan) and Bayesian Modeling of the Results

Thomas Higham, Johannes van der Plicht, Christopher Bronk Ramsey, Hendrik J. Bruins, Mark Robinson, and Thomas E. Levy

Abstract

A series of AMS radiocarbon determinations have been obtained from the site of Khirbet-en-Nahas, Jordan. An initial suite of samples dated in Oxford and a subsequent and much larger suite from Groningen were obtained to determine the onset of copper and iron production in the Faynan district. The determinations came from two different areas at the site. Bayesian modeling was used to improve the chronometric resolution. This showed that copper production expanded from ca. 950 BCE. The challenge at sites such as this is to obtain samples of short-lived age and thereby avoid 'inbuilt age'. Several of the AMS determinations were, in all likelihood, affected by this, and the Bayesian modeling enabled us to determine outliers and question their reliability. Further work is planned.

Introduction

This chapter concerns the analysis of the radiocarbon chronology of Khirbat en-Nahas (hereafter KEN), Jordan, the largest Iron Age copper production site in the Faynan district. It is, therefore, a partial contribution to the Jabal Hamrat Fidan Project, which is engaged in extensive archaeological investigations in this region. Details of the archaeology of the site is discussed elsewhere in this volume (Levy et al. [Chapter 10, this volume]) and in a recent publication (Levy et al. 2004). The aims of the radiocarbon dating program were initially focussed upon two key areas. First, to date one of the large buildings and part of a gate complex at the site. Second, to date samples from the slag mounds to determine more reliably both the onset and span of metal production. We wanted to place the site into its proper chronological context and test whether iron and copper production was a local incipient development or whether it was influenced by external stimuli, such as the Assyrian empire in the 8th–6th centuries BCE. A key aim was to investigate the time span of manufacturing and copper processing at the site.

Sample Selection

A number of scholars have cautioned against dating wood or wood charcoal whose species composition is unknown, or which contains material derived from long-lived trees (Anderson 1991; Higham 1994; McFadgen 1982; Trotter 1968). Since KEN was a large copper production site, abundant charcoal was found within the area excavated. Excavated charcoal was identified using high-powered light microscopy by one of us (M.R.). Tamarix sp. (probably *T. jordanis*) was the most abundant taxon. In the absence of clearly short-lived material, such as seeds, we initially selected the outermost rings to reduce the influence of inbuilt age as much as possible. In each case, 1–3 tree rings were sampled from the exterior of the plants. Unfortunately, there is no guarantee in each case that this represents 1–3 years of inbuilt age, it could simply represent the outermost rings of a piece of branchwood whose peripheral wood has been removed or eroded away post-depositionally.

Radiocarbon Dating and Pre-treatment

Samples of identified charcoal from three areas of KEN were Accelerator Mass Spectrometry (AMS) dated at the Oxford Radiocarbon Accelerator Unit (ORAU), University of Oxford. Four samples came from the Area A fortress, four from the Area S building complex and two from the Area M slag mound.

Archaeological materials may be affected by a variety of natural processes within their depositional environment (Schiffer 1987). In addition to these formation processes, there are two major contaminants present in soils that may affect radiocarbon dating of organic samples from archaeological sites; humic acids and fulvic acids. Both are organic compounds derived from the decayed remains of plants in the surface layers of the soil. Their presence in archaeological charcoals may constitute error of unknown magnitude and is highly site specific. Humic substances within the soil have been classified according to the ease with which they can be removed from soils using alkaline solutions (Head 1987). Humic acid is defined as the fraction extracted by alkaline solution which becomes insoluble after acidification (Head 1987: 144). Fulvic acids are soluble in both acid and alkaline solutions (Head 1987). The residue soluble and insoluble in alkaline solutions is termed humin and is usually the fraction targeted for radiocarbon dating. Samples of charcoal dated initially at Oxford were pretreated using the acid-base-acid method (Hedges *et al.* 1989). In all cases, humin carbon was isolated for AMS dating.

Calibration and Analysis

We used the program OxCal (v3.10; Bronk Ramsey 1995, 2001) and the INTCAL04 calibration curve (Reimer *et al.* 2004) to calibrate the radiocarbon dates. The individual radiocarbon dates have been described and interpreted by Levy *et al.* (Chapter 10, this volume). In order to analyse the results with a greater level of sophistication it is useful to use a Bayesian approach. A general overview of the method is described in this volume by Bronk Ramsey. Put simply, it allows the incorporation of associated archaeological information to be combined within the chronometric analysis, in an explicit manner. Stratigraphic constraints, for example, can be applied to the calibrated dates in instances where material inferred to have been excavated in its primary context is submitted for radiocarbon dating. The data are made explicit in the analysis via a probability distribution, termed the *prior*, which weights the calibrated dates towards values in line with prior archaeological expectations. The data act through a distribution called the *likelihood*. A calibrated value that makes the observed radiocarbon age a likely outcome of the radiocarbon observation process has a high likelihood. The prior and likelihood distributions together determine a new probability distribution known as the *posterior*. Sets of calibrated dates agreeing with the data, and at the same time plausible in the light of prior information, yield a large posterior probability. Bayesian analysis is performed by constructing a suitable posterior that reflects our understanding of the archaeological record and the temporal relationship between the dated events and those observed in the archaeological record (Higham and Jones 2004).

Area A Results

Table 11.1. AMS determinations from the Oxford Radiocarbon
Accelerator Unit (ORAU) for samples from Area A at KEN.

Stratum	Area A Gatehouse	Lab. Number	Radiocarbon age BP
Stratum A4a	KEN A L95 Ashy layer below surface over bedrock.	OxA-12365	2825 ± 32
Stratum A3	KEN A L94 Surface connected to original gate structure	OxA-12366	2783 ± 31
Stratum A2b	KEN A L92 Massive smelting inside chamber	OxA-12367	2689 ± 31
Stratum A2a	KEN A L61 Installation with human remains, outside gate	OxA-12368	2719 ± 33

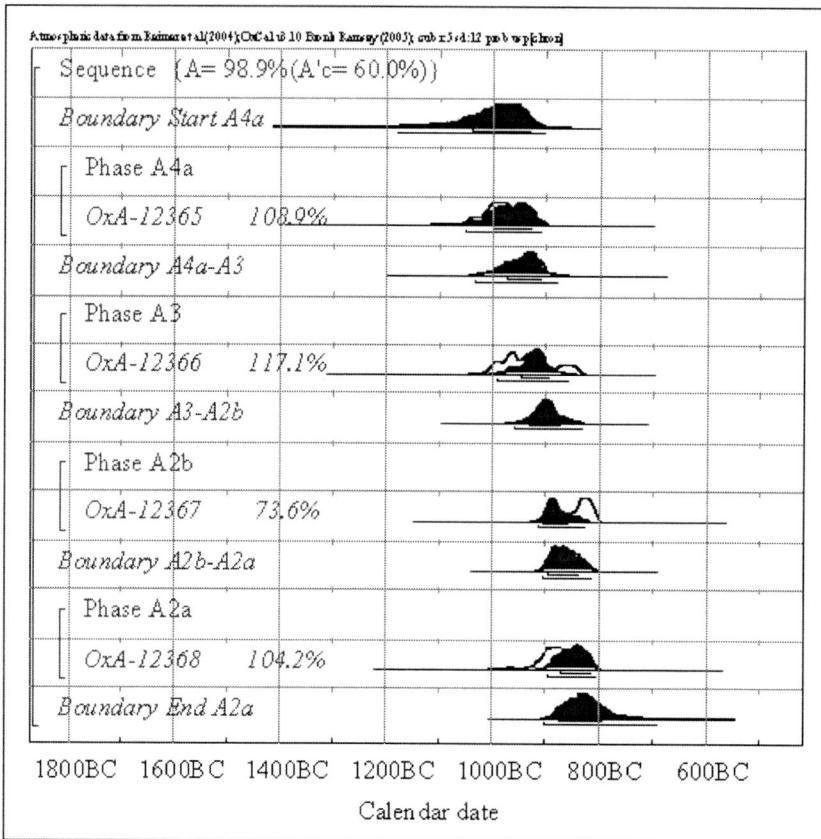

Figure 11.1. Bayesian model for the initial suite of radiocarbon determinations produced at the Oxford laboratory. The outline distributions represent the likelihoods derived from the calibration of the radiocarbon dates. The solid distributions show the results after stratigraphic constraints are imposed on the dates using OxCal. The bars beneath the distributions show the 68.2 and 95.4% ranges from the analysis. The agreement index (A) must be greater than 60.0% for confidence to be expressed in the overall model.

Area A represents the four-room gate in the fortress area of the site (Levy *et al.* [Chapter 10, this volume]). The initial series of radiocarbon results are shown in Figure 11.1 and Table 11.1. The samples were excavated from four discrete phases: Stratum A4 is a sterile layer and radiocarbon dated material from within it acts as a *terminus post quem* for subsequent human activity; Stratum A3 represents the initial construction phase; and Strata A2a and A2b represent the main occupation. OxA-12365 from Stratum A4, then, is a date for the earliest phase prior to the construction of the fortress, while the remainder, despite the lack of clear stratigraphic connections, can be argued to fall in sequence above this determination. We incorporated these data within a chronological model assuming this imposition within the fortress structure (Fig. 11.1).

The Oxford results show that the modeling has had a limited influence. The posterior distributions show little difference when compared with the original radiocarbon likelihoods themselves. The Area A sequence appears to span about 200 years, and within this there are only 4 determinations and from few stratigraphic horizons, therefore the archaeological prior adds little in terms of constraining the likelihoods themselves. Generally speaking, the dates suggest that the gate was constructed towards the end of the 10th century BCE and that metal processing was expanding by the beginning of the 9th century BCE. Further fine-grained analysis could be obtained with more radiocarbon results, but the initial series did provide good evidence to suggest that Edomite societies were extracting copper ore and producing copper well before the influence of Assyrian imperialism became apparent in the region (Levy *et al.* [Chapter 10, this volume]).

Area S Results

The key deposit in the Area S excavations is Stratum 3, because it represents the start of extensive metal processing in this area of KEN. Our principal questions in examining the chronology here were: (1) When did this metal-processing activity commence? and (2) Was it contemporary with similar activities at Area A, specifically, with Stratum A3? Of similar importance is Stratum S2b, which represents a phase of building construction allied with metal processing. Stratum S2b is the main occupation phase within the building. It comprises a major phase of copper processing that is attested to by hammerstones, pestles, tuyere pipe fragments, partially processed copper ore, slag with copper and grindstones. Its foundations are built over Stratum S3. When was this building constructed and how long was it used for?

The initial series of four determinations is shown in Table 11.2. The Bayesian analysis yielded little additional chronometric data compared with that derived from the radiocarbon likelihoods (Fig. 11.2). The dates suggest that the initial phase of slag deposition and metalworking activities took place just after 1000 BCE and the activity in the house structure ceased before 800 BCE.

Table 11.2. Radiocarbon determinations from the Area S house at KEN.

Stratum	Area S	Lab. Number	Radiocarbon age BP
Stratum S4	KEN S L356 Cooking installation; basal layer	OxA-12169	2899 ± 27
Stratum S3	KEN S L341 Earliest industrial slag layer; under building foundations	OxA-12342	2830 ± 27
Stratum S2b	KEN S L36 Main occupation phase of building	OxA-12168	2747 ± 26
Stratum S2a	KEN S L331 Re-use of Room 2	OxA-12274	2682 ± 34

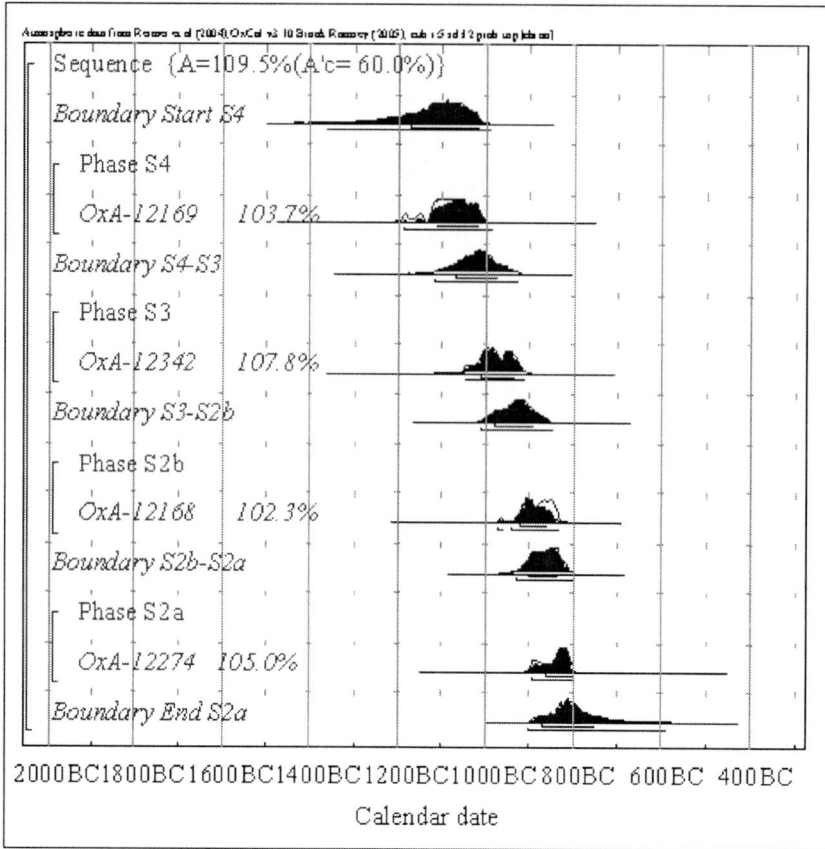

Figure 11.2. Posterior probability distributions for the Area S house excavated at KEN.

To increase dating precision and enhance the Bayesian model parameters described above, a further series of samples from KEN was dated at the Center for Isotope Research—Groningen (Levy *et al.* [Chapter 10, this volume: Table 10.1]). Like Oxford, Groningen is an accelerator facility (see van der Plicht *et al.* 2000).

Area A—New Analyses

The new Groningen determinations obtained from Area A were added to the calibration model. The initial run of the model showed a low agreement index (A) associated with some of the dates (Fig. 11.3). Some of these are lower than is normally considered acceptable (i.e. <60%). Statistically speaking, 5% of the dates would be expected to fail this test (i.e. 1 date), but in this instance there are 7 dates that fail (GrA-25320 [6.7%], GrA-25318 [2.2%], GrA- 25354 [43.6%], GrA-25321 [31.4%], GrA-25322 [52.3%], GrA-25316 [22.4%] and GrA-25334 [0.4%]). There is likely to be a range of reasons for this. However, we think that there are two that are the most likely. The first is inbuilt age. We have good reason to think that some of the determinations are likely to be affected by this, since the site is industrial and substantial quantities of timber were required for fuel. One would expect a variety of types of wood to be processed, not simply those of short-lived duration. The error will be to make the results of certain samples too old by a non-systematic amount. GrA-25318 for example, was not able to be confidently identified. GrA-25334 was also a date of an unknown species. This could be a young, short-lived specimen, but we are not able to determine this with any surety. GrA-25354 was only tentatively identified as tamarisk. Approximately 8 rings were identified, but this could not be confidently associated with exterior wood. Bruins and van der Plicht (Chapter 21, this volume) consider that for arid areas such as Jordan, the age of most wood is not likely to be more than 10–30 years, usually less. If this is case, inbuilt age is likely to be less significant than we think. Further work is required. The second potential problem affecting the reliability of the radiocarbon results is the possibility (as in many archaeological cases) that there is some bioturbation or mixing of material within the excavated areas at the site (see Levy *et al.* [Chapter 10, this volume]). There is a chance, then, that some dated material could be younger for its context as well as older. Finally, there are some caveats that must be attached to the stratigraphic modeling since in different areas there was no direct cross-correlation possible between stratigraphic units argued to be contemporary or superposed. Rather, this was based upon the similarities noted between the depositional sequences in different loci. This is hardly a unique experience in archaeology, but it is worth acknowledging as a possible source for uncertainty. At any rate, these may be the principal contributing reasons for the low agreement indices in the first iteration of the modeling for Area A.

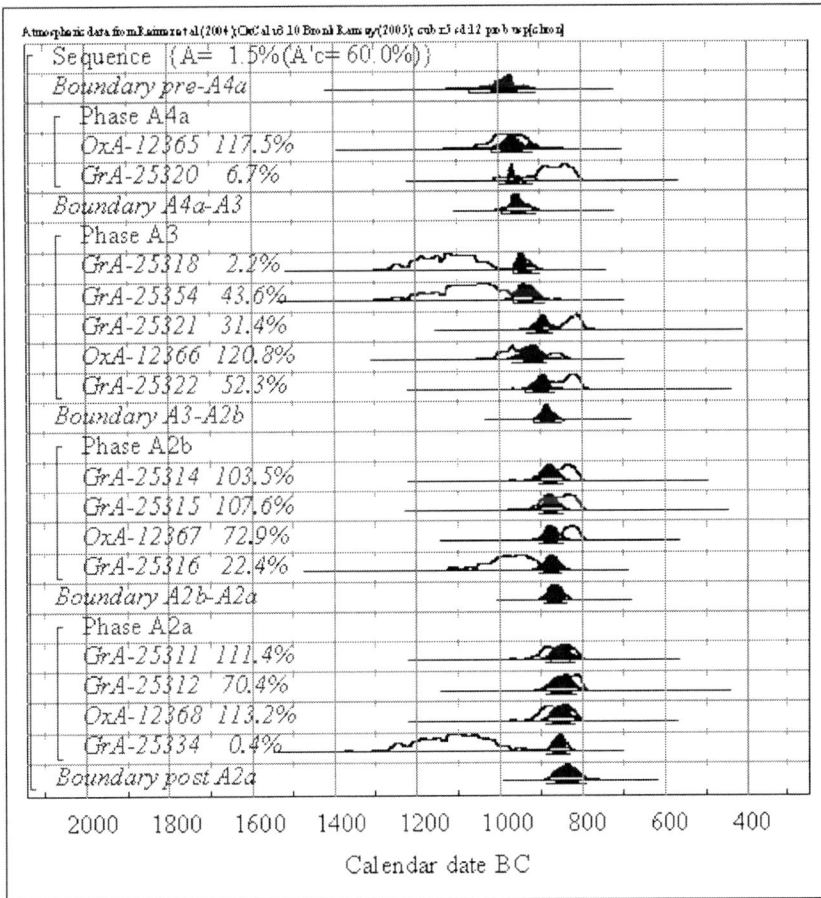

Figure 11.3. The initial Bayesian model for Area A. The first run of this model showed a poor agreement index (1.5%) and some determinations (e.g. GrA-25318, 25316 and 25334) that did not fit acceptance criteria. See text for details.

We downweighted results appearing to be anomalous in the sequence by questioning their position within it (using OxCal's Question command). The overall agreement index in the second model run in the light of removing GrA-25334 and GrA-25316 was 10.2%—still lower than acceptable. With the exception of GrA-25322 (59.9%) which just failed the agreement index, the remainder of the dates that produced low agreement indices in the first run of the model were also questioned subsequently in further iterations. We eventually questioned the accuracy of GrA-25320 from Stratum A4a, GrA-25318, 25354 and 25321 from Stratum A3, and GrA-25316 from Stratum A2b, as well as GrA-25334 from Stratum A2a on the basis of their low agreement indices in subsequent runs of the model. The final run of the model is shown in Figure 11.4. It shows that 6 dates were eventually excluded due to low agreement indices. This model produced a final acceptable agreement index of 78.6%.

The inclusion of the new Groningen series for Area A and the modeling work produced some extremely informative results compared with the initial modeling. Stratum A3 is the first building layer in the gate. Stratum A4 is bedrock and the stratum that we have termed here as A4a represents the basal occupation. In the light of the low agreement index for GrN-25320, this phase is dated only by OxA-12365. The probability distribution marking the boundary between Strata A4a and A3 (effectively a *terminus post quem* for occupation A3) is 930–875 BCE (68.2% probability), with a highest relative probability of 900 BCE (Fig. 11.5).

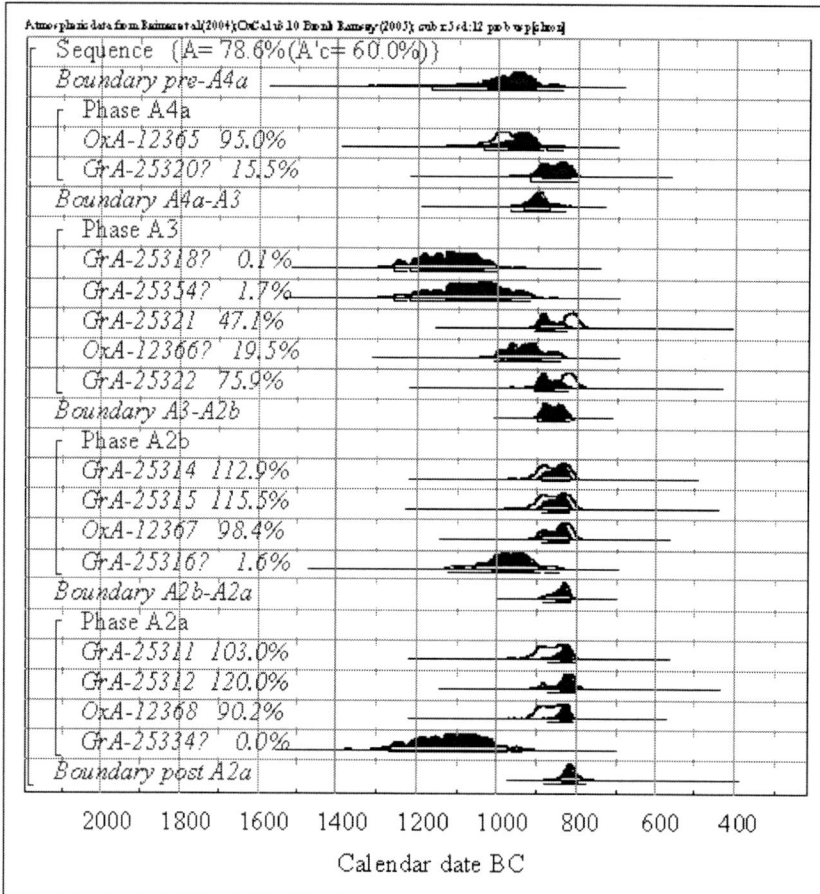

Figure 11.4. Final Bayesian model for Area A.

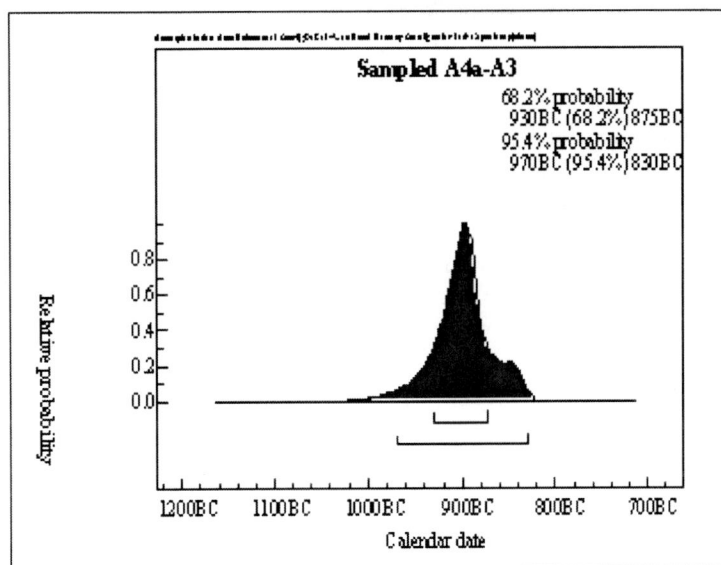

Figure 11.5. Probability distribution for the boundary between Strata A4a and A3, in Area A at KEN. This distribution effectively acts as a *terminus post quem* for the construction of the Area A gate.

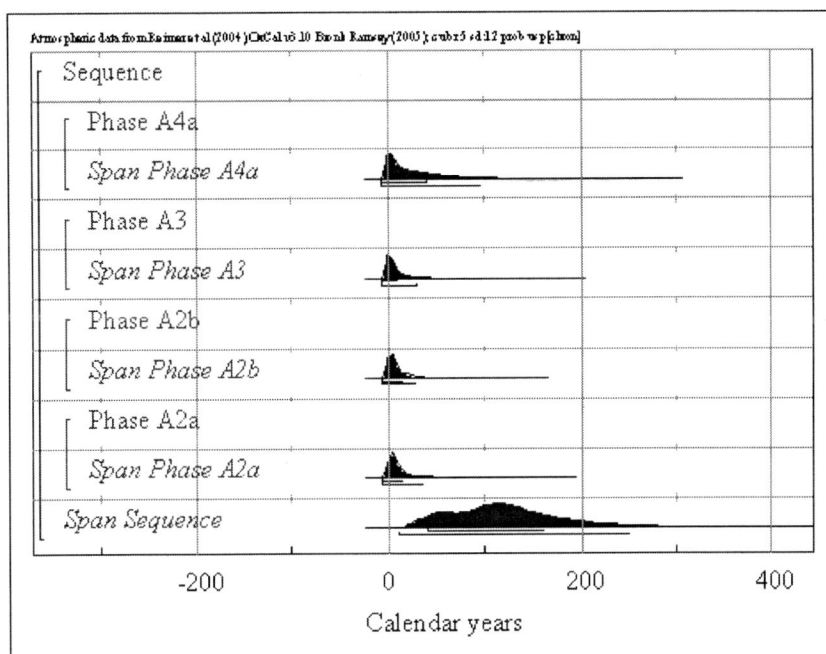

Figure 11.6. Probability distributions for the span of time in years for each of the four phases in Area A and KEN. See text for details.

Since the gate was founded during Stratum A3, we can state on the basis of the boundary probability distribution for A4a–A3 that this took place *after* about 900 BCE (Fig. 11.5). The construction of such an impressive feature was not, apparently, associated with a long phase of actual use and the gate was used instead later for metal processing, as attested to by the archaeology of Stratum A2b and the final Stratum A2a deposit. The Stratum A2b activity appears to have begun after the mid-9th century BCE (890–860 BCE [37.1% probability] or 855–830 BCE [31.1%]). We modeled the spans of time associated with each of the strata excavated in Area A and found that each was brief (Fig. 11.6). Stratum A3, for instance, spanned only 0–10 years (at 68.2% probability). Both Strata A2b and A2a, like A3 before it, appear to be relatively brief phases of activity (Fig. 11.6). Our analysis suggests that activity in this part of the site, as represented by the uppermost boundary probability distribution, ceased before the first few decades of the 9th century BCE (i.e. before 835–795 BCE [68.2%]).

Taken together, the Bayesian analysis sharpens the available chronometric data considerably. First, it enables us to consider the question of outliers and potentially inaccurate results within an explicit model in a probabilistic manner. This results in the identification of a number of determinations that we consider are almost certainly influenced either by taphonomy and mixing within the confines of the site, or are affected by inbuilt age. Once these aberrant determinations are questioned within the sequence, a coherent interpretation of the actual chronology emerges. Second, the analysis of that chronology suggests a surprisingly brief span of use of the gate, which itself appears as one of the larger installations of its type in the region (Levy *et al.* [Chapter 10, this volume]). The overall span of time represented by the gate and the subsequent metal-processing activities that took place is about a century (40–160 years [68.2%] with a highest probability of 110 years). The gate spans at most 10 years use from its construction to a change when the rooms within it were used instead in metal-working activities. By the late 9th century BCE, the area appears to have been abandoned. Whether this indicates a more general abandonment of the site as a whole is not able to be ascertained without further excavation and chronometric analysis of other occupational areas of the site. This brings us on to a more detailed analysis of the Area S sequence.

Area S—New Analyses

New determinations for Area S were added to the calibration model for the sequence described above. These are shown in Levy *et al.* (Chapter 10, this volume: Table 10.1). The overall agreement index for the first run of the model was 55.5%, which again is less than acceptable. In addition, three dates had agreement indices lower than the normally acceptable value of 60% (Fig. 11.7). OxA-12169 from Stratum S4 produced a low agreement index of 43.4%, GrN-25331 produced a value of 21.0%, while GrN-25342 resulted in an index of 51.0%. As mentioned previously, however, 5% of samples would be expected to fail this test (i.e. 1 date from the group in Fig. 11.7). Again, inbuilt age possibilities lead us to expect some results to be too old, as these indeed are, and so we questioned them in OxCal. The final run of the model resulted in a much higher agreement index (140.3%), with no discernible outliers (Fig. 11.8).

The Bayesian analysis suggests that Stratum S3, which represents the beginnings of large-scale metal production, commenced after 970–930 BCE (68.2% probability) with the highest probability associated with 950 BCE. The actual time span represented is brief (0–20 years, with the highest probability associated with 5 years). It is thought likely on archaeological grounds that Stratum A3 in Area A and Stratum S3 in Area S are probably contemporaneous, since they document similar expansions in copper processing.

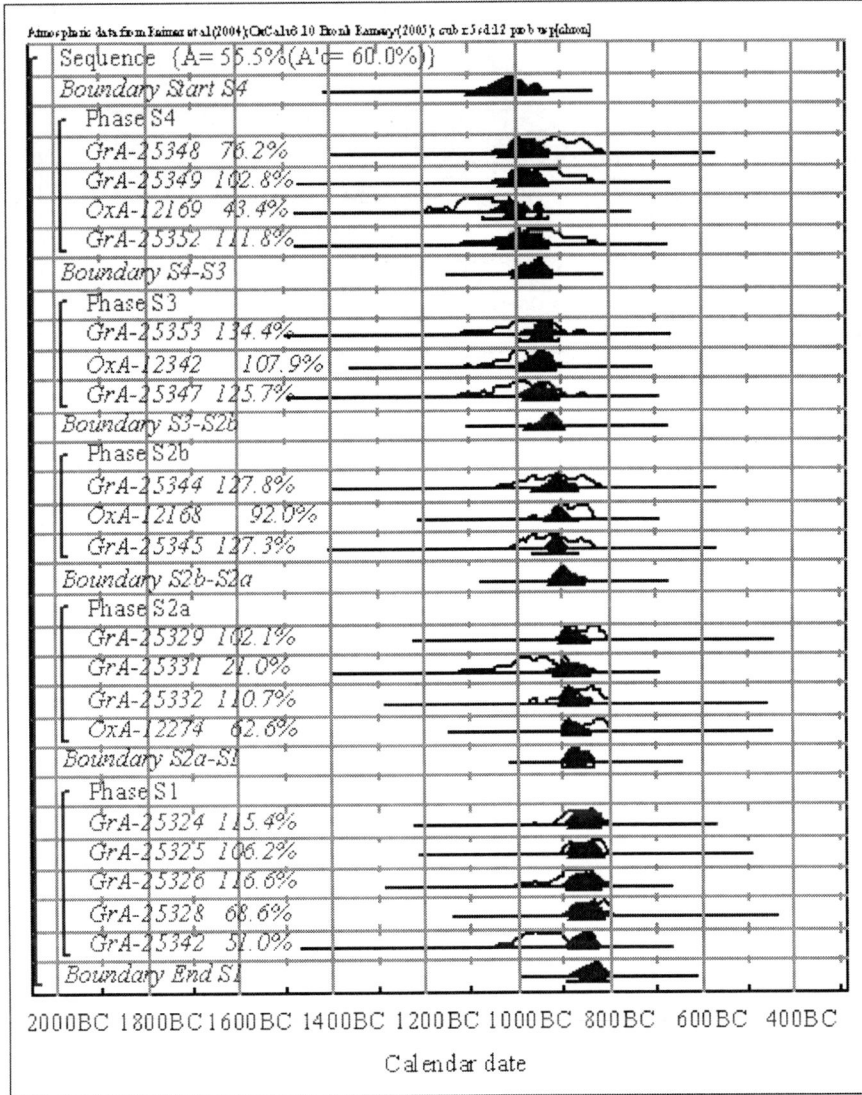

Figure 11.7. Bayesian model for Area S, comprising the new determinations obtained from the Groningen laboratory. See text for details.

The commencement date for the Stratum A3 occupation was shown in Figure 11.5. It shows that this took place after 930–875 BCE, with the highest probability favouring 900 BCE. This appears to be slightly later than Stratum S3 in Area S. Stratum S2b, representing the building construction and phase of use of the house, commenced after ~920 BCE and, like Stratum S3, lasted for a similarly brief period. The end of the sequence is represented by the boundary distribution for Stratum S1 (boundary end S1), which has a range of 860–800 BCE (63.0%) and represents a *terminus ante quem* for human activity in Area S.

Taken together, each phase in Area S could represent a brief period of time, ranging between 5 and 20 years. Our analysis suggests a total time span for this area of KEN of approximately 150 years (105–195 years at 68.2% probability) (Fig. 11.9).

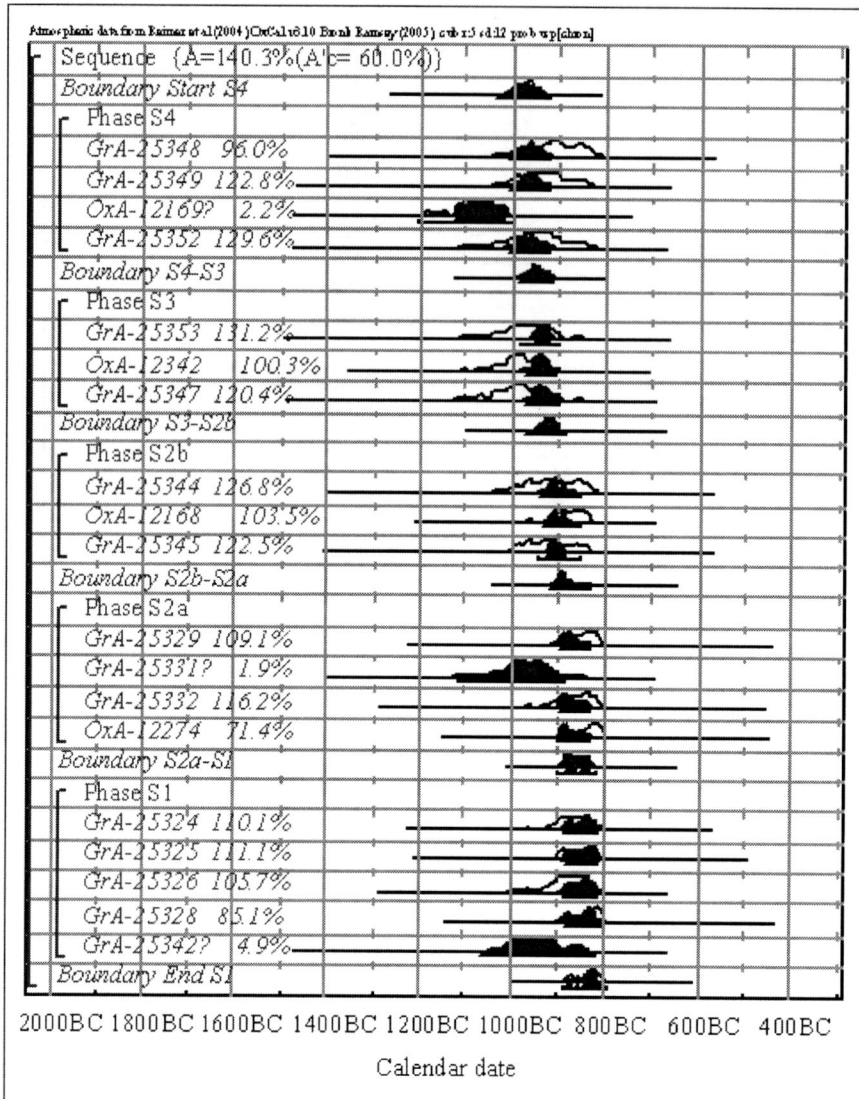

Figure 11.8. Final Bayesian model for Area S at KEN.

Levy *et al.* (Chapter 10, this volume) have considered the range in the radiocarbon ages obtained from Stratum 4. Clearly, OxA-12169 is demonstrably earlier than the three other determinations here and our analysis suggested this to be an outlier. There are two possible explanations. First, as already mentioned, OxA-12169 is affected by a degree of inbuilt age. Second, the selected samples are not dating a single period of archaeological activity. Levy *et al.* (Chapter 10, this volume) argue that in their view OxA-12169 is more likely to date the initial occupation in this stratum and that the three other Groningen determinations date later phases of human activity, perhaps mixed with earlier S4 material. Stratum 4, according to them, must be Iron I in age since scarabs dating to this phase are present within it. We decided to test both scenarios and examine the sensitivity of the modeling of post-S3 phases to changing priors in the earlier two phases.

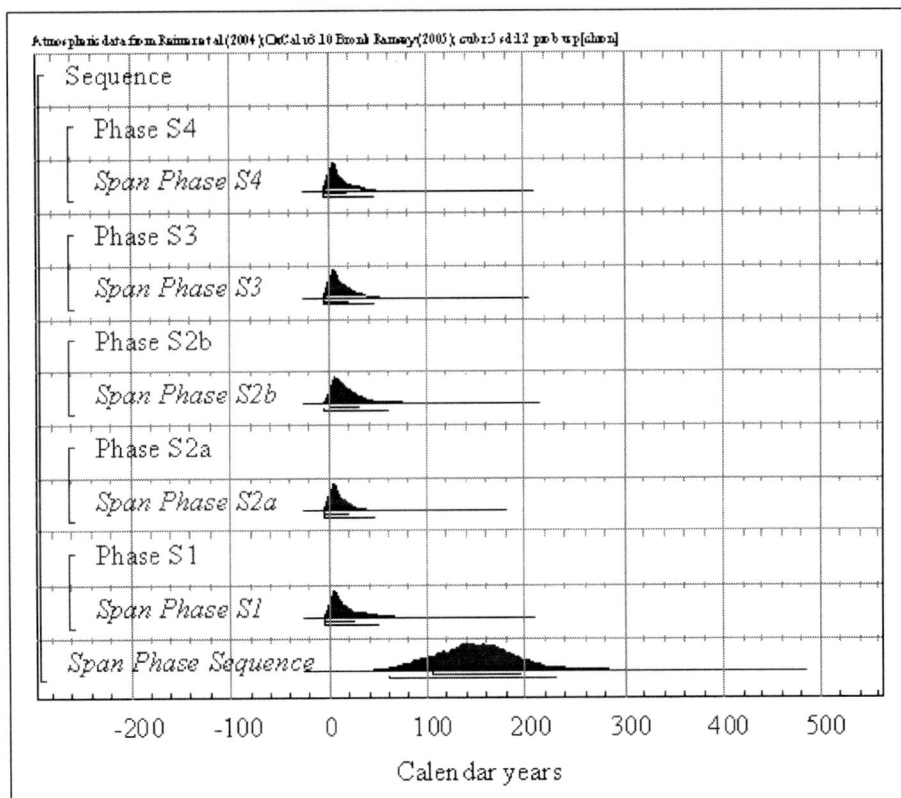

Figure 11.9. Probability distributions for the span of time in years in each of the four phases in Area S at KEN.

In our second model, we placed the three Groningen determinations from Stratum S4 as coming instead from the phase above (i.e. S3). The results show once again that there are two dates with low agreement indices (GrA-25331 and 25342) (Fig. 11.10). Downweighting these in the sequence, the posterior probabilities show that, as might be expected, the most important differences between the two models relate to the lowest strata (S3 and S4), while the modeled distributions for the upper strata remain largely identical. The principal difference is the starting date for Stratum S3, which shifts to 1025–960 BCE (highest probability at 1000 BCE), which is about 50 years earlier than that originally modeled. Similarly, the boundary probability associated with the start of Stratum S4 is earlier than previously modeled, between 1130–1010 BCE, with the highest probability at 1050 BCE. The results show generally, then, that the initial model is insensitive to changes in the Stratum S4 determinations when the younger phases of the site are considered, but is sensitive when strata S3 and S4 are considered. Both are pushed earlier within the overall sequence. Which of these two priors is appropriate is dependent upon more archaeological excavation and dating, particularly from Stratum 4. It is clearly important for determining both the start dates of strata S3 and S4, and their duration. If we accept the archaeological interpretation, that only OxA-12169 reliably dates Stratum S4, then extensive metal production in Area S appears to have begun around 1000 BCE.

Balanced against this interpretation, of course, is that if one considers A3 and S3 to be essentially contemporaneous, then the most parsimonious explanation is that the Groningen dates do in fact reliably date Stratum S4, and OxA-12169 is an outlier. Further dating is needed.

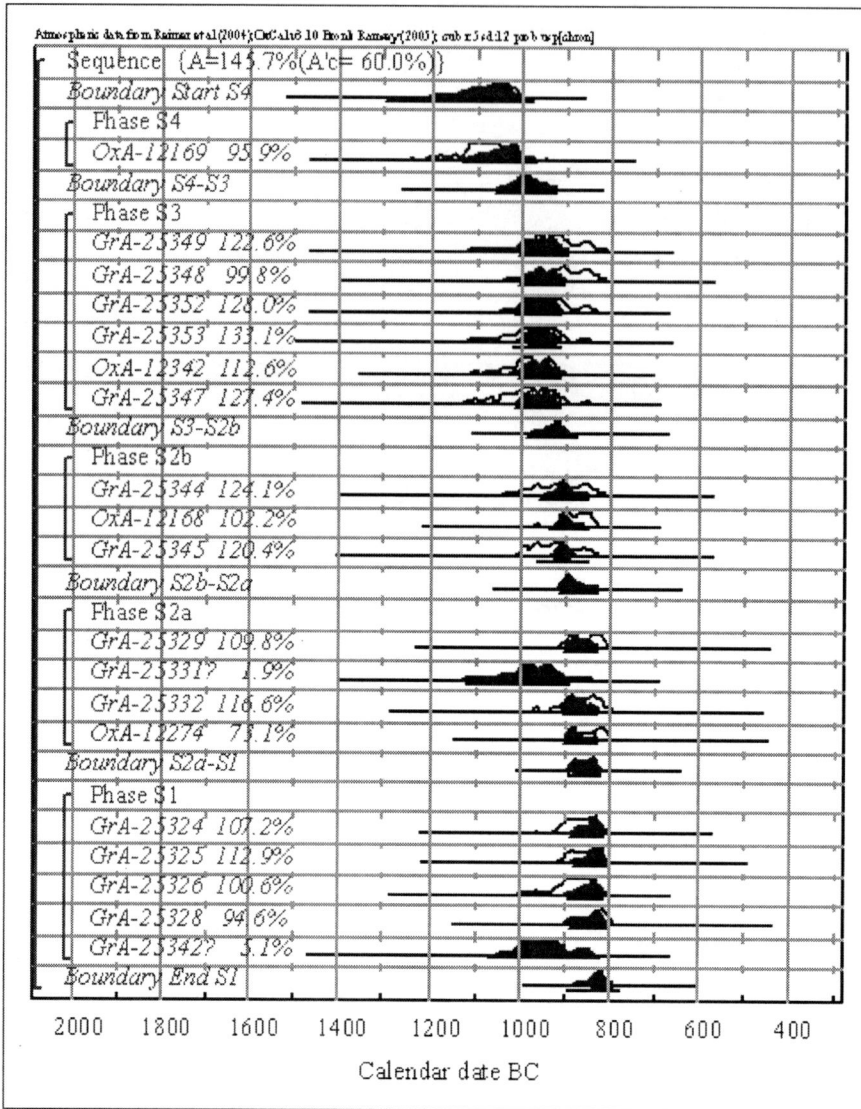

Figure 11.10. Model for Area S, with the original Groningen determinations from Stratum 4 moved to Stratum 3. See text for details.

Conclusions and Summary

The dating work undertaken at KEN thus far in the gate complex in Area A and the slag processing building in Area S have demonstrated incipient copper production from at least the early 10th century BCE in the Faynan area. It is clear that the areas of KEN that have been excavated do not date to the 8th–6th centuries BCE. We obtained close agreement with shorter-lived specimens dated at the radiocarbon facilities at ORAU and Center for Isotope Research—Groningen. However, problems in obtaining universally short-lived species resulted in some samples, comprising probable old wood, being dated. The Bayesian analysis of the radiocarbon dates supported this, and showed that there were more outliers in the data compared with what one might expect were the variation purely derived from statistical uncertainty alone.

The results of the modeling show that there is an expansion in copper production evident at the site from about 950 BCE. The impressive gate structure in the fortress at KEN appears to have been utilised for its intended purpose for a brief period (ca. 5–10 years) after which it too was devoted to the processing of copper. In both areas, we determined an overall span of time of about 100–150 years. Towards the end of the 9th century BCE, activity in both areas ceased but further excavation and dating is required to determine whether this occurred across the site as a whole, or was more circumscribed.

Further work is planned. Many more dating samples are needed to more adequately test questions rooted in historical problems such as those connected with archaeology and the Hebrew Bible. We are particularly interested in the identification of other botanical specimens for AMS dating and improving calibrated ranges in the models developed so far by selecting further material for analysis. The results presented here suggest that the adoption of Bayesian modeling for investigating the dating of sites in this and other regions is most profitable and enables higher levels of dating resolution to be obtained in the study of archaeological chronologies.

Acknowledgments

We are grateful to members of the ORAU and Groningen AMS laboratories for their careful laboratory work on preparing the samples dated in this project.

References

Anderson, A.J. (1991) The Chronology of Colonisation in New Zealand. *Antiquity* 65: 767-95.
Bronk Ramsey, C. (1995) Radiocarbon Calibration and Analysis of Stratigraphy: The OxCal Program. *Radiocarbon* 37(2): 425-30.
—(2001) Development of the Radiocarbon Calibration Program OxCal. *Radiocarbon* 43: 355-63.
Head, M.J. (1987) Categorisation of Organic Sediments from Archaeological Sites. In *Archaeometry: Further Australian Studies*, edited by W.R. Ambrose and J.M.J. Mummery (Canberra: Department of Prehistory, Research School of Pacific Studies, ANU): 143-59.
Hedges, R.E.M., *et al.* (1989) The Oxford Accelerator Mass Spectrometry Facility: Technical Developments in Routine Dating. *Archaeometry* 31: 99-113.
Higham, T.F.G. (1994) Radiocarbon Dating New Zealand Prehistory with Moa Eggshell: Some Preliminary Results. *Quaternary Geochronology (Quaternary Science Reviews)* 13: 163-69.
Higham, T.F.G., and M.D. Jones (2004) Settlement and Chronology. In *Change through Time: 50 Years of New Zealand Archaeology*, edited by L. Furey and S. Holdaway (Auckland: Publishing Press): 215-34.
Levy, T.E., *et al.* (2004) Reassessing the Iron Age chronology of Biblical Edom: New Excavations and [14]C Dates from Khirbat en-Nahas (Jordan). *Antiquity* 863-76.
McFadgen, B.G. (1982) Dating New Zealand Archaeology by Radiocarbon. *New Zealand Journal of Science* 25: 379-92.

Reimer, P.J. *et al.* (2004) INTCAL04 Terrestrial Radiocarbon Age Calibration, 0–26 kyr BP. *Radiocarbon* 46(3): 1029-58.

Schiffer, M.B. (1987) *Formation Processes of the Archaeological Record* (Albuquerque: University of New Mexico Press).

Trotter, M.M. (1968) On the Reliability of Charcoal for Radiocarbon Dating New Zealand Archaeological Sites. *New Zealand Archaeological Association Newsletter* 11: 86-88.

Van der Plicht, J., *et al.* (2000) The Groningen AMS Facility: Status Report. *Nuclear Instruments and Methods B* 172: 58-65.

12 Mesha, the Mishor, and the Chronology of Iron Age Mādabā

Timothy P. Harrison and Celeste Barlow

Abstract

Delineating the process by which the Iron Age communities in the central highlands of Jordan coalesced into the culturally and territorially defined polities referred to in ancient Near Eastern sources is not an easy task. By the mid-9th century BCE, however, a mosaic of autonomous regional communities appears to have emerged, as tacitly acknowledged in the contemporary Mesha Inscription. This study presents a summary of the Tall Mādabā Archaeological Project's (TMAP) ongoing investigations of the Iron Age levels at Mādabā, consistently identified in the documentary record as a prominent settlement in the central highland region during this period, including the results of recently analyzed radiocarbon evidence. Though preliminary, it is hoped that these results will contribute toward the continuing effort to gain a better understanding of the historical development of this region, and its broader role in the cultural and political history of the southern Levant.

Introduction

The task of delineating the process by which the Iron Age communities in the central highlands of Jordan coalesced into the culturally and territorially defined polities referred to in the Hebrew Bible and contemporary textual sources is not an easy one. By the mid-9th century BCE, however, a mosaic of autonomous regional communities appears to have emerged, as tacitly acknowledged in the Mesha Inscription by references to 'the land of Medeba', 'the land of 'Atarot', and Mesha's own identification with Dibon and its surrounding territory. Although there may have been incipient attempts at political unification prior to Mesha's reign, as reflected for example in the story of Balak (Numbers 22–24), which assumes the existence of a Moabite monarchy, the contrasting account in 2 Kings (1.1; 3.4-27) seems to confirm the pivotal nature of the political events memorialized on his stela. Moreover, the rhetoric (and formal syntax) of the inscription suggests a carefully crafted attempt to construct a broader national identity by invoking an older collective image, 'the land of Moab', while subtly shifting the locus of regional identities from kinship to that of geography.

Unfortunately, despite more than seventy years of exploration, the archaeology of Iron Age Moab is still relatively poorly documented and understood. Although the pioneering surveys of Nelson Glueck in the 1930s and the landmark excavations at Dhiban in the 1950s first drew attention to the existence of important Iron Age remains east of the Jordan River many years ago, these remains were examined almost exclusively as they related to the more thoroughly studied cultural sequences of Cisjordan. Subsequent characterizations of Iron Age Moab have tended to perpetuate this western interpretive bias, further impeding the delineation of Moabite cultural traditions based on internally secured cultural sequences. The past decade, however, has witnessed the launching of numerous field projects initiated with the explicit aim of documenting the archaeological record of Iron Age Moab more systematically, and on its own terms. Concurrent with this concerted documentation effort, there has been a growing awareness of the need to identify issues and themes specific to the Moabite (and central highland) context, and to craft an explicitly Moabite perspective on its experience in state formation and cultural development; an ambitious challenge undertaken most recently by Routledge (2004).

For such an endeavor to be successful, however, robust cultural sequences for the principal settlements in the region are critical. Moreover, these 'local histories' must be linked to a regional chronological framework that draws on multiple lines of evidence, including chronometric data, if meaningful comparative analyses and regional syntheses are to be possible. Accordingly, this study seeks to present a summary of the TMAP's ongoing investigations of the Iron Age levels at Mādabā, consistently identified in textual sources as a prominent settlement in the central highlands during this period, as well as the results of recently analyzed radiocarbon evidence. Though preliminary, it is hoped that these results will contribute toward the broader effort to gain a better understanding of the historical development of the region.

Historical and Archaeological Context

The textual record is unequivocal about the regional importance of Mādabā and its fertile hinterland, the biblical *Mishor* (or tableland; cf. Joshua 13.9, 16-21), during the Iron Age. Despite the many intractable issues that have been raised concerning the historical veracity of these disparate sources, they nevertheless are consistent in portraying the region as a highly prized and contested zone. In the Hebrew Bible, for example, we are told that the Israelites fought and won a pitched battle against a coalition of Aramaeans and Ammonites in the vicinity of Mādabā, or Medeba as it was then called, during the reign of David, early in the 10th century BCE (1 Chronicles 19.6-15; cf. 2 Samuel 10.6-14).

According to the Mesha Inscription, Mādabā was still under Israelite control ('the house of Omri') when Mesha captured (lines 7-8) and rebuilt the town (line 30) along with a series of other settlements on the tableland in the mid- to late 9th century BCE (either during or shortly after the reign of Ahab, the son of Omri). Little is known historically about the region during the remainder of the Iron Age, though the town appears to have been considered a part of the Moabite realm at the end of the period, since it is listed with other cities in Isaiah's oracle forecasting the devastation of Moab (Isaiah 15.2).

The Mesha Inscription

The Mesha Inscription, dated paleographically to the mid-9th century BCE, represents an unparalleled contemporary account from an explicitly Moabite (or perhaps more accurately, a 'Dibonite') perspective of the political struggle between Israel and Moab for control of the central highland region. Despite the contrasting perspectives, it also broadly corresponds with the later biblical account of the unsuccessful attempt by Jehoram (Ahab's successor) to restore Israelite hegemony over Mesha and his kingdom (2 Kings 3.4-27). In this well-known and widely studied document, Mesha describes Moab's lengthy oppression by Omri, 'king of Israel', and his unnamed son (probably Ahab), followed by his successful liberation of the towns and lands of the northern plateau (i.e. the Mādabā Plain region) at the direction of Kemosh. In conjunction with the repossession of these territories, we are told that Mesha embarked upon an ambitious building program, constructing public monuments (including temples), fortification systems, roads, and water reservoirs throughout the region.

As a royal inscription memorializing the principal accomplishments of Mesha's reign, the political and propagandistic character of the stela is undisputed. Nevertheless, the historically specific nature of the events described, together with the open acknowledgment of foreign domination, argue against viewing the inscription as simply a transparent rhetorical exercise in the legitimization of royal authority. Rather, as Routledge has recently argued (2000: 226-27; 2004), the Mesha Inscription gives a surprisingly sophisticated and subtle articulation to the more ambitious goal of transforming the existing political realities of its day. To achieve this objective, the narrative of the inscription had to be embedded within a recognized political discourse that could authenticate and give meaning to this transformation. For it to have done otherwise would have undermined the very motivation for its creation.

Recent linguistic analysis of the Mesha Inscription has identified a two-part syntactic structure in the text, with the inscription subdivided into sections (or paragraphs) characterized by alternating verbal constructions (*waw*-x-*qatal* + *wayyiqtol* and x-*qatal* + *waw*-x-*qatal*) (Niccacci 1994; see also Routledge 2000: 227-28; 2004). Not surprisingly, the thematic progression of the text closely follows this dualistic syntactic composition. Recognition of this, in turn, has prompted the proposal that the inscription be read as a series of alternating biographical and narrative sections, with the surviving portion of the inscription organized in a five-paragraph sequence that moves progressively from north to south (Routledge 2000: 228-30; 2004). According to this reading, the inscription begins with an introductory biographical statement (lines 1-4), followed by a narrative section (lines 5-21a) that describes campaigns conducted by Mesha north of the Wadi Mujib (the biblical *Arnon*). The third section (lines 21b-31a) returns to the biographical format, and provides an account of building projects accomplished by Mesha north of the Wadi Mujib. The sequence is then repeated for southern Moab, beginning with a narrative of Mesha's campaigns south of the Wadi Mujib (lines 31b-34), and ending with an abbreviated biographical statement (lines 34-?) recounting his building activities in this southern region.

The syntax and thematic structure of these individual sections or paragraphs also preserve patterns that appear to have social and political significance. The sites of Ba'al Ma'on (probably modern Ma'in) and Qiryatēn (possibly Quraya, located west of Mādabā [see Fig. 12.1]; for further discussion of these and other Moabite toponyms, see Dearman 1989: 170-89; MacDonald 2000: 171-83), and the building activities associated with them, for example, are syntactically positioned within the paragraph that also describes 'the land of Medeba' (lines 7b-10a). Since these sites are located within a circumscribed geographical area, it seems reasonable to infer that this paragraph describes Mesha's actions within a specific territorial and sociopolitical unit, 'the land of Medeba', which included the regional center and a number of secondary settlements (cf. Dearman 1989: 189-91, 194-96; 1992: 73; Routledge 2000: 230-32). Similar territorial units are also implied in the references to 'the land of 'Atarot' (line 10b), 'all of Dibon' (line 28), and possibly Jahaz (lines 19-20). Thus, an implicit acknowledgment of the prevailing political organization of the region appears to be embedded within the narrative of the Mesha Inscription, as well as the recognition that this organization was constructed largely of autonomous sub-regional polities.

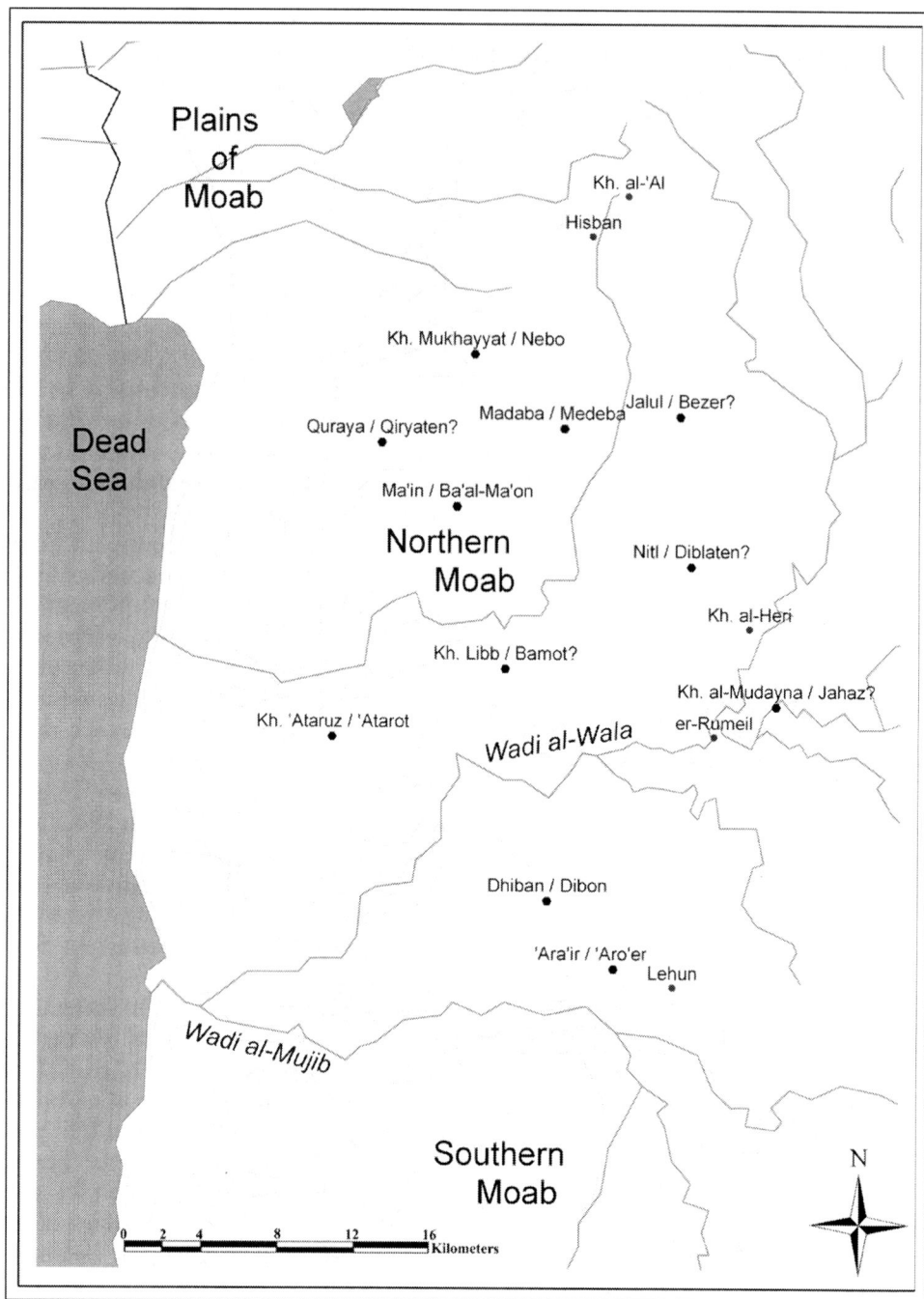

Figure 12.1. Map of Iron Age northern Moab, with the probable locations of towns mentioned in the Mesha Inscription marked with a hexagon (the topography has been adapted from the Digital Chart of the World).

Rather than attempt to eradicate or supplant the deeply rooted loyalties that structured these polities, however, Mesha's strategy appears to have been to shift the locus of political discourse from the intra-regional level, with its orientation toward local identities and alliances, to the trans-regional level. This was accomplished by invoking an older, collective image, the 'land of Moab'. The result, as commemorated on his memorial stela, was the forging of a territorial nation-state that subsumed (but did not necessarily suppress) existing regional polities within a nested political hierarchy, with Mesha positioned as the overall ruler (or king), and Dibon, his ancestral home, as the political center (or capital) (for a similar view, emphasizing the segmentary nature of this political strategy, see Routledge 2000: 235-39, Fig. 3; 2004). While there may have been prior attempts at political unification, as noted earlier, the corresponding biblical account would appear to substantiate the transformative impact of the political actions taken by Mesha, and commemorated on his memorial stela. It seems reasonable, therefore, to credit Mesha with the creation of the first territorially integrated Moabite state, achieved through the annexation and unification of the sub-regional polities that previously had dominated the political landscape of the central highland region.

Following his political victories, we are told that Mesha embarked upon an ambitious building program. He embellished the regal character of his capital (constructing a palace and apparently a park or royal garden [lines 21b-23]), established religious complexes dedicated to Kemosh, and commissioned a wide range of public works. These actions clearly were designed to further consolidate the political gains he had achieved. The eradication of Israelite cultic installations and paraphernalia (e.g. at 'Atarot [line 12b; probably Khirbat 'Ataruz] and Nebo [lines 17c-18a; Khirbat al-Mukhayyat]), for example, coupled with the construction of temples (rendered 'bet' + PN) in key settlements on the northern plateau (e.g. Bamot [modern Libb?; line 27a], possibly Medeba, Diblaten [line 30a], and Ba'al Ma'on [line 30b]), and the elevation of Kemosh as patron deity of all Moab, are actions that appear aimed specifically at the creation of a shared national religious identity. The construction of fortification systems, roads, and water storage facilities, meanwhile, suggest an attempt to build an infrastructure that would facilitate expanded economic production, and centrally controlled redistribution of the surplus. References to purges (e.g. the inhabitants of 'Atarot [line 11] and Nebo [lines 14-17]), population relocation (e.g. the Sharonites and Maharotites [line 13b]), and the rebuilding of settlements (e.g. Ba'al Ma'on [line 9b], Qiryaten [lines 9b-10a], 'Aro'er [line 26b], and Bezer [line 27b]) even imply a carefully crafted resettlement policy.

The Archaeology of the Mādabā Plain Region

More concretely, these activities, if indeed part of a systematic effort to transform the political and socioeconomic realities of the day, might be expected to have left traces in the archaeological record, such as the remains of fortification systems, cultic structures, and palatial complexes. Corresponding shifts in settlement patterns and the organization of craft industries should also reveal the extent to which Mesha's political reforms succeeded in reorganizing the social and economic structures of Iron Age Moab. The archaeological record, therefore, should help to clarify the extent to which the political claims articulated in the rhetoric of the Mesha Inscription were realized in the physical landscape of Iron Age Moab.

While the textual and inscriptional evidence appear to suggest extensive land use and settlement activity in the Mādabā Plain region during the 10th and 9th centuries BCE, however, syntheses of the archaeological record generally have characterized it as a period of limited settlement, with flourishing sedentary activity concentrated during the era of Assyrian and Babylonian hegemony, or the Late Iron II period (cf. Sauer 1986; Herr 1997; Herr and Najjar 2001; Routledge 2004: 191-92). The Hesban Survey, for example, succeeded in identifying only 16 sites with early Iron II pottery (Ibach 1987: 163). Nevertheless, early Iron II tomb assemblages have been reported for

Sahab (Dajani 1970; Harding 1948), Mādabā (Piccirillo 1975; Thompson 1984, 1986) and Khirbat al-Mukhayyat (Saller 1966), while excavations at Tall al-'Umayri (Herr *et al.* 1994: 149-50), Jawa (Daviau 1996: 84-90), Hisban (Ray 2001: 53-57, 121-26), Jalul (Herr *et al.* 1996: 71-74; 1997: 154-57), Nitl (Hamarneh 1999: 489), Khirbat al-Mudayna on the Wadi ath-Thamad (Chadwick *et al.* 2000: 260-61), and Dhiban (Morton 1989; Routledge 2004; Tushingham 1990) have all produced early Iron II material. It seems more likely, therefore, that this period remains under-represented in the archaeological record that has been documented for the region.

Iron Age Mādabā

The remains of Iron Age Mādabā presently form part of a visible rise in the downtown core of the modern town, located 30 km southwest of Amman. The ancient mounded settlement, or tall, lies on a natural rise created by branches of the Wadi Mādabā, which flows south to the cavernous Zarqa Ma'in. The TMAP, as part of a broader, regional research effort that seeks to test prevailing theories about the development of centralized institutions and the rise of early state-ordered societies in the southern Levant, was initiated for the specific purpose of gathering archaeological data from this important urban center for comparison with data sets from other settlement sites in the region. Two preliminary field seasons were conducted in 1993 and 1996 in order to create an integrated base map delineating the settlement parameters of the site, and to establish a stratigraphic profile of the lower mound of the tall (Field A). In 1998, large-scale excavations were initiated along the western slope of the upper mound (or 'acropolis') of the tall (Fields B and C). These excavations continued on an annual basis, except in 2001, until 2002. The primary objective of these field seasons was to develop a detailed record of the major cultural strata present at Tall Mādabā (for a detailed description of the project's research objectives, and preliminary reports of these field seasons, see Foran *et al.* 2004; Harrison 1996, 1997; Harrison *et al.* 2000, 2003).

Substantial Iron Age remains have been encountered in each of the fields investigated by TMAP. The most extensive remains have been uncovered in Field B, and include a monumental fortification wall preserved to a height of 5 m and a width of 7 m at its greatest extent; its circumference has been traced for approximately 25 m. The wall separates Fields B and C, and represents the earliest structure uncovered thus far along the western slope of the upper mound. Its external face had been exposed prior to the TMAP excavations, and in its original phase was constructed directly on bedrock. Our excavations suggest a complex construction history that included at least two separate efforts to reinforce the original wall, which measured approximately 2 m in width. The earlier of these two events expanded the width of the wall to 7 m, while the superimposed later renovation widened it to 5 m. The limited vertical exposure achieved thus far along the inner face of this wall prevents a more precise dating of its construction history. Nevertheless, excavations of a depositional sequence that sealed against the later renovation indicate that this effort to widen the wall occurred during the Iron IIB (ca. 9th–8th centuries BCE), or earlier. The date of the earlier rebuild is still not known.

Although excavations have not yet reached the bottom of the Iron Age sequence, thus far two architectural phases (Field Phases [FP] 6 and 7) have been identified in Field B, with a series of occupational surfaces associated with each. Both architectural phases date to the Iron IIB, according to the pottery and material culture recovered from their associated soil deposits, with the earlier field phase (FP 7) appearing to seal against the earlier of the two rebuilds identified in the construction history of the fortification wall. FP 7 was divided further into two occupational sub-phases (FPs 7.1 and 7.2), while the stratigraphic sequence associated with the later FP 6 was sub-divided according to four occupational surfaces (FPs 6.1–6.4), with FP 6.1 representing the latest phase in the combined sequence. Extensive rock tumble and heavily burnt brick material furnished evidence that the end of FP 7.1 was marked by destruction (Foran *et al.* 2004).

A thick deposit of thinly laminated layers of gray, ashy sheet wash sealed the Iron IIB remains in Field B. Micromorphological analyses (both bulk sediment and thin section analysis) conducted on samples from these layers indicate that they probably represent post-abandonment debris accumulation, resulting from the progressive erosion of abandoned structures during the annual rains (Harrison *et al.* 2003). This deposit of thinly laminated sheet wash, in turn, was sealed by a substantial Late Hellenistic complex. The Field B excavations failed to produce any stratified evidence of later Iron II occupation, although isolated Late Iron II sherds were recovered from fills associated with the founding levels of the Late Hellenistic complex, suggesting that a reduced settlement did exist elsewhere on the site during this later period.

The 1993 survey of Mādabā supports the view of a flourishing settlement during the Iron IIB period, with the distribution of surface sherds indicating a site size between 13 and 16 hectares, easily rendering Mādabā one of the largest Iron II sites in Jordan (Harrison 1996, 1997). The existence of Iron II deposits in Fields A and B, as well as adjacent to the Church of the Prophet Elijah in the Archaeological Park to the north, provides stratified evidence substantiating the spatial extent delineated by the surface survey. Although our excavations in the Iron Age levels in Field B are still at an early stage, it is tempting to link the renovation and expansion of the fortification wall to the building program commemorated by Mesha on his memorial stela. While the results excavated thus far in Field B are preliminary, and therefore must remain tentative, they nevertheless point unambiguously to a major building and occupational phase that dates to the Iron IIB period. Moreover, the ceramic evidence points to close cultural ties with other sites mentioned in the Mesha Inscription, or generally associated with the Moabite realm to the west and south of Mādabā, such as Khirbat al-Mukhayyat (Nebo), Maʿin (Baʿal Maʿon), Libb (Bamot?), Nitl (Diblatēn?), Khirbat al-Mudayna on the W. Thamad (Jahaz?), and Dhiban (Dibon) (Foran *et al.* 2004; Harrison *et al.* 2003).

Field B Radiocarbon Analytical Results

Charcoal and carbonized seeds were collected whenever sealed soil loci were encountered during the excavations in Field B. Following the 2002 field season, a suite of 17 samples were selected from key loci associated with each of the principal sub-phases in the Iron IIB stratigraphic sequence, and submitted to the IsoTrace Radiocarbon Laboratory at the University of Toronto for radiocarbon analysis. The analysis was performed by R.P. Beukens in the Accelerator Mass Spectrometry Facility at the University of Toronto. The results presented here represent the average of two separate analyses (at normal precision), and were corrected for natural and sputtering isotope fractionation, using the measured $^{13}C/^{12}C$ ratios. All of the samples were of wood charcoal, with the exception of three carbonized seeds, which had high ash content, and therefore produced very low pretreatment yields. Consequently, two of these samples (TM10 [TO-11207] and TM12 [TO-11209]) were analyzed at a lower precision, and the third (TM11 [TO-11208]) was not analyzed at all. The radiocarbon analytical results are presented in Table 12.1.

The radiocarbon evidence from Field B indicates that the occupational activity associated with the depositional sequence preserved in FPs 7 and 6 occurred over a time period spanning the late 10th to early 8th centuries BCE, or during the early part of the Iron IIB, which corresponds well with the relative chronological dates assigned to these deposits based on their associated material cultural remains. More specifically, with the exception of a few outliers, the calibrated dates cluster tightly in the mid- to late 9th century BCE. Moreover, an ascending progression of dates can be observed when the samples are organized according to their stratigraphic position in the sequence, as illustrated in Figure 12.2, using the OxCal Program, Version 3.9 (Bronk Ramsey 1995, 2001, 2003).

Table 12.1. Radiocarbon data from Field B, Tall Mādabā, Jordan.

Field Phase	Sample No.	IsoTrace Lab. No.	Sample Description	Weight Used (mg)	Age (years BP)	Age (BCE)	68.3% (1 Sigma)	95.5% (2 Sigma)
7.2	TM 5	TO-11202	wood charcoal	660	2780 ± 80	915	1005–830	1125–800
7.1	TM 12	TO-11209	charbonized seeds	61	3380 ± 120	1665	1775–520	1975–1410
7.1	TM 10	TO-11207	charbonized lentils (?)	21	2780 ± 120	915	1050–810	1260–780
7.1	TM 17	TO-11214	wood charcoal	603	2720 ± 50	880	905–820	940–800
7.1	TM 4	TO-11201	porous charcoal	639	2690 ± 50	825	895–800	920–795
6.4	TM 16	TO-11213	wood charcoal	264	2660 ± 50	810	830–795	900–785
6.4	TM 3	TO-11200	wood charcoal	356	2620 ± 50	800	820–790	835–760
6.4	TM 2	TO-11199	wood charcoal	344	2680 ± 80	825	900–795	1000–760
6.3	TM 9	TO-11206	wood charcoal	732	2630 ± 50	800	825–790	835–760
6.3	TM 15	TO-11212	wood charcoal	148	2800 ± 50	960	1000–895	1050–830
6.3	TM 14	TO-11211	wood charcoal	444	2690 ± 50	825	895–800	920–795
6.2	TM 13	TO-11210	wood charcoal	257	2630 ± 50	800	825–790	835–760
6.2	TM 8	TO-11205	wood charcoal	—	2670 ± 50	820	835–800	915–790
6.2	TM 7	TO-11204	wood charcoal	984	2610 ± 50	795	810–785	830–760
6.2	TM 6	TO-11203	wood charcoal	451	2810 ± 80	955	1045–890	1130–805
6.1	TM 1	TO-11198	wood charcoal	184	2750 ± 80	895	975–820	1055–795

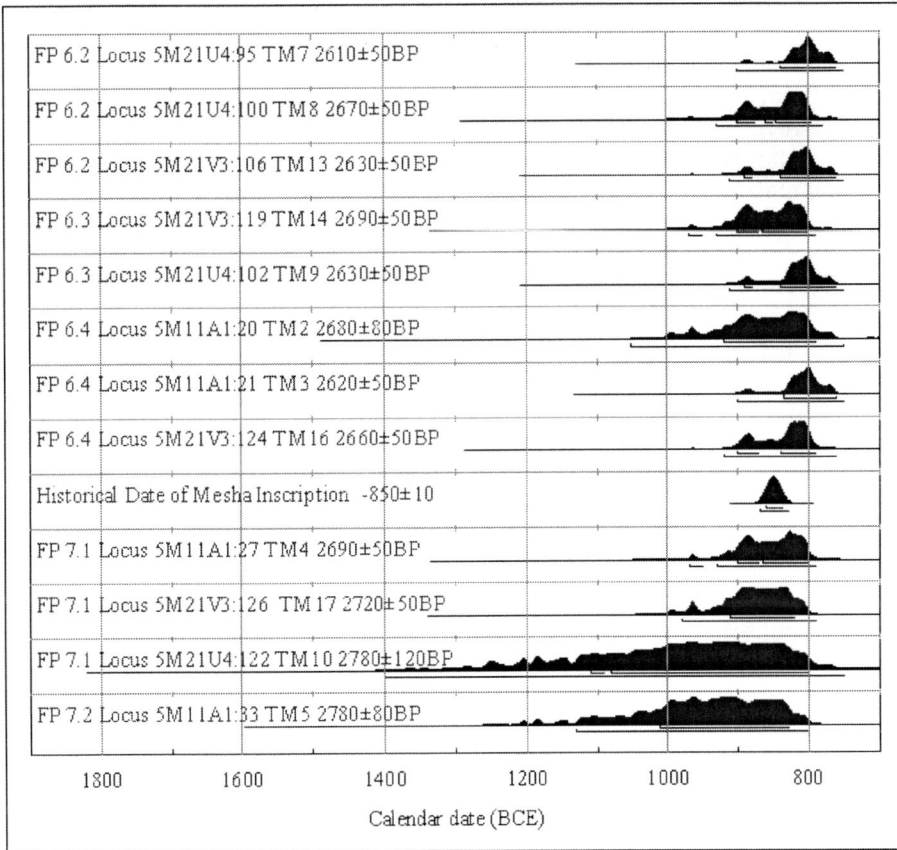

Figure 12.2. Stratigraphic sequence of calibrated dates from Field B, as
determined by the OxCal Program, Ver. 3.9 (Bronk Ramsey 2003),
using atmospheric data from Stuiver *et al.* (1998).

Samples TM12, TM15, TM6, and TM1 clearly do not synchronize with the rest of the sequence.
TM12 (TO-11209), a carbonized seed, was recovered from a pottery vessel after it had been
washed, and therefore is probably corrupted. Samples TM1 (TO-11198) and TM6 (TO-11203)
were collected from the eroded sheet wash layers that sealed the Iron IIB remains, and therefore
may represent earlier depositional activity. No obvious explanation can be given for the early date
of sample TM15 (TO-11212).

Despite these anomalies, the radiocarbon evidence clearly identifies FPs 7 and 6 as chronologically distinct architectural phases, and thus also part of two discrete cultural phases. The calibrated
modal dates for FP 7 range between 915 and 825 BCE, with an average date of 884 BCE, while
those for FP 6 range between 825 and 795 BCE, with an average date of 807 BCE, separating their
construction phases by as much as eighty years, the first dating to the first half of the Iron IIB
period (the early 9th century BCE), and the second dating to the second half (late 9th–8th centuries
BCE). Since these date ranges were drawn largely from wood samples, however, the potential for a
relatively lengthy growth cycle must be factored into each calculation, and some latitude therefore
given to the calendar years assigned to each sample. The possibility that the sampled wood
remained in circulation for significant periods of time before entering the archaeological record
must also be kept in mind.

Nevertheless, as demonstrated in Figure 12.2, the two clusters of radiometric dates, and their associated field phases, straddle the relative historical date (ca. 850 BCE) usually assigned to Mesha's campaigns and building activities, including his proclaimed reclamation of Mādabā and its hinterland. In light of the evidence for destruction that marks the end of FP 7, it is tempting to attribute this destruction to his reclamation project. Given the limited scope of the Iron Age exposure achieved thus far, however, and the preliminary nature of the analyses completed to date, such a conclusion must remain tentative, contingent on further excavations and an expansion of the radiocarbon sample base.

Summary Observations

Despite the preliminary nature of the results presented in this study, the prospect of a convergence between the archaeological, epigraphic, and radiometric evidence represents a significant step toward realization of the project goal to establish a secure internal chronology for the cultural sequence preserved at Tall Mādabā, as well as the wider goal to gain a better understanding of the cultural and political development of the region. Though preliminary and tentative, these results also give credence to the broader historical significance attributed to the events described in the Mesha Inscription. As we have argued, the documentary record suggests the emergence of a political landscape in the early Iron II (i.e. 10th and 9th centuries BCE) comprised of small, autonomous sub-regional polities. Although not dealt with in this study, the settlement patterns for this period present a similar, supporting view.

In the end, what can we say of Mesha's claim to have consolidated power in the central highland region, and his apparent attempt to shift the locus of political discourse from the local to the trans-regional level, thereby forging a broader Moabite national identity in the latter part of the 9th century BCE? Did his actions in fact result in a transformation of the social, economic, and political institutions of Iron Age Moab? While it is still too early to answer these questions with confidence, the long trajectory of historical experience in the region would suggest that the measure of his success will ultimately weigh more substantively in the realm of the imagination than in that of the physical world. The persistent tenacity with which highland communities have adhered to subsistence strategies that favor flexibility and autonomy, while resisting hierarchical relationships that facilitate integration and the maximization of production, is a well-documented fact (cf. Harrison 1995; Harrison and Savage 2003; LaBianca 1990). It is a key to understanding the remarkable resilience and longevity of the cultures that have thrived in the uncertain environment of the highland region, and almost certainly will prove to have been crucial in giving shape to the experience of Iron Age Moab as well.

Acknowledgments

The TMAP excavations have been supported by research grants from a number of funding sources, including the Social Sciences and Humanities Research Council of Canada, the Connaught Fund of the University of Toronto, the Harris Fund of the American Schools of Oriental Research, and the National Geographic Society. The excavations have been conducted in collaboration with the Department of Antiquities of Jordan, which has helped provide workers and equipment. The successful outcome of each field season would not have been possible without the dedicated help of Dr Ghazi Bisheh, former Director General of Antiquities, Dr Fawwaz al-Khraysheh, the present Director General of Antiquities, and the staff of the Mādabā Museum. We wish also to acknowledge the past and present mayors of Mādabā, who have unhesitatingly offered their assistance and freely made available the resources of the municipality, and the people of Mādabā for their extended hospitality throughout our field work.

References

Bronk Ramsey, C. (1995) Radiocarbon Calibration and Analysis of Stratigraphy: The OxCal Program. *Radiocarbon* 37: 425-30.
—(2001) Development of the Radiocarbon Program OxCal. *Radiocarbon* 43: 355-63.
—(2003) OxCal Program, Version 3.9 <http://www.rlaha.ox.ac.uk/O/oxcal.php#intro>.
Chadwick, R., P.M.M. Daviau, and M. Steiner (2000) Four Seasons of Excavations at Khirbat al-Mudayna on Wādī ath-Thamad, 1996–1999. *ADAJ* 44: 257-70.
Dajani, R.W. (1970) A Late Bronze-Iron Age Tomb Excavated at Sahab, 1968. *ADAJ* 15: 29-34.
Daviau, P.M.M. (1996) The Fifth Season of Excavations at Tall Jawa (1994): A Preliminary Report. *ADAJ* 40: 83-100.
Dearman, J.A. (1989) Historical Reconstruction and the Mesha' Inscription. In *Studies in the Mesha Inscription and Moab*, edited by J. Dearman (Atlanta: Scholars Press): 155-210.
—(1992) Settlement Patterns and the Beginning of the Iron Age in Moab. In *Early Edom and Moab: The Beginning of the Iron Age in Southern Jordan*, edited by P. Bienkowski (Sheffield Archaeological Monographs 7; Sheffield: J.R. Collis): 65-75.
Foran, D., *et al.* (2004) The Tall Mādabā Archaeological Project: Preliminary Report of the 2002 Field Season. *ADAJ* 48: 79-96.
Hamarneh, B., S. de Luca, and V. Michel (1999) Campagna di scavi a Nitl- Mādabā—1999. *Liber Annuus* 49: 489-94.
Harding, G.L. (1948) An Iron-Age Tomb at Sahab. *Quarterly of the Department of Antiquities of Palestine* 13: 92-102.
Harrison, T.P. (1995) *Life on the Edge: Human Adaptation and Resilience in the Semi-Arid Highlands of Central Jordan During the Early Bronze Age* (Doctoral dissertation, University of Chicago).
—(1996) The Surface Survey. In *Mādabā: Cultural Heritage*, edited by P.M. Bikai and T.A. Dailey (Amman: American Center of Oriental Research): 18-23.
—(1997) Intrasite Spatial Analysis and the Settlement History of Mādabā. *Studies in the History and Archaeology of Jordan* 6: 137-42.
Harrison, T.P., and S. Savage (2003) Settlement Heterogeneity and Multivariate Craft Production in the Early Bronze Age Southern Levant. *Journal of Mediterranean Archaeology* 16: 33-57.
Harrison, T.P., *et al.* (2000) Urban Life in the Highlands of Central Jordan: A Preliminary Report of the 1996 Tall Mādabā Excavations. *ADAJ* 44: 211-29.
Harrison, T.P., *et al.* (2003) The Tall Mādabā Archaeological Project: Preliminary Report of the 1998–2000 Field Seasons. *ADAJ* 47: 129-48.
Herr, L.G. (1997) The Iron Age II Period: Emerging Nations. *BA* 60: 114-83.
Herr, L.G., and M. Najjar (2001) The Iron Age. In *The Archaeology of Jordan*, edited by B. MacDonald, R. Adams, and P. Bienkowski (Levantine Archaeology 1; Sheffield: Sheffield Academic Press): 323-45.
Herr, L.G., *et al.* (1994) Mādabā Plains Project: The 1992 Excavations at Tell el-'Umeiri, Tell Jalul, and Vicinity. *ADAJ* 38: 147-72.
Herr, L.G., *et al.* (1996) Mādabā Plains Project 1994: Excavations at Tall al-'Umayri, Tall Jalūl, and Vicinity. *ADAJ* 40: 63-81.
—(1997) Mādaba Plains Project 1996: Excavations at Tall al-'Umayri, Tall Jalūl, and Vicinity. *ADAJ* 41: 145-67.
Ibach, R.D., Jr (1987) *Archaeological Survey of the Hesban Region: Catalogue of Sites and Characterization of Periods* (Hesban 5; Berrien Springs, MI: Andrews University Press).
LaBianca, O. (1990) *Sedentarization and Nomadization; Food System Cycles at Hesban and Vicinity in Transjordan* (Hesban 1; Berrien Springs, MI: Andrews University Press).
MacDonald, B. (2000) *'East of the Jordan': Territories and Sites of the Hebrew Scriptures* (Boston, MA: American Schools of Oriental Research).
Morton, W. (1989) A Summary of the 1955, 1956, and 1965 Excavations at Dhiban. In *Studies in the Mesha Inscription and Moab*, edited by J. Dearman (Atlanta: Scholars Press): 239-46.
Niccacci, A. (1994) The Stele of Mesha and the Bible: Verbal System and Narrativity. *Orientalia* 63: 226-48.

Piccirillo, M. (1975) Una tomba del Ferro I a Madaba (Madaba B). *Liber Annuus* 25: 199-224.

Ray, P. (2001) *Tell Hesban and Vicinity in the Iron Age* (Hesban 6; Berrien Springs, MI: Andrews University Press).

Routledge, B. (2000) The Politics of Mesha: Segmented Identities and State Formation in Iron Age Moab. *Journal of the Economic and Social History of the Orient* 43: 221-56.

—(2004) *Moab in the Iron Age: Hegemony, Polity, Archaeology* (Philadelphia: University of Pennsylvania Press).

Saller, S.J. (1966) Iron Age Tombs at Nebo, Jordan. *Liber Annuus* 16: 165-298.

Sauer, J.A. (1986) Transjordan in the Bronze and Iron Ages: A Critique of Glueck's Synthesis. *BASOR* 263: 1-26.

Stuiver, M. *et al.* (1998) INTCAL98 Radiocarbon Age Calibration, 24,000-0 Cal BP. *Radiocarbon* 40: 1041-83.

Thompson, H.O. (1984) Mādabā—An Iron Age Tomb. In *The Answers Lie Below*, edited by H. Thompson (Lanham, MD: University Press of America): 147-83.

—(1986) An Iron Age Tomb at Mādabā. In *The Archaeology of Jordan and Other Studies Presented to Siegfried H. Horn*, edited by L.T. Geraty and L.G. Herr (Berrien Springs, MI: Andrews University Press): 331-63.

Tushingham, A.D. (1990) Dhiban Reconsidered: King Mesha and his Works. *ADAJ* 34: 183-92.

V.
ISRAEL IN THE IRON AGE

13 Ladder of Time at Tel Reḥov

Stratigraphy, archaeological context, pottery and radiocarbon dates

Amihai Mazar, Hendrik J. Bruins, Nava Panitz-Cohen and Johannes van der Plicht

Abstract

Six excavation seasons conducted between 1997–2003 at Tel Reḥov south of Beth Shean revealed rich data related to the 12th–8th centuries BCE. In Area D, six stratigraphic phases (D-7 to D-3) relate to the Iron Age I. Occupation layers of the Iron Age IIA were explored in Areas B, C, D, E, F and G. In each of these areas, three to four stratigraphic phases from this period were found. The correlation between the various areas is not an easy task, yet we suggested strata numbers which, though tentative, provide a general stratigraphic framework for the entire site. All three strata, VI–IV, produced typical pottery assemblages. The pottery of Stratum VI differs from the later two later in details, yet all three belong to the Iron IIA horizon. The rich assemblages from Strata V–IV are identical to those found in Strata VB and VB–IVA at Megiddo and related sites and thus the correct dating of Tel Reḥov strata is crucial for the ongoing debate over the chronology of the Iron Age in the Southern Levant.

^{14}C dates of samples from Tel Reḥov were measured at three laboratories. Altogether, 70 dates are now available: 15 at the Weizmann Institute, 9 at the University of Arizona (both published in Radiocarbon 2001), 34 at Groningen laboratories (published in the journal *Science* [April 2004]) and 30 additional dates from Groningen. An additional five are being prepared at the Weizmann Institute. This paper will present the nature and contexts of the samples and discuss the various questions raised in this research. Some major points are:

1. The dates measured at the Weizmann Institute during the late 1990s are consistently too low by 50–100 years when compared to those from Arizona and Groningen.
2. The stratigraphic sequence and ^{14}C dates from Area D are in accord with the conventional chronology of the Iron Age I in Israel. The uppermost phase in this sequence (concentration of pits from level D-3) yielded a limited pottery assemblage which appears to belong to the end of this period. The ^{14}C dates and other archaeological considerations call for the termination of the Iron Age I somewhere in the first quarter of the 10th century BCE.
3. The few dates from Stratum VI and many from the destruction of Stratum V fall in the last quarter of the 10th century BCE. Wiggle matching enables to date Stratum VI close to the mid-10th century and Stratum V to the later half of that century. The ^{14}C dates from Stratum IV indicate that its violent destruction occurred during the 9th century, not later than ca. 830 BCE, yet a more precise date within this time depends on archaeological and historical considerations. These dates at Tel Reḥov fit the 'extended conventional chronology' for the Iron IIA in Israel (ca. 980–840/830 BCE).
4. Historical events like the raid of Shoshenq I and the Aramean wars may be taken into consideration as causing some of the destruction layers at Tel Reḥov, though such identifications remain tentative.

5.   The dates measured at Tel Reḥov are important for substantiating the chronology of Phoenicia, Cyprus and Greece, since imported pottery from all three regions was found at Tel Reḥov in stratigraphic contexts.

Introduction

Tel Reḥov is a large site, covering 10 hectares, situated at an important geographic junction in the Jordan Valley, 5 km south of Beth Shean (Figs. 13.1–3).

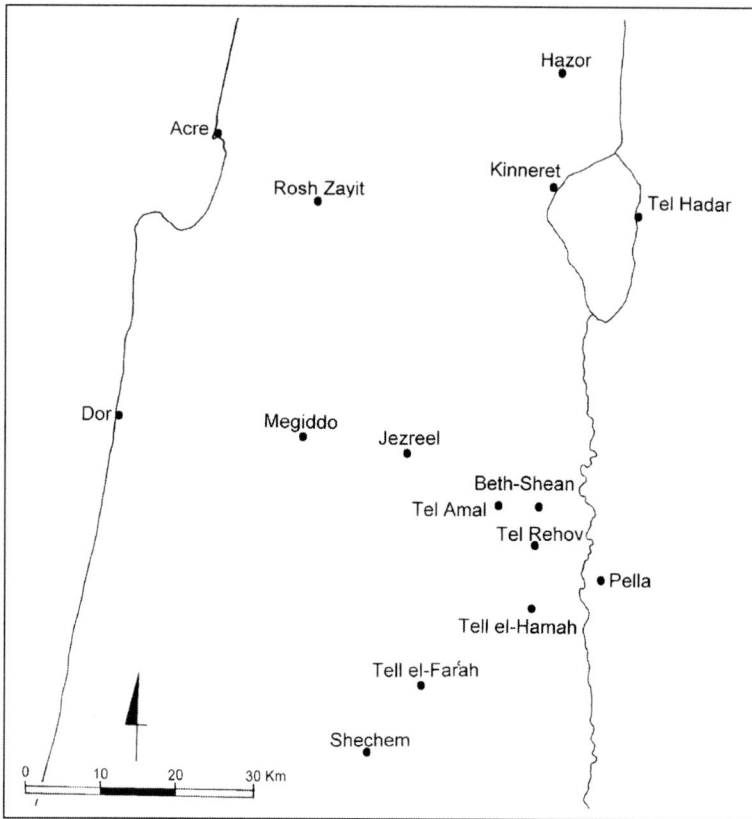

Figure 13.1. Location map of Tel Reḥov.

Six excavation seasons between the years 1997 to 2003 revealed complex stratigraphic sequences in seven excavation areas, yielding rich material assemblages from the end of the Late Bronze to the end of the Iron Age IIB. The most widely exposed and explored period is the Iron Age IIA (10th–9th centuries BCE),[1] which was excavated in six excavation areas (Mazar 1999, 2003b, in press a, in press b).[2] The rich material culture assemblages from Tel Reḥov provide a major contribution to

---

1.   The definition of Iron IIA in this article follows that of Mazar and others, relating to most of the 10th and 9th centuries BCE as one integral cultural unit (Coldstream and Mazar 2003: 40-44; see Mazar [Chapter 2, this volume]).

2.   The excavations at Tel Reḥov, directed by A. Mazar, have been conducted since 1997 under the auspices of the Institute of Archaeology of the Hebrew University and generously sponsored by Mr John Camp. Our thanks to Mr Harm-Jan Streurman, Mrs Anita T. Aerts-Bijma and Mr Stef Wijma for carefully preparing and measuring the radiocarbon samples in the Centre for Isotope Research of Groningen University.

many aspects of material culture relating to northern Israel in the 12th–8th centuries BCE. Large well stratified and restorable pottery assemblages and a large number of ^{14}C dates based on short-lived organic samples from a sequence of well stratified loci provide important data for the currently debated subject of Iron Age chronology. The main results were already published earlier (Bruins, van der Plicht and Mazar 2003a; Mazar and Carmi 2001) and raised controversy (Bruins, van der Plicht and Mazar 2003b; Finkelstein and Piaseztky 2003a, 2003b; Gilboa and Sharon 2003; Mazar 2004).

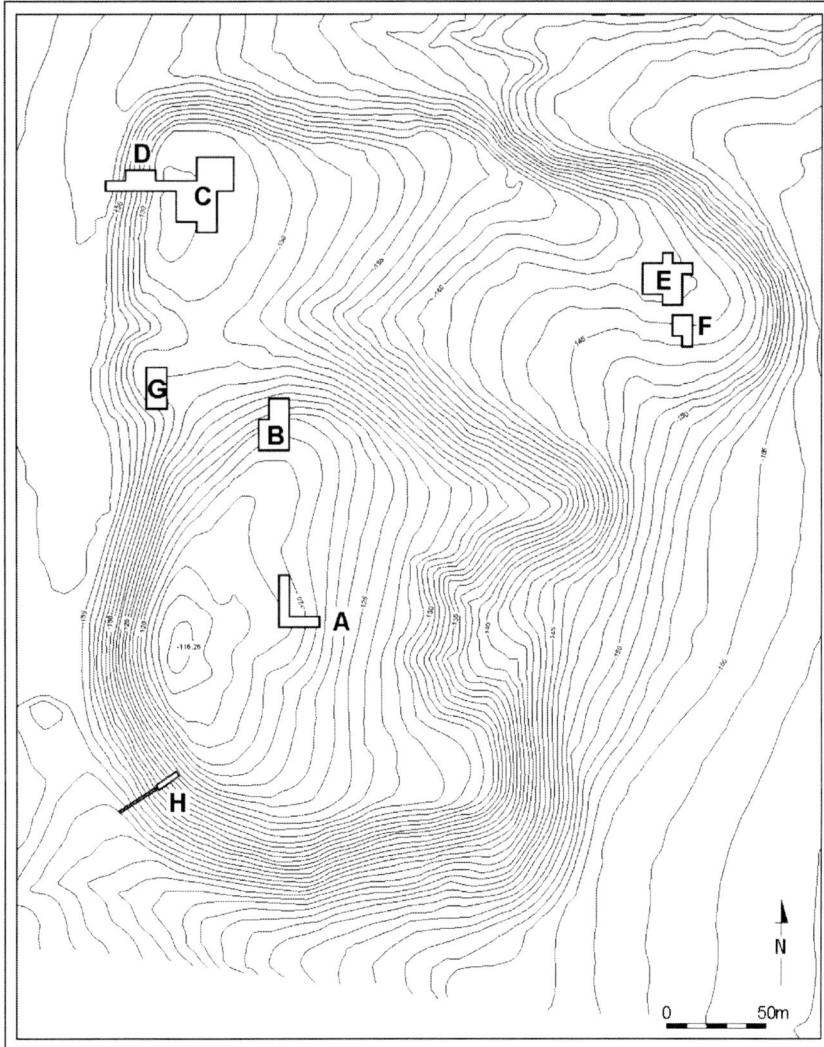

Figure 13.2. Tel Rehov: topographic map and areas of excavation.

Figure 13.3. Tel Reḥov (looking to the north-east).

In the current paper, we present in considerable detail the major features of the architecture, stratigraphy and pottery assemblages in Areas D, C and B, from which ^{14}C dates were obtained. We explain the context of each sample used for ^{14}C dating and present the large Groningen radio-carbon series of 64 dates. Moreover, a comparison is made with published dates obtained from two other radiocarbon laboratories—Rehovot and Arizona. Finally, the implications of the results are discussed with respect to the Iron Age chronology in the Southern Levant.

The stratigraphic phases (termed here 'strata') in each excavation area at Tel Reḥov were numbered separately; thus Stratum D-1 is the uppermost stratum in Area D, and so on (Table 13.1). Since layers of the Iron Age IIA were excavated in six different excavation areas, we attempted to correlate these local stratigraphic phases into a comprehensive overall framework. These final strata numbers are marked in Roman numerals in Table 13.1. Yet it should be pointed out that this correlation is tentative and insecure in several cases, and its details might be changed or refined in the future. In view of local stratigraphic developments in each of the excavation areas and the correlation uncertainty between areas C, B and E with respect to Iron IIA, we use final Roman numeral strata mainly in relation to Area C, but maintain the local phase stratigraphy in most other cases.

Table 13.1. Stratigraphic table of Tel Reḥov, showing the correlation
between the different excavation areas.

Genera Stratum	Local Strata in Individual Excavation Areas							Period	Conventional Time frame (BCE)
II	-	-	-	-	-	B-2	A-2	Iron Age IIB/C	After 732
III	-	-				B-3	A-3a	Iron Age IIB	Until 732
							A-3b		
IV	-	C-1a	E-1a	F-1	G-1	B-4*	A-4		Until ca. 830–840
V	D-1(?)	C-1b	E-1b	2	2	5a* 5b			
VI	D-2	C-2	E-2	F-3-4	G-3	B-6		Iron Age IIA	From ca. 980
VII	D-3	C-3							Until 990–980
	D-4							Iron Age IB	
	D-5								ca. 1130 (?)
	D-6							Iron Age IA	12th century
	D-7								
	D-8							Late Bronze IIB	13th century
	D-9a								
	D-9b								
								Late Bronze I-IIA	15th–14th century
	D-10								
	D-11							MB/LBI	16th century

* Needs further clarification in the future. It is possible that 5a should be correlated with general Stratum IV.

^{14}C Dates from Tel Reḥov: An Overview[3]

The following groups of ^{14}C dates from Tel Rehov were published previously:
(a) A total of 15 dates from seven loci, measured during the years 1998–99 in the ^{14}C Laboratory of the Weizmann Institute in Rehovot (hereafter: Rehovot, laboratory code RT) measured conventionally by Liquid Scintillation Counting (LSC) (Mazar and Carmi 2001; cited in the present paper, Tables 13.2 and 13.4). Nine of these were charred grain samples from Locus 2425 of Area C; three were samples of olive stones from various phases in Area D, and an additional three samples consisted of charred timber used for construction in Areas C and E. Also included is one date from Stratum D-3 prepared at Rehovot and measured at Tucson (RTT-3805).
(b) Nine dates of charred grain from Locus 2425 were measured in the AMS laboratory of the University of Arizona (hereafter: Arizona, laboratory code AA; Mazar and Carmi 2001: 1338; cited in the present paper, Table 13.4).
(c) A series of 34 dates of charred grains and olive stones from 14 loci, measured during 2001–2002 at the Radiocarbon Laboratories of the University of Groningen were published in 2003 (Bruins, van der Plicht and Mazar 2003a, 2003b; Tables 13.2 and 13.3 in the present paper). The two Groningen ^{14}C labs, situated at the Centre for Isotope Research (hereafter Groningen), have separate pre-treatment and different measurement procedures: (1) conventional radiometry by Proportional Gas Counting (PGC); (2) AMS. The laboratory radiocarbon date codes are GrN and GrA, respectively (see van der Plicht and Bruins [Chapter 14, this volume] for a more extensive treatment of laboratory procedures).

---

3.   All 14 dates in this paper were calibrated in OxCal 3.9 (Bronk Ramsey 2003).

Table 13.2. Radiocarbon dating results from Iron Age I Strata in Area D at Tel Rehov.

GrN: Groningen PGC method.; GrA: Groningen, AMS method; RT: Rehovot LSC method (cited from Mazar and Carmi 2001); RTT: Rehovot, AMS (see footnote 9).

Stratum and Period	Locus	Basket	Charred Organic Material	Lab. No.	14C Date (BP)	δ13C (‰)	14C Date BP or Average used in calibration	1σ Calibrated Date 1998 Curve OxCal v3.9 (year BCE)	2σ Calibrated Date 1998 Curve OxCal v3.9 (year BCE)
	1858	28395	Olive stones	RT-3120	2670 ± 40	–20.80	Same	892–880 (11.4%) 836–799 (56.8%)	900–795 (95.4%)
	2862	28493	Olive stones	RTT-3805	2800 ± 20		Same	1000–985 (6.7%) 975–950 (24.8%) 945–905 (36.7%)	1010–890 (95.4%)
	2862	28493	Olive stones	GrA-19033 GrN-26119	2835 ± 45 2720 ± 30	–23.03 –22.33	2835 ± 45	1046–920 (68.2%)	1128–896 (93.5%) 877–857 (1.9%)
	4815	48105	Olive stones	GrA-16757	2820 ± 50	–22.51	same	1042–1031 (3.8%) 1022–901 (64.4%)	1126–891 (87.0%) 881–835 (8.4%)
D-3	4816	48103	Olive stones Charcoal	GrA-12889 GrA-16848	2870 ± 70 2895 ± 40	–25.29 –24.41	2870 ± 70	1188–1181 (2.1%) 1150–1144 (1.6%) 1128–970 (55.2%) 960–928 (9.3%)	1260–1228 (3.8%) 1221–894 (88.8%) 878–839 (2.9%)
Iron IB	4830	48115	Olive stones	GrA-21044 GrA-21056 GrA-21183 GrA-22302a GrA-22302b GrA-22329a GrA-22329b	2845 ± 35 2825 ± 35 2820 ± 50 2730 ± 50 2820 ± 40 2810 ± 50 2760 ± 40	–22.05 –23.30 –23.35 –23.00 same –22.63 same	first 3 dates 2832 ± 22 5 coherent dates 2827 ± 18	1004–970 (40.0%) 959–934 (28.2%) 1001–971 (39.9%) 958–937 (28.3%)	1044–918 (95.4%) 1018–916 (95.4%)

Context	Reg. no.	Lab no.	Material	Sample	¹⁴C BP	δ¹³C	Combined	Calibrated 1σ	Calibrated 2σ
D-4 Iron IB	1836	48450	Olive stones	GrN-26121 GrA-18825	2890 ± 30 2870 ± 50	−22.95 −22.99	2885 ± 26	1125–1119 (3.3%) 1112–1098 (10.0%) 1087–1059 (18.0%) 1053–1005 (36.9%)	1189–1179 (2.9%) 1154–1143 (2.2%) 1129–996 (86.3%) 990–974 (2.5%) 955–943 (1.6%)
	1845	48556	Seeds	GrA-21046 GrA-21057 GrA-21184	2905 ± 35 2945 ± 35 2920 ± 50	−22.49 −23.10 −24.12	2924 ± 22	1208–1202 (3.6%) 1189–1179 (7.2%) 1154–1142 (8.1%) 1129–1108 (15.1%) 1102–1067 (23.7%) 1065–1050 (10.4%)	1254–1244 (2.3%) 1212–1199 (6.2%) 1192–1139 (25.7%) 1132–1020 (61.2%)
	1845	28243	Olive stones	RT-3121	2800 ± 40	−21.10	same	999–902 (68.2%)	1044–887 (81.6%) 884–833 (13.8%)
	1876	28536	Olive stones	RT-3119	2685 ± 40	−20.70	same	896–876 (18.1%) 858–852 (4.2%) 841–802 (45.9%)	905–797 (95.4%)
D-6 Iron IA	2836	28352	Olive stones	GrN-26118 GrA-18826	2920 ± 30 2950 ± 50	−22.28 −22.46	2928 ± 26	1209–1201 (5.1%) 1190–1178 (7.9%) 1159–1141 (11.3%) 1130–1108 (13.8%) 1102–1067 (20.8%) 1066–1050 (9.2%)	1257–1239 (4.9%) 1213–1197 (7.4%) 1194–1138 (28.1%) 1133–1018 (55.0%)
	2874	28701	Olive stones	GrA-19034 GrN-26120	2935 ± 45 2880 ± 30	−22.14 −22.36	2897 ± 25	1126–1040 (60.6%) 1032–1020 (7.6%)	1210–1200 (2.0%) 1191–1177 (4.5%) 1161–1141 (4.6%) 1130–1000 (84.3%)

Table 13.3. Calibrated Groningen radiocarbon dates from Iron IIA Strata of Tel Reḥov.

Local Stratum & General Stratum	Architectural Unit	Locus	Basket	Charred Organic Material	Lab. No.	¹⁴C Date (BP)	$\delta^{13}C$ (‰)	¹⁴C Date BP or Average used in calibration	1σ Calibrated Date 1998 Curve OxCal v3.9 (year BCE)	2σ Calibrated Date 1998 Curve OxCal v3.9 (year BCE)
C-1a IV	Building F Destruction	5498	54702	Cereal grains	GrA-21152 GrA-21154 GrA-21267 GrA-22301a GrA-22301b GrA-22330a GrA-22330b	2770 ± 50 2730 ± 50 2760 ± 35 2710 ± 45 2775 ± 40 2760 ± 50 2785 ± 40	-22.54 -22.28 -22.74 -22.34 same -22.32 same	3 dates 2755 ± 2.5 all 7 dates 2758 ± 16	918–893 (25.0%) 879–837 (43.2%) 918–895 (28.2%) 877–840 (40.0%)	970–959 (6.0%) 934–830 (89.4%) 969–960 (4.7%) 926–833 (90.7%)
E-1b ? ?	Courtyard in Sanctuary	2618	46281	Olive stones	GrA-17260	2745 ± 40	-21.98	2745 ± 40	915–833 (68.2%)	997–988 (1.4%) 974–953 (7.4%) 945–811 (86.5%)
B-5 IV or V ?	Below Destruction Layer	6229	62430	Seeds	GrA-24108 GrA-24109 GrA-24111 GrA-24112 GrN-28368	2765 ± 45 2770 ± 45 2780 ± 45 2750 ± 45 2735 ± 30	-23.60 alkali -23.60 alkali -24.30 seeds -26.40 seeds -23.60 total	all 5 dates 2755 ± 18	915–895 (24.1%) 877–839 (44.1%)	968–961 (3.8%) 925–832 (91.6%)
B-5 ? V ?	0.2 m above Wall 1241 of Stratum B-5	1224	41016	Olive stones	GrN-27365	2765 ± 15	-22.98	2765 ± 15	967–962 (5.2%) 922–896 (37.9%) 876–858 (16.8%) 852–842 (8.3%)	970–959 (8.6%) 934–890 (48.0%) 882–835 (38.8%)
B-5 V	Stratum V Destruction Layer	4218	42236	Olive stones Olive stones Olive stones Charcoal Charcoal Charcoal	GrA-21034 GrA-21047 GrA-21179 GrA-21042 GrA-21053 GrA-21180	2760 ± 35 2820 ± 35 2770 ± 50 2765 ± 35 2750 ± 35 2690 ± 50	-21.86 -21.76 -22.43 -23.80 -25.62 -26.36	Olive stones 2786 ± 22	995–991 (1.9%) 973–956 (19.4%) 942–899 (46.9%)	999–895 (83.7%) 877–841 (11.7%)
C-1b V	Building E Floor surface in room	6449	64756	Olive stones	GrA-24455 GrA-24456 GrA-24497	2775 ± 45 2750 ± 45 2745 ± 45	-23.73 n/a n/a	2757 ± 26	919–893 (26.5%) 879–837 (41.7%)	971–957 (7.1%) 938–830 (88.3%)

C-1b V	Stratum V Destruction Layer	2422	24408	Cereal Grains	GrN-27361 GrN-27362 GrN-27412	2764 ± 11 2777 ± 13 2785 ± 28	-22.11 -22.15 -22.43	2771 ± 8	969–961 (11.2%) 925–897 (55.7%) 872–870 (1.3%)	970–959 (12.7%) 935–894 (62.0%) 878–840 (20.7%)
C-1b V	Stratum V Destruction Layer Building G Southern room	2441	24579	Cereal Grains / Coarse Middle / Fine fraction	GrN-26116 GrN-26117 GrN-27363 GrN-27385 GrN-27386	2810 ± 20 2775 ± 25 2745 ± 15 2771 ± 15 2761 ± 15	-22.64 -23.14 -22.66 -22.31 -22.37	all 5 dates 2767 ± 7	967–962 (6.6%) 922–896 (52.1%) 874–864 (9.5%)	969–960 (8.7%) 930–893 (57.3%) 879–838 (29.4%)
C-1b or a V or IV	Destruction Layer Building G Middle room	2444	24647	Cereal Grains Fine fraction	GrN-27364 GrN-27413	2764 ± 11 2866 ± 21	-22.15 -22.04	2764 ± 11	966–963 (3.5%) 921–896 (42.0%) 876–860 (16.5%) 850–844 (6.3%)	969–960 (7.0%) 930–891 (49.3%) 881–836 (39.1%)
C-1b or a V or IV	Destruction Layer Building G Middle room	2425 Continuation of 2444	24306	Cereal Grains	GrN-26114 GrN-26115	2775 ± 20 2800 ± 20	-22.42 -21.45	2788 ± 14	971–959 (20.7%) 935–903 (47.5%)	998–981 (5.7%) 976–896 (86.9%) 876–860 (2.8%)
C-2 VI	Building A Below bowl above floor	4426	44166	Cereal Grains Fine Charcoal Fine Charcoal Fine Charcoal Bone	GrN-27366 GrA-21043 GrA-21054 GrA-21182 GrA-21417	2761 ± 14 2755 ± 35 2805 ± 35 2800 ± 50 2840 ± 45	-22.48 -25.50 -24.74 -24.68 -19.64	all 5 dates 2772 ± 11	969–960 (12.4%) 928–897 (52.2%) 873–868 (3.6%)	971–958 (14.0%) 936–893 (59.5%) 879–839 (21.9%)
D-2 V/VI	Refuse debris	1823	18183	Olive stones	GrN-26113 GrA-19030	2760 ± 30 2750 ± 50	-22.15 -23.29	2757 ± 26	919–893 (26.9%) 879–837 (41.3%)	971–957 (7.3%) 939–830 (88.1%)
D-2 V/VI	Refuse deposits	1802	18119	Olive stones	GrN-26112	2805 ± 15	-22.46	2805 ± 15	997–989 (8.5%) 974–954 (25.9%) 944–919 (33.8%)	999–913 (91.8%) 912–905 (3.6%)

Moreover, 30 additional Groningen dates from Tel Reḥov are presented in this paper (included in Tables 13.2 and 13.3). Therefore, the entire Groningen series of Tel Reḥov totals an impressive 64 radiocarbon dates, the largest lab series available for a single Iron Age site in the Levant (see also van der Plicht and Bruins [Chapter 14, this volume], for intercomparison and quality control assessment of the Groningen series; and Bruins *et al.* [Chapter 15, this volume], for Bayesian modelling of the Groningen Tel Reḥov dates through statistical stratigraphic analysis, with emphasis on the Iron Age IIA destruction events).

Virtually all organic samples used in the ^{14}C age determinations from Tel Reḥov (except the three mentioned in section [a] above) are short-lived and came generally from the best stratigraphic contexts available in each stratum, as explained in detail below.[4] Tables 13.2–4 provide details concerning all these dates.[5] There are 23 Groningen dates of Iron Age I strata (derived from 8 different loci) and 41 Groningen dates of Iron IIA strata (from 13 different loci). Moreover, published ^{14}C dates from other labs are also included in the tables and the text.[6]

The Iron Age I

The Iron Age I was explored at Tel Reḥov mainly in Area D (Figs. 13.4–5), where a step trench was excavated on the western slope of the lower city (Mazar 1999: 9-16). The first excavations resulted in a 5 m wide trench, which was subsequently widened to 10 m in certain parts. Eleven strata were determined in this section, numbered D-11 to D-1 (Table 13.1). Strata D-11 to D-8 belong to the Late Bronze Age, D-7 to D-3 to the Iron Age I and D-2 and D-1 to the Iron Age IIA. The latest three strata can be correlated with the stratigraphy in the adjacent Area C, as indicated in Table 13.1. The steep slope of the tell in this area limited the spatial exposure of each stratum to no more than about 20–40 m².

Stratum D-6. The underlying Stratum D-7 contained several walls and floors, while D-6 included only several floor surfaces but very little architecture. The pottery from both these strata is similar to that of Tel Beth Shean Level VI (University of Pennsylvania excavations) and Strata S-4 and S-3 (Hebrew University excavations; Mazar 1993, 2003a: 324, 333-37). Therefore, it is safe to date Stratum D-6 to the Iron Age IA,[7] parallel to the time of the Egyptian XXth Dynasty (most probably between the time of Ramesses III and Ramesses VI). It is noteworthy to mention that the small amount of pottery from D-6 included two sherds of imported Mycenaean IIIC ceramics.

Samples of charred olive stones from three loci of Stratum D-6 were dated, one locus at Rehovot and two at Groningen (both PGC and AMS techniques). The results are as follows:

Locus 1876. Accumulation of floor surfaces (striations) in Square P4. The surfaces were between levels 82.19–82.93 m; the particular sample came from level 82.77 m. Dated at Rehovot (RT-3119) to 2685 ± 40 BP, which is 243 BP years younger than the average of two Groningen dates presented below. The calibrated age of the Rehovot date lies in the 9th century BCE. This is much too young by all standards, as already stated in the initial publication (Mazar and Carmi 2001: 1336), and the above date is consequently rejected.

---

4.   Finkelstein and Piaszetky (2003a, 2003b) criticize some of our contexts as unreliable. We reject this criticism, and explain the nature of each context in some detail in the following paragraphs.

5.   Much of the data and following discussion, mainly concerning the Iron Age I, appears also in Bruins, Mazar and van der Plicht (in press).

6.   The tables don't include three dates of charred beams published previously by Mazar and Carmi 2001: 1337, Table 5.

7.   We use here the term Iron IA for the period of the Egyptian 20th Dynasty, following the terminology in Stern (ed.) 1993. It is worth pointing out that some Israeli scholars include this period in the Late Bronze Age (Ussishkin 1985; Gilboa and Sharon 2003).

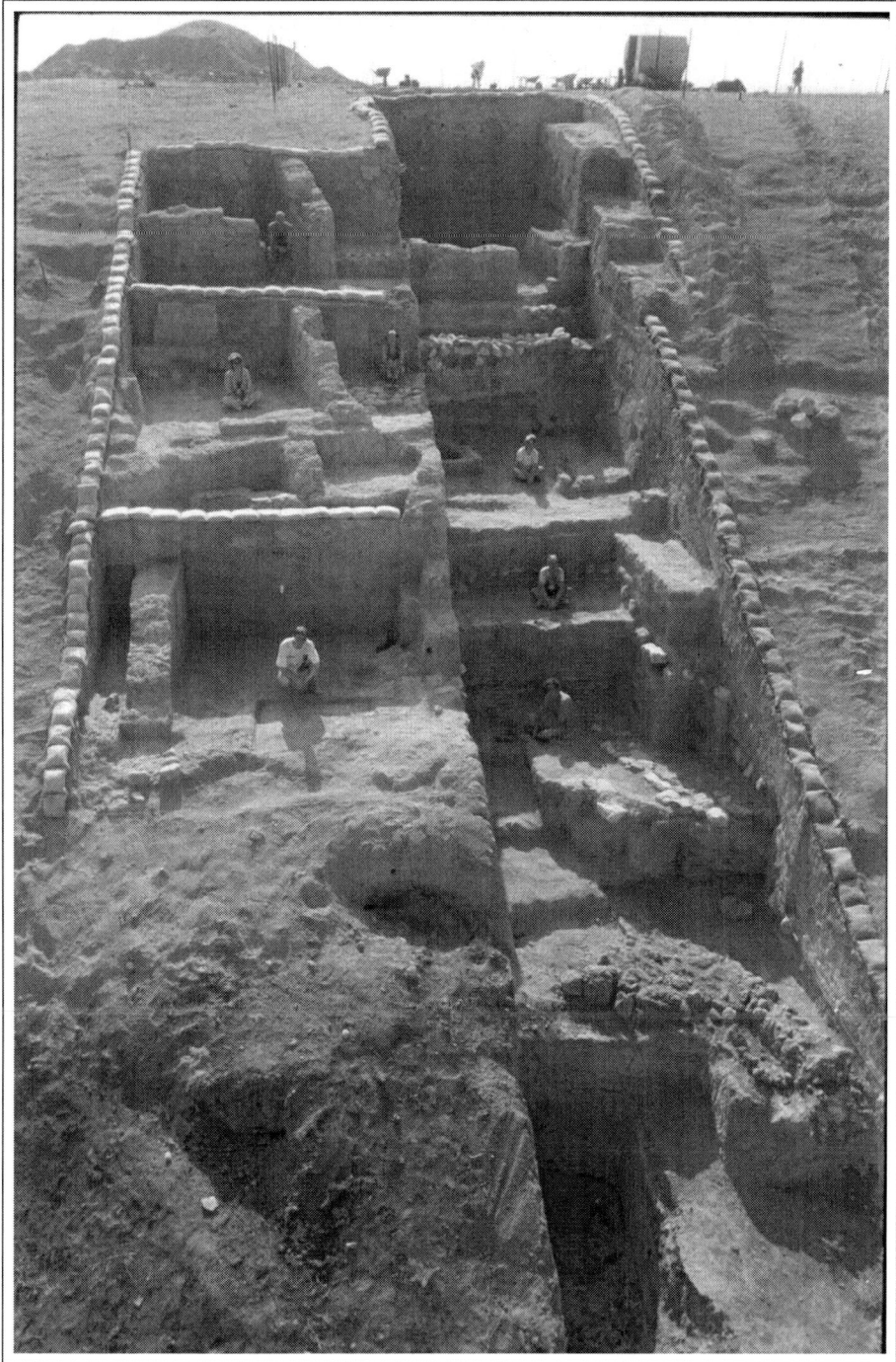

Figure 13.4. Area D: general view (looking east).

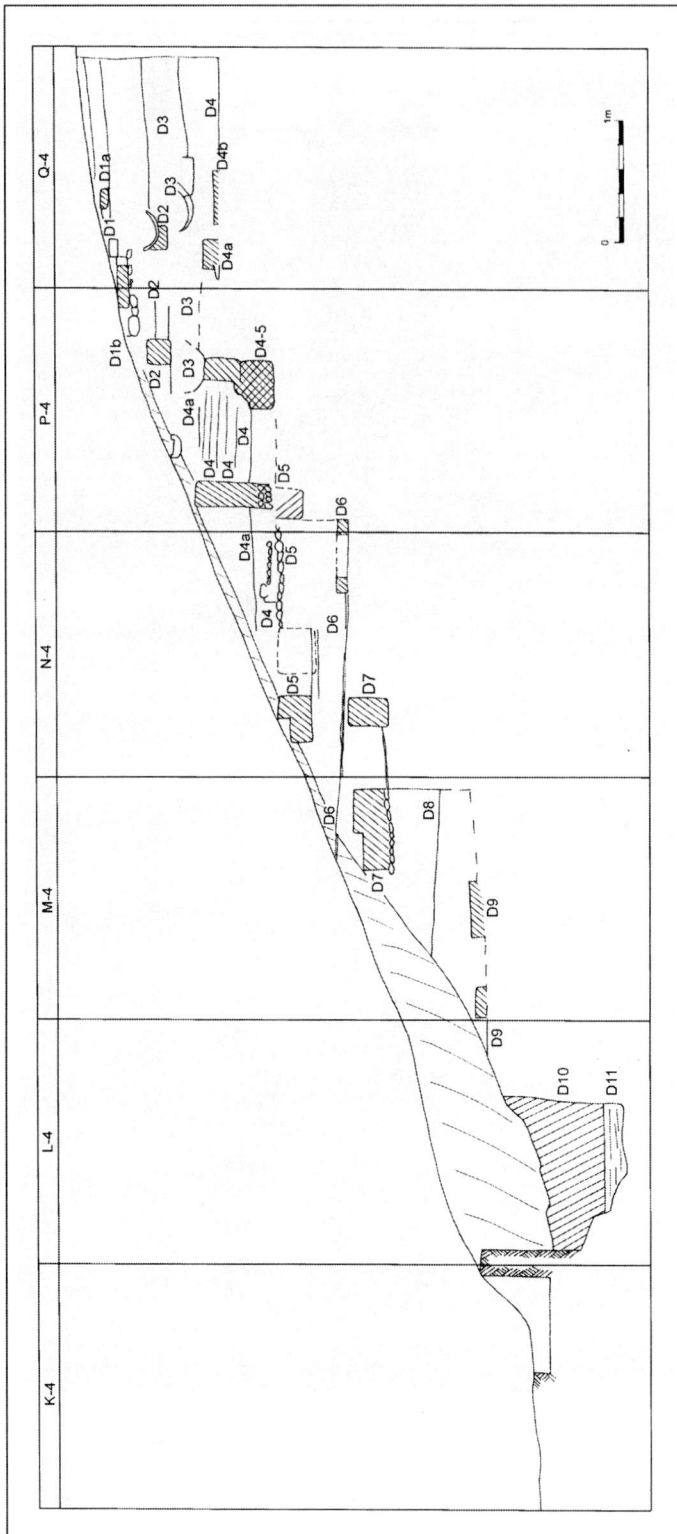

Figure 13.5. Area D: schematic section.

Locus 2874. A plastered basin sunk from a floor in Square P4 (level 83.00 m) was sealed by brick debris. The Groningen dates are 2935 ± 45 BP (GrA-19034) and 2880 ± 30 BP (GrN-26120), measured by AMS and PGC, respectively (Table 13.2). The results are within 1σ (one standard deviation) from each other and therefore acceptable. The weighted average has a smaller standard deviation: 2897 ± 25 BP.

Locus 2836. A layer of occupation debris and floor surface that includes organic deposits and ash patches in Square N4. The AMS date, 2950 ± 50 BP (GrA-18826), and the PGC date, 2920 ± 30 BP (GrN-26118), are within 1σ from each other. The average date is 2928 ± 26 yr BP.

The calibration curve (Fig. 13.6) remains at a rather similar level, albeit with many wiggles, for much of the 13th to 11th centuries BCE (radiocarbon year period of about 3020–2880 BP). Therefore, the calibration of individual loci will inevitably result in wide age ranges. More precise ^{14}C calibration is usually not feasible in a single layer approach, but stratified archaeological wiggle matching (Bruins, van der Plicht and Mazar 2003a) and Bayesian modelling (Bruins *et al.* [Chapter 15, this volume]) does select a narrower calibrated time range. The undifferentiated 2σ calibrated range for the average date of Locus 2874 is 1210–1000 BCE while the more coherent average BP date of Locus 2836 yields a 1σ calibrated age of 1209–1050 BCE (Fig. 13.6) in which the period 1159–1108 BCE has the highest relative probability of 25.1%. This result fits nicely with the available archaeological–historical age criteria, based on comparisons with Tel Beth Shean and Egyptian chronology, suggesting a date in the 12th century BCE with emphasis on the second half of this century.

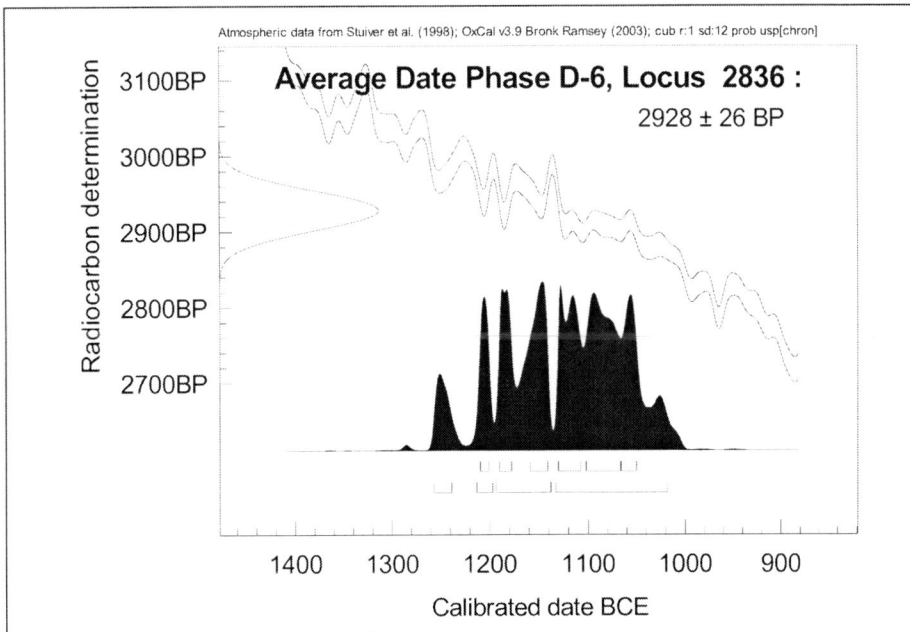

Figure 13.6. Stratum D-6, Locus 2836. Calibration of the weighted average Groningen date (2928 ± 26 BP), resulting in a 1σ age range of 1209–1050 BCE, in which the period 1159–1108 has the highest relative probability of 25.1%.

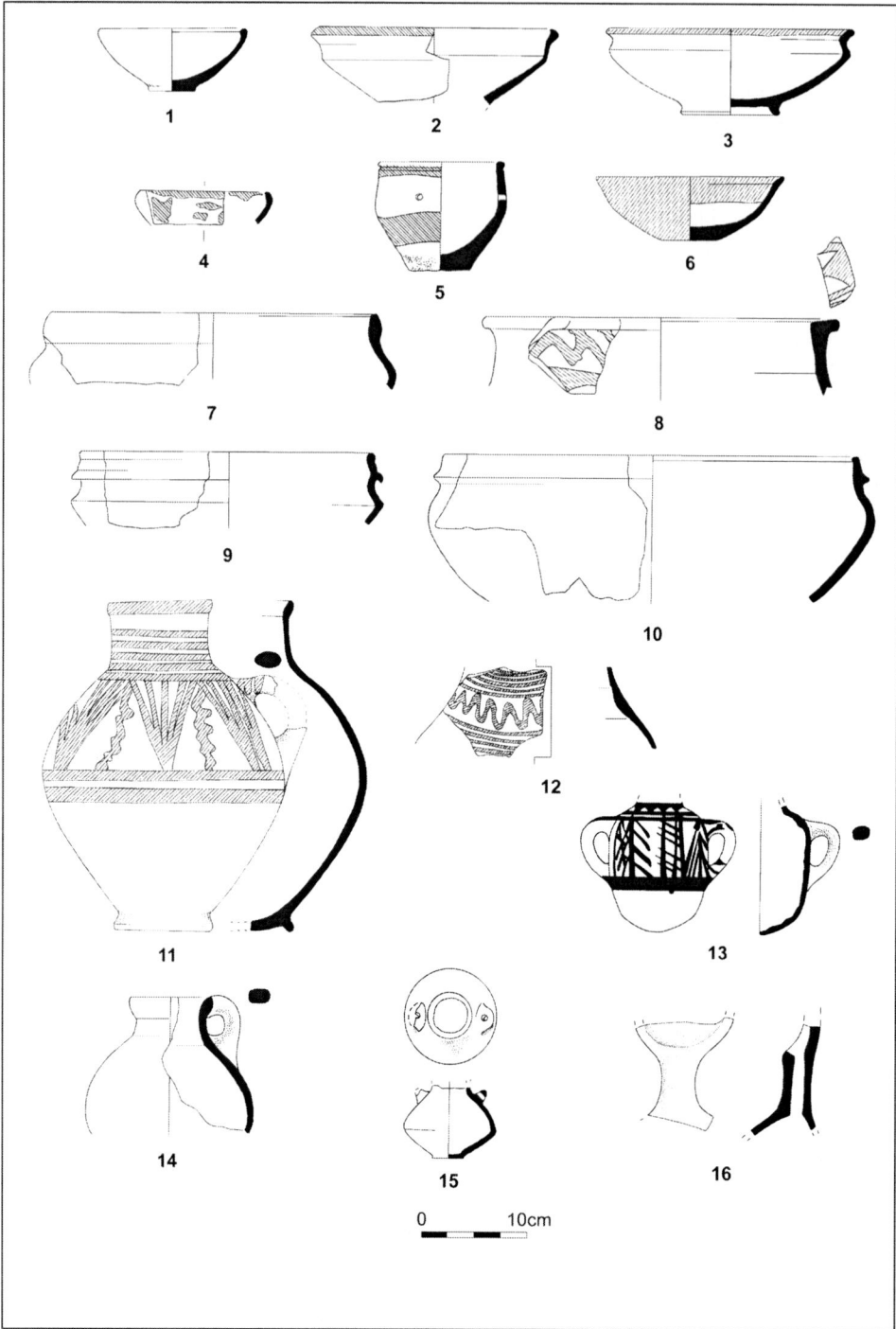

Figure 13.7. Area D: selected pottery from Stratum D-4.

*Strata D-5 and D-4.*Going up in the stratigraphy, Strata D-5 and D-4 constitute two distinct architectural periods. Both relate in spatial–urban terms to a north–south oriented street that is flanked by buildings on both sides. The occupation debris of D-5, which is sealed by that of D-4, has hardly been excavated. However, a substantial area of Stratum D-4 was exposed, yielding a well-defined Iron Age IB pottery assemblage (Fig. 13.7 presents the main pottery types represented in this assemblage). Pottery vessels are often painted in red, but in this pottery assemblage red slip is very rare and burnish does not appear at all. Floor surfaces of Stratum D-4 were excavated in the street as well as in a courtyard paved with cobble stones. The original floor surfaces in both cases were raised from time to time during the lifespan of this city, resulting in a succession of striated floor surfaces, some of which could be dated by ^{14}C.

Locus 1845 (Phase D-4b). A cluster of charred seeds found on the Stratum D-4b cobble floor of the courtyard, below thick accumulation of occupation striations.[8] The seeds were dated by both the Rehovot and Groningen labs. The Rehovot date (RT-3121) is 2800 ± 40 BP and the calibrated age lies in the 10th century BCE, which would fit the 'low chronology' (Mazar and Carmi 2001: 1336, Table 3). The three AMS dates from Groningen are older than the Rehovot date by more than a century: 2905 ± 35 (GrA-21046), 2945 ± 35 (GrA-21057) and 2920 ± 50 BP (GrA-21184). The Groningen results are close to each other, mostly within 1σ, indicating high-quality dates with robust repeatability (Scott [ed.] 2003). The weighted average for these dates is 2924 ± 22 yr BP, while the chi-squared test (Bronk Ramsey 2003) underlines the high degree of coherence of the three AMS dates, T = 0.7, which is very low compared to the 5% confidence limit of 6.0, above which T should not rise. The calibrated 1σ age range is 1208–1050 BCE.

Locus 1836 (Phase D-4a). Locus 1836 marks a series of striated floor surfaces accumulated above cobble floor 1845. A cluster of charred olive stones was found at the bottom of this accumulation, close to cobble floor 1845 (level 84.18 m). The two Groningen dates, measured by both PGC and AMS, gave very similar results: 2890 ± 30 yr BP (GrN-26121) and 2870 ± 50 yr BP (GrA-18825), respectively (Table 13.2). The chi-squared test shows the high level of coherence between the dates: T = 0.1, which is well below 3.8, the 5% confidence level (Fig. 13.8). The weighted average is 2885 ± 26 yr BP, being 39 radiocarbon years younger than the average of the sample found on cobble floor 1845, which neatly fits the stratigraphy. This difference in the BP dates may reflect the time that passed between the accumulation of these respective floor surfaces. The calibrated 1σ date of Locus 1836 (Fig. 13.8) is 1124–1120 (2.8%), 1112–1098 (9.9%), 1086–1060 (17.7%) and 1053–1005 (37.8%) BCE.

Taking the stratigraphic sequence into consideration, a date in the 11th century BCE for Stratum D-4 is most likely. The lowest floor (1845) may be dated to the early or mid-11th century and the striations on top of it (Locus 1836) were accumulated during the second half of the 11th century. Indeed the highest relative probability (37.8%) of the 1σ calibrated age range of the higher floor surfaces in Stratum D-4 (Locus 1836) is the period 1053–1005 BCE (Fig. 13.8). The Groningen dates for both D-4 loci support the conventional archaeological age for Iron IB period, to which this stratum belongs in terms of pottery typology (see Fig. 13.7). The single Rehovot date is much younger than all five Groningen dates of D-4.

---

8. Basket 28243 came from squares N-P-4 at level 83.80 m; basket 48556 came from Square N5 at level 84.05 m.

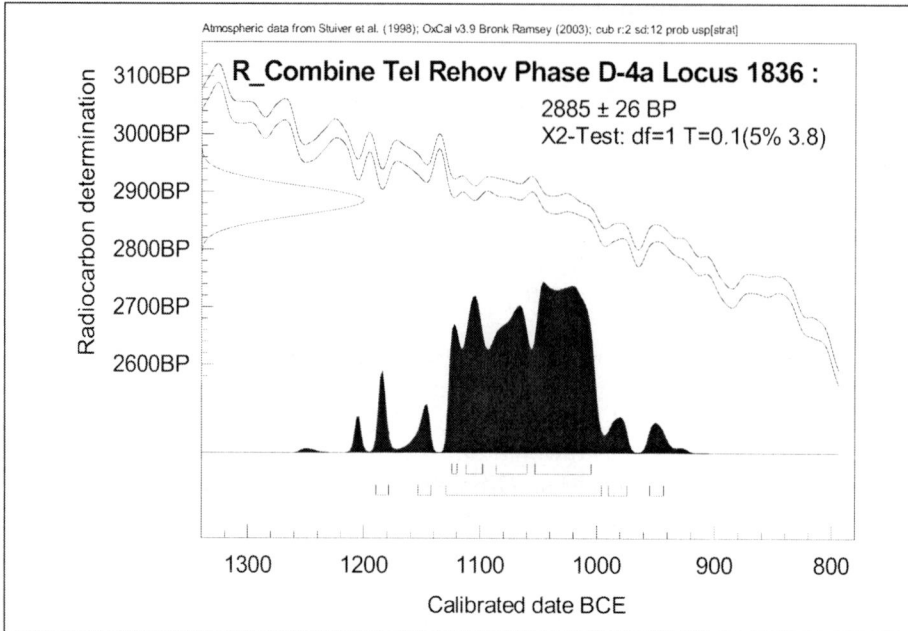

Figure 13.8. Stratum D-4a, Locus 1836. Calibration of the weighted average Groningen date (2928 ± 26 BP), resulting in a 1σ age range of 1124–1005 BCE, in which the period 1053–1005 has the highest relative probability of 37.8%.

Stratum D-3. More than 30 small and shallow pits concentrated in an accumulation layer less than one meter thick make up Stratum D-3. Some of the pits penetrated the underlying destruction debris of Stratum D-4 and some cut each other. Thus, the activity represented by these pits might have lasted quite some time. Some of the pits were covered with thin white plaster while others were not. The function of these pits remains obscure; it seems that they were used for storage or refuse, with the former option appearing more reasonable. The small amount of pottery sherds found in the pits are of similar types as the pottery from Stratum D-4 (Fig. 13.9 presents a selection of the main types). The pits were sealed by a thick layer of debris (Locus 1802, Stratum D-2) containing Iron IIA pottery.

Ten ^{14}C dates of charred olive stones from five different pits are available (Table 13.2). The olive stones were always found together in clusters inside the pits. Thus, their stratigraphic context should be considered reliable.

Pit 4830. A shallow, unplastered and ill-defined pit in Square Q-4. The concentration of olive pits found here at level 85.15 m could also belong to an occupation layer between the pits. In any event, this locus is above the uppermost brick debris of Stratum D-4, and is cut by Pit or Bin 2872, attributed to Stratum D-3 or D-2. Seven AMS dates were measured at Groningen, in two sets. The triplicate results of the first AMS series are as follows: 2845 ± 35 BP (GrA-21044), 2825 ± 35 BP (GrA-21056) and 2820 ± 50 BP (GrA-21183). These results are very close, within 1σ from each other. The chi-squared test underscores the high quality of this first series of three AMS measurements, as T = 0.2, which is very small compared to the 5% confidence limit of 6.0. The weighted average date is 2832 ± 22 BP.

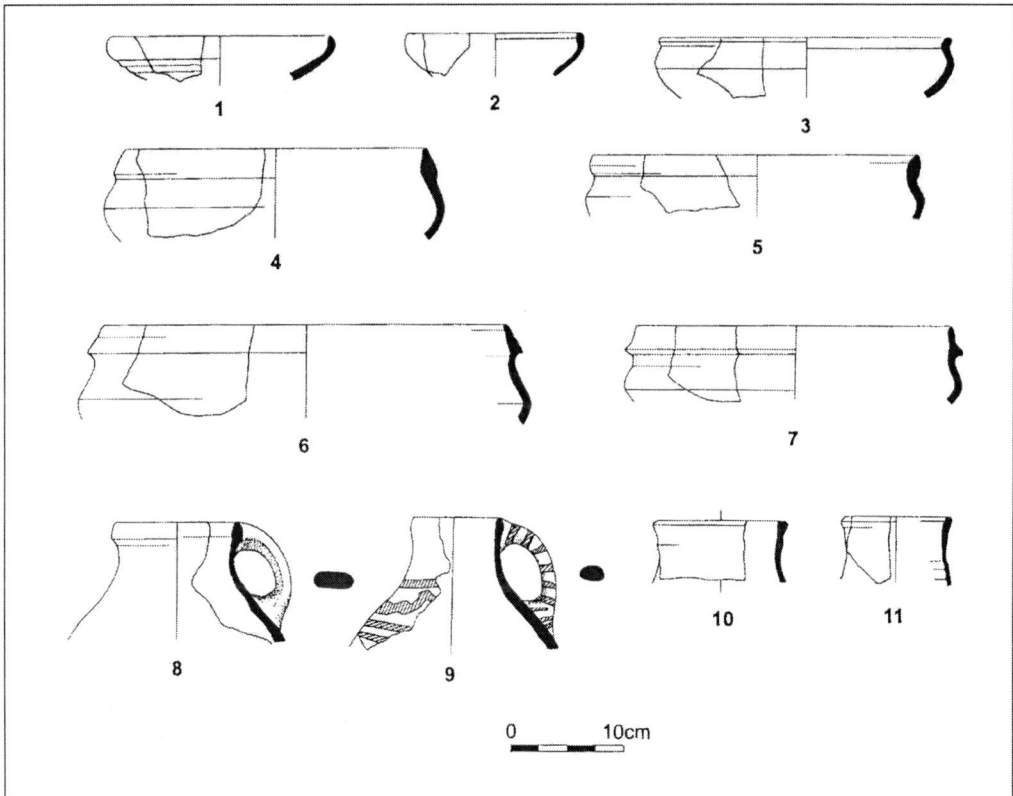

Figure 13.9. Area D: selected pottery from Stratum D-3.

The calibrated age (Fig. 13.10) gives two possible options in the 1σ range: 1004–970 (40.0%) and 959–934 (28.2%) BCE. The first period (1004–970 BCE) has the highest relative probability. Notice that the date is too old for the 975–955 BCE wiggle, which is excluded in the 1σ range (Fig. 13.10). The latter wiggle fits very well with Stratum VI of Area C (presented below). Since Stratum VI overlies Stratum VII, which can be equated with Stratum D-3 in ceramic terms, the period 1004–970 BCE is also preferable in sequential stratigraphic terms.

The second set of four measurements resulted in two dates similar to the first series, 2820 ± 40 BP (GrA-22302b), 2810 ± 50 BP (GrA-22329a), and two younger dates, 2730 ± 50 BP (GrA-22302a), 2760 ± 40 BP (GrA-22329b). The youngest and oldest dates of the two series are still within the 2σ overlap range. Hence, in physical–statistical terms all dates are acceptable. Here we are at the limit of measurement resolution and measurement variability inherent in radiocarbon dating (Mook and Waterbolk 1985: 10), discussed by van der Plicht and Bruins (Chapter 14, this volume). Taking the weighted average of all seven dates, 2807 ± 16 BP, the chi-squared test shows the lower coherence between the dates, as T = 5.3, but still well acceptable in comparison to the 5% confidence limit of 12.6. The calibrated age of 2807 ± 16 BP still favours the latter half of the 10th century BCE, but the younger range has only a slightly lower relative probability: 997–953 (34.9%), 945–920 (33.4%) BCE (Fig. 13.11).

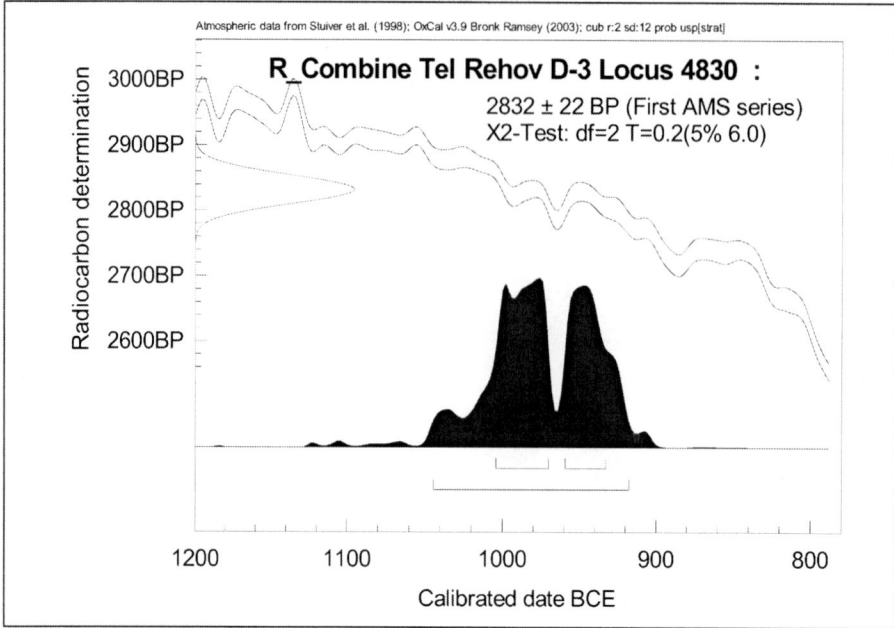

Figure 13.10. Stratum D-3, Locus 4830. Calibration of the weighted average Groningen date (2832 ± 22 BP) of the first AMS series (3 dates). The period 1000–970 BCE has the highest relative probability of 40.0%. Notice that the date is too old for the 975–955 BCE wiggle, which is excluded in the 1σ range. The latter wiggle fits very well with Stratum VI of Area C, overlying Stratum VII which is similar in terms of ceramics to Stratum D-3.

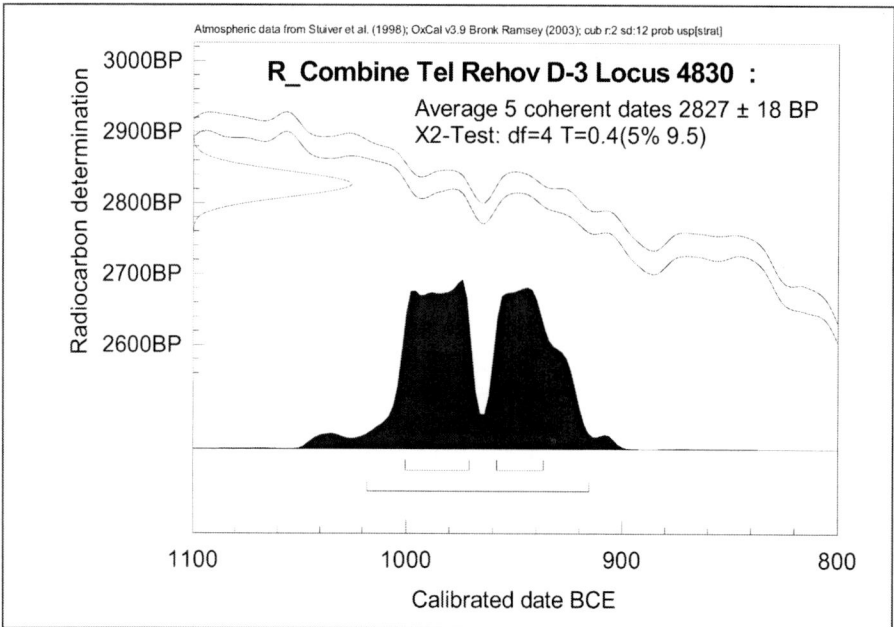

Figure 13.11. Stratum D-3, Locus 4830. Calibration of the weighted average Groningen date (2827 ± 18 BP) of 5 coherent AMS dates of two series. Notice again the exclusion of the 975–955 wiggle.

It is clear that the difference of 115 midpoint BP years between the oldest date 2845 ± 35 BP (GrA-21044) and the youngest date 2730 ± 50 (GrA-22302a) is quite large. The repeatability of the second series is clearly inferior to that of the coherent first series. Since two dates of the second series are similar to the results of the first series, we have altogether five coherent dates. The two young dates are outliers, not in the classical sense as they are within the 2σ overlap range, but in comparative terms. If one only takes the consistent five dates of Locus 4830, the weighted average becomes 2827 ± 18 BP, while the chi-squared test shows an excellent coherence, T = 0.4, which is very low in comparison to the 5% confidence limit of 9.5. The calibrated date of 2827 ± 18 BP is 1001–971 (39.9%) and 958–937 (28.3%) BCE, again favouring the oldest three decades of the 10th century BCE, while the wiggle of 971–958 BCE (fitting Stratum VI) is excluded in the 1σ range. In conclusion, the most probable date of Stratum D-3 Locus 4830, both in terms of calibration and sequential stratigraphy, is the period 1000–970 BCE.

Pit 4816. This is a plastered pit cut into mudbrick wall 4859 of Phase D-4. The olive stones were found between two plastered surfaces in the pit, at level 85.40 m. The amount of material was small, even for AMS, resulting in a date with a somewhat larger standard deviation (2870 ± 70 BP [GrA-12889]). The 1σ calibrated range is 1188–1181 (2.1%), 1150–1144 (1.6%), 1128–970 (55.2%), 960–928 (9.3%) BCE. Fine charcoal from the same layer was dated separately, also by AMS, giving a date of 2895 ± 40 BP (GrA-16848). The results are close to each other, within 1σ, while the charcoal is slightly older than the olive pit fragments, as might be expected. The calibrated results favour the 11th and 10th centuries BCE.

Pit 4815. This is a large and deeply cut pit, with many layers of debris. A cluster of 15 charred olive stones was found at levels 85.15–85.30 m. A single Groningen measurement gave a date of 2820 ± 50 BP (GrA-16757), which is identical to one of the dates from Pit 4830. The relatively large standard deviation of 50 BP years results in a rather wide 1σ calibrated age range: 1042–1031 (3.8%), 1022–901 (64.4%) BCE. A date from 1000–950 BCE has the highest relative probability, being the principal area of intersection of the mid-point of the BP date with the calibration curve, resulting in the highest peaks.

Pit 2862. This is a shallow plastered pit. Olive stones were found at level 85.70 m. An AMS measurement from Groningen gave a date of 2835 ± 45 BP (GrA-19033), which is very similar to the dating results for Pit 4815 and Pit 4830 (Fig. 13.12). However, a PGC date from Groningen of the same material is much younger, 2720 ± 30 BP (GrN-26119). This is a rare outlier with a difference of about 4σ, which is too much. The reason for the discrepancy is due to the small amount of material, which was too little for normal PGC measurement, as presented in detail by van der Plicht and Bruins (Chapter 14, this volume).

A sample from the same organic material from Pit 2862 was more recently measured at Rehovot by AMS resulting in a date of 2800 ± 20 BP (RTT 3805; average of three dates).[9] This result is only slightly younger than the above Groningen AMS date, remaining within the 2σ range and therefore similar in physical–mathematical terms. The Groningen date has a calibrated 1σ age range of 1046–920 (68.2%) BCE and the Rehovot–Tucson date covers the entire 10th century BCE.

9.   This result was obtained by E. Boaretto (Weizmann Institute of Science), A. Gilboa (Haifa University) and I. Sharon (Hebrew University) as part of a research project on 'A New, ^{14}C-Based, Chronology for the Early Phoenician Iron Age—Implications for the Regional and Supra-Regional Spheres' supported by the Israel Science Foundation of the Israel Academy of Sciences and Humanities (grant no. 778/00).

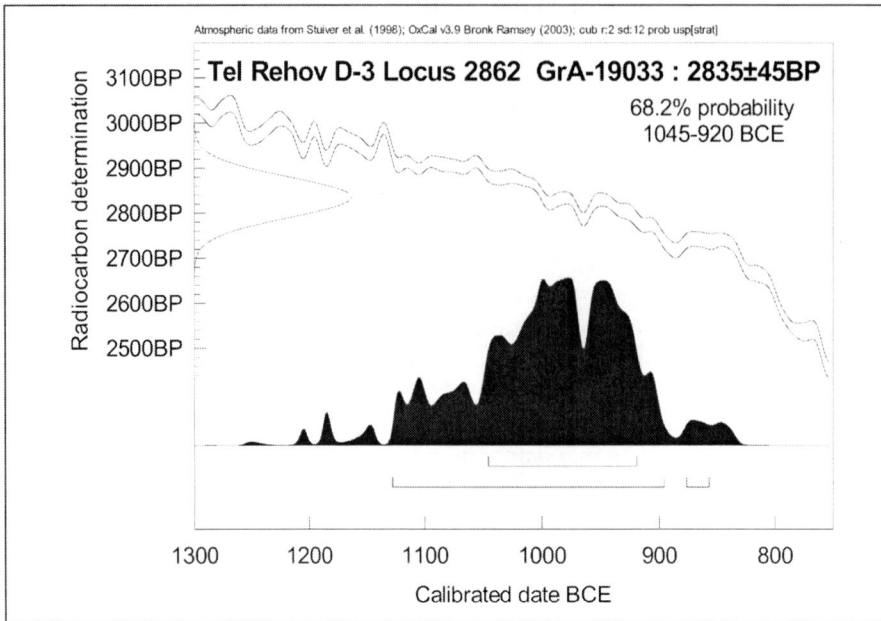

Figure 13.12. Stratum D-3, Locus 2862. Calibration of a single AMS date with a typical standard deviation of 45 years, which results in a rather wide time range. The 11th and 10th centuries BCE are most probable in the 2σ range. The graph shows that the central part of the 1σ range, the first 30 years of the 10th century BCE, has the highest relative probability. Notice the substantial drop in probability in relation to the 975–955 BCE wiggle.

Pit 1858. This is one of the largest and well-defined pits in this stratum. A single measurement of olive stones at Rehovot during the 1990s provided a low date of 2670 ± 40 (RT-3120), resulting in a calibrated age range in the 9th century BCE (Mazar and Carmi 2001: 1336; see also Table 13.2 in the present paper). This low date stands in contrast to the other dates from the Stratum D-3 pits and should be rejected.

In conclusion, the calibrated dates from Stratum D-3 loci provide a wide range of possibilities in the 11th and 10th centuries BCE. The youngest average coherent dates in the series have their highest calibrated relative probability in the first three decades of the 10th century (1000–970 BCE), which supports the suggestion by Mazar (above p. 210, this volume) to place the boundary for the transition from Iron I to Iron IIA at about 980 BCE.

The Iron Age IIA

The excavation of Iron Age IIA strata at Areas B, C, D, E, F and G at Tel Rehov has yielded a vast amount of data concerning this period. Separate stratigraphic phases were counted in each of these excavation areas, and the correlation of these local phases into a comprehensive stratigraphic frame is not easy due to the complex development of the city during this time. The three general strata numbers VI, V and IV (Tables 13.1 and 13.3) are terms used to describe three major stratigraphic phases detected in most of the excavation areas. Yet the local stratigraphy in each excavation area or part of an area is sometimes more complex; in certain places there were more than three Iron IIA phases, and in others less than three. Thus, the correlation between the different areas is complex and should be taken as tentative. Radiocarbon dates from this period are available from Area C, D, B and E.

Radiocarbon Dating in the 10th and 9th Centuries BCE: Introduction to Problems and Solutions

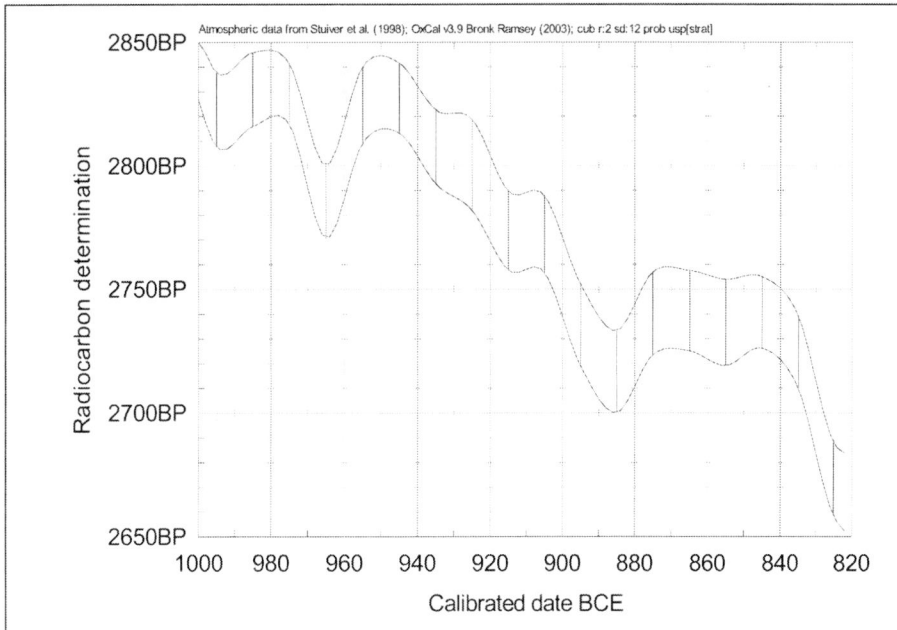

Figure 13.13. Detailed shape of the calibration curve, linking the historical period 1000–820 BCE on the x-axis, covering the Iron Age IIA period, with the corresponding radiocarbon BP time-scale on the y-axis.

The detailed calibration curve covering the Iron Age IIA period (Fig. 13.13) shows a fundamental problem for radiocarbon dating in the 10th and 9th centuries BCE. Radiocarbon dates in the range of about 2770–2750 BP, with a standard deviation (σ) of 20 or higher, can be related to three different historical periods (975–955, 930–890 and 880–835 BCE). This means that short-lived organic samples (charred seeds) from these three historical periods will have similar radiocarbon BP dates. It is clear that arranging radiocarbon dates only according to their BP dates in terms of older or younger (Finkelstein and Piasetzky 2003c) does not work in such cases. Indeed, the paradox is that the comparatively *older* part of the 10th century BCE, 975–955 BCE, has *younger* radiocarbon BP dates than the period 955–935 BCE. How then can one decide whether a radiocarbon date in the range of 2770–2750 BP belongs to the early–middle 10th century, late 10th century or middle 9th century BCE? One possible solution is to lower the standard deviation (σ, or sigma value). This can be accomplished in Groningen by high-precision radiometry (PGC), which can give a standard deviation as low as about 12 BP years, provided the sample is sufficiently large (>10 grams of C). A σ of about 12 BP years is the absolute lower limit on single measurements, due to the σ of the oxalic acid standard. However, multiple measurements of the same sample material, including AMS on small samples, may enable the calculation of a weighted average that can result in very low standard deviations, below 10. For example, five Groningen PGC dates were obtained from charred cereal grains within a secure destruction layer of Iron Age IIA Stratum V (Locus 2441), which resulted in a weighted average of 2767 ± 7 BP (Fig. 13.29). The BP date in the above example is in the problematic range of 2750–2770, as outlined above, usually having three possible historical dates (975–955, 930–890 or 880–835 BCE). Looking at Figure 13.29

shows that the 2767 ± 7 BP date, because of its small σ, is largely below the 975–955 BCE wiggle and above the 880–835 BCE plateau, while it hits the calibration curve in the historical range of 922–896 BCE, which has by far the highest relative probability of 52.1% out of 68.2% in the 1σ range.

The additional advantage in the latter case is that the average date is likely to be more accurate as well. Single ^{14}C measurements may be some time distance away from the actual date, as indicated by the standard deviation (Mook and Waterbolk 1985: 10). Multiple measurements of the same sample are likely to result in an average date with a higher precision (smaller σ) and also a higher accuracy, in other words, closer to the real age (van der Plicht and Bruins 2001), provided the radiocarbon lab does not have a systematic bias towards older or younger dates. Indeed, laboratory quality becomes of paramount importance in our use of radiocarbon dating, pushing the method to its very limit of resolution. Systematic dating errors do sometimes occur, as happened in the radiocarbon laboratory of the British Museum during 1980–84 (Bowman, Ambers and Leese 1990), when dates were systematically too young.

The ^{14}C results of a number of Iron IIA Stratum V destruction dates measured in Groningen are unambiguous with regard to their position on the calibration curve and provide the pivotal anchor of radiocarbon dating at Tel Reḥov (Bruins *et al.* [Chapter 15, this volume]; Bruins, van der Plicht and Mazar 2003a; Finkelstein and Piasetzky 2003a). Based on the secure dates for the Stratum V destruction, radiocarbon results from other strata can now be placed on the calibration curve in successive stratigraphic order (Fig. 13.45) by logical deduction (Bruins, van der Plicht and Mazar 2003a) or by Bayesian statistics (Bruins *et al.* [Chapter 15, this volume]), if the stratigraphic order is clear.

Area D: Radiocarbon Dates from Iron IIA Refuse Debris

The uppermost layers in Area D (Strata D-1 and D-2) consist of thick refuse debris (Loci 1802 and 1823) which must be earlier than Stratum IV (Local Stratum C-1a) in the adjacent Area C since structures of this city were found in a higher level. The refuse debris could be related to either or both Strata VI and V in the adjacent Area C (local Strata C-1b and C-2), on the basis of relative levels, though there is no direct stratigraphic contact with these strata. Stratum D-2 contains homogeneous Iron IIA pottery, including a unique red-slipped juglet and a globular jug painted with red concentric circles. This layer, which accumulated above the pits of Phase D-3, was probably dumped from the nearby buildings in Area C (Strata VI and V). Two clusters of charred olive stones from Stratum D-2 were dated.

The sample Stratum D-2, Square P4, Locus 1802, Basket 18119, level 86.11 m is from a layer of occupation debris south of Wall 1820; it included a one meter thick accumulation (87.19–86.10 m) close to the slope of the mound. A cluster of charred olive stones was found in the lowest level of this layer. The sample of olive stones was large enough for PGC radiometry in Groningen, resulting in a high-precision date with a low standard deviation: 2805 ± 15 BP (GrN-26112). The calibration of this date gives an age exclusively situated in the 10th century BCE (Fig. 13.14). The 1σ range is 997–989 (8.5%), 974–954 (25.9%), 944–919 (33.8%) BCE and the 2σ range is 999–913 (91.8%) and 912–905 (3.6%) BCE. The actual date for Locus 1802 from these possible options could be either older or younger than the 975–955 BCE wiggle on the calibration curve.

The second cluster of charred olive seeds (Stratum D-2, Square P4, Locus 1823, Basket 18183, level 86.07 m) is from 90 cm thick refuse debris (levels 86.35–85.67 m), partly below Locus 1802. The sample was dated in Groningen by both PGC and AMS. The results are almost identical: 2760 ± 30 BP (GrN-26113) and 2750 ± 50 BP (GrA-19030). The weighted average date is 2757 ± 26 BP, while the chi-squared test confirms the extremely high coherence, as T = 0, whilst the 5% confidence limit is 3.8. The 1σ calibrated age is 919–893 (26.9%), 879–837 (41.3%) BCE and the

2σ age is 971–957 (7.3%), 939–830 (88.1%) BCE. The ^{14}C dates for Locus 1823 are precisely in the problematic range of 2770–2750 BP (Fig. 13.13), similar to some of the dates for Strata VI, V and IV in Area C (see next section). The standard deviation of the above average is still 26 yr BP, which makes the date rather wide: 2783–2731 BP in the 1σ range. Both the 10th and the 9th centuries BCE are possible calibration options. Hence, it is difficult to correlate these refuse layers on the basis of the ^{14}C dates with Strata VI, V or IV, as very small changes in the BP date may shift the ^{14}C correlation to either Stratum. Here we have reached intrinsic limitations of both field archaeology and radiocarbon dating.

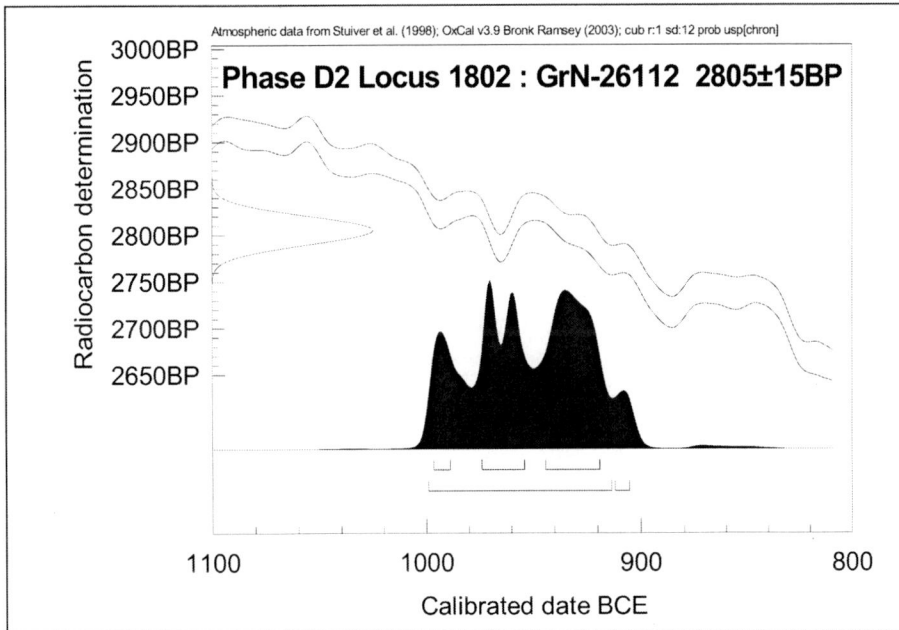

Figure 13.14. Stratum D-2, Locus 1802. Calibration of the high-precision PGC date (2832 ± 22 BP) of a refuse layer with Iron IIA ceramics overlying Iron I Stratum D-3. The calibrated date is exclusively in the 10th century BCE.

Area C: The Iron IIA Stratigraphy, Architecture, Pottery Assemblages and Radiocarbon Dates

Area C is located at the north-western end of the lower city (Fig. 13.15). Here a total area of ca. 560 m^2 was exposed during five seasons of excavations. A maximum depth of 3.5 m was reached going from the soil surface to the lowest point of excavation. Four main strata were identified: denoted in local stratigraphic terms as Phases C1a, C1b, C2 and C3. These are correlated with the comprehensive stratigraphic terminology of Tel Reḥov as Strata IV–VII, mainly applied so far in Area C (see Table 13.1).

Stratum VII, the oldest layer in Area C, was reached only in a very limited section. This stratum corresponds to Stratum D-3 in Area D (latest Iron Age I phase). Strata VI–IV were widely exposed during the excavations. Following the final destruction of Stratum IV, the lower city was entirely abandoned. The excavation of Area C revealed material remains in a way as desired by every archaeologist: buildings destroyed with their entire contents intact. A particular advantage is provided by the existence of two consecutive destruction levels (Strata V and IV) in several places.

Hundreds of complete restorable vessels from these sealed contexts present us with a secure ceramic sequence. Charred seeds and olive stones from some of these very contexts provided a stratigraphic sequence of ^{14}C dates of great significance. The integration of this rich and comprehensive data constitutes a robust chronological framework, both in relative and absolute terms.

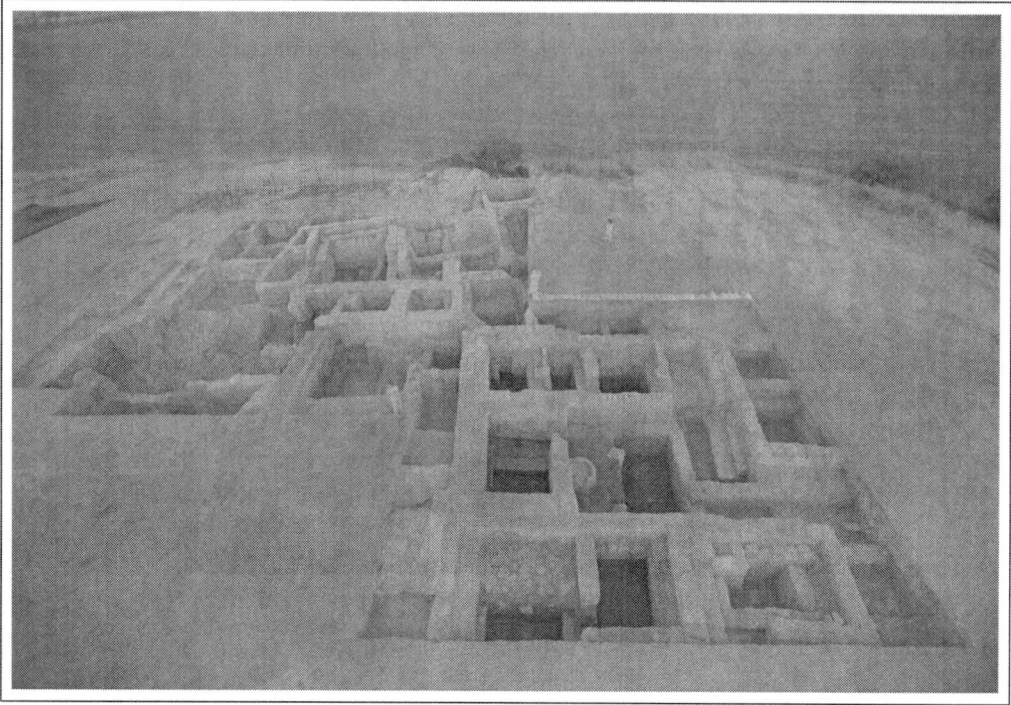

Figure 13.15. Area C: general view (looking west).

In the following, we present the stratigraphic contexts of the secure loci from which charred organic samples were collected for ^{14}C dating, along with their representative ceramic assemblages. It should be realised that the ceramics described here form only a part of the much wider typological repertoire from this period found at Tel Reḥov.

The nature of the architectural remains in Area C is consistent in all the three Strata VI–IV. Excavated buildings were solely composed of mudbricks without any use of stones even in their foundations. The town plan consists of densely built, intricate series of inter-related structures; many of these had shared walls, or were constructed as 'back to back' units. A feature typical of all Stratum V construction is the massive use of wooden beams in the foundations of the walls, as well as in the floor makeup (Mazar 1999: 21-22). No streets or alleyways were detected, though a few courts and open areas are known. It appears that the area excavated is part of a densely built and well planned urban block of buildings. The architecture, both in terms of construction technique, as well as in terms of planning, is virtually unique in comparison to known architecture of this period in other parts of the country.

The three consecutive Strata VI–IV show a great deal of continuity, as buildings were reconstructed along similar lines, while some elements were re-used with only minor renovations and floor raisings. It must be emphasized that the architectural history of the buildings in Area C is complex and entails repairs, restorations, additions and renovations alongside new constructions, so that it is not always possible to correlate these actions with the main strata. However, the stratigraphic picture is clear in those contexts that were terminated by a violent destruction. The contexts that underwent multiple renovations are somewhat less definitive.

Stratum VI (Fig. 13.16). The remains of Stratum VI in Area C include at least four main units—Building A, at the north-western part of the area; Building B, south of Building A, with a large rectangular room and entrances leading to additional parts of the building to the east and north; part of Building C in the south of the area; and a large building only partly exposed under Buildings E and F of Stratum V–IV at the north-eastern extension of Area C. Only Building A and its ceramic finds will be presented below, as ^{14}C dates are available only from this structure.

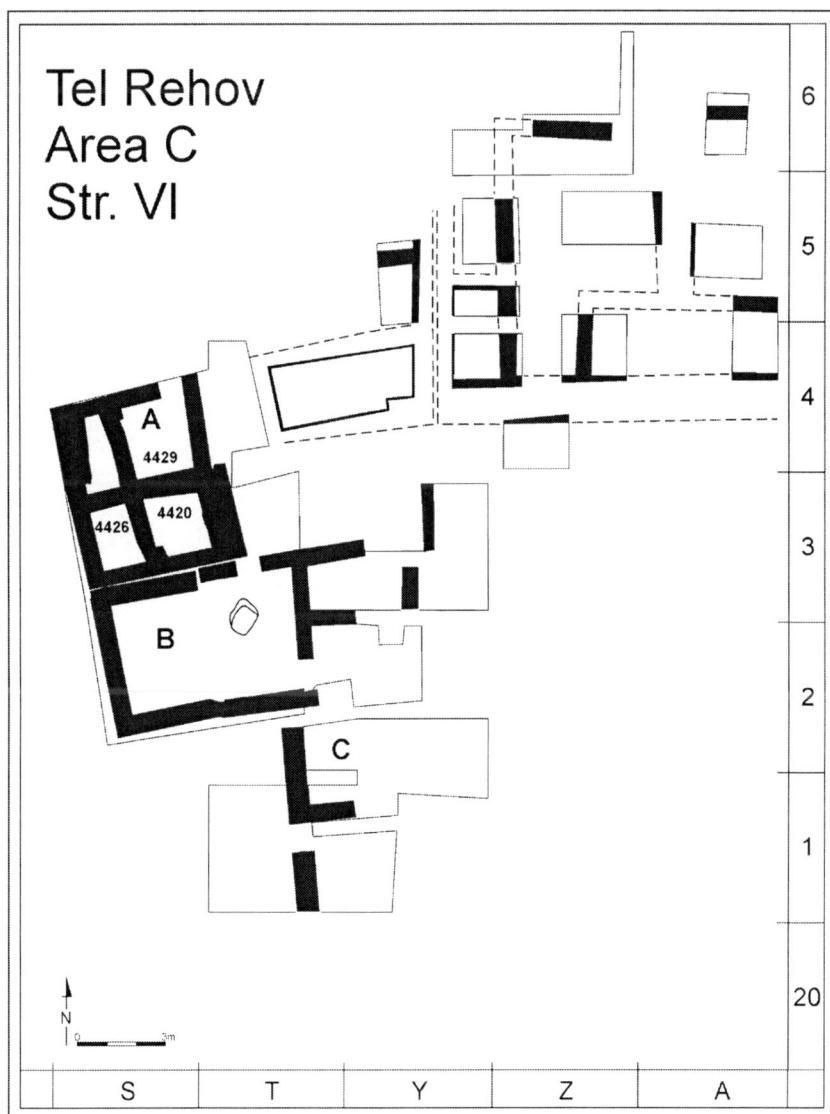

Figure 13.16. Area C: plan of Stratum VI—Buildings A and B.

Building A measures ca. 5 m × 6 m. It consists of an entrance in its north-eastern corner, which led into a square room (Locus 4429). To the south of this room was a slightly smaller room (Locus 4420); a wide wall separates these two eastern rooms from two small, narrow chambers on the west, which possibly functioned as storage cells. The stratigraphic attribution of this building to Stratum VI is based on several considerations: the walls were built of hard yellow bricks, typical of Stratum VI; the western wall was constructed above a wall of Stratum VII. The poor preservation of the walls, showing signs of brick slippage and cracks, indicate that the building might have been damaged by an earthquake. Prior to its reconstruction and renovation during Stratum V (designated Building D), the building was levelled off and filled in. A clear line of 'repair' can be seen, levelling the uneven tops of the walls, above which are the rebuilt walls of Building D (Fig. 13.17).

Figure 13.17. Repair line in Building A (looking south).

The finds in the building were scanty and it seems that it was abandoned with its contexts removed. The pottery recovered included one complete and one almost complete vessel (Fig. 13.18:4, 13) and a variety of sherds, a large proportion of which were red-slipped and burnished, while several were painted in red. Additional finds in this building are bones, flints, grindstones, as well as a seal, a bead and a faience pendant.

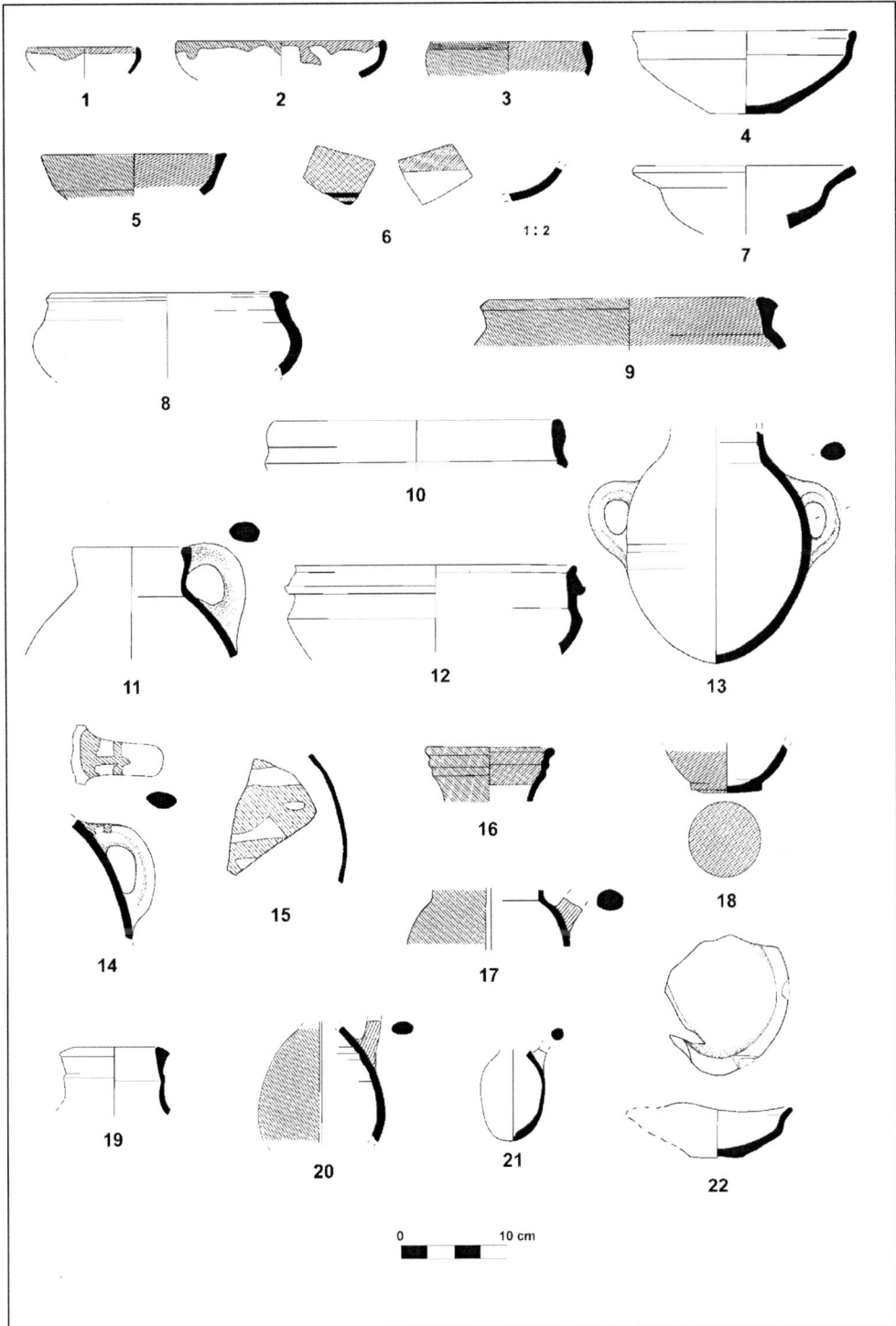

Figure 13.18. Pottery from Building A, Area C, Stratum VI.

The pottery from Building A (Fig. 13.18).

Bowls: Alongside a few hemispherical bowls (Fig. 13.18:1-3), the majority are carinated, with a soft, blunt carination usually just above mid-body, a plain or everted rim and a flat base (Fig. 13.18:4-5). This carinated bowl type continues into Strata V–IV. The bowls with red slip also bear hand burnish inside and outside. Several bowls have a red band on the rim interior and exterior, which drips down.

Chalices: One chalice has a wide everted rim and shallow softly carinated bowl (Fig. 13.18:7). This shape is typical of the numerous chalices uncovered throughout Area C in all three Iron Age IIA strata, though its rim is slightly longer.

Kraters: Two main krater types are represented in this building: a wide-necked krater with thickened rim (Fig. 13.18:8-9) and a krater with a short rounded vertical neck (Fig. 13.18:10), which on analogy to more complete examples (i.e. Fig. 13.23:8), has a body with a high rounded carination. Both types continue in Strata V–IV.

Amphoriskos: An almost complete amphoriskos (Fig. 13.18:13) is well made, but undecorated, though many vessels of this type at our site were red-slipped or painted in red. Such amphorae are found in Strata V–IV as well, though the later examples often had a rounder body.

Cooking pots: The cooking pot rims from this building are varied, some with straight exteriors and some with up-turning ends (Fig. 13.18:12). The cooking jugs mostly have slightly concave necks and slightly thickened inner rims (Fig. 13.18:11). The cooking pots and cooking jugs continue unchanged in Strata V–IV.

Closed vessels: It is impossible to determine whether the following sherds belong to amphoriskoi, storage jars or jugs: the main characteristic is the rather careless red painted design with mainly straight or wavy horizontal bands, as well as amorphic patterns (Fig. 13.18:14-15). Such sherds were quite common in Stratum VI, and continue to be found throughout Strata V–IV.

Jugs: The most typical jug is a narrow neck with a grooved rim exterior (Fig. 13.18:16); some are wider, with a ridge at mid-neck (Fig. 13.18:19). The body is mostly rounded with a short shoulder (Fig. 13.18:17), though a few are oval (Fig. 13.18:20). The base is always a disc base (Fig. 13.18:18). The jugs are almost all covered with a deep red slip and polished burnish, often with visible vertical burnish lines.

Juglets: The juglets have short bodies with wide rounded bases and sloping shoulders (Fig. 13.18:21). Many had red slip and vertical burnish.

Lamps: The only lamp found in Building A has an everted rim and a wide flat base (Fig. 13.18:22).

General: No storage jars were found in Building A. It should be noted that no 'Hippo'-type storage jars have been found in any Stratum VI context in Area C so far. It is not clear whether this is a chronological or functional issue, in light of the fact that such jars become common in the subsequent Strata V–IV.

This pottery assemblage differs from that of the previous Stratum VII (represented mainly by the pits of Area D, Stratum D-3) in the appearance of several new forms and specifically in the appearance of red slip and irregular hand burnish, which is unknown in Stratum Phase D-3, but became the hallmark of the Iron IIA period. Thus, the transition between these two pottery periods (late Iron I and Iron IIA) is quite distinct.

The ^{14}C dates from Stratum VI, Building A.

Basket 44166, Locus 4426, level 85.45 m (Table 13.3). A concentration of charred grains, fine charcoal powder and a small piece of bone were found covered by a bowl above a beaten earth floor in the south-western room of Building A. The amount of grains was large enough to make one PGC measurement in Groningen, which resulted in a high-precision date having a small standard deviation: 2761 ± 14 yr BP (GrN-27366). A remaining fraction of the sample, composed of charred broken grains and fine black charcoal powder was dated in triplicate by AMS. This fine black powder amongst the broken grains is most likely derived from the seeds or associated short-lived material (threshing remains, husks). No wood remains were detected. Two of the AMS dates gave similar results: 2805 ± 35 yr BP (GrA-21054) and 2800 ± 50 yr BP (GrA-21182). A third AMS measurement yielded a somewhat younger date: 2755 ± 35 yr BP (GrA-21043). The small piece of bone, which is also short-lived organic material, gave a date of 2840 ± 45 BP (GrA-21417).

The weighted average of all five Groningen dates from Stratum VI is 2772 ± 11 BP (Fig. 13.19). The chi-squared test shows that combining the five dates into a weighted average is acceptable in statistical terms (Bronk Ramsey 2003), as T = 4.4, which is smaller than the maximally allowed value of 9.5 (5% confidence limit). The 1σ calibrated result is 969–960 (12.1%), 927–897 (52.1%), 873–867 (4.0%) BCE and the 2σ range is 971–958 (14.0%), 936–893 (59.5%), 879–839 (21.9%) BCE. The calibration figure (Fig. 13.19) clearly shows that there are three distinct possible dating options—two main peaks in the 10th century BCE and a minor peak in the 9th century BCE. Though the period 969–960 BCE does not have the highest relative probability, due to the comparatively narrow time area of the wiggle, it is in our view the only possible option. Stratum V has many secure dates for its destruction in the period of about 930–900 BCE, as presented below. Since Stratum VI is older than Stratum V, on the basis of relative stratigraphy, it cannot be placed on the younger side of the calibration curve, to the right of Stratum V, but only on the left side of Stratum V, where it matches with the wiggle of 975–955 BCE (Bruins, van der Plicht and Mazar 2003a).

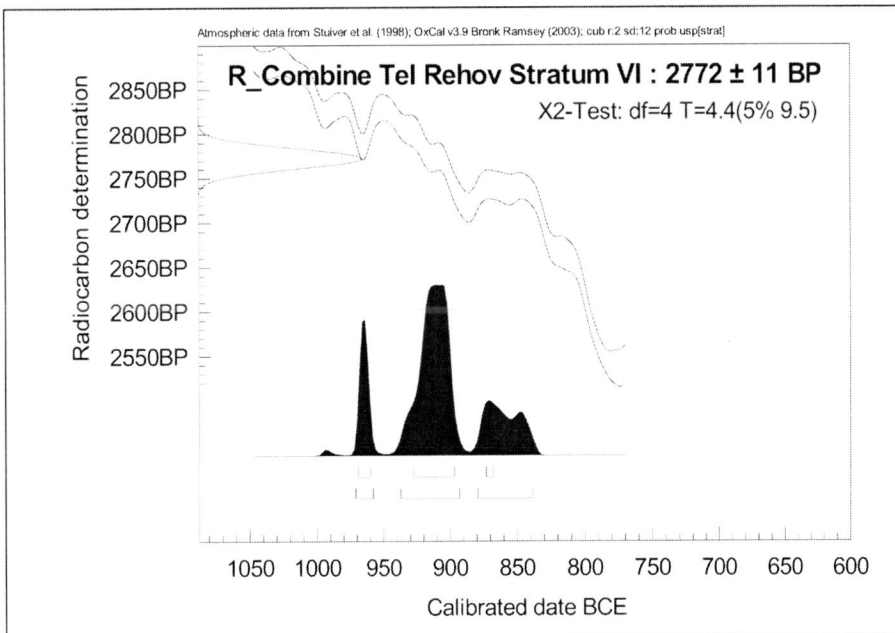

Figure 13.19. Area C, Stratum VI, Locus 4426. Calibration of the weighted average (2772 ± 11 BP) of five Groningen dates. The first hit with the calibration curve, with the 975–955 wiggle, is the most likely dating option in sequential stratigraphic terms, as explained in the text. This option is also supported by Bayesian statistics (see Bruins *et al.* [Chapter 15, this volume]).

The alternative is to date Stratum VI to the last 28 years of the 10th century BCE, in about the same time frame as Stratum V (see next section). Indeed, Finkelstein and Piasetsky (2003b: 289, Fig. 2) suggest condensing both Strata VI and V to the years between 925 and 900 BCE. However, squeezing Stratum VI and Stratum V into a mere 25 years is not tenable since the duration of Stratum VI, the subsequent construction of Stratum V, its lifespan and its final destruction, including the changes observed in the pottery between these two strata require a longer time period. Indeed, Bayesian modelling in relation to the stratigraphy supports the selection of the wiggle around 965 BCE as the preferred dating option for Stratum VI (Bruins *et al.* [Chapter 15, this volume]). Moreover, the underlying Stratum VII corresponds with Stratum D-3 in Area D, which is dated to the late 11th to early 10th centuries BCE, fitting very well on the calibration curve to the left (older part) of the 975–955 wiggle.

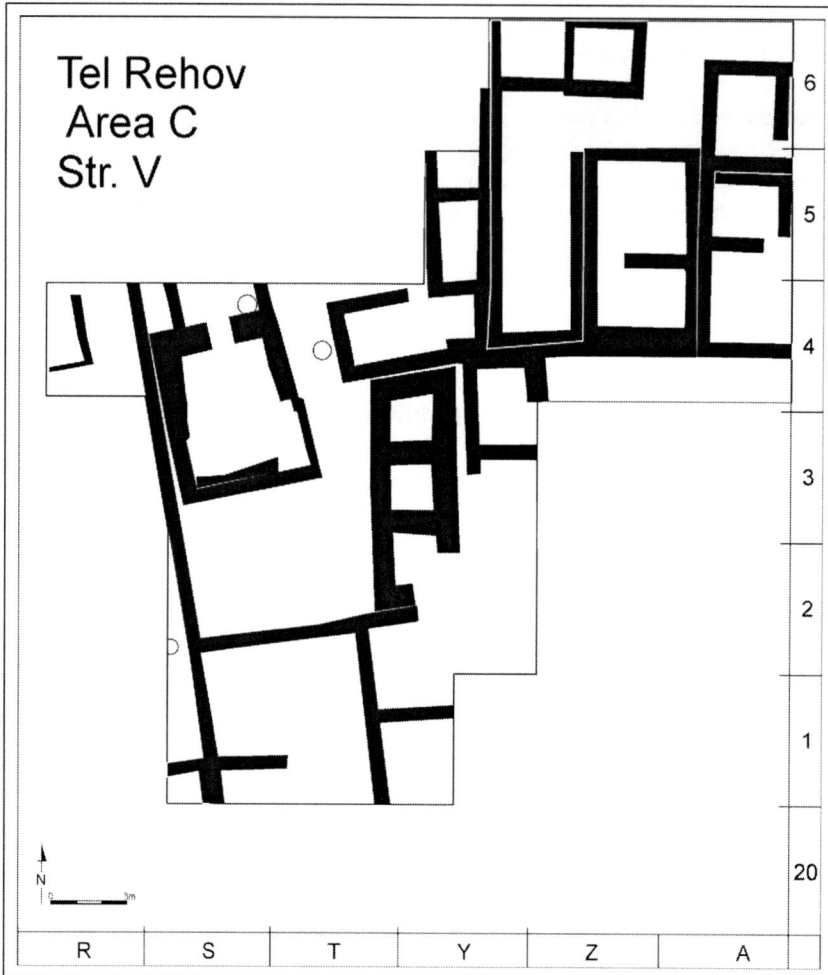

Figure 13.20. Area C: plan of Stratum V.

Stratum V in Area C (Fig. 13.20). The finds from Stratum V come mainly from two adjoining buildings located in the south-eastern part of Area C: Buildings G and H. They were both built with wooden beams incorporated into their foundations, as well as running under the floor makeup. Such wooden beams form an architectural hallmark of the Stratum V construction throughout Area C. Both buildings were destroyed by a fierce conflagration, leaving rich restorable pottery assemblages and numerous other objects as well. Though the pottery assemblages from both buildings are similar, a typological representation of each is presented below separately (Figs. 13.23–24). Samples of charred grain from both buildings (Locus 2422 from Building H and Loci 2425, 2444 and 2441 from Building G) were dated at Groningen. Eighteen additional samples from Locus 2425 were previously dated at Rehovot and Tucson.

Building H. This building occupies the south-eastern part of Area C. Its attribution to Stratum V is clear since two of its walls were constructed above Stratum VI architecture; the building was destroyed in fierce fire and in Stratum IV a new building (Building L) was constructed on top of the destruction layer, with a different plan. The plan of Building H is only partially known, as its entire eastern part was cut by later construction in Stratum IV and its southern part is beyond the limit of the excavation area. Parts of two rooms or large spaces were exposed and though no connection between them was uncovered, it seems that indeed they belong to one building. In the north, this building abuts Building G.

Figure 13.21. Collapsed Wall 2426 (looking south).

A unique trait in Building H was the nature of its destruction, which essentially is the result of its initial construction: while the floors and destruction debris of the western part of the building were found to be horizontal, the eastern part was found collapsed down at an angle of almost 45% to the east (Fig. 13.21). It seems that this eastern part collapsed into a sub-floor space, perhaps a basement of some kind, roofed by the wooden beams which also supported the floor above (Figs. 13.21–22). The burning of the building resulted in a massive collapse of destruction debris with numerous vessels[10] and whole fallen bricks, onto this lower level. Excavation of the floor of this lower level in the southern part of the building yielded a 'cultic corner' with a pottery altar ('cult stand'), a painted 'petal' chalice and a number of chalices and bowls. A concentration of burnt grain found near a Hippo-type storage jar in the southern part of the northern room (Locus 2422) is one of the samples discussed below.

Figure 13.22. Construction with wood beams in Building H (looking west).

Following the destruction of Building H, its western part remained an open area, while a new building (Building L) was constructed in Stratum IV directly above the collapsed destruction debris on the east.

Building G. This building is located north of Building H. It is an unusual building: rectangular in shape, the building measures 3.8 m × 8.4 m and is composed of three small square chambers that had no entrances and most likely were accessed by ladders from a higher level. This implies its use as a storage building or granary and, indeed, the central chamber (Loci 2425/2444) and southern-most chamber (Locus 2441) both contained a large amount of burnt grain, investigated by ^{14}C dating.

The attribution of this building to Stratum V is based on its relationship to Building H to the south and Building M to the east, and especially its superposition above Stratum VI architecture (Building B, see Fig. 13.16). The south-eastern part of the southern room (Locus 2441) of this building suffered the same collapse down to the east as that noted above in Building H. The burnt collapsed layer penetrated underneath the northern part of Building L of Stratum IV and thus this destruction layer clearly belongs to Stratum V (Fig. 13.27). No later element was constructed above the central and northern rooms of Building G following its destruction and yet there is

10. See Mazar 1999: 22, Fig. 11 for a photo of selected vessels from the northern room.

evidence for re-use of this part of the building in Stratum IV, as courtyard floors of Stratum IV abutted the top of the walls on both the east and west. There are three possible scenarios for the fate of this building during the time of Stratum IV:

1. The building was burnt at the end of Stratum V. The southern room collapsed to the south-east, the other two chambers remained standing. In Stratum IV the building itself remained as a useless ruin, though floors abutted the preserved top of the walls of the ruined building. In that case the finds in the chambers should be attributed to Stratum V.

2. The same, but with an assumption that the inhabitants of Stratum IV constructed floors on a higher level inside the northern two chambers of the building. These floors were above the present topsoil and disappeared due to erosion. In that case, too, the finds inside the chambers should be attributed to Stratum V.

3. Stratum IV people reutilized the original two northern chambers of the building, without changing the floor level. In that case, the finds in the destruction layer of these two rooms should be attributed to Stratum IV.

As described above, the charred grain from Building G that was subjected to ^{14}C analysis comes from both the southern chamber (Locus 2441), whose destruction debris definitely belongs to Stratum V, as well as from the central chamber (Loci 2425 and 2444) whose stratigraphic attribution to Strata V or IV is open to interpretation as detailed above. This latter chamber yielded a large quantity of charred grain (Locus 2425) found above a beaten earth floor (Locus 2444), under a thick layer of collapsed and burnt bricks. Samples from Locus 2425 are from the grain heap itself; samples from Locus 2444 are from the bottom of the heap, just above the floor. Locus 2441 (the destruction layer of the southern room) yielded an extremely rich pottery assemblage of ca. 50 vessels of various types, while Room 2425 contained very small amounts of pottery. An additional group of pottery was revealed in the northern chamber (Locus 2460).

The pottery assemblage of Stratum V, Buildings G and H (Figs. 13.23–25).
Bowls: Rounded bowls are relatively rare (Fig. 13.23:1) and the majority of bowls have a blunt carination slightly above mid-body, mostly with a short everted rim and flat base (Figs. 13.23:2; 13.24:1), as well as other rim and base variations (Figs. 13.23:3-5; 13.24:2-3). Note also the large bowl with thickened rim and low ring base; some of these have bar handles and are distorted (Fig. 13.24:5). Bowls with a short vertical rounded rim/neck and body with a round carination (Fig. 13.23:6) are also found, though not common. A unique type is a small deep rounded bowl with rounded base (Fig. 13.24:6). The majority of bowls are red-slipped inside and outside, or just outside. Most of these also have irregular or horizontal hand burnish.

Chalices: Chalices of a similar type and size were plentiful in both Buildings G and H. Their bowl is rounded with a soft carination below the everted rim and the foot has a pronounced ridge above the flaring base (Figs. 13.23:7; 13.24:4). Most chalices were red-slipped and some were also burnished.

Kraters: Two basic krater types were found: a krater with a short rounded neck/rim, with a soft high carination (Fig. 13.23:8), and a krater with a straight wide neck with a slight ridge, and a carinated body; these have thickened rims, two or four handles and a ring base (Fig. 13.24:7). The kraters too were mostly red-slipped and hand burnished.

Cooking pots: Cooking pots and cooking jugs were found in both buildings, while one large cooking amphora comes from Building H (Fig. 13.24:9). There are a number of variations of cooking pot rims, including long straight triangular rims, as well as a thickened rounded exterior triangle (Fig. 13.24:8) and a 'pinched' or upturned exterior (Fig. 13.23:9). The cooking jugs generally have sack-shaped bodies and slightly concave necks (Figs. 13.23:10; 13.24:10).

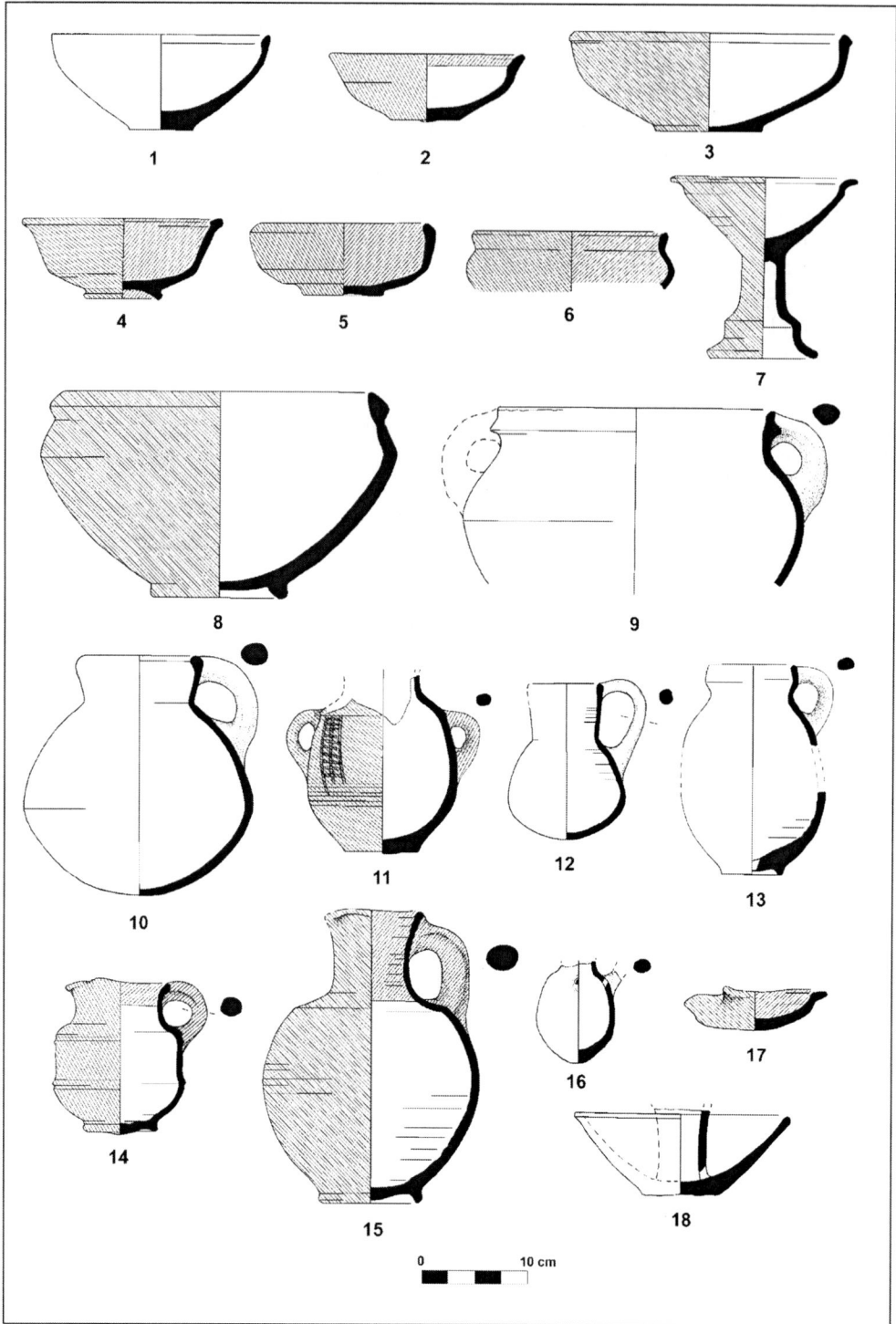

Figure 13.23. Pottery from Building G, Area C, Stratum V.

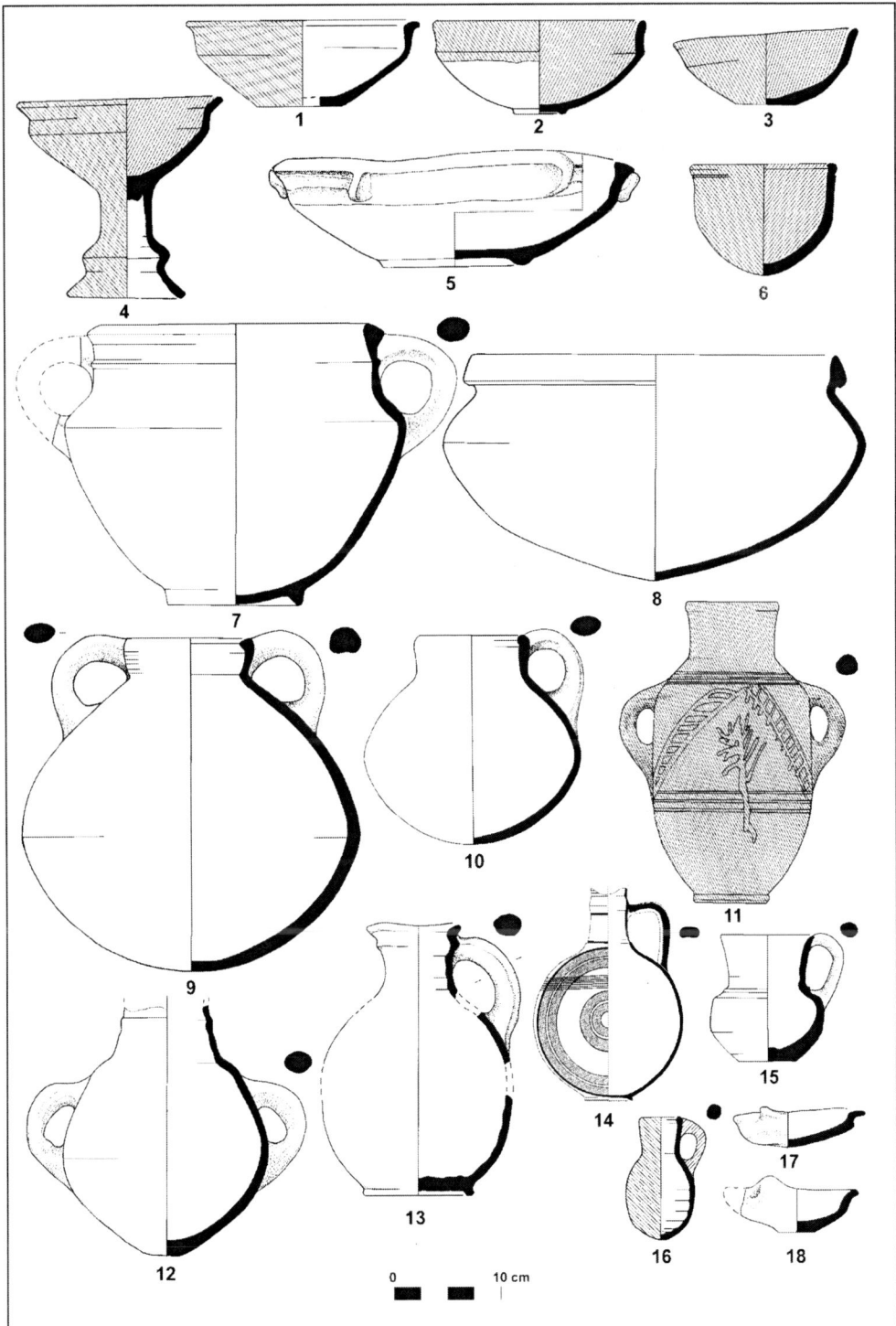

Figure 13.24. Pottery from Building H, Area C, Stratum V.

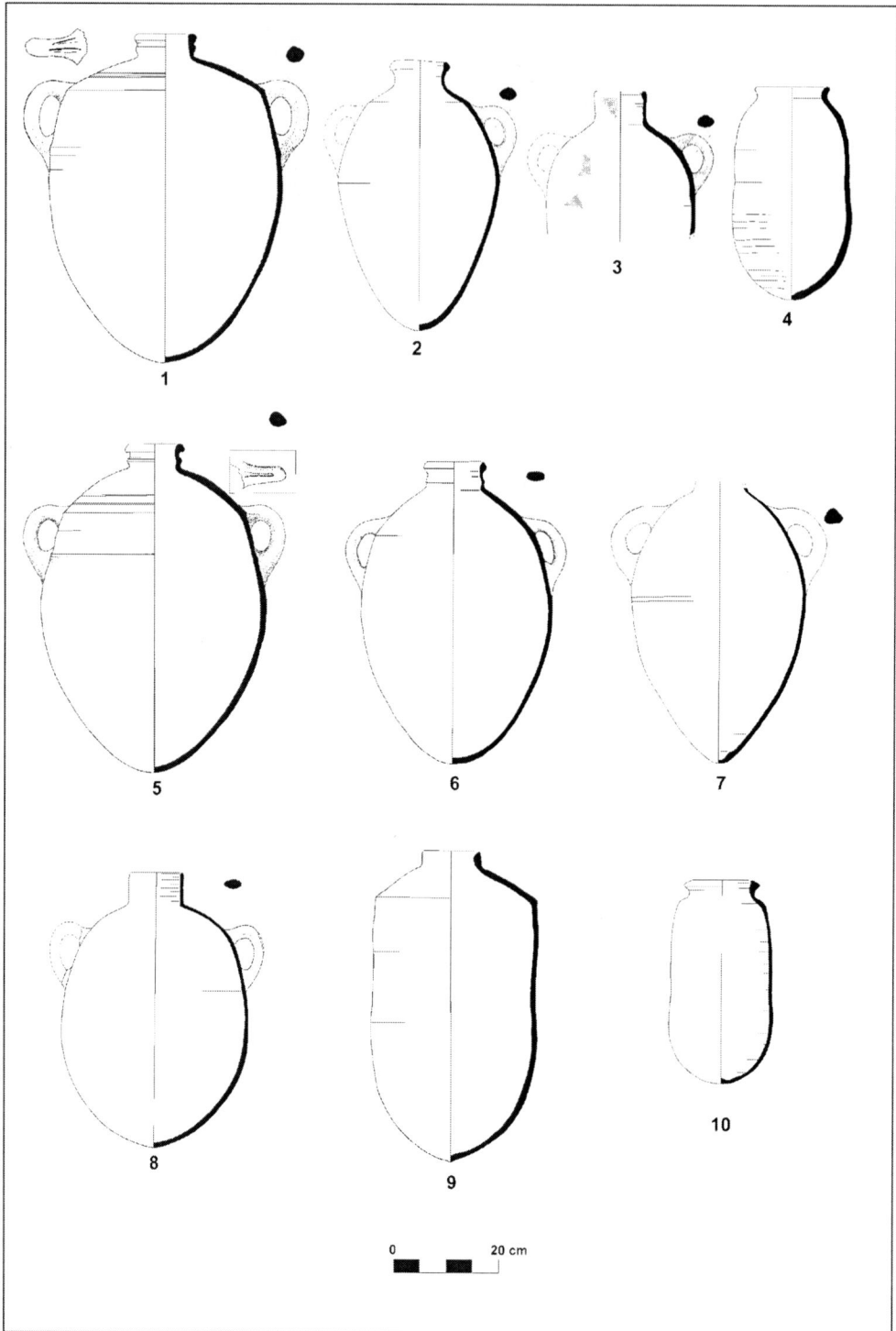

Figure 13.25. Storage jars from Buildings G and H, Area C, Stratum V.

Amphoriskoi: Small to medium sized amphoriskoi were common in Stratum V. The two basic types that were found are: an amphoriskos with an oval body, short shoulders and wide medium sized neck, disc base and two loop handles from the shoulder to the body (Figs. 13.23:11; 13.24:11). Most of these are red-slipped, hand burnished and some also bear a red painted design on top of the red slip, which sometimes include debased 'Canaanite' motifs such as vertical ladders and even a stylized palm tree (Figs. 13.23:11; 13.24:11). The second amphoriskos type has a small round or sack-shaped body with a wide neck and two large loop handles (Fig. 13.24:12); it is very similar to the one found in Stratum VI Building A (see above). These are either red-slipped and/or red painted with rather careless horizontal straight or wavy bands (see Fig. 13.36:4, Stratum IV, for an example).

Storage jars: Numerous storage jars were found in Buildings G and H and essentially, almost all the Iron Age IIA storage jar types found at Tel Rehov are represented in these two buildings. The most common jar is the Hippo-type storage jar (Fig. 13.25:1, 5). Other storage jars include those with an oval shaped body, a tapering base, a short neck and a rounded rim (Fig. 13.25:2, 7); some of these have wider and rounder bodies (Fig. 13.25:6). A common jar type is characterised by a short round body and a long straight neck; many of these jars are covered with a reddish wash (Fig. 13.25:3, 8). Rarer is a jar with pronounced sloping shoulders, a short plain neck and a straight body (Fig. 13.25:9; in this example the handles were not preserved). A common type is the cylindrical hole-mouth jar, with two rim variations: a plain everted rim (Fig. 13.25:4) and a short neck with a thickened hammer-head rim (Fig. 13.25:10).

Jugs: No typology can be formed for the jugs in these buildings as each one is represented basically by one example (Figs. 13.23:12-15; 13.24:13, 15). Most have flat or low ring bases and all have handles that extend from the rim to the shoulder. They are well formed and about half are red-slipped; of these only about half are also burnished.

Juglets: The juglets all have short rounded bodies and rounded bases; some are quite squat (Fig. 13.23:16) and others are slightly more oval (Fig. 13.24:16). Most have a trefoil mouth and are covered with red slip, but not all are burnished.

Lamps: Lamps were common in these two buildings. Most are of the shallow wide saucer bowl type with an everted shelf rim (Figs. 13.23:17; 13.24:17), while a less common type is deeper and has a flattened base (Fig. 13.24:18). Some of the lamps were red-slipped inside and outside. A cup and saucer in Building G (Fig. 13.23:18) is one of two found in Stratum V.

Imports: A Cypriot Bichrome jug, found intact aside from its rim, was found in the destruction debris above the floor in the north-western part of Building H (Locus 1465; Fig. 13.24:14).

General: The ceramic assemblages of Buildings G and H are characterized by a wide variety of vessel classes and types, including vessels for food preparation and serving, as well as for storage and cult. A very rough estimate, pending more exact quantitative registration, shows that ca. 35% of the vessels are red-slipped and burnished, while painted traditions do continue, either in rather careless red geometric patterns and sometimes in combination with the red slip. Though no Cypro-Phoenician Black on Red or White Painted vessels were found in these buildings, other Stratum V contexts (in Area C and other areas as well) did yield such sherds (for comparative discussion see below, pp. 242-43).

Radiocarbon dates from Stratum V in Area C (Table 13.3).

Construction date. Two wood samples used in the construction of Stratum V buildings in Area C were dated at Rehovot (Mazar and Carmi 2001: 1337, Table 5). The first is an olive tree from Locus 1479, Building J, dated to 3070 ± 40 BP (RT-2995) with a calibrated age of 1395–1264 BCE (1σ). This date is at least 200 years earlier than the construction date of Stratum V and thus is an example of the 'old wood effect'. Indeed, an olive tree can be very long-lived. The second sample was from an elm tree (Locus 1465, Building H) dated in Rehovot to 2875 ± 25 BP (RT-2997).[11] The calibrated age ranges are 1124–1000 (1σ) and 1188–940 BCE (2σ). This radiocarbon date is credible as an elm tree has a life span of up to 100 years. Thus, this last date strengthens the possibility that Stratum V was constructed during the 10th century BCE.

Figure 13.26. Stratum V pottery assemblage.

Figure 13.27. Stratum IV, Building L, above Stratum V destruction debris (looking south).

11.   Attention that in Mazar and Carmi 2001: 1337 there is a typing mistake: the locus number in Table 5 should be 1465 rather than 1475.

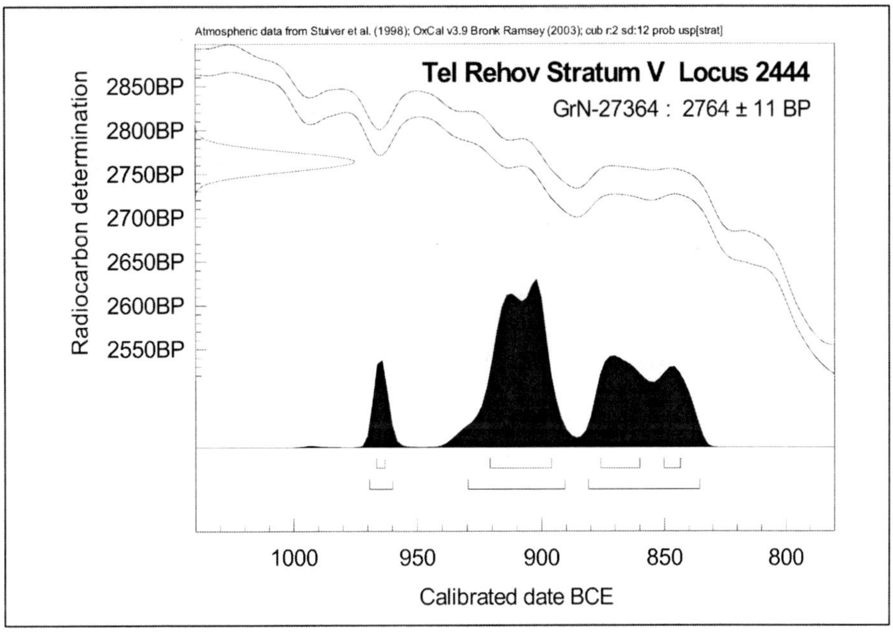

Figure 13.28. Area C, Stratum V, Locus 2444. Calibration of the destruction of Stratum V. The most probable date, 921–896 (42.0%) BCE, is virtually the same as for Loci 2441 and 2425.

Loci 2444 and 2425 (Building G). A large concentration of charred cereal grains (several litres) was found below a 0.8 m thick layer of fallen and burnt mudbricks in the central chamber of Building G (for the description of this building see above, pp. 224-25).

The cluster of charred cereal grains (Basket 24647, level 86.20 m) was found as a layer (Locus 2425) above a beaten earth floor (Locus 2444) laid on a layer of charred wooden beams. The floor itself was most likely constructed in Phase C1b (Stratum V), but it could have been re-used in the subsequent Phase C1a (Stratum IV) (see the three alternatives suggested above, p. 225). Therefore, it is difficult to decide based on stratigraphic reasoning whether the charred cereal grains belong to Stratum V or Stratum IV.

Locus 2444 (Basket 24647, level 86.21 m). Since the beaten earth floor in Locus 2444 was thin and crumbling, the charred wood was exposed just below the grain layer. Black powder found together with the grain might have originated from these charred wooden beams. Therefore the Groningen lab measured independently the charred grain and the black powder. The amount of charred grains was quite large, enabling conventional radiometry. The two Groningen PGC dates from this locus are of special interest in relation to the above stratigraphic uncertainty. The sample of charred cereal grains was passed through a 0.18 mm sieve in the Groningen lab, in order to separate the bulk grains from finer charred organic particles. The cereal grains (particle size larger than 0.18 mm) gave a high-precision date of 2764 ± 11 (GrN-27364), resulting in a 1σ calibrated age range of 966–844 BCE, whereby the range 921–896 BCE (42.0%) has the highest relative probability (Fig. 13.28). This radiocarbon result would allow for both the Stratum V and IV stratigraphic options, though the highest relative probability period of 921–896 BCE favors Stratum V.

The fine material (< 0.18 mm) gave a much older date of 2866 ± 21 BP (GrN-27413) with a 1σ calibrated age of 1108–976 BCE. Although a laboratory error concerning the older date cannot be entirely excluded, another possible explanation is that the sample consisted of non-homogeneous material. The fine material had a similar date as the wood from the elm tree dated at the Rehovot lab (2875 ± 25 BP; RT-2997).

Locus 2425. (Basket 24306, level 86.57 m). The large amount of charred grains was analyzed in three different radiocarbon labs, yielding a total of 20 dates (Tables 13.3 and 13.4): nine dates were measured in Rehovot, nine in Arizona (Mazar and Carmi 2001: 1338, Table 6) and two in Groningen (Bruins *et al.* 2003a; Table 13.3, this paper). Statistical examination of the results showed that the average Rehovot date (excluding one outlier in order to pass the chi-squared test) is 2699 ± 7 BP (T = 13.2, 5% = 14.1). The chi-squared value is high (13.2) with respect to the 5% confidence level, indicating that the Rehovot series is not coherent. The calibrated age lies entirely in the 9th century BCE. The average Arizona date for this locus is 2749 ± 16 BP (T = 7.1, 5% = 15.5), a difference of 50 BP years. The 1σ calibrated range is 905–835 BCE and the 2σ range is 930–830 BCE, giving most probability to the 9th century BCE, though the 10th century is still marginally feasible. The chi-squared value of 7.1 indicates that the Arizona series is significantly more coherent than the Rehovot series. The Arizona dates seem to support an association of the grains with Stratum IV on chronological considerations. However, the average of the two Groningen PGC dates from this locus is 2788 ± 14 BP, which is 89 BP years older than Rehovot and 39 BP years older than Arizona (Bruins *et al.* 2003b). The 1σ calibrated age range is 971–959 (20.7%), 935–903 (47.5%) BCE and the 2σ range is 998–981 (5.7%) 976–896 (86.9%) 876–860 (2.8%) BCE. Thus, a 10th-century BCE date for Locus 2425 is clearly determined by Groningen, with the highest relative probability in the period 935–903 BCE. This option is possible according to the Arizona date in the 2σ range, while the Rehovot dates are by far the youngest, a tendency also noted for the Iron Age I dates, described above.

Table 13.4. Comparison of 21 ^{14}C dates from Locus 2425, measured at Rehovot (1998–99), Arizona (1998–99) and Groningen (2003).

Rehovot (LSC)		Arizona (AMS)		Groningen (PGC)	
RT-3122	Year BP	AA-30431-U3-	Year BP		Year BP
A	2700 ± 0	11	2830±55	GrN-26114	2775 ± 20
A1	2655 ± 25	12	2745±50	GrN-26115	2800 ± 20
A2	2655 ± 25	13	2730±45		
B	2720 ± 25	21	2815±50		
B1	2700 ± 25	22	2770±50		
B2	2650 ± 30	23	2710±45		
BB	2725 ± 15	31	2685±45		
C	2860 ± 20	32	2760±60		
D	2710 ± 20	33	2740±50		

Locus 2441 (Building G). This locus marks a one meter thick collapse and destruction layer of the southern room in the three-chamber structure to which Locus 2425 also belongs. A relatively large amount of charred cereal grains was found in this thick destruction layer (Baskets 24441, 24579, 24580 all at level 86.60 m This collapse layer is sealed by walls of Building L that was founded in Stratum IV (see above, pp. 223-24, and Fig. 13.27). Moreover, Stratum VI remains were found below both the destruction layer 2441, as well as below Room 2444/2425. Hence, the charred grains can be clearly related to the destruction of Stratum V (local C-1b).

All three baskets contained sufficient grains for PGC radiometry measurements. Basket 24441 gave a date of 2810 ± 20 BP (GrN-26116). Basket 24580 gave a similar date of 2775 ± 25 BP (GrN-26117). It is important to note that the dating results of these two baskets are *identical* to the two Groningen PGC dates of Locus 2425 from the same building (Table 13.4) and thus it may be possible to conclude that the charred grains from Locus 2425 also belong to the destruction of Stratum V, supporting option 1 and 2 of the three possible archaeological interpretations (see p. 225).

Basket 24579 was a particularly large sample of charred cereal grains. In Groningen, during the pretreatment process, the material was separated into three size fractions (coarse: > 0.85 mm, fine: < 0.18 mm and medium: in between these values) by sieving. Each size fraction was dated separately, in order to evaluate the homogeneousness of the charred sample material. The results are as follows: 2745 ± 14 BP (GrN-27363) coarse, 2771 ± 15 BP (GrN-27385) medium and 2761 ± 15 BP (GrN-27386) fine. The coarse material is the youngest, but still within 1σ of the oldest date for the medium-sized grains, while the date for the fine material is in between the two. Therefore, the results are the same in physical terms. Combining the three dates into a weighted average results in a date of 2758 ± 8 BP which is acceptable according to the chi-squared test (Bronk Ramsey 2003), as T = 1.7, which is well below the 5% confidence limit of 6.0. This average BP date of Basket 24579 from Stratum V is similar as the average date for Stratum D-2 Locus 1823, some dates for Stratum VI and the average date of Stratum IV (2758 ± 16 BP), presented below. The results from Basket 24579 are younger than for the two other baskets of Locus 2441.

Since the destruction layer of Locus 2441 marks a single event, and in the absence of archaeological errors with regard to the three baskets, the spread in radiocarbon dates is probably due to the inherent variability in the reproducibility of radiocarbon dating (Mook and Waterbolk 1985: 10). Thus, we may combine all the dates from the three baskets of Locus 2441 into an overall weighted average (Fig. 13.29). The chi-squared test (Bronk Ramsey 2003) accepts the averaging of all dates, as T = 7.4, which is below the 5% maximally allowed confidence limit of 9.5. The weighted average of Locus 2441 is 2767 ± 7 BP. The 1σ calibrated age is 967–962 (6.6%), 922–896 (52.1%), 874–864 (9.5%) BCE and the 2σ calibrated age is 969–960 (8.7%), 930–893 (57.3%), 879–838 (29.4%) BCE (Fig. 13.29).

The period 930–893 BCE has by far the highest relative probability (57.3%) in the 2σ range for the destruction of Stratum V, based on the weighted average of all radiocarbon dates from Locus 2441.

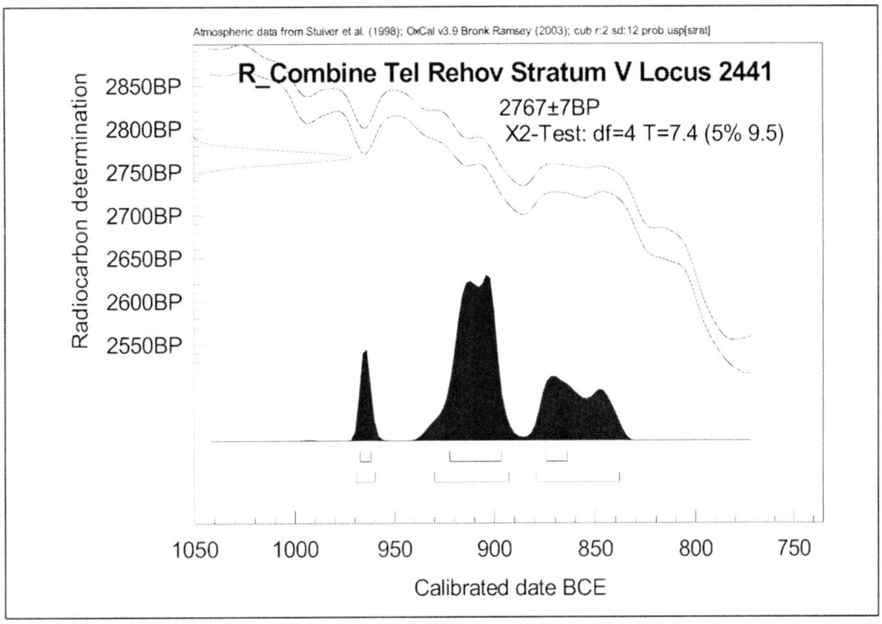

Figure 13.29. Area C, Stratum V, Locus 2441. Calibration of the destruction of Stratum V according to the weighted average of all five dates from Locus 2441: 2767 ± 7 BP. This overall result clearly favours the middle peak, which has by far the highest 1σ relative probability: 922–896 (52.1%) BCE. The first peak, related to the wiggle of 975–955 BCE, fits with Stratum VI.

Locus 2422 (Building H). A large concentration of charred grains (Basket 24408, level 86.40 m) was found close to the floor level of Building H, below a ca. 1 m thick destruction layer. The amount of grains was large enough to make three sub-samples in the lab, one making up the fine material (< 0.18 mm). The three Groningen PGC dates are coherent, also showing that the material is homogeneous in age: 2764 ± 11 BP (GrN-27361), 2777 ± 13 BP (GrN-27362) and for the fine parts of the charred grains 2785 ± 28 BP (GrN-27412). The weighted average of Locus 2422 is 2771 ± 8 BP (Fig. 13.30). The calculated chi-squared value, T = 0.9, is very low in comparison to the 5% confidence limits of 6.0, which underlines the excellent internal consistency of the three dates. The 1σ calibrated age is 969–961 (11.0%), 925–897 (56.2%), 871–870 (1.0%) BCE and the 2σ range is 970–959 (12.4%), 934–894 (61.7%), 878–840 (21.3%) BCE (Fig. 13.30). Evidently, the period 934–894 BCE has by far the highest relative probability for the destruction of Stratum V in Locus 2422.

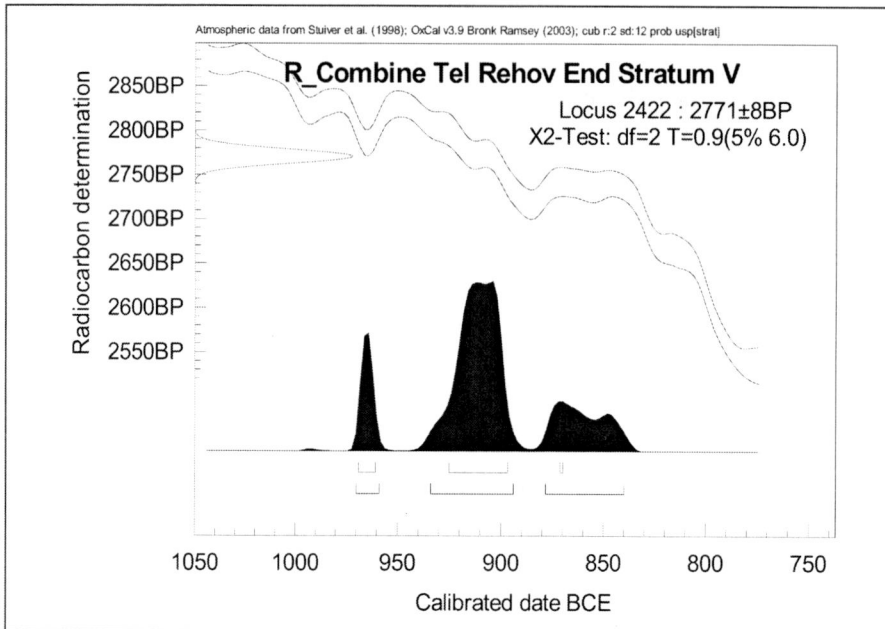

Figure 13.30. Area C, Stratum V, Locus 2422. Calibration of the destruction of Stratum V. The most probable date, 925–897 (56.2%) BCE, is virtually the same as for Locus 2441.

Conclusion: the destruction date of Stratum V in Loci 2422, 2441, 2425, 2444. The average Groningen dates for Loci 2425, 2441 and 2422 are all rather similar: 2788 ± 14 BP, 2767 ± 7 BP, 2771 ± 8 BP, respectively, while the single date for Locus 2444, 2764 ± 11 BP, is also in the same range. These radiocarbon results strongly suggest that the destruction of Buildings H and G of Stratum V in Area C occurred probably simultaneously in a severe conflagration, which is quite possible in relation to the stratigraphic evidence. The overall weighted average of the four destruction loci results in an extremely precise date of 2770 ± 4 BP, well accepted by the chi-squared test, as T=2.2 versus the 5% confidence limit of 7.8. The 1σ calibrated age range is 968-961 (9.4%), 924-897 (58.8%) BCE and the 2σ calibrated range is 969-959 (11.2%), 932-894 (64.4%), 878-841 (19.9%) BCE. Thus the period 924-897 BCE has by far the highest relative probability in the 1σ range. The alternative period of 968-961 (9.4%) is unlikely, since this wiggle fits with Stratum VI in the correct stratigraphic order (Fig. 13.31).

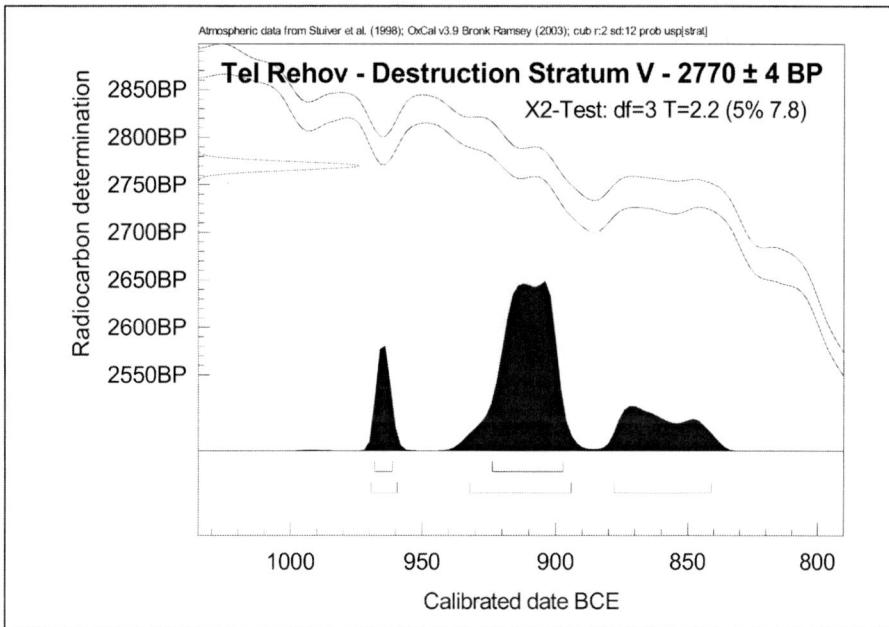

Figure 13.31. Area C, Stratum V. Destruction of Stratum V, based on the combined average of Loci 2425, 2441, 2422, 2444. The most probable date is 924–897 (58.8%) BCE, which is almost all the 68.2% in the 1σ range.

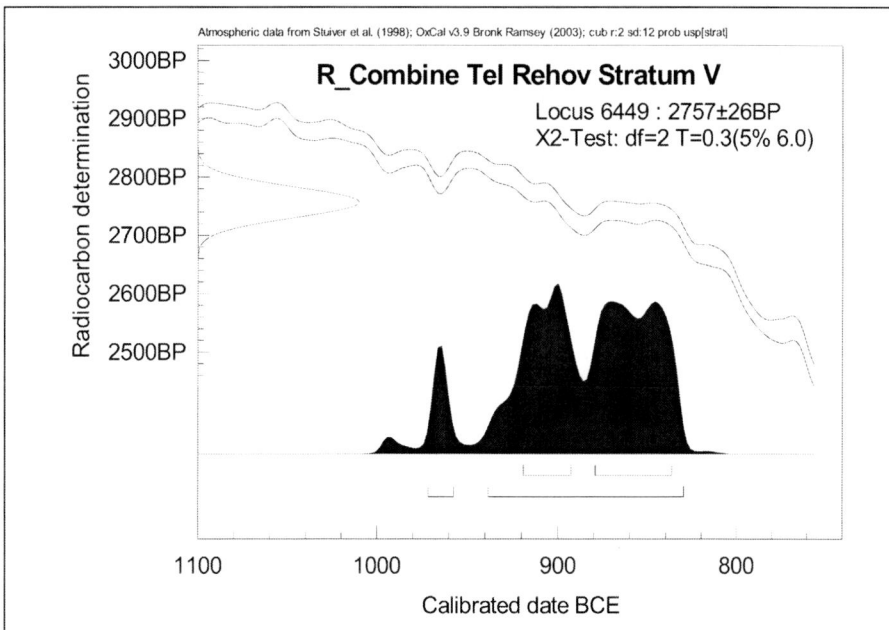

Figure 13.32. Area C, Stratum V, Locus 6449. The average date of this Locus is similar to Stratum IV. The period 879–837 (41.7%) BCE has the highest relative probability, though the period 919–893 (26.5%) BCE is still significantly represented.

Locus 6449 (Building E). This locus belongs to a building located in the north-western part of Area C (Square T-5), which has only been partly excavated. Locus 6449 forms a floor surface in a room; it was covered by destruction debris and sealed by a higher floor, attributed to Stratum IV, which was also covered by destruction debris. Charred olive stones were found together (Basket 64756, level 86.17 m) on the lower floor surface, related to Stratum V. Three Groningen AMS dates were measured: 2775 ± 45 BP (GrA-24455); 2750 ± 45 BP (GrA-24456) and 2745 ± 45 BP (GrA-24497). The results are very coherent, within 1σ from each other, underscored by the very low chi-squared value, T = 0.3, in relation to the 5% confidence limits of 6.0. The weighted average date is 2757 ± 26 BP (Fig. 13.32), which is slightly younger than other Stratum V loci in Area C. Although the midpoint of the average date is identical to the average dates of Locus 5498 of Stratum IV, located nearby, and Basket 24579 of Stratum V Locus 2441, the standard deviation is larger. Thus, the calibration results are somewhat different, favouring the 9th century more than the 10th century BCE. The 1σ calibrated age range is 919–893 (26.5%), 879–837 (41.7%) BCE and the 2σ range is 971–957 (7.1%) and 938–830 (88.3%) BCE.

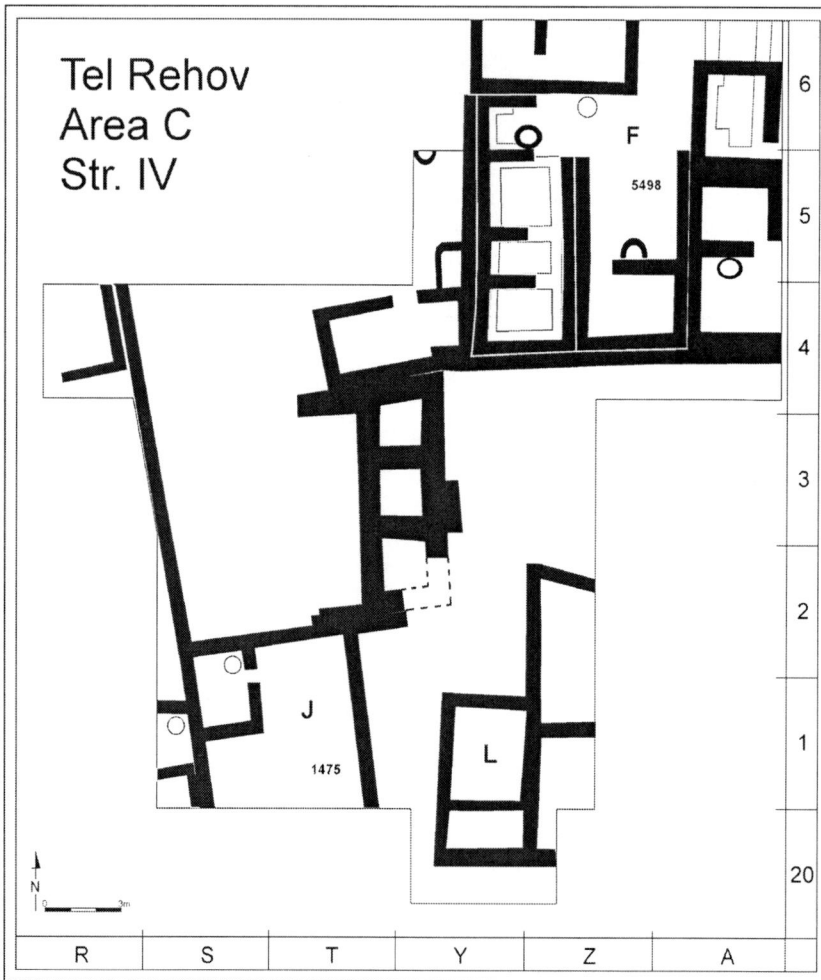

Figure 13.33. Area C: plan of Stratum IV.

Stratum IV, Area C, Building F (Fig. 13.33–34). The sudden destruction that terminated Stratum IV and the abandonment of the lower city following this catastrophe created a destruction layer, which yielded very rich and complete pottery assemblages in a number of buildings. In this article we only refer to Building F in the north-eastern part of Area C, because this is the only structure that provided samples for ^{14}C dating from Stratum IV. The architecture and pottery typology of this building are briefly described below. These pottery characteristics are representative of Stratum IV in other buildings as well.[12]

Figure 13.34. Area C, Stratum IV Building F (looking west).

Building F is composed of three main parts: a western wing, an eastern wing and a northern space (Figs. 13.33–34). It was originally constructed in Stratum V, when its walls were built on top of a large building of Stratum VI. Wood was incorporated in the foundations of both floors and walls, as in all other Stratum V buildings. This phase suffered destruction and in Stratum IV the building was re-utilized and renovated. The floors of Stratum IV were constructed just above those of Stratum V, apparently after clearing the rooms from most of the Stratum V destruction debris. Most of the walls were repaired, others were removed and some new walls were added, so that the terminal phase of the building in Stratum IV represents more of a re-use and alteration than a re-build. This phenomenon of re-use of Stratum V buildings in Stratum IV is also known from other places in Area C (note the above discussion of this possibility in Building G, pp. 224-25).

The entrance into the building was from the northeast, through a wide corridor or street(?). The entrance led into the eastern wing of the building, which included a larger hall and a smaller room to its south. Both rooms contained thick layers of destruction debris with numerous vessels of all types, as well as many other objects. The northern hall had a large grinding installation,

---

12. See Mazar 2003: 153-55, Figs. 18–19, for an additional typological presentation of the Strata V–IV ceramic assemblage.

dozens of loom weights were found and burnt wooden beams of what appears to have been a loom. An oven was found at its north-western corner. This room also yielded a unique pottery 'model shrine' decorated with an animal (bull or feline figure?) grasping two human heads in its claws. A pottery vessel found on the floor of this room (5498) contained charred grain, which was radiocarbon dated. The southern room was nicely plastered; it contained a large number of storage jars and other vessels, as well as a pottery object known as a 'footbath' type.

The western wing is comprised of four consecutive small rooms. The northernmost room was wide open to the main hall. It included a grinding installation identical to the one in the main hall, though smaller. A very large concentration of pottery was found here, including the fragmentary remains of a pottery altar, decorated with three female figures made in a mold. From this room one could gain access to three additional rooms, arranged in a row, each of which was entered through its north-eastern corner and each of which was lined with brick benches. These benches and the floors that abutted them were built on top of the remnants of the Stratum V destruction debris that abutted the lowest courses of the buildings' walls. These rooms contained large quantities of pottery. The southernmost room also contained a large heavy pottery box with a lid, found resting on a brick shelf. The plan of this western wing is unique in the architecture of the Iron Age II in Israel, and thus this building probably had some special function in addition to the utilitarian functions of grinding, baking and weaving, indicated by the various finds.

The pottery from Building F (Figs. 13.35–37).

Bowls: Round side bowls are rare (Fig. 13.35:1) and the shallow wide open bowl with ring base in Fig. 13.35:2 is unique in our corpus. Carinated bowls of various types are the most common, usually with a blunt carination, everted rim and a flat or concave disc base, though other types include a low carination with a rounded or high ring base (Fig. 13.35:4-7). Large open bowls with hammer head rims and low ring bases are found as well; these are sometimes distorted (Fig. 13.35:3). Bowls with a short rounded rim/neck and a body with a round carination and a disc or flat base are also found (Fig. 13.35:8). A little over 50% of the bowls are red-slipped; of these about half are also burnished. Sometimes the red slip is rubbed away and visible only in small patches.

Chalices: Chalices are very common in Stratum IV, all with a shallow bowl, everted rim and a foot with a ridge above the flaring base (Fig. 13.35:9). In a similar manner to the bowls, about 50% of these chalices are red-slipped, though they are rarely burnished.

Kraters: Two basic krater types are found: a medium-large sized krater with a vertical neck, hammer head rim, two or four handles,[13] a deep rounded body and a ring base (Fig. 13.35:10-11). The other krater type has a short rounded neck/rim and a deep body with high rounded shoulders and a ring base (Fig. 13.35:12). The kraters are mostly red-slipped, though the distribution between the two krater types differs: only about 40% of the necked type are red-slipped, often lacking burnish, while almost 90% of the round rimmed type are red-slipped and generally burnished as well, with horizontal hand burnish.

Cooking pots: Cooking pots, cooking jugs and cooking amphorae were common in Stratum IV. The cooking pots show two basic variations: a vertical rim stance, with a triangular exterior that is straight or up-turned (Fig. 13.35:13), and more rarely, an inverted upper stance, with an up-turned rim (Fig. 13.35:14). The cooking jugs have slightly concave necks and sack-shaped bodies (Fig. 13.35:15). Cooking amphorae are somewhat less common than the other types (Fig. 13.35:16).

---

13.   Several kraters of this type, with large deep barrel-shaped bodies, had as many as 9 handles in Stratum IV; such a phenomenon was not noted in Stratum V, though this might be a contingency of exposure as of now.

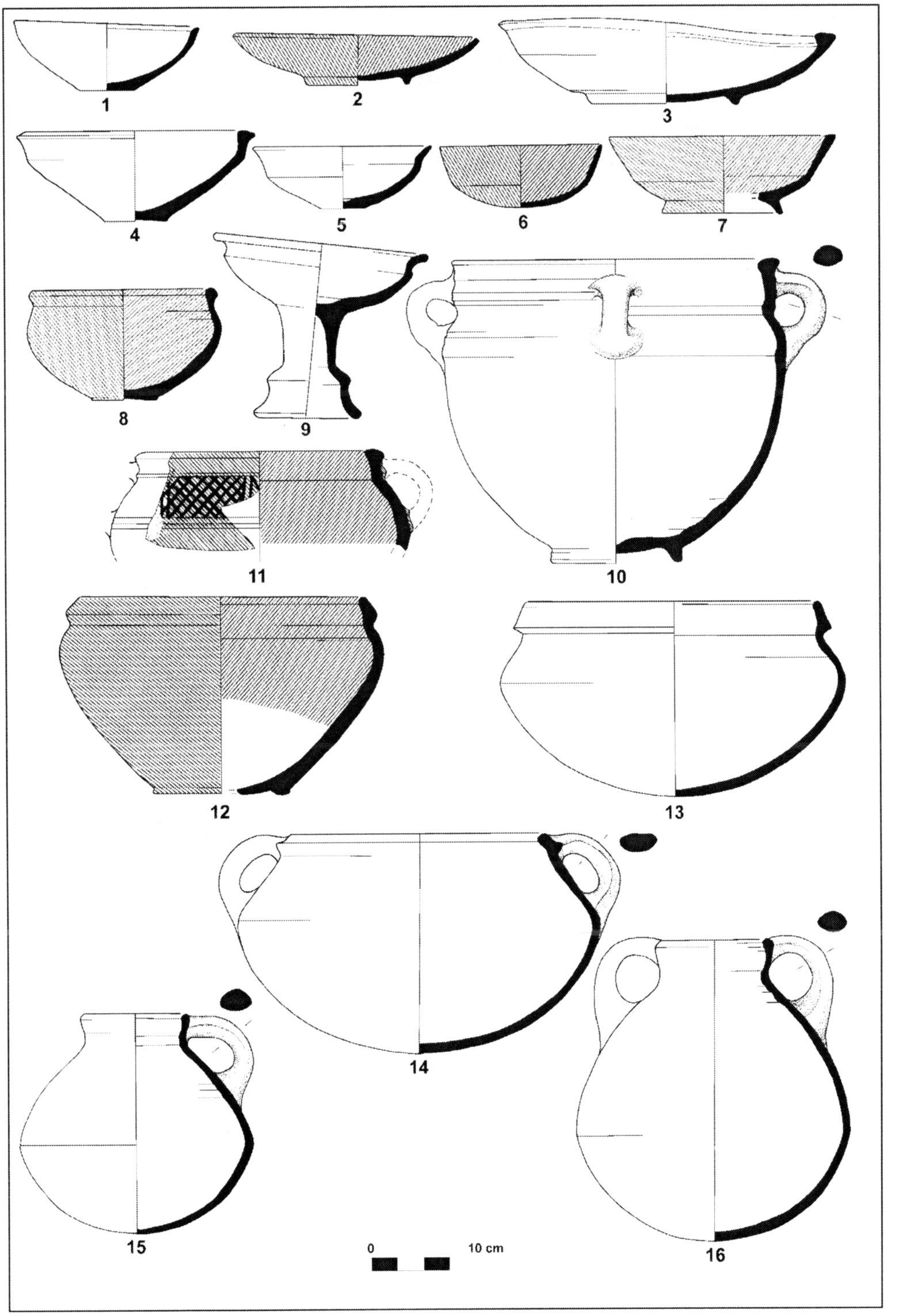

Figure 13.35. Pottery from Building F, Area C, Stratum IV.

Figure 13.36. Pottery from Building F, Area C, Stratum IV (continued).

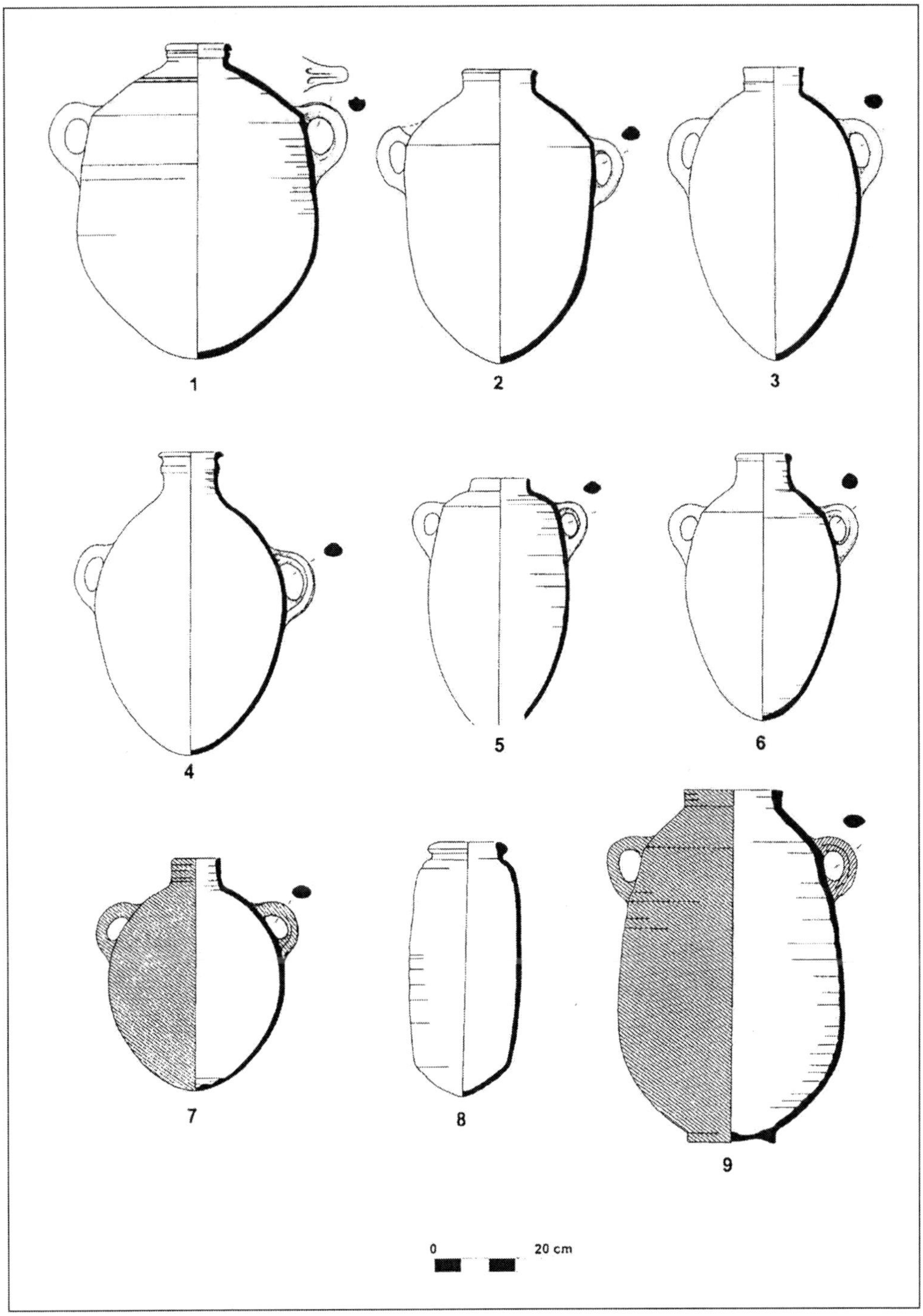

Figure 13.37. Pottery from Building F, Area C, Stratum IV (continued).

Amphoriskoi and Amphorae: Small and medium sized amphorae are common in Stratum IV. Three basic types were found: a small vessel with an oval shaped body and a flat or disc base. These are generally decorated, either with red slip or painted in red (Fig. 13.36:1); a medium sized amphora with a long neck and ridged exterior rim. Two loop handles extend from the neck and it has a ring base (Fig. 13.36:2).[14] These are often red-slipped but seldom burnished; a third type has a wide round body and base and a vertical neck (Fig. 13.36:3-4). These are always decorated— either red-slipped or painted with rather careless geometric designs in red (i.e. Fig. 13.36:4). The examples shown here from Building F are quite large, though other such amphorae were smaller.

Storage jars: The most common jar is the Hippo-type (Fig. 13.37:1). One of these carried an inscription incised after firing (Mazar 2003c: 178-81). Other common types are the oval shaped body with a thickened rim (Fig. 13.37:6) and the jar with a wide round body, round base and long vertical neck (Fig. 13.37:7); the latter is almost always covered with a thin red wash. Cylindrical holemouth jars are common as well, with both everted and thickened rims (Fig. 13.37:8). Less common are a variety of jars that are in fact related to each other in details of body shape or rim/neck shape, but differ in the combination of these elements (Fig. 13.37:2-5).

Large, thick walled closed vessels with ring bases ('krater/jars') were used as storage vessels in Stratum IV.

Jugs: The most common jug type in Stratum IV is an oval shaped jug with a wide vertical neck, trefoil mouth and ridged rim exterior (Fig. 13.36:5). These are mostly undecorated, though some bear traces of red slip but generally are not burnished; in some cases, red lines are painted on top of the red slip (i.e. Fig. 13.36:6). Other types are similar (Fig. 13.36:6), or differ in handle placement, base or body shape (Fig. 13.36:7). Figure 13.36:8 is a small squat jug with carinated shoulder and lower body; this type is rare, but was also found in Stratum V (Fig. 13.23:14).

Juglets: Juglets too were very common in Stratum IV. Most have short rounded bodies and bases, though several are squatter (Fig. 13.23:9-10). Black juglets are not common and most have a rounded body with narrow neck and handle that joins at mid-neck (Fig. 13.36:11). The one shown in Fig. 13.36:12, with its pointed base and handle from the neck, is unique in this stratum. It was found on Floor 5498, under a large wooden beam (of a loom?).

Pyxis: Several small pyxides were found in Stratum IV, with a sack shaped body, narrow vertical neck and two small horizontal handles. They are all red-slipped but not burnished (Fig. 13.36:13).

Lamps: Lamps are shallow, with everted shelf rims and wide rounded bases (Fig. 13.36:14); other buildings included flat-based lamps as well.

Imports: Greek Sherds: Figure 13.36:15 shows a reconstruction of an Attic Early Middle Geometric I skyphos; two sherds of this vessel were found in the southern and middle rooms of the western wing of Building F (Coldstream and Mazar 2003: 35, Fig. 7). A body sherd of a Cypro-Phoenician closed vessel was found in Locus 5429 (not illustrated).

Summary. The pottery assemblage of Stratum IV is extremely varied and includes mostly types that continue from Stratum V, and some from Stratum VI as well. Isolated shapes begin to appear in Stratum IV, but the typological differences with previous strata are mainly quantitative. The amount of red slip slightly declines, comprising ca. 30% of the assemblage; hand burnish is still common. The painted tradition continues mainly on amphorae and other closed vessels, though in much smaller amounts. Though only one small sherd of Cypro-Phoenician Black on Red ware was found in Building F, other Stratum IV contexts (in Area C and other areas as well) did contain a number of high quality sherds and vessels of this ware, as well as White Painted sherds.

---

14.   Though not shown in the contexts of Buildings H and G, this amphora type was found in Stratum V as well, though it was an infrequent type at that time as opposed to in Stratum IV.

The pottery of Strata VI–IV: general conclusions. The pottery assemblages of Strata VI–IV demonstrate a basic similarity of the pottery industry in typology, technology and decoration throughout the entire Iron IIA period. There is a modicum of continuity of ceramic types from Stratum VI to V, while the overwhelming majority of ceramic types of Stratum V continue into Stratum IV. Modes of decoration continue as well, primarily red slip and hand burnish, but also the notable red painted tradition that is still present in Stratum IV. However, despite this similarity, there are subtle differences that express themselves in the quantities of types and decoration modes, technological change and distribution of imports. These differences will become clearer with further research.

The basic homogeneity of the ceramic assemblages of Strata VI–IV allows us to compare it as a unit to assemblages from other Iron Age IIA northern sites, in particular Tel 'Amal Strata 3–4 (Levy and Edelstein 1972), Tell el-Hama (unpublished assemblage from a destruction layer), Megiddo VB and VA–IVB (Finkelstein, Zimhoni and Kafri 2000), Yoqne'am Strata XV–XIV (Zarzecki-Peleg 1997), Ta'anach Periods IIa–IIb (Rast 1978), Horvat Rosh Zayit, Strata III–IIa-b (Gal and Alexandre 2000), Tell el-Far'ah (Tirzah) Stratum VIIb (Chambon 1984) and Jezreel (both the pre-Omride fills and the destruction layer, Zimhoni 1997: 13-56).

Though regional differences exist, comparisons may also be made to Hazor Strata X–VIII (see comparative discussion in Zarzecki-Peleg 1997: 275-82). Thus, a framework of relative chronology is established that covers a number of strata at various sites, emphasizing the longevity of this ceramic assemblage. Based on the stratigraphic data combined with the ^{14}C dates, we estimate the duration of this assemblage to be ca. 150 years. Such a duration of pottery types is known from other contexts as well, such as the Canaanite Late Bronze Age, when ceramic types and decorative modes continue from the 15th century BCE well into the 13th century BCE virtually unaltered. The cultural, social, economic and demographic implications of this homogeneity and longevity will be explored in future studies of these rich assemblages.

Imported pottery in these and other Iron IIA contexts at Tel Rehov include Greek Proto-Geometric, Sub-Proto-Geometric and Middle Geometric sherds (Coldstream and Mazar 2003; Mazar 2004), Cypro-Phoenician Black on Red, Cypriot Bichrome and White Painted (Smith forthcoming) and Phoenician Bichrome. Establishing dates as precise as possible for the Tel Rehov context is thus a valuable contribution to elucidate the questionable ages of these Mediterranean pottery groups.

Destruction date of Stratum IV, based on radiocarbon dates from Building F.
Basket 54702, Locus 5498, level 86.10 m. Charred grain was found inside a pottery jug above the beaten earth floor in the eastern side of the main room of Building F, under a 1.18 m thick layer of destruction debris. This is the best possible context for an homogeneous sample of grains. Seven AMS measurements of the charred cereal grains were made in Groningen and the results (Table 13.3) range from a low of 2710 ± 45 (GrA-22301a) to a high of 2785 ± 40 (GrA-22330b), while the other five dates are in between this range within 1σ overlap from each other. It is noteworthy to mention that these dates were prepared and measured in two different periods. The weighted average of the first three measurements is virtually the same as the weighted average of the later series of four measurements, which underlines the robustness of reproducibility in the Groningen AMS lab, which is an important element of quality control. The excellent archaeological context of this sample also underlines the possible level of inherent variability of individual ^{14}C measurements (Mook and Waterbolk 1985: 10) of the same sample, up to 75 midpoint BP years in this case. These midpoint differences are covered by the standard deviation levels, which form an integral part of each BP date.

The overall weighted average of the seven dates is 2758 ± 16 yr BP and the chi-squared test (Bronk Ramsey 2003) underlines the good level of coherence between the individual dates (Fig.

13.38). The value for T = 2.1, which is much less than the critical 5% confidence limit of 12.6. Calibration of the average date gives a 1σ age range of 918–895 (28.2%), 877–840 (40.0%) BCE and a 2σ range of 969–960 (4.7%), 926–833 (90.7%) BCE (down to 833 BCE in the 2σ range). Thus, the 9th century period of 877–840 BCE has the highest relative probability. The alternative is the last quarter of the 10th century BCE, which does not make sense in stratigraphic terms, as the destruction of Stratum IV must be younger in age than the destruction of Stratum V.

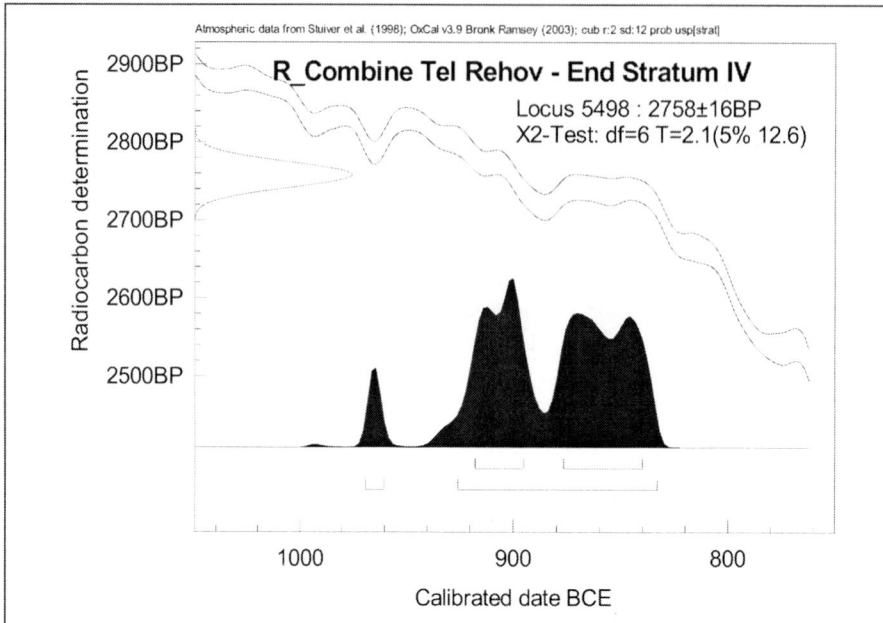

Figure 13.38. Area C, Stratum IV, Locus 5498. Calibration of the destruction of Stratum IV. The period 877–840 (40.0%) BCE has the highest relative probability, while the period 918–895 (28.2%) BCE remains significant.

Iron IIA samples in Area B

Stratigraphy. Area B was excavated on the northern slope of the upper mound, overlooking the lower city (Fig. 13.39).

Stratum B-6 was exposed in small probes only; floor surfaces and few fragmentary walls were revealed. The pottery is typical of the Iron Age IIA.

Stratum B-5 (Fig. 13.40) contained the remains of four structures. Two buildings at the western and eastern edges of the area were only partly exposed; both were destroyed by heavy fire. Four rooms were partly excavated in the eastern building. The two southern rooms in this building were preserved to a height of over one meter; the walls were found covered by plaster and there were wooden beams at the foundations, as well as below the floors and walls, similar to Stratum V in Area C. Concerning the western building, only the eastern outer walls and small parts of three rooms were exposed, while the rest is beyond the limit of the excavation area. Remains of an additional structure were exposed between these two buildings, showing evidence of two building phases, denoted Phase B-5b and B-5a. Part of a fourth building was recovered in the southern part of Area B. Thus, Phase B-5 represents part of a densely built and well planned block of buildings, recalling the densely built quarters in Areas C and E. Both the eastern and western buildings were destroyed by heavy fire, but no indication of fire was detected in the central area or in the southern building.

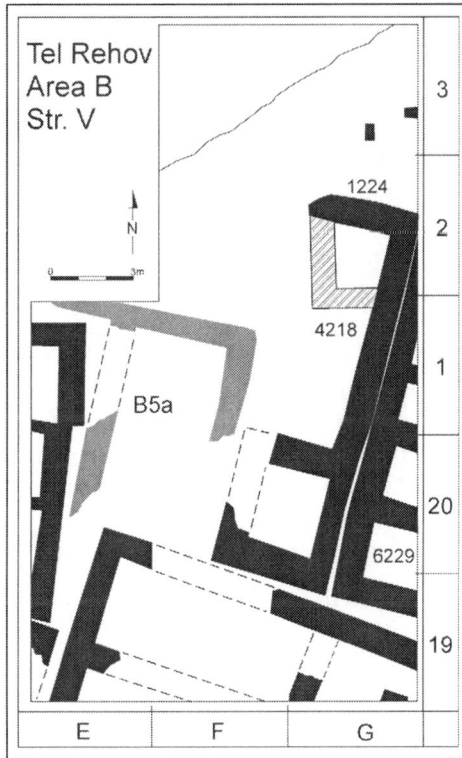

Figure 13.40. Area B: plan of Stratum B-5.

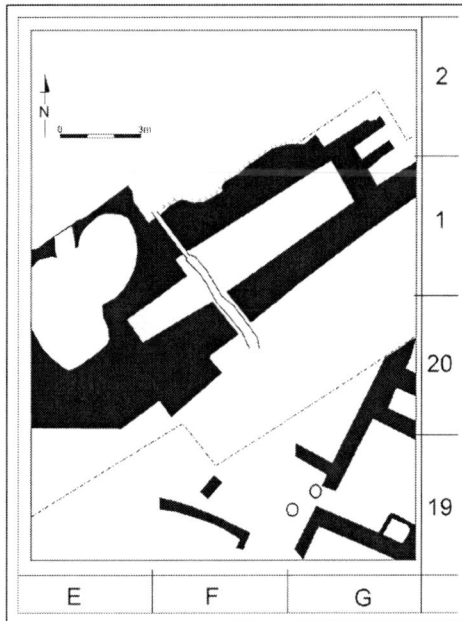

Figure 13.41. Area B: plan of Stratum B-4.

The pottery found in all these buildings is typical for the Iron IIA period, yet there were no restorable assemblages like those of Areas C and E.

In Stratum B-4 (Fig. 13.41) a major change in town planning occurred. The buildings of Stratum V went out of use and were replaced by two new features: a double wall system with a drain crossed the area from north-east to south-east; a badly preserved tower was related to this wall at the western part of the area. Both were perhaps part of a fortification system of the upper city. South of these remains appeared parts of dwellings and courtyards, having a surprisingly different spatial orientation than the fortification line. Though no restorable assemblages were found in this phase, all pottery sherds are typical of the Iron Age IIA period, as described in the previous section on Area C.

During Stratum B-3, a 9 m wide city wall made of bricks was constructed, retaining the orientation of the previous double wall system and reutilizing the tower related to it as part of the new wall. The dwellings of the previous city continued to be in use, though altered, while the floors were raised. The small amount of pottery found on these floors is typical of the Iron IIB period. The violent destruction of this city, attested especially in Area A, can be safely attributed to the Assyrian conquest in 732 BCE. The subsequent Stratum B-2 showed remains of a few squatters and a grave containing an intact Assyrian ceramic bottle.

Our original stratigraphic correlation between Area C and Area B was as follows:

Area C		Area B		General Stratum No.
C-1a	=	B-4	=	IV
C-1b	=	B-5b and B-5a	=	V
C-2	=	B-6	=	VI

Indeed, the pottery in all these layers is typical for Iron Age IIA. Yet this correlation may be questioned in light of the different urban developments in the two areas. As described above, in Area C there is a great deal of continuity in the urban planning between Strata V and IV. Area B, on the contrary, revealed a significant change in urban planning between Strata B-5 and B-4, while there is much architectural continuity between B-4 and B-3. Therefore, it seems possible that the destruction by fire of B-5 corresponds to the conflagration of Stratum IV in Area C, followed by the abandonment of the lower city. In such a case, Stratum B-4, though still belonging to Iron Age IIA, could have been constructed slightly after the destruction of the lower city. This might explain the construction of a fortification wall (the double wall system) in B-4.

Thus, the following alternative stratigraphic correlation may be suggested:

Area C		Area B		General Stratum No.
Abandoned lower city	=	B4	=	IIIB
C1a	=	B5a	=	IV
C1b	=	B5b	=	V
C2	=	B6	=	VI

At this stage, it is difficult to decide which of the two options is the correct one.

^{14}C dates from Area B.

Stratum B-5b, Locus 4218 (Basket 42236, level 90.75 m). Charred olive stones were found in the middle of a 40 cm thick layer of occupation debris in Square G-1, the central block in Area B. Locus 4218 is sandwiched between brick debris of Locus 4250 below and brick debris of Locus 3242 above. There were higher floor surfaces of Stratum B-5 above this surface.

Basket 42236 contained 10 charred olive stones and also one small piece of charcoal; both types were dated separately in the Groningen lab. Three AMS measurements were made of the olive stones (Table 13.3): 2760 ± 35 (GrA-21034); 2820 ± 35 (GrA-21047); 2770 ± 50 (GrA-21179). The weighted average is 2786 ± 22 BP, approved by the chi-squared test that underlines the coherence of the series, as T = 1.6, well below the 5% confidence limit of 6.0. The 1σ calibrated date is 994–991 (1.7%), 973–956 (19.5%), 942–899 (47.0%) BCE and the 2σ range is 999–895 (83.9%), 877–842 (11.5%) BCE. Clearly, the period 942–899 has the highest relative probability (Fig. 13.42).

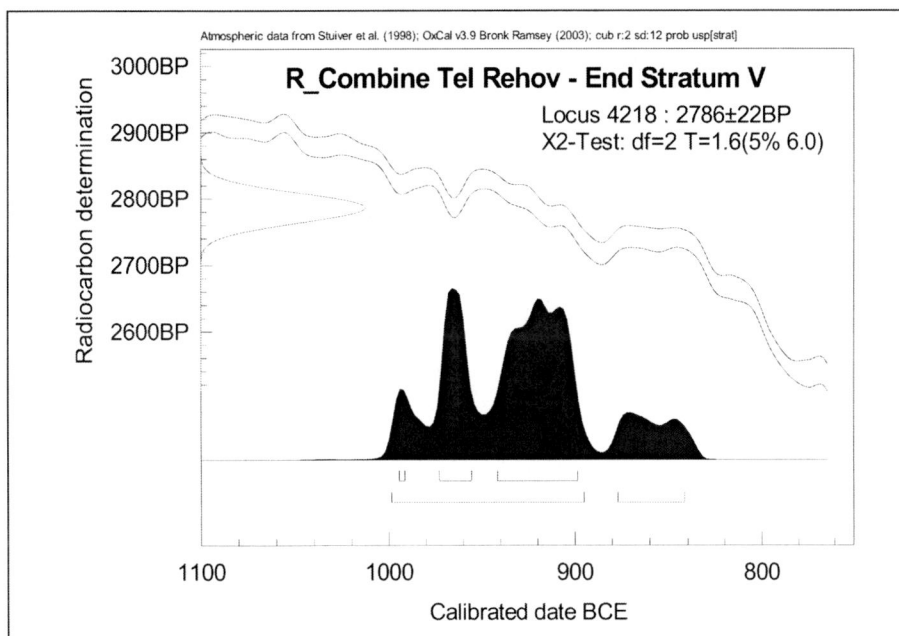

Figure 13.42. Area B, Stratum V, Local Stratum B-5, Locus 4218. Calibration of the destruction of Stratum V in Area B, based on the combined date of three AMS measurements of charred olive stones. The period 942–899 (47.0%) BCE has the highest relative probability.

Besides the olive stones, the charcoal piece was also subjected to three AMS measurements: 2765 ± 35 (GrA-21042), 2750 ± 35 (GrA-21053), 2690 ± 50 (GrA-21180). The weighted average date of the charcoal is 2744 ± 22 BP, which is significantly younger than the above average date for the charred olive stones. The chi-squared test approves the series of individual dates on which the average date for the charcoal is based, as T = 1.5, while the 5% confidence limit is 6.0. The 1σ calibrated date for the charcoal is 902–891 (12.4%), 880–835 (55.8%) BCE and the 2σ range is 967–962 (1.8%), 922–830 (93.6%) BCE. Thus, the highest relative probability is in the 9th century BCE. On the other hand, the average date for the olive pits (2786 ± 22 BP) is in the 10th century BCE, being very similar to the results of other Stratum V dates. The reason for the comparatively young date of the charcoal is not clear and may relate to a number of options, including occasional excessive radiocarbon measurement variability inherent to the system, as well as archaeologically-related uncertainties such as burrowing by animals. The coherent dates based on the cluster of 10 short-lived olive stones are to be preferred from any perspective in comparison to the dates based on one piece of charcoal.

Stratum B-5a, Locus 6229 (Basket 62430, level 91.23 m). A concentration of charred grains was found on the floor of the southern room of the eastern building in Area C, under a layer of burnt destruction debris, more than one meter in thickness. The grains were dated in Groningen by both AMS and PGC. The four AMS measurements gave the following results: 2765 ± 45 (GrA-24108), 2770 ± 45 (GrA-24109), 2780 ± 45 (GrA-24111), 2750 ± 45 (GrA-24112). The AMS dating reproducibility of the cereal grains is outstanding, as all results are very close together within 1σ. This high quality is reflected in the very low chi-squared value of $T = 0.2$, with respect to the 5% value of 7.8, in relation to the weighted average AMS date of 2766 ± 23 BP (Fig. 13.43). The calibrated age for 1σ is 968–961 (6.8%), 923–895 (33.1%), 877–857 (17.6%), 853–841 (10.7%) BCE. The 2σ calibrated age range is 973–956 (10.9%), 941–832 (84.5%) BCE. The highest relative probability is the period 923–895 BCE, but a date in the 9th century, before 832 BCE is also possible. The single PGC date (2735 ± 30 BP, GrN-28368) is somewhat younger than all four AMS dates, though within 1σ overlap. Its 1σ calibrated date is 899–887 (12.7%), 884–833 (55.5%) BCE situated entirely within the 9th century BCE, though the 2σ range also includes the 10th century BCE: 969–960 (2.6%), 928–816 (92.8%).

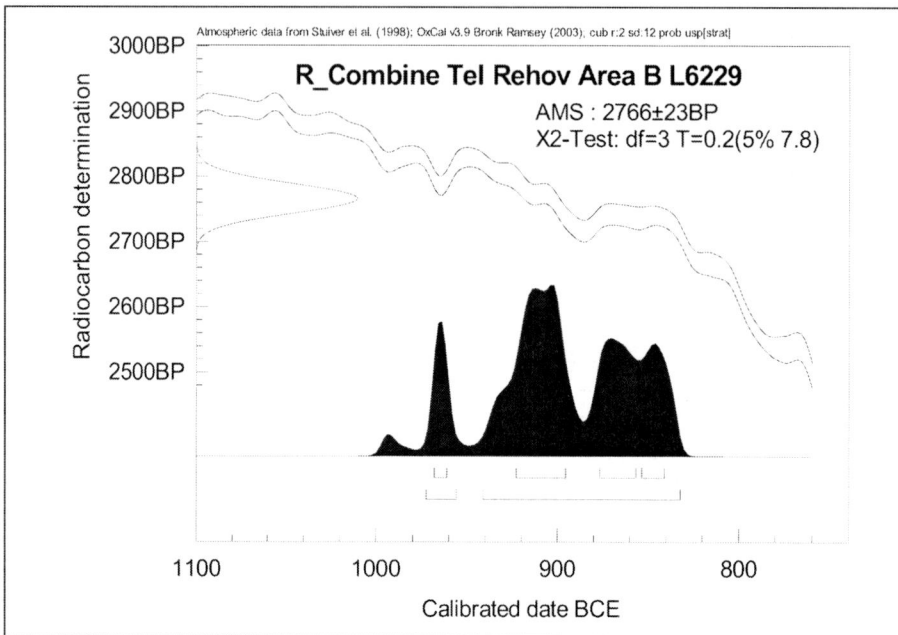

Figure 13.43. Area B, Locus 6229. Calibration based on the combined date of four AMS measurements of charred grains. The period 923–895 (33.1%) BCE has the highest relative probability, favouring linkage with Stratum V.

Combining all the dates, AMS and PGC, gives a weighted average of 2755 ± 18 BP. The chi-squared value $T = 0.9$ (5% 9.5) is also very much acceptable (Fig. 13.44). The 1σ calibrated date is 915–895 (24.1%), 877–839 (44.1%) BCE, in which both the 10th and 9th centuries BCE are significant options, but the highest relative probability is in the 9th century BCE. The 2σ calibrated range is 968–961 (3.8%), 925–832 (91.6%) BCE. In conclusion, Locus 6229 of Phase B-5 could belong to either general Stratum IV or V on stratigraphic grounds, and the ^{14}C dates allow for both options. The more tenable option is that the heavy destruction of the building occurred with the destruction of general Stratum IV.

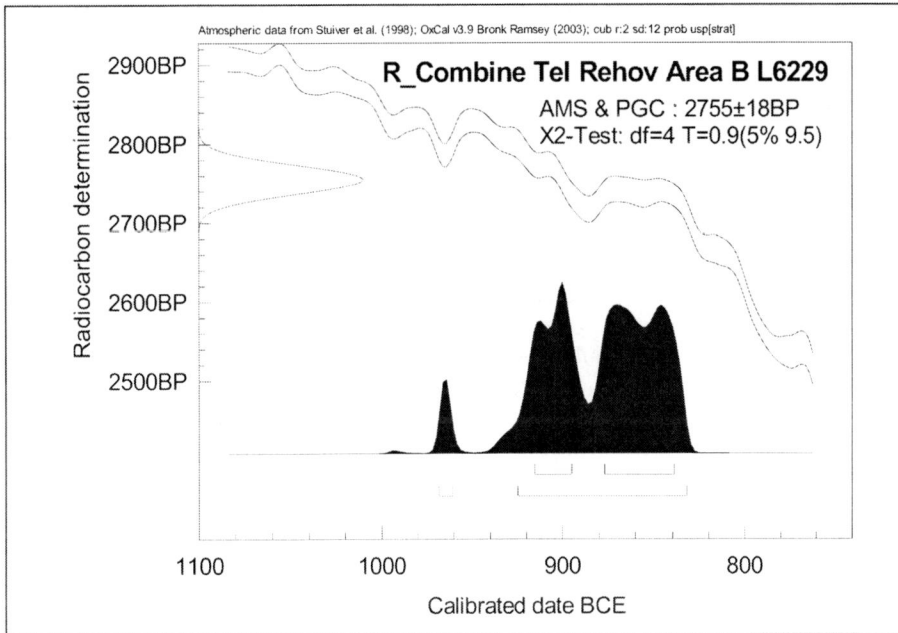

Figure 13.44. Area B, Locus 6229. Calibration based on four AMS dates and one PGC measurement, all of charred grains. The younger PGC date affects the calibration result and now the period 877–839 (44.1%) BCE is more likely, though the period 915–895 (24.1%) BCE remains important. Linkage with Stratum IV is favoured according to this result.

Locus 1224, Square G-2, Basket 41016, Level 90.60 m. This context is not a good one; a concentration of olive pits was found in cleaning the western section of Square G2, about 0.2 m above the bricks of Wall 1241 of Stratum B-5. All remains of B-4 were washed away in this area, and thus the layer can be attributed to Stratum B-5 with some confidence.

Sample GrN-27365 the BP date is 2765 ± 15 BP. The 1σ calibrated age is 967–962 (5.2%), 922–896 (37.9%), 876–858 (16.8%), 852–842 (8.3%) BCE and the 2σ age range is 970–959 (8.6%), 934–890 (48.0%), 882–835 (38.8%) BCE. The period with the highest relative probability in the 1σ range is 922–896 BCE.

Iron IIA samples in Area E

Area E, at the eastern part of the lower city of Tel Rehov, was identified as an open sanctuary (Mazar 1999: 23-28). It includes a spacious courtyard and several structures related to it. One sample from this area was dated.

Locus 2618, Square E16, Basket 46281, Level 71.92 m, Stratum E-1b. The locus is a surface in the open courtyard of the sanctuary. In this courtyard occupation debris accumulated during a long time, up to a thickness of about 1 m. The olive stones in this sample were found at the lowest levels of this accumulation, which we tend to attribute to Stratum E-1b (probably to be correlated with general Stratum V). The AMS date is 2745 ± 40 BP (GrA-17260). Though the mid-point BP date is comparatively young, the large standard deviation covers many options concerning the actual date. The 1σ calibrated age is 915–833 (68.2%) BCE. Both the late 10th and the 9th centuries BCE are included. The 2σ age range covers a wider time span: 997–988 (1.4%), 974–953 (7.4%), 945–811 (86.5%) BCE. This is an example of a single date with a rather large standard deviation, normal for AMS measurements, which cannot give a definite dating answer, due to the shape of the calibration curve.

A piece of olive wood found in Locus 1664 in Area E (local Stratum E1a, correlated with Stratum IV) was dated at Rehovot to 2770 ± 25 BP (RT-2996), calibrated in the 1σ range to 970–840 BCE (Mazar and Carmi 2001: 1337, Table 5).

Conclusions

The Groningen dates of Tel Reḥov are almost exclusively based on short-lived samples, found in a detailed stratigraphic sequence that covers both the Iron Age I and IIA cultural periods. The samples were pre-treated and measured in Groningen by conventional PGC radiometry (GrN) for large samples and AMS (GrA) for small samples. Therefore, results from the two Groningen labs enable ongoing intercomparison and quality control under the same roof, which is a great advantage for chronological studies in historical Near Eastern archaeology. The ^{14}C method is pushed to the very limit of its time resolution capability—both precision and accuracy—in physical scientific terms. The repeatability of the measurements, which is a most important indicator of quality and accuracy, is generally outstanding, both within the AMS lab and in comparison with the PGC lab, although there are a few exceptions, mentioned above and also treated by van der Plicht and Bruins (Chapter 14, this volume).

The 64 ^{14}C dates from Tel Reḥov measured in Groningen, the 13 dates measured at Rehovot and the 9 dates measured at Tucson, were evaluated in relation to the stratigraphic sequence and the typological development of pottery, as presented above. The following concluding remarks can be made:

1. Stratum D-6 of the late Iron Age IA in Area D may be dated to a time span that covers the entire 12th and part of the 11th centuries BCE, based on three coherent dates from Groningen. The slightly younger date for Locus 2874 (GrN-26120) is still within the 1σ overlap range of the other D-6 samples. Ceramic types in both Strata D-7 and D-6 seem to favour a date in the 12th century BCE, possibly contemporary with the end of the Egyptian presence at Beth Shean during the late 20th Dynasty (Mazar 2003a: 324 Table 1; 333-37).

2. Stratum D-4 of the Iron Age IB has a calibrated 1σ age range that covers both the 12th and 11th centuries BCE. *None* of the calibrated dates from this level are younger than 1000 BCE, either in the 1σ or 2σ age range. In fact most dates are not later than the mid-11th century BCE. The rather flat calibration curve and many wiggles in this time period make more precise dating difficult. The radiometric dates overlap with many of the Stratum D-6 dates. Considering the stratigraphic relations between D-6 and D-4, the existence of the additional Stratum D-5 between them, as well as the pottery typology, place D-4 in the 11th century BCE.

3. Stratum D-3 includes pits which are generally dated, according to the small amount of pottery (mainly small sherds) found in them, to the end of the Iron Age I. The youngest series of coherent Groningen dates of Stratum D-3 (Locus 4830) has the highest relative probability in the period 1000–970 BCE. The calibrated date in the 1σ range clearly excludes the 975–955 BCE wiggle, which requires younger BP dates, fitting Stratum VI of Area C, which overlies Stratum VII. The latter stratum is equivalent to Stratum D-3, marking the last phase of the Iron Age IB, just before the introduction at Tel Reḥov of red-slipped and hand burnished ware at the beginning of Iron Age IIA. This transition occurred at Tel Reḥov most probably during the first three decades of the 10th century BCE, according to the radiocarbon dates. The suggestion by Finkelstein and Piasetzky (2003a) that the transition from Iron I to Iron IIA took place around 920 BCE, contradicts the radiocarbon dating results as presented above.

4. The 43 dates from Groningen related to Iron IIA contexts in three different strata at Tel Rehov provide extensive radiocarbon coverage of this controversial period. A fundamental problem of radiocarbon dating in the 10th and 9th centuries BCE is evident from the detailed calibration curve in Figure 13.13. Charred seeds from three different historical periods, 975–955, 930–890 and 880–835 BCE, will have similar radiocarbon dates in the range of about 2770–2750 BP, particularly if the standard deviation σ is above 20. As explained above, the comparatively *older* part of the 10th century BCE, 975–955 BCE, has *younger* radiocarbon BP dates than the period 955–935 BCE. Therefore, arranging radiocarbon dates according to their BP dates as older or younger (Finkelstein and Piasetzky 2003c) is in our view wrong in such cases.

How then can one decide whether a radiocarbon date in the range of 2770–2750 BP belongs to the early–middle 10th century, late 10th century or middle 9th century BCE? The destruction of Stratum V provided large quantities of charred seeds that could be dated in Groningen by PGC radiometry, which can give very low standard deviations of individual measurements, with a standard deviation as low as about 12 BP years. Moreover, multiple measurements of the same sample material, including AMS on small samples, enabled the calculation of a weighted average that resulted in very low standard deviations (below 10). Thus, we obtained very precise results for the destruction of Stratum V for various loci, which almost exclusively favour the period 925–895 BCE. The many Groningen dates for the destruction of Stratum V provide the *pivotal anchor* of radiocarbon dating at Tel Rehov, enabling the positioning of the other Strata on the calibration curve in successive stratigraphic order (Fig. 13.45) by logical deduction (Bruins, van der Plicht and Mazar 2003a) or by Bayesian statistics (Bruins *et al.* [Chapter 15, this volume]).

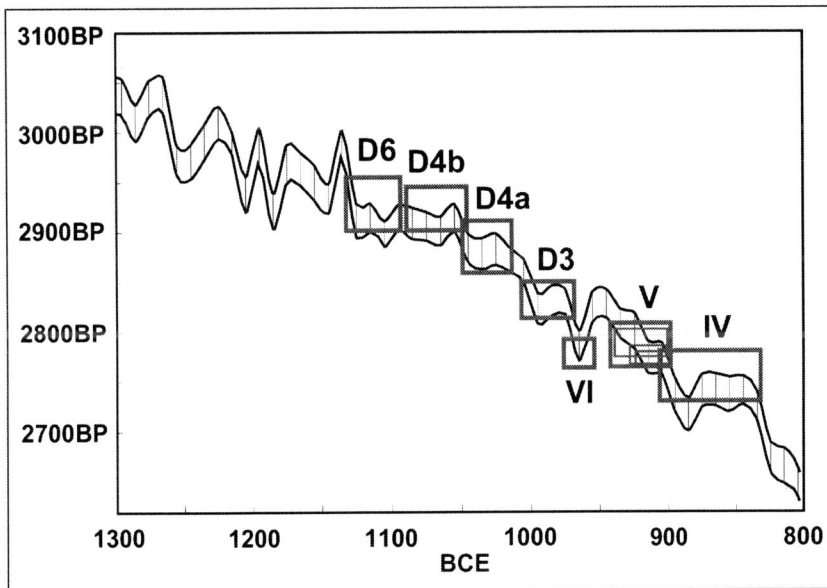

Figure 13.45. Placing the calibrated dates of the successive strata in stratigraphic order on the calibration curve (after Bruins, van der Plicht and Mazar 2003a).

5. The additional advantage of multiple measurements of the same sample source is not only an increase in precision but also in accuracy. Single ^{14}C measurements may be some time distance away from the actual date, as indicated by the standard deviation (Mook and Waterbolk 1985: 10). Multiple measurements are likely to result in a weighted average that is closer to the real age (van der Plicht and Bruins 2001), provided the radiocarbon lab does not have a systematic bias towards older or younger dates.

6. Since Stratum VI (= C-2) is older than Stratum V (= C1b), based on the stratigraphic sequence, its radiocarbon results must be placed on the calibration curve to the left (older) of Stratum V. The weighted average of all Stratum VI dates is 2772 ± 11 BP, which is almost the same as for Stratum V in BP years. The 1σ calibrated date gives three possible age ranges: 969–960 (12.4%), 928–897 (52.2%), 873–868 (3.6%) BCE. It is clear that the period 928–897 BCE has the largest relative probability of 52.2%, which is the same period as determined for Stratum V. However, on stratigraphic archaeological grounds Stratum VI cannot be coeval with Stratum V, but must be older. Now we might argue that within this period of 928–897 BCE, the first half, 928–913 BCE, is the date of Stratum VI and the second half, 913–897 BCE, is the date of Stratum V, as more or less suggested by Finkelstein and Piasetzky (2003a). There are several problems with this option. The first is that the precise dates for Stratum V relate to its destruction, which, as a point date, has the highest relative probability around 910–914 BCE (Bruins *et al.* [Chapter 15, this volume]). Taking the period 928–913 BCE for Stratum VI does not leave any time whatsoever for the duration of the city of Stratum V, if it was destroyed around 913 BCE. Moreover, there are ceramic differences between Stratum VI and V that cannot be accounted for within such a very short period of only 5 or 10 years separation between the two strata.

Concerning the two alternative dating options for Stratum VI, we can ignore the period 873–868 BCE, because it is younger than Stratum V, and its relative probability is very low (3.6%). However, the third dating option of 969–960 BCE is realistic, because it reflects a direct hit of the BP date with the calibration curve (Fig. 13.45) in a period that is older than Stratum V. Since Stratum VI overlies Stratum VII, which is similar to Stratum D-3, this radiocarbon option for Stratum VI fits very well indeed. The most probable radiocarbon date for the end of Stratum D-3 is the period 1000–970 BCE, which neatly predates the most realistic average date for Stratum VI, namely, 969–960 BCE. Considering the fact that the radiocarbon dates for Stratum VI come from only one locus, the actual duration of Stratum VI could have been the period 980–950 BCE, while that of Stratum V would be 950–910 BCE.

7. The sample from Building F, Stratum IV in Area C relates to the final destruction of the lower city at Tel Reḥov. The 1σ calibrated date has one option in the last part of the 10th century BCE and a more likely option in the 9th century BCE, but not later than 840 BCE (in 2σ: 833 BCE). Any date between ca. 900 and 833 BCE is thus legitimate for the end of Stratum IV.

8. The problem of contradictory results obtained at different laboratories should be addressed. In our case, it can be clearly shown that most of the dates from Tel Reḥov measured at the Weizmann lab during the late 1990s were younger by 100–150 years (BP years) as compared to the dates obtained at Groningen.

These serious discrepancies raise suspicion that some of the Weizmann dates on samples from other sites like Dor and Megiddo, which were prepared during the 1990s (Finkelstein and Piasetzky 2003a, 2003b, 2003c; Gilboa and Sharon 2001, 2003; Mazar 2004; Sharon 2001), may also represent results that are too young. These dates should now be examined by other ^{14}C laboratories. Thus, the far reaching conclusions of Gilboa and Sharon (2003) and the criticism of our results by Finkelstein and Piasetzky (2003a, 2003b), which is based to a large extent on dates measured at the Rehovot lab during the late 1990s, should be dismissed (Mazar 2004: 31-35).

9. The implication of our research on the Iron Age chronology of the Levant should be noted. The stratigraphy, pottery sequence and radiometric dates at Tel Rehov as well as at other sites support a long duration for Iron Age IIA, from ca. 980 to ca. 840/830 BCE, in line with the view of Aharoni and Amiran (1958), Barkay (1992: 303), Ben-Tor (1992: 2) and Mazar (since 1997—Mazar 1997: 163-64; 1990: 40-42; Mazar and Carmi 2001: 1340; Coldstream and Mazar 2003: 40-44; Mazar [Chapter 2, this volume]); this system was accepted lately also by Herzog and Singer-Avitz (2004) and Ben-Shlomo, Shai and Maeir (2004).

10. Imported Phoenician, Cypriot and Greek pottery in the Iron Age IIA strata at Tel Rehov can be dated to the 10th–9th centuries BCE, and thus provide important links for dating pottery groups in these countries. In our view, the Cypriot chronology should be slightly raised in time, and the Cypriot Geometric II period should probably be obliterated (Gilboa and Sharon 2004; Smith forthcoming). The Greek chronology as suggested by Coldstream in 1968 can be maintained, provided that we utilize the extended dates for the Iron Age IIA as suggested here (see Coldstream and Mazar 2003; Mazar 2004 for further discussion). The suggestion of Gilboa and Sharon to lower the chronology of Cyprus and Greece by about 100 years in light of the ^{14}C dates from Dor should be questioned in light of the noticed tendency at the Weizmann lab during the 1990s to produce dates that are too young, as explained above (Mazar 2004).

11. Some historical questions should be addressed here briefly. Rehov is mentioned aside Beth Shean and 'the valley' in the topographic list of Pharaoh Shoshenq I (biblical Shishak) at Karnak (Kitchen 1986: 187-239; B. Mazar 1986: 146). This is the only mention of Rehov in written documents of the first millennium BCE. Most scholars believe that Shoshenq destroyed (partly or completely) sites mentioned in his list (see, e.g., Finkelstein 2002), though Na'aman (1998) suggested that perhaps no destructions accompanied this raid. We claim that a total or partial destruction of the city during this event is a very possible scenario, and thus it is legitimate to locate a destruction layer that would fit the event. The only candidate is the partial destruction by fire of Stratum V in Areas C and perhaps B. It should be noted, however, that this destruction was not total: not all the buildings were burnt, and many were renovated in the following Stratum IV. In Area C, some buildings went out of use, others continued from Stratum V to Stratum IV with very little change and still others were renovated, changed, and so on. The precise time of Shoshenq's campaign is unclear: the date 925 BCE suggested by Kitchen (1986: 187-239; 2000: 40-41) is most widely cited, but his argumentation depends to a large extent on biblical chronology and leaves the door open for a somewhat higher or lower date. Andrew Shortland (Chapter 4, this volume) suggests a date ca. 920 BCE, based on internal Egyptian data. The best average date for the destruction of Stratum V based on the Groningen dates is within the last quarter of the 10th century BCE. Most of this range is slightly later than 925 and would better fit the date 917 BCE. We thus conclude that though the end of Stratum V and the transition to IV was a complex process, at least parts of the Stratum V city could have been destroyed during Shoshenq's attack.[15] Of course, one may claim that the partial destruction of Stratum V occurred as a result of some local event, for example an earthquake that caused local fires. Yet, if these were local events, they must have occurred close to the years when Shoshenq's army passed through the Beth-Shean Valley and recorded at Rehov in the official Egyptian records as a raided town.

---

15. Finkelstein and Piasetzky (2003b: 286-77) suggested that the end of Stratum V should be correlated with Jeroboam's I conquest of the so far Canaanite Beth Shean valley. This is a most untenable suggestion, since the material culture of Stratum V (as well as that of the previous Stratum VI) is identical to that of sites like Tell el-Far'ah (Tirzah) VIIb, Ta'anach IIA–IIB, Megiddo IVB–VA etc. which are defined as Israelite by all scholars, including Finkelstein. Defining Tel Rehov V as a Canaanite city (contemporary with Megiddo Stratum VIA according to Finkelstein) is an absurd suggestion, since these two assemblages represent totally different material cultures (see also Mazar [Chapter 2, this volume]).

12. The calibrated average radiocarbon date for the destruction of Stratum IV, according to the seven Groningen AMS dates of charred cereal grains from Building F, comprises the possible periods 918–895 (28.2%) and 877–840 (40.0%) BCE in the 1σ range. The calibrated dates in the 2σ range are 969–960 (4.7%) and 926–833 (90.7%) BCE. The lowest end of this time range may allow us to relate the destruction and abandonment of the lower city at Tel Reḥov to one of the historical events following the end of the Omride Dynasty. The invasions of Hazael king of Damascus between ca. 840–830 BCE are a possibility. Yet the resemblance of the pottery in Strata V and IV may allude to an even earlier date during the 9th century BCE for the destruction of Stratum IV.

The significance of our results for the debate concerning the archaeological nature of the United Monarchy and the northern kingdom of Israel is discussed by Mazar elsewhere in this volume (see Chapter 2).

References

Aharoni, Y., and R. Amiran (1958) A New Scheme for the Subdivision of the Iron Age in Palestine. *IEJ* 8: 171-84.

Barkay, G. (1992) The Iron Age II–III. In *The Archaeology of Ancient Israel*, edited by A. Ben-Tor (New Haven: Yale University Press): 302-73.

Ben-Shlomo, D., I. Shai and A. Maeir (2004) Late Philistine Decorated Ware ('Ashdod Ware'): Typology, Chronology, and Production Centers. *BASOR* 335: 1-34.

Ben-Tor, A. (1992) Introduction. In *The Archaeology of Ancient Israel*, edited by A. Ben-Tor (New Haven: Yale University Press): 1-9.

Bowman, S.G.E., J.C. Ambers and M.N. Leese (1990) Re-evaluation of British Museum Radiocarbon Dates Issued between 1980 and 1984. *Radiocarbon* 32(1): 59-79.

Bronk Ramsey C. (2003). *OxCal Program v3.9, Radiocarbon Accelerator Unit* (Oxford: Oxford University Press).

Bruins, H.J., J. van der Plicht and A. Mazar (2003a) [14]C Dates from Tel Reḥov: Iron Age Chronology, Pharaohs, and Hebrew Kings. *Science* 300: 315-18.

—(2003b) Response to Comment on '[14]C Dates from Tel Reḥov: Iron-Age Chronology, Pharaohs and Hebrew Kings'. *Science* 302: 568c.

Bruins, H.J., A. Mazar and J. van der Plicht (in press) The End of the 2nd Millennium BCE and the Transition from Iron I to Iron IIA: Radiocarbon Dates of Tel Reḥov, Israel. In *The Synchronization of the Civilization in the Second Millennium BCE*, edited by M. Bietrak (Vienna: Austrian Academy).

Chambon, A. (1984) *Tell el-Far'ah I, L'Age du Fer* (Paris: Édition Recherche sur les Civilisations).

Coldstream, N., and A. Mazar (2003) Greek Pottery from Tel Reḥov and Iron Age Chronology. *IEJ* 53:29-48.

Finkelstein, I. (2002) The Campaign of Shoshenq I to Palestine. *ZDPV* 118: 109-35.

Finkelstein, I., and E. Piasetzky (2003a) Comments on '[14]C Dates from Tel Reḥov: Iron Age Chronology, Pharaohs and Hebrew Kings'. *Science* 302: 658b.

—(2003b) Wrong and Right: High and Low, ^{14}C dates from Tel Reḥov and Iron Age Chronology. *Tel Aviv* 30: 283-95.

—(2003c) Recent Radiocarbon Results and King Solomon. *Antiquity* 77: 771-79.

Finkelstein, I., O. Zimhoni and A. Kafri (2000) The Iron Age Pottery Assemblages from Areas F, K and H and Their Stratigraphic Implications. In *Megiddo III. The 1992–1996 Seasons*, edited by I. Finkelstein, D. Ussishkin and B. Halpern (Tel Aviv: Institute of Archaeology, Tel Aviv University): 244-324

Gal, A., and Y. Alexandre (2000) *Horbat Rosh Zayit: An Iron Age Storage Fort and Village* (IAA Reports 8; Jerusalem: Israel Antiquities Authority).

Gilboa, A., and I. Sharon (2001) Early Iron Age Radiometric Dates from Tel Dor: Preliminary Implications for Phoenicia and Beyond. *Radiocarbon* 43: 1343-52.

—(2003) An Archaeological Contribution to the Early Iron Age Chronological Debate: Alternative Chronologies for Phoenicia and their Effects on the Levant, Cyprus and Greece. *BASOR* 332: 7-80.

Herzog, Z., and L. Singer-Avitz (2004) Redefining the Centre: The Emergence of State in Judah. *Tel Aviv* 31: 209-44.

Kitchen, K.A. (1986) *The Third Intermediate Period in Egypt* (Warminster: Aris & Phillips, 2nd edn).

—(2000) The Historical Chronology of Ancient Egypt: A Current Assessment. In *The Synchronization of Civilizations in the Eastern Mediterranean in the Second Millennium B.C.*, edited by M. Bietak (Vienna: Österreichische Akademie der Wissenschaften): 39-52.

Levy, S., and G. Edelstein (1972) Cinq années de fouilles à Tel Amal (Nir David). *RB* 79: 325-67.

Mazar, A. (1993) Beth Shean in the Iron Age: Preliminary Report and Conclusions of the 1990–1991 Excavations. *IEJ* 43: 201-29.

—(1997) Iron Age Chronology: A Reply to I. Finkelstein. *Levant* 29: 157-67.

—(1999) The 1997–1998 Excavations at Tel Reḥov: Preliminary Report. *IEJ* 49: 1-42.

—(2003a) Beth Shean in the Second Millennium B.C.E.: From Canaanite Town to Egyptian Stronghold. In *The Synchronization of Civilizations in the Eastern Mediterranean in the Second Millennium B.C.*, edited by M. Bietak (Vienna: Österreichische Akademie der Wissenschaften): 323–40.

—(2003b) The Excavations at Tel Reḥov and their Significance for the Study of the Iron Age in Israel. *Eretz Israel* 27: 143-60 (Hebrew).

—(2003c) Three 10th–9th Century Inscriptions from Tel Reḥov. In *Saxa loquentur: Studien zur Archäologie Palästinas/Israels. Festschrift für Volkmar Fritz zum 65. Geburtstag*, edited by C.G. Hertog, U. Hübner and S. Münger (Alter Orient und Altes Testament 302; Münster: Ugarit Verlag): 171-84.

—(2004) Greek and Levantine Iron Age Chronology: A Rejoinder. *IEJ* 54: 24-36.

—(in press a) Tel Reḥov: The Contribution of the Excavations to the Study of the Iron Age in Northern Israel. In *Proceeding of the Second International Congress on the Archaeology of the Ancient Near East* (Winona Lake, IN: Eisenbrauns).

—(in press b) Tel Reḥov. In *The New Encyclopedia of Archaeological Excavations in the Holy Land, Supplementary Volume*, edited by E. Stern (Jerusalem: Israel Exploration Society).

Mazar, A., and I. Carmi (2001) Radiocarbon Dates from Iron Age Strata at Tel Beth Shean and Tel Reḥov. *Radiocarbon* 43: 1333-42.

Mazar, B. (1986) Pharaoh Shishak's Campaign to the Land of Israel. In *The Early Biblical Period, Historical Studies*, by B. Mazar (ed. S. Ahituv and B.A. Levine; Jerusalem: Israel Exploration Society): 139-50.

Mook, W.G., and H.T. Waterbolk (1985) *Handbook for Archaeologists. III. Radiocarbon Dating* (Strasbourg: European Science Foundation).

Na'aman, N. (1998) Shishak's Campaign to Palestine as reflected by the Epigraphic, Biblical and Archaeological Evidence. *Zion* 63: 247-76 (Hebrew).

Rast, W.E. (1978) *Ta'anach I: Studies in the Iron Age Pottery* (Cambridge, MA: Harvard University Press).

Scott, E.M. (ed.) (2003) The Third International Radiocarbon Intercomparison (TIRI) and the Fourth International Radiocarbon Intercomparison (FIRI), 1990–2002. *Radiocarbon* 45(2): 135-408.

Sharon, I. (2001) 'Transition Dating'—A Heuristic Mathematical Approach to the Collation of Radiocarbon Dates from Stratified Sequences. *Radiocarbon* 43: 345-54.

Smith, J.S. (forthcoming) Evidence for Restructuring the Early Cypriot Iron Age from the Finds of Cypriot Ceramics at Tel Reḥov. *Tel Reḥov*, Volume I.

Stern, E. (ed.) (1993) *The New Encyclopedia of Archaeological Excavations in the Holy Land* (New York: Simon & Schuster, rev. edn).

Stuiver, M., *et al.* (1998) INTCAL98 Radiocarbon Age Calibration, 24,000-0 cal BP. *Radiocarbon* 40(3): 1041-84.

Ussishkin, D. (1985) Levels VII and VI at Tell Lachish and the end of the Late Bronze Age in Canaan. In *Palestine in the Bronze and Iron Ages: Papers in Honor of Olga Tufnell*, edited by J.N. Tubb (London: The Institute of Archaeology): 213-30.

Van der Plicht, J., and H.J. Bruins (2001) Radiocarbon Dating in Near-Eastern Contexts: Confusion and Quality Control. *Radiocarbon* 43(3):1155-66.

Zarzecki-Peleg, A. (1997) Hazor, Jokneam and Megiddo in the Tenth Century B.C.E. *Tel Aviv* 24: 258-88.

Zimhoni, O. (1997) *Studies in the Iron Age Pottery of Israel* (Tel Aviv: Institute of Archaeology, Tel Aviv University).

14 Quality Control of Groningen ^{14}C Results from Tel Reḥov

Repeatability and intercomparison of Proportional Gas Counting and AMS

Johannes van der Plicht and Hendrik J. Bruins

Abstract

Stratified radiocarbon dates provide a scientific chronological framework independent of cultural assessments. In both Groningen ^{14}C labs (conventional and Accelerator Mass Spectrometry [AMS]), a total of 64 radiocarbon dates were measured from Tel Reḥov, derived from 21 Iron Age loci. This is the largest Iron Age series available at present for any site in the Near East. We present, evaluate, and discuss in this article our methodology in terms of quality assurance, reliability and reproducibility.

Introduction

Radiocarbon dating plays a key role in (pre)historic research, because it provides a scientific yardstick (quite often the only objective) for the measurement of time. This yardstick is independent of cultural deliberations and enables chronological comparisons, for example, of different areas at an excavation site, or between sites and regions. This is essential for proper interpretation of archaeological layers and association with other data (van der Plicht and Bruins 2001).

Our ^{14}C Iron Age chronology established for Tel Reḥov, Israel, unambiguously favors a 'high chronology' (Bruins, van der Plicht, and Mazar 2003a, 2003b). However, our findings are contested by Finkelstein and Piasetzky (2003; Chapter 16, this volume). It is of crucial importance to be aware of perceived or real quality problems of dating results. The present Iron Age chronology discussion takes place at the limits of resolution of the ^{14}C method, as issues need to be resolved with a temporal resolution well within a century. Here even small errors may have important consequences. Mistakes can be made by the ^{14}C laboratory (methodology and accuracy), and/or in the field (sampling and association).

In this paper we discuss the ^{14}C dates from Tel Reḥov in terms of quality control, as measured by the two Groningen radiocarbon laboratories: conventional by means of Proportional Gas Counting (PGC) and AMS. This is necessary in order to evaluate the coherence and robustness of our radiocarbon series, composed of 64 dates, based on two separate measurement systems (for all these dates, refer to the tables in Mazar *et al.* [Chapter 13, this volume]). Our dates are contested by proponents of the 'low chronology' theory. They refer to other ^{14}C dates, which are comparatively younger than the Groningen series, as far as Tel Reḥov is concerned (Bruins, van der Plicht, and Mazar 2003b, 2004).

The ^{14}C Dating Method

Radiocarbon (^{14}C) is a natural isotope of the element Carbon, which is produced by cosmic radiation and occurs in minute concentrations in living organisms. Since this isotope is radioactive (with a half-life of 5730 years) the ^{14}C concentration gradually declines after the death of the organism. Thus, by measuring the remaining ^{14}C content in (pre)historic samples one can date these samples, or more precisely, calculate the moment of death of the organism.

Although the principle of ^{14}C dating is based on this straightforward model, in practice the theory is complicated by many factors. First, the natural ^{14}C concentration has not been constant through time; the exact value of the half-life to be used for ^{14}C age calculations is not transparent; furthermore, isotopic effects in natural processes change the ^{14}C content for various sample materials, thereby changing the age. Second, measuring the ^{14}C radioactivity in natural concentrations is not simple, and requires specialized laboratories and measuring procedures. Here we summarize briefly the issues relevant for this paper. For more detailed accounts we refer to the specialized literature.

The theoretical complications are solved by a number of conventions (e.g. Mook and Waterbolk 1985). The ^{14}C measurements are reported in a specially defined unit BP. This definition comprises: (a) the ^{14}C radioactivity is measured relative to an international standard (i.e. oxalic acid with a ^{14}C activity corresponding to 1950 AD); (b) the ^{14}C age is calculated using the original half-life value of 5568 years; (c) the ^{14}C age calculation includes correction for isotopic fractionation using the ^{13}C content of the sample (to the standard value of $\delta^{13}C = -25\text{‰}$).

This convention is valid for all measuring techniques used for ^{14}C dating. Thus, the ^{14}C timescale is *defined*; a ^{14}C chronology (in BP) is different (and varying over time) from a calendar chronology (in BC/AD). The relation between the two timescales is established by calibration, which is the process of translating ^{14}C dates into calendar ages. Calibration curves are established by high precision ^{14}C measurements of wood samples dated absolutely by dendrochronology. The present calibration curve recommended by the ^{14}C community is INTCAL98 (Stuiver *et al.* 1998) to be replaced by INTCAL04 (Reimer *et al.* 2004). The part of the calibration curve relevant for this volume, 1500–500 BCE, is shown in Figure 14.1.

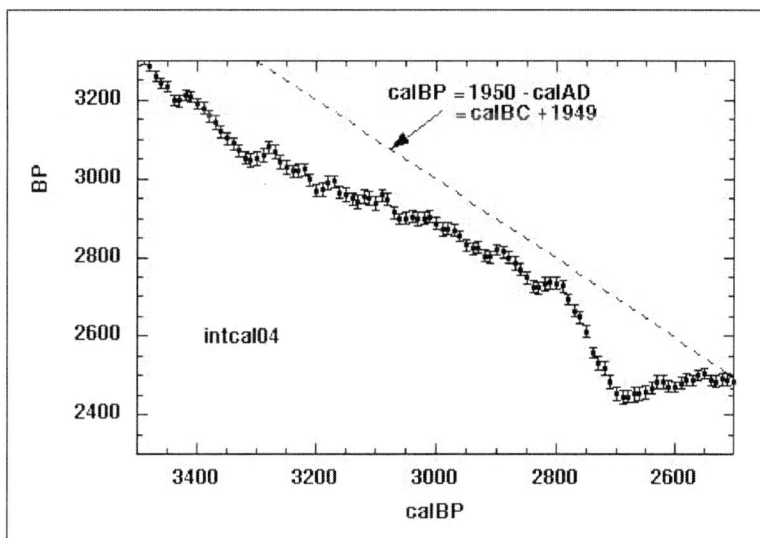

Figure 14.1. Radiocarbon calibration curve (Reimer *et al.* 2004) for the timerange 1500–500 BCE.

Calibrated age range distributions for individual or stratified series of ^{14}C dates can be obtained using computer programs like OxCal (Bronk Ramsey 1995).

The measuring process of the ^{14}C content of archaeological samples such as bone, charcoal, wood, and so on, can be viewed from two perspectives: measuring technique and sample preparation. For ^{14}C, three different measuring techniques have been developed—PGC, Liquid Scintillation Spectrometry (LSC), and AMS. The first two, PGC and LSC, are called 'conventional techniques' and are based on radiometry; they require ca. 1 gram of carbon (e.g. Kromer and Münnich 1992; Theodorsson 1996). Larger sample amounts may result in a more precise measurement with a smaller standard deviation. The technique of AMS is based on mass spectrometry, for which mg size C is sufficient (e.g. Bayliss, McCormac, and van der Plicht 2004; Tuniz *et al.* 1998). The radiocarbon laboratory in Groningen houses both a conventional (PGC-based) and an AMS laboratory, with both facilities operating independently.

Sample preparation follows similar procedures for all three measuring techniques (Mook and Streurman 1983). The general rules are that contaminants have to be removed (physically and chemically) and that a reliable datable fraction has to be isolated. The latter is then combusted into CO_2 gas, which needs to be purified. For PGC, the $^{14}CO_2$ is counted in terms of radiometry; for AMS, the CO_2 needs to be transferred into graphite. Stable isotope mass spectrometers are used to measure the δ^{13}C content of the same CO_2 gas. Apart from fractionation information, the δ^{13}C is a measure for quality of the sample material—as well as the carbon content.

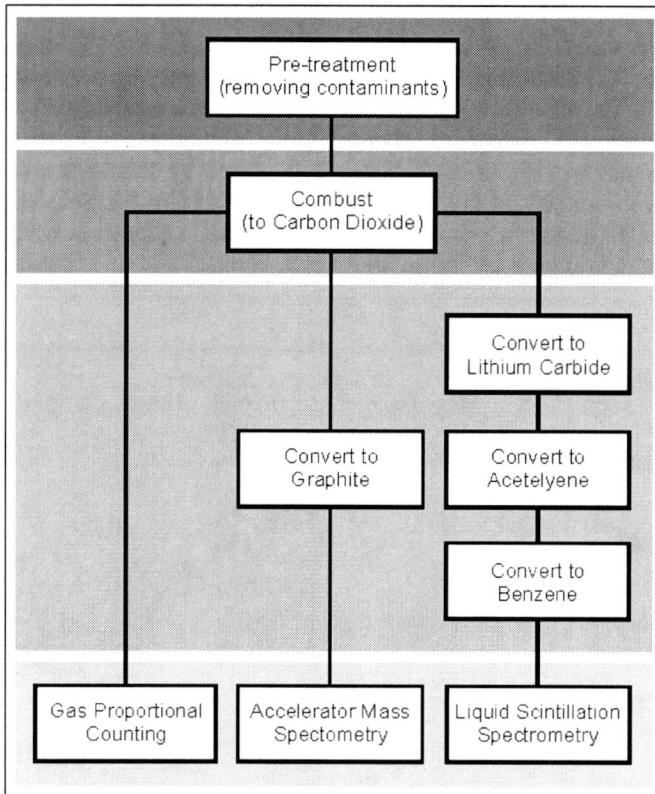

Figure 14.2. Schematic illustration for measuring archaeological samples (Bayliss, McCormac, and van der Plicht 2004; Mook and Streurman 1983): (a) overview of methods for measurements of ^{14}C; (b) method of pre-treatment for an archaeological charcoal sample.

The pre-treatment for an archaeological charcoal sample is shown as an example in Figure 14.2. Only the ¹⁴C that was part of the organism when it died should be measured. Therefore the first task is to remove any foreign carbon that has entered the sample material since that time. Such contamination comes mainly from the burial environment. We mention the two most common contaminants for charcoal samples: rootlets (usually from higher strata and thus younger) may be present in the collected material; soil carbonate (containing fossil carbon, thus older than the sample). We refer to Mook and Streurman (1983) for more details.

Quality Control Issues

Radiocarbon (¹⁴C) is the most common radiometric dating tool applied in disciplines such as archaeology, geosciences, and environmental research. Stringent quality control is required to build up reliable ¹⁴C chronologies, in particular for the (pre)historical periods in the Levant. Important aspects of quality control involve regular laboratory intercomparisons, multiple analyses of selected samples, sample material selection, archaeological association, and sample size (i.e. conventional versus AMS as measuring technique). These aspects will be discussed below.

General Aspects

True point dates cannot be achieved with ¹⁴C dating, as there will always be a standard deviation. Both equipment resolution and measurement stability, as well as the random nature of radioactive decay (Mook and Waterbolk 1985: 10) 'causes the results of repeated measurements to spread around a "true" value. The possible discrepancy between a measured value and the "true" value is indicated by the standard deviation (σ)'. Hence one measurement of a sample may result in a date that is very close to the real date, in terms of the mid-point Gaussian value, but may also be older or younger, depending on the value of the standard deviation. Concerning radiocarbon research in Near Eastern historical archaeological periods in which an accuracy and precision is required within a 100 year BP range, multiple measurements of the same sample were suggested (van der Plicht and Bruins 2001). Such multiple measurements will theoretically result in an average date that is both more accurate and precise than can be achieved with single measurements, provided that the ¹⁴C laboratory does not have a systematic bias towards older or younger dates. The issue of multiple measurements is further discussed below.

The quality of the BP date—before calibration—always forms the basis for every radiocarbon age determination. It must be realized that a ¹⁴C date *does* provide a very important universal physical measurement of time, independent of cultural–historical viewpoints and associative reasoning.

Sample selection is a critical component in the ¹⁴C dating process. The layers from which archaeological or geological samples are taken during excavations have not always remained static and may have been affected by different kinds of post-depositional processes. Perturbation by plants, animals or human activities (e.g. digging) may cause migration or contamination of carbon in samples used for ¹⁴C dating.

Another key question is the relationship between the age of the sample and the archaeological or historical question addressed: 'How is the ¹⁴C event related to the human event to be dated?' (van Strydonck *et al.* 1999). A well known problem in this respect is the so-called 'old wood effect'. Wood used (or re-used) to construct a building may have a ¹⁴C date that differs from the human construction event by several centuries, depending on the age of the wood. It must be emphasized that the ¹⁴C date of the wood in such a case is *not* a measurement mistake. Rather the age of the wood sample is older than the age of the archaeological layer or building in which it was found.

Another important matter related to sample selection is the respective choice of 'conventional dating versus AMS'. There can be a temptation to collect and submit all isolated seeds and tiny flecks of charcoal. The dating of such isolated samples by AMS should be discouraged, if larger samples (seed or charcoal clusters) are present in the same layer. If sufficient material is available, samples can be dated more cheaply and often more accurately by conventional means. The possibility of dating erratic post-depositional influences is considerable when isolated small fragments of charcoal or seeds are used, which are liable to movement by faunal or human digging activity. Such tiny samples have to be derived from a clearly defined context or association to justify dating. Lanting and van der Plicht (1994) presented a detailed discussion about these issues, including examples. It is a 'myth' that AMS is better than conventional radiocarbon dating: standard deviations are usually not smaller.

Time-width effects represented by a sample have to be considered. Bulk samples of peat layers, for example, are centimeters thick for conventional ^{14}C analysis. Such a sample comprises many years of sedimentation or growth. Isolated seeds, macrofossils, and grains represent single-year samples and are typical AMS material, due to their small sample size, but the stratigraphic context must be clear, as noted above.

The correct calibration procedure of ^{14}C dates from multi-year or single-year samples needs to be carefully contemplated. Smoothed curves are recommended for multi-year samples, while single-year samples ought to be calibrated with the most detailed calibration curve available (Mook and Waterbolk 1985).

The 975–955 BCE wiggle, so important in the Iron Age (Bruins, van der Plicht, and Mazar 2003a, 2003b; Mazar et al. [Chapter 13, this volume]) is based on dendrochronological data through radiocarbon measurements of groups of 10 tree rings (decadal) or 20 tree rings (bidecadal) (Stuiver et al. 1998). The radiocarbon measurements of Tel Rehov Stratum VI are based on short-lived samples (seeds, bone) with a time span of a few years or even less (growing season). Past ^{14}C variations in the atmosphere are not captured in such detail by the calibration curve itself, due to the comparatively 'coarse' decadal and bidecadal measurements. Therefore, it might be important to make a special primary study of this 975–955 BCE wiggle through ^{14}C measurements of each individual tree ring in the available dendrochronological series for the period 980–940 BCE or even for the entire 10th century BCE. Such detailed measurements have been carried out for older Bronze Age periods (Vogel and van der Plicht 1993).

Intercomparison

Intercomparison is a major part of quality assurance. In an intercomparison, the same samples are dated by different laboratories. This may involve either samples of known age or blind samples. Thus a laboratory can 'check' its performance—in particular, the sample (pre)treatment and ^{14}C measurement procedures. Intercomparison is a well recognized issue in the ^{14}C community, and various exercises form a continuing process. The latest large scale intercomparison is FIRI (Fourth International Radiocarbon Intercomparison) in which 84 laboratories participated worldwide. Several publications are generated by this program (Boaretto et al. 2003; Scott et al. 2004), and the final report is a special publication of the *Radiocarbon* journal (Scott [ed.] 2003).

This FIRI had the following aims:

1. Evaluation of the comparability of routine analysis of both AMS and conventional laboratories.
2. Quantification of the extent of and the sources for any variation.
3. Investigation of the effects of sample size, precision, and pre-treatment on the results (Scott [ed.] 2003).

Groningen Intercomparison and Quality Aspects

We show here the results for the two Groningen laboratories (conventional and AMS) in Table 14.1. The FIRI samples are named A–J. 'AMS-extra' were optional samples (not officially part of the FIRI exercise). The consensus value is the resulting value as determined by analysis of the FIRI measurements, except for the wood samples which are dated by dendrochronology.

Table 14.1. FIRI results for the Groningen ^{14}C laboratories (conventional [lab. code GrN] and AMS [lab. code GrA]). The ^{14}C ages are reported in BP or as ^{14}C activities in %. All errors are 1σ. 'AMS-extra' were optional samples (not officially part of the FIRI exercise).

	Sample	Conventional	AMS	AMS-extra	Consensus Value
A	Kauri	52400(+1830, −1500)	>50000		0.24%
	cellulose			>50000	
B	Kauri	53140(+2030, −1620)	>50000		0.24%
	cellulose			>50000	
C	Turbidite	18270(70)	17930(60)		18176
D	wood	4510(20)	4485(40)		4508
	cellulose			4470(40)	
E	humic	11850(40)	11800(50)		11780
	1 mg			11860(60)	
	0.2 mg			11650(80)	
	0.06 mg			12050(330)	
F	wood	4490(20)	4525(40)		4508
	cellulose			4550(40)	
G	barley	111.08(0.22)%	110.91(0.31)%		110.7%
H	wood	2190(20)	2240(40)		2232
	cellulose			2230(40)	
I	cellulose	4505(35)	4490(30)		4485
J	barley	110.76(0.22)%	110.72(0.31)%		110.7%

A second class of intercomparison was done by high precision laboratories. This is a 'subset' of laboratories, traditionally active in the field of calibration of the radiocarbon timescale (Seattle, Belfast, Heidelberg, Groningen [conventional], Pretoria, and Tucson [conventional]). These laboratories produced the calibration curves, recommended by the ^{14}C conferences (Reimer *et al.* 2004; Stuiver and Kra [eds.] 1986; Stuiver, Long, and Kra [eds.] 1993; Stuiver and van der Plicht [eds.] 1998). By exchanging dendro-dated wood and standards, the interlaboratory differences yield offsets in the 0–20 ^{14}C year range (Stuiver *et al.* 1998), and sometimes smaller. The interlaboratory difference between Groningen and Pretoria, for example, appears to be 7.1 ± 6.4 ^{14}C years, Pretoria being the older of the two. This allowed us to construct a calibration curve with a high temporal resolution (1–4 years) for the 4th–3rd millennia BC (Vogel and van der Plicht 1993).

Thirdly, we mention the development of working standards for the ^{14}C community. The Groningen laboratory developed the IAEA standards C3, C7 and C8. The latter two have designed activities of 15 and 50%, respectively; C3 is modern (Rozanski *et al.* 1992). The final activities of the material have been measured as an intercomparison between 7 laboratories: Seattle, Belfast, Heidelberg, Groningen (both conventional and AMS), Waikato, and Tucson (conventional). The measured results can be found in LeClercq, van der Plicht, and Gröning (1998).

The Groningen Centre for Isotope Research is in a unique position because it has two radiocarbon laboratories—one conventional and one AMS—which operate independently. Exchange of samples between the two laboratories—as an 'internal intercomparison'—does take place. Often this happens to test or check the extreme limits of the ^{14}C method. As an example, we mention the ^{14}C date of 55,000 BP for a mammoth from Siberia (Arilakh) based on 4 age measurements

(2 conventional, 2 AMS) on 2 types of material (bone marrow and bone collagen). Three of the 4 individual dates would result in an infinite radiocarbon age (Mol *et al.* forthcoming).

More common is the cross-checking of standards and backgrounds. For the conventional laboratory, a few liters of the original standard Oxalic Acid (Ox1) is kept, used, and re-used as the primary standard activity for the conventional laboratory with a radioactivity of 226 ± 1 Bq/kgC (Mook and van der Plicht 1999). The new Oxalic Acid (Ox2) with a ^{14}C activity of 134.06% is used as a working standard for both the conventional and the AMS laboratories.

For AMS, a batch of measurements consists of 57 samples, including typically 5 backgrounds and 8 standards (Aerts, van der Plicht, and Meijer 2001; van der Plicht *et al.* 2000). These standards are Ox2—a mixture of Ox2 combusted by the AMS preparation line following the same route as the unknown samples, and Ox2 from a large volume prepared by the conventional laboratory. This way, the conventional and AMS preparation lines are checked against each other. Similar exchanges between conventional and AMS take place occasionally for background material, which is CO_2 prepared from ^{14}C-free anthracite. We note that the CO_2 gas as prepared by the conventional laboratory is very pure, because this is required for the gas counters (van der Plicht, Streurman, and Schreuder 1992).

In addition, performance of the ^{14}C quality over a long time period is checked using IAEA-C7 and C8. These materials (LeClercq, van der Plicht, and Gröning 1998) are also working standards but treated as unknowns; the Ox2 average ^{14}C measured activity ratio value per batch determines the standard measurement, which is set to 134.06%.

Multiple Analysis

Duplicate measurements of samples may confirm each other, if both results are similar, thus ensuring quality control. But it may also lead to different results. Waterbolk (1990: 148) stated: 'If a sample has been measured twice, be it by the same or by another laboratory, and the results are not congruent, we cannot know which date to reject'. In such cases a third measurement on the same sample should be conducted, in order to determine the correct ^{14}C date.

The standard deviation σ of the radiocarbon date is usually based on the uncertainty in the ^{14}C counts for sample, standard and background. A measure of the reproducibility of the result is another very important factor that influences the standard deviation. Reproducibility is generally estimated by using in-house standards (known age material) and may often be negligible. Nevertheless, this factor is crucial in quality control. Laboratories may be tempted to report a small standard deviation based on radiometry counting only, but neglecting the reproducibility of the date. The latter may also be related to other factors in standard lab routine and performance, including the quality of equipment, and so on.

The calibrated age range is not only defined by counting statistics, but is also 'wiggle' dependent. The calibrated age range for a series of dates can be narrowed down by 'wiggle matching' (Pearson 1986) or using special statistics (Bronk Ramsey 1998). 'High Precision' measurements are usually defined as those with errors (1 σ) < 0.2%. For very large samples containing more than 10 grams of C and measured with Proportional Gas Counting, the smallest feasible limit is 10–15 BP. This lower limit of precision results from the following constraints:
1. The error margins of standards and backgrounds are only slightly smaller.
2. The error margins of the calibration curve are not smaller, as the ^{14}C measurements of the dendro-dated wood are 'high precision' by themselves. The INTCAL98 curve is decadal (i.e. one data-point per 10 tree rings, representing 10 calendar years).

Combined stratified series of short-lived samples and multi-year charcoal are better than only a few isolated short-lived dates (see for examples Bruins and van der Plicht 1995; Bruins *et al.*

concerning Tel Dan [Chapter 19, this volume]). A *paramount requirement* for the establishment of a high-quality radiocarbon chronology of Near Eastern archaeology involves the ¹⁴C data acquisition of as many archaeological layers as possible.

Tel Reḥov: The ¹⁴C Dates

Following an initial series of datings by the ¹⁴C laboratory at Rehovot, Israel (Mazar and Carmi 2001), a series of dates, now reaching 64 (Table 14.2), from 21 loci were measured in Groningen (Bruins, van der Plicht, and Mazar 2003a, 2003b, 2004; Mazar *et al.* [Chapter 13, this volume]). The conventional laboratory in Groningen operates a set of 9 proportional gas counters, with one counter especially suitable for very large samples such as grains (tens of grams). The counter operates for 25 liters of CO_2 and is capable of high precision ¹⁴C dating with errors (1σ) down to 10–15 BP. This enabled the unique high precision dates for sites like Jericho (Bruins and van der Plicht 1995, 2001). Smaller gram-size samples were measured in other proportional counters, and intrinsically small samples were measured by AMS. Thus, both conventional and AMS measurement techniques were used, according to sample size and for quality control reasons. Altogether, the dates for Tel Reḥov constitute the largest group of radiometric measurements from a single Iron Age site in the Levant.

Table 14.2. List of all 64 radiocarbon dates from Tel Reḥov with related stratigraphic and laboratory information. The ¹⁴C dates are measured in Groningen (GrN—conventional [PGC]; GrA—AMS). For a detailed discussion, see Bruins, van der Plicht, and Mazar (2003a, 2004) and particularly Mazar *et al.* (Chapter 13, this volume).

Area, Stratum and Period	Locus	Basket	Charred Organic Material	sample weight ratio	%C organic fraction	Lab. No.	¹⁴C Date (BP)	$\delta^{13}C$ (‰)
C-1a IV Iron IIA	5498	54702	Cereal Grains	26.9	55.9	GrA-21152	2770 ± 50	–
				same	57.1	GrA-21154	2730 ± 50	22.54
				same	55.6	GrA-21267	2760 ± 35	–
				same	55.5	GrA-22301a	2710 ± 45	22.28
				same	same	GrA-22301b	2775 ± 40	–
				same	55.2	GrA-22330a	2760 ± 50	22.74
				same	same	GrA-22330b	2785 ± 40	–
								22.34
								same
								22.32
								same
E-1b ? IV or V ? Iron IIA	2618	46281	Olive stones	36.2	62.0	GrA-17260	2745 ± 40	–
								21.98
B-5 IV or V ? Iron IIA	6229	62430	Total	20.0	66.3	GrN-28368	2735 ± 30	–
			Alkali			GrA-24108	2765 ± 45	23.60
			Alkali			GrA-24109	2770 ± 45	–
			Seeds			GrA-24111	2780 ± 45	23.60
			Seeds			GrA-24112	2750 ± 45	–
								23.60
								–
								24.30
								–
								26.40

B-5 ? V ? Iron IIA	1224	41016	Olive stones	54.3	66.9	GrN-27365	2765 ± 15	-22.98
B-5 V Iron IIA	4218	42236	Olive stones Olive stones Olive stones Charcoal Charcoal Charcoal	39.3 same same 47.6 same same	62.5 61.0 60.7 57.9 58.1 58.0	GrA-21034 GrA-21047 GrA-21179 GrA-21042 GrA-21053 GrA-21180	2760 ± 35 2820 ± 35 2770 ± 50 2765 ± 35 2750 ± 35 2690 ± 50	– 21.86 – 21.76 – 22.43 – 23.80 – 25.62 – 26.36
C-1b V Iron IIA	6449	64756	Olive stones	8.6 same same	53.9 53.7 52.9	GrA-24455 GrA-24456 GrA-24497	2775 ± 45 2750 ± 45 2745 ± 45	– 23.73 n/a n/a
C-1b V Iron IIA	2422	24408	Cereal Grains middle fine fraction	27.0 17.6 8.9	67.5 68.2 67.6	GrN-27361 GrN-27362 GrN-27412	2764 ± 11 2777 ± 13 2785 ± 28	– 22.11 – 22.15 – 22.43
C-1b V Iron IIA	2441	24579	Cereal Grains coarse middle fine fraction	22.6 33.5 23.2 16.4 9.6	69.2 66.8 67.8 68.2 68.4	GrN-26116 GrN-26117 GrN-27363 GrN-27385 GrN-27386	2810 ± 20 2775 ± 25 2745 ± 15 2771 ± 15 2761 ± 15	– 22.64 – 23.14 – 22.66 – 22.31 – 22.37
C-1b or a V or IV Iron IIA	2444	24647	Cereal Grains fine fraction	14.0 19.2	67.8 67.3	GrN-27364 GrN-27413	2764 ± 11 2866 ± 21	– 22.15 – 22.04
C-1b or a V or IV Iron IIA	2425 Continuation of 2444	24306	Cereal Grains	22.9 33.4	67.6 67.4	GrN-26114 GrN-26115	2775 ± 20 2800 ± 20	– 22.42 – 21.45
C-2 VI Iron IIA	4426	44166	Cereal Grains Fine charcoal Fine charcoal Fine charcoal Bone	50.0 58.4 same same 2.0	67.9 63.3 63.6 64.8 36.8	GrN-27366 GrA-21043 GrA-21054 GrA-21182 GrA-21417	2761 ± 14 2755 ± 35 2805 ± 35 2800 ± 50 2840 ± 45	– 22.48 – 25.50 – 24.74 – 24.68 – 19.64
D-2 IV/V/VI Iron IIA	1823	18183	Olive stones	38.9 same	67.6 61.2	GrN-26113 GrA-19030	2760 ± 30 2750 ± 50	– 22.15 – 23.29

D-2 IV/V/VI Iron IIA	1802	18119	Olive stones	47.1	67.7	GrN-26112	2805 ± 15	– 22.46
D-3 Iron IB	2862	28493	Olive stones	44.2 same	58.3 67.1	GrA-19033 GrN-26119	2835 ± 45 2720 ± 30	– 23.03 – 22.33
	4815	48105	Olive stones	*	59.7	GrA-16757	2820 ± 50	– 22.51
	4816	48103	Olive stones Charcoal	* 37.0	57.0 65.5	GrA-12889 GrA-16848	2870 ± 70 2895 ± 40	– 25.29 – 24.41
	4830	48115	Olive stones	21.6 same same same same same same	62.9 62.0 63.3 64.4 same 60.8 same	GrA-21044 GrA-21056 GrA-21183 GrA-22302a GrA-22302b GrA-22329a GrA-22329b	2845 ± 35 2825 ± 35 2820 ± 50 2730 ± 50 2820 ± 40 2810 ± 50 2760 ± 40	– 22.05 – 23.30 – 23.35 – 23.00 same – 22.63 same
D-4 Iron IB	1836	48450	Olive stones	43.6 same	72.3 58.3	GrN-26121 GrA-18825	2890 ± 30 2870 ± 50	– 22.95 – 22.99
	1845	48556	Seeds	21.6 same same	61.4 61.8 60.8	GrA-21046 GrA-21057 GrA-21184	2905 ± 35 2945 ± 35 2920 ± 50	– 22.49 – 23.10 – 24.12
D-6 Iron IA	2836	28352	Olive stones	49.4 same	68.3 54.8	GrN-26118 GrA-18826	2920 ± 30 2950 ± 50	– 22.28 – 22.46
	2874	28701	Olive stones	38.0 same	58.9 72.9	GrA-19034 GrN-26120	2935 ± 45 2880 ± 30	– 22.14 – 22.36

* = pre-treatment conventional, measured by AMS.

The list of all 64 ^{14}C dates are shown in stratigraphic order in Table 14.2 (see also Mazar *et al.* [Chapter 13, this volume], for more archaeological data and the calibration of the dates). The Tel Reḥov dates measured in the Rehovot ^{14}C laboratory (RT) (Gilboa and Sharon 2004; Mazar and Carmi 2001) are shown in the tables in Mazar *et al.* (Chapter 13, this volume). It appears from these tables that there is a systematic difference between RT and GrN/GrA, as RT is consistently younger. This is a significant observation, because the low/high chronology debate is partly caused by this interlaboratory deviation. Examples are discussed below.

A sample of charred olive pits from the oldest Iron I Stratum in Area D (D-6, Iron IA) was dated in Rehovot to 2685 ± 40 BP (RT-3119); this result is much too young by all standards as already noted by Mazar and Carmi (2001). The same stratum also yielded 4 Groningen dates

(2 conventional, 2 AMS), which are older by more than 200 BP (GrA-18826, 19034; GrN-26118, 26120).

Seeds from phase D-4b were dated at Rehovot to 2800 ± 40 BP (RT-3121), while the same seeds were dated in triplicate by AMS in Groningen yielding consistently older (ca. 100 BP) results (GrA-21046, 21057, 21184).

Another sample of olive stones from phase D-3 was dated at Rehovot to 2670 ± 40 BP (RT-3120), which is also considered much too young (Mazar and Carmi 2001).

We note that most Tel Rehov samples measured in Groningen originate from a clear archaeological context, that is, there is no association problem. All samples (seeds, olive pits) represent truly single year material. The entire series forms an excellent set of material from the ^{14}C point of view. Table 14.2 shows the Groningen dates (GrN and GrA) for the Iron Age IIA strata, in relation to the stratigraphy. The archaeological interpretations are discussed elsewhere (Bruins *et al.* 2004; Bruins *et al.* [Chapter 19, this volume]; Mazar *et al.* [Chapter 13, this volume]).

The strong point of the Groningen set of dates (Table 14.3) is the quality control aspect; two independent laboratories, one conventional including a high precision counter for large quantities of single year sample material, and one AMS. The AMS cannot achieve high precision but triplicate analyses were performed (both pre-treatment and measurement were performed in triplicate!). This enables the calculation of a weighted average of the dates in order to increase the precision and possibly also the accuracy, resulting in a measurement that is closer to the 'true age'.

Table 14.3. Specific tests for the ^{14}C methodology of additional Groningen Radiocarbon dates (GrN—conventional; GrA—AMS) for Tel Rehov.

Phase and Stratum	Locus	Basket	Charred Organic Material	Lab. No.	^{14}C Date (BP)	$\delta^{13}C(‰)$ Fraction
C-1a IV	5498	54702	Charred seeds	GrA-22301	2710(45)	−22.34
				GrA-22301	2775(40)	same
				GrA-22330	2760(50)	−22.32
				GrA-22330	2785(40)	same
D-3	4830	48115	Olive pits	GrA-22302	2730(50)	−23.00
				GrA-22302	2820(40)	same
				GrA-22329	2810(50)	−22.63
				GrA-22329	2760(40)	same
C V	2441	24579	Cereal grains	GrN-27363	2745(15)	−22.66 coarse
				GrN-27385	2770(15)	−22.31 middle
				GrN-27386	2760(15)	−22.37 fine
C-1b V	2444	24647	Cereal grains	GrN-27364	2765(15)	−22.15 coarse
				GrN-27413	2865(20)	−22.04 fine
C-2 VI	4426	44166	Bone	GrA-21417	2840(45)	−19.64 collagen
	6229	62430	Charred seeds	GrA-24108	2765(45)	−23.60 alkali
				GrA-24109	2770(45)	−23.60 alkali
				GrA-24111	2780(45)	−24.30 seeds
				GrA-24112	2750(45)	−26.40 seeds
				GrN-28368	2735(30)	−23.60 total
B-5 V b	4218	42236	Charcoal	GrA-21042	2765(35)	−23.80
				GrA-21053	2750(35)	−25.62
				GrA-21180	2690(50)	−26.36

Moreover, this (costly) exercise is also a quality check: practically all individual dates of the same sample material (basket) are within 1σ of each other. Such consistent results are indicative of high quality with robust repeatability (Scott [ed.] 2003).

In addition, the two Groningen techniques (conventional and AMS) enable internal intercomparison. Occasionally, samples were measured by both techniques, yielding consistent results. This is in accordance with other internal quality procedures which are performed routinely, and is a strong indication for quality and reliability (Scott [ed.] 2003).

Table 14.2 shows that many samples are dated by multiple analyses. The duplicates overlap very well, mostly within 1σ, which justifies the calculation of weighted averages. This applies to both AMS (typical single date errors 35–50 BP) and conventional (mostly high precision, errors ≈ 15 BP). Therefore, the Groningen ^{14}C results from Tel Reḥov constitute a high quality dataset from all physical/chemical perspectives.

Table 14.3 highlights additional dates, measured in a later stage as a test exercise for the ^{14}C methodology. The first eight measurements (baskets 54702 and 48115) constitute a 'double duplication' test: charred seeds and olive pits are treated in duplicate (GrA-22301/22330 and GrA-22302/22329), and these four samples were measured again at a later time (AMS measurement duplicate, same graphite targets). All measured ^{14}C dates show excellent reproducibility. Note that one set (basket 54702) had been dated earlier in triplicate as well (Table 14.2), yielding the same ^{14}C dates within error.

Homogeneity tests were performed for samples from baskets 24579 and 24647. This concerns large samples, measured by the conventional laboratory. The sample material was divided into parts, according to size fractions, by sieving: coarse (>850 μm), middle (<850 μm, >180 μm) and fine (<180 μm). The coarse fraction is probably the most reliable in terms of ^{14}C analysis; the recognizable seeds are obviously present in this fraction. The fine fraction may contain charred soil organic matter, and if so, it should be older. Indeed, for basket 24647, GrN-27413 is older than GrN-27364. It was suggested by Mazar *et al.* (Chapter 13, this volume) that the fine material indeed is probably derived from charred wooden beams.

However, the other samples that were split in terms of size fractions do not show an age difference. For basket 24579 the three fractions yield the same ^{14}C date. Note that also basket 24408b (Table 14.2) consists of such a measurement—GrN-27412 corresponds to the fine fraction, and GrN-27362 to the coarse fraction of the same sample material. Also here the ^{14}C dates are the same within the σ error.

Concerning basket 44166, besides the charred seeds, a bone sample was available for dating. Collagen is extracted from the bone material as the datable fraction (Mook and Streurman 1983). Both types of organic material yielded the same ^{14}C date, within the error.

Finally, a pre-treatment test was performed. Seeds from basket 62430 were dated both in terms of the alkali fraction and the residue (the 'normal' fraction). The chemical part of this experiment was done by the conventional laboratory. However, the separate alkali and residue fractions appeared too small for a precise conventional radiometric measurement. Hence they were sampled and transferred to the AMS laboratory for further analysis. At the end, both fractions were put together again and measured by the conventional laboratory (total fraction, GrN-28368). The AMS measurements were done in duplicate to test reproducibility. The overall total of five ^{14}C measurements is in excellent agreement in physical terms.

Problem Analysis—Is there a Way Out ?

We believe that our ^{14}C methodology, as applied to Tel Reḥov, is robust and coherent, representing the best that ^{14}C has to offer by using stringent quality control. Nevertheless, some problems remain to be solved. For example, there appears to be a significant offset between the ^{14}C dates from Groningen and the earlier dates obtained by Rehovot. Below is a list of possible causes for 'wrong' [14]C dates (e.g. van Strydonck *et al.* 1999):

1. A wrong archaeological association in the field.
2. Mislabeling of samples (in the field, storehouse or ^{14}C laboratory).
3. Contamination of the sample (in the field or in the laboratory).
4. The sample is not homogeneous or otherwise problematic.
5. The ^{14}C measurement is wrong (e.g. standards, background problems).
6. The sample pre-treatment is erroneous or not adequate.
7. The fractionation (δ^{13}C value) correction is not correct.
8. A combination of the above.

We note that all of the above mishaps do occasionally happen, as the volume of samples going through a ^{14}C laboratory can be very large (e.g. in Groningen, around 4000 samples annually). As an illustrative example, we can calculate (Mook and van der Plicht 1999) that an error of around 100 BP for a Levantine Iron Age sample is introduced by an error of 6‰ in δ^{13}C, or by contamination with 1% fossil (^{14}C free) or 3% modern material.

The δ^{13}C value serves as a quality parameter for the sample material. It can be seen from the measurements listed in Tables 14.2 and 14.3 that for Tel Reḥov, these values are usually in the −22 to −23 range for seeds, and around −24 for charcoal (see also Bruins *et al.* concerning Tel Dan [Chapter 19, this volume]). The one bone sample (GrA-21417) clearly has a different δ^{13}C = −19.64‰, which is a normal value for bone material.

The second quality parameter used in the ^{14}C laboratory is the organic content or the carbon content of the sample. In Table 14.2, two numbers are listed. The first column states the weight ratio (in %) of the original sample after/before the pre-treatment procedure. The carbon content of the organic fraction (%C), however, is the best sample material quality parameter. For seeds and charcoal, this value should be around 60%. From this perspective, all samples dated qualify as good datable material. Note that some samples were routed in an unusual way: for example, GrA-16757 and GrA-12889 (*) were pretreated by the conventional laboratory, but combusted and measured by the AMS laboratory.

Besides the deviating dates from Rehovot, there is one Groningen date which is an outlier: GrN-26119 from Stratum D-3 is too young, also by about a century (Table 14.2). This particular sample was submitted as a conventional sample, but appeared too small and hence was rerouted to the AMS laboratory (GrA-19033). Nevertheless, the sample could be measured conventionally by adding fossil (^{14}C free) CO_2 (Mook and Streurman 1983). We suspect the source of error is caused by this procedure. If so, this qualifies as a 'systematic error'.

The errors quoted for ^{14}C measurements only include measurement errors, which are determined from statistics (i.e. the number of ^{14}C counts), and scatter of standards and/or backgrounds. Other errors are difficult to quantify because they are not known; they can be assessed by sample quality parameters like the δ^{13}C value and organic carbon content, or tests concerning homogeneity and pre-treatment (see examples in Table 14.3). Multiple analysis is a good way to test reproducibility and reliability; intercomparison between different laboratories is a way to resolve possible discrepancies. This is one of the goals of intercomparison exercises like FIRI. As for Tel Reḥov, an intercomparison between Rehovot/Groningen/Tucson is underway for current measurements. This intercomparison will not necessarily be able to resolve the reason for the rather young dates of the Rehovot lab, measured during the 1990s, in comparison to Groningen dates from the same material or strata from Tel Reḥov.

Conclusions

In general, it is obvious that quality control in ^{14}C dating is essential in order to obtain meaningful results in the historical archaeological periods of the Near East (van der Plicht and Bruins 2001; Scott [ed.] 2003). Both archaeological and scientific elements are involved. The Groningen dates of Tel Rehov come from a detailed stratigraphic series of reliable sequenced contexts, each providing short-lived samples. These are perfect materials for dating from the radiocarbon point of perspective (van Strydonck *et al.* 1999). Internal quality assessment and internal intercomparison were performed between the two independent Groningen laboratories (conventional: PGC and AMS). The repeatability of the various dates is generally excellent, with only very few exceptions.

Reproducibility of a radiocarbon measurement on the same sample is both a check and confirmation of accuracy and reliability. It is, therefore, important that key samples are measured to the highest possible precision, that is, they should be short-lived, large in size and preferably subject to duplicate or triplicate analysis. In some cases, the same samples or loci were dated earlier by a third laboratory, Rehovot. Our research resulted, therefore, in an unplanned intercomparison with this laboratory. It appears that for Tel Rehov, the results from the Rehovot lab are systematically younger than those from both Groningen laboratories.

Since the consistent Groningen dates are based on both PGC and AMS measurements, we are inclined to consider them as reliable, while the Rehovot dates from Tel Rehov are too young by a century or more. The reason for the apparent systematic offset between the Radiocarbon laboratories of Rehovot and Groningen remains to be solved. An independent intercomparison for the current lab operation in 2004 is underway. Ultimately, in order for the Rehovot lab to check the comparatively low dates mentioned above, it would be necessary for the lab to date this material again in its current operational setup and working procedures in order to evaluate the possible problems in former measurements.

References

Aerts, A.T., J. van der Plicht, and H.A.J. Meijer (2001) Automatic AMS Sample Combustion and CO_2 Collection. *Radiocarbon* 43: 293-98.

Bayliss, A., F.G. McCormac, and J. van der Plicht (2004) An Illustrated Guide to Measuring Radiocarbon from Archaeological Samples. *Physics Education* 39: 137-44.

Boaretto, E., *et al.* (2003) How Reliable are Radiocarbon Dates? A Report on the Fourth International Radiocarbon Intercomparison (FIRI) (1998–2001). *Antiquity* 295: 146-54.

Bronk Ramsey, C. (1995) Radiocarbon Calibration and Analysis of Stratigraphy: The OxCal Program. *Radiocarbon* 37: 425-30.

—(1998) Probability and Dating. *Radiocarbon* 40: 461-74.

Bruins, H.J., and J. van der Plicht (1995) Tell Es-Sultan (Jericho): Radiocarbon Results of Short-lived Cereal and Multi-year Charcoal Samples from the End of the Middle Bronze Age. *Radiocarbon* 37: 213-20.

—(2001) Radiocarbon Challenges Archaeo-historical Time Frameworks in the Near East: The Early Bronze Age of Jericho in Relation to Egypt. *Radiocarbon* 43: 1321-32.

Bruins, H.J., J. van der Plicht, and A. Mazar (2003a) ^{14}C Dates from Tel Rehov: Iron-Age Chronology, Pharaohs, and Hebrew Kings. *Science* 300: 315-18.

—(2003b) Response to Comment on '^{14}C Dates from Tel Rehov: Iron-Age Chronology, Pharaohs, and Hebrew Kings'. *Science* 302: 568c-d.

—(2004) The End of the 2nd Millennium BCE and the Transition from Iron I to Iron IIA: Radiocarbon Dates of Tel Rehov, Israel (Vienna: SCIEM).

Finkelstein, I., and E. Piasetzky (2003) Comment on '^{14}C Dates from Tel Rehov: Iron-Age Chronology, Pharaohs, and Hebrew Kings'. *Science* 302: 568b.

Gilboa, A., and I. Sharon (2004) An Archaeological Contribution to the Early Iron Age Debate: Alternative Chronologies for Phoenicia and their effects on the Levant, Cyprus, and Greece. *BASOR* 322: 7-80.

Kromer, B., and K.O. Münnich (1992) CO_2 Gas Proportional Counting in Radiocarbon Dating—Review and Perspective. In *Radiocarbon after Four Decades: An Interdisciplinary Perspective*, edited by R.E. Taylor, A. Long, and R.S. Kra (New York: Springer Verlag): 184-97.

Lanting, J.N., and J. van der Plicht (1994) ^{14}C-AMS: Pros and Cons for Archaeology. *Palaeohistoria* 35/36: 1-12.

LeClercq, M., J. van der Plicht, and M. Gröning (1998) New [14]C Reference Materials with Activities of 15 and 50 pMC. *Radiocarbon* 40: 295-97.

Mazar, A., and I. Carmi (2001) Radiocarbon Dates from Iron Age Strata at tel Beth Shean and Tel Reḥov. *Radiocarbon* 43: 1333-42.

Mol, D., *et al.* (forthcoming) Results of the Cerpolex/Mammuthus Expeditions on the Taimir Peninsula, Arctic Siberia, Russian Federation. *Quaternary International* 142–43: 186-202.

Mook, W.G., and H.J. Streurman (1983) Physical and Chemical Aspects of Radiocarbon Dating. In *Proceedings of the First International Symposium ^{14}C and Archaeology, Groningen*, edited by W.G. Mook and H.T. Waterbolk (PACT 8; Strasbourg: Council of Europe): 31-55

Mook, W.G., and J. van der Plicht (1999) Reporting [14]C Activities and Concentrations. *Radiocarbon* 41: 227-39.

Mook, W.G., and H.T. Waterbolk (1985) *Handbook for Archaeologists. III. Radiocarbon Dating* (Strasbourg: European Science Foundation).

Pearson, G.W. (1986) Precise Calendrical Dating of known Growth-period Samples using a 'Curve Fitting' Technique. *Radiocarbon* 28: 292-99.

Reimer, P.J., *et al.* (2004) INTCAL04 Terrestrial Radiocarbon Age Calibration, 26–0 ka BP. *Radiocarbon* 46: 1029-58.

Rozanski, K., *et al.* (1992) The IAEA [14]C Intercomparison Exercise. *Radiocarbon* 34: 506-19.

Scott, E.M. (ed.) (2003) The Third International Radiocarbon Intercomparison (TIRI) and the Fourth International Radiocarbon Intercomparison (FIRI). *Radiocarbon* 45: 135-408.

Scott, E.M., *et al.* (2004) Precision and Accuracy in Applied [14]C Dating: Some Findings from the 4th International Radiocarbon Comparison. *Journal of Archaeological Science* 31: 1209-13.

Strydonck, M. van, *et al.* (1999). What's in a [14]C Date. *Proceedings of the Third International Symposium ^{14}C and Archaeology, Lyon, France, 6–10 April 1998* (Paris: Société Préhistorique Française): 433-448.

Stuiver, M., and R.S. Kra (eds.) (1986) Calibration Issue. *Radiocarbon* 28(2B): 805-1030.

Stuiver, M., A. Long, and R.S. Kra (eds.) (1993) Calibration Issue. *Radiocarbon* 35(1).

Stuiver, M., and J. van der Plicht (eds.) (1998) INTCAL98, Calibration Issue. *Radiocarbon* 40(3).

Stuiver, M., *et al.* (1998) INTCAL98 Radiocarbon Age Calibration, 24,000-0 cal BP. *Radiocarbon* 40: 1041-84.

Theodorsson, P. (1996) *Measurement of Weak Radioactivity* (Singapore: World Scientific Publishing).

Tuniz, C., *et al.* (1998). *Accelerator Mass Spectrometry* (Boston/London/New York/Washington, DC: CRC Press).

Van der Plicht, J., and H.J. Bruins (2001) Radiocarbon Dating in Near-Eastern Contexts: Confusion and Quality Control. *Radiocarbon* 43: 1155-66.

Van der Plicht, J., H.J. Streurman, and G.R. Schreuder (1992) A New Data Acquisition System for the Groningen Counters. *Radiocarbon* 34: 500-505.

Van der Plicht, J., *et al.* (2000) The Groningen AMS Facility: Status Report. *Nuclear Instruments and Methods B* 172: 58-65.

Vogel, J.C., and J. van der Plicht (1993) Calibration Curve for Short-lived Samples, 1900–3900 BC. *Radiocarbon* 35: 87-91.

Waterbolk, H.T. (1990) Quality Differences between Radiocarbon Laboratories Illustrated on Material from SW Asia and Egypt. *Proceedings of the Second International Symposium ^{14}C and Archaeology, Groningen*, edited by W.G. Mook and H.T. Waterbolk (PACT: Journal of the European Study Group on Physical, Chemical and Mathematical Techniques Applied to Archaeology 29; Strasbourg: Council of Europe): 141-58.

15 The Groningen Radiocarbon Series from Tel Reḥov

OxCal Bayesian computations for the Iron IB–IIA Boundary and Iron IIA destruction events

Hendrik J. Bruins, Johannes van der Plicht, Amihai Mazar, Christopher Bronk Ramsey, and Sturt W. Manning

Abstract

The stratified series of Iron Age radiocarbon dates from Tel Reḥov, based on short-lived samples, measured in Groningen, is the most detailed and dense chronometric record currently available for the Levant in this period. The more detailed IntCal98 calibration curve was used, though some comparisons were made with the smoothed IntCal04 curve. The current Bayesian stratigraphic model for Tel Reḥov gave a number of significant results. The data strongly favour an early Iron Age IB–IIA transition, as the statistically sampled boundary in the 1σ range is 992–961 BCE (68.2%). Considering the 2σ range, the older time option, 998–957 BCE, further increases in probability to 75.2%, but a second option also appears, 953–921 BCE, albeit with a significantly lower relative probability of 20.2%. Our Bayesian model was also tested with the IntCal04 calibration curve, which gave similar but slightly older results: the 1σ range is 993–961 BCE (68.2%) and the 2σ range is 1001–927 BCE (95.4%). The peak probability remains the same at ca. 970 BCE. The Stratum VI dates have the most likely position within the 1σ range 971–958 BCE (62.4%). The City of Stratum V had a possible duration of 26 to 46 years, in the 1σ and 2σ ranges, respectively. The 1σ sampled destruction of City V is 924–902 BCE (68.2%). This time range could fit a possible association with the Asian campaign of Shoshenq I (Shishak), solely based on Egyptian criteria (see Shortland [Chapter 4, this volume]). Running the Bayesian model with the IntCal04 calibration curve yielded a slightly older date in the 1σ range: 929–906 BCE (68.2%). The latter range does include the date 925 BCE for the Shoshenq campaign as suggested by Kitchen (1986, 2000). The City of Stratum IV had a possible duration of 28–55 years, in the 1σ and 2σ ranges, respectively. The 1σ sampled destruction of City IV is 903–892 (13.4%), 885–845 BCE (54.8%). Thus, the Bayesian statistical computation results of the Tel Reḥov stratigraphic model generally strengthen earlier conclusions concerning a revised traditional chronology, and do not indicate support for the low chronology viewpoint.

Introduction

The purpose of this paper is to show the results of Bayesian statistical analysis of the Groningen radiocarbon dates from Tel Reḥov, which form the most detailed Iron Age chronometric record currently available from a single site for the Levant (Mazar *et al.* [Chapter 13, this volume]; van der Plicht and Bruins [Chapter 14, this volume]). The results are compared with previous results and conclusions (Bruins, van der Plicht and Mazar 2003a, 2003b), in which Bayesian statistics were not employed. The critique of this work by Finkelstein and Piasetzky (2003a, 2003b) is also evaluated in light of the Bayesian results.

The OxCal program (Bronk Ramsey 1995, 2001, 2003) provides the important ability to engage in Bayesian statistical analysis of radiocarbon datasets where other, prior, information is available, such as a stratigraphic sequence; see also Buck and Millard (2004). Thus, the program enabled the development of a Bayesian model that incorporated as well as possible the detailed available stratigraphic information of Tel Reḥov. Essentially, a succession of 'Phases' and 'Boundaries' needs to be defined in the correct stratigraphic order (note: 'Boundaries' are horizons we wish to be able to date between the identified 'Phases' with their ^{14}C dating information—these boundaries or transitions are quantified through the analysis). The program will assume *a priori* that the period from which the dates are selected has no limits. Therefore, the 'Boundary' command has to be used in the correct way in order to place limits in the model, according to the stratigraphy and other relevant information available. Any coherent group of dates should be contained within boundaries to signal to the program that they all belong to one period. A sequence is defined in the program as a group of successive phases with no possibility of overlap in time.

An OxCal Bayesian Model for the Stratigraphy of Tel Reḥov

The building of an appropriate Bayesian model that reflects as satisfactorily as possible the observed Iron Age stratigraphy at Tel Reḥov cannot incorporate all the 64 Groningen dates from Tel Reḥov. There are archaeological constraints in terms of some stratigraphic uncertainties (Mazar *et al.* [Chapter 13, this volume]). The dates used, therefore, are mainly from Area D and Area C on archaeological grounds. Moreover, the ^{14}C dates from a certain Locus or 'Phase' should be internally coherent in the sense that recognisable outliers should be removed *before* the Bayesian analysis. Yet samples that seem to have every stratigraphic reason to be correct but appear to have less ^{14}C coherence should not be arbitrarily withheld from the model. Such samples may end up as not agreeing *after* the Bayesian analysis. Their low agreement index indicates a problem (maybe instances of reworked material, humic acid infiltration, erroneous stratigraphic interpretation, and so on). Nevertheless, a few of such erroneous samples will have little impact on the overall Bayesian dating results, if the number of coherent dates is sufficiently large. This is an important strength of employing a holistic analytical framework.

The model that has been developed is presented in Table 15.1, showing all stratigraphic and ^{14}C date components. A concise description of the model is given below, as extensive information about each Stratum and Locus is available (Bruins, Mazar and van der Plicht, in press; Bruins, van der Plicht and Mazar 2003a; Mazar 1999, 2003; Mazar *et al.* [Chapter 13, this volume]; van der Plicht and Bruins [Chapter 14, this volume]). Most Groningen radiocarbon dates from Tel Reḥov are based on seeds. Therefore, a calibration curve based on single year dendrochronological measurements would have been preferable, as stated by Mook and Waterbolk (1985: 22): 'the ^{14}C sample and the calibration data should have the same time-width (growth-period)'. Such a curve is not available for the approximate time-period 1200–600 BCE of the Levantine Iron Age. Since the 1998 calibration curve (Stuiver *et al.* 1998; Stuiver and van der Plicht [eds.] 1998) is more detailed than the smoothed 2004 version (Reimer *et al.* 2004), the former has been used rather than the latter. The dendrochronological database for the IntCal04 curve is largely similar to the dataset of the IntCal98 curve, but also includes new measurements for the Iron Age period, for example, on German Oak samples run for the East Mediterranean Radiocarbon Intercomparison Project (see also Manning *et al.* [Chapter 10, this volume]). A trial run of the model against the IntCal04 calibration curve gave essentially similar results, albeit that the dates become slightly older. A few examples of these IntCal04 results are included for comparison in relation to the Iron IB–IIA boundary and the Stratum V destruction event.

There is another basic aspect that should be mentioned here briefly in relation to the Groningen ^{14}C dates of Tel Reḥov: 'The statistical (random) nature of radioactive decay causes the results of repeated measurements to spread around a "true" value. The possible discrepancy between a measured value and the "true" value is indicated by the standard deviation (σ)' (Mook and Waterbolk 1985: 10). Therefore, the midpoint value of a single date may be 1σ (68.2%) or 2σ (95.4%) away from the 'true' value. Making two or three measured values of the same sample (subsamples), each with its own pre-treatment, results in a much firmer dating basis, which we consider important in Near Eastern archaeology, as the ^{14}C dating method is pushed to its very limit of resolution (van der Plicht and Bruins 2001). Though two midpoint dates on both ends of a mutual 2σ range are considered the same in physical–mathematical terms, the calibrated age of each of them may be substantially different from an archaeological–historical perspective. It is imperative in our methodology of duplicate or triplicate measurements of single samples, employed for many of the Tel Reḥov Loci, to calculate the weighted average of the separate dating measurements. Thus, the outcome will be more precise and possibly also more accurate, closer to the 'true' value, if the radiocarbon laboratory involved does not have any systematic measurement bias (van der Plicht and Bruins [Chapter 14, this volume]). Hence the 'R_Combine' command is often used in the developed Bayesian model, so that the weighted average results of multiple measurements of one sample of a certain Locus are calculated by the model prior to the Markov Chain Monte Carlo sampling process (Bronk Ramsey 2003; Gilks, Richardson and Speigelhalter 1996). The underlying assumption for calculation of the weighted average is that the organic materials from the Locus are truly contemporary.

The oldest Iron Age layer at Tel Reḥov is Stratum D-6, containing Iron IA ceramics. This Stratum is represented in the model as 'Phase D6'. The term 'Phase' here is the OxCal model language terminology to characterise an archaeological layer that cannot overlap in time with another 'Phase', due to stratigraphic succession (Bronk Ramsey 2003). Hence, each Phase is contained within an upper and lower boundary in the model. 'Phase D6' is represented by two Loci (2874 and 2836), as each Locus has two coherent radiocarbon dates. The sample of charred olive stones from Locus 2874 was split and subsequently separately pre-treated and dated by the two different radiocarbon dating systems available at Groningen (van der Plicht and Bruins [Chapter 14, this volume]): Proportional Gas Counting (PGC) and Accelerator Mass Spectrometry (AMS). Thus, we have two dates from the same sample (Basket 28701) and, therefore, the 'R_Combine' command is used in the Bayesian model, as only the calculation of the weighted average of the same sample renders the correct representation for this Locus. The same procedure was followed for Locus 2836, as the charred olive stones from Basket 28352 were dated by both PGC and AMS. Such a procedure does not only increase precision but probably also accuracy, because two independent pre-treatment and radiocarbon dating systems are involved. Both Groningen systems having an ongoing record of accuracy against one another and against other high precision laboratories active in the field of calibration of the Radiocarbon timescale (Seattle, Belfast, Heidelberg, Groningen-conventional, Pretoria, and Tucson-conventional). Differences between the above laboratories are in the range of 0–20 ^{14}C years, with the difference between Pretoria and Groningen (conventional) being only 7 ^{14}C years, Groningen being slightly younger. The results of an intercomparison (LeClercq, van der Plicht and Gröning 1998) between Seattle, Belfast, Heidelberg, Groningen (both conventional and AMS), Waikato and Tucson (conventional) are available (see van der Plicht and Bruins [Chapter 14, this volume] for more details).

No ^{14}C dates are available for Stratum D-5, but the layer has been represented in the model in its stratigraphic order as 'Interval Phase D5', placed within boundaries. The introduction of the 'Interval' query in the model does not by itself alter the outcome of the computation results—the significant addition being the two 'Boundaries', which indicate that some time (period unknown) must have elapsed between Strata D-6 and D-4.

Stratum D-4, belonging to Iron Age IB in terms of material remains, yielded five radiocarbon dates from two Loci (1845 and 1836). This layer is termed 'Phase D4' in the model, contained within boundaries. Each Locus has coherent ^{14}C results. Locus 1845 yielded a sample of charred seeds (Basket 48556), which were dated by AMS in triplicate. A sample of charred olive stones (Basket 48450) was found at a somewhat higher level in Locus 1836. The sample was split, pre-treated separately and subsequently measured by PGC and AMS, respectively. The somewhat younger coherent dates fit well with the relative stratigraphy within Stratum D-4. The calculation of the weighted average of the available dates for each Locus is again signified by the 'R_Combine' command, which is appropriate in each case. Thus, the increased dating precision for each Locus (before calibration and Bayesian analysis) is based on multiple dates of the same sample material, respectively.

The refuse or storage pits of Stratum D-3 contain material remains that seem typical of the last part of Iron Age IB. Boundaries contain this stratigraphic period, defined as 'Phase D3' in the model. There are nine coherent radiocarbon dates available for Phase D3, derived from three Loci (4830, 2862 and 4815). The two dates for Locus 4816 are internally consistent but appear to be significantly older than the other D-3 Loci. Yet there is no obvious stratigraphic reason not to include this Locus in the model. Thus, we allow the Bayesian analysis to make the judgement and eleven D-3 dates are included. However, one date for Locus 2862 (GrN-26119) is clearly too young, because the sample was too small for Proportional Gas Counting, as explained by van der Plicht and Bruins (Chapter 14, this volume). This date is not included in the model. The same sample was subsequently measured by AMS and this result (GrA-19033) matches with the other dates and is included to represent Locus 2862. It was appropriate here to use the 'R_Combine' command in the model, as in previous cases, for each Locus that has multiple dates of the *same* sample.

The lower boundary of Phase D3 is of special importance, because it signifies the boundary between Iron I and Iron II. The Bayesian model calculates a time value for each boundary.

The oldest Iron IIA layer in the model is 'Phase Stratum VI City', contained within boundaries. Notice that the two Loci of Stratum D-2 are not placed in the model, because it cannot be decided on stratigraphic archaeological grounds whether these refuse layers belong to Stratum VI or V, all being Iron IIA. There are five radiocarbon dates from Stratum VI, all organic sample material coming from exactly the same position below a bowl above a floor in Locus 4426. The five dates pass the chi-squared test for a hypothesis of contemporaneity and, therefore, a weighted average seems a reasonable time representation for Stratum VI, as signalled to the model with the 'R_Combine' command. The organic materials at this stratigraphic spot (Basket 44166) consist of charred cereal grains, fine charcoal and a small bone. Since they were all found together below a bowl and above a floor, the three organic constituents could well have been from a single meal. The fine charcoal involved is certainly not old wood, as is clear from the radiocarbon dates, but may possibly relate to the grains. The very small bone is also short-lived. These organic constituents below the bowl might represent the same time period, but this is only one possible interpretation. Therefore, two alternative Bayesian model options were tested: (1) each date included separately, (2) the three triplicate dates on the fine charcoal with 'R_Combine' but the grains and bone dates separately. The Bayesian computations of the three model options were hardly different in outcome with regard to the Iron IB–IIA boundary and the destruction events that terminated City V and City IV.

Stratum V represents the next Iron IIA City at Tel Rehov, overlying Stratum VI. Most secure ^{14}C dates available relate in stratigraphic terms to the destruction at the end of its lifespan. However, the duration of City V must also be represented in the model. Its lifespan can in fact be queried by inserting a line 'Interval Duration City V', separated by a boundary from the destruction phase. Only Locus 4218 from Area B seems to belong stratigraphically to the duration of City V and its three ^{14}C dates on charred olive stones are placed within the same 'Phase' as the 'Interval Duration City V' (see Table 15.1). The olive stones were split in three sub-samples, each pre-treated and dated separately by AMS. The results are coherent and the 'R_Combine' command gives the best possible time representation for Locus 4218.

Concerning the destruction Phase of City V, the charred cereal grains from Loci 2425, 2441 and 2444 are all from the same topographic level from building G (Mazar *et al.* [Chapter 13, this volume]). The Groningen radiocarbon results for Loci 2425 and 2441 are very similar and seem to suggest that the charred cereal grains from these Loci represent the same archaeological layer and destruction event, as also indicated by the similar height level. However, there may be a possibility (Mazar *et al.* [Chapter 13, this volume]) that Loci 2425 and 2444 belong to Stratum IV, and Mazar advised us not to include these Loci in the Bayesian model. Locus 2441 of building G has been included in the model. The weighted average (R_Combine) is the best time representation of the charred cereal grains of Locus 2441, which were split into two complete sub-samples, each pre-treated and dated separately by PGC.

Locus 2422 from a different building in Area C, with three coherent dates on charred cereal grains, is also placed in the model. Here we have an exceptional case of calculated precision that requires some additional explanation. The amount of charred cereal grains (Basket 24408) was quite large and three sub-samples were dated separately by PGC. Concerning the standard deviation of individual radiocarbon dates, the Proportional Gas Counters at Groningen (Mook 1983; van der Plicht, Streurman and Schreuder 1992) and Heidelberg (Kromer and Münnich 1992) are radiocarbon dating systems capable of delivering the highest possible precision (i.e. the smallest possible standard deviation). The lowest possible limit of about 10–15 ^{14}C years BP is determined by scatter, precision in standards, as well as the amount of available sample material, its age and measurement time. A sample consisting of 25 grams C that is measured routinely for two days (2700 minutes) in specific counters of the Groningen laboratory can give a low standard deviation of 9 ^{14}C years BP for modern samples and 12 ^{14}C years BP for samples of about 5000 years old (Mook and Waterbolk 1985: 12). The three PGC dates of Locus 2422 have standard deviations of 11 ^{14}C years BP (GrN-27361), 13 ^{14}C years BP (GrN-27362) and 28 ^{14}C years BP (GrN-27412), which are all within the capability of the Groningen PGC system and there is nothing extraordinary here (see also Bruins and van der Plicht 1995). However, averaging these dates does decrease the error to only 8 ^{14}C years BP. Since we have one single archaeological sample of charred cereal grains that was split into three sub-samples, the weighted average (R_Combine command in the model) calculation is appropriate.

Concerning the destruction phase of Stratum V, there are altogether five secure radiocarbon dates for this important event, which was tentatively associated with the campaign of Shoshenq I (Shishak), as discussed previously (Bruins, van der Plicht and Mazar 2003a). A line 'Event Destruction City V' was added into the model together with the above ^{14}C dates in order to signal to the model to make a specific calculation for this event.

Stratum IV was the last Iron Age IIA City at Tel Rehov. Datable organic material was only found in Locus 5498 in the form of charred cereal grains, representing the destructive end of City IV. The seven AMS dates from this single sample of cereal grains (Basket 54702) are placed in the model, with the 'R_Combine' command determining the weighted average. Similar in procedure to the stratigraphic situation for City V, a separate Phase was placed in the model, albeit without ^{14}C dates, representing the duration of City IV, while an 'Event Destruction City IV' was placed together with the seven ^{14}C dates.

Table 15.1. A Bayesian model of the secure Groningen ^{14}C dates arranged according to the stratigraphy of Tel Reḥov.

```
Plot
{
Sequence
{
Boundary;
Phase 'D6'
{
R_Combine 'D6b Locus 2874'
{
R_Date 'GrN-26120' 2880 30;
R_Date 'GrA-19034' 2935 45;
};
R_Combine 'D6a Locus 2836'
{
R_Date 'GrN-26118' 2920 30;
R_Date 'GrA-18826' 2950 50;
};
};
Boundary;
Interval 'Phase D5';
Boundary;
Phase 'D4'
{
R_Combine 'D4b'
{
R_Date 'GrA-21046' 2905 35;
R_Date 'GrA-21057' 2945 35;
R_Date 'GrA-21184' 2920 50;
};
R_Combine 'D4a'
{
R_Date 'GrN-26121' 2890 30;
R_Date 'GrA-18825' 2870 50;
};
};
Boundary;
Phase 'D3'
{
R_Combine 'Locus 4816'
{
R_Date 'GrA-12889' 2870 70;
R_Date 'GrA-16848' 2895 40;
};
R_Combine 'Locus 4830'
{
R_Date 'GrA-21044' 2845 35;
R_Date 'GrA-21056' 2825 35;
R_Date 'GrA-21183' 2820 50;
R_Date 'GrA-22302a' 2730 50;
```

R_Date 'GrA-22302b' 2820 40;
R_Date 'GrA-22329a' 2810 50;
R_Date 'GrA-22329b' 2760 40;
};
R_Date 'L2862 GrA-16757' 2820 50;
R_Date 'L4815 GrA-19033' 2835 45;
};
Boundary;
Phase 'Stratum VI City'
{
R_Combine 'Locus 4426'
{
R_Date 'GrN-27366' 2761 14;
R_Date 'GrA-21043' 2755 35;
R_Date 'GrA-21054' 2805 35;
R_Date 'GrA-21182' 2800 50;
R_Date 'GrA-21417' 2840 45;
};
};
Boundary;
Phase 'Stratum V City'
{
Interval 'Duration City V';
R_Combine 'Locus 4218'
{
R_Date 'GrA-21034' 2760 35;
R_Date 'GrA-21047' 2820 35;
R_Date 'GrA-21179' 2770 50;
};
};
Boundary;
Phase 'Stratum V Destruction'
{
R_Combine 'Locus 2422'
{
R_Date 'GrN-27361' 2764 11;
R_Date 'GrN-27362' 2777 13;
R_Date 'GrN-27412' 2785 28;
};
R_Combine 'Locus 2441'
{
R_Date 'GrN-26116' 2810 20;
R_Date 'GrN-26117' 2775 25;
};
Event 'Destruction City V';
};
Boundary;
Phase 'Stratum IV City'
{
Interval 'Duration City IV';
};
Boundary;
Phase 'Stratum IV Destruction'
{
R_Combine 'Locus 5498'
{
R_Date 'GrA-21152' 2770 50;

```
R_Date 'GrA-21154' 2730 50;
R_Date 'GrA-21267' 2760 35;
R_Date 'GrA-22301a' 2710 45;
R_Date 'GrA-22301b' 2775 40;
R_Date 'GrA-22330a' 2760 50;
R_Date 'GrA-22330b' 2785 40;
};
Event 'Destruction City IV';
};
Boundary;
};
;
```

Bayesian Modelling Results

The computation results are shown in Table 15.2. The standard calibrated ages appear in the first half of the table, often with a calculation of the weighted average and the related chi-squared test results. T is the chi-squared value calculated and the value given in brackets is the level above which T should not rise in order to be acceptable. The degrees of freedom are given by df (the number of dates minus one). All T results in Table 15.2 are well below the respective values for rejection of the contemporaneity hypothesis at 95% confidence.

The Bayesian computation results appear in Table 15.2 after the line MCMC, which is the acronym for the Markov Chain Monte Carlo sampling process (Gilks, Richardson and Speigelhalter 1996). The MCMC technique allows samples to be taken that properly reflect the probability distributions and constraints. The program uses a mixture of the Metropolis-Hastings algorithm and the more specific Gibbs sampler (Bronk Ramsey 2003). In our case the program made 227,094 iterations for the sampling computations.

Table 15.2. The computation results of the above Bayesian model of secure Groningen ^{14}C dates arranged according to the stratigraphy of Tel Reḥov.

INFORM: References—Atmospheric data from Stuiver *et al.* (1998); OxCal v3.9 Bronk Ramsey (2003); cub r:1 sd:12 prob usp[chron]

```
(Sequence
Boundary _Bound
(Phase D6
R_Combine D6b Locus 2874: 2897.04±24.9616BP
 68.2% probability
 1125.7BC (60.6%) 1040.3BC
 1031.9BC (7.6%) 1020.1BC
 95.4% probability
 1209.5BC (2.0%) 1200.5BC
 1190.5BC (4.5%) 1177.2BC
 1160.7BC (4.6%) 1141.1BC
 1130.3BC (84.3%) 999.6BC
 X2-Test: df=1 T=1.0(5% 3.8)
R_Combine D6a Locus 2836: 2927.97±25.7248BP
 68.2% probability
 1209.4BC (5.1%) 1201.1BC
 1190.1BC (8.0%) 1177.9BC
 1158.8BC (11.3%) 1141.1BC
 1130.2BC (13.9%) 1107.7BC
 1102.2BC (20.7%) 1067.1BC
```

1065.5BC (9.1%) 1050.2BC
95.4% probability
1256.7BC (4.8%) 1238.6BC
1213BC (7.4%) 1197BC
1193.6BC (28.1%) 1137.9BC
1132.9BC (55.1%) 1018.5BC
X2-Test: df=1 T=0.3(5% 3.8)
) Phase D6
Boundary _Bound
Interval Phase D5
Boundary _Bound
(Phase D4
R_Combine D4b: 2924.08±22.1804BP
68.2% probability
1208.1BC (3.7%) 1202.3BC
1189.2BC (7.2%) 1179.1BC
1153.8BC (8.1%) 1142.1BC
1129.4BC (15.0%) 1107.7BC
1102.3BC (23.7%) 1066.8BC
1065.7BC (10.5%) 1050.1BC
95.4% probability
1254.6BC (2.4%) 1243.4BC
1211.6BC (6.2%) 1198.6BC
1192.1BC (25.7%) 1139.2BC
1131.8BC (61.0%) 1019.8BC
X2-Test: df=2 T=0.7(5% 6.0)
R_Combine D4a: 2884.72±25.7248BP
68.2% probability
1124.5BC (3.1%) 1119.4BC
1112BC (9.9%) 1097.8BC
1086.7BC (17.7%) 1059.6BC
1052.8BC (37.4%) 1004.6BC
95.4% probability
1189.1BC (2.8%) 1179.1BC
1153.3BC (2.0%) 1142.7BC
1129.2BC (86.7%) 996.3BC
989.4BC (2.4%) 974.3BC
954.7BC (1.5%) 943.9BC
X2-Test: df=1 T=0.1(5% 3.8)
) Phase D4
Boundary _Bound
(Phase D3
R_Combine Locus 4816: 2888.87±34.7298BP
68.2% probability
1125.4BC (4.9%) 1116.5BC
1114.7BC (33.4%) 1056.7BC
1055.1BC (29.9%) 1006.2BC
95.4% probability
1210.7BC (2.3%) 1199.4BC
1191.3BC (4.4%) 1175.5BC
1167.3BC (5.5%) 1140BC
1131.1BC (80.1%) 971.5BC
958BC (3.1%) 937.9BC
X2-Test: df=1 T=0.1(5% 3.8)
R_Combine Locus 4830: 2807.26±15.6507BP
68.2% probability
997BC (10.3%) 987.7BC

974.6BC (11.2%) 965.9BC
963.8BC (13.3%) 952.8BC
945.7BC (33.3%) 920BC
95.4% probability
999.9BC (92.6%) 913.9BC
911.4BC (2.8%) 905.3BC
X2-Test: df=6 T=5.3(5% 12.6)
L2862 GrA-16757: 2820±50BP
68.2% probability
1042.2BC (3.8%) 1030.8BC
1021.5BC (64.4%) 901.2BC
95.4% probability
1126BC (87.0%) 890.8BC
880.9BC (8.4%) 835.1BC
L4815 GrA-19033: 2835±45BP
68.2% probability
1045.6BC (68.2%) 919.5BC
95.4% probability
1128BC (93.5%) 895.6BC
876.5BC (1.9%) 856.9BC
) Phase D3
Boundary _Bound
(Phase Stratum VI City
R_Combine Locus 4426: 2772.33±11.4494BP
68.2% probability
969.3BC (12.7%) 960BC
927.8BC (52.3%) 897BC
873BC (3.3%) 868.3BC
95.4% probability
970.8BC (14.4%) 958BC
937.2BC (59.2%) 893.2BC
879BC (21.8%) 838.2BC
X2-Test: df=4 T=4.4(5% 9.5)
) Phase Stratum VI City
Boundary _Bound
(Phase Stratum V City
Interval Duration City V
R_Combine Locus 4218: 2786.21±22.1805BP
68.2% probability
995BC (2.2%) 991.2BC
972.9BC (19.4%) 955.6BC
941.8BC (46.7%) 898.7BC
95.4% probability
998.6BC (83.8%) 895.3BC
876.9BC (11.6%) 841.6BC
X2-Test: df=2 T=1.6(5% 6.0)
) Phase Stratum V City
Boundary _Bound
(Phase Stratum V Destruction
R_Combine Locus 2422: 2770.72±8.04333BP
68.2% probability
968.6BC (11.0%) 960.7BC
925BC (55.7%) 897.1BC
871.9BC (1.5%) 869.9BC
95.4% probability
969.9BC (12.5%) 959BC
934.2BC (61.6%) 894.1BC

878.3BC (21.3%) 839.9BC
X2-Test: df=2 T=0.9(5% 6.0)
R_Combine Locus 2441: 2796.4±15.6174BP
68.2% probability
972.6BC (23.7%) 956.3BC
940.9BC (44.5%) 904.9BC
95.4% probability
998.6BC (95.4%) 900.4BC
X2-Test: df=1 T=1.2(5% 3.8)
) Phase Stratum V Destruction
Boundary _Bound
(Phase Stratum IV City
Interval Duration City IV
) Phase Stratum IV City
Boundary _Bound
(Phase Stratum IV Destruction
R_Combine Locus 5498: 2758.06±16.3079BP
68.2% probability
917.7BC (28.8%) 895.3BC
876.9BC (23.9%) 856BC
854.2BC (15.5%) 840.2BC
95.4% probability
968.7BC (4.7%) 960.5BC
925.7BC (90.7%) 833.3BC
X2-Test: df=6 T=2.1(5% 12.6)
) Phase Stratum IV Destruction
Boundary _Bound
) Sequence
(MCMC
Sampled _Bound
68.2% probability
1133.8BC (68.2%) 1060.8BC
95.4% probability
1198.2BC (95.4%) 1042.7BC
Sampled D6b Locus 2874: 2897.04±24.9616
68.2% probability
1125.4BC (67.1%) 1067.9BC
1066.2BC (1.1%) 1065BC
95.4% probability
1188.6BC (2.4%) 1179.8BC
1156BC (4.5%) 1141.7BC
1130.2BC (88.5%) 1036.3BC
Agreement 109.9%
Sampled D6a Locus 2836: 2927.97±25.7248
68.2% probability
1122.2BC (61.3%) 1068.8BC
1061BC (6.9%) 1053.6BC
95.4% probability
1190BC (2.4%) 1177BC
1162.2BC (6.6%) 1139BC
1132.8BC (86.4%) 1036.3BC
Agreement 110.6%
Sampled _Bound
68.2% probability
1105BC (68.2%) 1047.1BC
95.4% probability
1151BC (3.0%) 1133.7BC

    1129BC (92.4%) 1021.9BC
Sampled Phase D5
 68.2% probability
 -0.5 (68.2%) 27.9
 95.4% probability
 -0.5 (95.4%) 66.3
Sampled _Bound
 68.2% probability
 1076.9BC (68.2%) 1024.8BC
 95.4% probability
 1112.8BC (95.4%) 1011.9BC
Sampled D4b: 2924.08±22.1804
 68.2% probability
 1063.9BC (31.9%) 1044BC
 1039.1BC (36.3%) 1015.7BC
 95.4% probability
 1090.5BC (95.4%) 1004.9BC
 Agreement 70.7%
Sampled D4a: 2884.72±25.7248
 68.2% probability
 1053.9BC (68.2%) 1009.8BC
 95.4% probability
 1088.8BC (95.4%) 1000.5BC
 Agreement 120.1%
Sampled _Bound
 68.2% probability
 1040.6BC (68.2%) 992.5BC
 95.4% probability
 1073.6BC (95.4%) 972.7BC
Sampled Locus 4816: 2888.87±34.7298
 68.2% probability
 1018.6BC (40.2%) 995BC
 992.3BC (28.0%) 973.9BC
 95.4% probability
 1046.8BC (90.7%) 968.9BC
 957.6BC (4.7%) 941.9BC
 Agreement 76.4%
Sampled Locus 4830: 2807.26±15.6507
 68.2% probability
 999.7BC (57.5%) 979.8BC
 974.9BC (10.7%) 969.6BC
 95.4% probability
 1003.9BC (95.4%) 938.5BC
 Agreement 91.6%
Sampled L2862 GrA-16757: 2820±50
 68.2% probability
 1007BC (68.2%) 970BC
 95.4% probability
 1035.1BC (95.4%) 938.9BC
 Agreement 130.2%
Sampled L4815 GrA-19033: 2835±45
 68.2% probability
 1008.6BC (68.2%) 971.2BC
 95.4% probability
 1036.5BC (95.4%) 939.7BC
 Agreement 134.2%
Sampled _Bound

68.2% probability
991.8BC (68.2%) 961.3BC
95.4% probability
997.5BC (75.2%) 957.1BC
953.1BC (20.2%) 920.6BC
Sampled Locus 4426: 2772.33±11.4494
68.2% probability
970.8BC (62.4%) 958.3BC
933.6BC (5.8%) 929.2BC
95.4% probability
972.4BC (67.3%) 955.5BC
940.5BC (28.1%) 912.1BC
Agreement 86.7%
Sampled _Bound
68.2% probability
967.2BC (40.0%) 948.8BC
934.8BC (28.2%) 917BC
95.4% probability
968.6BC (95.4%) 910.7BC
Sampled Duration City V
68.2% probability
0.3 (68.2%) 26.1
95.4% probability
-0.5 (95.4%) 46.4
Sampled Locus 4218: 2786.21±22.1805
68.2% probability
941.2BC (68.2%) 910.9BC
95.4% probability
964.6BC (95.4%) 907.1BC
Agreement 116.5%
Sampled _Bound
68.2% probability
931.3BC (68.2%) 906.5BC
95.4% probability
957.9BC (95.4%) 902.1BC
Sampled Locus 2422: 2770.72±8.04333
68.2% probability
920.1BC (68.2%) 902.9BC
95.4% probability
934BC (95.4%) 896.9BC
Agreement 127.6%
Sampled Locus 2441: 2796.4±15.6174
68.2% probability
922.9BC (68.2%) 902.9BC
95.4% probability
939.4BC (95.4%) 898BC
Agreement 98.3%
Sampled Destruction City V
68.2% probability
924.2BC (68.2%) 901.6BC
95.4% probability
945BC (95.4%) 887.4BC
Sampled _Bound
68.2% probability
918.5BC (68.2%) 895.8BC
95.4% probability
931.7BC (95.4%) 873BC

Sampled Duration City IV
68.2% probability
-0.5 (68.2%) 27.7
95.4% probability
-0.5 (95.4%) 54.7
Sampled _Bound
68.2% probability
907.9BC (68.2%) 866.2BC
95.4% probability
919.2BC (95.4%) 844.1BC
Sampled Locus 5498: 2758.06±16.3079
68.2% probability
902.7BC (10.3%) 895.5BC
878.9BC (57.9%) 842.6BC
95.4% probability
911.1BC (24.5%) 886.1BC
885.1BC (70.9%) 834.9BC
Agreement 104.4%
Sampled Destruction City IV
68.2% probability
903.2BC (13.4%) 891.6BC
884.9BC (54.8%) 845.1BC
95.4% probability
917.5BC (95.4%) 823BC
Sampled _Bound
68.2% probability
899.5BC (9.0%) 889.5BC
876.7BC (59.2%) 828.3BC
95.4% probability
914.7BC (95.4%) 792.7BC
Overall agreement 115.3%
) MCMC
227094 iterations used

The Bayesian computation results for this model give an overall agreement index of 115.3%, which is well above the lower limit of 60% to meet an approximate 95% confidence level. All individual results for the various Phases and Loci also show an agreement above the 60% agreement threshold. A graphical overview of the results is shown in Figure 15.1. The solid black fill in each calibration graph shows the time-section selected by the Bayesian computation from within the full calibrated range. Thus, Bayesian statistics narrow down the width of the calibrated dates according to the stratigraphic model (stratigraphic time succession), thereby giving more precise results in historical years. Only the results related to the subject of this article are briefly discussed below, while a more extensive account will be published elsewhere.

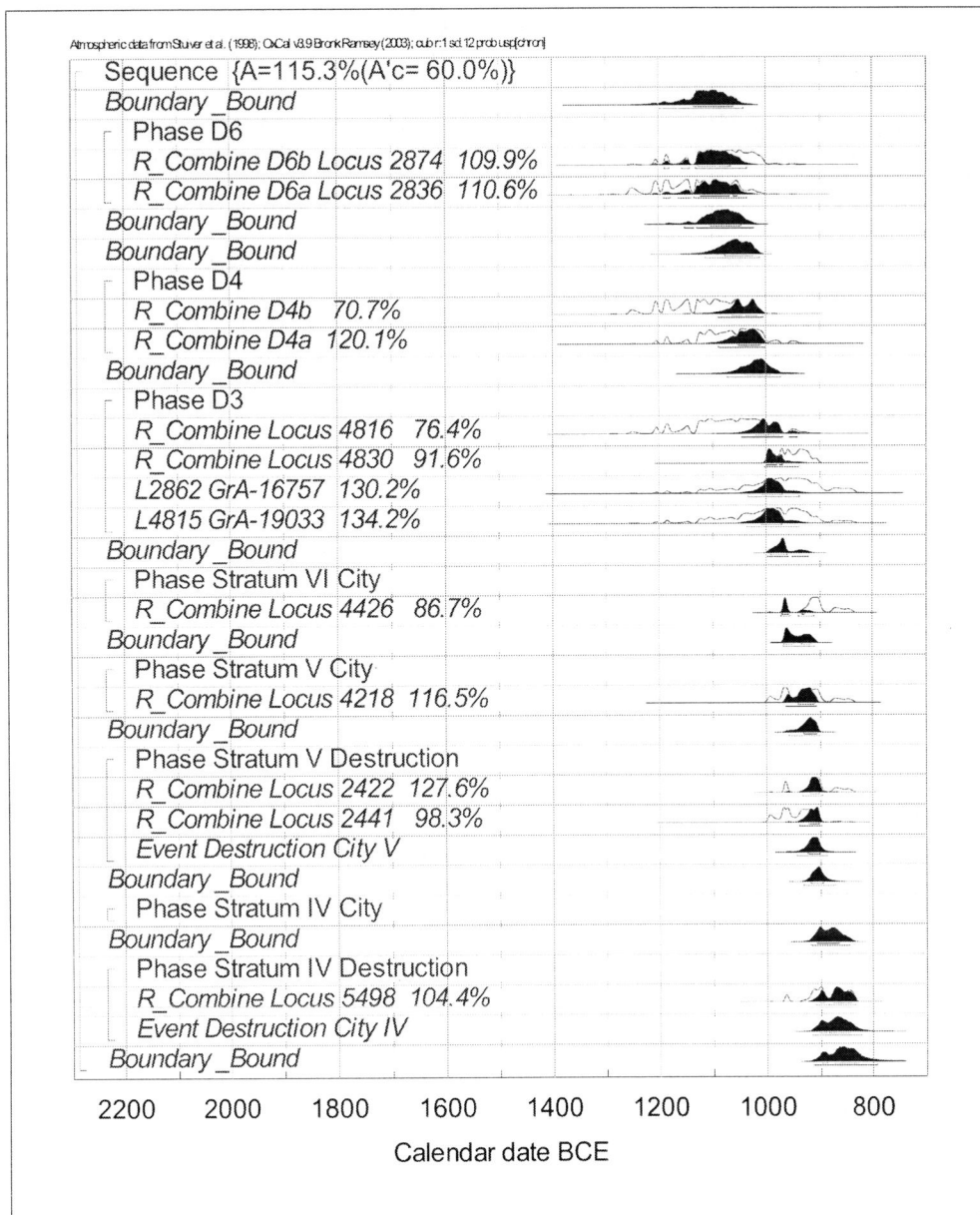

Atmospheric data from Stuiver et al. (1998); OxCal v3.9 Bronk Ramsey (2003); cub r:1 sd:12 prob usp[chron]

Sequence {A=115.3%(A'c= 60.0%)}
Boundary _Bound
  Phase D6
    R_Combine D6b Locus 2874 109.9%
    R_Combine D6a Locus 2836 110.6%
Boundary _Bound
Boundary _Bound
  Phase D4
    R_Combine D4b 70.7%
    R_Combine D4a 120.1%
Boundary _Bound
  Phase D3
    R_Combine Locus 4816 76.4%
    R_Combine Locus 4830 91.6%
    L2862 GrA-16757 130.2%
    L4815 GrA-19033 134.2%
Boundary _Bound
  Phase Stratum VI City
    R_Combine Locus 4426 86.7%
Boundary _Bound
  Phase Stratum V City
    R_Combine Locus 4218 116.5%
Boundary _Bound
  Phase Stratum V Destruction
    R_Combine Locus 2422 127.6%
    R_Combine Locus 2441 98.3%
    Event Destruction City V
Boundary _Bound
  Phase Stratum IV City
Boundary _Bound
  Phase Stratum IV Destruction
    R_Combine Locus 5498 104.4%
    Event Destruction City IV
Boundary _Bound

2200   2000   1800   1600   1400   1200   1000   800

Calendar date BCE

Figure 15.1. OxCal Bayesian statistical results showing the 1σ and 2σ calibrated age ranges (upper and lower horizontal black lines under each distribution, respectively), the sampled calibrated age ranges (solid black fill), as well as the sampled dates for boundaries and destruction events (solid black fill), according to the above stratigraphic model of Tel Rehov (the two boundaries between Phase D-6 and D-4 relate to Phase D-5 in between, lacking ^{14}C dates).

The Iron Age IB–Iron Age IIA Boundary

The youngest Iron Age IB layer at Tel Reḥov in Area D is Stratum D-3, composed of refuse pits. The Bayesian statistical computation results for Locus 4815 (Fig. 15.2) are shown in more detail as an example (see also Locus 4815 within the general overview of Fig. 15.1). The 1σ sampled calibration range is 1009–971 BCE, which means that somewhere within this time period appears the highest relative sampled probability for the last stage of Iron IB, as represented at Tel Reḥov.

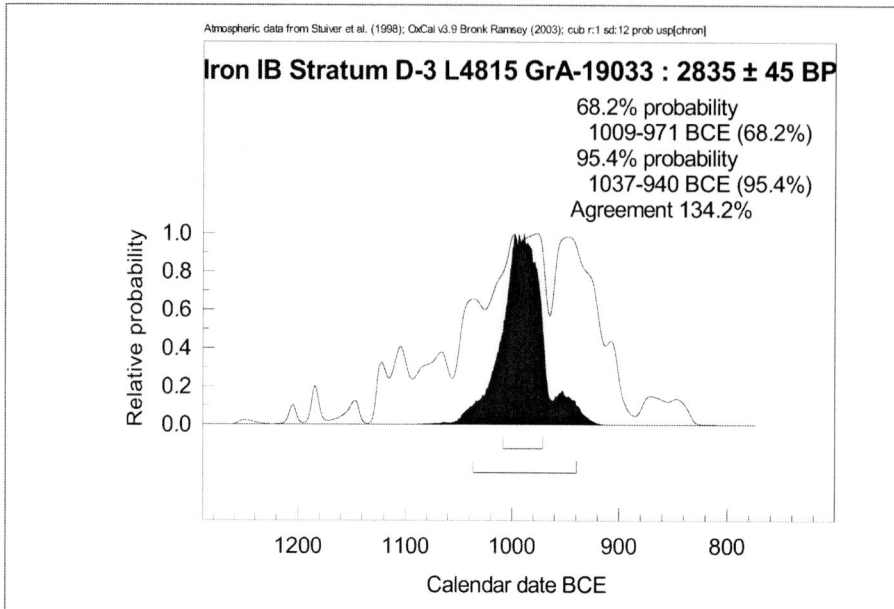

Figure 15.2. The Bayesian sampled date (solid black fill) from within the entire calibrated age range for Locus 4815 of Stratum D-3, the youngest Iron Age IB layer at Tel Reḥov. The upper and lower horizontal lines under each probability distribution indicate the 1σ and 2σ ranges, respectively.

The next youngest stratigraphic layer at Tel Reḥov is Stratum VI in Area C. The Bayesian model results from OxCal are shown in detail in Figure 15.3. The weighted average date for Stratum VI, 2772 ± 11 BP, hits the calibration curve at two places, reflected by the two peaks that reach a maximum relative probability level of 1 at the Y-axis. The Bayesian sampling computation according to the stratigraphic model selected the first peak as the most likely age range for Stratum VI, namely, 971–958 BCE. This result confirms the conclusions drawn by Bruins, van der Plicht and Mazar (2003a, 2003b), in which Bayesian statistics were not employed.

Alternative model options were also tested. Each radiocarbon date of Stratum VI was placed separately in the model, without using the R_Combine command. Thus, no weighted average was calculated and each date was separately evaluated by MCMC sampling. Another option that was also tested involved the inclusion of the three triplicate dates on fine charcoal by the R_Combine command, while the grains and bone date were included separately. Both alternative models gave essentially the same results for the Iron IB–IIA boundary and the destruction events of Strata V and IV. The model did indicate, however, that the only PGC grain date would drop just below 60% agreement (59% to 57% in different runs) with a standard deviation of 14 ^{14}C years BP. If the precision is relaxed to 20 ^{14}C years BP, the date becomes acceptable. There was no problem with the other four radiocarbon dates of Stratum VI. Moreover, the results of the above alternative models are very similar and the Bayesian computations remained remarkably stable and robust.

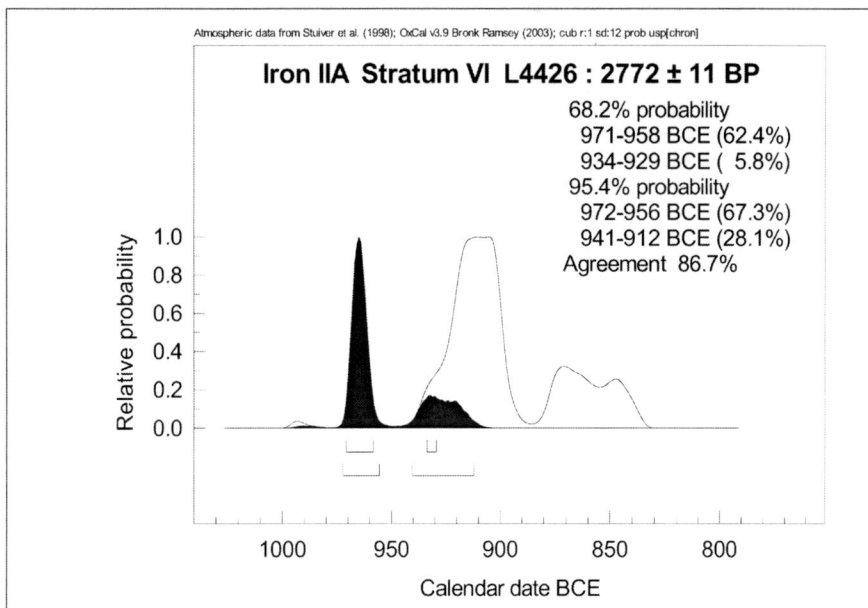

Figure 15.3. The Bayesian sampled date (solid black fill) from within the entire calibrated age range for Stratum VI, the oldest Iron Age IIA layer at Tel Reḥov.

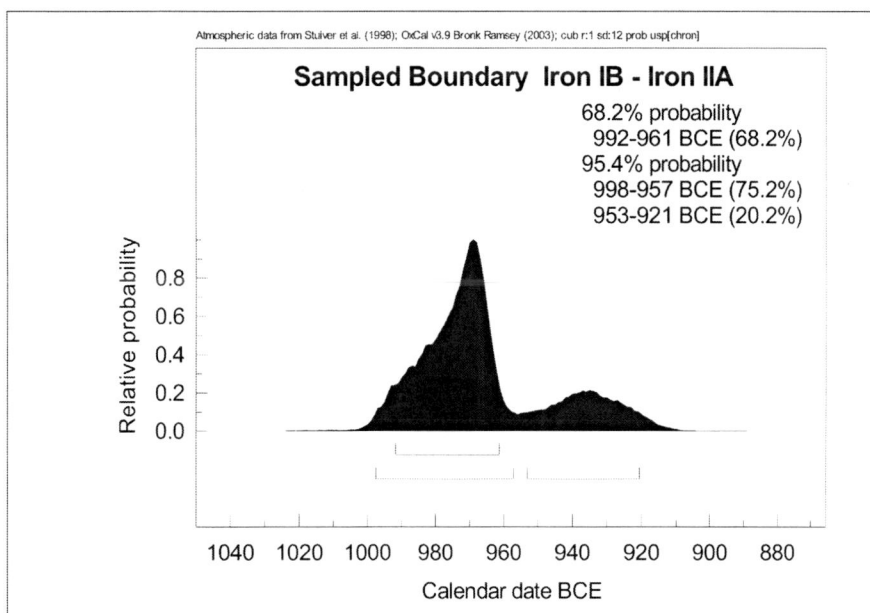

Figure 15.4. The Bayesian sampled date for the Iron IB–IIA Boundary between Stratum D-3 (youngest Iron IB) and Stratum VI (oldest Iron IIA) at Tel Reḥov.

Putting the most probable results for Stratum D-3 and Stratum VI in succession, it seems clear that the boundary between Iron IB and Iron IIA may well be placed around 980 BCE, as suggested by Mazar. On the other hand, placing this boundary around 900 or 920 BCE, as suggested by Finkelstein, seems very unlikely. Indeed, the sampled date for this boundary (Fig. 15.4) has the highest relative probability (1σ) within the period 992–961 BCE. The peak probability point is about 970 BCE (see Fig. 15.4, value of 1 on Y-axis), which is rather close to 980 BCE. The model was also tested vis-à-vis the IntCal04 calibration curve, which produced similar but slightly older results: the 1σ range is 993–961 BCE (68.2%) and the 2σ range is 1001–927 BCE (95.4%). The peak probability remains the same at ca. 970 BCE. Therefore, the Bayesian results, given the stratigraphic model, contradict the low chronology suggestions by Finkelstein and Piasetzky (2003a, 2003b) for both the IntCal98 and IntCal04 calibration curves.

The Destruction Event that Terminated the City of Stratum V

The detailed archaeological and radiocarbon date information for Stratum V are already described (Mazar *et al.* [Chapter 13, this volume]; van der Plicht and Bruins [Chapter 14, this volume]) and will not be repeated here. Concerning the destruction of City V, the Bayesian sampling result for the secure Locus 2422 is shown in detail (Fig. 15.5) as an example (see also the full sequence overview in Fig. 15.1). The highest relative probability (68.2%) for the destruction of Stratum V, in relation to Locus 2422 of Area C (Fig. 15.5), is the period 920–903 BCE. The agreement index with the stratigraphic model is 128%.

Notice that the weighted average ^{14}C date for Stratum VI and for the destruction phase of Stratum V are almost the same, 2772 ± 11 BP and 2771 ± 8 BP, respectively. Due to the wiggles in the calibration curve, it is difficult to decide whether radiocarbon dates in the range of about 2770–2750 BP, with a standard deviation (σ) of 20 or higher, belong to the 10th or 9th centuries BCE (see also Mazar *et al.* [Chapter 13, this volume]). Therefore, simple BP analysis (Finkelstein and Piasetzky 2003a, 2003b) without using the calibration curve and without wiggle-matching or Bayesian analysis cannot solve such a situation, because the radiocarbon time scale is not linear. The complex past reality of fluctuating concentrations of ^{14}C in the atmosphere and the resulting wiggles in the calibration curve *must* be taken into account through archaeological wiggle-matching (Bronk Ramsey, van der Plicht and Weninger [eds.] 2001; Bruins *et al.* 2003a; Manning and Weninger 1992) or Bayesian analysis (Bronk Ramsey 2003; Buck and Millard [eds.] 2004).

The 'Event Destruction City V' command line in the Bayesian model signalled the model to make a computation about this destruction event considering the five secure dates for the end of Stratum V (see Tables 15.1 and 15.2). The resulting sampled Bayesian date for the destruction of City V is 924–904 BCE in the 1σ range (Fig. 15.6). Previously, Bruins, van der Plicht and Mazar (2003a) had suggested a possible relationship between the destruction of Rehov City V and the Asian campaign of Pharaoh Shoshenq I (Shishak). The date of 925 BCE has been suggested by Kitchen (1986, 2000) for this campaign based on both Egyptian and biblical chronological data. The above year would be just outside the sampled 1σ Bayesian computation of 924–904 BCE in relation to our Tel Rehov stratigraphic model. However, the Bayesian result could fit chrono-logically with a novel historical dating assessment for Shoshenq I based on Egyptian texts only, in which a date around ca. 920 BCE for his campaign becomes feasible, as presented by Shortland (Chapter 4, this volume). Running our Bayesian model with the IntCal04 calibration curve yielded a slightly older date in the 1σ range: 929–906 BCE (68.2%). In fact the latter range does also now include the date 925 BCE for the Shoshenq campaign as suggested by Kitchen (1986, 2000).

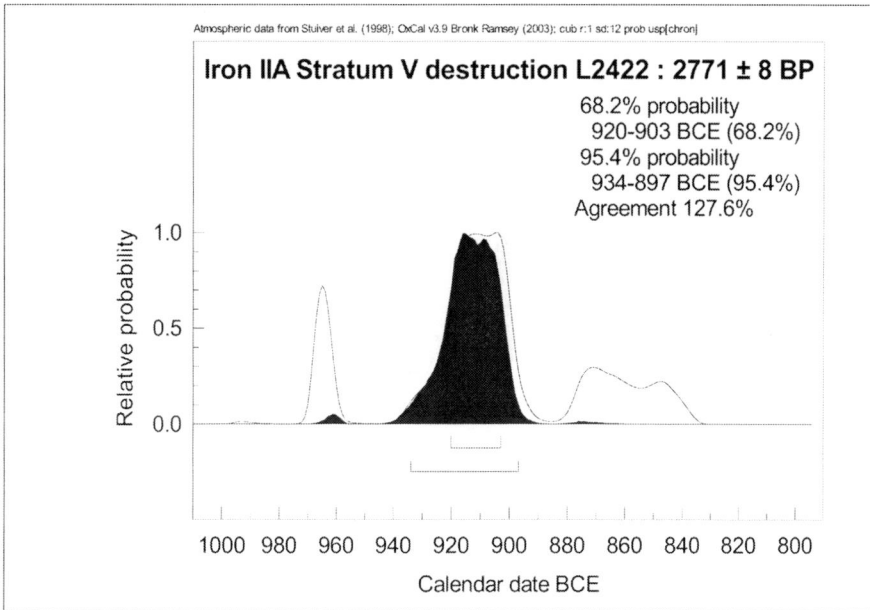

Figure 15.5. The detailed Bayesian sampled date (solid black fill) for the destruction of Iron IIA Stratum V, as shown for Locus 2422.

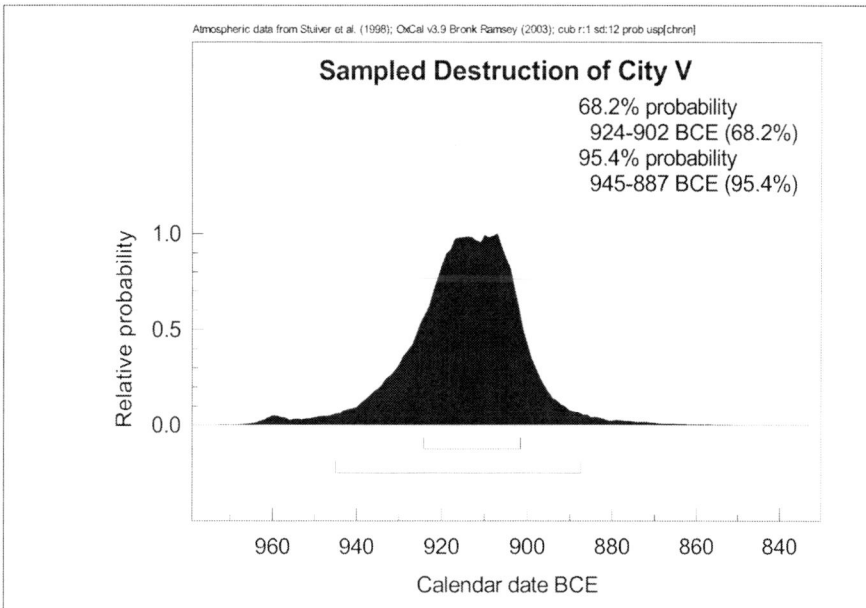

Figure 15.6. The sampled Bayesian date for the destruction of Stratum V, based on five secure radiocarbon dates from Area C.

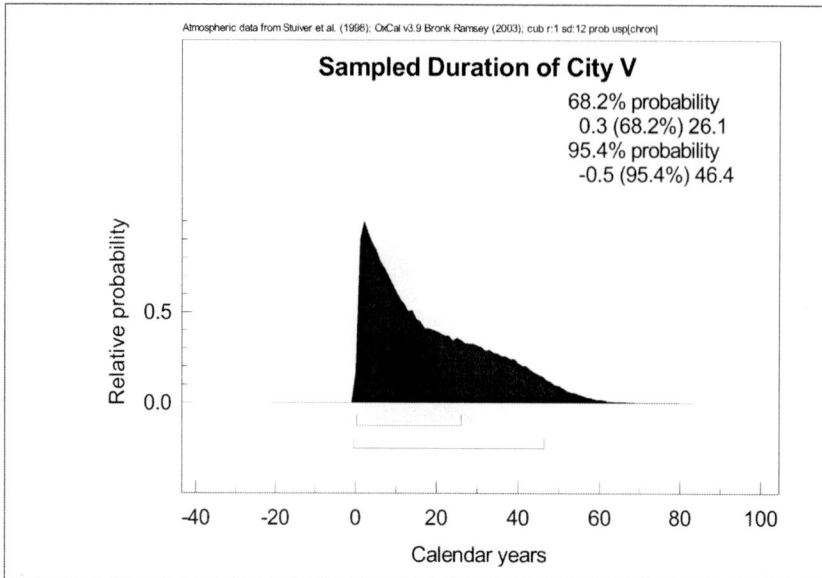

Figure 15.7. The Bayesian sampled date for the duration of City V, prior to its destruction.

Though the duration of City V is unknown, Finkelstein and Piasetzky (2003a) suggested a time-span for both City VI and City V of altogether 20 years in an attempt to squeeze the Groningen radiocarbon dates from Tel Reḥov into the young chronology theory. A duration of merely 10 years for City VI and another 10 years for City V seems very unlikely on archaeological grounds, besides ^{14}C evidence criteria (Bruins, van der Plicht and Mazar 2003b). What has Bayesian analysis to say on the subject? The line 'Interval Duration City V' signalled to the model to make a statistical computation about the duration of City V, prior to its destruction, as shown in Figure 15.7. The results suggest a time-span for City V of 26–46 years, in the 1σ and 2σ ranges, respectively.

The Destruction Event that Terminated the City of Stratum IV

The radiocarbon dates available for Stratum IV relate only to the destruction at the end of City IV's lifespan. The availability of samples for radiocarbon dating in archaeology are, unfortunately, more likely to come from fires or destruction events than from ordinary daily life. The sampled Bayesian destruction date of City IV (Fig. 15.8) has the highest probability in the 1σ range of 903–892 (13.4%), 885–845 BCE (54.8%), extended in the 2σ range to 918–823 BCE. Though it seems very unlikely that the Shishak campaign would have been responsible for the destruction of City IV, there are various other candidates later in time. As there are no younger Iron Age stratigraphic data from Tel Reḥov, the available ^{14}C data are insufficient to favour a certain decade within the above 2σ range of 920–815 BCE. The sampled Bayesian time-span for City IV is 28–55 years in the 1σ and 2σ ranges, respectively (Fig. 15.8).

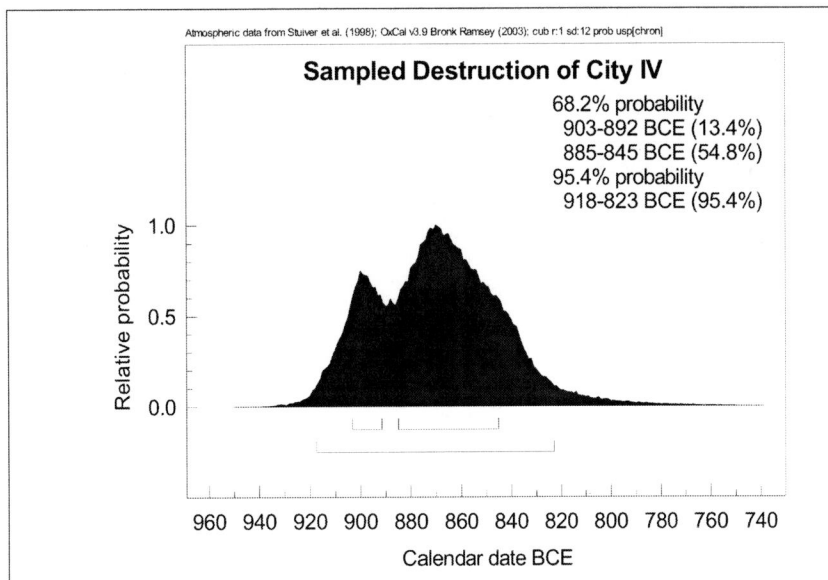

Figure 15.8. The sampled Bayesian date for the destruction of City IV, the last Iron Age settlement at Tel Reḥov.

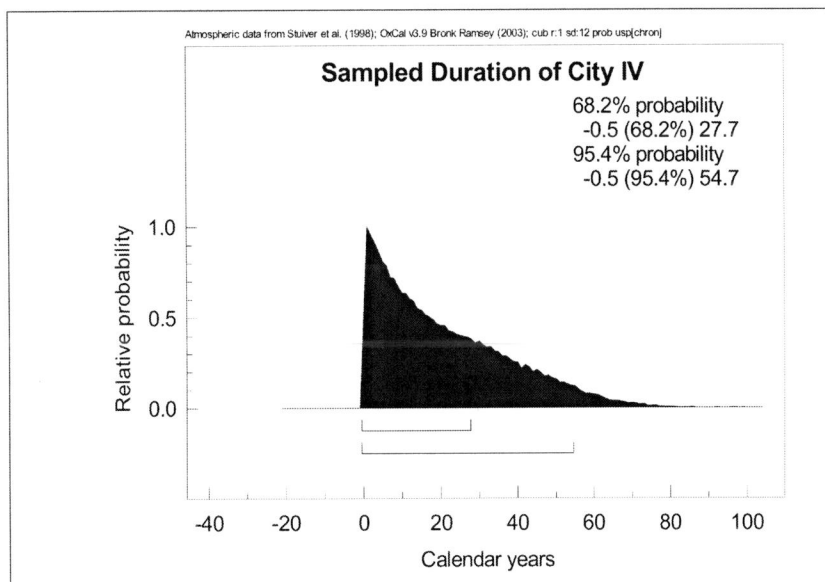

Figure 15.9. The Bayesian sampled date for the duration of City IV, prior to its destruction.

Conclusions

The Tel Reḥov excavations establish a detailed archaeological stratigraphy for the Iron Age with many finds of charred seeds in various Strata and Loci. A methodology of multiple radiocarbon measurements of single samples was used to increase precision and, very likely, also accuracy, as two independent Groningen dating systems were employed (PGC and AMS), each with independent criteria for accuracy (LeClercq, van der Plicht and Gröning 1998; van der Plicht and Bruins [Chapter 14, this volume]). The resulting dense dating basis embedded within a detailed stratigraphic sequence led to the development of a Bayesian model that proved to be remarkably stable and robust. Test runs of alternative model options gave similar results, also with respect to the IntCal98 and IntCal04 calibration curves. The latter curve resulted in slightly older dates. The above strategy considerably increased the time resolution and refinement of radiocarbon dating.

The current Bayesian stratigraphic model for Tel Rehov gives the following most probable statistical results:

1. An early Iron Age IB–IIA transition is strongly favoured by the data, as the sampled boundary (IntCal98 calibration curve) in the 1σ range is 992–961 BCE (68.2%), and in the 2σ range 998–957 (75.2%), 953–921 BCE (20.2%). The peak probability date is ca. 970 BCE. Running the model with the IntCal04 calibration curve gives similar but slightly older results: the 1σ range is 993–961 BCE (68.2%) and the 2σ range is 1001–927 BCE (95.4%). The peak probability remains the same at ca. 970 BCE.

2. Stratum VI has its most likely 1σ position in the range 971–958 BCE (62.4%). The three model options that were tested, with or without R_Combine, all selected more or less the above time period.

3. The City of Stratum V had a possible duration of 26–46 years, in the 1σ and 2σ ranges, respectively.

4. The destruction of City V occurred most likely in the full 1σ range of 924–902 BCE (68.2%). This time range could perhaps fit with the chronological assessments for the Asian campaign of Shoshenq I (Shishak), based only on Egyptian criteria (Shortland [Chapter 4, this volume]). Running the Bayesian model with the IntCal04 calibration curve yielded a slightly older date in the 1σ range: 929–906 BCE (68.2%). The latter range does also include the date 925 BCE for the Shoshenq campaign as suggested by Kitchen (1986, 2000).

5. The City of Stratum IV had a possible duration of 28–55 years, in the 1σ and 2σ ranges, respectively.

6. The destruction of City IV occurred at some time in the 2σ range of 918–823 BCE (95.4%).

References

Bronk Ramsey, C. (1995) Radiocarbon Calibration and Analysis of Stratigraphy: The OxCal Program. *Radiocarbon* 37(2): 425-30.

—(2001) Development of the Radiocarbon Program OxCal. *Radiocarbon* 43 (2A): 355-63.

—(2003) OxCal Program v3.9, Radiocarbon Accelerator Unit, University of Oxford.

Bronk Ramsey, C., J. van der Plicht and B. Weninger (2001) 'Wiggle Matching' Radiocarbon Dates. *Radiocarbon* 43 (2A): 381-89.

Bruins, H.J., and J. van der Plicht (1995) Tell es-Sultan (Jericho): Radiocarbon Results of Short-lived Cereal and Multi-year Charcoal Samples from the End of the Middle Bronze Age. *Radiocarbon* 37: 213-20.

Bruins, H.J., J. van der Plicht, and A. Mazar (2003a) ^{14}C Dates from Tel Rehov: Iron Age Chronology, Pharaohs, and Hebrew Kings. *Science* 300: 315-18.

—(2003b) Response to Comment on '^{14}C Dates from Tel Rehov: Iron Age Chronology, Pharaohs and Hebrew Kings'. *Science* 302: 568c.

Bruins, H.J., A. Mazar and J. van der Plicht (in press) The End of the 2nd Millennium BCE and the Transition from Iron I to Iron IIA: Radiocarbon Dates of Tel Rehov, Israel. In *The Synchronization of the Civilization in the Second Millennium BCE*, III, edited by M. Bietrak (Vienna: The Austrian Academy).

Buck, C.E., and A.R. Millard (eds.) (2004) *Tools for Constructing Chronologies* (London: Springer Verlag).

Gilks, W.R., S. Richardson and D.J. Speigelhalter (1996) *Markov Chain Monte Carlo in Practice* (London: Chapman & Hall).

Finkelstein, I., and E. Piasetzky (2003a) Comments on '^{14}C Dates from Tel Reḥov: Iron Age Chronology, Pharaohs and Hebrew Kings'. *Science* 302: 658b.

—(2003b) Wrong and Right, High and Low: ^{14}C Dates from Tel Reḥov and Iron Age Chronology. *Tel Aviv* 30: 283-95.

Kitchen, K.A. (1986) *The Third Intermediate Period in Egypt* (Warminster: Aris & Philips, 2nd edn).

—(2000) The Historical Chronology of Ancient Egypt: A Current Assessment. In *The Synchronization of Civilizations in the Eastern Mediterranean in the Second Millennium B.C.*, edited by M. Bietak (Vienna: Österreichische Akademie der Wissenschaften): 39-52.

Kromer, B., and K.O. Münnich (1992) CO_2 Gas Proportional Counting in Radiocarbon Dating—Review and Perspective. In *Radiocarbon After Four Decades. An Interdisciplinary Perspective*, edited by R.E. Taylor, A. Long and R.S. Kra (New York: Springer Verlag): 184-97.

LeClercq, M., J. van der Plicht and M. Gröning (1998) New ^{14}C Reference Materials with Activities of 15 and 50 pMC. *Radiocarbon* 40: 295-97.

Manning, S.W., and B. Weninger (1992) A Light in the Dark: Archaeological Wiggle Matching and the Absolute Chronology of the Close of the Aegean Late Bronze Age. *Antiquity* 66: 636-63.

Mazar, A. (1999) The 1997–1998 Excavations at Tel Reḥov: Preliminary Report. *IEJ* 49: 1-42.

—(2003) The Excavations at Tel Reḥov and their Significance for the Study of the Iron Age in Israel. *Eretz Israel* 27: 143-60.

Mook, W.G. (1983) International Comparison of Proportional Gas Counters for ^{14}C Activity Measurements. *Radiocarbon* 25: 475-84.

Mook, W.G., and H.T. Waterbolk (1985) *Handbook for Archaeologists. III. Radiocarbon Dating* (Strasbourg: European Science Foundation).

Reimer, P.J., *et al.* (2004) INTCAL04 Terrestrial Radiocarbon Age Calibration, 0-26 kyr BP. *Radiocarbon* 46: 1029-58.

Stuiver, M., and J.van der Plicht (eds.) (1998) Calibration Issue. *Radiocarbon* 40(3).

Stuiver, M., *et al.* (1998) INTCAL98 Radiocarbon Age Calibration, 24000-0 cal BP. *Radiocarbon* 40(3): 1041-83.

Van der Plicht, J., and H.J. Bruins (2001) Radiocarbon Dating in Near-Eastern Contexts: Confusion and Quality Control. *Radiocarbon* 43: 1155-66.

Van der Plicht, J., H.J. Streurman and G.R. Schreuder (1992) A New Data Acquisition System for the Groningen Counters. *Radiocarbon* 34: 500-505.

16 ¹⁴C Results from Megiddo, Tel Dor, Tel Rehov and Tel Hadar

Where do they lead us?

Eli Piasetzky and Israel Finkelstein

Abstract

All available data that correspond to ¹⁴C measurements of short-lived samples from two destruction horizons known from several key sites in Northern Israel (Megiddo, Tel Dor, Tel Rehov and Tel Hadar) have been used to judge which of the two Iron Age chronological hypotheses is correct. Unlike traditional methods, we have chosen not to calibrate each datum but rather to translate the two hypotheses into uncalibrated dates and compare them to the measurements. This method reduces the uncertainties and allows using normal distribution to evaluate the deviation between each datum and the prediction by each hypothesis. The procedure we have used shows unambiguously better agreement of the data with the 'Low Chronology' system. It allows us to determine that the 'High Chronology' system has little probability of being correct.

Introduction

The problem of absolute dating of the archeological finds from the Iron Age strata of the southern Levant has been fiercely debated in recent years (e.g. Ben-Tor 2000; Finkelstein 1996, 2001; Knauf 2000; Mazar 1997). A precise absolute dating (with a resolving power better than 50 years) may have far-reaching implications not only on the field of archaeology, but also on other, related disciplines such as biblical history and biblical exegesis. In this work we wish to concentrate on the ¹⁴C data and their analysis. Part of this study was published elsewhere (Finkelstein and Piasetzky 2003). In the short period of time that has passed since the publication of that article, the available data base has more than doubled. The new data are included in this paper (Table 16.1).

The Available Data

In recent years, a large number of samples from several key sites—such as Dor, Rehov, Beth-shean, Tel Hadar and Megiddo—were sent to different laboratories for ¹⁴C analysis. Sets of dates—from Dor (Gilboa and Sharon 2001; Sharon 2001), and from Tel Rehov and Beth-shean (Bruins, van der Plicht and Mazar 2003a, 2003b; Mazar 2004; Mazar and Carmi 2001)—have recently been published. Two more sets of data from Megiddo and Tel Hadar were also available for this study prior to their publication. The data correspond to two destruction horizons (each based on similarities in pottery assemblages) known from several key sites in Northern Israel. The first, referred to in this paper as 'the Megiddo VIA horizon', is dated according to the conventional dating system to ca. 1000 BCE and according to the Low Chronology system to ca. 930 BCE. The second, referred to here as 'the Megiddo VA–IVB destruction horizon', is dated to 925 BCE (Pharaoh Shoshenq I's campaign to Palestine) or to ca. 835 BCE (the assault of Aram Damascus on the Northern Kingdom [Na'aman 1997]) respectively.

All available data that correspond to short-lived samples from the Megiddo VIA and VA–IVB horizons are listed in Table 16.1. Long-lived samples, such as timber, wood and charcoal, establish early limits (*terminus post quem*) for the dating of the strata, and this can bias the conclusion toward the Low Chronology system. To avoid that, only short-lived samples have been considered.

Table 16.1. Short-lived samples from Iron Age strata.

No.	Site (stratum)	Horizon	Type of Sample	Number of Measurements	Technique	Laboratory
1	Tel Rehov V	VA–IVB	Charred grain	9	AMS	Arizona WI
2	(C1)			9	LSC	Gr
3	(L 2425)			2	GPC	
4	Tel Rehov V	VA–IVB	Charred grain	4	GPC+AMS	Gr
5	(C1)			3		
6	(L 2441, 2422, 4218)			3		
7	Tel Rehov V (area B)	VA–IVB	Grain	3	LSC	Gr
8	Tel Rehov IV	VA–IVB	Grain	3	AMS	Gr
9	Tel Rehov D3	VIA	Olive pits	1	LSC	WI
10	Tel Rehov D3	VIA	Olive pits	5	LSC	Gr
11	Tel Rehov D4	VIA	Olive pits	1	LSC	WI
12	Tel Rehov D4a	VIA	Olive pits	2	GPC+AMS	Gr
13	Tel Rehov D4b	VIA	Seeds	3	AMS	Gr
14	Tel Hadar IV	VIA	Charred grain	11	GPC	WI
	Tel Hadar IV	VIA	Charred grain	1	AMS	NZ
15	Tel Dor D2/10	VIA	Seeds	1	LSC	WI
16	Megiddo K-4	VIA	Olive pits	5	LSC	WI
17	Megiddo H-5	VA–IVB	Olive pits	2	LSC	WI

AMS—Accelerator Mass Spectrometry (Kutschera *et al.* 1999); LSC—Liquid Scintillation Counting (Aitken 1990); GPC—Gas Proportional Counting (Aitken 1990); Arizona—The AMS facility at the University of Arizona; WI—The Weizmann Institute laboratory in Rehovot, Israel; NZ—Rafter Radiocarbon Laboratory, New Zealand; Gr—University of Groningen, Holland

All in all, 67 measurements done by AMS and by conventional radiometric methods (LSC and GPC) were available to us. The data represent four sites and 15 different archeological contexts.

Tel Rehov

Charred grain samples were found in the destruction layer of Stratum C1 (Mazar 1999: 20-23), on the floor of a small chamber that had been sealed by fallen bricks (Locus 2425). The chamber contained a rich pottery assemblage of the Megiddo VA–IVB horizon.

The grain samples were analyzed by three laboratories. Nine samples were measured by the Weizmann Institute laboratory using LSC, nine samples were measured by AMS in the University of Arizona laboratory (Mazar and Carmi 2001) and two were measured by GPC the Center for Isotope Research, Groningen (Mazar 2004). The weighted average of the Weizmann Institute measurements was 2720 ± 7 BP, which corresponds to a 1 SD (standard deviation) calibrated range of 905–835 BCE. The Arizona weighted average was 2750 ± 16 BP and the calibrated 1 SD range is 900–830 BCE. The authors noted the consistency of the two different measurements and concluded a combined 900–830 BCE dating for the samples. If a constant is fitted to all the uncalibrated data a x_v^2 (x^2 per degree of freedom) of about 5 is obtained, indicating that the assumption of fully consistent measurements of the same age sample is wrong.[1] The Arizona data gives only a x_v^2 of about 1 and the Weizmann Institute of about 9. One measurement of the Weizmann Institute is about 7 SD above the average of the other 8. Removing single data point, which is clearly an 'outlier', one gets a weighted average of 2699 ± 10 BP for the Weizmann Institute measurements.[2] This is different by 2.7 SD from the Arizona results.

Results from 12 more samples of charred grain were measured by the Groningen Laboratory and published recently (Mazar 2004). Two samples are from the same locus (2425) as the above Weizmann and Arizona samples and 10 more come from 3 other loci, also corresponding to the end of Stratum V. The 12 Groningen measurements yielded an average of 2776 ± 5 BP. This average agrees with the Arizona average (it is older by about 1 SD only) but is in strong disagreement with the Weizmann average (Groningen is older than Weizmann by about 7 SD). In a recent paper Mazar (2004) has argued that this is an indication that all the Weizmann 1990s measurements (for other sites as well) are too low and should be considered with reservation. Sharon *et al.* (Chapter 6, this volume) have shown that there are no systematic differences between the Weizmann, Arizona and Groningen measurements.

Three charred olive pits were found in successive stratigraphic phases in Area D at Tel Reḥov and were dated by the Weizmann Institute laboratory using the LSC method (Mazar and Carmi 2001). Two of the pits, assigned to phases D3 and D4, which belong to the Megiddo VIA horizon, yielded uncalibrated dates of 2670 ± 40 BP and 2800 ± 40 BP. The third measurement, from phase D6, which is older than the Megiddo VIA horizon, is not quoted here. Mazar and Carmi referred to these data as 'unreliable', since the sequence of the ^{14}C dates does not fit the stratigraphic sequence (the D6 reading falls between the D3 and D4 ones, though it should be older than both). But this is only a 2 SD effect and hence does not indicate any significant problem with the data. Samples from different loci of Strata D3 and D4, analyzed by the Groningen Laboratory and published after our *Antiquity* article (Finkelstein and Piasetzky 2003), were added to the data base and analyzed in the present study. They include 5 LSC measurements of olive pits found in a Stratum D3 locus, 1 AMS and 1 GPC measurement of olive pits from a Stratum D4a locus and 3 AMS measurements of seeds from Stratum D4b.

Tel Hadar

The ^{14}C samples were taken from a large quantity of charred grain found sealed under a thick layer of brick collapse—evidence of the destruction of the site (Stratum IV) in a violent conflagration (Kochavi 1998: 470-71). The pottery assemblages of Stratum IV can clearly be associated with the Megiddo VIA horizon. Eleven samples were measured in the Weizmann Institute laboratory using its GPC system, which was later replaced by newer LCS equipment. One of the samples was analyzed using the AMS method in an accelerator laboratory in New Zealand. These data have never been published. The AMS measurement (2820 ± 80 BP), with a great degree of uncertainty, agrees well with the other 11 radiocarbon measurements. A fit to a constant for the 12 data points yields a date of 2780 ± 25 BP with $x_v^2 \sim 3$. We omitted two samples from the analysis, one that was not mechanically cleaned before measurement (contrary to the other samples) and another that was contaminated with burnt organic material from outside the granary.

---

1.   Reduced x_v^2 much larger than unity means that the actual distribution of results is larger than expected, or that the assigned errors are smaller than they should be.

2.   The SD for these points equals the 1 SD error of the fit to a constant multiplied by the square root of the x^2.

Tel Dor

The seed sample was found inside an elaborate public structure that is contemporary with the Megiddo VIA horizon. This sample was measured using the conventional LSC method by the Weizmann Institute laboratory. The result was 2735 ± 40 BP (Gilboa and Sharon 2001; Sharon 2001). This single measurement is consistent with other measurements of charcoal taken from the same context (Gilboa and Sharon 2001; Sharon 2001), but they are not considered here due to their long-range nature.

Megiddo

After the *Antiquity* article was published (Finkelstein and Piasetzky 2003), we received results of 5 new ^{14}C measurements of seeds from Megiddo. These measurements are part of a research project on ^{14}C and Iron Age chronology which is currently being conducted by Sharon *et al.* (see Chapter 6, this volume). Five samples were found on the floors of a Level K-4 building (Stratum VIA of the University of Chicago excavations), sealed by approximately one meter of destruction debris and collapse. The 5 samples yielded a weighted average of 2760 ± 40 BP, which is in good agreement with the data from the Megiddo VIA horizon at other sites discussed in this paper. Two more samples of olive pits were found in destruction debris from Level H-5 (Stratum VA–IVB) and analyzed by the LSC method in the Weizmann laboratory.

For this study we used all the data available as presented above. With only minor corrections, all explained above, we used the values and uncertainties as determined and published by the laboratories that performed the measurements.

Discussion

The difference between the two dating systems—the conventional one (called here the High Chronology) and the Low Chronology—is about 70 years (Table 16.2), which over 3000 years comes to about a 2% difference.[3]

Table 16.2. The two chronology hypothesis in absolute and uncalibrated (BP) dates. The translation to uncalibrated dates was done using the 1998 calibration curve (Stuiver *et al.* 1998).

Horizon		Low Chronology	High Chronology
Megiddo VIA		1025–925 BCE	1100–1000 BCE
	Uncalibrated BP	2900–2780 BP	2930–2830 BP
Megiddo VA–IVB		870–835 BCE	960–925 BCE
	Uncalibrated BP	2760–2710 BP	2845–2780 BP

A conventional radiometric measurement has a typical (1 SD) uncertainty of 15–20 years in determining the uncalibrated age of a sample from this period. The AMS uncertainty is about 50–70 years. Temporal fluctuations in the atmospheric concentration necessitate calibration of radiocarbon dates to known dendro-chronological dates (Kutschera *et al.* 1999: 20-22). The calibration curve has an uncertainty of about 10–20 years in this period. The non-linearity of the calibration curve and the possibility of more than one solution cause a fairly large non-regular uncertainty in the dating and destroy the normal distribution nature of the measured, uncalibrated dates (for a specific example see Reimer 2001, second figure).

---

3. By 'High Chronology' we refer to the traditional dating system (e.g. Mazar 1997; Dever 1997; Ben-Tor 2000; Stager 2003). Mazar has now lowered the dates (Chapter 13, this volume) and Dever too has recently sounded willing to accept a certain lowering of the dates (Chapter 25, this volume).

Given the sparse data available and the great uncertainties, it is clear that careful analysis is required to distinguish between the two dating systems for the Iron Age strata. Unlike traditional methods, we have chosen not to calibrate each datum. Rather, we have used the calibration curve to translate the two hypotheses to uncalibrated dates. We did this using the last published calibration curve (Stuiver *et al.* 1998). This procedure enabled us, for each sample, to use the measured (uncalibrated) data with smaller uncertainty and normal distribution.

The data and the two dating systems are shown in Figure 16.1. The Low Chronology horizon is presented by the band between the two dashed lines and the High Chronology by the band between the two full lines. Each datum is presented by its value and 1 SD range. The number attached to each point refers to the line number in Tables 16.1 and 16.3. Consistent measurements that correspond to the same archaeological context and time were combined to a single point.

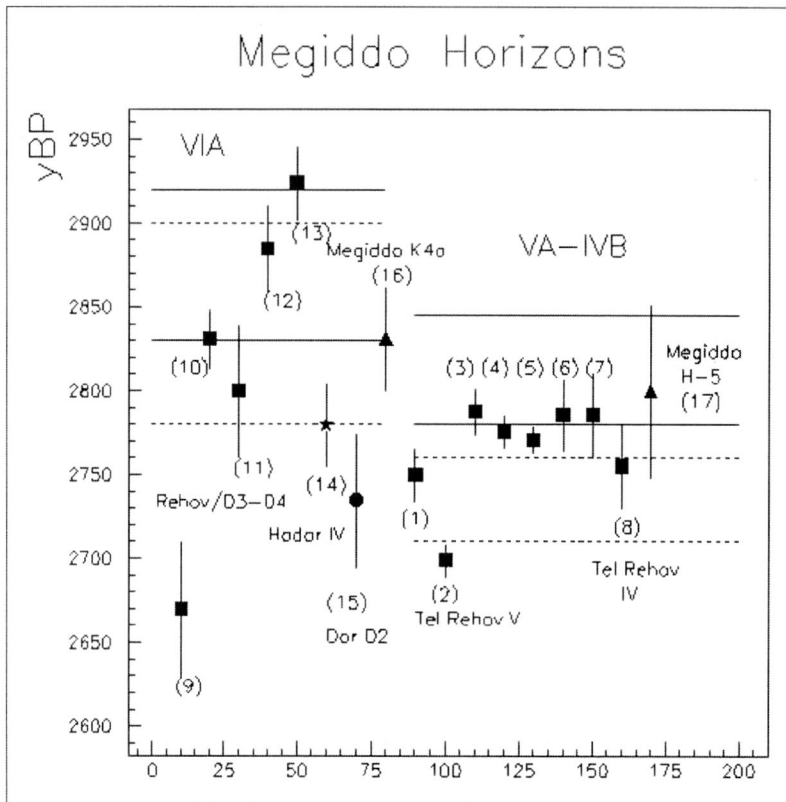

Figure 16.1. The uncalibrated ^{14}C measurements (BP) from the Megiddo VIA and Megiddo IVB–VA Horizons, all short-lived measurements. Consistent measurements from the same archaeological context have been combined. The High and Low Chronology hypotheses are shown as bands between full and dashed lines. The data are marked according to the line numbers in Tables 16.1 and 16.3. The numbers on the horizontal axis are meaningless.

For horizon VIA most of the data are lower than the High Chronology hypothesis band; some are even lower than the Low Chronology band. There is not even a single datum that is above the upper limit even for the Low Chronology band. Therefore, the agreement with the Low Chronology hypothesis is clearly better. The situation with the VA–IVB horizon is not as clear. The recently published Groningen measurements for Tel Rehov favor the High Chronology, while the Weizmann/Arizona results clearly favor the Low Chronology (but see below).

Overall it is clear from Figure 16.1 that all the data agree with the Low Chronology system better than they do with the High Chronology. To quantify this statement, we generalize the x^2 test used to compare data to a function so that it describes deviation from a band. For each dating system we calculate

$$x'^2 = \sum_{i=1}^{n} \left(d_i / \sigma_i \right)^2$$

where d_i is zero for a point inside the band and the distance from the upper (lower) band limit for points above (below) these limits. σ_i is the SD of the datum with index i measurement. The lower the value of the generalized x'^2, the better the hypothesis. x'^2_L and x'^2_H were calculated for the Low and High Chronology systems. Their values and the contribution of each datum are shown in Table 16.3 and Figure 16.2. Brackets with a positive/negative sign indicate datum above/below the band. At the bottom of Table 16.3 we summed all the contributions to x'^2 from deviations above the band (Line 18), all those from deviations below the band (Line 19) and x'^2 which is defined as the sum of all deviations below and above the band (Line 20).

Table 16.3. The contribution of each datum to x'^2_L and x'^2_H.

No.	Site (Stratum) (as in Table 16.1)	Measurement [BP]	x'^2_L	x'^2_H
1	Tel Rehov V(C1)	2750 ± 16	0	3.5 (–)
2	Tel Rehov V(C1)	2699 ± 10	1.2 (–)	65.6 (–)
3	Tel Rehov V(C1)	2788 ± 14	4.0 (+)	0
4	Tel Rehov V(C1)	2776 ± 10	2.6 (+)	0.2 (–)
5	Tel Rehov V(C1)	2771 ± 8	1.9 (+)	1.3 (–)
6	Tel Rehov V(C1)	2786 ± 22	1.4 (+)	0
7	Tel Rehov V(B)	2786 ± 25	1.1 (+)	0
8	Tel Rehov IV	2755 ± 25	0	1 (–)
9	Tel Rehov D3	2670 ± 40	7.6 (–)	16 (–)
10	Tel Rehov D3	2831 ± 18	0	0
11	Tel Rehov D4	2800 ± 40	~0	0.6 (–)
12	Tel Rehov D4a	2885 ± 26	0	0
13	Tel Rehov D4b	2924 ± 22	1.2 (+)	~0
14	Tel Hadar IV	2780 ± 25	0	4 (–)
15	Tel Dor D2/10	2735 ± 40	1.3 (–)	5.6 (–)
16	Megiddo K4a	2831 ± 31	0	0
17	Megiddo H-5	2800 ± 52	0.6 (+)	0
18	All data above the band's upper limit		12.8 (+)	0
19	All data below the band's lower limit		10.4 (–)	98 (–)
20	ALL DATA (= x'^2)		23	98

Comparing the data with the two hypotheses, apart from the clear difference in the size of x'^2, we call the reader's attention to two more points:

1. Several data points are in strong disagreement with the High Chronology (large contribution to x'^2). These are essentially measurements 2 (Tel Rehov), 9 (Tel Rehov), 14 (Tel Hadar) and 15 (Tel Dor). The collection of 12 new Groningen measurements (3–7) makes the strong deviations for the Low Chronology that favor the High Chronology. Yet, it is noteworthy that they all come from Stratum V, stratigraphically placed in the early

part of the VA–IVB horizon (Stratum IV is the one which closes the VA–IVB horizon at Reḥov). Therefore, the destruction of Stratum V should actually be somewhere in the center of the band. If this is so, the new Groningen samples are equally consistent with both hypotheses.

2. The amount of deviations above and below the Low Chronology band is what one expects from a correct hypothesis. For the High Chronology there are no deviations above the band and all the data that disagree are found below the band. This is a clear indication that the High Chronology is too high.

As can be seen in Table 16.3 and Figures 16.1–2, together the available measurements allow a clear conclusion to be drawn: the data unambiguously support the Low Chronology hypothesis. If the data would follow a Gaussian distribution, the probability that the High Chronology hypothesis is correct is well below 1%. Clearly far from the mean, the tail is not well described by a normal distribution so the 1% should be taken cautiously. It is, however, safe to argue that the data point to a small probability that the High Chronology is correct.

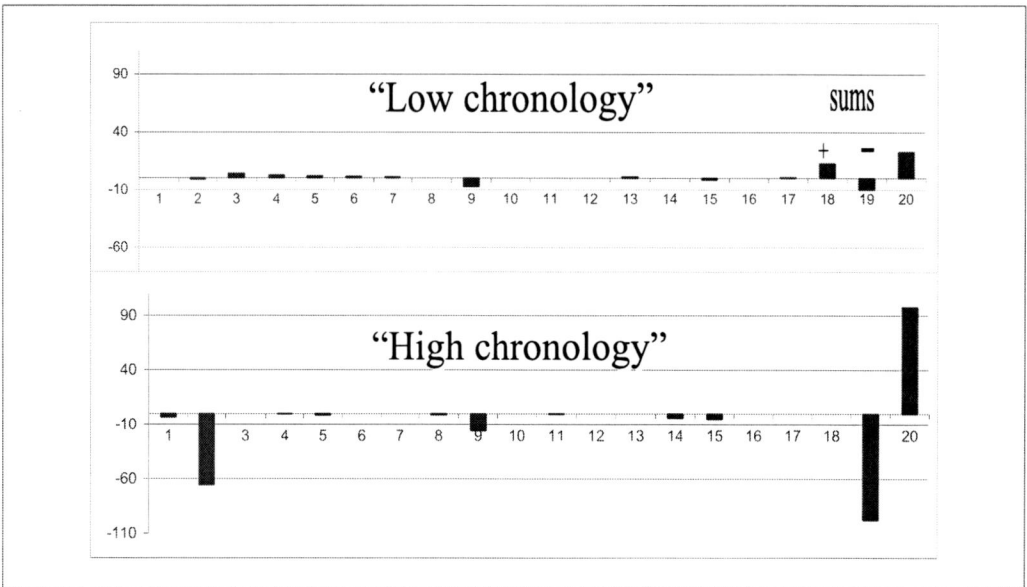

Figure 16.2. The x' for each measurement (1–17 as in Tables 16.1 and 16.3) calculated for the High and Low Chronologies as explained in the text. For results above/below the band the bars are above and below the horizontal axis. The sum of all contributions to x' from the data above/below the bands are shown as items 18 and 19 respectively. The sum of all contributions to x' (which is defined as x') is shown as the last entry marked 20.

To summarize, absolute dating based on ^{14}C measurements makes it possible to obtain a conclusive answer to the debate concerning the date of the Iron Age strata in the Levant. The data published so far unambiguously support the Low Chronology and disagree with the High Chronology. This conclusion is consistent with another study based on a much larger set of data (Sharon *et al.* [Chapter 6, this volume]).

Acknowledgments

The data from Megiddo are part of a research project which is supported by the Israel Science Foundation (grant 778/00), currently being conducted by Ilan Sharon of the Hebrew University, Elisabetta Boaretto of the Weizmann Institute and Ayelet Gilboa of the University of Haifa. We wish to thank them for allowing us to present the new data at this preliminary stage of their research. We also wish to thank David Ussishkin and Baruch Halpern, who co-direct the Megiddo Expedition with author Israel Finkelstein, for permitting us to refer to the new data. The authors are grateful to Moshe Kochavi and Israel Carmi for providing them with the Tel Hadar information prior to its publication.

References

Aitken, M.J. (1990) *Science-based Dating in Archaeology* (London: Longman).

Ben-Tor, A. (2000) Hazor and the Chronology of Northern Israel: A Reply to Israel Finkelstein. *BASOR* 317: 9-15.

Bruins, H.J., J. van der Plicht and A. Mazar (2003a) ^{14}C Dates from Tel Rehov: Iron-Age Chronology, Pharaohs, and Hebrew Kings. *Science* 300: 315-18.

—(2003b) Response to Comment on '^{14}C Dates from Tel Rehov: Iron-Age chronology, Pharaohs, and Hebrew Kings'. *Science* 302: 568c.

Dever, W.G. (1997) Archaeology and the 'Age of Solomon': A Case Study in Archaeology and Historiography. In *The Age of Solomon: Scholarship at the Turn of the Millennium*, edited by L.K. Handy (Leiden: Brill): 217-51.

Finkelstein, I. (1996) The Archaeology of the United Monarchy: An Alternative View. *Levant* 28: 177-87.

—(2001) The Rise of Jerusalem and Judah: The Missing Link. *Levant* 33: 105-15.

Finkelstein, I., and E. Piasetzky (2003) Recent Radiocarbon Results and King Solomon. *Antiquity* 298: 771-79.

Gilboa, A., and I. Sharon (2001) Early Iron Age Radiometric Dates from Tel Dor: Preliminary Implications for Phoenicia and Beyond. *Radiocarbon* 43: 1343-51.

Knauf, A.E. (2000) The 'Low Chronology' and How Not to Deal with It. *Biblische Notizen* 101: 56-63.

Kochavi, M. (1998) The Eleventh Century BCE Tripartite Pillar Building at Tel Hadar. In *Mediterranean Peoples in Transition*, edited by S. Gitin, A. Mazar and E. Stern (Jerusalem: Israel Exploration Society): 468-78.

Kutschera, W.R.A., *et al.* (1999) Proceeding of the Eighth International Conference on Accelerator Mass Spectrometry, Vienna, Austria. *Nuclear Instruments and Methods* B172: 1-977

Mazar, A. (1997) Iron Age Chronology—A Reply to Israel Finkelstein. *Levant* 29: 155-65.

—(1999) The 1997–1998 Excavations at Tel Rehov: Preliminary Report. *IEJ* 49: 20-23.

—(2004) Greek and Levantine Iron Age Chronology: A Rejoinder. *IEJ* 54:24-36.

Mazar, A., and I. Carmi (2001) Radiocarbon Dates from Iron Age Strata at Tel Beth Shean and Tel Rehov. *Radiocarbon* 43: 1333-42.

Na'aman (1977) Historical and Literary Notes on the Excavations of Tel Jezreel. *Tel Aviv* 24: 122-28.

Reimer, P.J. (2001) A New Twist in the Radiocarbon Tale. *Science* 294: 2492-95.

Sharon, I. (2001) 'Transition Dating'—A Heuristic Mathematical Approach to the Collation of Radiocarbon Dates from Stratified Sequences. *Radiocarbon* 43: 345-54.

Stager, L.E. (2003) The Patrimonial Kingdom of Solomon. In *Symbiosis, Symbolism, and the Power of the Past: Canaan, Ancient Israel, and their Neighbors from the Late Bronze Age through Roman Palestine*, edited by W.G. Dever and S. Gitin (Winona Lake, IN: Eisenbrauns): 63-74.

Stuiver, M., *et al.* (1998) INTCAL 98 Radiocarbon Age Calibration, 24,000-0 Cal BP. *Radiocarbon* 40: 1041-83.

17 High or Low: Megiddo and Tel Reḥov

Israel Finkelstein

Abstract

This chapter challenges the notion that Tel Reḥov can serve as the principal anchor for Iron Age chronology. It summarizes the main shortcomings in the analysis of the second series of ^{14}C determinations from Tel Reḥov and points to difficulties in the interpretation of the stratigraphy of the site. The chapter compares the stratigraphy of Megiddo and Tel Reḥov and shows that, in fact, the Tel Reḥov finds support the most important premise of the Low Chronology system—the dating of the ashlar palaces at Megiddo to the first half of the 9th century BCE.

Introduction

In recent years, Amihai Mazar has suggested making Tel Reḥov a principal anchor in the debate on the dating of the Iron Age strata in the Levant (Bruins, van der Plicht and Mazar 2003a; Coldstream and Mazar 2003; Mazar 1999a: 40-42; 2004; Mazar and Carmi 2001). In my opinion this cannot be the case. In what follows I wish to deal with the new data provided by Tel Reḥov and elaborate on the role of Megiddo in this discussion. Two facts call for a close look at Tel Reḥov and its stratigraphy: (1) An inter-laboratory test shows that the Weizmann and Groningen laboratories produce similar results (Sharon et al. [Chapter 6, this volume]); (2) The second Tel Reḥov series (Bruins, van der Plicht and Mazar 2003a) clearly diverts from the radiocarbon results provided by many other Iron I and early Iron II sites (Sharon et al. [Chapter 6, this volume]). Needless to say, what follows does not diminish in any way my respect for the importance of the site and the scholarship of its excavator Amihai Mazar.

The Second Series of [14]C Measurements from Tel Reḥov

Eliezer Piasetzky and I have shown that measured against the two main theories on the dating of the Megiddo VIA and the Megiddo VA–IVB horizons, previously published ^{14}C measurements from Tel Reḥov (Mazar and Carmi 2001) fit better the Low Chronology system (Finkelstein and Piasetzky 2003a). A second set of ^{14}C readings from Tel Reḥov has been described by Bruins, van der Plicht and Mazar (2003a) as supporting the conventional (High) chronology. In what follows I wish briefly to summarize and update the main points raised by Piasetzky and I against this notion (Finkelstein and Piasetzky 2003b, 2003c).

Other Measurements

Bruins, van der Plicht and Mazar (2003a) chose to overlook previously published radiocarbon measurements from the same strata and in some cases even the same loci at Tel Reḥov, which provide lower dates for the Iron IIA layers of this site (Mazar and Carmi 2001). They pointed to inconsistent results from three laboratories concerning the dating of short life samples from Locus 2425 at Tel Reḥov and decided not to include the dates determined by the Weizmann and Arizona laboratories and to base their entire analysis on results from the Groningen laboratory (see also Mazar 2004). Systematic differences between laboratories need to be studied carefully, but the procedure used by Bruins, van der Plicht and Mazar is unacceptable. One has either to resolve the problem that causes these inconsistencies or increase the uncertainty of the measurements. Excluding some measurements from the database leads to an unjustified bias. After all, in this situation one cannot really tell whether the Weizmann determinations are too low, Groningen too high, or, indeed, whether both laboratories divert from the true dates (and in which direction), and so on.

Possible Contamination

Some of the samples in the second Tel Reḥov series come from pits, refuse deposits and a street surface that may well be contaminated with old material. Strata VI–IV at Tel Reḥov yielded pottery assemblages which are very close typologically, meaning that contamination would be difficult to track. In other words, a sample from Stratum IV or V could have originated, in fact, in Stratum VI, and so on. As far as I can judge, only some of the second series of samples from Tel Reḥov can be considered sufficiently reliable (not to mention stratigraphic problems [see below]). In a delicate attempt to determine differences of a few decades in the Iron Age—an issue so crucial to historical and biblical studies—only absolutely 'safe' samples, that is, material from floors found under a thick accumulation of destruction debris (such as the Megiddo VIA or the Tel Hadar IV samples), should be submitted for ^{14}C analysis. The pits of Stratum D-3 do not answer these requirements. Pits are pits even if they can be affiliated stratigraphically, and Stratum D-3 will be mentioned later.

Historical Interpretation

Bruins, van der Plicht and Mazar's original statement, that 'There is only one known historical candidate that fits the destruction date of Tel Reḥov stratum V, 940 to 900 BCE, based on 12 high-quality ^{14}C dates: the invasion of Pharaoh Shoshenq I' (2003a: 318), was replaced, following our *Science* rejoinder (Finkelstein and Piasetzky 2003c), by a much softer language: 'It is tempting to relate our destruction dates of Reḥov Stratum V to this pharaoh' (Bruins, van der Plicht and Mazar 2003b). Indeed, clashes between the expanding kingdoms of Northern Israel and Aram Damascus should be considered equally good candidates for the *partial* destruction of this stratum. Pre-mid-9th century BCE hostilities between Israel and Damascus are recorded in the opening lines of the fragments of the Tel Dan stele (Biran and Naveh 1995: 12-13). In addition, Bruins, van der Plicht and Mazar (rightly) accepted that 'the precise historical date of Shoshenq I within the second half of the 10th century BCE remains a factor of uncertainty' (2003b). Indeed, the post-*Science* article lowering of the Stratum V dates to the end of the 10th century BCE (Mazar—presentation at the Yarnton conference, 6–9 September 2004) combined with the above statement shows how difficult it is to establish a clear Shoshenq I connection to any of the Reḥov strata.

Interpretation of the Calibration Curve

Bruins, van der Plicht and Mazar argued that the new data from Tel Reḥov are consistent with their historical interpretation, that is, with a Shoshenq I destruction of Stratum V at Tel Reḥov. Yet, they did not ask whether theirs is the only or the best historical reconstruction to fit the new measurements. Piasetzky and I used the same data, the same calibration curve and the same method and produced a different sequence, with Stratum V dating to the very late 10th century BCE, fitting it well within the Low Chronology system (Finkelstein and Piasetzky 2003b, 2003c; a somewhat similar interpretation for the new Tel Rehov readings was presented by Ayelet Gilboa and Ilan Sharon in The Second EuroConference on the Synchronization of Cultures in the Eastern Mediterranean, Vienna, May 2003). Two alternative interpretations for the dating of Strata VI–IV at Tel Rehov, both consistent with the data and the logic of the stratigraphic sequence, are therefore available. This has been acknowledged by Bruins, van der Plicht and Mazar in their reply to our *Science* rejoinder: their original statement speaks about 'one wiggle in the calibration curve from 950 to 980 BCE, which seems to fit the ^{14}C dating results for Stratum VI, in relation to the archaeological stratigraphy' (2003a: 317). In the rejoinder they say that 'The association between Stratum VI and the wiggle of 970 to 960 BCE seems more plausible in view of the tell stratigraphy' (2003b). In fact, the post-*Science* article lowering of the Rehov V dates (Mazar—presentation at the Yarnton conference, 6–9 September 2004) puts this stratum exactly where we suggest—in the late 10th century BCE.

Megiddo and Tel Rehov

Our central claim, which will be discussed below, is that Tel Rehov IV—not V—is the contemporary of Megiddo VA–IVB (*contra* Mazar, in Coldstream and Mazar 2003). This means that the new Tel Rehov readings actually support the Low Chronology system, according to which the Megiddo ashlar palaces date to the early 9th century BCE.

Stratigraphic Difficulties

The description of the Tel Rehov finds may lead scholars to conclude that it forms a solid basis for both relative and absolute chronology in the north. It is sufficient to refer to the following statement by Mazar in order to see that this is not the case: 'As in every stratigraphic excavation of a multi-layered mound, the excavation at Tel Rehov has its problems. Complicated stratigraphy resulting from continuous construction, partial destruction, and rebuilding of mudbrick structures creates difficulties not only in the correlation between the various local phases in each excavation area, but sometimes even between the different parts of a large excavation area itself' (Coldstream and Mazar 2003: 31). My only objection to this statement is that it does not characterize *every* stratigraphic excavation (see below); it does characterize brick-built mounds such as Tel Rehov.

One example of these 'problems'—regarding samples submitted to ^{14}C analyses—is given by Mazar: 'It is still an open question whether the heap of grain found in Locus 2425 should be attributed to the destruction of Stratum V or to the re-use of this chamber in Stratum IV' (Coldstream and Mazar 2003: 43 note 12). And this locus was one of the pivotal provenances for the ^{14}C dating of Stratum V (Bruins, van der Plicht and Mazar 2003a: Fig. 2)! Beth-shean provides another example of the risk of using material from unsafe stratigraphic contexts for ^{14}C measurements. The dates of charred linen seeds and grain from Bin 28817 there, which had originally been assigned to Stratum S-2, were interpreted as disproving the Low Chronology dates for this stratum (Mazar 1999b: 92). Yet, somewhat later, the bin was reassigned to Stratum S-3a (Mazar and Carmi 2001: 1335-36), which is not related to the chronology dispute. One should also note that the destruction of Stratum V was only partial, that in some places this phase was followed by reuse of the mudbrick walls (see, e.g., Coldstream and Mazar 2003: 43, note 12; Mazar 1999a: 17; also note the continuity between Strata VI and V in Area C [*ibid.*]), and that the whole sequence came to a close only with the destruction of Stratum IV.

I also wish to call attention to the description of the upper strata in Area D, which also figure prominently in the Tel Rehov radiocarbon results. Stratum D3 consists of an open space with pits for discarding refuse, Stratum D2 is a 'flimsy phase, which is difficult to detect' and Stratum D1 yielded mixed Iron I and Iron II pottery (Mazar 1999a: 15-16; more recently Stratum D2 has been described as consisting 'of refuse deposits from nearby Area C Strata V and VI' [Bruins, van der Plicht and Mazar 2003a: 317]). In this situation it can be quite difficult to fix the original stratigraphic affiliation of at least some of the samples.

It is doubtful, then, whether Tel Rehov can be treated as a key site in the debate over the chronology of the Iron IIA strata, which involves differences of 50–70 years. The spotlight should be turned back to Megiddo—the type-site for the Iron II in the north. In the century that has passed since the beginning of the Gottlieb/Schumacher excavations almost all theories on the chronology of the Iron Age strata have been formulated at that site (Guy 1931: 45-48; Watzinger 1929: 67-68, 91; Yadin 1970).

Megiddo has a significant advantage over most sites in the north, since it provides a relatively simple stratigraphic sequence. First, unlike the mudbrick construction of simple houses at Tel Rehov, Megiddo features large stone-built monuments, which are easier to place stratigraphically. Second, Megiddo provides a clear set of four destruction layers between the 12th and 8th centuries BCE: VIIA, VIA, VA and IVA. This series of destructions is the best available peg for the Iron Age chronology in the north. Third, the identification of the two Iron IIA strata at Megiddo (VB and VA–IVB) is relatively easy: everywhere at the site, two levels (sometimes with additional subphases) are 'trapped' between the total (and easy to identify) destruction of Stratum VIA and the characteristic features of Stratum IVA—the sets of pillared buildings (the Megiddo 'stables') and the offsets-insets City-Wall 325 (Cline forthcoming; Lamon and Shipton 1939: Figs. 5, 12; Lehmann, Killebrew and Gadot 2000; Loud 1948: Figs. 387–88; Yadin 1970: Fig. 8). Stratum VB represents the reconstruction of Megiddo after the destruction (possibly followed by a short gap) of Stratum VIA. This layer continued uninterrupted and 'became' an independent stratum in places where large monuments and sometimes simpler houses were added in the later days of this city (e.g. Cline forthcoming; Lamon and Shipton 1939: Figs. 5, 12). Stratum VA represents these monuments, mainly Palaces 6000 and 1723. It came to an end in a conflagration (see pictures in Fisher 1929: 66; Lamon and Shipton 1939: Fig. 11; Loud 1948: Fig. 99).

From all these perspectives, Megiddo must be the key site where the chronology debate is resolved (below).

The Greek Pottery

Mazar (2004) presented the Greek sherds from Rehov as contributing to the chronology debate, though he and Coldstream could not agree in what way. Any discussion of the Greek material from Tel Rehov (Coldstream and Mazar 2003) must start with the fact that it is comprised of sherds, not complete vessels. These sherds could have originated in an earlier stratum. For example, a sherd found in Stratum IV could theoretically have been part of a vessel that reached the site in the days of Stratum V or even in the time of Stratum VI. This is especially true for Tel Rehov, where most walls were made of mudbricks; their production no doubt involved the collection of tell material with discarded sherds (incidentally, Mazar specifically describes a fill laid for the construction of Stratum IV [Coldstream and Mazar 2003: 34]). Following are two specific examples:

1. Sherd no. 4 in Mazar and Coldstream's article, belonging to a Sub-Protogeometric I–IIIa *skyphos*, was found in a layer of destruction debris that contained many restorable vessels, which represents the end of Stratum IV (Coldstream and Mazar 2003: 33). But the sherd could have originated in Stratum V (or even VI). This would further extend the gap

between Levantine and Greek dating of this material: late 10th century BCE according to the current Mazar dating; early 9th century BCE according to Coldstream, who argued that the latter date is 'more easily reconciled with the internal Aegean chronology, based on association within several hundred single graves, associations of whole pots with painted decoration' (in Coldstream and Mazar 2003: 40).

2. The broader problems involved in making Tel Reḥov the axis for Levantine and Greek Iron Age chronology is demonstrated by Sherds nos. 5–6, which belong to a large *pyxis* (Coldstream and Mazar 2003: 34-35; I refer here to the two original sherds, before the discovery of a few more items from this vessel [Mazar 2004: 24-27]; as far as I can judge, the new items do not reflect on my description below). First, when Mazar and Coldstream wrote their article the stratigraphic affiliation of the two sherds—Stratum V or IV—was not clear. Second, they may have originated from a fill. Third, the 'scattering of the sherds over a wide area indicates that the vessel was already broken when these layers accumulated' (Coldstream and Mazar 2003: 35), meaning that the vessel arrived at Tel Reḥov earlier than the date given to the two sherds. Fourth, they come from a locus which could have been contaminated, according to Mazar (2003: 34), by erosion on the slope. In short, the stratigraphic and thus chronological origin of these sherds (identified by Coldstream as Euboean Sub-Protogeometric II–IIIa) is far from being clear.

Mazar describes the difficulty with the Greek connection at Tel Reḥov in the following words: 'The SPG II–IIIa Euboean *pyxis* (nos. 5–6) poses a problem. If indeed it belongs to Stratum V and if Stratum V was indeed destroyed by Sheshonq I, it would predate the date suggested by Coldstream…by some 50 years' (Coldstream and Mazar 2003: 44-45). But 50 years is the minimum in this case. If these sherds were part of a vessel that reached Tel Reḥov in the days of Stratum VI, the gap between Mazar and Coldstream, that is, between the traditional Levantine and Greek dating systems, would grow to about a century.

Tel Hadar and Tel Reḥov

According to Mazar, the pottery assemblage of Stratum IV at Tel Hadar 'could equally be dated to the tenth century BCE, at least to the middle of that century' (Coldstream and Mazar 2003: 29 note 1). Beck, Kochavi (1998) and others dated this assemblage to the late Iron I, to the Megiddo VIA horizon, which clearly predates the red-slipped, Iron IIA horizon in the north. Short-term ^{14}C dates from Tel Hadar IV, as well as from Dor and Megiddo VIA, fit well into the 10th century BCE (Finkelstein and Piasetzky 2003a; Gilboa and Sharon 2001). Yet, in the same breath Mazar dated Stratum VI at Tel Reḥov—which opens the red-slip, Iron IIA horizon—to 'the first part of the tenth century BCE' (Coldstream and Mazar 2003: 43). This turns the Iron Age pottery sequence upside down: It places a stratum characterized by Iron IIA pottery *before* a stratum which features a late Iron I assemblage! Labeling the Tel Hadar IV assemblage as 'transitional Iron I/Iron IIA' (Mazar—presentation at the Yarnton conference, 6–9 September 2004) does not change this awkward situation, as it still puts Hadar IV (no red-slip) after Reḥov VI with its early red-slip types.

Megiddo VA and Tel Reḥov

The major bone of contention in the Iron Age chronology debate is the dating of the Megiddo VA–IVB palaces to either the 10th century BCE (Dever 1997; Stager 2003; Yadin 1970) or the early 9th century BCE (Finkelstein 1996). Mazar still insists that they may be dated to the 10th century BCE. He does that by equating Megiddo VA with Reḥov V. But in doing so, he:

1. Arbitrarily disconnects Megiddo VA–IVB (and this stratum only) from a large group of contemporary strata in the north (Coldstream and Mazar 2003: 41, Table 2; incidentally, Mazar's updated view [Mazar—presentation at the Yarnton conference, 6–9 September 2004] would put it in the very late 10th century BCE, post-United Monarchy according to the traditional views…).

2. Leaves early 9th-century Megiddo uninhabited (see Coldstream and Mazar 2003: 41, Table 2), which is absolutely impossible historically.

But why not equate Megiddo VA–IVB with Rehov IV instead of Rehov V?

The pottery assemblages of Rehov V–IV, the Jezreel fill and compound, Taanach IIA–IIB, Yokneam XV–XIV and Megiddo VB and VA–IVB—all of which belong to the Iron IIA phase—are very similar (for Jezreel: Zimhoni 1997: 13-56; for Taanach: Rast 1978; for Yokneam: Zarzecki-Peleg 1997; for Megiddo: Finkelstein, Zimhoni and Kafri 2000). There is a stratigraphic logic in the sequence of each of these sites and in the equation between them (Table 17.1). At Rehov, Stratum IV closed the Iron IIA sequence (Strata VI–IV); it ended in a massive destruction which resulted in the abandonment of the lower mound (Coldstream and Mazar 2003: 31). At Jezreel, the casemate compound sealed the Iron IIA sequence; it ended in a destruction followed by a decline of the site (Ussishkin and Woodhead 1994: 46). At Taanach, Stratum IIB concluded the Iron IIA sequence; it ended in a major destruction which resulted in a severe decline of the settlement (Rast 1978: 41). At Yokneam, Stratum XIV, which came after the fragmentary XV, sealed the Iron IIA sequence (Ben-Tor 1993: 807). And at Megiddo, it is the city of Stratum VA which terminated the Iron IIA sequence (Strata VB and VA–IVB); it came to an end in a destruction that seems to have led to a short occupational gap (Finkelstein 1999: 63-64).

The logic, then, is crystal-clear. Detaching Megiddo VA–IVB from its contemporary strata (in order to preserve the affiliation of its ashlar palaces with Solomon?) contradicts all archaeological indications. Megiddo VA–IVB is the contemporary of Rehov IV. And both were *destroyed* in the course of the conflicts between Aram Damascus and the Northern Kingdom, ca. 835–830 BCE (Na'aman 1997).

But when were the ashlar palaces of Megiddo VA–IVB *built*? A clear, highly professional answer to this question had already been given as early as the beginning of the 20th century by Fisher (1929: 73) the excavator of Megiddo and Samaria, and Crowfoot (1940: 146), the second excavators of Samaria. Both pointed to the similarity in the building techniques between the palace of the Omrides at Samaria and ashlar buildings of Stratum VA–IVB at Megiddo. This observation, which was later replaced by the Solomonic frenzy (Dever 1997; Guy 1931: 45-48; Yadin 1970), has now been revived by Norma Franklin, who noticed the extraordinary similarity between the masons' marks found on ashlar blocks from the palace of Samaria and Palace 1723 at Megiddo (Chapter 18, this volume). Since the biblical evidence regarding the building of Samaria by the Omrides (1 Kings 16.24) is supported by the Assyrian records which refer to the Northern Kingdom as *Bit Humri*—probably in reference to the founder of its capital (Ephal 1991: 37-38)—there can hardly be any doubt that Palace 1723 at Megiddo was built in the first half of the 9th century BCE.

Table 17.1. Relative and absolute chronology of Iron IIA strata in the north.

Megiddo	Rehov	Hazor	Jezreel	Taanach	Pottery period	Dating
Short gap	Lower mound abandoned	VIII	Decline	Decline	Early Iron IIB	Late 9th century BCE
VA ↑ ↑ VB	IV ↑ ↑ VI	IX ↑ ↑ X	Compound ↑ ↑ Fills	IIB ↑ ↑ IIA	Iron IIA	Late 10th to ca. 835 BCE

Summary

All the difficulties discussed in this chapter may be resolved by one small step: lowering Strata VI and V at Tel Rehov to the late 10th and early 9th centuries BCE. This would result in a better harmony between the stratigraphy of all Iron IIA strata in the north, including those of Megiddo; it would put Tel Hadar IV and Rehov VI in a logical sequence; it would close the gap between Coldstream and Mazar regarding the dates of the Greek pottery groups; it would perfectly fit the new ^{14}C dates from Rehov (Finkelstein and Piasetzky 2003b); and it would fit even better all other ^{14}C dates which have been accumulated in recent years—from Tel Dor, Tel Hadar and Megiddo (Finkelstein and Piasetzky 2003a).

In any event, it is clear from the above that Tel Rehov alone cannot resolve the debate regarding the date of the late Iron I and Iron IIA strata in the Levant. In the north, the relative and absolute dating of the strata belonging to these horizons must be fixed at Megiddo, with synchronization to other central sites, such as Jezreel, Rehov and Dor.

References

Ben-Tor, A. (1993) Jokneam. In E. Stern (ed.), *The New Encyclopedia of Archaeological Excavations in the Holy Land* 3: 805-11.

Biran, A., and J. Naveh (1995) The Tel Dan Inscription: A New Fragment. *IEJ* 45: 1-18.

Bruins, H.J., J. van der Plicht and A. Mazar (2003a) [14]C Dates from Tel Rehov: Iron Age Chronology, Pharaohs, and Hebrew Kings. *Science* 300: 315-18.

—(2003b) Response to Comment on '[14]C Dates from Tel Rehov: Iron-Age Chronology, Pharaohs, and Hebrew Kings'. *Science* 302: 568c.

Cline, E.H. (forthcoming) Area L 1998–2000: Palace 6000 and the Northern Stables. In *Megiddo IV: The 1998–2002 Seasons*, edited by I. Finkelstein, D. Ussishkin and B. Halpern (Tel Aviv: Institute of Archaeology).

Coldstream, N., and A. Mazar (2003) Greek Pottery from Tel Rehov and Iron Age Chronology. *IEJ* 53: 29-48.

Crowfoot, J.W. (1940) Megiddo—A Review. *PEQ*: 132-47.

Dever, W.G. (1997) Archaeology and the 'Age of Solomon': A Case Study in Archaeology and Historiography. In *The Age of Solomon: Scholarship at the Turn of the Millennium*, edited by L.K. Handy (Leiden: Brill): 217-51.

Ephal, I. (1991) The Samaritan(s)' in the Assyrian Sources. In *Ah, Assyria...Studies in Assyrian History and Ancient Near Eastern Historiography Presented to Hayim Tadmor*, edited by M. Cogan and I. Ephal (Jerusalem: Magnes): 36-45.

Finkelstein, I. (1996) The Archaeology of the United Monarchy: An Alternative View. *Levant* 28: 177-87.

—(1999) Hazor and the North in the Iron Age: A Low Chronology Perspective. *BASOR* 314: 55-70.

Finkelstein, I., and E. Piasetzky (2003a) Recent Radiocarbon Results and Biblical History. *Antiquity* 77: 876-84.

—(2003b) Wrong and Right; High and Low: [14]C Dates from Tel Rehov and Iron Age Chronology. *Tel Aviv* 30: 283-95.

—(2003c) Comment on '[14]C Dates from Tel Rehov: Iron-Age Chronology, Pharaohs, and Hebrew Kings'. *Science* 302: 568b.

Finkelstein, I., O. Zimhoni and A. Kafri (2000) The Iron Age Pottery Assemblages from Areas F, K and H and their Stratigraphic and Chronological Implications. In *Megiddo III: The 1992–1996 Seasons*, edited by I. Finkelstein, D. Ussishkin and B. Halpern (Tel Aviv: Institute of Archaeology): 244-324.

Fisher, C.S. (1929) *The Excavation of Armageddon* (OIP 4; Chicago: The University of Chicago Press).

Gilboa, A., and I. Sharon (2001) Early Iron Age Radiometric Dates from Tel Dor: Preliminary Implications for Phoenicia and Beyond. *Radiocarbon* 43: 1343-51.

Guy, P.L.O. (1931) *New Light from Armageddon* (Chicago: The University of Chicago Press).

Lamon, R.S., and G.M. Shipton (1939) *Megiddo I: Seasons of 1925–34 Strata I–V* (OIP 42; Chicago: The University of Chicago Press).

Lehmann, G., A. Killebrew and Y. Gadot (2000) Area K: In *Megiddo III: The 1992–1996 Seasons*, edited by I. Finkelstein, D. Ussishkin and B. Halpern (Tel Aviv: Institute of Archaeology): 123-39.

Loud, G. (1948) *Megiddo II: Seasons of 1935–39* (OIP 62; Chicago: The University of Chicago Press).

Mazar, A. (1999a) The 1997–1998 Excavations at Tel Rehov: Preliminary Report. *IEJ* 49: 1-42.

—(1999b) Beth Shean during the Iron Age II: Stratigraphy, Chronology and Hebrew Ostraca. *Eretz-Israel* 26 (Frank M. Cross Volume): 91-100 (Hebrew).

—(2004) Greek and Levantine Iron Age Chronology: A Rejoinder. *IEJ* 54: 24-36.

Mazar, A., and I. Carmi (2001) Radiocarbon Dates from Iron Age Strata at Tel BethShean and Tel Rehov. *Radiocarbon* 43: 1333-42.

Na'aman, N. (1997) Historical and Literary Notes on the Excavations of Tel Jezreel. *Tel Aviv* 24: 122-28.

Rast, W.E. (1978) *Taanach I: Studies in the Iron Age Pottery* (Cambridge, MA: American Schools of Oriental Research).

Stager, L.E. (2003) The Patrimonial Kingdom of Solomon. In *Symbiosis, Symbolism, and the Power of the Past: Canaan, Ancient Israel, and their Neighbors from the Late Bronze Age through Roman Palestine*, edited by W.G. Dever and S. Gitin (Winona Lake, IN: Eisenbrauns): 63-74.

Ussishkin, D., and J. Woodhead (1994) Excavations at Tel Jezreel 1992–1993: Second Preliminary Report. *Levant* 26: 1-71.

Watzinger, K. (1929) *Tell el-Mutesellim II. Die Funde* (Leipzig: J.C. Hinrichs).

Yadin, Y. (1970) Megiddo of the Kings of Israel. *BA* 33: 66-96.

Zarzecki-Peleg, A. (1997) Hazor, Jokneam and Megiddo in the 10th Century B.C.E. *Tel Aviv* 24: 258-88.

Zimhoni, O. (1997) *Studies in the Iron Age Pottery of Israel: Typological, Archaeological and Chronological Aspects* (Tel Aviv: Institute of Archaeology).

18 Correlation and Chronology

Samaria and Megiddo Redux*

Norma Franklin

Abstract

Following a comprehensive reanalysis of Samaria and Megiddo, it can now be shown that at Samaria only Building Period I can be attributed to the 9th–century BCE Omride dynasty and that Building Period II must be downdated to the 8th century BCE, while at Megiddo it is Stratum V that must be attributed to the 9th century BCE and Stratum IV (IVA) that must be downdated to the 8th century BCE. In addition, Stratum IVB (VA–IVB) has now been proved non-existent. This new stratigraphic correlation revealed a number of similarities in the monumental architecture at both sites. These similarities provide a clear chronological correlation between the two 9th-century BCE cities, as well as the two 8th-century BCE cities, and so provide a firm link to the chronological anchor represented by Omride Samaria.

Introduction

The debate regarding the chronology of the Iron Age strata has been in the limelight for the last decade (see, among others, Ben-Tor 2000; Finkelstein 1996, 1999, 2000, 2002a, 2002b, 2004; Mazar 1997, 1999a, 1999b). Although crucial ^{14}C evidence for lowering the date of the Iron Age strata of some of the major archaeological sites in the Northern Kingdom of Israel (Hazor, Tel Hadar, Kinrot, Megiddo, Taanach, Dor, and Gezer) by ca. 100 years has recently become available (Finkelstein and Piasetzky 2003a, 2003b, 2003c; Sharon 2001) the debate continues to rage (Bruins, van der Plicht, and Mazar 2003a, 2003b).

During the Iron Age there are two key sites that hold the key to the chronological conundrum: Samaria, the royal capital, and Megiddo, the strategically located emporium. Together they epitomize the power of the Northern Kingdom of Israel during the 8th and 9th centuries BCE.

Before these two cities can be compared, however, it must first be established which strata—that is, which cities—in the stratigraphic sandwich correspond. Although both cities have been extensively excavated, the correct evaluation of the strata at both Megiddo and Samaria has been severely hindered by the excavation techniques employed, the pre-conceived conceptions of the excavators, and ill-founded interpretations based on circular reasoning. And until the relevant strata at both sites can be freed from the tangled thread that enmeshes them, no correlation can be made and no material at either site can be accurately compared. In short, the misallocation of

---

* This paper forms part of the author's doctoral dissertation to be submitted to Tel Aviv University. The figures were prepared by S. Stark.

certain crucial Iron Age loci has resulted in a faulty stratigraphic picture that has caused the two salient Iron Age cities to be seriously misinterpreted and therefore an accurate understanding of the Northern Kingdom of Israel during the 8th and 9th centuries BCE could not be achieved.

Megiddo Past

Megiddo is a multi-layered site that was occupied continuously from the 3rd millennium BCE until the Persian period. Its strata form the cornerstone of any discussion on Iron Age chronology.

Gottlieb Schumacher led the first excavation to Megiddo, from 1903 to 1905 (Schumacher 1908; Watzinger 1929). It was his excavation that first revealed the Iron Age strata that, until today, continue to fluctuate between the 10th and the 8th centuries BCE.

The second expedition, and the one that has been at the heart of my analysis of the Iron Age strata, was launched by the prestigious Oriental Institute of Chicago (OI), between the years 1925 and 1939. The results were published in *Megiddo I* (Lamon and Shipton 1939), *Megiddo II* (Loud 1948), and two preliminary publications (Fisher 1929; Guy 1931). Unfortunately, during its early days the expedition was beset by difficulties, starting with the chronic illness, and subsequent retirement, of the expedition's first director, Clarence Fisher, after just 18 months, during which time he excavated Strata I, II, sub-II, and III (the numbering system was later changed and Fisher's Stratum III was, in the main, re-allocated to Stratum V). The latter stratum included many key pottery-rich loci (Fisher 1929: 67, Fig. 45). P.L.O. Guy replaced Fisher as director in 1927, although due to prior commitments initially he could spend only three days a week at Megiddo (Guy 1931: 9). Robert Lamon took over Fisher's other function as excavation surveyor in 1928. Guy's pioneering work using balloon photography (Guy 1932) enabled Lamon the freedom to oversee the excavation of the water system (Lamon 1935). Also employed in 1928, contrary to the wishes of the OI, was the young, untutored Geoffrey Shipton who was entrusted by Guy to keep records. Shipton was the nephew of the excavation's administrator, Ralph Parker, who used his position to secure Shipton a job despite his total lack of training (unpublished correspondence, OI archives). The OI then insisted that a reluctant Guy make room for two other core members of staff, Robert Engberg (1930–34), and Herbert May (1931–34).

However, in 1929, well before their arrival, Guy had already identified the King Solomon 'stables', attributing them and other major architectural monuments to Stratum IV, which he dated to the 10th century BCE. Guy's reasoning: 'Who else could have built the stables?' (Guy 1931: 48). Guy's tenure became increasingly plagued by arguments and animosity due to the conflicting personalities of the now-enlarged excavation team, and this sorry situation was further exacerbated by the continuing demands of a disappointed OI that continuously urged Guy to proceed at a faster pace. Another contributing factor was that Guy was the only archaeologist with prior archaeological experience, for both Engberg and May were theologians who had acquired their archaeological skills while excavating the very strata at the center of this chapter. It was this discordant group that was responsible for the excavation of these crucial Iron Age strata, although not for their publication. The writing of the final report, *Megiddo I*, which dealt with the five uppermost strata, including the bulk of Stratum V, the sole elements of Stratum IVB, and the stables of Stratum IV, was reluctantly entrusted by the OI to Robert Lamon and young Geoffrey Shipton. Guy was finally discharged in 1934 and thereby explicitly denied the opportunity to participate in the volume's preparation (unpublished correspondence, OI archives), while both May and Engberg had already left the expedition to pursue their careers elsewhere. All this, combined with pre-conceived ideas regarding the factuality of the biblical references to Megiddo, proved a recipe for disaster, severely inhibiting until today our understanding of the Iron Age strata. It was only in the late 1960s that Yigael Yadin of the Hebrew University launched a number of small-scale archaeological forays to Megiddo (Yadin 1970, 1972). Following an earlier re-analysis by W.F. Albright (Albright 1943:

2-3), Yadin attributed the (post-Albright) now-amalgamated strata, Stratum VA–IVB, to the 10th century BCE (the period of Solomon) and the following strata, Stratum IV (consequently renamed Stratum IVA) to the 9th century BCE and the period of the Omride dynasty.

Thus, until now the conventional view has been that Stratum V and Stratum IVB, now known as Stratum VA–IVB, must be dated to the 10th century BCE, and Stratum IV, now known as Stratum IVA, be dated to the 9th century BCE. It is these crucial strata that fashion our comprehension of the historical development not only of Megiddo but of the Northern Kingdom of Israel as a whole, during the Iron Age.

Samaria Past

Unlike Megiddo, Samaria is not a multi-layered tell; rather, it is a rocky hill-top site whose primary architecture is Iron Age. Samaria also played an important political role during the Herodian period, when the site was rebuilt and renamed Sebaste. The later monumental buildings ploughed through the Iron Age strata to the bedrock, destroying stratigraphic connections and thereby blurring the chronological picture.

Gottlieb Schumacher, the original excavator of Megiddo, served initially as the temporary director (in 1908) of the Harvard Expedition, which operated from 1908 to 1910. However, before long, the experienced archaeologist George Reisner took over the directorship and Clarence Fisher (who later became the first director of the OI's expedition to Megiddo) was appointed excavation architect. They published their results in two volumes: *The Harvard Expedition to Samaria I and II* (Reisner, Fisher, and Lyons 1924). Intent on revealing the city founded by Omri in the 9th century BCE, they concentrated their excavation on the highest part of the summit. There they revealed a monumental building that they immediately identified as the 9th century BCE 'Palace of Omri', as it was clearly the earliest building founded on bedrock at the very summit of the hill (Reisner, Fisher, and Lyons 1924: I, 35, 60-61). Luckily, the actual palace building had been partially preserved due to the Herodian-period fill below the Temple to Augustus. The remains of other contemporaneous buildings west of the palace were merely hinted at by rock-cut foundation trenches and truncated walls. A large casemate wall system surrounded the palace and extended the available building area. However, it was considered to have been built after the 'Palace of Omri', although the latter continued to be used. This caused the Harvard Expedition, despite other clues to the contrary, to condense the possible timeframe. The deciding factor was the discovery of a large rock-cut basin located approximately 40 meters north of the 'Palace of Omri', adjacent to the northern stretch of the casemate wall. The basin was immediately identified as the 'Pool of Samaria', mentioned in 1 Kings 16.23-24 in reference to Ahab (Reisner, Fisher, and Lyons 1924: I, 112-13). Therefore, the (seemingly) adjacent casemate wall system was also attributed to Ahab, and the entire casemate complex was identified as the 'Palace of Ahab'. Strangely, the fact that the 'Pool of Samaria' was buried ca. 4 meters below the plaster courtyard that abutted and co-existed with the casemates was overlooked. This error and others were aggravated by the obligation to excavate using the 'strip' system, namely, filling in each succeeding excavation strip with the dump from the previous strip. This meant that the architectural elements were exposed piecemeal, reburied, and never viewed in their entirety. Thus, both the 'Palace of Omri' and the 'Palace of Ahab' were attributed to the Omride dynasty—a fact that has remained unchallenged until today.

The second expedition to Samaria, the Joint Expedition (1931 to 1935), was led by J.W. Crowfoot as overall director, while Kathleen Kenyon was responsible for the Iron Age (and later) remains on the summit. The stratigraphic results were published in *The Buildings at Samaria* (Crowfoot, Kenyon, and Sukenik 1942). The expedition attracted a great deal of attention and was touted as an exemplary excavation, even though it, too, had to adhere to the inhibiting strip system. The Joint Expedition adopted, on the whole, the stratigraphic picture presented by the Harvard Expedition, and they did not reinvestigate the areas already excavated. The Joint Expedition agreed that there was no monumental architecture prior to the 'Palace of Omri', which they renamed Building Period I, while they renamed the 'Palace of Ahab' Building Period II (Crowfoot, Kenyon, and Sukenik 1942). Crowfoot noted that these remains resembled the recently exposed 'Solomonic' stratum, Stratum IVB (VA–IVB) at Megiddo (Crowfoot 1940). They thus maintained that Building Periods I and II at Samaria must have been built some short time after Megiddo IVB (VA–IVB). This theory also strengthened the concept that Building Period II followed Building Period I within a very short time period. The scenario was adjusted slightly following Yadin's reappraisal of Megiddo, and scholars adopted the conventional view that Building Periods I and II were built at the same time as Megiddo Stratum IVB (VA–IVB).

Secure Stratigraphy is Paramount

It cannot be over-emphasized that the reliability of any dating technique is directly linked to the correct analysis of the stratigraphy of the site. If the stratigraphy of a site has been misinterpreted, or more precisely, if certain crucial loci have been allocated to the wrong stratigraphic horizon, then not only the absolute, but even the relative date of the stratum in question will be incorrect. At best, vital information will be lost; at worst, theories will arise that are not founded on any secure evidence.

If the stratigraphic context is secure then an inscription (*in situ* in its primary location), which can be associated with a historical event, is the ultimate tool for providing an absolute date. Unfortunately, at Megiddo there is only the inscribed Ramses VI's statue base, found minus its statue, buried below a Stratum VIIB wall (Loud 1948: 135 note 1), and a broken fragment of a stele of Shishak, retrieved from one of Schumacher's minor trenches that probed only as deep as Stratum IVA (Fisher 1929: 60-61).

Since Flinders Petrie's pioneer work on 'sequence dating', pottery has been used to establish the relative chronology of a site. The Megiddo pottery has formed the cornerstone of Levantine Bronze and Iron Age pottery typology as we know it today. Yet the typology established for the Iron Age II period was based on the pottery excavated during the directorships of Fisher and Guy. The typology was established according to the pottery's stratigraphic location vis-à-vis the architecture. In other words, if the stables were attributed to Solomon then the pottery was 10th century BCE as well. These pottery assemblages were later, after Yadin, downdated to the 9th century BCE. To further complicate matters, there was also an incongruity regarding the classification of the loci, and that too had a bearing on the affiliation of the pottery. For example, pottery contained in the fill below the stable courtyard (attributed to the 9th century BCE) was classified as 'Stratum IV fill' while the pottery contained in the fill below the adjacent courtyard (attributed to the 10th century BCE) was classified as 'minus-Stratum IVB'. Thus, although both fills were indistinguishable, the 'below stable courtyard' fill was believed to be later in date.

At Samaria, the Harvard Expedition recorded only the whole pottery forms associated with the earliest monumental architecture—Building Period I (their Omri Palace period) and Building Period II (their Ahab Palace period). Due to Harvard's interpretation of the absolute chronology the pottery typology was condensed to fit the narrow time span allowed it. In addition, neither the later Joint Expedition nor the scholars that followed could differentiate between the Building Period I and Building Period II pottery (Tappy 1992, 2001).[1] This was hardly surprising, since

1. Following a reappraisal by Wright (1959a, 1959b) these pottery loci are now more commonly known as Pottery Period 2 and Pottery Period 3.

1. the attribution of Building Period II to Ahab had no secure foundation.
2. the Joint Expedition incorrectly attributed certain Building Period II loci to Building Period I, in particular the loci associated with Wall 161 (Franklin 2004b: 197-98).

Thus, an apparent continuity of form between the pottery from Building Periods I and II was noted by the Joint Expedition and later researchers (e.g. Tappy 1992 and 2001). This fact was erroneously considered normal, especially as these two periods were supposed to encompass only the latter part of Omri's reign and Ahab's reign—a period of some 70 years.

In short, many of the important Iron Age II pottery typological studies cannot be used in their present format (e.g. Tappy 1992, 2001; Zimhoni 1997). The pottery from both these sites cannot be used to establish a relative chronology until the stratigraphy is reviewed and a new order imposed.

Megiddo Redux

In order to understand and re-establish the relative chronology of the Iron Age, the stratigraphy of Tel Megiddo from its inception had to be examined and understood.

First, an analysis of the profile of the original bedrock hill of Megiddo (Franklin and Peersmann forthcoming) provided an understanding of the pre-existing terrain and this was essential for comprehending how the builders of each successive city utilized the site. This technique allowed each consecutive city to be reconstructed, eventually providing an improved understanding of the macro-stratigraphy of the city in the 8th and 9th centuries BCE, and enabling a detailed topographic analysis of the remains, with special emphasis on the surface elevations of the Iron Age II cities.

Second, it soon became clear that the original premise for establishing a separate stratum, Stratum IVB, was based on an incorrect analysis of the monumental architecture in the south of the tell. This was exacerbated by the fact that the final report was not written by, or with the consultation of, the staff members responsible for the actual excavation of the area. Stratum IVB is an imaginary stratum, and therefore so is its composite successor, Stratum VA–IVB. Following an in-depth re-analysis the author was now re-assigned the architecture, from the erstwhile Stratum IVB to either Stratum V or to Stratum IV (IVA). The key element is Palace 1723, which can then be seen to be the earliest monumental building founded in Stratum V. The palace's foundations were dug deep into the burnt mudbrick debris of Stratum VI and there were no underlying Stratum V buildings. In other words, the palace belongs to the stratum that immediately supersedes Stratum VI. In addition, the plastered courtyard, originally thought to be the courtyard of the palace, in fact covered the southern part of the palace and abutted the Stratum IV (IVA) city wall. It can be clearly shown that Palace 1723 is sandwiched between Stratum VI and Stratum IV. Furthermore, Palace 1723 and its probable atrium, Platform 1728, were approached via the adjacent Sudlich Burgtor, a monumental building (excavated by Schumacher) whose foundations were also laid into the burnt mudbrick debris of Stratum VI (Schumacher 1908: 80). This building was inexplicably attributed to Stratum VII by the Chicago Expedition (Loud 1948: Fig. 410). Other important periphery buildings flanked the palace, for example, Buildings 1A and a newly re-discovered building, Building 1648. Subsequently, during the long history of Stratum V, other 'inner-city' buildings were interspersed in the remaining inner-city spaces. At some point later in the history of Stratum V a new monumental periphery building, Palace 6000, was erected on the north-east side of the mound (see Fig. 18.1).

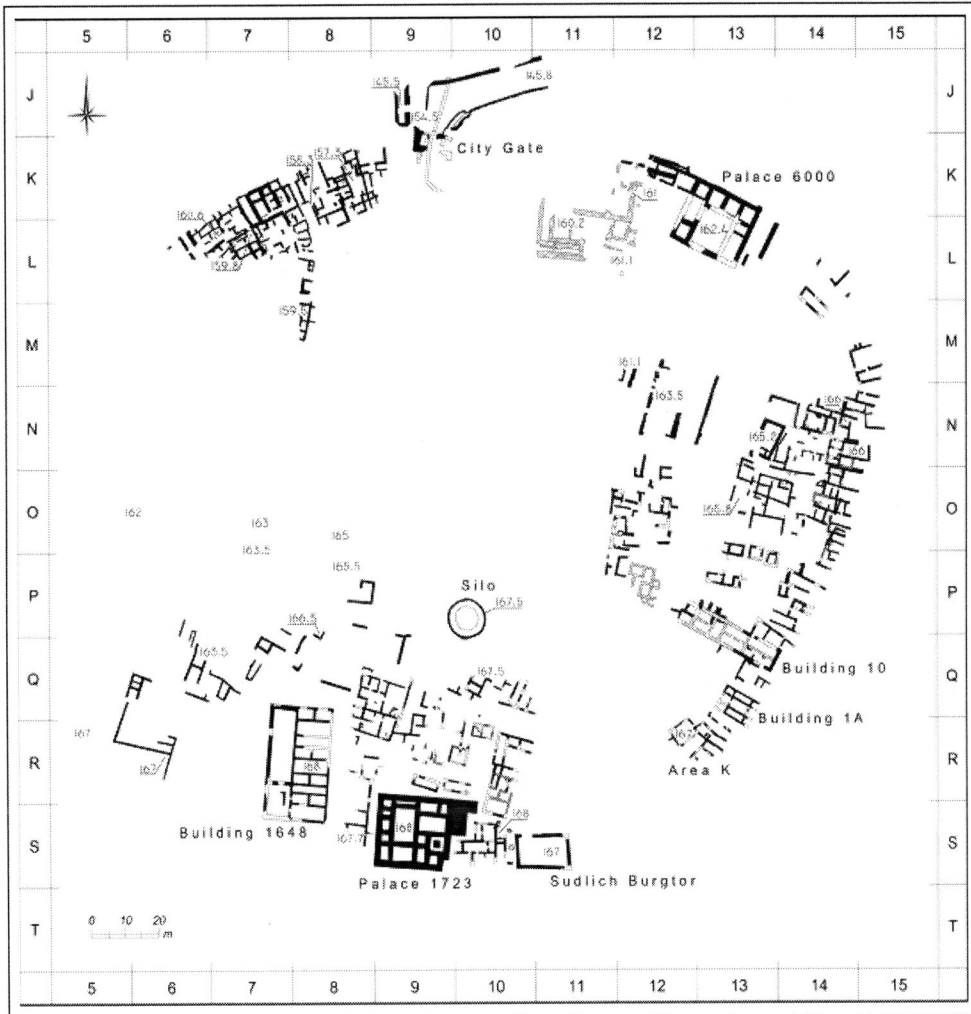

Figure 18.1. Stratum V.

Palace 6000 was built against a podium-like structure, originally thought to be a casemate city wall, which negated earlier Stratum V building remains (Yadin 1970; 1972: 156-58). This possibly coincided with the building of numerous pillared buildings around the now apparently defunct Palace 1723. These buildings must belong to the final phase of Stratum VA as they were buried, their stone support pillars still standing, when the Stratum IV builders transformed the area. In other words, Stratum V was not destroyed; rather, it was partially dismantled and buried by the Stratum IV builders (Franklin forthcoming). A new city with a very different topography arose. This Stratum IV city was a vast commercial center, with stables, storehouses, and courtyards, all built to a specific blueprint (see Fig. 18.2).

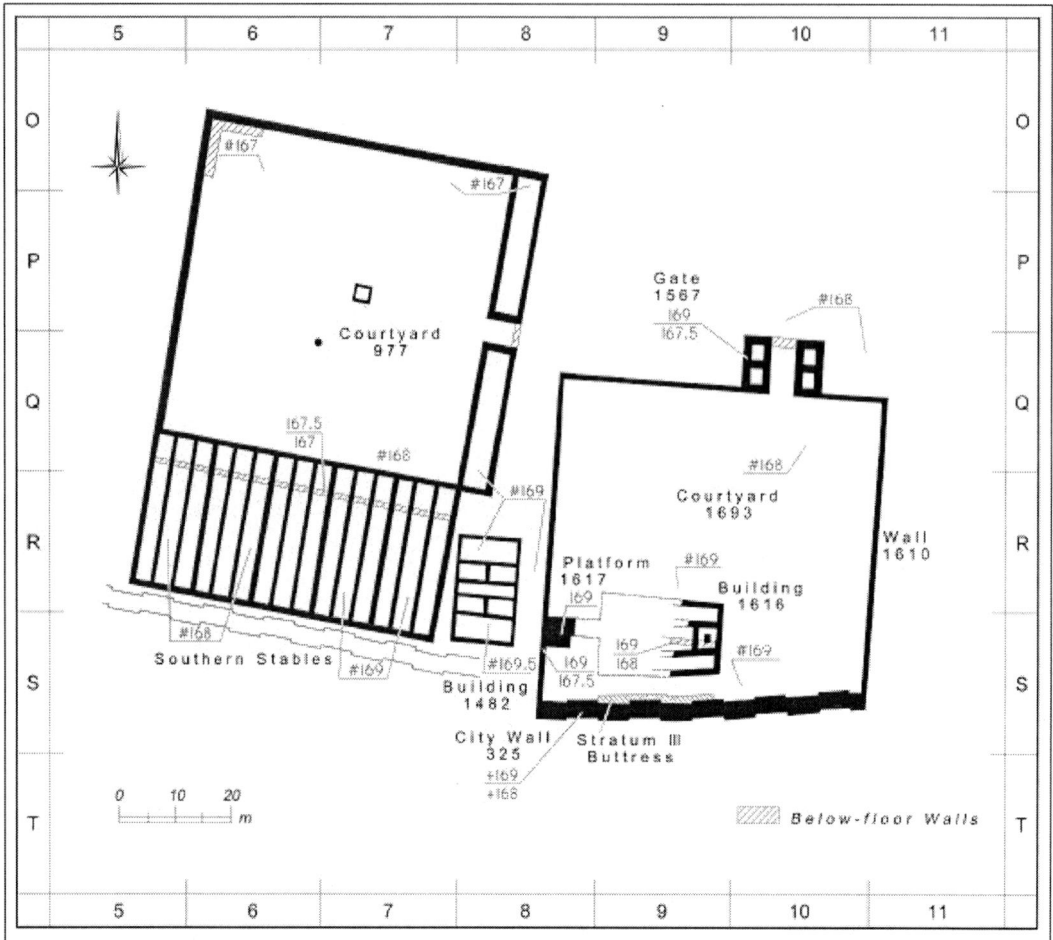

Figure 18.2. Stratum IV Area A.

Samaria Redux

Samaria, the capital of the Northern Kingdom of Israel, provides us with a chronological anchor, albeit one based on the biblical narrative. 1 Kings 16.23-24 relates that Omri purchased the hilltop site and established his capital there. This event is dated to ca. 880 BCE. The establishment of the Omride dynasty at Samaria is also documented in the Assyrian records (Eph'al 1991: 37-38), and the establishment of a new capital city parallels the Assyrian custom (e.g. Omri's contemporary, Ashurnasirpal, founded a new capital at Nimrud). Therefore, it was imperative to establish exactly which elements belonged to Building Period I (the strata that represented the foundation of Samaria as the Omride capital), and which elements belonged to Building Period II (the strata that had erroneously been attributed to Ahab). The earliest stratum was Building Period 0, consisting primarily of rock-cut cisterns and associated wine and oil preparation areas. A re-analysis of Building Period 0 also provided insight into the *raison d'être* for Omri's choice of location for the capital—the pre-existence of a lucrative oil and wine industry (Franklin 2004b; Stager 1990). A topographic plan of Building Period 0 combined with a topographic plan of Building Periods I and II clearly shows which elements were early and which were later, and Building Period I could at last be clearly defined as a separate entity. The acropolis in Building Period I consisted of a royal compound—the 'Palace of Omri' isolated from its surroundings by a 4-meter-high artificial rock-cut scarp. West of the royal compound, there was a newly re-discovered monumental ancillary building, and building traces that testified to the presence of other Building Period I buildings (Franklin 2004b). In addition, there were two rock-cut tombs that were hewn into the rock immediately below the Building Period I palace, identified as the tombs of the Omride kings (Franklin 2003). When these elements are viewed together it can be seen that Building Period I had to have been of a longer duration than previously thought and must be attributed to the Omride dynasty in its entirety and at least a part of the Jehu dynasty (Fig. 18.3.). Once Building Period I was clearly defined it became clear that Building Period II was not the continuation, embellishment, and execution of an unfinished Building Period I blueprint.

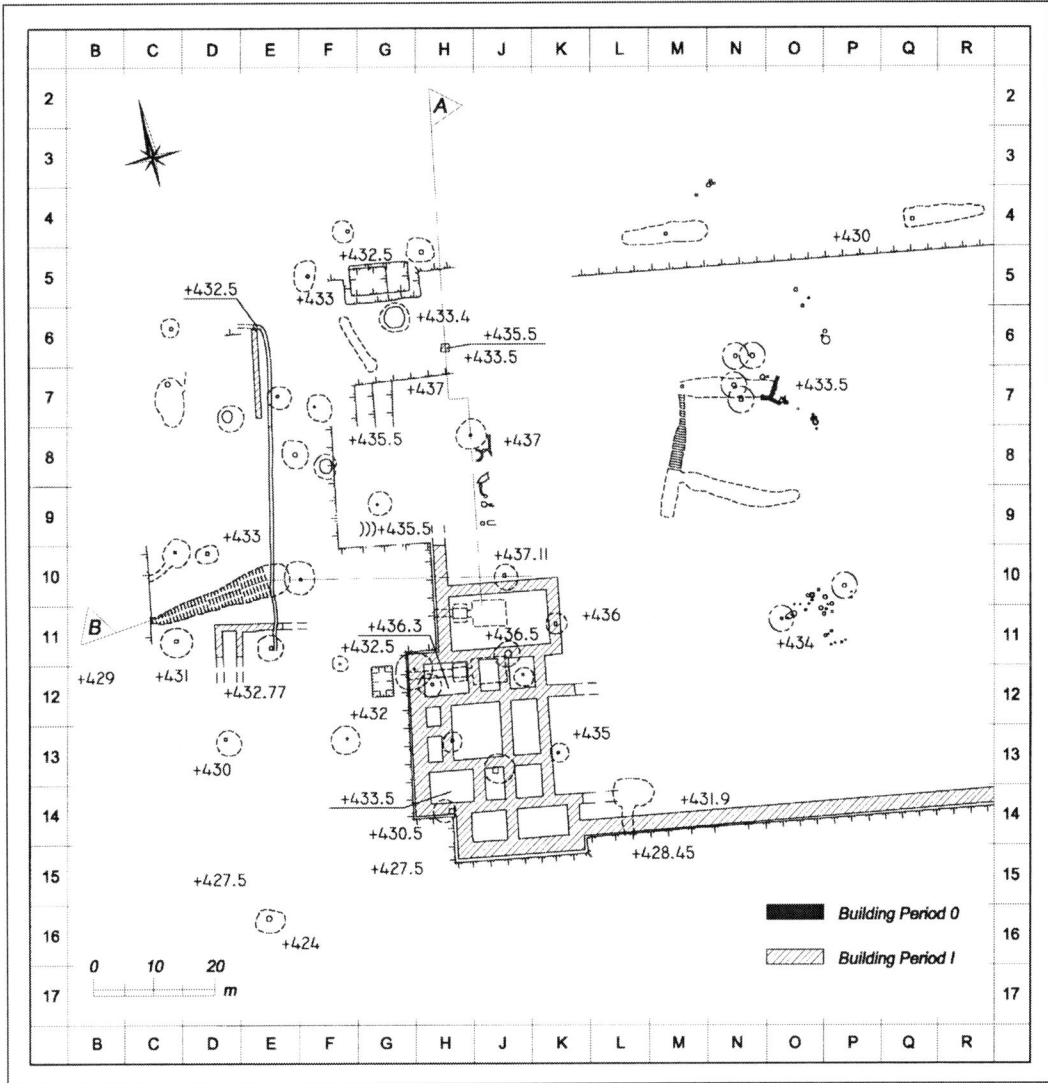

Figure 18.3. Samaria Building Period I.

Building Period II clearly signified a new era, a new regime, during which time the summit of Samaria became a strictly administrative center (Fig. 18.4.).

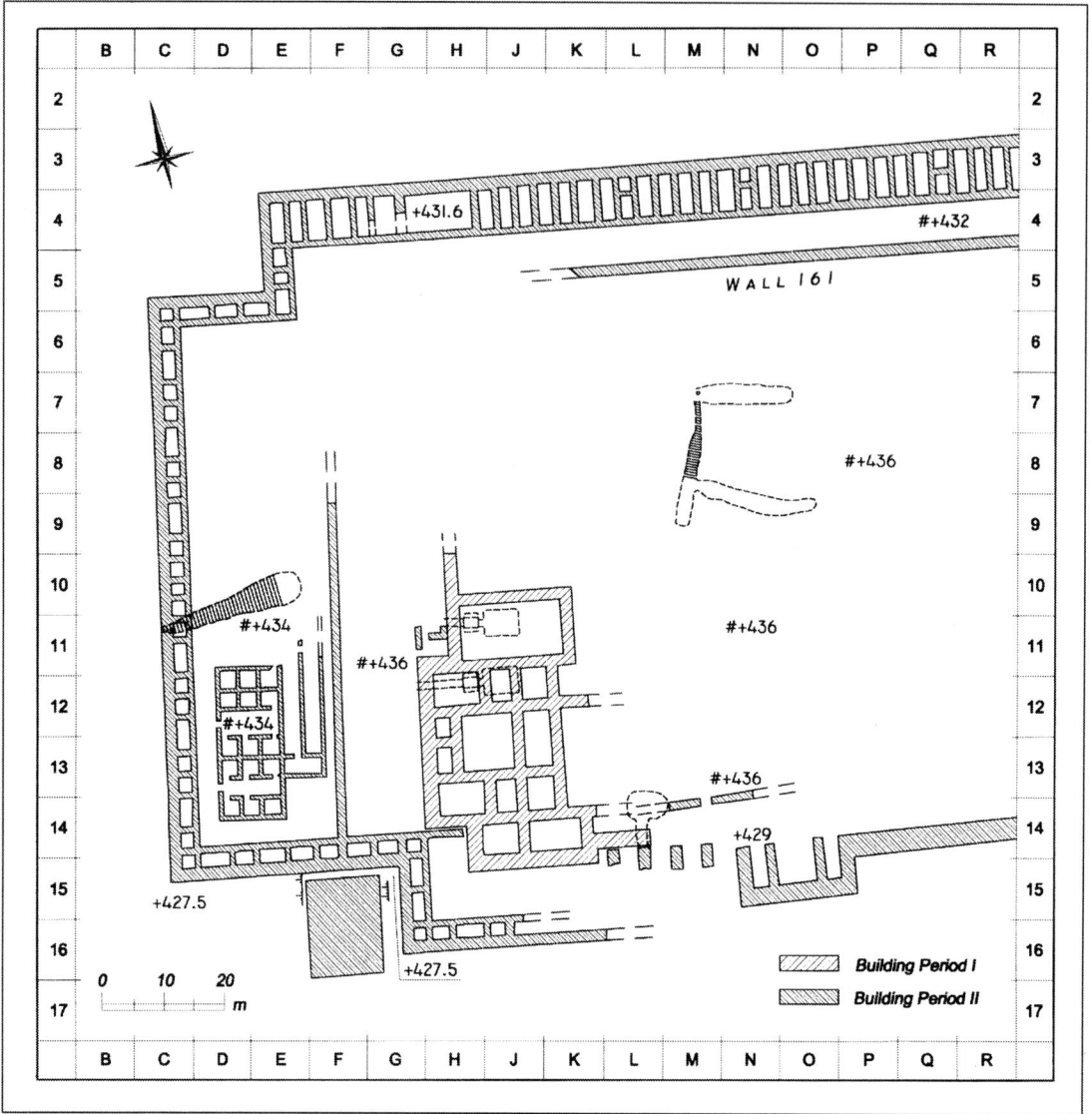

Figure 18.4. Samaria Building Period II.

Correlating Megiddo and Samaria

Once the strata at the two sites are rectified a number of similarities appear that enable a clear correlation to be made between Megiddo and Samaria.

Megiddo Stratum V and Samaria Building Period I

The most noticeable similarity is the unique series of masons' marks present at both sites. Schumacher excavated the first fourteen masons' marks at Megiddo in 1903. Two years later, he excavated identical masons' marks at Samaria. Today, more than seventy ashlars inscribed with twenty different masons' marks have been identified at both sites. Only nineteen of the fifty-three masons' marks at Megiddo were found *in situ*. They were all located in the foundations of Palace 1723—now known to belong to Stratum V. Only two of the twenty masons' marks at Samaria were *in situ*. They were both located in the foundations of the Building Period I Omride palace. The function of these unique marks is unknown; they may have served an atrophic purpose or reflect the presence of foreign construction workers, but their simultaneous use undoubtedly signifies a chronological correspondence (Franklin 2001).

Another feature of Stratum V at Megiddo and Building Period I at Samaria is that the monumental buildings were built using plain, roughly hewn ashlars. There were no interspersed fieldstones or marginal drafting; all the ashlars were plain, roughly hewn blocks (Franklin 2004b; forthcoming).

The next similarity is the common use of the short cubit of 0.45 meters. Its use is most noticeable when the ground plan of Palace 1723 at Megiddo is studied. The palace's foundations were preserved in their entirety and the complete plan of the building is known. The recognition of the short cubit of 0.45 meters as the unit of measurement is facilitated by the fact that the building has a number of faces, whose lengths all point to the use of the short cubit: lengths of 2, 6, 8, 10, 16, 48, and 50 short cubits. (Unfortunately Palace 6000 at Megiddo does not provide us with decisive measurements; it can only be said that it is a square building that appears to have been built using the short cubit.)

The use of the short cubit is again evident in the ground plan of the Building Period I palace at Samaria. Although most of the ashlar masonry did not survive, the fact that the palace was built on top of an artificially prepared 4-meter-high rock-scarp enables the extent of the palace to be defined. The palace is composed of lengths of 12, 16, 48, 60, and 100 short cubits (Franklin 2004a).

To summarize, at Megiddo and Samaria, both palaces attest to the use of the short cubit of 0.45 meters, both palaces are built using roughly hewn ashlars devoid of drafted margins or intervening fieldstone courses, and significantly both palaces have unique masons' marks inscribed on the ashlars contained in their foundation courses.

These three similarities testify to a clear technical, and therefore also a chronological, correlation between Samaria Building Period I and Megiddo Stratum V.

Megiddo Stratum IV (IVA) and Samaria Building Period II

The ashlar masonry at both sites, most of which were clearly in secondary use, were aligned with the aid of a drafted margin, a frame drafted *in situ*. The evidence for this final marginal drafting was a layer of limestone chips deposited at the base of these walls (Crowfoot, Kenyon, and Sukenik 1942: 99; Loud 1948: 47). In addition, the alignment of these ashlars was facilitated by the use of red guide lines. These were often preserved on the ashlar foundation courses and observed by the excavation teams at both sites (Crowfoot, Kenyon, and Sukenik 1942: 12, 98; Guy 1931: 37;

Loud 1948: 48; Reisner, Fisher, and Lyons 1924: I, 103-107, 111, Figs. 26, 30, 37). Furthermore, the load bearing walls and corners were built of integrated ashlars and fieldstones, often constructed in the Telalio pattern for added strength (Franklin forthcoming).

The next similarity is most noticeable when the southern Stable and Courtyard complexes at Megiddo and the city walls at both Samaria and Megiddo are studied. The ground plans of the monumental architecture at Megiddo Stratum IV and Samaria Building Period II were laid out using the cubit of 0.495 meters that originated in Mesopotamia, and is more commonly known as the Assyrian cubit. The two Megiddo courtyards, the Stable courtyard and its duplicate to the east, now known to belong solely to Stratum IV (IVA), both measure 120 by 120 Assyrian cubits. This square unit of measurement is known as an *IKU*, an Assyrian agricultural land measurement. In addition, all the Megiddo Stratum IV monumental architecture, the stables, gates, and city wall, are built in lengths of 8, 10, 12, 36, 40, 60, and 120 Assyrian cubits. At Samaria, although there are no stable complexes or city gates, there is a casemate wall system and the 'Ostraca House', and these architectural elements are all built using the Assyrian cubit of 0.495 meters, with lengths of 2, 4, 25, 30, and 50 Assyrian cubits (Franklin 2004a).

Chronology

Relative

To summarize, Stratum IV at Megiddo and Building Period II at Samaria both belong to a period that exhibits building methods very different from the previous strata. The ashlar masonry, much of it in secondary use, has drafted margins and was aligned with the aid of red guide lines. The ground plan of each city was laid out using the Assyrian cubit of 0.495 meters. Although the latter set of data do not provide a chronological anchor they do confirm what has previously been proved stratigraphically: that Samaria Building Period II is not a sequential addition to Building Period I. Rather, it can now be seen that during Building Period II, the summit of Samaria became a strictly administrative center, with a large plastered surface at a uniform elevation, and a new administrative building, the Ostraca House (Franklin 2004b). This occurred at approximately the same time as the city of Megiddo became a commercial center complete with stables, courtyard complexes, and large plastered surfaces at a uniform elevation (Franklin forthcoming). Thus, this simultaneous transformation of both sites must signify a new era, new influences, and probably a new regime.

Absolute

Now that a correlation between the two cities in two successive parallel periods has been established we must return to the earlier of the two periods in order to establish a chronological anchor. As mentioned above Samaria, the capital city, is universally acknowledged to have been founded by the Omride dynasty in the 9th century BCE. Furthermore, it has now been proven that Omride Samaria is only represented by Building Period I, that is, only Building Period I can be dated to the 9th century BCE. Furthermore, the Omride palace at Samaria and Palace 1723 at Megiddo (Stratum V) were both built using the same building techniques, including the use of unique masons' marks and the short cubit of 0.45 meters. And it is the use of the short cubit that provides us with another chronological anchor.

The first-known use of the short cubit is attested during the 3rd Intermediate period in Egypt. The 9th century BCE Omride dynasty coincides with the rule of the 22nd dynasty of the 3rd Intermediate period (Kitchen 1986). And it is this double-pronged chronological anchor that not only confirms the 9th-century BCE date for Building Period I at Samaria but also establishes that the inception of Megiddo Stratum V, marked by Palace 1723, must now also be dated to the 9th century BCE. This re-dating of two key Iron Age cities, Megiddo Stratum V and Samaria Building Period I, provides a new understanding of the 9th century BCE, and paves the way for new studies and new insights into this crucial period in the history of the Northern Kingdom of Israel.

References

Albright, W.F. (1943) *The Excavation of Tell Beit Mirsim*. III. *The Iron Age* (AASOR 21-22:2-3; New Haven: Yale University Press).

Ben-Tor, A. (2000) Hazor and the Chronology of Northern Israel: A Reply to Israel Finkelstein. *BASOR* 317: 9-15.

Bruins, H.J., J. van der Plicht, and A. Mazar (2003a) [14]C Dates from Tel Rehov: Iron-Age Chronology, Pharaohs, and Hebrew Kings. *Science* 300: 315-18.

—(2003b) Technical Comment: Response to Comment on '[14]C Dates from Tel Rehov: Iron-Age Chronology, Pharaohs, and Hebrew Kings'. *Science* 302: 568c.

Crowfoot, J.W. (1940) Megiddo—A Review. *PEQ*: 132-47

Crowfoot, J.W., K.M. Kenyon, and E.L. Sukenik (1942) *The Buildings at Samaria* (Samaria-Sebaste Reports I; London: Palestine Exploration Fund).

Eph'al, I. (1991) The Samaritan(s) in the Assyrian Sources. In *Ah Assyria... Studies in Assyrian History and Ancient Near Eastern Historiography Presented to Hayim Tadmor*, edited by M. Cogan and I. Eph'al (Jerusalem: Magnes): 36-45.

Finkelstein, I. (1995) The Date of the Philistine Settlement in Canaan. *Tel Aviv* 22: 213-39.

—(1996) The Archaeology of the United Monarchy: An Alternative View. *Levant* 28: 177-87.

—(1999) Hazor and the North in the Iron Age: A Low Chronology Perspective. *BASOR* 314: 55-70.

—(2000) Hazor XII-XI with an Addendum on Ben-Tor's Dating of Hazor X–VII. *Tel Aviv* 27: 231-47.

—(2002a) The Campaign of Shoshenq I to Palestine: A Guide to the 10th Century BCE Polity. *ZDPV* 118: 109-35.

—(2002b) Chronology Rejoinders. *PEQ* 134: 128-39.

—(2004) Tel Rechov and Iron Age Chronology. *Levant* 36: 181-88.

Finkelstein, I., and E. Piasetzky (2003a) Recent Radiocarbon Results and Biblical History. *Antiquity* 77: 771-79.

—(2003b) Wrong and Right; High and Low: [14]C dates from Tel Rechov and Iron Age Chronology. *Tel Aviv* 30: 283-95.

—(2003c) Comment on '[14]C Dates from Tel Rechov: Iron-Age Chronology, Pharaohs, and Hebrew Kings'. *Science* 302: 568b

Fisher, C.S. (1929) *The Excavation of Armageddon* (OIP 4; Chicago: The University of Chicago Press).

Franklin, N. (forthcoming) Revealing Stratum V at Megiddo. *BASOR*.

—(2004a) Metrological Investigations at 9th and 8th c. Samaria and Megiddo. *Journal of Mediterranean Archaeology and Archaeometry* 4/2: 82-92.

—(2004b) Samaria: From the Bedrock to the Omride Palace. *Levant* 36: 189-202.

—(2003) The Tombs of the Kings of Israel: Two Recently Identified 9th Century Tombs from Omride Samaria. *ZDPV* 119(1): 1-11.

—(2001) Masons' Marks from the 9th century BCE Northern Kingdom of Israel: Evidence of the Nascent Carian Alphabet? *Kadmos* 40: 107-11.

Franklin, N., and J. Peersmann (forthcoming) *The Megiddo Bedrock Project*.

Guy, P.L.O. (1931) *New Light from Armageddon. Second Provisional Report (1927–1929) on the Excavations at Megiddo in Palestine* (OIP 9: Chicago: The University of Chicago Press).

—(1932) Balloon Photography. *Antiquity* 6: 148-55.

Kitchen, K.A. (1986) *The Third Intermediate Period in Egypt (110–650 BC)* (London: Warminster).

Lamon, R.S. (1935) *The Megiddo Water System* (OIP 32; Chicago: The University of Chicago Press).

Lamon, R., and G.M. Shipton (1939) *Megiddo I: Seasons of 1925–1934, Strata I–V* (OIP 42; Chicago: University of Chicago Press).

Loud, G. (1948) *Megiddo II. Seasons of 1935–39* (OIP 62; Chicago: University of Chicago Press).

Mazar, A. (1997) Age Chronology: A Reply to I. Finkelstein. *Levant* 29: 157-67.

—(1999a) The 1997–1998 Excavations at Tel Rechov: Preliminary Report. *IEJ* 49: 20-23.

—(1999b) Beth Shean during the Iron Age II: Stratigraphy, Chronology, and Hebrew Ostraca. *Eretz-Israel* 26 (Frank M. Cross Volume): 91-100 (Hebrew).

Reisner, G.A., C.S. Fisher, and D.G. Lyons (1924) *Harvard Excavations at Samaria* 1908–1910 (HSS 1–2; 2 vols.; Cambridge, MA: Harvard University Press).

Sharon, I. (2001) 'Transition Dating'—A Heuristic Mathematical Approach to the Collation of Radiocarbon Dates from Stratified Sequences. *Radiocarbon* 43: 345-54.

Schumacher, G. (1908) *Tell el-Mutesellim I* (Leipzig: Haupt).

Stager, L.E. (1990) Shemer's Estate. *BASOR* 277/278: 93–107

Tappy, R. (2001) *The Archaeology of Israelite Samaria*. II. *The Eighth Century B.C.E.* (HSS 50; Winona Lake, IN: Eisenbrauns).

—(1992) *The Archaeology of Israelite Samaria: Early Iron Age through the Ninth Century B.C.E.*, I (HSS 44; Atlanta: Scholars Press).

Watzinger, K. (1929) *Tell el-Mutesellim*. II. *Die Funde* (Leipzig: J.C. Hinrichs).

Wright, G.E. (1959a) Israelite Samaria and Iron Age Chronology. *BASOR* 155: 13-29.

—(1959b) Samaria. *BA* 22/3: 67–78.

Zimhoni, O. (1997) *Studies in the Iron Age Pottery of Israel, Typological, Archaeological and Chronological Aspects*. Tel Aviv: Institute of Archaeology, Tel Aviv University).

Yadin, Y. (1970) Megiddo and the Kings of Israel. *BA* 33: 66-96.

—(1972) *Hazor* (The Schweich Lectures of the British Academy 1970; London: Published for the British Academy by Oxford University Press).

19 Iron-Age ¹⁴C Dates from Tel Dan

A high chronology

Hendrik J. Bruins, Johannes van der Plicht, David Ilan
and Ella Werker

Abstract

Organic samples have been collected from Tel Dan to establish an independent radiocarbon chronology of the site. In this paper we present and discuss 20 Iron-Age radiocarbon dates. Unfortunately, short-lived charred seeds were generally not excavated and charcoal formed the dominant sample material. However, two charred samples of olive pits, derived from Stratum V (Iron I) and IVA (Iron IIA), support the remarkably consistent charcoal dates, which are, of course, somewhat older. Another short-lived sample, consisting of charred seeds of *Vicia faba* and *Pisum sativum*, originally attributed to Stratum V, appeared to come from a Stratum III or II pit cut into Stratum V. The study underlines the importance of independent chronological measurements; the original stratigraphic assignment was sometimes adjusted on the basis of the radiocarbon results. Most radiocarbon dates are from Stratum V, which has been dated archaeologically by A. Biran and D. Ilan to ca. 1150–1050 BCE based on material culture analogy. The radiocarbon measurements of Stratum V (13th–11th centuries BCE on charred olive pits) confirm the above archaeological dating, but also allow for an even higher date. The ¹⁴C results are undeniably older than the 10th-century BCE date suggested by Finkelstein, who associated Dan Stratum V with Megiddo VIA in his low chronology theory. The radiocarbon date on charred olive pits from Stratum IVA yielded a calibrated age in the 11th–10th centuries BCE. Our dates clearly support a high chronology. But more short-lived dates from new excavations are required to enlarge the database and refine the present results.

Introduction

Tel Dan is situated at a choice location at one of the main sources of the Jordan River in the northernmost part of Israel between the Galilee and the Golan. The mound covers an area of 20 hectares and is composed of strata ranging from the Neolithic to the Islamic period. The site was first identified with the biblical city of Dan in 1838 by the American scholar–explorer Edward Robinson (1841). Archaeological excavations were carried out by Biran from 1966 to 1999. A bilingual dedicatory inscription of the Hellenistic period in ancient Greek and Aramaic mentions '...*the god who is in Dan*', confirming the identification of the site (Biran 1994: 221-24). A unique basalt stele discovered in 1993, inscribed with text in Old Aramaic dated to the 9th century BCE mentions both '*the king of Israel*' and the '*House of David*', the only extra-biblical example of the latter phrase (e.g. Biran and Naveh 1993, 1995; Schniedewind 1996).

Organic samples from Tel Dan were investigated in our continuing research to establish independent radiocarbon chronologies of selected sites in the Eastern Mediterranean region as a chronological basis for interdisciplinary studies (Bowman, Bruins, and van der Plicht 2001; Bruins and Mook 1989; Bruins, Mazar, and van der Plicht 2003a, 2003b, in press; Bruins and van der Plicht 1998, 2003; van der Plicht and Bruins 2001). In this paper we present 20 Iron-Age dates of Tel Dan, 16 from charcoal and 4 from charred seeds. Although short-lived organic material is clearly preferable, charcoal dates can still be meaningful and should be used in the absence of charred seeds. Most dates are derived from Stratum V, but Strata VI, IVB, IVA and III are also represented.

Materials and Methods

Charcoal samples exhibiting a wood structure were examined by microscope at the Department of Plant Sciences at the Hebrew University of Jerusalem to determine the wood species.

The organic samples from Tel Dan, charcoal and charred seeds, were dated at the Radiocarbon Laboratories of the Centre for Isotope Research at the University of Groningen. Samples of sufficient size (grams of carbon) were dated conventionally by Proportional Gas Counting (PGC; laboratory code GrN). The smaller (mg size) samples, containing too little carbon for conventional counting measurements, were measured by AMS (laboratory code GrA). The standard deviation for the conventional method is 15–50 BP, depending on sample size; for AMS the precision is 40–50 BP. All samples were first treated by the acid/alkali/acid (AAA) method (Mook and Waterbolk 1985). The larger samples were subsequently combusted to CO_2. The radioactivity of the ^{14}C was measured in gas counters for a number of days in order to obtain the best possible precision (small standard deviation). The purified organic matter of the small-sized samples was converted into CO_2 and then into solid carbon for measurement by Accelerator Mass Spectrometry (AMS) (van der Plicht *et al.* 2000).

Calibration of the radiocarbon dates from conventional radiocarbon years BP to calendar years BCE is based on dendrochronological atmospheric data from Stuiver *et al.* (1998), using the OxCal v3.9 program (Bronk Ramsey 1995, 2001, 2003), by which a resolution of 2 (r:2) and round-off age ranges of one year are specified in relation to the program calculations.

Iron Age Radiocarbon Dates of Tel Dan in Relation to the Archaeology

Stratum VI

The oldest Iron Age IA level of occupation at Tel Dan is Stratum VI, dated by Biran (1994: 134) to the 12th century BCE (Table 19.1). Pottery in this stratum includes the first appearance of collared-rim *pithoi*, the dominant *pithos* type. The body of this type of jar was made by hand, but the neck was manufactured on the potter's wheel. Painted decoration, common in the previous period, occurs mainly on alabastra and flasks. The imported Mycenaean and Cypriot pottery of the previous Late Bronze (LB) levels (Stratum VII) are no longer present (Ilan 1999).

One charcoal sample of wood (*Quercus ithaburensis/boissieri*) came from Stratum VI, from destruction debris associated with ash pits and metallurgy installations (Table 19.1). The radiocarbon date 2990 ± 50 BP (GrA-9610) gives a calibrated age of 1367–1129 cal BCE. The $\delta^{13}C$ value of –24.40 ‰ is typical for wood (Table 19.1). These ^{14}C results characterise the age of the wood, which is likely to be older by an unknown margin than the destruction event. The calibrated age range 1266–1188 cal BCE, having the highest relative probability (33.5%), is indeed slightly older but overlaps nicely with the 12th century BCE archaeological dating (Table 19.2) for Stratum VI by Biran (1994) and the more specific archaeological dating of 1200–1150 BCE by Ilan (1999).

Table 19.1. All Iron-Age radiocarbon dates of Tel Dan with stratigraphic and archaeological relationships. The column on palaeobotany includes the internal sample numbers of the charred wood.

Stratum	Area & Phase	Locus	Basket	Palaeobotany	Archaeological context and comments	Culture	Lab. No.	14C date BP	$\delta^{13}C$ (‰)	1σ Calibrated date (cal BCE)	2σ Calibrated date (cal BCE)
III?	Y 4b	3171	13718	Charcoal W-8 Olea europea	Destruction debris above floor. This surface appears as Stratum IVB, but the section shows a disturbance. The overlying Locus 3165 (Stratum IV–III) may have intruded.	Iron II	GrN-22533	2580 ± 30	−23.39	801–764 (68.2%)	822–759 (76.7%) 683–665 (8.3%) 632–618 (1.7%) 615–591 (5.7%) 578–558 (3.1%)
III or II	B	4718	25196/1	Seeds: 90% Vicia Faba var. minor, 10% Pisum Sativum, 1 Olive pit	Pit from Stratum III or II penetrating into Stratum V.	Iron II	GrN-25207 GrN-25299 (back-up date of the alkali extract)	2730 ± 30 2750 ± 120	−22.39 −23.29	897–887 (11.5%) 884–833 (56.7%)	968–961 (1.6%) 923–814 (93.8%)
IVA	B 6-7	570a	9394	Charred olive pits	1 complete pit & 3 pieces	Iron IIA	GrA-9619	2830 ± 50	−23.47	1046–914 (66.7%) 910–906 (1.5%)	1128–892 (89.6%) 880–836 (5.8%)
IVA	K	6453	22680	Charcoal W-5 Pistacia atlantica	The final stratigraphy has not been worked out for area K, so there is no phasing as yet. The pottery is clearly Stratum IVA. An oven in this locus used Iron I pottery as its lining, so the Stratum IVA people were accessing Stratum V or VI remains to recycle them, which may be the source of the charcoal.	Iron II (& Iron I)	GrA-9659	2990 ± 40	−25.42	1366–1363 (1.1%) 1296–1273 (9.7%) 1265–1207 (30.9%) 1203–1189 (7.0%) 1180–1152 (12.4%) 1143–1129 (7.1%)	1376–1335 (8.0%) 1320–1110 (83.9%) 1099–1075 (2.4%) 1062–1051 (1.1%)
IVB	A-B B 8	7114	23670	Charcoal (layered) W-12 Quercus ithaburensis	Debris associated with copper/bronze metallurgy—mainly melting and recasting scrap. From Basket 23663. This charcoal date of Stratum IVB is indeed younger than most charcoal dates of Stratum V	Iron I	GrN-22518	2945 ± 15	−25.75	1254–1244 (6.4%) 1212–1199 (11.9%) 1192–1139 (45.2%) 1132–1126 (4.7%)	1258–1235 (11.1%) 1214–1136 (62.4%) 1134–1109 (10.8%) 1100–1071 (7.7%) 1063–1051 (3.5%)

V	Y 6	3024	13103	Charred olive pits	On floor. This is a tamped earth surface with burnt destruction debris above it. As there was quite a bit of LB material, it was initially thought to be a layer of LB age with intrusions from Iron I pits from above. The radiocarbon date indicates that it is a Stratum V surface that seals Stratum VI pits.	Iron I	GrA-9624	2930 ± 50	−21.71	1256–1242 (4.7%) 1212–1198 (5.7%) 1192–1138 (21.8%) 1132–1045 (35.9%)	1296–1274 (2.3%) 1265–996 (92.0%) 990–974 (1.2%)
V	B-1 B 10	1204	10593	Mixture soil, charcoal	Destruction debris just above tamped earth floor in locus with metalworking furnace. Complete vessels. Horizon in between two pits.	Iron I	GrA-9616	2930 ± 50	−23.90	1256–1242 (4.7%) 1212–1198 (5.7%) 1192–1138 (21.8%) 1132–1045 (35.9%)	1296–1274 (2.3%) 1265–996 (92.0%) 990–974 (1.2%)
V	Y 5 or 6	3127a (3127)	13521	Charcoal W-3,-4 *Pistacia atlantica*	Sealed pit. The original pit 3127 was probably made in Phase Y7 (Stratum VI) but at least some of the contents are later—from Stratum V or IVB.	Iron I	GrN-22532	2985 ± 25	−24.50	1287–1282 (2.8%) 1261–1209 (37.7%) 1201–1190 (7.8%) 1178–1160 (11.6%) 1141–1130 (8.4%)	1368–1361 (1.4%) 1314–1186 (65.3%) 1183–1127 (28.7%)
V	B 9-10	593 (624)	10153/2	Charcoal (coarse fraction) W-18,-19 *Quercus boissieri*	In destruction layer above stone pavement. Square C-17	Iron I	GrN-22523	2960 ± 15	−24.94	1256–1240 (15.8%) 1213–1206 (6.4%) 1203–1198 (5.2%) 1193–1189 (4.0%) 1180–1151 (27.5%) 1143–1138 (5.3%) 1133–1129 (4.0%)	1261–1225 (22.7%) 1222–1124 (72.7%)
V	B 9-10	593 (624)	10153/2	Charcoal (fine fraction) W-18,-19 *Quercus boissieri*	In destruction layer above stone pavement. Square C-17	Iron I	GrN-22967	2995 ± 20	−25.56	1291–1279 (8.4%) 1262–1252 (7.9%) 1250–1211 (33.0%) 1200–1191 (6.6%) 1176–1167 (5.2%) 1140–1131 (7.2%)	1369–1360 (2.2%) 1315–1207 (64.3%) 1203–1189 (8.5%) 1180–1152 (11.6%) 1142–1129 (8.9%)

Phase	Area	Locus	Basket	Material/Sample	Description	Period	Lab No.	BP	δ13C	Calibration 1	Calibration 2
V	B 9-10	1203	10xxx	Charcoal W-9 *Platanus orientalis*	Initially associated with MB–IIA. However, the radiocarbon date suggests Iron I. The sample must be from Area B, where there is a L1203 (paved street excavated in 1975), and basket that begins with 10xxx, but the last 3 digits are wrong.	Iron I	GrN-22534	2960 ± 50	−24.76	1287–1283 (1.1%) 1261–1124 (56.6%) 1121–1111 (2.9%) 1099–1082 (5.0%) 1061–1052 (2.6%)	1370–1359 (1.6%) 1316–1012 (93.8%)
V	B 9-10	675	10376/1	Charcoal W-7 *Quercus boissieri*	In destruction layer on stone pavement.	Iron I	GrN-22530	2965 ± 15	−24.66	1257–1238 (19.0%) 1214–1208 (5.9%) 1202–1197 (5.0%) 1194–1189 (4.1%) 1179–1154 (24.5%) 1142–1137 (5.4%) 1134–1129 (4.2%)	1261–1226 (25.5%) 1222–1126 (69.9%)
V	B 9-10	675	10302/1	Charcoal (layered)	In destruction layer on stone pavement. Few soil crumbs adhered to charcoal	Iron I	GrN-22526	2980 ± 15	−24.85	1259–1231 (27.5%) 1218–1210 (8.5%) 1200–1191 (9.3%) 1177–1163 (12.3%) 1140–1131 (10.5%)	1291–1278 (4.3%) 1263–1188 (58.1%) 1181–1149 (20.2%) 1144–1128 (12.8%)
V	A-B B 9-10	7147	23867	Charcoal W-11 *Quercus ithaburensis*	Amongst collapsed mudbrick and plaster from destruction.	Iron I	GrN-22517	2985 ± 20	−25.09	1260–1210 (40.7%) 1200–1191 (8.1%) 1177–1163 (10.3%) 1140–1131 (9.1%)	1311–1273 (10.5%) 1265–1187 (56.0%) 1181–1149 (17.6%) 1144–1128 (11.3%)
V	B 9-10	593 (694)	10359/1	Charcoal W-6 *Quercus ithaburensis*	One large charcoal piece. In destruction layer above stone pavement, next to W4330.	Iron I	GrN-22527	2990 ± 15	−24.79	1287–1283 (2.9%) 1261–1253 (7.5%) 1248–1211 (35.9%) 1199–1191 (7.7%) 1175–1168 (5.4%) 1140–1131 (8.8%)	1310–1300 (1.6%) 1297–1273 (9.9%) 1265–1207 (49.4%) 1203–1188 (10.2%) 1180–1152 (13.6%) 1142–1129 (10.8%)

V	593 (624)	10307/1	Charcoal (layered) W-17 *Quercus ithaburensis* (apparently)	In destruction layer above stone pavement.	Iron I	GrN-22524	3000 ± 30	−24.97	1366–1363 (1.4%) 1304–1302 (0.9%) 1296–1273 (13.4%) 1265–1211 (35.6%) 1200–1191 (5.5%) 1176–1165 (5.7%) 1140–1131 (5.8%)	1372–1339 (8.6%) 1318–1188 (68.2%) 1181–1150 (11.2%) 1144–1128 (7.4%)
V	660	10148/1	Charcoal W-13 *Quercus ithaburensis* (apparently)	In destruction layer above stone pavement.	Iron I	GrN-22525	3000 ± 30	−24.97	1366–1363 (1.4%) 1304–1302 (0.9%) 1296–1273 (13.4%) 1265–1211 (35.6%) 1200–1191 (5.5%) 1176–1165 (5.7%) 1140–1131 (5.8%)	1372–1339 (8.6%) 1318–1188 (68.2%) 1181–1150 (11.2%) 1144–1128 (7.4%)
V	7208	24789	Mixture soil, charcoal	Youngest Iron-I; in destruction layer on lime-plaster floor	Iron I	GrA-9618	3020 ± 50	−25.42	1373–1337 (15.1%) 1319–1254 (30.8%) 1246–1211 (15.1%) 1199–1192 (2.8%) 1174–1170 (1.5%) 1139–1132 (3.0%)	1409–1125 (95.4%)
VI	7168	23974	Charcoal W-10 *Quercus ithaburensis/boissieri*	Destruction debris associated with ash pits and metallurgy installations; upright column or post surrounded by plaster floor	Iron I	GrA-9610	2990 ± 50	−24.40	1367–1362 (1.8%) 1313–1271 (14.9%) 1266–1188 (33.5%) 1180–1151 (11.6%) 1143–1129 (6.3%)	1385–1333 (10.5%) 1321–1049 (84.9%)

Stratum V

The next level of occupation, Stratum V (also Iron IA), was a densely built-up settlement, destroyed by a great fire (Biran 1994). The destruction layer was encountered in every excavated part of Tel Dan, usually over 50 cm thick. The pottery assemblage of Stratum V is very similar to that of Stratum VI, with one possible exception: a new 'Phoenician' type of *pithos* appears, originating from the Phoenician coast (Biran 1989: Fig. 4.7.9). This *pithos* was completely hand-made, characterised by an incised wavy decoration around the jar. Sherds of classic, white-slipped and bichrome Philistine ware and other pottery with 'Sea-People' motifs occur in all the Iron I levels, Strata VI–IVB (Ilan 1999: 93-95 [Table 19.2]).

Table 19.2. Stratigraphy and radiocarbon results of Tel Dan in relation to the conventional and low chronology. The radiocarbon dates on short-lived material contradict the low chronology. All archaeological age estimates and calibrated ^{14}C dates are in BCE

Tel Dan	Biran[1]	Biran[1]	Ilan[2]	Ilan[2]	Calibrated 1σ ^{14}C Dates Dan	Correlation Dan with Megiddo Finkelstein	Low Chronology Finkelstein
IVA	Iron II	ca. 875–950	ca. 850–950	Iron IIA	1046–906	VA–IVB [4]	ca. 900–835[3]
IVB	Iron I and II	ca. 950–1050	ca. 950–1050	Iron IB			
V	Iron I	ca. 1050 to 12th century	ca. 1050–1150	Iron IA	1256–1045	VIA [5]	ca. 1000–900[4]
VI	Iron I	12th century	ca. 1150–1200	Iron IA			
VIIA	LB II	13th century	ca. 1200–1300	Late LB IIB			

[1] Biran 1994: 11; [2] Ilan 1999: 137; [3] Finkelstein 1999: 61; [4] 1999: 67 note 14.

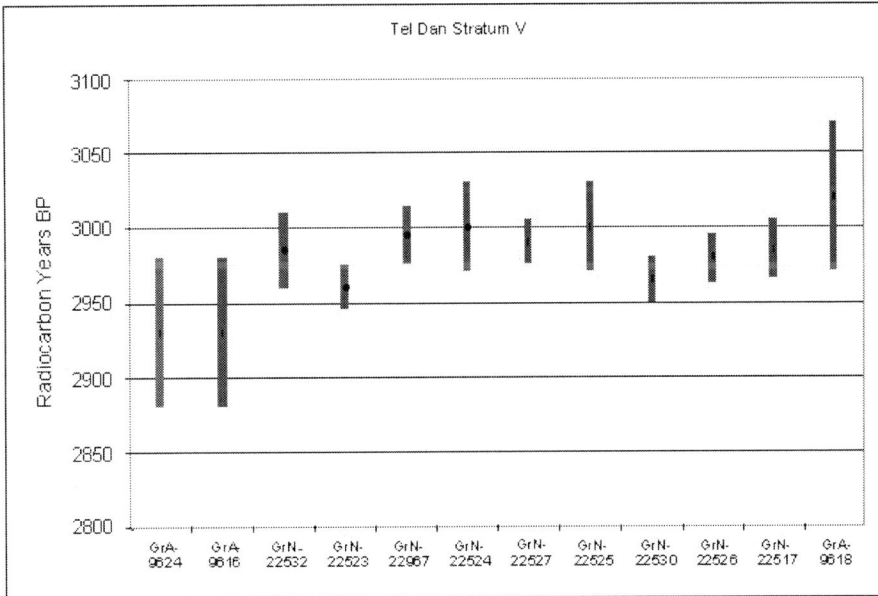

Figure 19.1. The 12 radiocarbon dates of Dan Stratum V are shown in conventional radiocarbon years BP (not calibrated). The first date on the left (GrA-9624) is derived from short-lived seeds (charred olive pits), while all the other dates are derived from multiyear charcoal. However, one charcoal date (GrA-9616) has the same age as the short-lived date. Indeed, the old-wood effect of charcoal can be very small or negligible. The internal correlation of the 10 older charcoal dates is excellent.

The consistent series of 12 radiocarbon dates from Stratum V (Table 19.1; Fig. 19.1) includes 11 dates on charcoal and one date on short-lived charred olive pits. The samples are derived from different parts of Tel Dan: Area B (most samples) and Area Y. The high internal consistency of the radiocarbon results, measured by both AMS and conventional gas counters (PGC), is an indicator of dating quality and reliability (Fig. 19.1). The AMS dates (GrA-9624, 9616, 9618) have a somewhat higher standard deviation (σ 50) than the best high-precision dates (GrN-22523, 22527, 22530, 22526) measured in gas counters (σ15).

The youngest charcoal date 2930 ± 50 BP (GrA-9616) is exactly the same as the age of the short-lived charred olive pits (GrA-9624). The former charcoal date is based on a sample that consisted of a mixture of soil and powdery charcoal from destruction debris just above a tamped earth floor with a metalworking furnace in Locus 1204. Complete Iron IA vessels were found here. Such powdery charcoal mixed with soil in destruction layers may be rather short-lived, as wood chunks are absent. The $\delta^{13}C$ value of –23.90 ‰ for GrA-9616 is an additional indicator, because real wood charcoal at Tel Dan tends to have values in the range of –25 to –26 ‰, while short-lived seeds are in the –21 to –23 ‰ range.

The detailed 1σ calibrated age range (Fig. 19.2) of both the charred olive pits (GrA-9624) and the powdery charcoal (GrA-9616) is 1256–1242 (4.7%), 1212–1198 (5.7%), 1192–1138 (21.8%), 1132–1045 (35.9%) cal BCE and the 2σ range is 1296–1274 (2.3%), 1265–996 (92.0%), 990–974 (1.2%) cal BCE. The highest relative probability in the 1σ range is 1132–1045 cal BCE (Fig. 19.2). This result fits very well indeed with the archaeological age estimate suggested by Biran (1994: 134), the 12th to the first half of the 11th centuries BCE, as well as by Ilan (1999): 1150–1050 BCE (Table 19.2). Nevertheless, the radiocarbon results for Stratum V would even allow for a higher chronology, as a cumulative 32.2% within 1σ is in the 1256–1138 cal BCE range. Anyway, the results clearly contraindicate a lowering of the date for Stratum V to the 10th century BCE, as advocated by Finkelstein (1999, 2000) who suggested a correlation between Dan VI–V, Hazor XII–XI and Megiddo VIA, which he re-assigned to the mid-10th century BCE (Table 19.2). In any event, Megiddo Stratum VIA correlates to Tel Dan Stratum IVB, not Stratum V (Ilan 1999: 137).

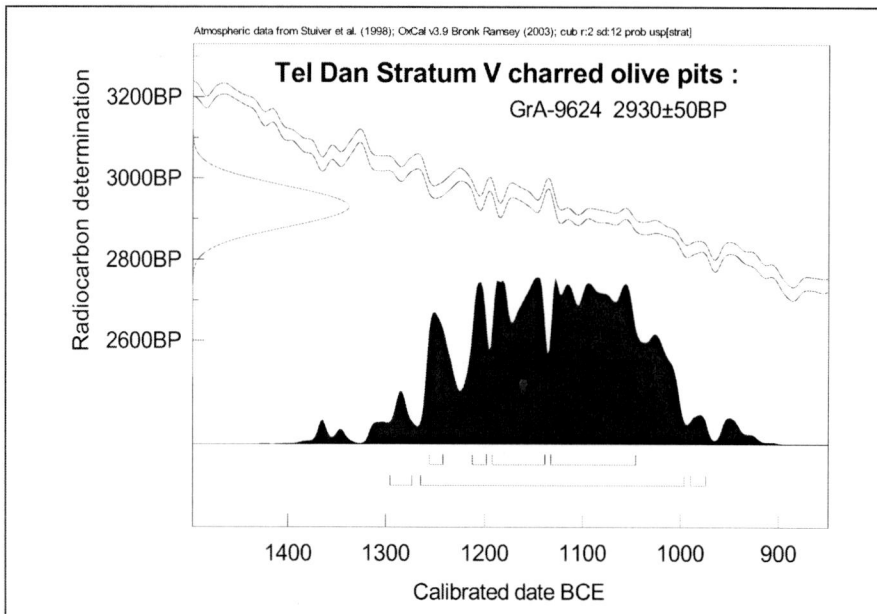

Figure 19.2. Calibration of the AMS date for the charred olive pits from Stratum V (2930 ± 50 BP, GrA-9624) into historical years BCE.

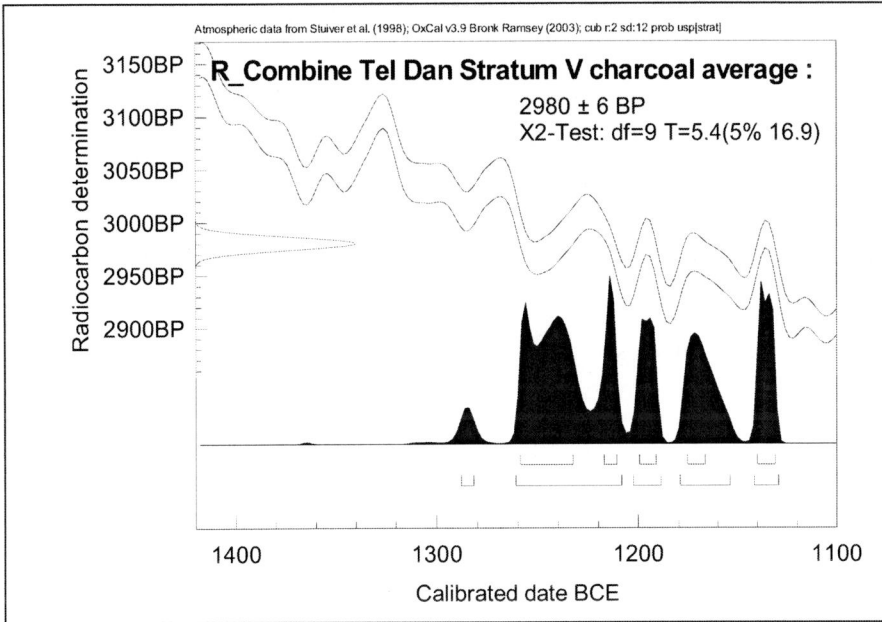

Figure 19.3. Calibration of the average of the 10 older charcoal dates from Stratum V (2980 ± 6 BP) into historical years BCE.

The calculated weighted average date 2980 ± 6 BP of the 10 older charcoal samples of Stratum V is 50 radiocarbon years older than the short-lived date of charred olive seeds, as well as the powdery charcoal of Locus 1204. These older charcoal dates, from different types of wood (Table 19.1), do not differ from each other beyond a few decades. The chi-squared test shows the high level of coherence between these charcoal dates: T = 5.4, which is well below 16.9, the 5% confidence level (Fig. 19.3). Though such a small σ of only 6 BP years seems unrealistic, as it is more precise than the oxalic acid standard used as a modern comparison of ^{14}C activity in individual ^{14}C measurements, we retain this value because it is derived from a weighted average calculation of 10 dates.

The age difference of about 50 BP years between short-lived seeds and multiyear charcoal at Tel Dan Stratum V is remarkably similar to results from MB IIC Jericho (Bruins and van der Plicht 1995). The detailed calibrated 1σ age range (Fig. 19.3) of the average multiyear charcoal date of Stratum V is 1259–1233 (29.0%), 1217–1211 (8.4%), 1199–1191 (9.5%), 1176–1167 (9.3%), 1140–1131 (12.1%) cal BCE and the 2σ age range is 1288–1282 (1.9%), 1261–1208 (48.2%), 1202–1189 (12.5%), 1179–1154 (18.7%), 1142–1129 (14.0%) cal BCE. This calibration result represents the average age of the wood used in Stratum V, which includes the following species: *Pistacia atlantica*, *Quercus boissieri*, *Quercus ithaburensis* (most common) and *Platanus orientalis*.

Stratum IVB

The destruction of Stratum V did not result in the abandonment of the site, as the city of Dan was soon rebuilt: Stratum IVB (Biran 1994). The outline and walls of the houses were retained in the rebuilding; few new walls were constructed. The archaeological age assignment of Stratum IVB, classified culturally as Iron IB, is given as the second half of the 11th century and the first half of the 10th century BCE (Biran 1994: 142; Ilan 1999: 137). The pottery types of Stratum IVB are much the same as those of the previous stratum, but the collared-rim and 'Galilean' *pithoi* were no longer being manufactured. A new element emerged: Phoenician bichrome jugs and flasks decorated with concentric circles or bands (Ilan 1999: 90-92, 102).

There is only one radiocarbon date from Stratum IVB, on charcoal from Tabor oak, *Quercus ithaburensis*: GrN-22518, 2945 ± 15 BP. The 1σ calibrated age range is 1254–1244 (6.4%), 1212–1199 (11.9%), 1192–1139 (45.2%), 1132–1126 (4.7%) cal BCE. The result is indeed slightly younger than most radiocarbon dates on charcoal for Stratum V. However, the most probable age range of 1192–1139 cal BCE is much older than the above archaeological date of ca. 1050–950 BCE. This is in fact a rare case in our charcoal dating results of Tel Dan that the old-wood effect is more extreme in terms of age difference. Another possibility is that the charcoal relates to Stratum V, because the stratigraphic differentiation between Stratum IVB and V is not always clear-cut, as the former is a kind of continuation of the latter.

Stratum IVA

The overlying Stratum IVA is classified as Iron IIA by Biran (1994: 143-46) and Ilan (1999). Pottery assemblages yielded a wealth of bowls (unlike earlier Iron I strata), many with yellow and red-slip decoration. Cypriot Black on Red juglets appear for the first time. The archaeological date of Stratum IVA is approximately the second half of the 10th century to the beginning of the 9th century BCE (Biran 1994) or ca. 950–850 BCE (Ilan 1999).

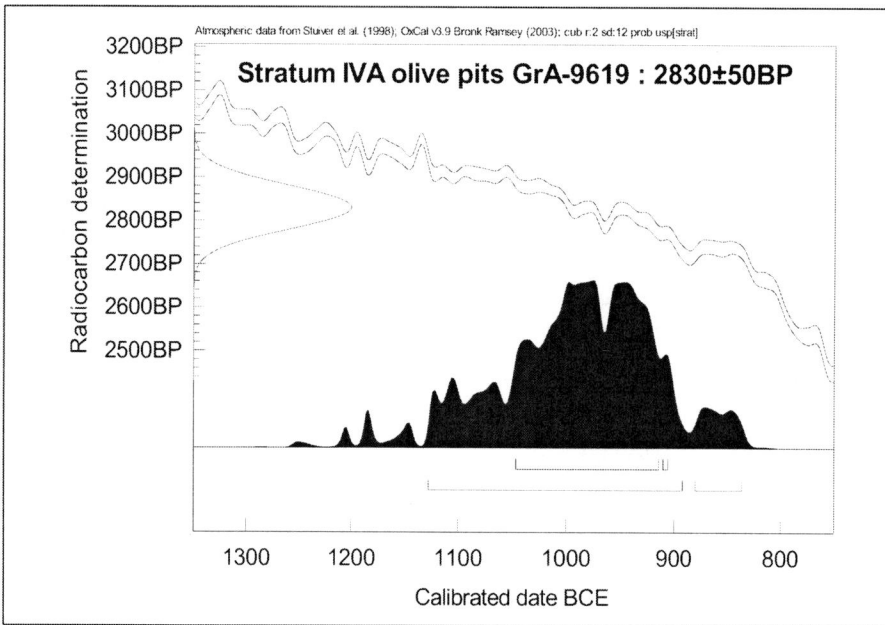

Atmospheric data from Stuiver et al. (1998); OxCal v3.9 Bronk Ramsey (2003); cub r:2 sd:12 prob usp[strat]

Stratum IVA olive pits GrA-9619 : 2830±50BP

Figure 19.4. Calibration of an AMS date on charred olive pits from Stratum IVA (2830 ± 50 BP, GrA-9619) into historical years BCE.

A very important sample of charred olive seeds from Stratum IVA, Locus 570 in Area B, gave an AMS date (GrA-9619) of 2830 ± 50 BP (Table 19.1). This short-lived sample associated with Stratum IVA is 100 radiocarbon years younger than the olive seeds from Stratum V and thus consistent in relative stratigraphic terms. The 1σ calibrated age range of the former date (Fig. 19.4) is 1046–914 (66.7%), 910–906 (1.5%) cal BCE, which fits quite well with the estimated archaeological age by Biran and Ilan but would also allow for a higher chronology. Though only one date is available at this stage, the result does not support a lowering of Dan Stratum IVA to the 9th century BCE (Table 19.2), as advocated by Finkelstein who correlates Dan IVA with Hazor Stratum IX (Finkelstein 1999: 61).

Stratum III or II

A sample of mixed charred seeds of *Vicia faba* and *Pisum sativum*, originally attributed to Stratum V, was supplied after the other samples were already measured. The sample of mixed seeds gave a very low date that does not fit the other results for Stratum V. The conventional PGC date of 2730 ± 30 BP (GrN-25207) with a calibrated age in the 9th century BCE (Fig. 19.5) is too low even for the low chronology (Finkelstein 1999: 67). This surprisingly young date raised some doubt about the validity of the ^{14}C dating result. Hence, an extra measurement was made of the alkali extract from the above sample, which gave essentially the same midpoint result (GrN-25299, 2750 ± 120 BP), verifying the former date.

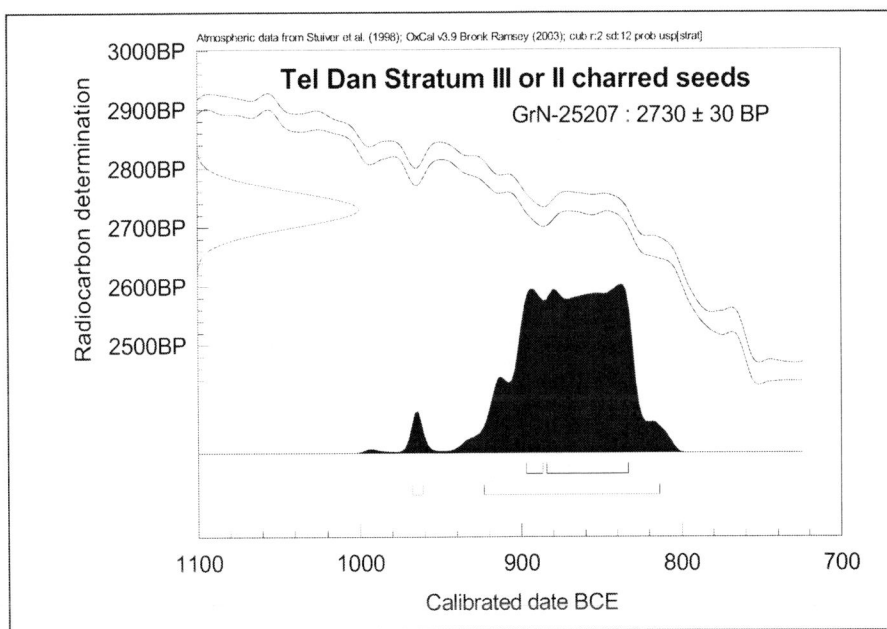

Figure 19.5. Calibration of a PGC date on charred seeds from a
Stratum III or II pit (2730 ± 30 BP, GrN-25207) into historical years BCE.

The stratigraphic archaeological context was re-evaluated as a result. Re-examination of field photographs allowed us to identify a pit originating in Stratum II or III at precisely the location of the charred seeds. The original stratigraphic attribution was erroneous. This particular instance illustrates the potential use of radiocarbon dating as a stratigraphic check, something that is not often mentioned in the literature.

The youngest radiocarbon date in our Iron Age series from Tel Dan came from charcoal of olive wood (*Olea europea*), measured by PGC: 2580 ± 30 BP (GrN-22533). The charcoal is derived from destruction debris above a floor, associated originally with Stratum IVB. The radiocarbon date in this case also suggests that at least part of the destruction debris is much younger, perhaps from Stratum II. The calibrated 1σ date (Fig. 19.6) is very precise, 801–764 cal BCE, due to the very steep slope of the calibration curve in this time trajectory. Association of this destruction layer with Assyrian incursions in the 8th century BCE is not unlikely.

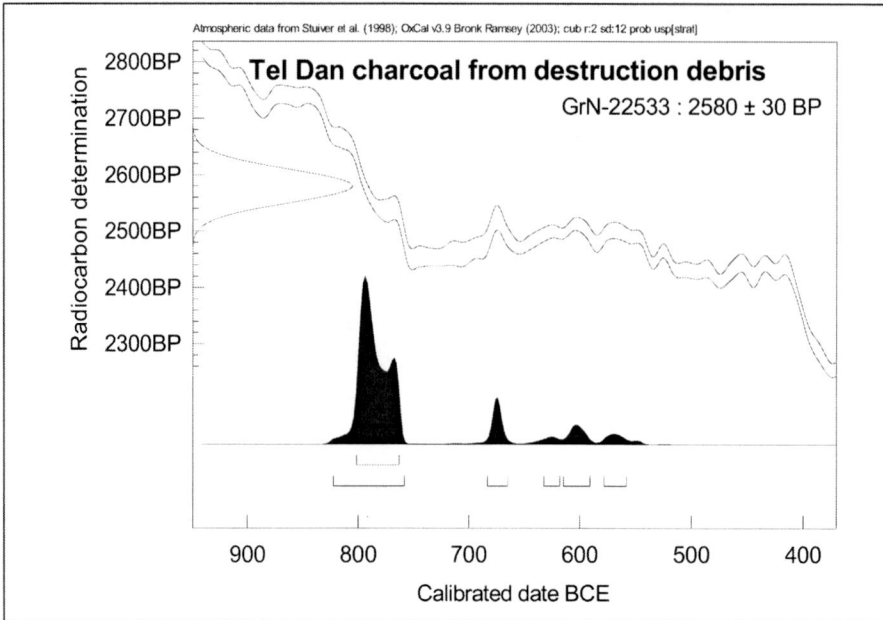

Figure 19.6. Calibration of a PGC date (2580 ± 30 BP, GrN-22533) on olive wood charcoal from destruction debris, perhaps related to Stratum II, into historical years BCE.

Conclusions

Conventional archaeological frameworks for the Iron Age as presented for example by Mazar (1992: 30) and Barkay (1992: 305) date the Iron I horizon from ca. 1200–1000 BCE and the Iron IIA to 1000–925 or 1000–800 BCE. Finkelstein (1996, 1999, 2000) has proposed a lowering of the chronology by some 70 years. Objections have been raised against the low chronology (Ben-Tor and Ben-Ami 1998; Mazar 1997). Some series of radiocarbon dates and some types of archaeological data appear to support the low chronology (e.g. in this volume, Franklin [Chapter 18]; Piasetsky and Finkelstein [Chapter 16]; Sharon *et al.* [Chapter 6]) which are largely based on dates from the Rehovot radiocarbon laboratory. The extensive and consistent series of radiocarbon results from Tel Rehov, measured at Groningen University (Bruins *et al.* 2003a, 2003b, in press; in this volume, Bruins *et al.* [Chapter 19]; Bruins *et al.* [Chapter 15]; Mazar *et al.* [Chapter 13]; van der Plicht and Bruins [Chapter 14]), support a high chronology.

The Groningen radiocarbon dates of Tel Dan also show a strong internal consistency, which provides robustness to the results, despite the lack of more short-lived samples. The calibrated ages for Stratum V and Stratum IVA, based on charred olive seeds, either support the conventional archaeological age assessment for the Iron I and IIA or allow for an even higher chronology. The ^{14}C results from Tel Dan contraindicate a lowering of the Iron Age chronology (Table 19.2). The radiocarbon dates on short-lived material place Stratum V in the 13th–11th centuries BCE range and Stratum IVA in the 11th–10th centuries BCE.

Future excavations will hopefully provide more short-lived charred organic material to verify, expand and refine the above results with more radiocarbon dates. In the meantime, additional measurements are planned on available animal bone samples from previous excavations. Radiocarbon dating of bones, also a short-lived organic material, can provide reliable dates. Moreover, a technique for dating burned bones was recently developed successfully in Groningen (Lanting, Aerts-Bijma and van der Plicht 2001), which might open further opportunities for dating destruction strata and loci related to religious ceremonies involving animal sacrifices.

Acknowledgments

We are grateful to A. Biran, the excavator of Tel Dan, for providing the stratified organic material; to M. Hershkowitz for assistance in sample selection; and to the technical staff of the Groningen laboratory for the ^{14}C measurements.

References

Barkay, G. (1992) The Iron Age II–III. In *The Archaeology of Ancient Israel*, edited by A. Ben-Tor (New Haven: Yale University Press): 302-73.

Ben-Tor, A., and D. Ben-Ami (1998) Hazor and the Archaeology of the 10th Century B.C.E. *IEJ* 48: 1-37.

Biran, A. (1989) The Collared-rim Jars and the Settlement of the Tribe of Dan. In Recent Excavations in Israel: Studies in Iron Age Archaeology, edited by S. Gitin and W.G. Dever (AASOR 49; Winona Lake, IN: Eisenbrauns): 71-96.

—(1994) *Biblical Dan* (Jerusalem: Israel Exploration Society).

Biran, A., and J. Naveh (1993) An Aramaic Stele Fragment from Tel Dan. *IEJ* 43: 81-98.

—(1995) The Tel Dan Inscription: A New Fragment. *IEJ* 45: 1-18.

Bowman, D., H.J. Bruins, and J. van der Plicht (2001) Load Structure Seismites in the Dead Sea Area (Israel): Chronological Benchmarking with ^{14}C Dating. *Radiocarbon* 43(3): 1383-90.

Bronk Ramsey, C. (1995) Radiocarbon Calibration and Analysis of Stratigraphy: The OxCal Program. *Radiocarbon* 37(2): 425-30.

—(2001) Development of the Radiocarbon Program OxCal. *Radiocarbon* 43(2A): 355-63.

—(2003) OxCal Program v3.9, Radiocarbon Accelerator Unit, University of Oxford (<http://www.rlaha.ox.ac.uk/O/oxcal.php>).

Bruins, H.J., and W.G. Mook (1989) The Need for a Calibrated Radiocarbon Chronology of Near Eastern Archaeology. *Radiocarbon* 31(3): 1019-29.

Bruins, H.J., and J. van der Plicht (1995) Tell Es-Sultan (Jericho): Radiocarbon Results of Short-lived Cereal and Multi-year Charcoal Samples from the End of the Middle Bronze Age. *Radiocarbon* 37: 213-20.

—(1998) Early Bronze Jericho: High-precision ^{14}C Dates of Short-lived Palaeobotanic Remains. *Radiocarbon* 40: 621-28.

—(2003) Assorting and Synchronizing Archaeological and Geological Strata with Radiocarbon: The Southern Levant in relation to Egypt and Thera. In *The Synchronization of Civilizations in the Eastern Mediterranean in the 2nd Millennium* BC, edited by M. Bietak (Vienna: Austrian Academy of Sciences): 35-42.

Bruins, H.J., J. van der Plicht, and A. Mazar (2003a) ^{14}C Dates from Tel Reḥov: Iron-Age Chronology, Pharaohs and Hebrew Kings. *Science* 300: 315-18.

—(2003b) Response to Comment on '^{14}C dates from Tel Reḥov: Iron-Age chronology, Pharaohs and Hebrew Kings'. *Science* 302: 568c.

—(in press) The End of the 2nd Millennium BCE and the Transition from Iron I to Iron IIA: Radiocarbon Dates of Tel Reḥov, Israel. In *The Synchronization of Civilizations in the Eastern Mediterranean in the 2nd Millennium BC*, III, edited by M. Bietak (Vienna: Austrian Academy of Sciences).

Finkelstein, I. (1996) The Archaeology of the United Monarchy: An Alternative View. *Levant* 28: 177-87.

—(1999) Hazor and the North in the Iron Age: A Low Chronology Perspective. *BASOR* 314: 55-70.

—(2000) Hazor XII–XI with an Addendum on Ben-Tor's Dating of Hazor X–VII. *Tel Aviv* 27: 231-47.

Ilan, D. (1999) Northeastern Israel in the Iron Age I (unpublished PhD thesis, Tel Aviv University).

Lanting, J.N., A.T. Aerts-Bijma, and J. van der Plicht (2001) Dating of Cremated Bones. *Radiocarbon* 43(2A): 249-54.

Mazar, A. (1992) The Iron Age I. In *The Archaeology of Ancient Israel*, edited by A. Ben-Tor (New Haven: Yale University Press): 258-301.

—(1997) Iron Age Chronology: A Reply to I. Finkelstein. *Levant* 29: 157-67.

Mook, W.G., and H.T. Waterbolk (1985) *Handbook for Archaeologists*. III. *Radiocarbon Dating* (Strasbourg: European Science Foundation).

Robinson, E. (1841) *Biblical Researches in Palestine*, III (London: Murray).

Schniedewind, W.M. (1996) Tel Dan Stela: New Light on Aramaic and Jehu's Revolt. *BASOR* 302: 75-90.

Stuiver, M., *et al.* (1998) INTCAL98 Radiocarbon Age Calibration, 24,000-0 cal BP. *Radiocarbon* 40(3): 1041-84.

Van der Plicht, J., and H.J. Bruins (2001) Radiocarbon Dating in Near-Eastern Contexts: Confusion and Quality Control. *Radiocarbon* 43(3): 1155-66.

Van der Plicht, J., *et al.* (2000) Status Report: The Groningen AMS Facility. *Nuclear Instruments and Methods* B172: 58-65.

20 Iron I Chronology at Ashkelon

Preliminary results of the Leon Levy expedition*

Daniel M. Master

Abstract

The Leon Levy Expedition to Ashkelon, directed by Lawrence E. Stager, has contributed to the history and chronology of periods ranging from the Early Bronze to the Crusader. In each epoch, the port of Ashkelon has been a bellwether for the important military and economic changes which transformed the southern Levant. The thirteenth and twelfth centuries BCE were periods of transformation throughout the Mediterranean, and recent excavations have brought to light a complete Iron I sequence with a host of implications for our understanding of the chronology of the Iron Age. While the radiocarbon studies of this sequence are ongoing, a preliminary report on the material culture assemblages, architectural layouts, and stratigraphic sequence can provide important anchors for the understanding of the end of the Late Bronze Age and beginning of the Iron Age in the southern Levant.

In the early twentieth century Duncan Mackenzie—followed by John Garstang and William Phythian-Adams—first attempted to understand the Late Bronze (LB) and Iron Ages at Ashkelon using sections scraped along the western and northern scarp of the mound (*al-Hadra*), in the center of Ashkelon. From these sections, Mackenzie and Phythian-Adams argued that the Late Bronze Age city had been destroyed in a massive conflagration and was succeeded by a Philistine city in the early Iron Age (Mackenzie 1913: 21-23, Plate II; Phythian-Adams 1923: 60-63, Fig. 3). It was left to the Leon Levy Expedition to confirm these observations by opening substantial areas adjacent to the sections cut by the teams from the Palestine Exploration Fund. Since the Iron Age strata lay below significant later buildup, it took more than a decade of intensive excavation to reach the Iron I remains with any breadth. A step trench excavated from 1985 to 1990 yielded tantalizing clues about the earliest Philistine settlement in the twelfth century (Stager 1991), but the evidence was, as in the case of Mackenzie and Phythian-Adams, quite limited in its scope.

The first broad excavation area to reach Iron Age I remains was immediately next to the sea—part of *Grid 50* according to the site-wide grid of the Leon Levy expedition (Fig. 20.1)—immediately adjacent to the area where Mackenzie first described a Late Bronze Age destruction in a

---

*   Early Radiocarbon results from 26 Iron Age samples accord well with the chronology presented here. Calibrated Phase 20 and Phase 19 results place the founding of Philistine Ashkelon in the late thirteenth to early twelfth centuries while calibrated Phase 17 results place the final Iron 1 stratum in the eleventh century (Bruins and van der Plicht: personal communication). These results will be discussed in full in a future forum.

scraping of the sea-side scarp. After fourteen seasons of modern excavation, the expedition discovered a single Iron I stratum from the eleventh century (equivalent to Miqne V, Tell Qasile XI), and below this, without a destruction, a stratum of the thirteenth century. While Mackenzie and Phythian-Adams presented a Late Bronze Age destruction as one of their chief conclusions (Mackenzie 1913: Plate I; Phythian-Adams 1923: Figs. 3–4), recent excavations have not found any evidence of a suitable destruction in any excavation area or probe in the vicinity.

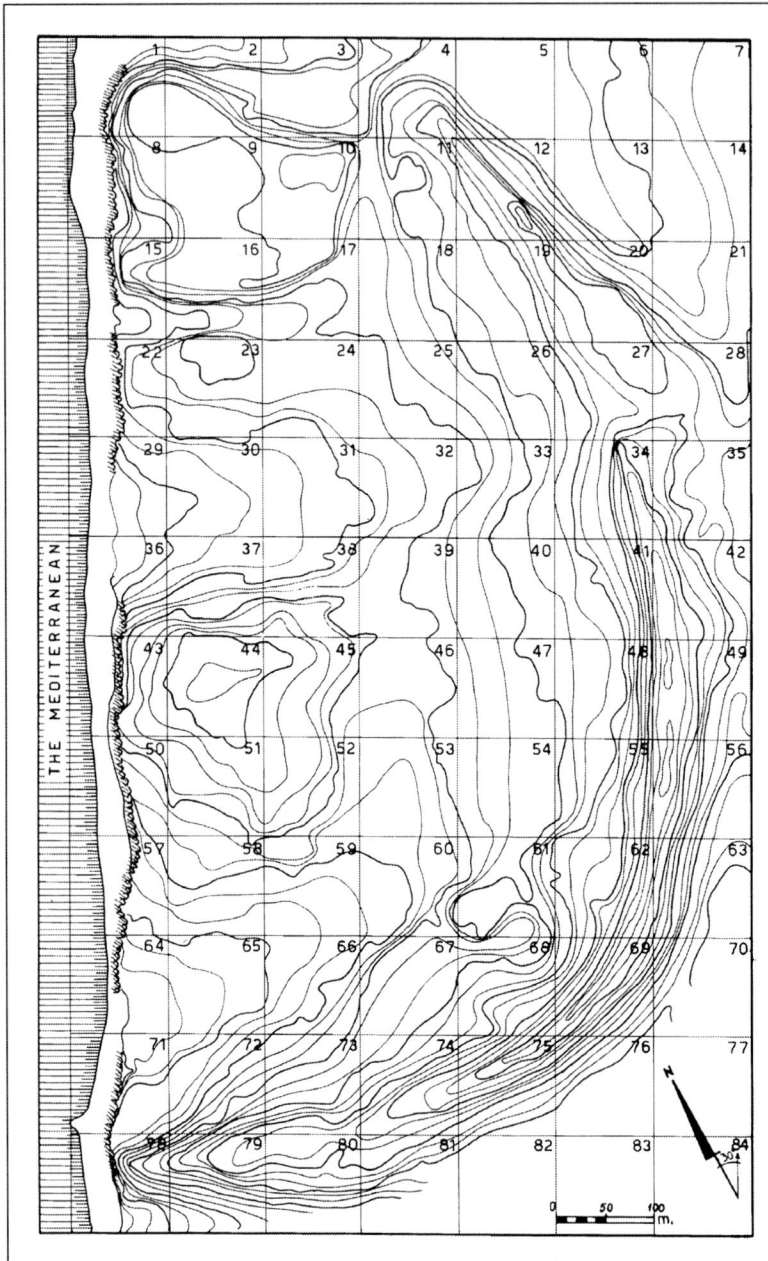

Figure 20.1. Plan of the Leon Levy Expedition to Ashkelon.

Although *Grid 50* did not depict the transition from the thirteenth to the twelfth centuries, its Late Bronze Age remains are a helpful baseline. In the Late Bronze Age, both in the tombs found in this area and in the occupational layers, excavations revealed a classic LBIIB assemblage containing typical thirteenth century Levantine forms along with contemporary imports from Cyprus and the Aegean (Baker 2003).

About 200 meters to the northeast, immediately adjacent to another step trench of Phythian-Adams, the excavation of *Grid 38* took slightly longer to reach the Iron I levels. But after the sixteenth year of excavation, a complete sequence was discovered from the end of the Late Bronze Age through the end of the Iron Age I.

The prominent feature of the latest Late Bronze stratum is a wide mudbrick wall (Fig. 20.2), made up of bricks identical in size to those at Deir el-Balah (Dothan 1993: 344). The wall is exactly four Egyptian cubits in width, with a sand foundation. While some have postulated that most 'Egyptian' remains in Late Bronze Age Canaan are merely 'Egyptianizing' (Higginbotham 2000: 131-38), the attribution of this wall to Egyptian builders relies on hard-to-imitate elements, such as a sand foundation or standard brick sizes, which are invisible to the eye of the casual observer. Furthermore, the pottery associated with this stratum is dominated by Egyptian-style ceramics made with Egyptian techniques including saucer bowls, flanged rim bowls, cup and saucer bowls, beer bottles, and a variety of storage vessels.

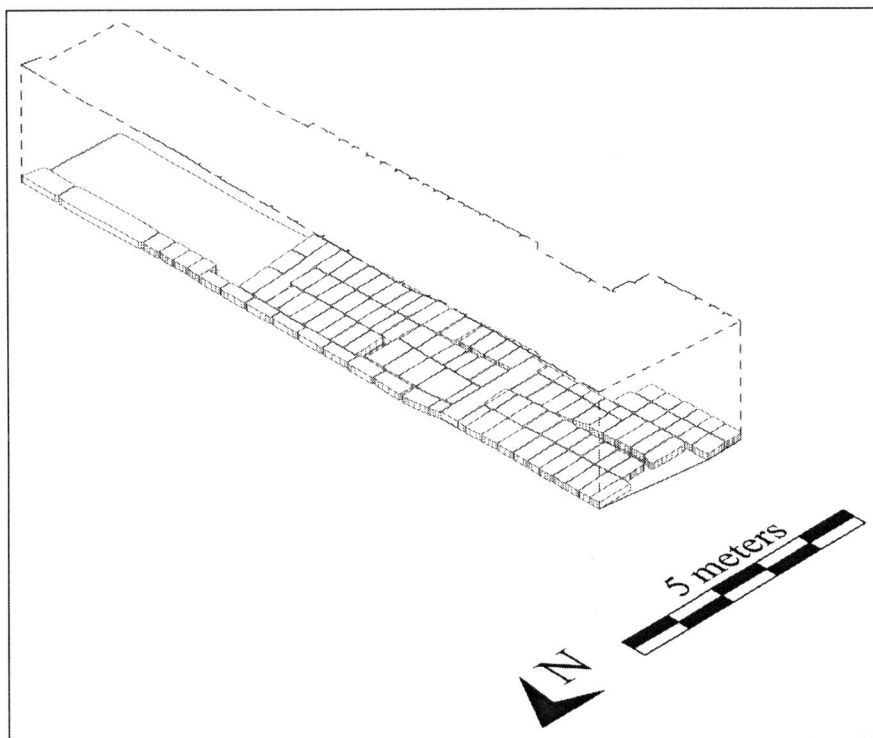

Figure 20.2. Reconstruction of *Grid 38*, Phase 21. Courtesy of the
Leon Levy Expedition to Ashkelon, reconstruction by G. Pierce.

This assemblage brings to mind several Egyptian inscriptions which mention Ashkelon at the end of the Late Bronze Age. Both in the Merneptah inscription and on the walls of the temple at Karnak, the Egyptians record a single conquest of Canaanite Ashkelon at the end of the thirteenth century (Stager 1985; Yurko 1986; *contra* Higginbotham 2000). The enforced Egyptian allegiance of Ashkelon is further reflected in three inscriptions from twelfth-century Megiddo, which mention a certain 'Kerker' who seems to have cultic or political ties with both Ashkelon and Egypt (summary in Higginbotham 2000: 68-69; Loud 1939: 12, Plate 63). It is likely that the recently uncovered remains at Ashkelon reflect the Egyptian control described in these texts.

By combining the picture presented by the two areas just excavated (Fig. 20.3), it appears that the Canaanite city of the mid-thirteenth century, visible in *Grid 50*, was conquered by Merneptah, and that an Egyptian precinct, visible in *Grid 38*, was constructed in the city, a precinct which perhaps supported the work of Kerker.

	Ashkelon Grid 50	Ashkelon Grid 38	Lachish	Gezer	Miqne/Ekron	Ashdod	Tel Qasile
1300							
	10		VII	XV	VIII	XIV	
		21					
1200							
	Ramses III ->	20	VI	XIV	VII	XIIIB	
		19		XIII	VI	XIIIA-XII	XII
1100				XII			
	9	18		XI	V	XI	XI
1000		17		X	IV	X	X

Figure 20.3. Comparative stratigraphy of selected sites.

The Egyptian precinct was soon abandoned. Throughout the excavation area, a thick layer of mudbrick detritus containing Egyptian pottery indicated that the water and time took their toll on the Egyptian precinct. Phythian-Adams found this same layer along with a Ramessid-period alabaster vase at roughly the same level in his trench (Phythian-Adams 1923: 162, 167).

Above these eroded walls, new walls were built without any regard for Egyptian convention (Fig. 20.4). In some places, as at Ashdod Area G, Stratum XIIIB, the builders filled in spaces next to and between a partially ruined Late Bronze Age building (Dothan and Porath 1993: 53). At Ashkelon, since a segment of the Egyptian wall was still standing, the new builders reinforced the remaining bricks and used the wall as an architectural element in their new constructions. However, just to the north, the architecture was entirely new: within the interior spaces defined by the new stone walls, a sequence of deliberately laid floors, each sealing the deposits below, marks the continuous use of these spaces.

The material culture of this phase is dramatically different from the preceding stratum. Phythian-Adams argued that this level should contain the earliest Philistine pottery, and in 1985 and 1986 a step trench supported his conclusions with the discovery of Myc IIIC pottery from the twelfth century BCE. These conclusions were published by Stager (1991, 1995) and formed the basis, along with the results from Ashdod XIIIB and Ekron VII, for his reconstruction of the chronology of the twelfth century. The more recent results, now exposed over an area of approximately three hundred and fifty square meters, support Stager's earlier chronological assertions (Stager 1995: 348, Summary 2–5).

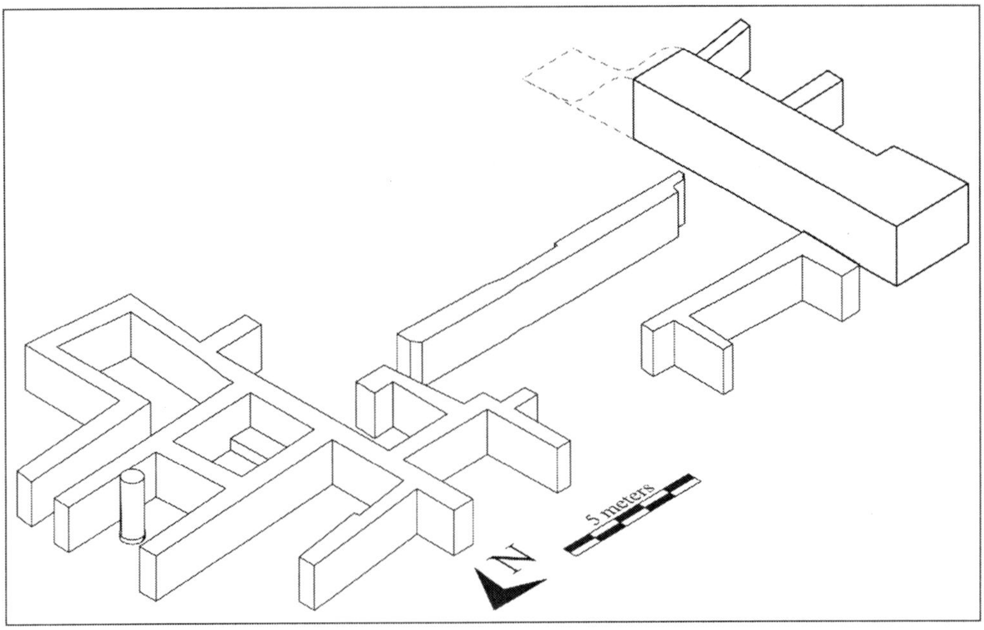

Figure 20.4. Reconstruction of *Grid 38*, Phase 20a. Courtesy of the Leon Levy Expedition to Ashkelon, reconstruction by G. Pierce.

Figure 20.5. Photo containing Mycenaean III C pottery.
Courtesy of the Leon Levy Expedition to Ashkelon, photo by D.M. Master.

The change in ceramic style from Phase 21 to Phase 20 is dramatic. The Egyptian styles and techniques were replaced by forms which follow the traditions of Late Bronze Age Canaanite Ashkelon. For much of the assemblage, the ceramic observations of Gezer Field II, Local Stratum 12 (overall Stratum XIV) can be echoed. The Ashkelon assemblage included 'ovoid storejars with more rounded bases', 'kraters with "T-rims" or sharply everted rims', 'cooking pots with the flanged rim', and 'carinated bowls with the "palm tree-and-panel" motif' (Dever *et al.* 1974: 51). Much of this assemblage also matches the non-Egyptian forms found in Lachish Stratum VI (Tufnell *et al.* 1958: Fig. 2:14-15, 17, 32-34; Ussishkin 1983: Figs. 15:8, 11-13; 16:7-17). In addition to pottery, finely carved ivories also have clear Canaanite parallels, even specific parallels in the Kerker hoard from the treasury of Megiddo Stratum VIIA.

But a new cultural trajectory appears alongside the Levantine (Fig. 20.5). Locally made shallow angular and bell-shaped bowls, rounded kraters with a ring base, kylixes, small cups, lids, stirrup jars, strainer jugs, and pyxides are new to the repertoire (Yasur-Landau, personal communication). In a few cases, precursors to these forms appeared in the Mycenaean imports' earlier strata, but in most cases the appearance of these Myc IIIC forms was without Late Bronze foundation. Simple monochrome bands are the most common decoration. But even the earliest stage in the Ashkelon assemblage contains some more elaborate decoration, including a variety of spiral motifs. It is not only distinctive fine wares which mark this stratum, Aegean-style cooking jugs and other forms not seen in the imported Mycenaean repertoire of the Late Bronze Age also appeared at Ashkelon—locally made—for the first time.

The Aegean-style cooking ware, which makes up roughly fifty percent of the total cooking pot assemblage, is indicative of new foodways. Preliminary zooarchaeological results show that for the first time pig appears as a substantial portion of the diet. And, once exploited, pig remained a part of the diet at Ashkelon throughout the Iron I period. In addition, dog bones with cut marks likely indicate canine consumption (Hesse, personal communication). While this is a rather rare practice, it has been noted in Crete by Snyder and Klippel (2003), who particularly describe the breakage and cutting necessary for the larger dogs to fit into smaller cooking jugs (p. 224). The details of bone records and the new smaller cooking jugs point to a new integrated foodway introduced without the predicate appearance of any of the individual elements.

There is significant evidence of industrial technology visible on the floors of the new buildings. Killebrew's studies (1998, 1999) show marked differences in clay exploitation and ceramic technology at Ekron. But perhaps one might argue that this was merely a technical leap forward as pottery techniques were diffused across the Mediterranean at the end of the thirteenth century (Sherratt 1998: 301-306). However, utilitarian explanations fail when applied to the changes in the weaving industry at Ashkelon. The perforated loomweight of Levantine looms and the newly introduced pinched spoolweight have no obvious functional difference: both come in variety of sizes; both seem to perform the same function equally well. Yet at Ashkelon we found 71 spoolweights on one floor and 52 on another; the perforated loomweight was replaced wholesale. Stager's assertions from more than a decade ago have been confirmed on a much larger scale; the inhabitants of this stratum simply did things like the early Iron Age inhabitants of Kition and Enkomi, like the earlier inhabitants of Tyrins, Pylos, or Mycenae (Stager 1991: 15).

The foodways, the industrial technology, and even much of the ceramic repertoire, appear fully developed from the beginning of this stratum. It is what Assaf Yasur-Landau has called 'deep change' (2002) and what Tristan Barako has demonstrated to be a migratory rather than mercantile phenomenon (2000). This stratum at Ashkelon is another vivid presentation of the migration of the Sea Peoples, particularly the Philistines, and their settlement in the southern Levant.

All of the material culture excavated from this stratum supports a date in the first half of the twelfth century (Fig. 20.3). The Levantine ceramics are stylistically similar to the assemblages at Lachish Stratum VI and Gezer Stratum XIV. While Lachish and Gezer have Egyptian forms not in the Ashkelon repertoire and Ashkelon has Aegean forms not at those cites, the Levantine ceramics that overlap are a close match. Ashkelon even has examples of the Anatolian Grey Ware that has been used to create a chronological separation between Lachish VI and the beginning of Myc IIIC in the southern Levant (Na'aman 2000). The Aegean-style ceramics (Myc IIIC) match the forms of Ashdod Stratum XIIIB, Locus 4106, and Ekron Stratum VII. As Dothan and Zukerman have recently shown, this assemblage parallels the Late Helladic IIIC Early or Early 2 and Late Cypriote IIIA. In terms of the stylistic subphasing of Ashkelon's forms, the decorative patterns are mostly linear. But complex decorative motifs, often judged to be slightly later, also appear in the earliest deposits (Dothan and Zukerman 2004: Table 2, 43; Yasur-Landau, personal communication).

One of the more important chronological clarifications which arose out of the renewed Lachish excavations was the observation that Philistine wares were not present in Lachish VI, and hence should be dated to after the collapse of the stratum (Ussishkin 1983, 1985). In 1985, Mazar and Stager independently observed that the Philistine assemblage should be subdivided into two distinct assemblages, first 'Myc IIIC' and then 'Philistine' (Mazar 1985a; Stager 1985). This important refinement strengthened Ussishkin's original conclusion since only the absence of the second phase of pottery at Lachish is notable in the first place. After all, no assemblages like the Myc IIIC assemblages at Ekron, Ashdod, and Ashkelon (and perhaps Tell Haror) exist anywhere in the Shephelah at any time, apart from a few stray sherds. No chronological shift of Myc IIIC will explain the absence of these assemblages at other sites because no matter when the Myc IIIC assemblages appear, they are still absent from every site outside the Philistine heartland. The oddity is that while Finkelstein has criticized Stager (1985) and Mazar's (1985a) sharp regional delineation of these forms, his own chronological shift does not solve the regional problem at all. Finkelstein ironically creates an odder, starker 'Pentapolis restriction' (Finkelstein 1996, 1998). If proposing a regional difference between Ashkelon *Grid 38*, Phase 20, and Lachish VI creates a problem, it is hardly solved by proposing an even more difficult regional difference between Ashkelon *Grid 38*, Phase 20, and Gezer XIII.

Figure 20.6. Scarab of Ramses III. Courtesy of the Leon Levy Expedition
to Ashkelon, photo by Z. Radovan.

In addition to the ceramic connections, excavations at Ashkelon revealed direct evidence for dating. Baruch Brandl identified a damaged Egyptian scarab found alongside the earliest Philistine material as bearing the name of Ramses III (Fig. 20.6). As at Lachish VI, this provides an important chronological datum for the onset of the Myc IIIC assemblage. While it is likely that this scarab is contemporary with the remains with which it was found, at the very least the Ramses III scarab provides a *terminus post quem* for the Iron I settlement at Ashkelon. This find places the onset of Myc IIIC at Ashkelon after the rough date of ca. 1200 (Sherratt [Chapter 9, this volume]), and relates the Ashkelon's settlement not only to long-term social and economic trends of the Mediterranean but also to the short-term political machinations that are part of a full-orbed human history. In that vein, this find reinforces the important link between the settlement observed in this region and the record of Sea People movement recorded in contemporary inscriptions by Ramses III (Bietak 1993).

The succeeding stratum at Ashkelon, Phase 19 (Fig. 20.7), is a fuller expression of the new cultural ideas that were first portrayed in Phase 20. The complete replacement of all earlier buildings allowed for the full architectural expression of the new affinities. For example, each interior room had a hearth at the center in typical Aegean fashion (Karageorghis 1998). Equid skull burials were placed in cairns to mark the new foundation. While not a new feature, it becomes more common. Other cultural features emerge such as the 'Ashdoda' figurines. And the ceramic repertoire continues to contain earlier Myc IIIC forms, now accompanied by Philistine Bichrome pottery as well.

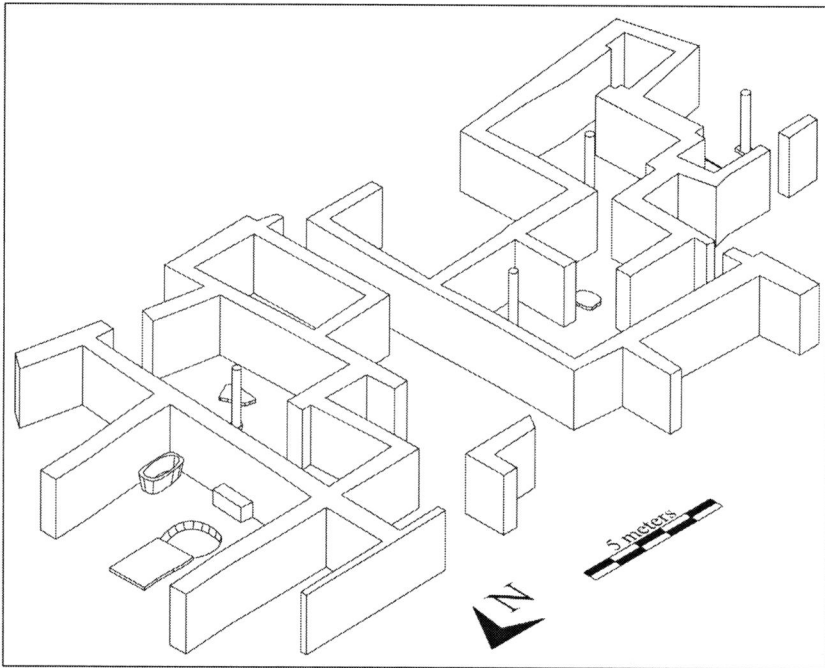

Figure 20.7. Reconstruction of *Grid 38*, Phase 19. Courtesy of the
Leon Levy Expedition to Ashkelon, reconstruction by G. Pierce.

These expressions parallel similar developments at Ashdod XIIIA–XII and Tel Miqne VI (Dothan and Zukerman 2004: 6, Table 2). The impression is one of strong continuity and development within a single trajectory. It is telling that among these cities of the southern coastal plain, we have found no Mediterranean imports. Certainly theirs was a land-based regional trade outside of the central Philistine cities, as evidenced by the relatively wide spread of Philistine Bichrome (Dothan 1982: Map 2). And perhaps, if the location of Tell Qasile is any indication (Mazar 1985b: 120), they engaged in local maritime trade. But unlike sites farther to the north, there is no direct indication of a connection to Cyprus or points west for some time (Barako 2000: Fig. 1, Table 1, 515-16).

Chronologically, the date of Phase 19 is not well anchored (Fig. 20.3). We rely on David Ussishkin's trenchant observation that the lack of Philistine Bichrome at Lachish Stratum VI strongly implies that this ceramic style only emerges following the collapse of Lachish Stratum VI (Mazar 1985a; Ussishkin 1983). This is a sound argument, since, unlike the earlier Myc IIIC pottery, Philistine Bichrome has a relatively wide distribution across the region.

At the end of this phase some of the early Philistine constructions collapsed. As often happens, the ruin next door took the whole neighborhood to seed, and what followed was a series of poorly planned industrial buildings (Fig. 20.8). A beautiful tub from an earlier phase was smashed to create pieces for a winepress; hovels, pits, and ash dot the area. But the features that first identified the Philistines as Aegean expatriates persist: a pictorial krater in Bichrome depicts Philistines in the distinctive headdress (Stager 1998: 164; Wobst 1977). A variety of hearths—round, square, and keyhole—recall the richness of these forms in Cyprus and the Aegean (Karageorghis 1998). An incised scapula, a stamp seal, and many 'Ashdoda'-type figurine fragments show a distinct cultural continuity. Alongside this distinctiveness, however, the red wash of the Iron I highlands becomes more prominent, and Levantine bread ovens appear alongside the hearths. Just as at Miqne V, Tell Qasile XI, or Ashdod XI, the process of acculturation to Levantine norms is eminently visible (Stone 1995).

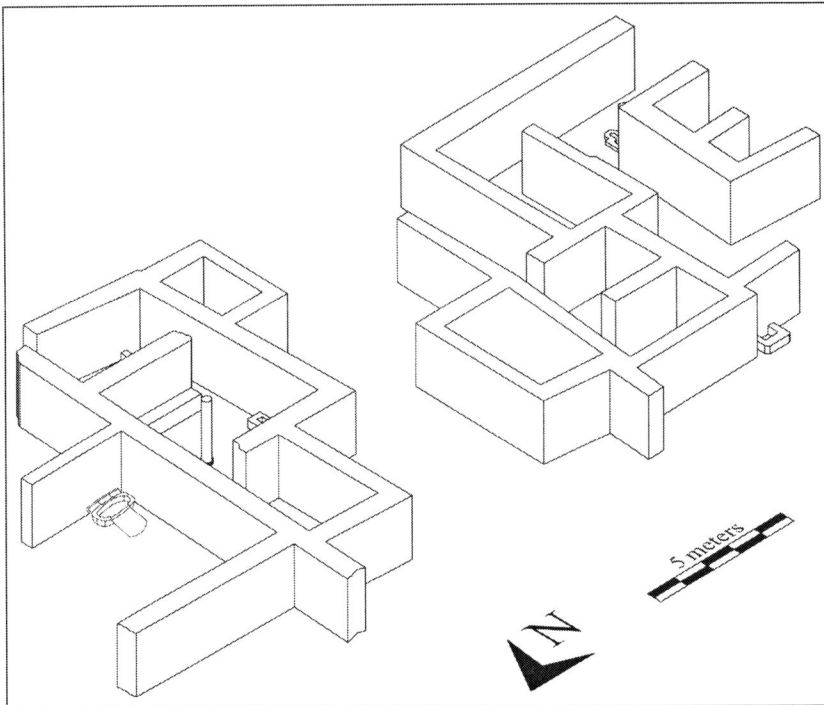

Figure **20.8.** Reconstruction of *Grid 38*, Phase 18a. Courtesy of the Leon Levy Expedition to Ashkelon, reconstruction by G. Pierce.

In the final Iron I phase (Fig. 20.9), the industry of the earlier period gave way to another well-planned residential area. Ceramically, Phase 17 begins with the white-slipped Philistine forms and concludes with red-slipped and burnished forms. The ceramic range is roughly equivalent to Miqne IV and Tell Qasile X (Mazar 1985b: Figs. 22–51).

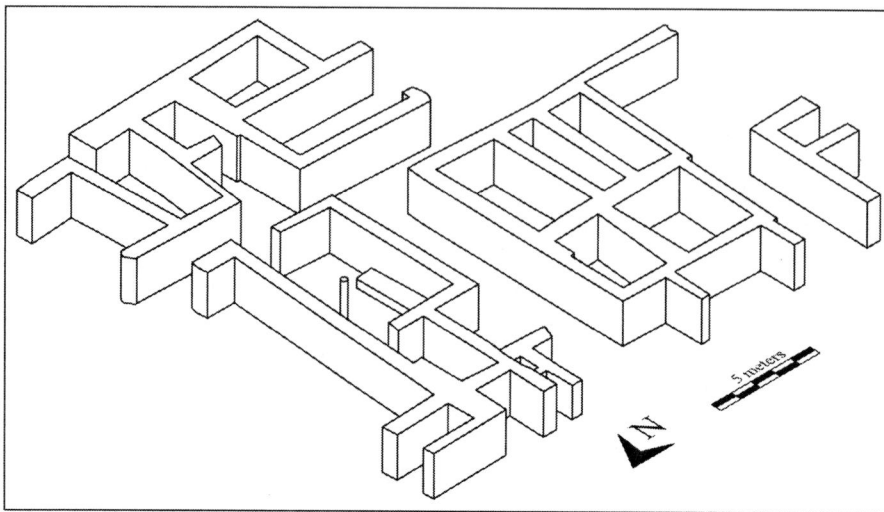

Figure 20.9. Reconstruction of *Grid 38*, Phase 17. Courtesy of the Leon Levy Expedition to Ashkelon, reconstruction by G. Pierce.

The characteristic cylindrical spool weights continued in use through Phase 17, nearly 200 years after the Sea Peoples settled the region. And a variety of iconic finds show continuity with previous forms even if the ceramic repertoire with its red-slipped and burnished forms became thoroughly Levantine.

It is not clear why Phase 17 ends, but it is followed by greatly diminished occupation in the major excavation areas of the central tell (fortifications along the northern tell of Ashkelon may persist until somewhat later). Diminished occupation at Ashkelon parallels the collapse of Miqne IV so closely that there must be a common explanation for the two sites. Just as at Miqne/Ekron, Ashkelon declines and reveals sparse remains until the end of the eighth century BCE.

While these results from the recent excavations of the Leon Levy Expedition are preliminary, with further ceramic and radiocarbon analysis to follow, even at this early stage the results for the earliest Philistine settlement mirror the stratigraphic and chronological results of the excavations at Ashdod, Ekron, and Tell Qasile (Dothan and Zukerman 2004; Mazar 1985a, 1985b; Stager 1995). The later strata, however, have few specific chronological parameters in the eleventh and tenth centuries BCE. As we continue our work with our scientific partners and pursue the results that radiocarbon can generate, we hope to be able to add new chronological dimensions to this rich Iron I sequence uncovered by the Leon Levy expedition to Ashkelon.

Acknowledgments

This report appears courtesy of the Leon Levy Expedition to Ashkelon directed by Lawrence E. Stager. I am grateful to Larry Stager for his help and collaboration. Special thanks are due to Adam Aja and Assaf Yasur-Landau who, along with the author, directed excavation of the twelfth century remains and to Elizabeth Bloch-Smith whose careful excavations (1985–90; 1997–99) provided the foundation for this study.

References

Baker, J. (2003) The Middle and Late Bronze Age Tomb Complex at Ashkelon, Israel: The Architecture and the Funeral Kit (Doctoral dissertation, Brown University).

Barako, T. (2000) The Philistine Settlement as Mercantile Phenomenon? *American Journal of Archaeology* 104: 513-30.

Bietak, M. (1993) The Sea Peoples and the End of Egyptian Administration in Canaan. In *Biblical Archaeology Today, 1990: Proceedings of the Second International Congress on Biblical Archaeology*, edited by A. Biran and J. Aviram (Jerusalem: Israel Exploration Society): 292-306.

Dever, W.G., *et al.* (1974) *Gezer II: Report of the 1967–1970 Seasons in Field I and II* (Jerusalem: Hebrew Union College).

Dothan, T. (1982) *The Philistines and Their Material Culture* (Jerusalem: Israel Exploration Society).

—(1993) Deir el-Balah. In *The New Encyclopedia of Archaeological Excavations in the Holy Land*, edited by E. Stern (New York: Simon & Schuster): 343-47.

Dothan, M., and Y. Porath (1993) *Ashdod V: Excavation of Area G. The Fourth–Sixth Seasons of Excavations 1968–1970* ('Atiqot 23; Jerusalem: Israel Antiquities Authority).

Dothan, T., and A. Zukerman (2004) A Preliminary Study of the Myccenaean IIIC:1 Pottery Assemblages from Tel Miqne-Ekron and Ashdod. *BASOR* 333: 1-54.

Finkelstein, I. (1996) The Archaeology of the United Monarchy: An Alternative View. *Levant* 28: 177-87.

—(1998) Philistine Chronology: High, Middle, or Low? In *Mediterranean Peoples in Transition*, edited by S. Gitin, A. Mazar, and E. Stern (Jerusalem: Israel Exploration Society): 140-47.

Higginbotham, C. (2000) *Egyptianization and Elite Emulation in Ramesside Palestine: Governance and Accommodation on the Imperial Periphery* (Leiden: Brill).

Karageorghis, V. (1998) Hearths and Bathtubs in Cyprus: A 'Sea Peoples' Innovation? In *Mediterranean Peoples in Transition*, edited by S. Gitin, A. Mazar, and E. Stern (Jerusalem: Israel Exploration Society): 276-82.

Killebrew, A. (1998) Ceramic Typology and Technology of the Late Bronze II and Iron I Assemblages from Tel Miqne-Ekron: The Transition from Canaanite to Philistine Culture. In *Mediterranean Peoples in Transition*, edited by S. Gitin, A. Mazar, and E. Stern (Jerusalem: Israel Exploration Society): 379-405.

—(1999) Late Bronze and Iron I Cooking Pots in Canaan: A Typological, Technological and Functional Study. In *Archaeology, History and Culture in Palestine and the Near East: Essays in Memory of Albert E. Glock*, edited by T. Kapitan (Atlanta: Scholars Press): 83-126.

Loud, G. (1939) *The Megiddo Ivories* (OIP 52; Chicago: The University of Chicago Press).

Mackenzie, D. (1913. The Philistine City of Askelon. *PEQ* 45:8–23.

Mazar, A. (1985a) The Emergence of Philistine Material Culture. *IEJ* 35: 95-107.

—(1985b) *Excavations at Tell Qasile, Part Two* (Qedem 12; Jerusalem: Hebrew University).

Na'aman, N. (2000) The Contribution of Trojan Grey Ware from Lachish and Tel Miqne-Ekron to the Chronology of the Philistine Monochrome Period. *BASOR* 317:1-7.

Phythian-Adams, W. (1923) Report on the Stratification of Askalon. *PEQ* 55:60–84.

Sherratt, S. (1998) 'Sea Peoples' and the Economic Structure of the Late Second Millennium in the Eastern Mediterranean. In *Mediterranean Peoples in Transition*, edited by S. Gitin, A. Mazar, and E. Stern (Jerusalem: Israel Exploration Society): 292-313.

Snyder, L., and W. Klippel (2003) From Lerna to Kastro: Further Thoughts on Dog as Food in Ancient Greece; Perceptions, Prejudices, and Reinvestigations. In *Zooarchaeology in Greece: Recent Advances*, edited by E. Kotjabopolulou, P. Halstead, C. Gamble, and P. Elefant (London: British School at Athens): 221-31.

Stager, L.E. (1985) Merenptah, Israel and the Sea Peoples: New Light on an Old Relief. *Eretz-Israel* 18: *56-*64.

—(1991) When Canaanites and Philistines Ruled Ashkelon. *BAR* 17.2: 24-43.

—(1995) The Impact of the Sea Peoples (1185–1050 BCE). In *The Archaeology of Society in the Holy Land*, edited by T. Levy (New York: Facts on File): 332-48.

—(1998) Forging an Identity: The Emergence of Ancient Israel. In *The Oxford History of the Biblical World*, edited by M. Coogan (Oxford: Oxford University Press): 123-76.

Stone, B.J. (1995) The Philistines and Acculturation: Culture Change and Ethnic Continuity in the Iron Age. *BASOR* 298: 7-32.

Tufnell, O., *et al.* (1958) *Lachish III: The Iron Age* (London: Oxford University Press).

Ussishkin, D. (1983) Excavations at Lachish 1978–1983: Second Preliminary Report. *Tel Aviv* 10: 97-75.

—(1985) Levels VII and VI at Lachish and the End of the Late Bronze Age in Canaan. In *Palestine in the Bronze and Iron Ages: Papers in Honor of Olga Tufnell*, edited by J.N. Tubb (London: Institute of Archaeology): 211-30.

Wobst, H.M. (1977) Stylistic Behaviour and Information Exchange. In *For the Director: Research Essays in Honor of James B. Griffin*, edited by C.E. Cleland (Museum of Anthropology Paper 61; Ann Arbor: University of Michigan): 317-42.

Yasur-Landau, A. (2002) Social Aspects of Aegean Settlement in the Southern Levant in the end of the 2nd Millennium BCE (Doctoral dissertation, Tel Aviv University).

Yurko, F. (1986) Merenptah's Canaanite Campaign. *Journal of the American Research Center in Egypt* 23: 189-215.

21 Desert Settlement through the Iron Age

Radiocarbon dates from Sinai and the Negev Highlands

Hendrik J. Bruins and Johannes van der Plicht

Abstract

Iron Age desert settlements in the Negev Highlands and the adjacent area of north-eastern Sinai are still enigmatic. Various theories have been developed to explain these settlements, particularly concerning the majority of the fortresses that are built in an elliptical or irregular shape. Chronology is obviously a crucial factor in archaeological theory-building. The time factor in Levantine Iron Age archaeology used to be like pottery clay that could be moulded to suit various theories. Radiocarbon dating, notwithstanding its limitations, provides an independent and scientific basis for chronology, though quality control is essential. Radiocarbon dates are presented from Iron Age strata at Tell el-Qudeirat in north-eastern Sinai, and from Nahal Ha'Elah and Horvat Haluqim in the Negev Highlands. Our main conclusion is that the establishment of the elliptical fortresses and related settlements appears to predate the Solomonic period.

Introduction

There are many remains of Iron Age settlements in the hilly desert of the Central Negev and adjacent area of north-eastern Sinai. Detailed archaeological surveys in part of the region have so far uncovered about 350 Iron Age sites, containing 58 fortresses, 1195 dwelling structures, 360 animal pens, many cisterns, 30 threshing floors and 80 silos dug into the ground, as reported by Haiman (1994). The climate of the region is arid; the average annual rainfall ranges from about 125 mm in the north to 75 mm in the south (Bruins 1986).

Geoarchaeological excavations at the site of Horvat Haluqim proved beyond doubt the existence of rainwater-harvesting agriculture in the Iron Age (Bruins and van der Plicht 2004). This was to be expected, as the region is too arid for normal rainfed farming. The many threshing floors and silos (Haiman 1994), if indeed dating to the Iron Age, are evidence of ancient farming that could only have been conducted successfully through irrigation by runoff rainwater, received from the surrounding catchments, arrested on each field by built terrace walls across the wadi. Wheat and barley require some 300 mm of rainfall to produce a reasonable yield and fruit trees even more. Only runoff water supply from local catchments could add sufficient water in addition to the low amounts (ca. 100 mm) of direct rainfall on the fields, in order to reach moisture levels in the soil comparable to 300–500 mm a year (Bruins 2003).

The age of these Iron Age settlements, particularly the date and character of the fortresses, are controversial issues. A detailed review was given by Cohen (1986), who interpreted most sites to have been short-lived within the 10th century BCE: established during the reign of King Solomon and destroyed by Pharaoh Shishak (Cohen 1980; Cohen and Cohen-Amin 2004). A similar interpretation was given by Haiman (1994), who dated all Iron Age sites in the surveys to Iron Age II in cultural terms, to the United Monarchy in political terms, and to the period 975–925 BCE in chronological terms. All settlements came to an end with the Shishak campaign. Other viewpoints, based on ceramic, architectural and Biblical considerations, range from about the 13th to the 7th centuries BCE. Most scholars considered the sites to be Israelite in one way or another, but Rothenberg (1967, 1972, 1988) and Finkelstein (1984, 1988) suggested a non-Israelite origin of these settlements.

An early date was proposed by Rothenberg (1967, 1972, 1988, 1999) on the basis of his extensive excavations at Timna. Besides Egyptian and Midianite pottery, Negev-ware (Negbite) pottery was also found in the Timna excavations, dating on Egyptian evidence from the late 14th to the 12th centuries (Ramesside): 'We are led to suggest that these local inhabitants of the Arabah and the Negev are the Amalekites mentioned in the Biblical narrative' (Rothenberg 1988: 276). Following a hiatus, represented by wind-blown loess deposition, the Egyptians returned to Timna during the 10th–9th centuries BCE (22nd Dynasty), as Timna Layer I yielded pottery vessels of the 22nd Dynasty, as well as Negbite ware, but no Midianite ceramics. This return of the Egyptians is related by Rothenberg (1999: 163) to the campaign by Pharaoh Shishak in ca. 920 BCE.

Aharoni considered these settlements of Israelite origin, ranging from the 10th to the 7th centuries BCE (Aharoni 1967). He changed his interpretation in a later publication (Aharoni 1978), suggesting that the settlements were established by Saul in relation to his wars with the Amalekites in the 11th century BCE. Herzog (1983) proposed an association of the Central Negev sites with the settlement of the tribe of Simeon, suggesting a date in the 11th century BCE. Meshel (1979) considered both the 11th and 10th centuries BCE as options, relating the fortresses possibly to Saul or David. However, both Meshel and Goren (1992) emphasize the basic problem of dating the fortresses and the lack of unambiguous criteria.

Finkelstein (1984, 1988) proposed a nomadic origin of these settlements, established by local desert tribes. These nomadic goat–sheep pastoralists became sedentary, in his view, due to supposed economic changes in the south, related to a revival of mining activity at Timna and prosperous Philistine centres along the southern coastal plain and the Shephelah. Finkelstein (1984, 1988) dated the settlements in the Negev Highlands to Iron Age I in cultural terms and to the 11th and early 10th centuries BCE in chronological terms.

It is clear that the use of ceramics and other archaeological criteria for dating Iron Age settlements in the Central Negev is problematic, enabling a wide range of scholarly opinion and a wide time range. The matter was summed up succinctly by Barkay (1992: 324): 'It is difficult to reach a conclusion concerning the fortresses, as their interpretation depends on their dating, and their dating involves serious difficulties. In many studies, scholars appear to be caught up in a circular argument, in which the dating is based on the general interpretation given to the fortress phenomenon and is in turn used to support the proposed interpretation of the character of the fortresses'.

What about radiocarbon dating in the region concerning the Iron Age? Bruins (1986) initiated research in the early 1980s in the Tell el-Qudeirat area in north-eastern Sinai (Fig. 21.1), but focussed mainly on geoarchaeological issues. Nevertheless, some ^{14}C results from the tell did *not* support a 10th-century BCE date for the Early Fortress, which appears to be older. The differences found here between radiocarbon dating and archaeological age assessment in the Iron Age convinced us of the necessity to establish an independent radiocarbon chronology for Near Eastern historical archaeology, particularly for the Bronze and Iron Ages (Bruins and Mook 1989). The

17th International Radiocarbon Conference held in Israel in 2000, on the initiative of Israel Carmi of the Weizmann Institute of Science, stimulated further interaction between Near Eastern archaeology and ^{14}C dating (Bruins, Carmi and Boaretto [eds.] 2001).

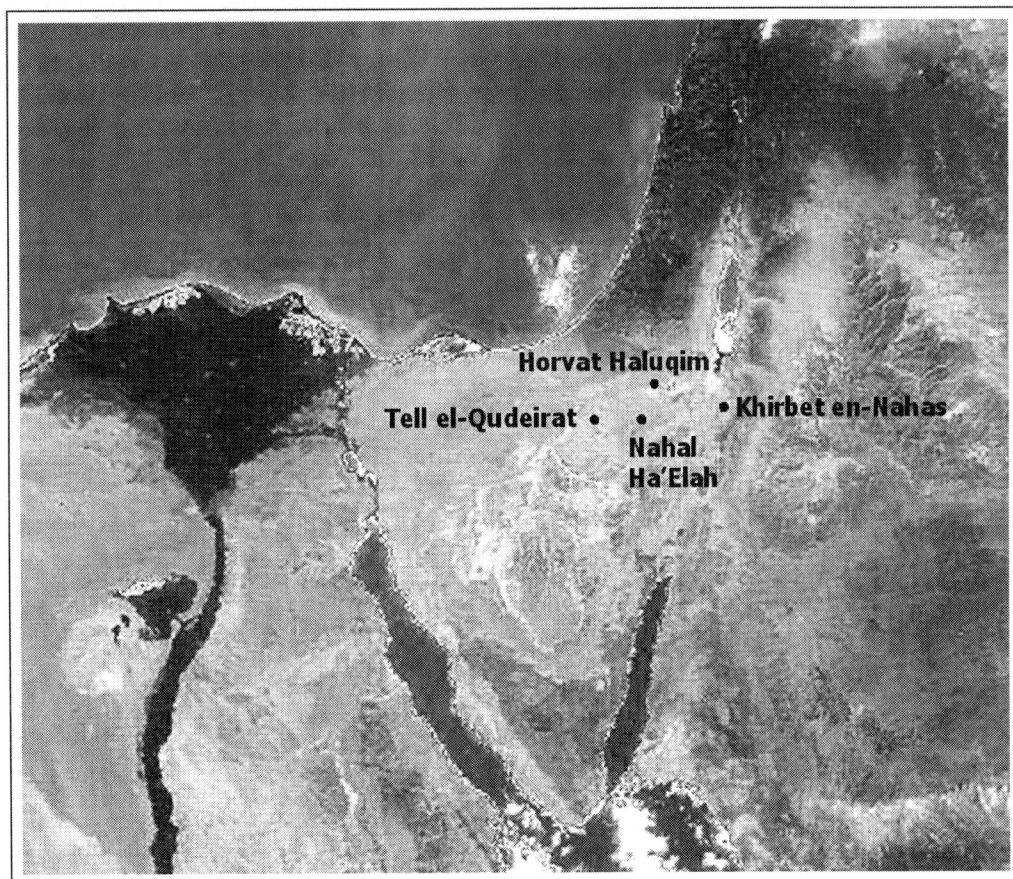

Figure 21.1. Location map of Tell el-Qudeirat, Nahal Ha'Elah, Horvat Haluqim and Khirbet en-Nahas based on a satellite image of 6 April 1998.

Ceramics undoubtedly carry the mark of time, but this mark should be established by independent dating (van der Plicht and Bruins 2001; Bruins, van der Plicht and Mazar 2003a; Mazar *et al.* [Chapter 13, this volume]). Moreover, some ceramic types, such as Negbite ware cannot be easily defined in time by traditional archaeological approaches. Perhaps also other pottery types may cover longer time spans than perceived.

An archaeological investigation involving radiocarbon dating on the eastern side of the Arabah Valley was conducted by Levy *et al.* (2004) in the ancient mining district of Faynan (Biblical Edom) at Khirbat en-Nahas, which is the largest Iron Age copper-smelting site in the southern Levant. Hitherto it was assumed that Iron Age settlement in the region, as well as the establishment of the Kingdom of Edom, occurred in the 8th–6th centuries BCE. However, the ^{14}C dates from Khirbat en-Nahas give evidence of Iron Age occupation already in the early Iron Age (ca. 1200–1000 BCE) and also in the 10th–9th centuries BCE. It is important to compare these ^{14}C dates from neighbouring south-western Jordan with the dates from Sinai and the Negev, presented in the current article.

The radiocarbon dates from Iron Age strata in north-eastern Sinai and the Central Negev were measured at the University of Groningen (Table 21.1). All samples were pre-treated with the acid/alkali/acid (AAA) method (Mook and Waterbolk 1985). The purified organic matter of each sample was subsequently converted into CO_2. Conventional radiometry of the CO_2 gas was conducted by Proportional Gas Counter (PGC). The samples from north-eastern Sinai were all measured in the 1980s by PGC, as the Accelerator Mass Spectrometry (AMS) facility in Groningen was not established until 1994. Recent small samples from Horvat Haluqim were dated by AMS. The CO_2 gas derived from those samples underwent additional treatment to convert it into solid graphite to enable AMS measurement (van der Plicht *et al.* 2000).

Table 21.1. Iron Age radiocarbon dates from north-eastern Sinai and the Central Negev.

Site and Stratigraphy	Material	Lab. code	^{14}C date BP	$\delta^{13}C$ ‰	Calibrated date BCE 1σ range	Calibrated date BCE 2σ range
Tell el-Qudeirat Upper Fortress grains in jar	Charred cereal grains	GrN-15551	2515 ± 15	–21.93	780–772 (4.3%) 766–760 (4.0%) 681–666 (10.9%) 634–591 (34.2%) 578–557 (14.7%)	788–757 (15.1%) 697–658 (16.5%) 649–542 (63.8%)
Tell el-Qudeirat Upper Fortress destruction layer	Charcoal	GrN-12329	2535 ± 50	–22.89	796–758 (17.9%) 685–660 (9.9%) 647–542 (40.4%)	803–515 (92.8%) 464–450 (1.5%) 440–428 (1.2%)
Tell el-Qudeirat Middle Fortress destruction layer	Charcoal	GrN-11948	2740 ± 110	–23.42	1020–798 (68.2%)	1259–1232 (1.0%) 1217–758 (91.3%) 581–544 (1.2%)
Tell el-Qudeirat Lower Fortress destruction layer	Charcoal	GrN-12330	2930 ± 30	–22.53	1210–1200 (5.5%) 1191–1177 (8.1%) 1162–1141 (12.7%) 1131–1107 (13.3%) 1103–1050 (28.6%)	1258–1235 (6.5%) 1215–1016 (88.9%)
Nahal Ha'Elah fortress	Charcoal in casemate room	GrN-15552	2840 ± 15	–22.39	1006–972 (46.2%) 957–940 (22.0%)	1043–1028 (4.7%) 1023–969 (57.7%) 961–923 (33.0%)
Horvat Haluqim Terraced field WE-13 Anthropogenic soil layer	Sheep/goat bone	GrA-14398	2860 ± 40	–20.00	1124–1121 (0.9%) 1111–1099 (4.7%) 1080–1061 (7.5%) 1052–971 (45.7%) 958–938 (9.4%)	1189–1179 (1.9%) 1154–1142 (1.5%) 1129–915 (92.0%)
Horvat Haluqim Terraced field WE-13 Anthropogenic soil layer	Charcoal	GrA-12448	2590 ± 60	–17.75	828–759 (41.2%) 682–666 (6.6%) 634–591 (14.1%) 578–557 (6.4%)	896–875 (1.8%) 842–519 (93.6%)

Tell el-Qudeirat Fortresses

Woolley and Lawrence (1914–15) suggested associating the relatively well-watered area of Tell el-Qudeirat in north-eastern Sinai with Biblical Kadesh Barnea, the main place of sojournment of the ancient Israelites in the desert following the Exodus from Egypt (Figs. 21.1, 2). Though many scholars have accepted the above suggestion, there is so far no independent evidence to confirm this viewpoint. The extensive excavations by Cohen (1980, 1981a, 1981b, 1983, 1986, 1993a) uncovered three different Iron Age fortresses at the tell, which followed each other in time.

Geoarchaeological research by Bruins (1986) showed that the fortresses were established on a firm natural foundation: a Pleistocene deposit composed of slightly cemented coarse gravel and rounded boulders up to 40 cm in diameter. Similar deposits in the area contained Middle Palaeolithic discoid cores (Goldberg 1984). Prior to the building of the oldest fortress, the stony Pleistocene deposits probably appeared as a slightly elevated hillock rising just above the general level of the valley plain, which at this point is 164 m wide. This geomorphic surface provided a logical choice and firm foundation for the site-location of the successive fortresses in the valley of Wadi el-Qudeirat, as floods during the rainy winter season sometimes cover the entire width of the valley (Bruins 1986).

Figure 21.2. View of Tell el-Qudeirat looking SSW across the width of the valley (photo by H.J. Bruins 1981).

The Upper Fortress

Dothan (1965) excavated a small part of the upper fortress in 1956. He dated the construction of the fortress to the 9th century BCE and its violent destruction to the Babylonian military campaign of the early 6th century BCE (Fig. 21.2). Cohen (1981a, 1983, 1993a) discovered the more complex situation that the Upper Fortress was built on the remains of the Middle Fortress. Cohen (1981a, 1983, 1993a) suggested dating the construction of the Upper Fortress to King Josiah ca. 640–609 BCE, and its destruction to the Babylonian onslaught, possibly coinciding with the destruction of Jerusalem and the First Temple in 586 BCE.

The uppermost destruction layer in the centre of the tell was exhibited clearly in the western profile of Square K-67. The black layer was situated at a depth of 50 cm below the surface of the tell. A sample of fine powdery charcoal mixed with soil was taken from this destruction layer by one of us (H.B.) in December 1981 in cooperation with Cohen, who considered this layer to represent the destruction of the Upper Fortress. The sample was measured in Groningen and yielded a radiocarbon date of 2535 ± 50 BP (GrN-12329).

The calibrated age relates to one of the most problematic sections of the calibration curve (Fig. 21.3), as the historical timescale of about 780–420 BCE (x-axis) corresponds to the same BP date on the radiocarbon timescale (y-axis), around 2500 BP. The calibrated date of GrN-12329 in the 1σ range is 796–758 (17.9%), 685–660 (9.9%), 647–542 (40.4%) BCE and the 2σ range is 803–515 (92.8%), 464–450 (1.5%), 440–428 (1.2%) BCE. This result is quite meaningful, because the highest relative probability (40.4%) in the 1σ range is in the period 647–542 BCE, which fits well with the period of the wars between Egypt (Pharaoh Necho II, 610–595 BCE) and the Babylonians (Nebuchadnezzar II, 604–562 BCE), in which Judah became involved, eventually leading to its destruction in 586 BCE. There are several correlations and synchronisms between Biblical and historical textual data concerning this period (Finegan 1979).

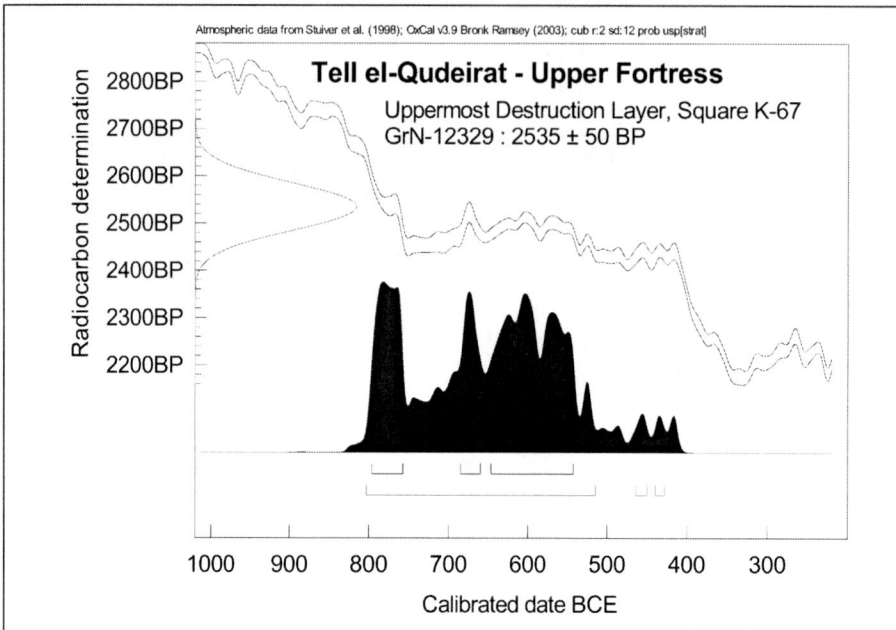

Figure 21.3. Dating of the uppermost destruction layer in Square K-67, related to the destruction of the Upper Fortress, based on fine charcoal.

The southern casemate room in the western side of the Upper Fortress yielded five complete storage jars in a thick ash layer. One of the jars was full of charred cereal grains (Cohen 1983). The sample received for radiocarbon dating (Square P5, Locus 523) was large enough for high-precision dating in the large PGC counter, resulting in a date for the charred cereals of 2515 ± 15 BP (GrN-15551, Fig. 21.4). Notice how well these two BP dates of destruction layers from different parts of the Upper Fortress agree with one another: the results overlap within 1σ. The charred cereal grains from a jar are 20 midpoint BP years younger than the powdery charcoal, which shows that the fine charcoal in the latter destruction layer is also rather short-lived. The 1σ calibrated date of the cereal grains is 780–772 (4.3%), 766–760 (4.0%), 681–666 (10.9%), 634–591 (34.2%), 578–557 (14.7%) BCE and the 2σ range is 788–757 (15.1%), 697–658 (16.5%), 649–542 (63.8%) BCE.

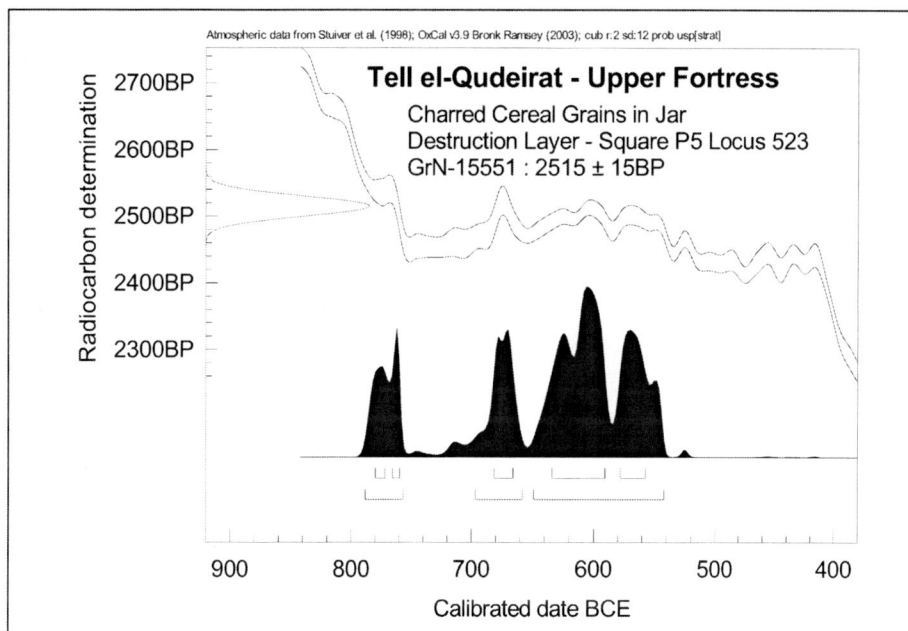

Figure 21.4. Dating of a destruction layer in Square P-5, related to the destruction of the Upper Fortress, based on charred cereal grains found inside a jar.

The calibrated 2σ results usually show less detail than the 1σ calibrated date. The period 649–542 BCE has the highest relative probability (63.8%) in the former range. However, the high-precision BP date results in five possible calibrated periods in the 1σ range, due to the plateau and wiggles in the calibration curve. Notice that the period 591–578 BCE is excluded in the 1σ calibrated date, due to a small wiggle (Fig. 21.4). This result is perhaps significant, because it leaves out the date 586 BCE, during which Nebuchadnezzar destroyed Jerusalem and the First Temple. The period 634–591 BCE has the highest relative probability (34.2%) in the 1σ range, which would favour, in fact, the destruction of the Upper Fortress at Tell el-Qudeirat in north-eastern Sinai during the earlier military campaign of the Babylonians, as they marched to Egypt in 601 or 600 BCE, according to Finegan (1979: 126).

The Middle Fortress

The outline of the Middle Fortress was similar to the Upper Fortress with a rectangular ground plan of ca. 60 × 40 m and eight protruding towers (Cohen 1983, 1993a, 1993b). The remains of the 4 m thick broad solid walls of the Middle Fortress were preserved to a height of about 1.80 m. An earthen rampart surrounded the fortress, resting on a revetment wall, 2.5 m high, which was completely excavated along the eastern side of the fortress (Cohen 1983, 1993a, 1993b).

A black ash layer was found on the eastern side in Square Q-9, sloping down from the revetment wall (Wall 207) at 12° towards the east. The black ash layer touches the revetment wall at a level of 18.96 m, which is about 60 cm above its base level of 18.35 m. The ash layer, ca. 10 cm thick, formed the ancient surface on top of a layer of fine yellowish-brown loessial sediment, about 60 cm thick, overlying the Pleistocene gravel deposits that also form the foundation for the revetment wall. The dark ash layer, a former living floor just east of the eastern revetment wall, seems to signify a destruction event that postdates the construction of the Middle Fortress on stratigraphic grounds. If the revetment wall was built later than the formation of this destruction layer, a direct stratigraphic contact between the two would have been virtually impossible. It would have been necessary to remove part of the destruction layer and dig down to the gravel deposits to build the first course of the revetment wall. However, the direct stratigraphic contact is evidence that the destruction layer postdates the building of the revetment wall.

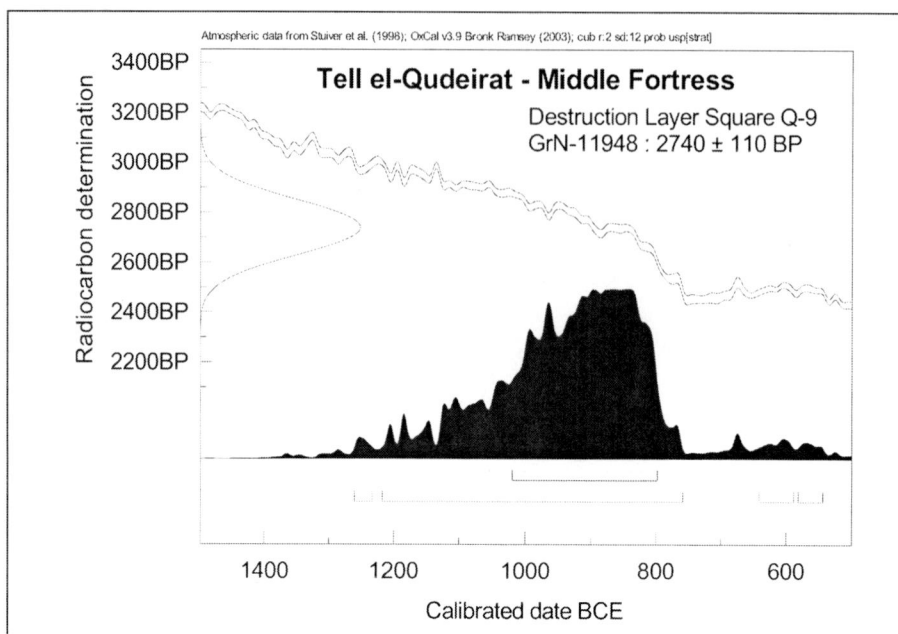

Figure 21.5. Dating of a destruction layer in Square Q-9, probably related to the destruction of the Middle Fortress, based on fine charcoal.

A sample for radiocarbon dating was taken by Bruins (1981) from this ash layer at a level of 18.73 m and at a distance of 80 cm east from the revetment wall. The amount of fine charcoal was comparatively small, and the AMS facility in Groningen had not yet been established. Hence, the PGC date (GrN-11948) had a rather large standard deviation: 2740 ± 110 BP (Fig. 21.5). The result of the 1σ calibrated age range is 1020–798 (68.2%) BCE. The 2σ age range is very wide: 1259–1232 (1.0%), 1217–758 (91.3%), 642–588 (1.9%), 581–544 (1.2%) BCE. The relevant 1σ result, indicating the narrowest time range with the highest relative probability, covers both the 10th and 9th centuries BCE. Cohen suggested that the Middle Fortress was built during the time of King Uzziah, ca. 769–733 BCE, and destroyed towards the end of the reign of Manasseh (ca. 698–642 BCE). The above radiocarbon date is clearly older, by about 150 to 200 years.

The Lower Fortress
The oldest archaeological remains discovered at Tell el-Qudeirat were found at a depth of about 5 m below the surface of the mound. The Lower Fortress had an elliptical ground plan, about 27 m in diameter, with casemate rooms around a central courtyard. In addition, several buildings and silos were found to the west of the fortress. Many types of pottery vessels were found in the ash covered floors of the casemate rooms (Cohen 1983, 1993a). The excavator (Cohen 1980, 1983, 1993a) suggested that the Lower Fortress was established during the reign of Solomon and destroyed in the course of Pharaoh Shishak's campaign, all in the 10th century BCE.

The western profile of Square K-67 in the centre of tell el-Qudeirat, which exhibited the uppermost destruction layer 50 cm below the surface of the tell, also exposed the lowermost destruction layer at a depth of about 5 m. A sample of fine powdery charcoal mixed with soil was taken from this destruction layer by the first author, again in 1981, in cooperation with Cohen, who considered this layer to represent the destruction of the Lower Fortress. The dark ash layer, about 10 cm thick, covered a 20 cm thick layer of loessial soil, also containing a few pieces of charcoal, indicating past human activity predating the dark ash layer. Below the loessial soil lies a 'virgin' layer of fine gravel mixed with sandy loam (Bruins 1986).

The fine charcoal sample from the ash layer was measured in Groningen and yielded a radiocarbon date of 2930 ± 30 BP (GrN-12330, Fig. 21.6). The 1σ calibrated age ranges are 1210–1200 (5.5%), 1191–1177 (8.1%), 1162–1141 (12.7%), 1131–1107 (13.3%), 1103–1050 (28.6%) BCE. The 2σ calibrated ages are 1258–1235 (6.5%), 1215–1016 (88.9%) BCE. The most probable calibrated age range of 1103–1050 BCE would place the destruction layer in the first half of the 11th century BCE, which is about 150 years older than the suggested destruction, according to Cohen, by Shishak around 925 BCE. Alternative ^{14}C dating options, albeit of lower relative probability, include the 12th century and even the 13th century BCE, while the 11th century BCE is the youngest possible date in the 2σ range. A possible old-wood effect of the charcoal is unlikely to move the date into the first half of the 10th century BCE, as this would require a lowering of the date by about 150 BP years. It was shown from the Upper Fortress at Tell el-Qudeirat that the difference between charred seeds and fine charcoal can be quite small, that is, only 20 BP years!

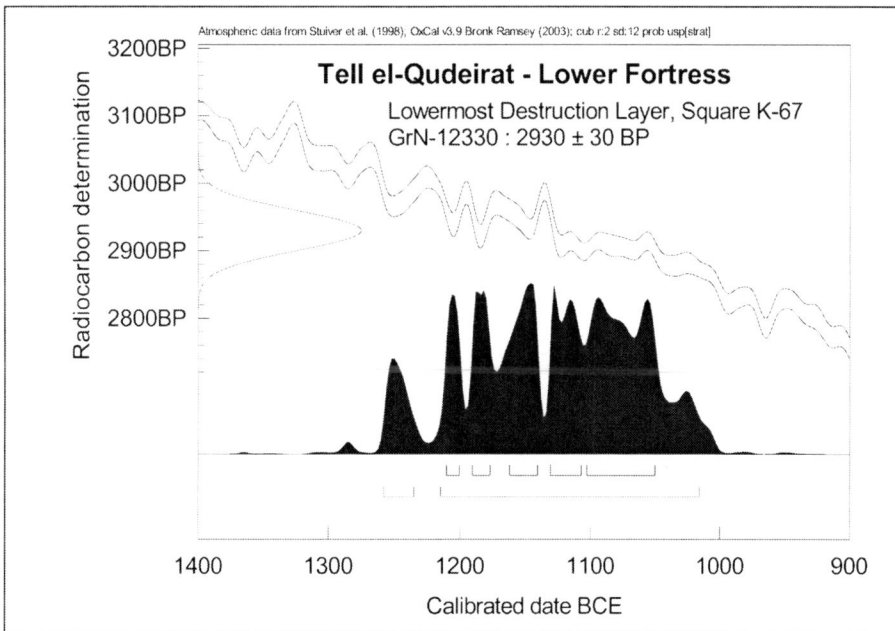

Figure 21.6. Dating of the lowermost destruction layer in Square K-67, probably related to the destruction of the Lower Fortress, based on fine charcoal.

Nahal Ha'Elah Fortress

The site lies about 13 km north-west of the modern town of Mizpe Ramon and about 10 km due north of the Makhtesh Ramon cirque (Fig. 21.1). The fortress is located on a lofty hill (685 m) west of nahal Ha'Elah (nahal is the Hebrew word for a dry stream valley or wadi). A cistern is situated eastwards below the fortress, above the western bank of nahal Ha'Elah. Hillside conduit channels carried runoff water to the cistern. Remnants of an Iron Age settlement, consisting of 10 structures, including a 4-room house and single room dwellings, are situated 1 km north of the fortress (Cohen 1986).

Excavations at the fortress were conducted in 1983 by Cohen (1986, 1993b). The fortress has an elliptical shape, being 34 m long and 20 m wide. It consists of 13 casemate rooms and a gate, surrounding a central courtyard. The walls of local hard limestone were found to be 0.60 to 0.90 m wide, based on bedrock and still standing to a height of 1.50 m. Many of the casemate rooms were excavated, often showing a thin ash layer. Cohen (1986, 1993b) dated the fortress and its destruction to the 10th century BCE. A large sample of fine charcoal (28.6 g) was given by Cohen for radiocarbon dating, derived from one of the casemate rooms (Locus 1235/64). The weight of the sample was sufficient for high-precision measurement with PGC, yielding a date of 2840 ± 15 BP (GrN-15552, Fig. 21.7). The 1σ calibrated age is 1006–972 (46.2%), 957–940 (22.0%) BCE and the 2σ calibrated age is 1043–1028 (4.7%), 1023–969 (57.7%), 961–923 (33.0%) BCE. The date seems too old for association with the Shishak campaign (ca. 920 BCE), as favoured by Cohen (1980). But uncertainty regarding a possible old-wood age of the charcoal requires caution.

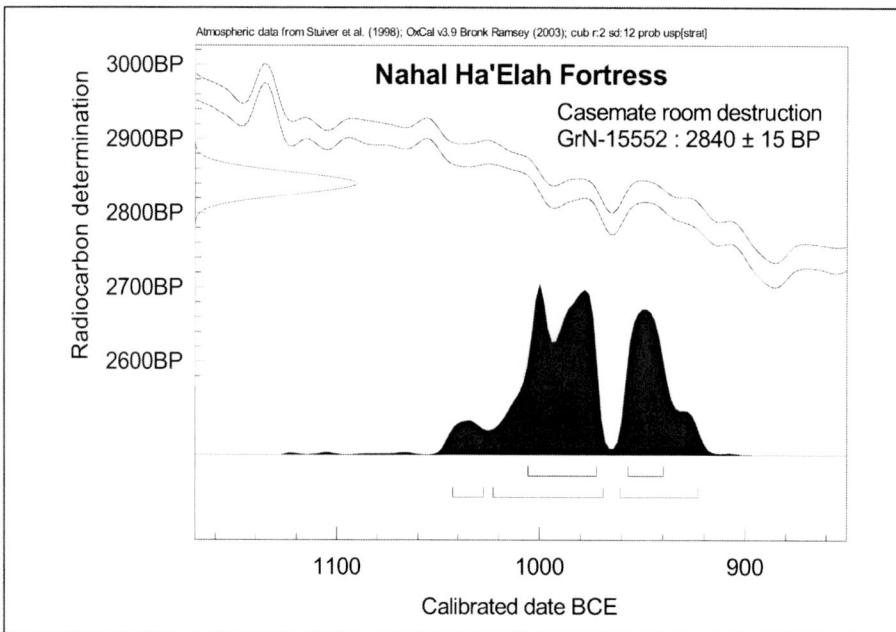

Figure 21.7. Dating the destruction of a casemate room in the
Nahal Ha'Elah fortress, based on fine charcoal.

Horvat Haluqim Agricultural Terraces

The site of Horvat Haluqim is an excellent example of an Iron Age desert village, located along three parallel dry stream valleys (wadis) at the south-eastern slopes of the Haluqim Anticline, 2 km north-west of Kibbutz Sede Boker (Figs. 21.1, 8). The site comprises 25 structures, including a fortress, seven 4-room houses, other buildings and 4 cisterns. Cohen (1976) excavated the fortress and a number of buildings at the site. The elliptical fortress (23 m long and 21 m wide) has virtually the same size as the Lower Fortress at Tell el-Qudeirat (see above).

Cohen (1976) suggested that Horvat Haluqim was established, together with most other Iron Age fortresses and sites in the region, during the reign of King Solomon and destroyed during the campaign of Pharaoh Shishak. Thus, according to the above viewpoint of Cohen, the settlements were inhabited for only 30 to 40 years within the 10th century BCE. Much later in time, during the Roman period, two buildings were constructed at the site, probably in the 2nd–3rd centuries CE, according to ceramics and a coin found at the site (Cohen 1986).

Bruins (1986) carried out a survey in the three wadis of Horvat Haluqim and found more than 70 terrace walls with adjacent fields. Geoarchaeological excavations in the 12th terraced field of the eastern wadi led to the discovery of a buried anthropogenic layer (accumulative palaeo A horizon), beginning at a depth of about 45–50 cm below the present surface (Fig. 21.9). This anthropogenic soil layer has a remarkable thickness of about 75 cm, spanning the entire terraced field (Bruins and van der Plicht 2004). It has unique significance as an archive of past human agricultural activity at the site through time. This type of information is irreplaceable within the site, as such data cannot be obtained from the building or ceramic remains.

Figure 21.8. The elliptical fortress at Horvat Haluqim, looking ESE at some of the casemate rooms (photo by H.J. Bruins 2004).

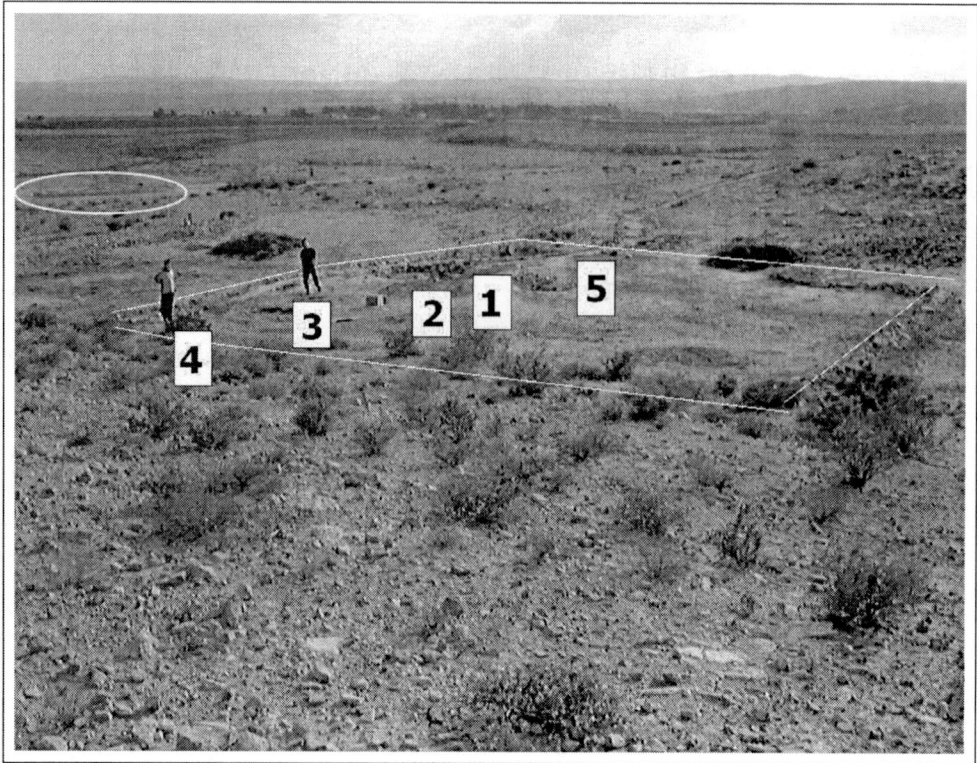

Figure 21.9. Geoarchaeological excavations in the 12th terraced field (outline field marked in white) of the eastern wadi at Horvat Haluqim, showing the location of the pits in which the dark anthropogenic soil layer was found at a certain depth below the present surface. The location of the fortress is indicated by the white elliptical line. The view is WSW towards the Zin Canyon and Avdat.

The anthropogenic layer yielded small Iron Age pottery sherds, small animal bones, charcoal flecks, as well as some pieces of flint in its lower part. Radiocarbon measurement of a bone from a sheep or goat gave an AMS date of 2860 ± 40 BP (GrA-14398). The 1σ calibrated age (Fig. 21.10) is 1124–1121 (0.9%), 1111–1099 (4.7%), 1080–1061 (7.5%), 1052–971 (45.7%), 958–938 (9.4%) BCE, and the 2σ range is 1189–1179 (1.9%), 1154–1142 (1.5%), 1129–915 (92.0%) BCE. The most likely period within all these options is 1052–971 BCE with a relative probability of 45.7% in the 1σ range.

The above date, derived from a human-made agricultural soil layer, is the first independent scientific evidence that rainwater-harvesting agriculture at Horvat Haluqim was carried out relatively early in the Iron Age (Bruins and van der Plicht 2004). The bones entered the anthropogenic soil layer due to manuring practices by the ancient farmers. They used home refuse to improve soil fertility, as established by detailed micromorphological research by Bruins and Jongmans (to be published elsewhere). Bone dates from sheep or goats are based on short-lived organic material and no 'old-wood arguments' can be used in this case to advocate a younger age. Comparing this date with the detailed Iron Age radiocarbon sequence from Tel Rehov (Bruins, van der Plicht and Mazar 2003) suggests that we are dealing here in chronological terms with the later part of the Iron Age I period.

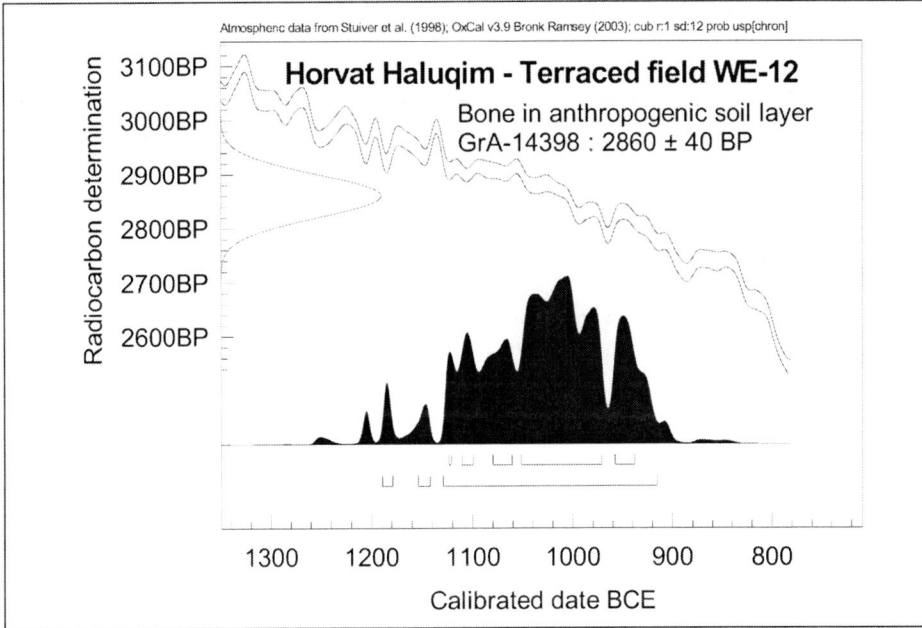

Figure 21.10. Dating part of the anthropogenic agricultural soil layer in terraced field 12 of the eastern wadi at Horvat Haluqim, based on a sheep or goat bone.

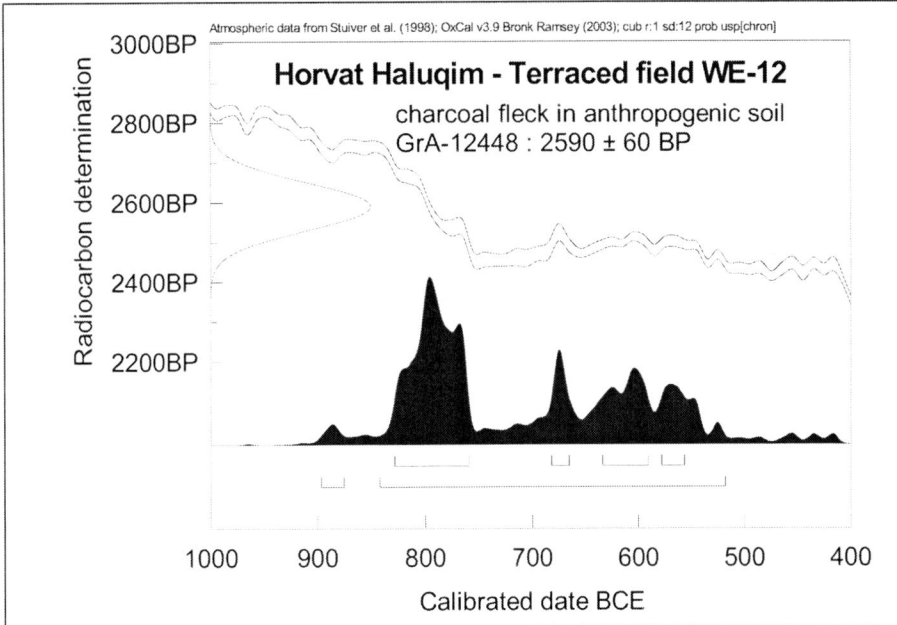

Figure 21.11. Dating another part of the anthropogenic agricultural soil layer in terraced field 12 of the eastern wadi at Horvat Haluqim, based on a speck of powdery charcoal.

A small but distinct charcoal fleck from another part of the anthropogenic layer gave a radiocarbon date of 2590 ± 60 BP (GrA-12448). The $\delta^{13}C$ value of −17.75 ‰ is higher than for wood (usually around −25‰), which indicates that the charcoal is more likely derived from short-lived shrubs, annual plants or animal dung. The 1σ calibrated date (Fig. 21.11) is 828–759 (41.2%), 682–666 (6.6%), 634–591 (14.1%), 578–557 (6.4%) BCE and the 2σ calibrated date is 896–875 (1.8%), 842–519 (93.6%) BCE. The highest relative probability in the 1σ range is for the period 828–759 BCE. The result suggests human activity at the agricultural terrace *also* during the later Iron Age. Settlement in the Negev–Sinai region during the later Iron Age is also known from the Middle and Upper Fortress at Tell el-Qudeirat (Fig. 21.1) and the two successive fortresses at Hazeva in the Arabah Valley (Cohen 1993c). However, notice that the above date from the human-made agricultural soil at Horvat Haluqim is older than the two dates (charcoal and charred cereal grains) for the destruction of the Upper Fortress at Tell el-Qudeirat.

Discussion and Conclusions

Cohen (1983, 1993a) suggested that the Upper Fortress at Tell el-Qudeirat was built during the reign of King Josiah (ca. 639–609 BCE). If so, then its existence was short—probably less than 40 years. In 609 BCE, Pharaoh Necho II moved the Egyptian army through Judah on his way to Mesopotamia to assist the Assyrians against the Babylonians. Josiah decided to confront the Egyptians near Megiddo, but was killed in battle (2 Kings 23; 2 Chronicles 35). Later Johoiakim (608–598 BCE) was placed on the throne by Pharaoh Necho II, instead of Jehoahaz (2 Kings 23), indicating considerable Egyptian influence over Judah. Some of the ostraca found by Cohen (1983, 1993a, 1993b) in the Upper Fortress show both ancient Egyptian hieratic numerals and Hebrew words, which might fit the above political picture. In 605 BCE the Egyptian army in Mesopotamia was decisively defeated by the Babylonians in the famous battle at Carchemish near the Euphrates River.

The commander of the Babylonian troops, Nebuchadnezzar, became king in 604 or 603 BCE. He marched his army to Egypt in 601 or 600 BCE and fierce battles took place, as the Babylonians and the defending Egyptians inflicted heavy losses on each other (Finegan 1979). Johoiakim changed allegiance twice, first to Nebuchadnezzar and then back again to Necho, and he died in about 598 BCE. It is at this point that 2 Kings 24.7 gives an interesting geopolitical state of affairs: '*And the king of Egypt did not come out of his land anymore, for the king of Babylon had taken all that belonged to the king of Egypt from the Brook of Egypt to the River Euphrates*'. The fortress at Tell el-Qudeirat was the closest Judean presence near Egypt, located only 25 km west of Wadi el-Arish. Perhaps the Upper Fortress was destroyed during these fierce battles between the Babylonians and Egyptians in 601 or 600 BCE, maybe punishing Johoiakim for changing alliance. This historical age fits somewhat better with the calibrated radiocarbon date (charred cereal grains in a jar) for the destruction of the Upper Fortress than the year 586 BCE, the Babylonian destruction of Jerusalem.

The ^{14}C date associated with the destruction of the Middle Fortress at Tell el-Qudeirat is considerably older (10th–9th centuries BCE in the 1σ range) than the age suggested by Cohen (1983, 1993a) in the mid-7th century BCE. One radiocarbon date of a destruction layer outside the eastern revetment wall is certainly a reason to regard the result as preliminary with regard to the Middle Fortress. Yet the four radiocarbon dates of the three fortresses are internally coherent in terms of stratigraphy and must be taken into account.

In terms of possible regional correlations between architecture and governmental planning, it should be noted that both Stratum V and IV of Tel Beer Sheva had a solid wall, like the Middle Fortress at Tell el-Qudeirat. Casemate walls built on top of the remains of the previous solid walls occur at Tel Beer Sheva in Stratum III (Herzog 1993) and at Tell el-Qudeirat with the Upper

Fortress (Cohen 1983, 1993a). Herzog (1993) suggested that Stratum V of Tel Beer Sheva—characterised by a solid wall—might have been destroyed by Pharaoh Shishak. The only ^{14}C date from Tell el-Qudeirat that might fit the Shishak campaign is the destruction layer associated with the Middle Fortress, which also had a solid wall.

The elliptical Lower Fortress was smaller and had a different shape than the rectangular Middle and Upper Fortresses at Tell el-Qudeirat, which are decisively younger in age. Most Iron Age settlements in the Negev–Sinai region are characterised by elliptical or irregular shaped fortresses, including Horvat Haluqim, Nahal Ha'Elah and the Lower Fortress at Tell el-Qudeirat. The most probable calibrated ^{14}C date of 1103–1050 BCE for the destruction of the Lower Fortress is about 150 years older than the suggested date for its destruction by Cohen (1980, 1983, 1993a). The above ^{14}C date would place the Lower Fortress firmly in the Iron I period, as favoured by Rothenberg (1972, 1988), Aharoni (1978), Herzog (1983), Finkelstein (1984, 1988) and considered possible by Meshel (1979).

We note that the old-wood effect may lower the date to some extent at Tell el-Qudeirat. However, the powdery charcoal mixed with soil from the destruction layer of the Lower Fortress is generally not characteristic for old wood. Large trees of an old age tend to give chunks of recognizable woody charcoal, such as found often at Tel Dan. But even the radiocarbon results from such woody charcoal at Tel Dan are only rarely older than 50 or 60 years in comparison to short-lived seeds (Bruins et al. [Chapter 19, this volume]). Therefore, particularly in arid regions, usually devoid of trees, the inherent age of fine charcoal is in most cases probably not more than 10–30 years, or even much less. Annual vegetation growing after the winter rains withers in the spring. Burning of such vegetation would give short-lived powdery charcoal similar in age to seeds. Desert shrubs are older than annual plants and charcoal derived from such shrubs may have an age of ca. 2 to 20 years, occasionally even older, but on average below 10 years. Though the exception may always be present, a small to medium old-wood effect is probably the rule.

The destruction date for the elliptical Nahal Ha'Elah fortress in the Central Negev seems on the face of it too old for the Shishak campaign, as the most probable age range is 1006–972 (46.2%) BCE in the 1σ range.

The 75 cm thickness of the anthropogenic agricultural soil layer at Horvat Haluqim, situated in a field terraced to catch runoff water, could not have been formed in just 40 years within the 10th century BCE. The Iron Age radiocarbon date on a small piece of bone from a sheep or goat, found in this soil layer, indicates that the terraced field was already established *before* the period of Solomon. The most probable age range is 1052–971 (45.7%) BCE, favouring the second half of the 11th century or the first decades of the 10th century BCE.

The younger Iron Age date on a small fleck of charcoal gives a most probable age range within the period 828–759 (41.2%) BCE and a second most likely age within the period 634–591 (14.1%) BCE. The result confirms that the thick anthropogenic soil layer was not formed in just one generation during the 10th century BCE, but could have begun in the 11th century (animal bone) or even well before. Agriculture and manuring continued, or were resumed after possible gaps, in the 9th, 8th or 7th centuries BCE (charcoal fleck). Micromorphological research of many thin sections from this soil layer showed the common presence of very small charcoal and bone fragments, even below 0.01 mm in size, pointing to home refuse as the source of the fertilizer.

Comparing the Iron Age ^{14}C dates from Sinai and Negev with those from Khirbet en-Nahas in the eastern Arabah Valley in Jordan (Levy et al. 2004), it is quite remarkable that *grosso modo* a similar BP time range is found for the older part of the Iron Age. The oldest dates are 2930 ± 30 BP (GrN-12330) in relation to the Lower Fortress at Tell el-Qudeirat and 2906 ± 39 BP (HD-14057) concerning the Slag Mount East (Hauptmann 2000). Moreover, also the period 2880–2825 BP appears in both areas. The oldest Iron Age date so far from the agricultural terrace at Horvat Haluqim (2860 ± 40 BP, GrA-14398) and a destruction date for the elliptical fortress at

Nahal Ha'Elah (2840 ± 15 BP, GrN-15552) are rather similar to three dates (2880 ± 28, HD-14302; 2876 ± 38, HD-14308; 2864 ± 46, HD-14113) from the Slag Mound West (Hauptmann 2000) and to Stratum A4a in Gate 2002 of the Khirbat en-Nahas Area A (2825 ± 32, OxA-12365). These chronological data are most significant, showing the regional scale of Iron Age settlement and activities in north-eastern Sinai, the Negev Highlands and the eastern Arabah Valley (Levy *et al.* 2004) for the early part of the Iron Age. These four sites are relatively close to each other, as can be seen in Figure 21.1.

In conclusion, the radiocarbon dates from the three successive fortresses at Tell el-Qudeirat are internally consistent in stratigraphic terms. The results indicate that the Upper Fortress was probably destroyed by the Babylonian campaigns, as suggested by Cohen, though a 601/600 BCE historical destruction date would fit better than the alternative 586 BCE option. The Middle Fortress appears older than suggested by Cohen. It is the only radiocarbon date that can possibly be linked, in chronological terms, with the Shishak campaign. The thick solid wall of this fortress appears similar in architectural construction to that of Stratum V of Tel Beersheba, the destruction of which is also associated with the Shishak campaign (Herzog 1993). The Lower Fortress at Tell el-Qudeirat and the Nahal Ha'Elah Fortress, both elliptical in shape, have destruction layer dates that appear older than the Solomonic period. The possible old-wood effect must be taken into consideration, but fine charcoal tends to be rather short-lived. If the old-wood effect is minimal, even the 12th century BCE is a reasonable option for the Lower Fortress at Tell el-Qudeirat in terms of its radiocarbon date.

Considering all the different theories proposed for the elliptical Iron Age fortresses and related settlements, briefly presented in the introduction, it seems that the suggested chronologies and historical associations by Cohen and Haiman are the most unlikely, while the 11th and early 10th centuries BCE appear most probable. However, even older dates for the beginning of these settlements cannot be ruled out, as the radiocarbon dates were derived from destruction layers. Indeed, the oldest date obtained so far, from the agricultural soil layer at the site of Horvat Haluqim, backs the above picture. Here the old-wood effect cannot be used as an excuse, because the date is based on a sheep or goat bone from within the anthropogenic agricultural soil layer. Nevertheless, more dates are necessary to substantiate and refine this preliminary radiocarbon dating assessment.

Acknowledgments

We thank Dr Rudolph Cohen and the Israel Antiquities Authority for their cooperation in the sampling and provision of the organic material and the permit for the geoarchaeological excavations at Horvat Haluqim. Despite disagreements concerning chronology, we acknowledge the great value of the large amount of fieldwork and excavations conducted in the region by Dr Cohen and his colleagues, including Dr Haiman. We thank the technical staff of the Centre for Isotope Research (University of Groningen) for performing the radiocarbon measurements.

References

Aharoni, Y. (1967) Forerunners of the Limes: Iron Age Fortresses in the Negev. *IEJ* 17: 1-17.

—(1978) *The Archaeology of Eretz Israel* (Jerusalem: Shakmonah).

Barkay, G. (1992) The Iron Age II–III. In *The Archaeology of Ancient Israel*, edited by A. Ben-Tor (New Haven: Yale University Press): 302-73.

Bruins, H.J. (1986) Desert Environment and Agriculture in the Central Negev and Kadesh-Barnea during Historical Times (PhD Dissertation, University of Wageningen; Nijkerk: Stichting Midbar Foundation).

—(2003) Man and Landscape in the Negev Highlands: Runoff Systems. *Horizons in Geography* 57–58: 146-58 (Hebrew).

Bruins, H.J., I. Carmi, and E. Boaretto (eds.) (2001) Near East Chronology: Archaeology and Environment. *Radiocarbon* 43(3): 1147-54.

Bruins, H.J., and W.G. Mook (1989) The Need for a Calibrated Radiocarbon Chronology of Near Eastern Archaeology. *Radiocarbon* 31(3): 1019-29.

Bruins, H.J., and J. van der Plicht (2004) Desert Settlement in the Central Negev: First [14]C Indication of Rainwater-harvesting Agriculture in the Iron Age. In *Radiocarbon and Archaeology: Proceedings of the 4th International Symposium*, edited by T.F.G Higham, C. Bronk Ramsey and D.C. Owen (Oxford University School of Archaeology Monograph 62; Oxford: Oxford University Press): 83-98.

Bruins, H.J., J. van der Plicht and A. Mazar (2003) [14]C Dates from Tel Rehov: Iron Age Chronology, Pharaohs and Hebrew Kings. *Science* 300: 315-18.

Cohen, R. (1976) Excavations at Horvat Haluqim. *Atiqot* 11: 34-50.

—(1980) The Iron Age Fortresses in the Central Negev. *BASOR* 236: 61-79.

—(1981a) Excavations at Kadesh-barnea 1976–1978. *BA* 44: 93-107.

—(1981b) Did I Excavate Kadesh-Barnea? *BAR* 7(3): 20-33.

—(1983) *Kadesh-barnea* (Jerusalem: The Israel Museum).

—(1986) The Settlement of the Central Negev in light of Archaeological and Literary Sources during the 4th–1st Millennia BCE (PhD dissertation, The Hebrew University of Jerusalem [Hebrew]).

—(1993a) Kadesh-Barnea: The Israelite Fortress. In *The New Encyclopaedia of Archaeological Excavations in the Holy Land*, III, edited by E. Stern (New York: Simon & Schuster): 1123-33.

—(1993b) Middle Bronze Age I and Iron Age II Sites in the Negev Highlands. In *The New Encyclopaedia of Archaeological Excavations in the Holy Land*, III, edited by E. Stern (New York: Simon & Schuster): 843-47

—(1993c) Hazeva, Mezad. In *The New Encyclopaedia of Archaeological Excavations in the Holy Land*, II, edited by E. Stern (New York: Simon & Schuster): 593-94

Cohen, R., and R. Cohen-Amin (2004) *Ancient settlement of the Negev Highlands*, II (Jerusalem: The Israel Antiquity Authority).

Dothan, M. (1965) The Fortress at Kadesh Barnea. *IEJ* 15: 134-51.

Finegan, J. (1979) *Archaeological History of the Ancient Middle East* (New York: Dorsett Press).

Finkelstein, I. (1984) The Iron Age 'Fortresses' of the Negev Highlands: Sedentarization of Nomads. *Tel Aviv* 11: 189-209.

—(1988) Arabian Trade and Socio-political Conditions in the Negev in the Twelfth–Eleventh Centuries B.C.E. *JNES* 47(4): 241-51.

Goldberg, P. (1984) Late Quaternary History of Qadesh Barnea, Northeastern Sinai. *Zeitschrift für Geomorphologie N.F.* 28(2): 193-217.

Haiman, M. (1994) The Iron Age II sites of the western Negev Highlands. *IEJ* 44: 36-61.

Hauptmann, A. (2000) *Zur frühen Metallurgie des Kupfers in Fenan* (Der Anschnitt 11; Bochum: Deutsches Bergbau-Museum).

Herzog, Z. (1983) Enclosed Settlements in the Negeb and the Wilderness of Beer-sheba. *BASOR* 250: 41-49.

—(1993) Tel Beersheba. In *The New Encyclopaedia of Archaeological Excavations in the Holy Land*, I, edited by E. Stern (New York: Simon & Schuster): 167-73.

Levy, T.E., *et al.* (2004) Reassessing the Chronology of Biblical Edom: New Excavations and [14]C Dates from Khirbat en-Nahas (Jordan). *Antiquity* 78: 863-76.

Meshel, Z. (1979) Who Built the Israelite Fortresses in the Negev Hills? *Kathedra* 11: 3-29 (Hebrew).

Meshel, Z., and A. Goren (1992) The 'Aharoni Fortress' Near Quseima—Another 'Israelite Fortress' in the Negev and the Problem of these 'Fortresses'. *Eretz-Israel* 23: 196-215.

Mook, W.G., and H.T. Waterbolk (1985) *Handbook for Archaeologists*. III. *Radiocarbon Dating* (Strasbourg: European Science Foundation).

Rothenberg, B. (1967) *Zefunot Negev: Archaeology in the Negev and the Arabah* (Tel-Aviv: Massada [Hebrew]).

—(1972) *Timna, Valley of the Biblical Copper Mines* (London: Thames & Hudson).

—(1988) *The Egyptian Mining Temple at Timna* (London: Institute for Archaeo-Metallurgical Studies, University College London).

—(1999) Archaeo-metallurgical Researches in the Southern Arabah 1959–1990. Part 2: Egyptian New Kingdom (Ramesside) to Early Islam. *PEQ* 131: 150-76.

Van der Plicht, J., *et al.* (2000) Status Report: The Groningen AMS Facility. *Nuclear Instruments and Methods* B172: 58-65.

Van der Plicht, J., and H.J. Bruins (2001) Radiocarbon Dating in Near-Eastern Contexts: Confusion and Quality Control. *Radiocarbon* 43(3): 1155-66.

Woolley, C.L., and T.E. Lawrence (1914–15) *The Wilderness of Zin* (London: Committee for the Palestine Exploration Fund).

22 Trajectories of Iron Age Settlement in North Israel and their Implications for Chronology

Anabel Zarzecki-Peleg

Abstract

This article discusses models of settlement development in Iron Age II at selected sites in North Israel, contributing a somewhat different aspect to the chronological debate on Iron Age IIA and the subdivision of Iron Age II. The tracing of trajectories of settlement development at various sites enables the identification of several settlement models, sometimes very different from one another. Each model contains several periods/settlement episodes, each with its own particular characteristics. The models are primarily based on the architectural and urban features of each period as expressed in the plans of the settlements, on the internal development during that period in comparison with other periods at the same site, and the pottery vessels that are typical of each period. A geographical distinction between the models can be discerned, emphasizing the histories of different regions. A comparison of this kind refines our understanding of different stages in continuous settlement and enables us to distinguish transitional stages within the Iron Age II, both at its beginning and at the transition between Iron Age IIA and IIB. I am convinced that distinctions of this kind have far-reaching implications, providing an additional dimension to the issues concerning the chronology of the Iron Age II.

The following exposition of settlement development models accords a different perspective to the current debate concerning the subdivision and chronology of Iron Age IIA. A comparison between the models enhances our understanding of the development continuum, and allows us to distinguish between the various phases within Iron Age II, both at its outset and at the transition between Iron Age IIA and IIB. I believe that these distinctions have far-reaching chronological implications, and enable us to consider the issues from a novel point of view.

Tracing the developmental trajectories connected with the various sites permits us to identify similar lines of growth between them, and comprises a basis for proposing a number of sometimes quite dissimilar models. The settlement processes delineated by these models continue across most of the Iron Age IIA–B. Each model features two main stages of settlement, each with its distinctive characteristics. These models are based chiefly upon architectural and urban features, as expressed in settlement layout, internal development (both over the period concerned and in relation to the second period at the same site), and the ceramic assemblage associated with each period. I have focused upon the relationship between the occupation levels and the nature of their differences. Continuity or discontinuity in layout and the time required to reach the apex of the trajectory are the parameters defining the model, whereas other criteria, such as the settlement's absolute compass, are less relevant (for definitions such as 'Major and Secondary Administrative Cities', 'Provincial Towns', etc., see, e.g., Herzog 1992: 250-65). It should be noted that these models evince a marked geographical division, which stresses how different sections of the country experienced different historical vicissitudes.

I should like to present three models, each of which offers a special contribution to constructing a common chronological continuum, as well as two additional sites which correspond, albeit not exactly, to the framework of the models. Owing to limitations of scope, I will refrain from presenting a comprehensive discussion of ceramics; I will merely note a few characteristics in order to illustrate my thesis (for recently studies on this issue see Ben-Tor and Zarzecki-Peleg forthcoming; Zarzecki-Peleg forthcoming; Zarzecki-Peleg, Cohen-Anidjar, and Ben-Tor 2005).

Model A

This includes Megiddo and Jokneam in Jezreel Valley (Zarzecki-Peleg 2005; for a new stratigraphic and architecture analysis of Megiddo and bibliography see Zarzecki-Peleg forthcoming). Although these cities are stable in terms of area from one period to the next, they evince substantial differences (see Graph 22.1). The first period includes the following strata: Megiddo VC (i.e. K-3b in the excavations of Tel Aviv University; Lehmann, Killebrew, and Gadot [eds.] 2000: 126-28; Zarzecki-Peleg forthcoming), VB, and VA–IVB (Finkelstein, Ussishkin, and Halpern [eds.] 2000; Lamon and Shipton 1939; Loud 1948; Yadin 1972); and Jokneam XVI, XV, and XIV (Zarzecki-Peleg 2005: 90-168). Over the course of Iron Age II, it is possible to follow their gradual development: beginning as interim settlements, they evolve into permanent settlements, and then into actual cities. Only at an advanced phase of this early period are there clear indications of central organization and administrative–governmental buildings: administrative buildings and/or palaces 1723 and 6000 in Megiddo VA–IVB, and a massive casement wall and an installation for supplying water in Jokneam XIV.

The pottery is characteristic of Iron Age IIA, but changes can be observed over the course of the period (Finkelstein, Zimhoni, and Kafri 2000: 265ff.; Zarzecki-Peleg 2005: Figs. I.36–I.69; Zarzecki-Peleg forthcoming; Zarzecki-Peleg, Cohen-Anidjar, and Ben-Tor 2005). The cooking-pots, for example, provide an excellent index of these changes (Zarzecki-Peleg, Cohen-Anidjar, and Ben-Tor 2005: 294-95). The sampling of pottery from this first phase is relatively small. Nevertheless, new features, not in evidence in the rich assemblages from the end of Iron Age I (Megiddo VIA and Jokneam XVII), occur now. Red slip and irregular, discontinuous burnishing are innovations, and appear, albeit seldom, at the outset (Finkelstein, Zimhoni, and Kafri 2000: Fig. 11.18:11; Zarzecki-Peleg 2005: Fig. I.36:1). Considering that the first phase of Iron Age IIA at these settlements was interim and brief, it is possible to affirm that a number of years elapsed between the end of Iron Age I and the beginning of Iron Age II. Pottery of the Black-on-Red Family appears in Jokneam XV in small quantities, and is typical of the period's end: Jokneam XIV and Megiddo VA–IVB (Schreiber 2003: 94-103, 187-89; Zarzecki-Peleg forthcoming; Zarzecki-Peleg, Cohen-Anidjar and Ben-Tor 2005: 250-51, 334). It is unclear whether this family occurs in Megiddo VB (Gilboa and Sharon 2003: 57).

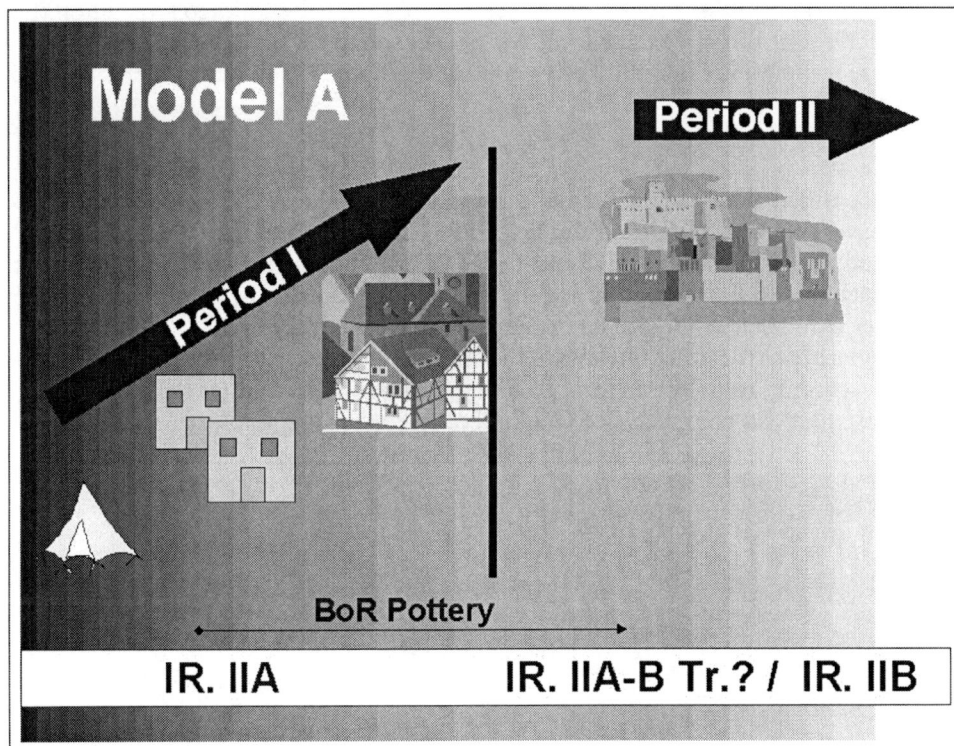

Graph 22.1. Trajectory of Model A—Megiddo and Jokneam.

The close of the period was sudden. Sign of destruction were discerned at Megiddo, although not everywhere. The second period—Megiddo IVA and Jokneam XII—presents a city with a comprehensive, well-developed, and obviously pre-planned layout. Megiddo IVA experienced a momentous turning-point in terms of the city's function (Herzog 1992: 251-53; 1997: 226-29; Lamon and Shipton 1939); it became a governmental centre *par excellence* (Zarzecki-Peleg forthcoming). This change is expressed in the reallocation of its resources, whereby wide tracts were devoted to the construction of ambitious official complexes. This new planning took scant account of the buildings from the previous period. The cities reached their developmental apex in the second period, that is to say, at the end of the trajectory.

Generally speaking, the pottery of this second period can be ascribed to Iron Age IIB; its terminus corresponds to the campaign of Tiglath-Pileser III, the Assyrian king, in 732 BCE (Finkelstein, Zimhoni, and Kafri 2000: 300ff.; Zarzecki-Peleg 2005: Figs. I.77–I.84; forthcoming; Zarzecki-Peleg, Cohen-Anidjar, and Ben-Tor 2005: 256ff.). Its beginning is more difficult to date, and conceivably varied from site to site. Jokneam XIIb was preceded by the so-called 'pit' phase, Stratum XIII, which is not linked to the urban layout of Stratum XII (Zarzecki-Peleg 2005: 169-83). The pottery from the pits represents the transition between Iron Age IIA and IIB. At Megiddo IVA it is also possible to discern secondary phases in the stratum (in the stable assemblage, for instance; Zarzecki-Peleg forthcoming), but no earlier pit stratum has been identified. It appears that a clue to dating the beginning of Stratum IVA is afforded by the sparse fragments retrieved from the plaster floor of Building 434 in Yadin's excavations at Megiddo (Zarzecki-Peleg forthcoming: Fig. 34). He assigned the building to Stratum VA–IVB (Yadin 1966: 279), but, following a careful re-examination, there can be no doubt that Wightman was correct in reassigning it to

Stratum IVA (Wightman 1984: 136-37) as formerly proposed by the Chicago Expedition (Lamon and Shipton 1939: 44ff.). It appears that the few sherds found on the floor, generally typical of Iron Age IIA, are responsible for Yadin's erroneous stratigraphy. I shall return to this issue below.

Model B

This has been identified chiefly in the Beth-Shean and Jordan Valleys, and includes both rural and urban settlements: Tel 'Amal (Edelstein and Feig 1993; Levy and Edelstein 1972), Rehov (Mazar 1999, 2003), and Tell el-Hammah (Cahill and Tarler 1993). These settlements, in contrast to those of Model A, reach their fullest extent during the first period, contracting considerably during the second. Another significant difference is connected with their history in the first period. The sites of Model B evince two destruction levels: the first, after which the settlement was largely reconstructed according to its precursor's groundplan; and the second (at the period's end), in which the devastation was complete (see Graph 22.2).

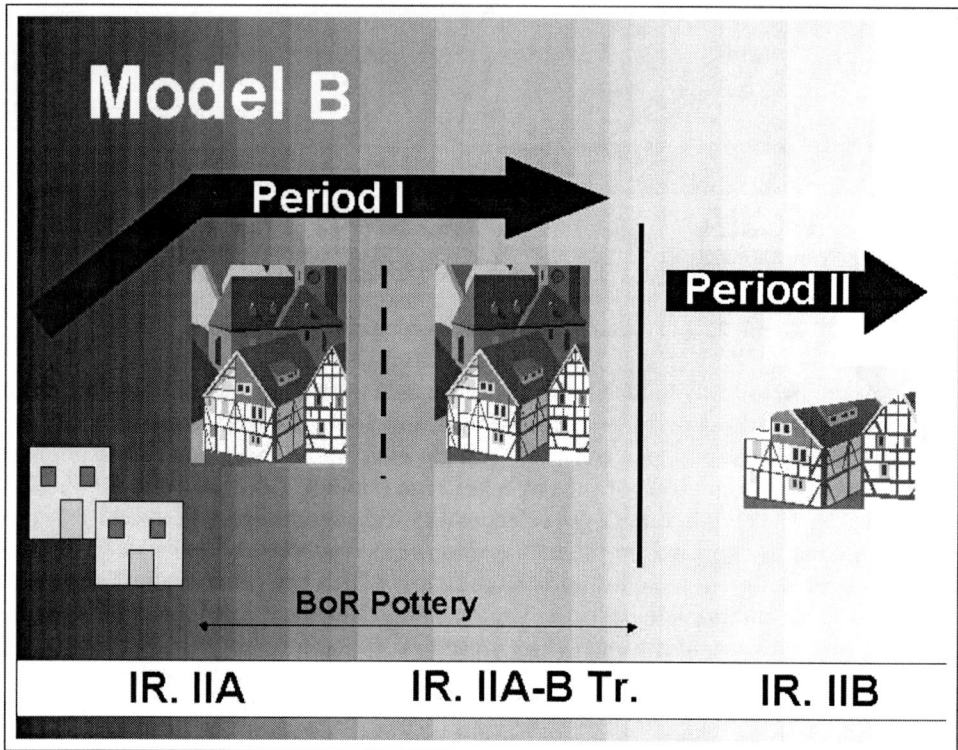

Graph 22.2. Trajectory of Model B—Rehov, Tel 'Amal, and Tell el- Hammah.

The excavations of the sites ascribed to this model are not sufficiently adequate to allow us to draw a general picture of their urban features during Iron Age II. Nevertheless, it is possible to observe continuity in the architectonic vestiges in the strata from the first period, which is quite surprising, considering the destruction of the earlier level. At Rehov, where three strata (VI–IV) were discerned, the continuity between the two later strata is striking (Mazar 2003: 147-48, Figs. 5, 7 and Table 2), which also applies to Tel 'Amal IV–III (Edelstein and Feig 1993: 1448) and Tell el-Hammah, L terrace (Cahill and Tarler 1993: 561-62).

The pottery from this period can be defined broadly as Iron Age IIA. However (at Tel 'Amal, for instance), it is possible to observe differences between the two strata (Levy and Edelstein 1972: 335ff.; Figs. 8–15). The later stratum evinces signs of ceramic development, including several traits characteristic of Iron Age IIB (e.g. bowls and cooking-pots; as Levy and Edelstein 1972: Figs. 10:4; 14:9). Thus, the later strata (Tel 'Amal III, Reḥov IV, and Tell Ḥammah) of the first period in Model B attest to the transition between the pottery of Iron Age IIA proper and IIB.

During the second period, as stated above, the Model B settlements (in contrast to those of Model A) decline in power and their area contracts considerably. At Reḥov, for instance, the settlement withdraws to the tell's upper terrace (Mazar 2003: 157). The pottery of this period is characteristic of Iron Age IIB (p. 156).

The identification of several Model B sites in the Beth-Shean and the Jordan Valleys indicates that many settlements here failed to recover from the destruction that befell them at the end of the first period—during the Iron Age IIA–IIB Transition.

Model C

Hazor represents the archetype of this model, which is crucial for understanding the settlement trajectory and for the chronological debate (Ben-Tor 1996, 1999; Ben-Tor et al. [eds.] 1997; Ben-Tor and Ben-Ami 1998; Yadin et al. 1958, 1960, 1961, 1989). Hazor's developmental model is rather different from that of the previous sites (see Graph 22.3).

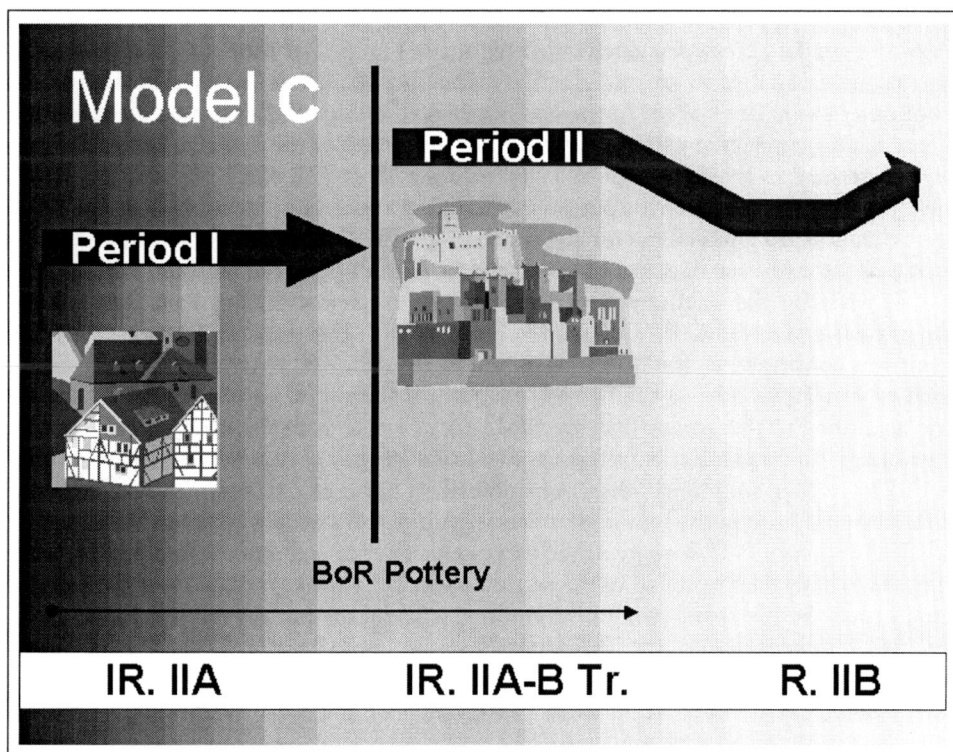

Graph 22.3. Trajectory of Model C—Hazor.

Even at the outset of the first period (Stratum Xb), it is already possible to distinguish a partially pre-planned urban layout. The size of the city then was relatively small. It was confined to the tell's western half, and only part of this area was actually settled (Yadin 1972:140-42; Ben-Tor 1996: 77, Fig. 11). This urban layout was retained throughout all four phases (Xb–IXa) ascribed to the first period, while a gradual increase in size was observed only in the occupied areas within the city limits (Yadin *et al.* 1989: 30ff.). The pottery is typically Iron Age IIA (Ben-Tor and Ben-Ami 1998; Yadin *et al.* 1961: Pls. CLXXI–CLXXIX; Zarzecki-Peleg 1997: 270-84). At the very beginning of this period, vessels of the Black-on-Red Family appear (see Yadin *et al.* 1961: Pl. CLXXII:1). Towards its end (IXa), one can already discern several indices of Stratum VIII pottery (Zarzecki-Peleg 1997: 281; see below).

In the second period (Strata VIII–Va), the city increases in size, spreading over the entire tell (Yadin 1972: 165). Even at its outset (Stratum VIII) the layout changes, and Hazor becomes an administrative-governmental centre, which includes, *inter alia*, the citadel, storehouses, and granaries (Ben-Tor 1993: 253, fig. 1; 1999: 34, 37; Bonfil 1997: 126, Plan II.13; Yadin *et al.* 1960: 6-9, Pl. CC). There is no connection between the new structures and the previous city, apart from partial reuse of the fortifications. Later, in Stratum VI, Hazor underwent a significant change of status, as expressed in its urban disposition, through the utilization and repartition of its districts, especially in reference to the storage facilities. It is not merely a question of their transfer to the area adjoining the city's entrance (Area G), as Yadin averred (Yadin 1972: 184). The change was more significant, and affected the settlement's entire design. The alteration in the citadel access and the secondary use of the proto-Aeolian columns which had formerly adorned the complex (Yadin *et. al* 1989: 93), provide a further illustration of the same phenomenon (for a new reconstruction of the citadel access, see Zarzecki-Peleg forthcoming). In Model C, the peak of urban development can be ascribed to the outset of the second period. It was followed by decline, despite partial continuity in the city layout. At the end of period (Stratum Va), it is possible to distinguish changes here mainly connected with preparations for the assault of the Assyrian army. The period's conclusion is ascribed to the campaign of Tiglath-Pileser III in 732 BCE.

The pottery from the outset of the period is still mainly typical of the end of Iron Age IIA; later, however, it changes into types characteristic of Iron Age IIB. Already Aharoni and Amiran (1958) ascertained that the transition between the two ceramic periods occurred between Stratum VIII and Stratum VII, whereby the beginnings of the main types characterising Iron Age IIB (or III, according to their system) initially appeared in Stratum VII (Aharoni and Amiran 1958: 174ff.). Their claim was confirmed in the fifth season and in the renewed excavations under Ben-Tor's direction (Ben-Tor 1996: 69-71; Bonfil 1997: 129ff.). It should be noted that the subdivision of the period according to the urban trajectory *does not coincide* with the subdivision according to ceramic typology. The transition between the two urban phases occurs between Stratum IXa and Stratum VIII (a further secondary phase was identified between Stratum VII and Stratum VI), whereas the turning-point in the typology of Iron Age II pottery occurs between Stratum VIII and Stratum VII. Thus, Hazor VIII is represented by vessels still connected to the first period, while the urban planning signals the beginning of the second period. If we take into account the fact that the architectonic phase betokens the stratum's founding, whereas the pottery retrieved from the floors of its structures betokens its end, the 'dichotomy' becomes even greater. Thus, Model C provides an illustration of the phenomenon in which the indices attesting to clear changes in infrastructure, such as the establishment of a governmental centre, precede the same indices in pottery.

Additional Settlement Models: Rosh Zayit and Jezreel

I should now like to consider two further sites, Rosh Zayit and Jezreel, which can be related partially to the models described above.

The character and developmental history of Rosh Zayit differ from those of the sites considered hitherto (Gal and Alexandre 2000). Three occupation periods have been discerned here over the course of Iron Age II (see Graph 22.4). The first comprises a rural settlement with dwellings and scattered installations (2000: 8-11). Its pottery is Iron Age IIA, and includes a vessel of the Black-on-Red Family (2000: 33, Figs. III.1:8; III.3:5). The second is represented by the citadel on the top of the hill (2000: 12ff.). This administrative-governmental structure bespeaks a notable difference in the function and planning of the settlement, whereby Stratum II is the peak of its trajectory. I take exception to the excavators' conclusions regarding the stratigraphy and architectonic reconstruction of the citadel. Owing to limitations here, I shall focus on one point only, but it is of considerable moment for the present discussion (a detailed stratigraphic and architectonic analysis was presented in Zarzecki-Peleg forthcoming). The excavators affirm that the citadel in its entirety served only Stratum II (Phases b and a), and that it was wholly destroyed at the period's end. Only sections of the structure continued to host squatters in Stratum I (Gal and Alexandre 2000: 8, 23, 200). However, an examination of its vestiges in all its wings and a comparison of the heights of its enclosing walls indicate that the citadel was rebuilt after the destruction marking the end of Stratum II, and that the central space was reorganized and divided into cells. If so, it continued in existence until the end of Stratum I. The second period at Rosh Zayit is represented by pottery characteristic of the end of Iron Age IIA and the transition between Iron Age IIA and IIB (2000: 34ff., Figs. III.72–III.95; III.121–III.122). In the third period, the site reverted to its rural cast, and the associated pottery is Iron Age IIB (2000: 152ff.).

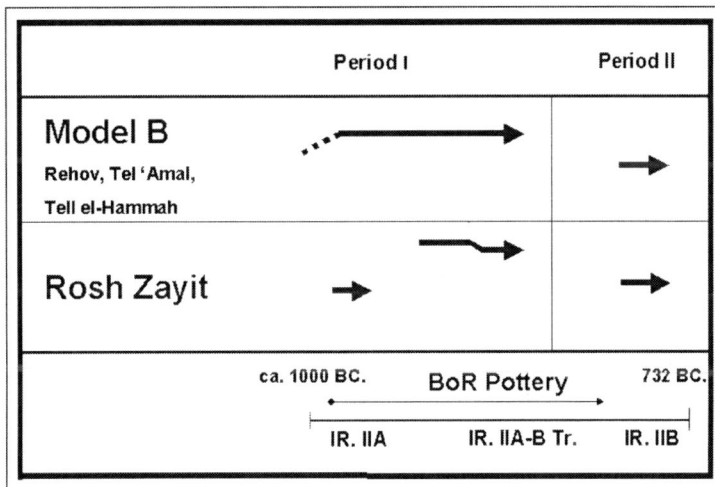

Graph 22.4. Comparison between trajectories of Model B and Rosh Zayit.

The developmental trajectory of Rosh Zayit, which comprises several buildings (including the citadel), differs from that of a densely populated village or true city belonging to the class of the three models I defined above. Nevertheless, one can recognize a common denominator in the initiative to erect a public edifice (such as the citadel) by some central authority at an advanced phase of Iron Age IIA. The process at Rosh Zayit bears a certain resemblance to that marking the end of the first period in Model A, especially the erection of Structures 1723 and 6000 at Megiddo VA–IVB (see above).

The trajectory at Rosh Zayit can also be compared to that of Model B, even though the sites are located at opposite ends of the northern valleys. In both instances, significant destruction was followed by rapid recovery and continuity in the architectural layout. It was only another 'blow' that brought about the period's end and a drastic reduction in the status of the site. And in both this period is dated to Iron Age IIA and the Iron Age IIA–IIB Transition.

Jezreel exhibits two occupation periods over the course of Iron Age IIA–B (Ussishkin and Woodhead 1992, 1994, 1997; see Graph 22.5). We lack information concerning the nature of the settlement in the first period, and most of our knowledge is based on the fills underneath the compound containing Iron Age IIA pottery (Zimhoni 1997: 83, 86-89, Figs. 3–4).

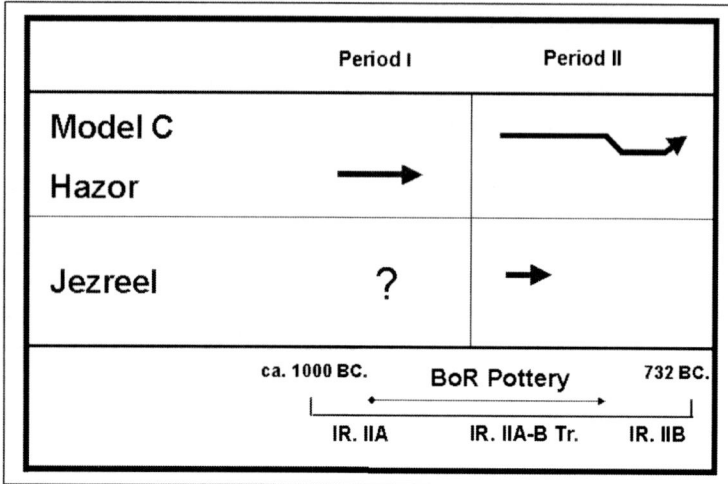

Graph 22.5. Comparison between trajectories of Model C—Hazor—and Jezreel.

The second period is represented by the extensive compound attributed to Omri's Dynasty (Ussishkin and Woodhead 1992: 53). Its vestiges are poorly preserved, but one cannot fail to be impressed by the notable investment of resources involved in its construction. It was a new administrative–governmental centre, well-planned from the beginning, and with no relation to the previous remains. The excavators ascribe it to Iron Age IIA. The pottery assemblages from both periods were similar (Zimhoni 1997: 89-91, Figs. 5-14), but the second includes several vessels whose traits suggest a slightly later date (Zarzecki-Peleg 1997: 284-87).

The analogy between Jezreel and the models described above is partial only, since the present site was not restored in Iron Age IIB. Nevertheless, it is possible to distinguish the same trajectory typifying Models A and C, that is to say, the establishment of a well-planned governmental centre entailing a substantial investment of resources, and totally divorced from the prior settlement. Here, too, the 'new order' represents the peak of the trajectory. The resemblance between the beginning of the second period at Jezreel and that of Hazor VIII is striking (*contra* Finkelstein [2000: 117-18], who proposed a corollary between the compound at Jezreel—second period in our category—and Hazor X). In both instances, this period is still marked by pottery linked to the tradition of the first period (Iron Age IIA), whereas the urban layout betokens the onset of a new and ongoing era, one which characterises the governmental centres of Iron Age IIB. Thus, as at Hazor VIII, the second period at Jezreel is Iron Age IIA–IIB Transition.

The vessels accompanying the initial phase of these new complexes—Hazor VIII and the compound of Jezreel, and the last phase of Model B (Reḥov IV, Tel 'Amal III, and Tell el- Ḥammah)— are still closely linked to the Iron Age IIA assemblage. Although there are new types, these are rare: straight-walled bowls—prototype of the *'dishes'* bowls (Gal and Alexandre 2000: Fig. III.90:26;

Yadin *et al.* 1958: Pl. XLVII:7; Zimhoni 1992: Fig. 2:2); hemispherical bowls (Bonfil 1997: Fig. II.37:4; Gal and Alexandre 2000: Fig. III.90:24; Yadin *et al.* 1960: Pl. LV:10;); bowls with a delicate ridge below the rim (Levy and Edelstein 1972: Fig. 15:9; Yadin *et al.*1960: Pl. LIV:25); grooved-base bowls (Yadin *et al.* 1960: Pl. LV:22; Zimhoni 1992: 61, 67, Figs. 1:18, 8:5; 1997: Fig. 5:3); profile big bowls—'*plates*' (Zimhoni 1997: Fig. 8:11); cooking pots with short thick triangular rim, short shoulder, and sharp carination—a transitional type (Ben-Tor *et al.* [eds.]: Fig. II.35:10; Gal and Alexandre 2000: Fig. III.85:23; Mazar 2003: Fig. 20, second cooking pot from right; Zimhoni 1992: Fig. 6:11); cooking pot with short, triangular grooved rim—regular or particularly thin walls (Gal and Alexandre 2000: Fig. III.79:25; Levy and Edelstein 1972: Fig. 10:4; Yadin *et al.* 1960: Pls. LVII:25; LVIII:1; for discussion see Bonfil 1997: 129-31; Yadin *et al.* 1960: 9-14; Zarzecki-Peleg 1997: 285-87; forthcoming; Zarzecki-Peleg, Cohen-Anidjar, and Ben-Tor 2005: 255-56, 293-95).

Summary

The analysis of the settlement trajectories of several selected Iron Age II sites in northern Israel allows us to trace their distinctive developments with greater precision. It reveals similar processes among diverse settlements, and aids us in reconstructing the occupation pattern over the course of the time-frame concerned.

The three basic models, in addition to their variations, illustrate various proceedings, sometimes contrary in their tendencies, among the different groups (see Graph 22.6).

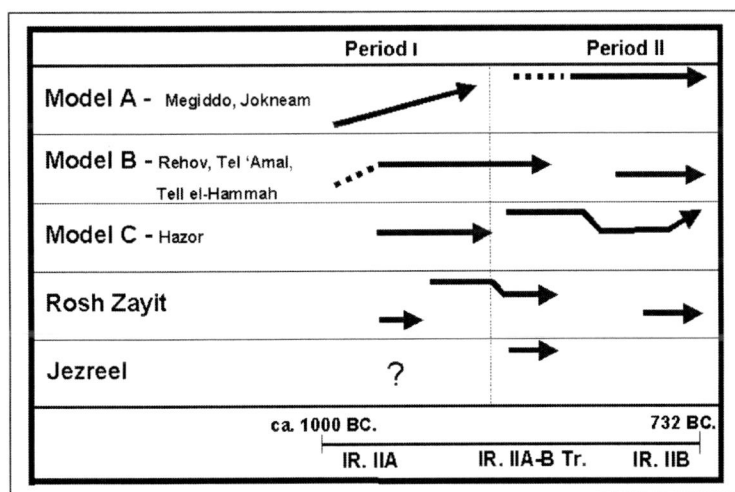

Graph 22.6. Comparison between the trajectories.

The settlements of Model A evince gradual and continuous growth during the first period. Towards its conclusion (the end of Iron Age IIA), they 'lurch forward', as revealed by civil constructions, on a comparatively modest scale. It is only in the second period, however, that one observes complex and pre-planned development. These settlements experience an urban efflorescence, which the Assyrian invasion terminates.

In Model B, this efflorescence occurs during the first period. In terms of layout, there is a tendency towards settlement continuity, especially between the later strata. Even after conflagration and general destruction, there is an evident desire to abide by the existing pattern, as opposed to 'turning over a new leaf', as in the other models. The first period of Model B extends beyond that of Model A, including the Iron Age IIA–IIB Transition. It is possible that the aforementioned destruction during the first period in Model B coincides with the end of this period in Model A.

Already at the start of the first period, the settlements of Model C were established according to a partially pre-planned urban scheme, and public building on a modest scale is already in evidence (recalling the mature state of the first period in Model A). The layout was preserved throughout the entire first period. Only in the second does the long-term planning change: an administrative-governmental centre is established, and the city's area is virtually doubled. The peak of urban development can be assigned to the beginning of this period, after which a decline sets in, in spite of partial continuity in terms of layout. The beginning of the second period occurs during the Iron Age IIA–IIB Transition, thus overlapping the end of the first period in Model B. It is conceivable that the inception of Megiddo IVA in Model A is similar to that of Model C.

This article has considered two phenomena connected with the beginning and end of Iron Age IIA which are relevant to the chronological issue now under review and these are discussed below.

The Beginning of Iron Age II

The identification of an interim and short-lived occupation level at the beginning of Iron Age II in Model A (Jokneam XVI and Megiddo VC) is of real significance. It is usually very difficult to distinguish such sparse remains in a multilayered tell characterized by wide-ranging building activity. Their exposure allows us to study the inception of the settlement trajectory, which has not been possible heretofore for Iron Age II. This phase is important chronologically, since its pottery exhibits certain traits which are later than those of the foregoing stratum (Jokneam XVII and Megiddo VIA). Thus, at both sites, one should interpose an occupation gap between the destruction at the end of Iron Age I (ca. 1000 BCE) and the beginning of Iron Age II.

The Iron Age IIA–IIB Transition

This transitional phase is crucial to the urban development of Iron Age II, which is characterized by the appearance of new and well-planned governmental centers, entailing the erection of substantial and unprecedented official edifices. By contrast, one is struck by other sites, sometimes central in themselves, which were rebuilt in the 'old' mode, and which continued in existence, if not for very long. The new centers of the transitional phase adhered to the building tradition of several structures which had already appeared as individual units at the end of Iron Age IIA. Now, however, they became complexes forming the core of the main cities arising in Iron Age IIB. Their establishment required an infrastructure and sizeable economic investment, which posits the initiative of a governmental power. They were conscientiously planned and attest to an overall spatial conception. It is clear that the architectural vision was inspired by an ideology. These cities betoken the 'new order' coming into being at that time and whose power was embodied by these monumental administrative centers.

In marked contrast to the innovation on the urban–architectural plane is continuity exhibited by the pottery, and a meaningful change occurs only at a later phase. Under such circumstances, I am of the opinion that evidence of socio-political change should be sought, first of all, on the plane of urban layout and architecture, since it was only later that the 'gap' was closed on the ceramic plane.

The division into two main periods—Iron Age IIA and IIB (or II and III)—was appropriate when, some fifty years ago, Aharoni and Amiran wrote their article. But it no longer suffices! A comprehensive ceramic study, which considers the typological details together with a quantitative analysis (as in Jokneam; see Zarzecki-Peleg, Cohen-Anidjar, and Ben-Tor 2005), enables us to identify shifts and trends in the repertoire from the beginning, middle, and end of the Iron Age IIA, as well to distinguish between Iron Age IIA assemblages proper and those of the IIA–IIB Transition.

The Iron Age IIA–IIB Transition phase must be attributed to Omri's Dynasty, in the second and the beginning of the third quarter of the 9th century BCE. This nomenclature, separated from the Iron Age IIA, represents our desire to isolate a distinctive phase in which the changes between the 'old' and 'new' order came about. This transition is thus crucial for the crystallisation of the social, economic, and geopolitical transformations which shaped most of Iron Age IIB. It seems to me that even now the complexity of this phase has not received the attention it deserves.

References

Aharoni, Y., and R. Amiran (1958) A New Scheme for the Sub-Division of the Iron Age in Palestine. *IEJ* 8: 171-84.

Ben-Tor, A. (1993) Tel Hazor: Notes and News. *IEJ* 43: 253-56.

—(1996) The Yigael Yadin Memorial Excavations at Hazor: Aims and Preliminary Results of 1990–1992 Seasons. *Eretz Israel* 25: 67-81.

—(1999) Excavating Hazor—Part One: Solomon's City Rises from the Ashes. *BAR* 25: 26-37, 60.

Ben-Tor, A. *et al.* (eds.) (1997) *Hazor V: An Acount of the Fifth Season of Excavation, 1968* (Jerusalem: Israel Exploration Society and Hebrew University).

Ben-Tor, A., and D. Ben-Ami (1998) Hazor and the Archaeology of the Tenth Century B.C.E. *IEJ* 48: 1-37.

Ben-Tor, A., and A. Zarzecki-Peleg (forthcoming) The Pottery of Iron IIA–IIB in the Northern Valleys and the Upper Galilee. In *The Ancient Pottery of Israel and its Neigbours from the Neolithic through the Hellenistic Period*, edited by S. Gitin (Jerusalem: Israel Exploration Society).

Bonfil, R. (1997) Middle Bronze Age to Persian Period: Area A. In *Hazor V: An Account of the Fifth Season of Excavation, 1968*, edited by A. Ben-Tor *et al.* (Jerusalem: Israel Exploration Society and Hebrew University): 25-176.

Cahill, J., and D. Tarler (1993) Hammah, Tell el-. In *The New Encyclopaedia of Archaeological Excavations in the Holy Land*, edited by E. Stern *et al.* (Jerusalem: The Israel Exploration Society): 561-62.

Edelstein, G., and N. Feig (1993) Tel 'Amal. In *The New Encyclopaedia of Archaeological Excavations in the Holy Land*, edited by E. Stern *et al.* (Jerusalem: The Israel Exploration Society): 1447-50.

Gal, Z., and Y. Alexandre (2000) *Horbat Rosh Zayit: An Iron Age Fort and Village* (Israel Antiquities Authority Reports 8; Jerusalem: Israel Antiquities Authority).

Gilboa, A., and I. Sharon (2003) An Archaeological Contribution to the Early Iron Age Chronological Debate: Alternative Chronologies for Phoenicia and Their Effects on the Levant, Cyprus, and Greece. *BASOR* 332: 7-80.

Finkelstein, I. (2000) Omride Architecture (10th-Century BCE Monumental Building Activities of the Northern Kingdom). *ZDPV* 116: 114-38.

Finkelstein, I., D. Ussishkin, and B. Halpern (eds.) (2000) *Megiddo III: 1992–1996 Seasons*, I–II (Tel Aviv: Institute of Archaeology).

Finkelstein, I., O. Zimhoni, and A. Kafri (2000) The Iron Age Pottery Assemblages from Area F, K and H and their Stratigraphic and Chronological Implications. In *Megiddo III: 1992–1996 Seasons*, I–II, edited by I. Finkelstein, D. Ussishkin, and B. Halpern (Tel Aviv: Institute of Archaeology): 244-324.

Herzog, Z. (1992) Settlement and Fortification Planning in the Iron Age. In *The Architecture of Ancient Israel*, edited by A. Kempinsky and R. Reich (Jerusalem: Israel Exploration Society): 231-74.

—(1997) *Archaeology of the City: Urban Planning in Ancient Israel and its Social Implications* (Tel Aviv: Institute of Archaeology).

Lamon, R., and G. Shipton (1939) *Megiddo I* (OIP 42; Chicago: The University of Chicago Press).

Lehmann, G., A. Killebrew, and Y. Gadot (2000) Area K. In *Megiddo III: 1992–1996 Seasons*, I–II, edited by I. Finkelstein, D. Ussishkin, and B. Halpern (Tel Aviv: Institute of Archaeology): 123-39.

Levy, S., and G. Edelstein (1972) Cinq années de fouilles à Tel 'Amal (Nir David). *RB* 79: 325-67.

Loud, G. (1948) *Megiddo*, II (OIP 62; Chicago: The University of Chicago Press).

Mazar, A. (1999) The 1997–1998 Excavations at Tel Reḥov: Preliminary Report. *IEJ* 49: 1-42.

—(2003) The Excavations at Tel Reḥov and Their Significance for the Study of the Iron Age in Israel. *Eretz-Israel* 27: 143-60 (Hebrew).

Schreiber, N. (2003) *The Cypro-Phoenician Pottery of the Iron Age* (Culture and History of the Ancient Near East 13; Leiden/Boston: Brill).

Ussishkin, D., and J. Woodhead (1992) Excavations at Tel Jezreel 1990–1991: Preliminary Report. *Tel Aviv* 19: 3-56.

—(1994) Excavations at Tel Jezreel 1992–1993: Second Preliminary Report. *Levant* 26: 1-48.

—(1997) Excavations at Tel Jezreel 1994–1996: Third Preliminary Report. *Tel Aviv* 24: 6-72.

Wightman, G.J., (1984) Building 434 and Other Public Buildings in the Northeastern Sector of Megiddo. *Tel Aviv* 11: 132-45.

Yadin, Y. (1966) Megiddo—Notes and News. *IEJ* 16: 278-80.

—(1972) *Hazor, The Head of All Those Kingdoms* (The Schweich Lectures of the British Academy 1970; London: Oxford University Press).

Yadin, Y., *et al.* (1958) *Hazor I: An Account of the First Season of Excavations, 1955* (Jerusalem: Magnes Press).

—(1960) *Hazor II: An Account of the Second Season of Excavations, 1956* (Jerusalem: Magnes Press).

—(1961) *Hazor III–IV (Plates): An Account of the Third and Fourth Seasons of Excavation, 1957–1958* (Jerusalem: Magnes Press).

—(1989) *Hazor III–IV (Text): An Account of the Third and Fourth Seasons of Excavation, 1957–1958* (Jerusalem: Israel Exploration Society and Hebrew University).

Zarzecki-Peleg, A. (1997) Hazor, Jokneam and Megiddo in the Tenth Century B.C.E. *Tel Aviv* 24: 258-88.

—(2005) Stratigraphy and Architecture. In *Yoqne'am II: The Iron Age and the Persian Period, Final Report of the Archaeological Excavations (1977–1988)*, edited by A. Ben-Tor, A. Zarzecki-Peleg, and S. Cohen-Anidjar (Jerusalem: Institute of Archaeology, Hebrew University): 5-232.

—(forthcoming) Tel Megiddo during the Iron I and II Age: The Excavations of the Yadin Expedition at Megiddo and their Contribution for Comprehending the History of this Site and other Contemporary Sites in Northern Israel (PhD Dissertation, Hebrew University, Jersualem [submitted in March 2005, Hebrew]).

Zarzecki-Peleg, A., S. Cohen-Anidjar, and A. Ben-Tor (2005) Pottery Analysis. In *Yoqne'am II: The Iron Age and the Persian Period, Final Report of the Archaeological Excavations (1977–1988)*, edited by A. Ben-Tor, A. Zarzecki-Peleg, and S. Cohen-Anidjar (Jerusalem: Institute of Archaeology, Hebrew University): 235-344.

Zimhoni, O. (1992) The Iron Age Pottery from Tel Jezreel—An Interim Report. *Tel Aviv* 19: 57-90.

—(1997) Clues from the Enclosure-Fills: Pre-Omride Settlement at Tel Jezreel. *Tel Aviv* 24: 83-109.

VI.
HISTORICAL CONSIDERATIONS

23 Stamp-Seal Amulets and Early Iron Age Chronology

An update

Stefan Münger

Abstract

This study is intended to be a follow-up of an article published in the journal *Tel Aviv* (Münger 2003), which dealt with a group of seemingly mass-produced stamp-seal amulets and their chronological implications. In the author's opinion, these seals originated in Egypt and were initially produced during the reigns of Siamun and Sheshonq I in the middle years of the 10th century BCE. Thus, such amulets may be considered as supra-regional chronological anchors. This view has, however, been challenged (Ben-Tor, forthcoming). Therefore, the case—illustrated with additional material from Palestine and Egypt—is presented again and the opinion will be upheld that Egypt should be considered as the place of origin and that the 10th century BCE is the most probable chronological timeframe for the group's initial production. Furthermore, this study discusses the typology of the seals and gives an outline of the iconographical development, thus trying to present new arguments for the view that the seals in question should be considered as a reasonably homogeneous lot. Finally, examples of alleged chronological outliers are given and their relevance for the relative chronology is discussed.

1. Prolegomena

Two obstacles seriously hamper the search for primary sources in the reconstruction of the history of the first kings of Israel and Judah (for the necessity in differentiating the value of historical sources in biblical historiography, cf., e.g., Knauf 1991; Uehlinger 2001: esp. 28-39). The first hindrance is the lack of any substantial information about the regnal years of the first Israelite and Judahite kings (cf. Dietrich and Münger 2003: 48-49 with further literature). The second obstruction is the fact that to date modern archaeology has not been able to find generally accepted, non-biblically related evidence in order to date the material remains of the era in question.

The following is intended to offer a possible solution for the latter problem based on a group of Egyptian stamp-seal amulets. These tiny finds are promising candidates for becoming interregional chronological pegs within the material culture of the late Iron Age I in Israel/Palestine, as they are independent of both information retrieved from the biblical texts as well as correlation of inscriptional and archaeological data (as, e.g., in the case of Arad). However, this can only happen under the premise that the accepted chronology of the Egyptian 21st and 22nd dynasties is viewed as a valid chronological reference system (Gilboa, Sharon and Zorn 2004: 49-51; Kitchen 1996, 2000; Shortland [Chapter 4, this volume]).

2. Introduction

Among the known stamp-seal groups of the Early Iron Age, the so-called '(Post-Ramesside) mass-produced stamp-seal amulets' form the largest coherent glyptic class known to date. It was Sir W.M. Flinders Petrie who was the first to recognize it as a distinct group typical of the Eastern Delta in Egypt. He described such seals in the wake of the 19th century CE with the following words (Petrie 1888: 27-28, but see also Petrie 1925: 29 for an alternative dating of the stamp-seals in question):

> The Tanis scarabs, on the other hand, are nearly always of schist [i.e. Enstatite—burned Steatite—cf. Keel 1995a: §387], and are often still smaller... The lower Delta scarabs are much on the same level as the later ones [the mass-produced stamp-seal amulets; S.M.], about the XXIInd dynasty; there is a coarse deep--cut work of that time which seems to belong to the whole Delta, but which is absent from Memphis and the south.

Yet, another excavator of Tanis provided a more detailed description of the glyptics in question. The Frenchman P. Montet noted (1942: 219):

> Nombreux sont les scarabées ornés au revers d'un nom royal, surtout du prénom de Thoutmès III... Le répertoire comprend en outre des animaux, lions, chevaux, crocodiles et des ornements géométriques. Un certain nombre de scarabées semblent sortis du même atelier. Le décor d'un dessin sommaire est toujours gravé profondément. Il représente par exemple deux lions près d'une chèvre renversée, ou près d'un chasseur, ou près d'un arbre ou encore un lion qui semble dévorer un chasseur tandis qu'un autre homme s'approche de leur groupe [...] [une scène] est reproduite à plusieurs exemplaires. Un personnage est assis sur un siège à haut dossier. Il tient, semble-t-il, un fléau et un sceptre. Un homme tout petit est debout devant lui ou sur ses genoux...

The last motif mentioned by Montet—the enthroned pharaoh with an adorant (cf. No. 30)—was analyzed much later by A. Wiese, who attributed this iconeme to the Ramesside period. Wiese also realized the great homogeneity of the group in question and concluded that such seals were presumably crafted in a mass-production process (Wiese 1990: 89-95). In a response to Wiese, O. Keel, who already previously recognized the typical iconography (Keel 1977: 153-54 with note 56 = *idem*, in Keel, Shuval and Uehlinger 1990: 41-42 with note 56 and an addendum on p. 272; Keel 1982: 458 with notes 179-81, updated in *idem* 1994: 106 with notes 179-81) questioned Wiese's high dating of the group on the basis of the find contexts of the items from Israel/Palestine. Keel further enlarged the set of motifs substantially and elaborated on the religio-historical importance of the mass-produced stamp-seals as a primary source for the history of religions of Early Israel (Keel, in Keel, Shuval and Uehlinger 1990: 337-67 and 396-421; Keel 1994a: 1-52; see also *idem* 1995b: 128-29; Keel and Uehlinger 1998: §61-79 *passim*). Yet, by that time, the question of the group's dating and its provenance was still unsolved.

3. Mass-produced Seals—An Overview

Mass-produced amulets can easily be isolated in the glyptic material of the Southern Levant and Egypt (in addition to the references above, the group was recognized, e.g., by Hornung and Staehelin 1976: 192 note 3; A. Mazar 1985: 18-20; Shuval, in Keel, Shuval and Uehlinger 1990: 67-161 did not separate the specific items as a distinct group). They are characterized by their coarse work, deep schematic engraving, and a clearly defined, rather poor, but highly standardized iconographic repertoire. Such seals are often grouped with other amulet types sharing some common iconographic features. Examples are (1) 'oval pieces with sheaf shaped handles' made of composition—a form most typical of the 21st dynasty (1075-945 BCE) in Egypt (Keel, in Keel, Shuval and Uehlinger 1990: 355-60) as well as (2) 'truncated pyramids' decorated on all five sides, possibly related to the Philistine culture (Keel 1994b; A. Mazar 2000: 227-28). According to the find contexts such types, as well as exceptionally large 'rectangular pieces' (e.g. Timnah [South]: Schulmann in Rothenberg 1988: 137-38, Eg. cat. no. 184, 310, fig. 46.10, pl. 123.5; see also Gilboa, Sharon and Zorn 2004: fig. 1.2) and individual scarabs made of composition/faience showing similar motifs, may slightly forerun the mass-produced amulets (cf., e.g., the scarab from Tell Qasile, stratum XII, mentioned in Münger 2003: 73 note 7; it should be noted, however, that the otherwise strict distinction between items made of Enstatite and those made of composition/faience cannot be upheld regarding the lion-shaped and possibly human face scaraboids).

a. Typology

The shape of the seals in question is usually the scarab—in accordance with the base engraving cut on a low artistic level (the following is based on the corpus from Israel/Palestine—a representative selection is given on Plates 23.1-9—for which the necessary data are normally available; but see, e.g., Nos. 10.44-45). However, other forms like (a) rectangular or (b) round pieces with a geometrically decorated domed top are common. Fifteen rectangular pieces from Israel/Palestine are known to date. They all are comprised in Keel's sub-type b (cf. Nos. 3, 12, 34, 37; see also Fig. 23.1:7, 8, 11, 12; cf. Keel 1995a: §229-32). Of the 8 round pieces with a domed back 6 belong to Keel's subtype II—a simple form with a star-shaped decoration (No. 25; see also Fig. 23.1:26). A slightly more sophisticated variant—Keel's subtype IV—with an additional barred strand pattern is represented by 2 items (cf. Keel 1995a: §196-201; note that the base engraving of those two seals are not very typical for the group; see, e.g., Fig. 23.1:29). Rarely, mass-produced amulets were used to seal bullae (e.g. Tell Keisan: Keel, in Briend and Humbert [eds.] 1980: pl. 90:26, 31; Ekron: Ben-Shlomo, forthcoming) or handles of vessels (e.g. Bethany: Saller 1953: 23-24, fig. 10; Jericho: Sellin and Watzinger 1913: 157 with pl. 42-43).

Amulets in the shape of (c) a recumbent lion (Nos. 18, 19, 22, 26, 31; cf. Keel 1995a: §159-61; note that Brandl, in Keel 1997 [Achsib no. 125 = No. 18] assumes a non-Egyptian production, dating to the 9th century BCE, for some of these seals; however, the iconography is indistinguishable from the mass-produced glyptic) or (d) a striding ibex (No. 14; cf. Keel 1995a: §147) are attested rather rarely: 13 and 1, respectively. (e) Human face scaraboids (Keel 1995a: §170) bearing motifs typical of the mass-produced items are missing completely from the material found in legal excavations in Israel/Palestine (but cf. Keel in Briend and Humbert [eds.] 1980: 265 fig. 72 for an item allegedly coming from Ta'anach; a specimen which is said to come from the area of Zagazig in the Egyptian delta is No. 17; human headed scarabs are typical elements in the Egyptian iconography of the 21st dynasty encountered on coffins and papyri, cf. Niwiński 2000: fig. 11a; note that a human face scaraboid from Tell Qasile found in an ambiguous context does not have a base engraving characteristic for the group discussed here, cf. B. Mazar 1951: pl. 35D; A. Mazar 1986: 12 note 14). (f) Regarding the scarabs it has to be stated that no clear-cut typology can be offered (see also Wiese 1990: 92 types b-d and f-h; a similar situation can be found, e.g., in the group of the 'rectangular stylized enthroned figure' [cf. Keel 1995a: §68]). Generally, the scarab amulets are very clumsily carved without paying attention to a naturalistic rendering of the dung beetle itself. Nevertheless, a few typological outlines can be traced. Vis-à-vis the shaping of the head and the back, three main groups can be discerned (note that information on the scarab shape is available only for 140 out of more than 180 mass-produced scarabs found in Israel/Palestine). See note on catalogue at the end of this chapter.

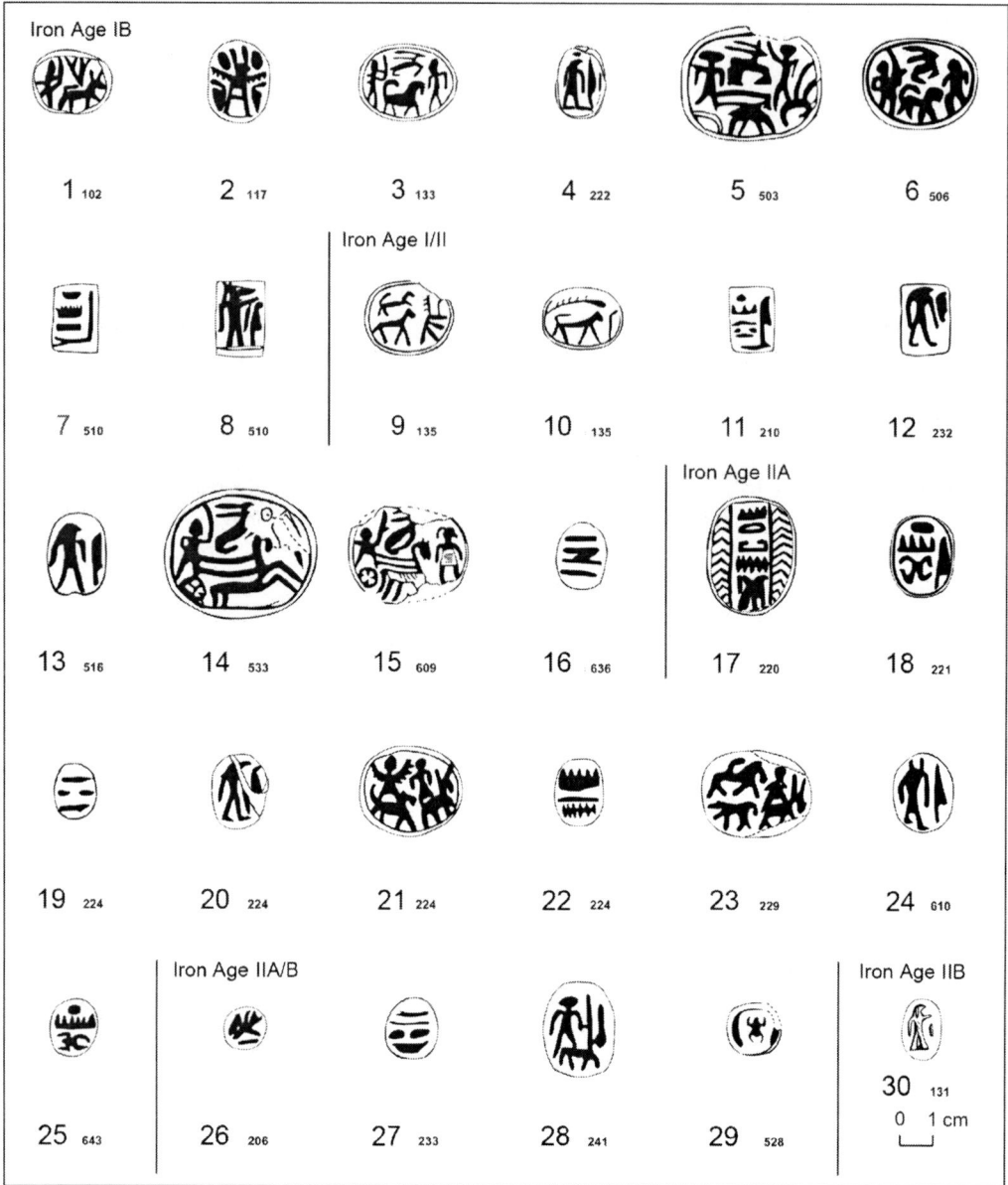

Figure 23.1. The iconographic development according to the sequence in the cemeteries at Tel el-Far'ah South. The small figures indicate the tomb numbers. (1) Petrie 1930: pl. 33. 353 (2) see No. 13 (3) pl. 29.272 (4) pl. 33.364 (5) pl. 31.287 (6) pl. 31.324 (7) pl. 35.396 (8) pl. 35.394 (9) pl. 29.282 (10) pl. 29.283 (11) see No. 3 (12) pl. 35.392 (13) pl. 31.315 (14) see No. 43 (15) pl. 31.304 (16) pl. 31.313 (17) see No. 9 (18) pl. 41.290 (19) pl. 43.536 (20) see No. 11 (21) see No. 15 (22) unpublished (UCL London, Inv. no. E.VII.83/9) (23) see No. 16 (24) pl. 33.380 (25) pl. 35.400 (26) pl. 33.350 (27) pl. 33.343 (28) pl. 43.513 (29) pl. 33.332 (30) pl. 31.316.

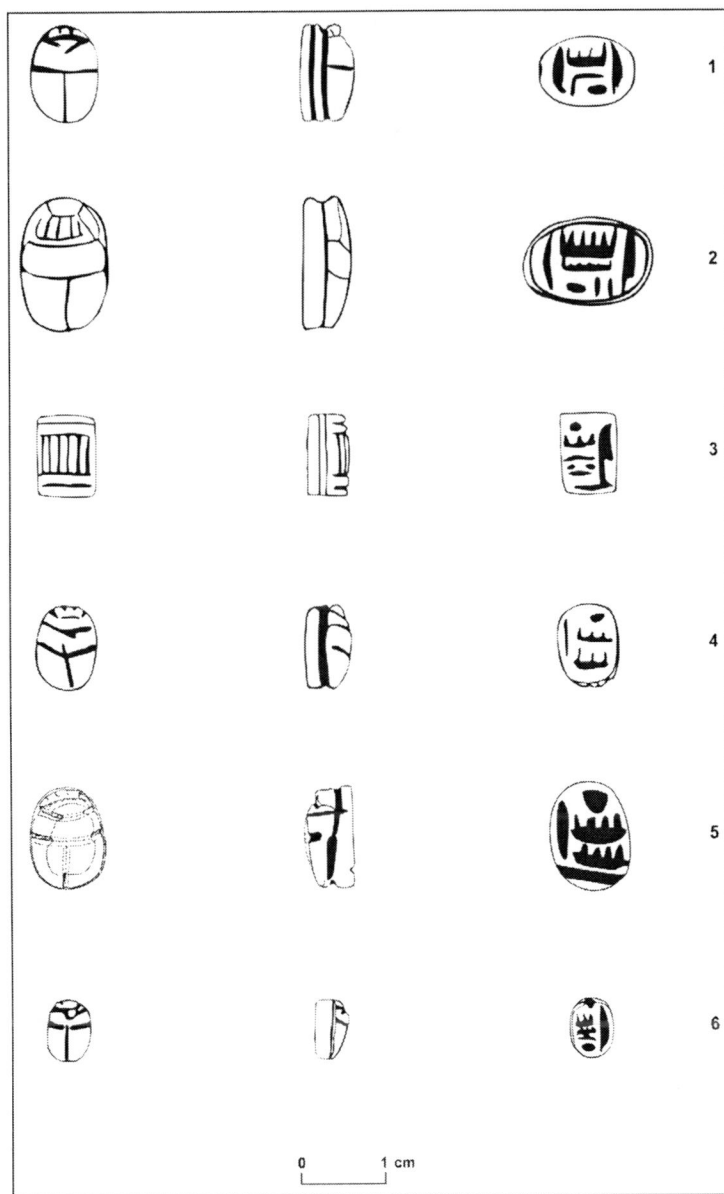

Plate 23.1. (1) Scarab: Dor, area G, phase 7a, locus 9300, reg. no. 94427. 11.4 × 8.7 × 6.1 mm (Gilboa, Sharon and Zorn 2004: fig. 1,3) (2) Scarab: Acco, unknown context. 15.6 × 10.9 × 6.1 mm (Keel 1997: Akko no. 269 [Lit]) (3) Rectangular piece with domed top: Tell el-Far'ah South, cemetery 200, tomb 210. 9.7 × 6.7 × 5.2 mm (Petrie 1930: pl. 35.393) (4) Scarab: Ashkelon, Grid 38, reg. no. 45835. 10.0 × 7.5 × 5.4 mm (Keel 1997: Aschkelon no. 100 [Lit]) (5) Scarab: el-Aḥwat, area C, main phase, locus 1314, reg. no. 13144. 12.0 × 9.5 × 6.0* mm (Keel 1997: el-Aḥwat no. 1 [Lit]) (6) Scarab: Beth-Shean, Block B-6, stratum Lower V, locus 1183. 7.2 × 5.4 × 4.1 mm (James 1966: 332 fig. 109.1; cf. A. Mazar 1993: 205 Table 1, regarding chronology and stratigraphy).

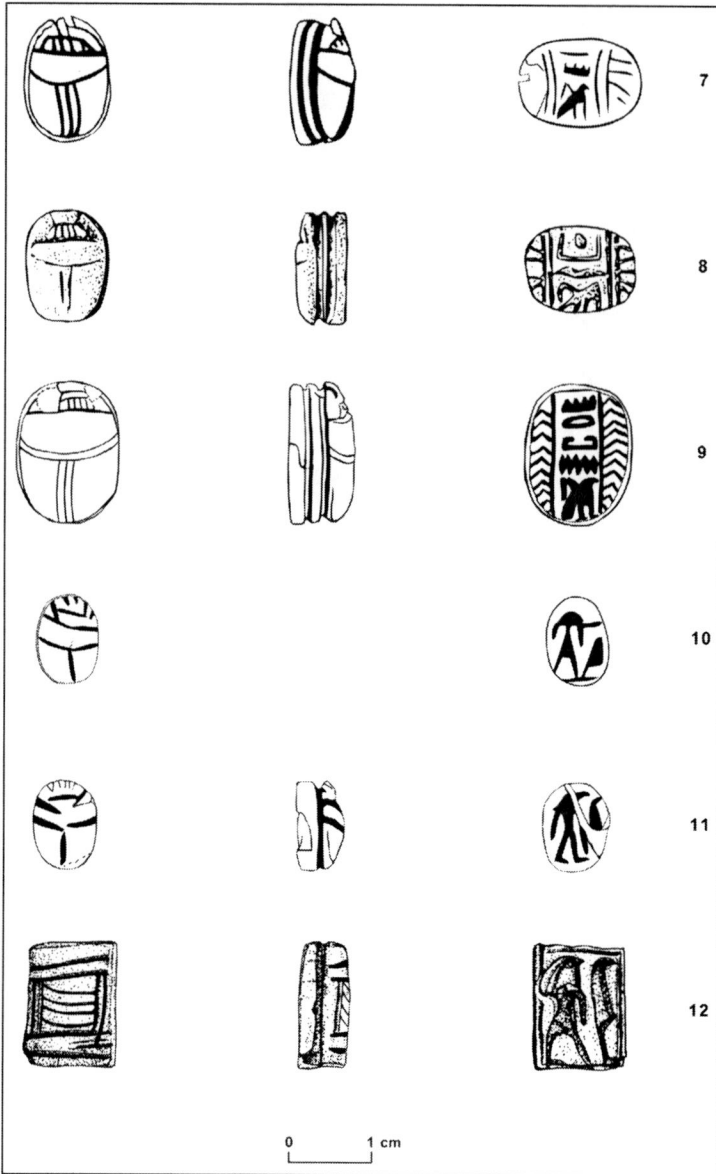

Plate 23.2. (7) Scarab: Tell en-Naṣbeh, tomb 32C, reg. no. M 2328. 15.0 × 11.0 × 9.0 mm (McCown *et al.* 1947: 295 no. 13, pl. 54.13) (8) Scarab: Tell es-Saʿidiyeh, cemetery BB 200, tomb 65, reg. no. T65.5. 14.3 × 11.0 × 6.8 mm (Tubb 1988: 65, 75, fig. 51) (9) Scarab: Tell el-Farʿah South, cemetery 200, tomb 220. 17.2 × 13.0 × 8.0 mm (Petrie 1930: pl. 35.385) (10) Scarab: Megiddo, hoard below palace 6000, stratum VIA, locus 6206, reg. no. B241/7. 10.8 × 7.8 × 6.0 mm (Yadin 1970: fig. 6 [back shown only]; Münger 2003: fig. 1.3) (11) Scarab: Tell el-Farʿah South, cemetery 200, tomb 224. 10.8 × 8.0 × 5.6 mm (Petrie 1930: pl. 43,535) (12) Rectangular piece with domed top: Tel Dan, area T, unclear Early Iron Age context, locus 2328, basket 12168. 13.0 × 9.2 × 5.0 mm (Keel 1995a: §229 fig. 159).

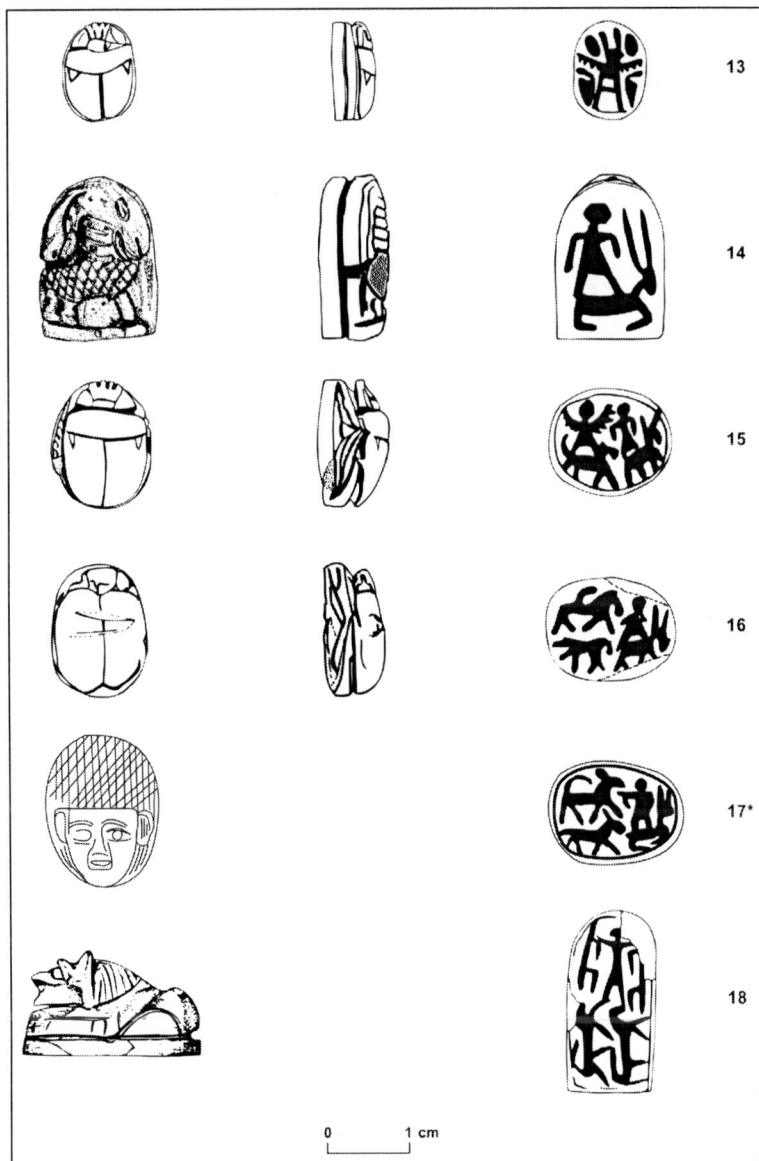

Plate 23.3. (13) Scarab: Tell el-Far'ah South, cemetery 100, tomb 117. 12.0 × 9.4 × 5.5 mm (Petrie 1930: pl. 35.398) (14) Ibex scaraboid: Tell en-Naṣbeh, tomb 32N, reg. no. M 2306. 20.0 × 15.0 × 7.0 mm (McCown *et al.* 1947: 149, 295 no. 34, pl. 54.34) (15) Scarab: Tell el-Far'ah South, cemetery 200, tomb 224. 15.5 × 12.4 × 8.4 mm (Petrie 1930: pl. 43.534) (16) Scarab: Tell el-Far'ah South, cemetery 200, tomb 229. 16.2 × 12.0 × 6.4 mm (Petrie 1930: pl. 39.439) (17) Human face scaraboid: Zagazig, bought on the market. No measurements available (Petrie 1906: pl. 33.67) (18) Lion scaraboid: Achzib, Southern cemetery, tomb 979. 22.0 × 11.0 × 12.0 mm (Keel 1997: Achsib no. 115 [Lit]).

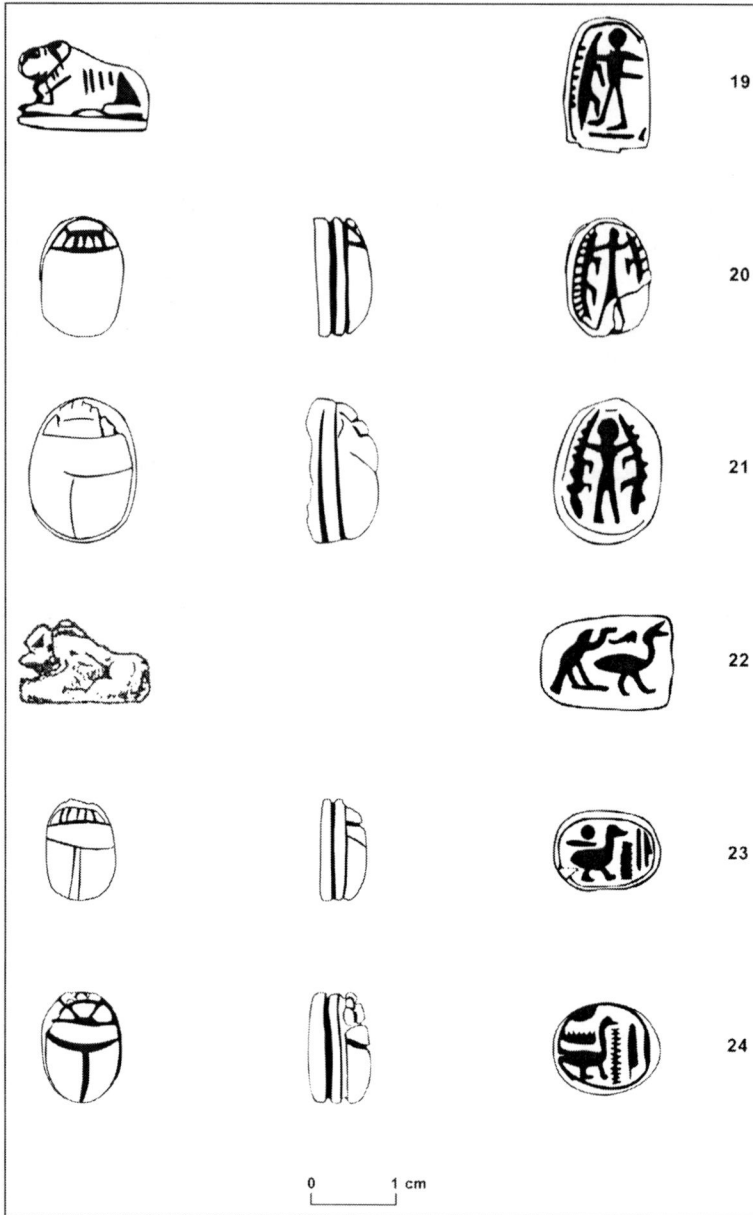

Plate 23.4. (19) Lion scaraboid: Beth-Shean, Northern cemetery, tomb 107. 16.0 × 11.0 × 11.0 mm (Oren 1973: 125 no. 6) (20) Scarab: Beth-Shemesh, Northwestern cemetery, tomb 1. 14.0 × 10.2 × 7.4 mm (Mackenzie 1912–13: 61, pl. 29A,1) (21) Scarab: Tell el-'Ajjul, unknown context. 17.0 × 12.0* × 8.0 mm (Keel 1997: Tell el-'Aǧul no. 200 [Lit]) (22) Lion scaraboid: Megiddo, 'nördliche Brandstätte, vierte Schicht', ambiguous context. 16.2 × 11.5 × 9.7 mm (Keel 1994a: 24 pl. 11.26 [Lit]) (23) Scarab: Megiddo, tomb 3143, reg. no. b1012. 13.0 × 8.7 × 5.7 mm (Keel 1995a: §657 [Lit]; Münger 2003: fig. 4,1) (24) Scarab: Dor, area G, phase 7a, locus 9259, reg. no. 92604. 13.0 × 10.2 × 7.2 mm (Münger 2003: fig. 4.2; Gilboa, Sharon and Zorn 2004).

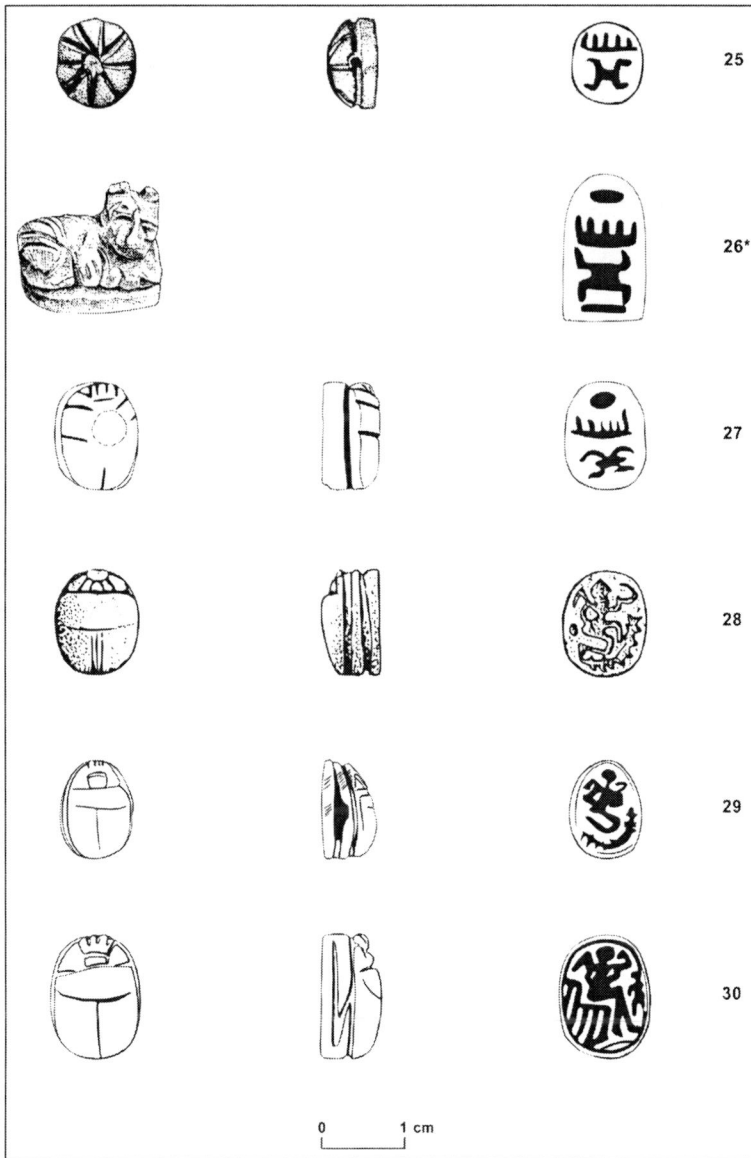

Plate 23.5. (25) Round piece with domed top: Megiddo, Schumacher's hoard, 'nördliche Brandstätte, vierte Schicht', ambiguous context. 10.1 × 9.5 × 5.3 mm (Keel 1994a: 33 no. 15 with plates 1b, no. 15.2 no. 24 and 9.15, note p. 52 [Lit]) (26) Lion scaraboid: Dor, foundation of the four-chambered gate. No measurements available (Stern 2000: 114 fig. 58) (27) Scarab: Tell el-Far'ah South, unknown context, cemetery 600. 13.0 × 10.2 × 6.7 mm (Petrie 1930: pl. 43.539) (28) Scarab: Tell es-Sa'idiyeh, cemetery BB 200, tomb 65, reg. no. T65.2. 12.3 × 10.4 × 7.1 mm (Tubb 1988: 65, 75, fig. 51) (29) Scarab: Tell el-'Ajjul, cemetery VI, tomb 1029. 12.0 × 9.0 × 7.0 mm (Keel 1997: Tell el-'Aǧul no. 210 [Lit]) (30) Scarab: Tell el-'Ajjul, area T, 'stratum TCQ, level 965', ambiguous context. 15.0 × 12.0 × 7.0 mm (Keel 1997: Tell el-'Aǧul no. 798 [Lit]).

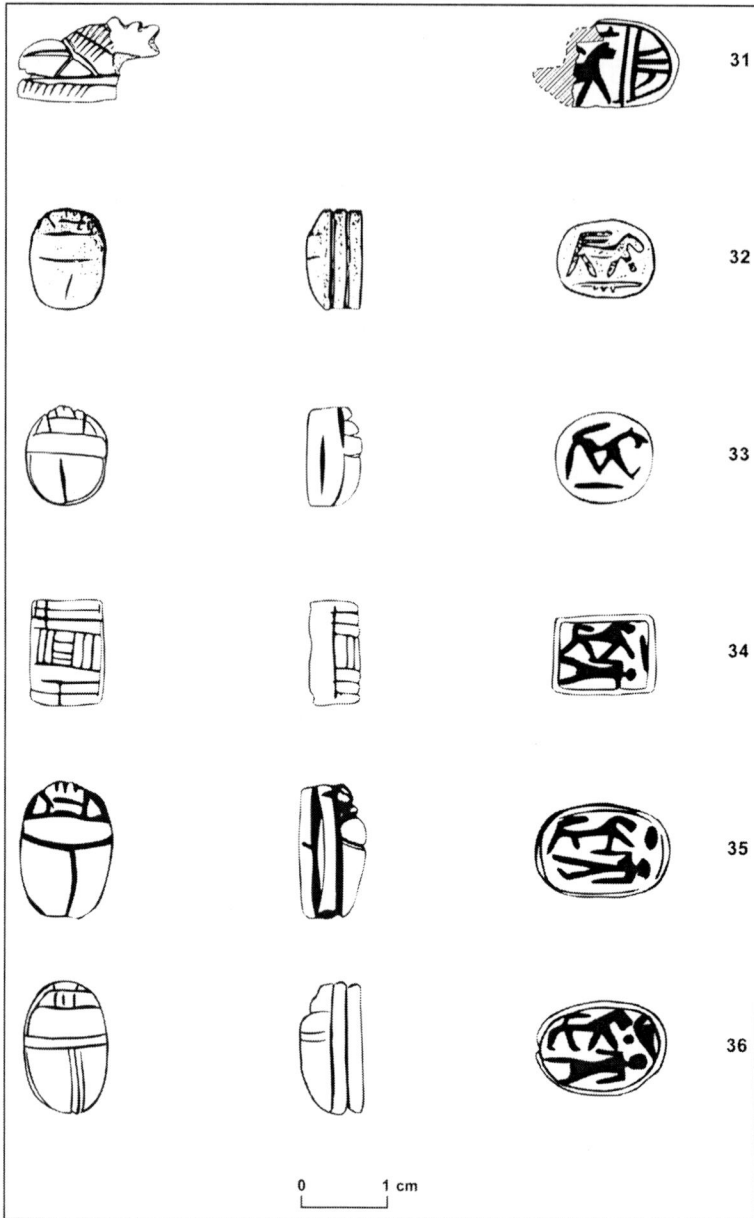

Plate 23.6. (31) Lion scaraboid: Arad, fortress, stratum XII, locus 903, reg. no. 6500/50. 17.2* × 10.2 × 9.6* mm (Keel 1997: Arad no. 21 [Lit]) (32) Scarab: Tell es-Saʿidiyeh, cemetery BB 200, tomb 65, reg. no. T65.4. 12.2 × 10.0 × 6.0 mm (Tubb 1988: 65, 75, fig. 51) (33) Scarab: Acco, surface find. 11.5 × 10.0 × 7.0 mm (Keel 1997: Akko no. 142 [Lit]) (34) Rectangular piece with domed top: Acco, surface find. 12.0 × 9.0 × 6.0 mm (Keel 1997: Akko no. 121 [Lit]) (35) Scarab: Beersheba, area A1, stratum VII, locus 1683, reg. no. 15114/50. 15.5 × 11.0 × 7.5 mm (Giveon, in Herzog *et al*. 1984: 120-21, fig. 38.2, pl. 15.3) (36) Scarab: Tel Rekesh, surface find. 15.0 × 10.5 × 7.4 mm (unpublished).

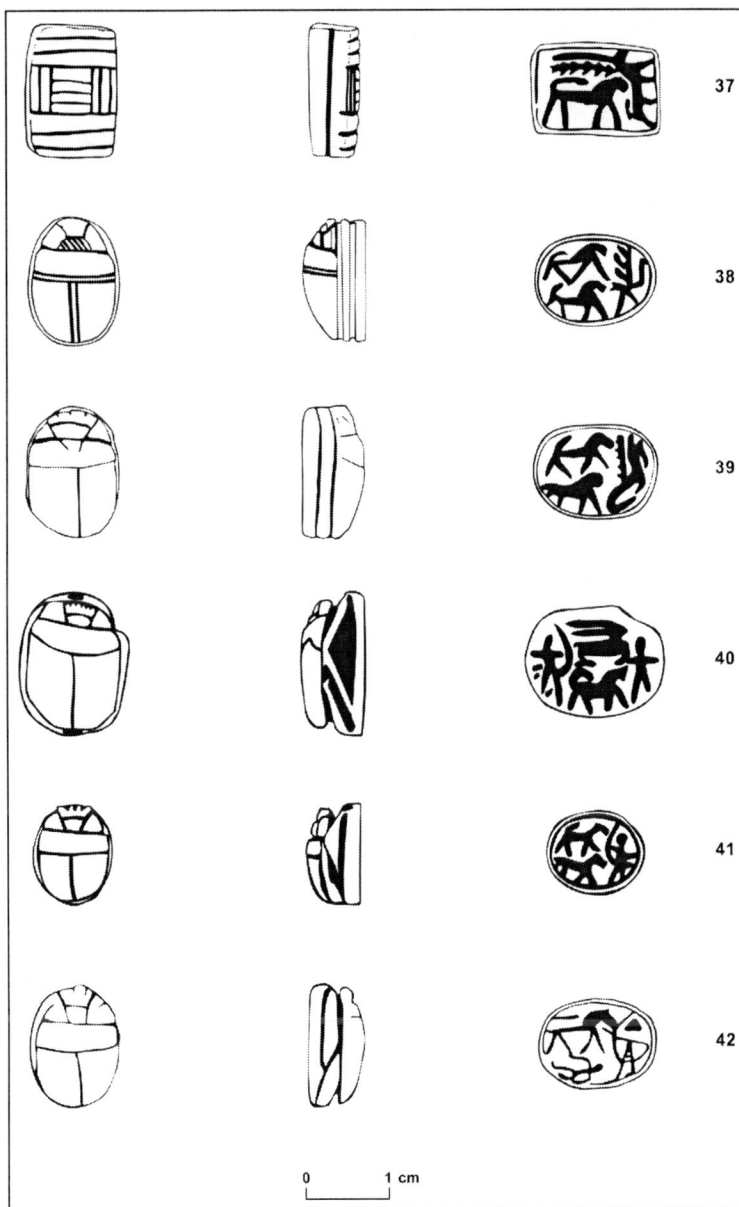

Plate 23.7. (37) Rectangular piece with domed top: Tell el-Far'ah South, 'stratum V/W, level 374'. 15.8 × 11.0 × 6.5 mm (Macdonald, Starkey and Harding 1932: pl. 61 [photo], top right, 3rd row) (38) Scarab: Nazareth, burial cave, reg. no. 4. 15.0 × 11.0 × 7.0 mm (Vitto 2001: 162-64, 166 fig. 3) (39) Scarab: Acco, surface find, 15.5 × 12.3 × 7.9 mm (Keel 1997: Akko no. 90 [Lit]) (40) Scarab: Tell Jemmeh, unknown context. 17.0 × 13.0 × 8.0 mm (Petrie 1928: pl. 17.44; pl. 19.47) (41) Scarab: Ta'anach; area B; stratum IB, locus 27, reg. no. TT 701. 12.1 × 9.8 × 7.1 mm (Lapp 1967: 34-35, fig. 24 top left, 2nd item from right) (42) Scarab: Acco; surface find. 14.5 × 11.2 × 7.0 mm (Keel 1997: Akko no. 233 [Lit]).

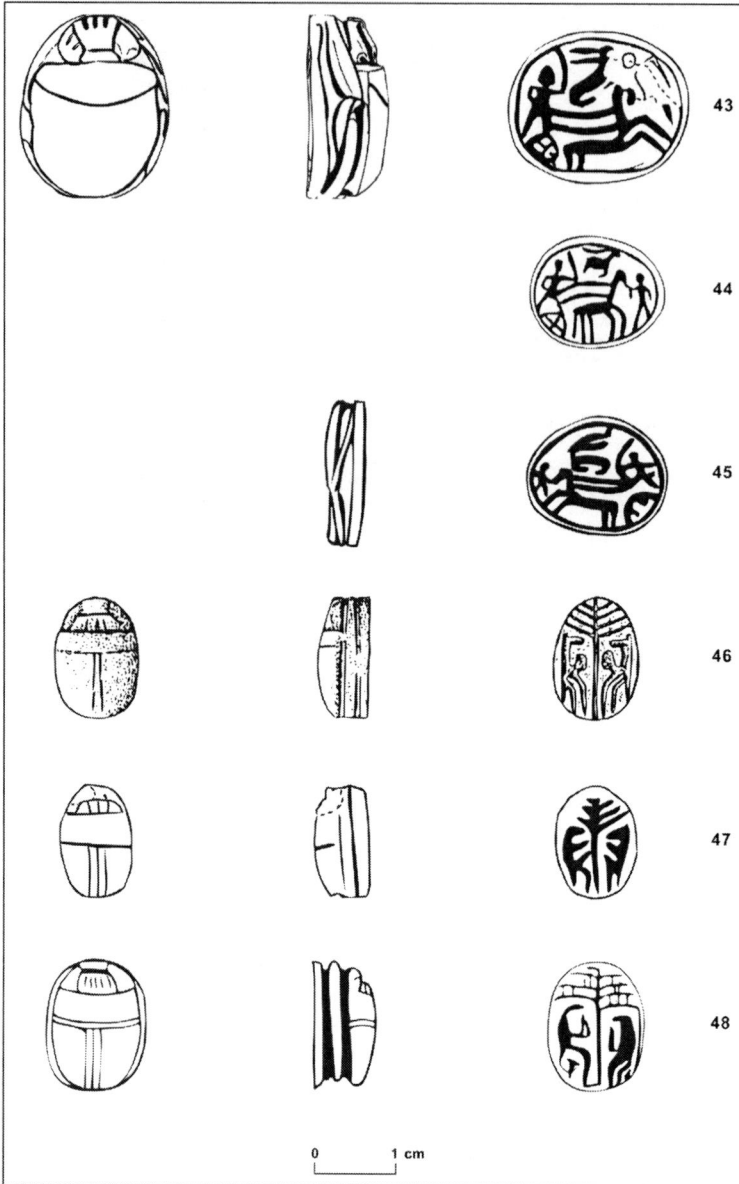

Plate 23.8. (43) Scarab: Tell el-Far'ah South, cemetery 500, tomb 533. 22.9 × 18.8 × 10.3 mm (Petrie 1930: 10, pl. 31.284; pl. 69) (44) Scarab: Tell Qasile; area A; stratum VIII (B. Mazar)/ stratum XI–X (A. Mazar), locus L2. 14.7 mm (B. Mazar 1951: 204, fig. 13a and pl. 37.8; A. Mazar 1985: 18-20; fig. 6.2; 1986: 12 note 14 [mentioned]) (45) Scarab: Gezer, '4th Semitic Period', 18.0 × 15.0 × 5.0 mm (Macalister 1912: II: 327-28, no. 364 and III: pl. 208.51) (46) Scarab: Tell es-Sa'idiyeh, cemetery BB 200, tomb 65, reg. no. T65.6. 13.9 × 10.8 × 6.4 mm (Tubb 1988: 65, 75, fig. 51) (47) Scarab: Megiddo, area A, stratum IV, locus 1650, reg. no. M 5470. 14.0 × 10.0 × 7.5 mm (Lamon and Shipton 1939: 144 pl. 69/70.32) (48) Scarab: Acco, surface find. 16.0 × 12.0 × 8.0 mm (Keel 1997: Akko no. 202 [Lit]).

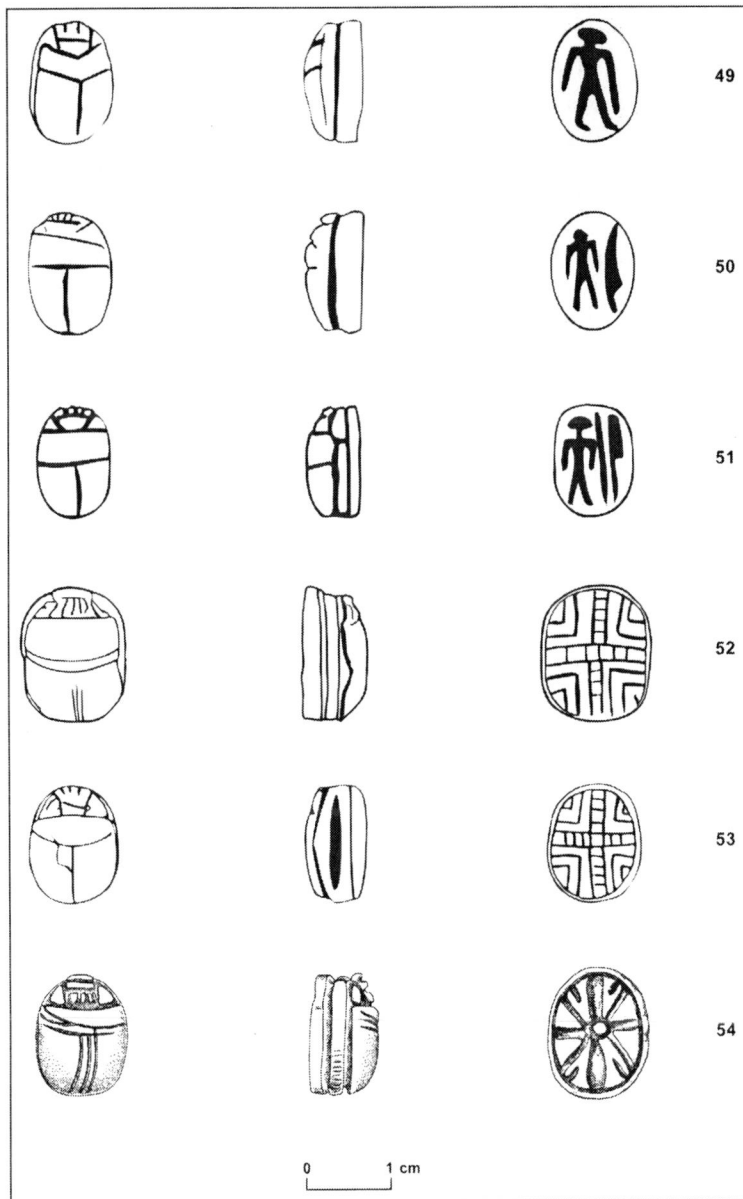

Plate 23.9. (49) Scarab: Acco, surface find. 14.5 × 10.5 × 6.5 mm (Keel 1997: Akko no. 113 [Lit]). (50) Scarab: Megiddo, surface find, square R5, reg. no. M 2340. 14.5 × 10.0 × 7.0 mm (Lamon and Shipton 1939: pl. 67.17 and 68.16) (51) Scarab: Megiddo, Schumacher's hoard, 'nördliche Brand-stätte, vierte Schicht', ambiguous context. 13.4 × 10.4 × 6.7 mm (Keel 1994a: 23-24 no. 6 with pls. 1b no. 6, 2 no. 8 and 7,6, note p. 52 [Lit]) (52) Scarab: Tell el-'Ajjul, unknown context. 16.0 × 13.0 × 8.0 mm (Keel 1997: Tell el-'Aǧul no. 872 [Lit]) (53) Scarab: Acco; surface find. 14.0 × 12.0 × 7.0 mm (Keel 1997: Akko no. 161 [Lit]) (54) Scarab: Khirbet Nisya, tomb 65, locus 2, basket 3, reg. no. 24. 14.0 × 11.0 × 8.0 mm (Brandl 2002: 40-42 fig. 5).

Group A (Nos. 2, 7–9, 20, 23, 28, 36, 38, 46–48, 52). There is a specific, vertically hatched head-type which Petrie called 'ribbed head' and which he dated to the 25th–26th dynasties (728–525 BCE; cf. Petrie 1917: 5 with pl. 68 esp. nos. 70, 74, 78, 86; I thank B. Brandl for pointing me to this reference). This type comes close to a head/clypeus type which is—according to Rowe—generally common to New Kingdom scarabs (Rowe 1936: pl. 32, types HC 15-16; according to Keel 1995a: §87 and Brandl 2003: 255-57, it cannot be dated prior to the 19th dynasty). However, contrary to Rowe's types HC15 and HC16 (the latter is actually closer to our type as it lacks an additional dividing line between the head and the pronotum) the 'ribbed heads' of the mass-production items are round in shape and not trapezoidal like their possible archetypes (note that Brandl [2003] views head-type HC15 to be of Southern Canaanite origin). Equally, in many instances the clypeus—if at all present—is shorter than that of the HC15/16 type. In most cases such heads are accompanied by an equally typical back-type with multiple, roughly cut dividing lines between the elytra (wing-cases) and the pronotum. In no instances are the humeral callosities indicated with v-shaped marks (in this respect this type has clearly to be differentiated from Hölbl's Asiatic types of the 1st millennium BCE [1986: 172-73, Typentafel 1: nos. 15-16, 18-20, 23]). As a rule, the combination of such back- and head-types—which is only attested on approximately 25% of the assemblage—is complemented by a very debased side-type that only shows one or two revolving horizontal lines instead of the naturalistic three legs on each side (Type e11, according to the typology of Tufnell 1984: 37 fig. 14).

Group B (Nos. 1, 4–6, 10–11, 21, 24, 27, 30, 32-33, 35, 39–42, 49–51, 53). The lion's share—approximately 55% of the mass-produced scarabs—has a very generic v- or u-shaped combination of the head and—in some cases—the corrugated clypeus. Such a type is actually absent from Rowe's typology. Its fabrication corroborates the assumption that these seals have been crafted in a rationalized production process in so far, as the basic features of the beetle have been cut with a few single strokes only. Contrary to the above-mentioned scarab subtype of Group A, single lines divide the pronotum and the elytra on the backs of Group B. Again, the v-shaped notches are missing. Nevertheless, a variety of different side-types occur. As in Group A, the legs may be represented with horizontal lines (Nos. 1, 4-6, 11, 21, 24, 27, 32-33, 35, 39, 49-51, 53), but there are also seals with legs indicated with two offset notches/kerfs (similar to Tufnell's side type e5 [1984: 37 fig. 14] or Rowe's types 37-38 [1936: pl. 35]; cf. Nos. 30, 41-42). Finally, in Group B, scarabs with plastically worked legs can be found as well (similar to Tufnell's type d5 [1984], or type 27 following Rowe [1936]; cf. No. 40; no information is currently available for No. 10).

Group C (Nos. 13, 15, 43). Only a few scarabs—approximately 7%—are close to the Ramesside glyptic (see the overview in Keel 1995a: figs. 56-58, 62-64) with a properly worked head and a more or less correct and naturalistic rendering of the back and the legs. It should be noted that such scarabs are in some cases larger than the other mass-produced scarab-types (the average length is 14.0 mm with a range from 7.2 mm [No. 6] to 22.9 mm [No. 43]). Also because of their base engravings they might mark the first stage in the production process (cf. e.g. No. 43; Keel 1997: Aschdod no. 54). The remaining scarabs—approximately 13%—are cut very individually and cannot be grouped into further subtypes (Nos. 16, 29, 54).

b. Iconography

The iconography of the base engravings in the group under question can be divided into a few main themes (note that the individual motifs are slightly differently distributed in Egypt as compared to Israel/Palestine; cf. Münger 2005, esp. fig. 6). The divine sphere includes the genuine

Egyptian gods: Amun, who is never depicted figuratively and represented either by the hieroglyphs *Jmn (-R')* (Nos. 1–3, defectively written: Nos. 4-6; see also Fig. 23.1:7, 22², 27²) or in cryptographic writing (Nos. 7–9; note that the single striding lion, sometimes associated with a sign similar to the hieroglyph 'flowering reed' [M17 in Gardiner's sign list, 1957], can also be interpreted as the cryptographic rendering of the divine name Amun; cf. Keel, in Keel, Shuval and Uehlinger 1990: 405-10; Keel and Uehlinger 1998: §64); the falcon-headed god Horus (Nos. 10–12 see also Fig. 23.1:4, 8², 12, 13, 20, 30); the originally Asiatic deities Baal (in Sethian stance; No. 13), Reshef (No. 14, see also Fig. 23.1:28, as well as Nos. 16–17)—the latter two either alone or paired (No. 15); and a 'Lord of the crocodiles' (Nos. 18–21). Goddesses are seemingly absent, apart from one very vague allusion to the name of the Egyptian goddess Mut on the base of a lion-scaraboid found by Schumacher in a hoard at Megiddo (No. 22). The base shows (from left to right) the vulture (G15 in Gardiner's sign list, ideogram for the goddess *Mwt*), *t* (X1) and a pintail duck (G39, phonetic for *z3*, 'son') that can be read as the name *z3(t) Mwt* ('son/daughter of Mut') (Ranke 1935: 282.3, 289.1; see already Watzinger 1929: 52). Furthermore, there is a sequence of hieroglyphs that the present author proposed to read as the name of the pharaoh Siamun (Nos. 23–24; cf. Münger 2003: 72-73; see below). Other hieroglyphic combinations are scarce, except for *Mn-ḫpr-r'*, the throne-name of the famed pharaoh Thutmosis III (1479–1426 BCE), whose high level of representation within the set of motifs will prove to be significant (Nos. 25–27; see also Fig. 23.1:18, 25, 29²). Furthermore, the royal sphere embodies the anonymous king kneeling on a branch (Nos. 28–29) or sitting on his throne accompanied by an adorant (No. 30).

However, the most frequent base engravings are various scenes with the lion as a central motif (see also Nos. 16–18), be it the single striding lion (Nos. 31–33; see also Fig. 23.1:10), the lion trampling upon a man stretched on the ground (Nos. 34–36, see also No. 42) or hunting a fleeing caprid (No. 37), or finally two lions, one atop the other, stalking an ostrich (Nos. 38–39; see also Fig. 23.1:9). Furthermore, the lion plays a central role in hunting scenes, where it is, sometimes in company with a resting caprid and a human figure (No. 40; see also Fig. 23.1:3, 6), now in turn tracked by a standing or kneeling archer (Nos. 41–42; for another hunting scene see Fig. 23.1:1). These last motifs and especially the charioteer scenes (Nos. 43–45; see also Fig. 23.1:5, 15)—among others—clearly show the dependency of the iconography of the Egyptian 19th–20th dynasties (1292–1075 BCE; Keel in Keel, Shuval and Uehlinger 1990: 290 fig. 0130). This is the reason why some scholars dubbed the group as 'Ramesside' (Wiese 1990: 90) or 'Post-Ramesside' (Keel 1994a: 49), depending on their respective dating (as will be shown below, the designation 'Tanite' is more appropriate in view of the group's chronological horizon and presumed place of production).

Beside the above, there are other motifs, for example, the two apes flanking a tree or pillar (Nos. 46–48), which show a clear nexus to the Egyptian culture (Hornung and Staehelin 1976: 108; Keel 1995a: §724). But there are also new iconographic features such as the more generic motif displaying a standing human figure with sloping shoulders (Nos. 49–51 and possibly Fig. 23.1:24²; sometimes with additional elements on its side) or a geometric pattern with a central cross (Nos. 52–53), which seems to belong exclusively to the group in question. Only cautiously mentioned should be the motif with a four-leafed rosette with intersecting curls or *uraei* (No. 54). This motif has a long tradition that also continues, as in the case of, for example, the enthroned pharaoh, into later periods (e.g. Tell el-Far'ah South: Petrie 1930: pl. 43.502-503; cf. the overview given by Keel in Keel, Shuval and Uehlinger: 352-53, but note that not all of these mentioned or illustrated scarabs should be grouped with the mass-production seals, esp. nos. 40 [Mt. Ebal], 41 [Javneh], 42 [Beth-Shemesh] and 42a [Tell Keisan]; see also Brandl 2002: 41-42). An attribution to the mass-produced seals is, in such individual cases, thus dependent on the seal type rather than on the motifs displayed on it.

c. Identifying the Group

After having presented the main iconographic motifs and the different seal types, the question might be raised as to whether this large assemblage actually forms one homogeneous group (Ben-Tor, forthcoming). As may be deduced from the illustrated examples (Fig. 23.1 and Plates 23.1–9), there are various interlocking elements that justify the hypothesis that all these seals are connected to each other and that they most probably originate from one single place of production. The following mutual characteristics can be summarized as follows:

1. In all cases the bases are engraved in a very typical coarse and deep-cut style (e.g. in Fig. 23.1:28 the engraving is 1.2 mm deep). Purely linear or hollowed-out engraving with hatching is absent.

2. All the different amulet types bear motifs from one common iconographic pool. Hardly any type is restricted to iconemes that cannot be found on other types as well.

3. There are many ties that link the two main scarab subtypes (Group A and B, see above), thus suggesting that these types were in use at the same time and possibly fabricated not too distant geographically or chronologically from each other.

d. Distribution and Place of Production

Isolated mass-produced stamp seals have been found all over the Mediterranean and Greater Syria. However, significant numbers have been collected, mainly as surface finds (cf., e.g., Montet 1942: 216; there are some items reported that were bought on the market in Zagazig; cf. Petrie 1906: pl. 33.67-68, 70), in Egypt, at Third Intermediate Period sites in the Eastern Delta, such as Tell Nebesheh (Petrie 1888: pl. 8.19; possibly the earliest context in Egypt documented; the tomb contained pottery parallel to Tell Qasile X, Megiddo VIA and Beth Shean VI; cf. also Aston 1996: 25-26), Saft el-Henna (Petrie 1906: pl. 37.20, 56), er-Retabeh (Petrie 1917: pl. 33.21) and Tell-Yehudiyah (Griffith 1890: pl. 16.15; Petrie 1906: pl. 9.153; *idem*. pl. 9.188-89 = *idem* 1925: pl. 19 no. 1527-28; *idem* 1906: pl. 11.209 = *idem* 1925: pl. 19 no. 1585; *idem* 1906: pl. 11.210-11; *idem* 1906: 222 = *idem* 1925: pl. 19 no. 1561; *idem* 1925: pl. 11.242). Further to the South, some seals were found in Memphis (Petrie and Walker 1909: pl. 34.92; Petrie 1925: pl. 19 nos. 1449, 1464; Petrie and Walker 1909: pl. 34.93 = Petrie 1925: pl. 19 no. 1483; Petrie and Walker 1909: pl. 34.108.). One item originates from el-Lahun (Petrie 1925: pl. 19 no. 1518; see also Petrie 1891: pl. 29.2, side B). Unfortunately, Medinet Habu—one of the rare sites with stratified material—yielded not a single mass-produced seal with one possible exception that was found—among other seals—in a 22nd to 26th dynasty context (Teeter 2003: 39 no. 36 with pl. 13c [as this is a *Mn-ḫpr-rˤ* scarab, utmost caution should be exercised regarding an attribution with the group in question]). The bulk of the material, however, comes from Tanis—the newly founded capital of the 21st and 22nd dynasties. From this site only a few items have been published, by Petrie (1888: pl. 8.72-73, 79, 82-83) and Montet (1942: fig. 63.1, 3). According to the records at Centre Wladimir Golenischeff in Paris ca. 25 items collected during Montet's expedition are now hosted in the Louvre (Inv. nos. E14764, E14773, E14775, E14776, E14786, E14790, E14798, E14933, E14964, E15862, E15863, E15866, E15875, E15880, E15881, E15886?, E15887, E15892, E15896, E15922, E15925, E15935, E15941, E15964, E15977), four additional ones are located in the museum at Cairo (JE 67053, JE 67060 = Montet 1942: fig. 63.1, JE 87870, JE 87874) and more than 30 additional items are documented on registration cards only at Centre Wladimir Golenischeff and await publication. These figures, however, have recently been contested by D. Ben-Tor who counted not more than 23 in the Montet archive in Paris (Ben-Tor, forthcoming). But, seemingly, she overlooked various motifs (e.g. the lord of the animals [like Nos. 19–21], the enthroned pharaoh [like No. 30], the king kneeling on a branch [like Nos. 28–29] or variants of *Mn-ḫpr-rˤ* [similar to Nos. 25–27]) or seal types typical for the group in question (lion scaraboids, rectangular or round pieces with a domed top). In sum, it should not be disputed that Tanis produced by far the greatest amount of the stamp-seals in question and could thus be considered in first place as the original place of production. This suggestion is supported by the fact that such seals are almost uniquely made of Enstatite—a material that was at the time mainly available in Egypt (Keel 1995a: §386). It is true, for example in the case of Israel/Palestine, that partly worked, unfinished or blank scarabs—attested, for example, at Beit Mirsim or at Tell el-'Ajjul—suggest local workshops (Keel 1995a: §59f.; for Levantine scarab productions cf., e.g., Ben-Tor 1997, 2003; Keel 1995b; see also Brandl 2003). However, it is rather unlikely that seals made of Enstatite were re-imported in such large quantities (Münger 2003: 71) and one would expect a lower ratio of such foreign seals in Egypt (e.g. compare the number of examples in Mlinar 2001 *passim*; Mlinar, in Fischer and Sadeq 2002: esp. 149-51 for Middle Bronze Age scarabs or Brandl 2003: esp. 257-58 for Late Bronze Age types). Additionally, a further—though not archaeological—argument for an Egyptian origin of the seals in question could be put forward, but with the highest caution. Major scarab collections, such as the former collection of Fouad S. Matouk, now hosted at the Department for Biblical Studies at Fribourg University, which were mainly assembled in Egypt, seem to support the hypothesis that such seals were indeed very common in Egypt (cf., e.g., Matouk 1977: nos. 559-76, 642-61, 750-55, 1312a–c.1511-24, 1581-86, 2248, 2267 and many more; note that Matouk—though of Syrian origin and later based in the Lebanon—spent most of his life in Egypt; cf. Uehlinger 1996: 58). Equally, P.E. Newberry's catalogue of seals kept in the Museum of Cairo—though outdated and incomplete—provides a glimpse of the inventory (Newberry 1907: pl. 4.36198; 7.36606, 36317, 36419, 37337; pl. 10.36372, 36595, 36640; pl. 13.36811, 36810, 36804-36805; pl. 14.36329 to name safe examples; cf. also the many items from the Cairo museum cited, e.g., in Wiese 1990: 41-50 and 89-104, esp. 44 and 94). As for the location of the workshop (or workshops; Münger 2003: 67 clearly referred to individual motifs) producing such seals, the suggestion was made by Keel that this was the temple of Amun at Tanis (Keel and Uehlinger 1998: §254). That seal amulets indeed have been produced in temple compounds is clearly attested at Memphis where in the courtyard of the Ptah-temple a scarab workshop dating to the end of the 13th century BCE with many unfinished items has been uncovered (cf. now Keel and Page Gasser 2003: 14-15 with fig. Ib and further references).

e. Relative and Absolute Dating

A comprehensive study of the find context of all items found in Cis- and Transjordan—well over 200 seals—has shown that regarding the *relative* chronology the amulets in question generally have not been found prior to a ceramic horizon which is defined by so-called late Philistine ware, Cypriot White-Painted I and wheelmade 'Black-slip'/Bucchero Ware and Phoenician Bichrome Ware. Thus, settlement layers that correspond to the well-defined Early Iron Age IB horizon mark the initial stage of the appearance of the mass-produced stamp-seal amulets in the Levant (Table 1). This stage includes the material culture of Northern sites such as Tell Qasile X, phase 7a-b in area G or phase 9b in area D2 at Dor, Jokneam XVII, Megiddo VIA or Kinneret V, among others. The sequence of the find contexts from the cemeteries of Tell el-Far'ah South furthermore—and in accordance with other sites—suggests that the deposition of the mass-produced seal came to an end with the appearance of imported pottery types of a later time, primarily with the arrival of Cypriot Black-on-Red and White-Painted III ware—hallmarks of the Iron Age IIA horizon that includes settlement layers like Rosh Zayit III–II, Hazor X–VIII, Megiddo V–IVB and Tel Rehov VI–IV (Münger 2003: 73 with further references; for ostensible outliers, see below). Tell el-Far'ah South is, therefore, possibly the only—though, because of the hardly usable documentation, a not very suitable—place to study the iconographic development of the mass-produced seals (Fig. 23.1; note the degenerated base-engravings in the later phases, e.g., Fig. 23.1:16, 19, 22, 26-27, 29). In this sequence it can be observed that seals bearing the name of Thutmosis III (*Mn-ḫpr-rʿ*), in fact appear only at a somewhat later stage, corresponding to the beginning of the Iron IIA. This might prove chronologically significant. Datable scarabs (i.e. bearing the names of pharaohs) using this name/title are not attested after Ramses IV (1156–1150 BCE) and only reappear much later in connection with the 10th-century BCE pharaohs Siamun and especially Sheshonq I, who actually could have been the promoter of the *Mn-ḫpr-rʾ* seal production (Münger 2003: 73-74 with further references and additional arguments; for the cultural historical background of this period see now Schipper 2005, esp. 299-324).

Table 1. Main deposits in Israel/Palestine in chronological order.

Archaeological Periods		*Transitional Periods or Contexts with a Long Range*	
Iron Age IB = 33.0%	el-Ahwat (main phase), Tell es-Saʿidiyeh (tombs 65, 118, 444), Taʿanach IB *** Tell el-ʿAjjul (tombs 1029, 1101), Beth Shean (tomb 107), Tel Dan (area T), Dor 9b (area D2)/7a (area G), Tell el-Farʿah South ('Strata' C and V–W, tombs 102, 117, 133?, 222, 503, 506, 510?), Megiddo VIA, Nazareth (burial cave), Kh. Nisya (tomb 65), Pella (tomb 89), Tell Qasile X?	Iron IB/IIA = 29.1% Megiddo (Schumacher's hoard) *** Arad XII, Beersheba VII, Dor 6b (area G), Tell el-Farʿah South (tombs 135, 210, 232, 516, 533?, 609, 636), Tell en-Nasbeh (tomb 32), et-Tayibeh (burial cave 6)	
Iron Age IIA = 9.4%	Achzib (tomb 979), Beth Shean Lower V, Dor 6a (area G), Tell el-Farʿah South (tombs 220, 221, 224?, 610, 643), Tel Gerisa		Iron IIA/B = 8.7% Achzib (tomb ZR9), Ashkelon, Beth Shemesh (tomb 1), Tell el-Farʿah South (tombs 206, 229, 233, 241, 528)
Iron Age IIB = 10.2%	Tell Abu Salima (SW-graves, 'stratum' K), Beth Shean Upper V, Tell Deir ʿAlla (phase IX), Tell el-Farʿah South (burial 131), Gezer (4th Semitic Period), Lachish (tombs 191, 218, 1002), Megiddo IV		
Later deposits = 9.4%	Akko II, Aphek X–4, Ashkelon, Bethany (columbarium), Dor (Persian pits), Tell Jemmeh ('stratum' E–F), Megiddo F2		

The *absolute* chronological chief witness regarding the dating of the group is a scarab found in a late Iron Age IB context in phase 7a at Dor (No. 24; cf. also No. 23 said to originate from a Middle Bronze Age tomb at Megiddo). The scarab was discovered in one and the same room together with three other mass-produced seals and one seal that is closely related to the seals in question. Fortunately, a meticulous and careful report on these finds, their archaeological context, the accompanying pottery assemblage of the last phase of the Iron Age I and the position of the finds in the ^{14}C-sequence of Dor is at hand (Gilboa, Sharon and Zorn 2004). It is noteworthy to mention that the pottery horizon of phase 7a at Dor generally corresponds to the *earliest* appearance of the mass-produced seals (according to the radiometric data from Dor this horizon ends shortly before 880 BCE; see also Gilboa and Sharon 2003 for a thorough characterization of the Early Iron Age material culture at Dor and its dating). The main question, however, is whether the clearly readable hieroglyphs on this very scarab's base (No. 24) really denote the name of pharaoh Siamun, who according to the prevalent Egyptian chronology reigned between 978–959 BCE (alternatively 975–956 BCE; Kitchen 2000: 41 with table 2). In fact, two different spellings of the king's birth name exist. The first, significantly more frequent, variant is written with two opposed sitting figures representing Amun (C12), an egg (H8) and *mr(j)* 'beloved' (N36). The second spelling consists of the pintail duck (G38), the flowering reed (M17), *men* (Y5) and *n* (N35) and is never accompanied by an epithet (Beckerath 1999: 181 *sub* Siamun, E2; see also Bonhême 1987: 87-94 and Gauthier 1914: III, 294-98). Note, however, that not every combination of the pintail duck with the divine name *Jmn* should be viewed as referring to the name of Pharaoh Siamun (see the overview in Hölbl [1979: fig. 1] for various combinations). This is especially true for the formula *nfr z3 Jmn-rʿ* 'perfect (is) the son of Amun-Re' which was particularly common during the New Kingdom (cf. Jaeger 1982: §217 and 1221 no. 11; Keel 1995a: Tell el-ʿAğul no. 251 with further references and Rowe 1936: no. 771 = Guy 1938: pl. 131.10).

Whereas the first of the above-mentioned spellings is the normal ideographic rendering, the second one is phonetically written. Nevertheless, both variants appear in monumental inscriptions—the latter, for example, in a text from the priestly annals from Karnak (cf. Kruchten 1989: 47-48 text 3b). Moreover, it is obviously the case that the position of the individual signs could be interchanged without affecting the literal sense—even on media where a rearrangement is not necessarily to be expected due to restricted space (cf. a graphito from near Abydos; see Gauthier 1914: 295, VII; Berlev 1997: 6 on a papyrus in the Golenischeff collection; I thank K. Jansen-Winkeln for pointing me to these references). Both notations thus should be viewed as equally valid, especially in view of the generally poor and defective rendering of hieroglyphs on royal scarabs during the Third Intermediate Period (Kruchten 1989: 87-94). Therefore, the reading of the hieroglyphs on the base of the Dor scarab as the pharaonic name Siamun (see already Gauthier 1914: 298 esp. XXII, seemingly accepted by Kitchen 1996: 279 note 220) should be given precedence to a cryptographical reading of the divine name Amun (Hornung and Staehelin 1976: 73.177).

4. Chronological Implications

If one accepts that the scarab group in question is a homogeneous lot originating from Egypt and most probably dating to the reign of Siamun and later the reign of Sheshonq the following consequences are implied (for the sake of brevity, references are given only, if information on the objects and their find context cannot be deduced from the captions of the respective plates).

Settlement layers containing mass-produced seals should not be dated prior to the reign of Siamun, most probably not even before 960 BCE (in order to allow a certain time-span for their initial deposition). Such deposits in the North are, for example, found at Dan (No. 12; found in an Early Iron Age phase in area T [D. Ilan, personal communication], Nazaret (No. 38), Megiddo VIA (No. 10, found in a hoard below palace 6000; cf. Yadin 1970: 77-79), Dor (Nos. 1, 24; phase 7a in area G; see also No. 26 found in the foundation of the four-chambered gate together with Iron Age IB pottery; cf. Stern 2000: 114 with fig. 58), Tell Qasile XIʾ–X (No. 44; for the correction of the stratigraphic attribution of the room it was found in, cf. A. Mazar 1986: 12), Kh. Nisya (No. 54) or Beth Shean (tomb 107, No. 19). Similarly, a stratigraphically secured hoard attributed to stratum IB at Taʿanach contained a mass- produced seal (No. 41). Stratum IB was originally dated to the mid/late 12th century BCE (Rast 1978: 6). This date, however, should be lowered in accordance with the above-described general relative chronological horizon of the seals in question (see also Finkelstein 1998, with different arguments). Likewise, the date of the one period site of el-Aḥwat—according to its excavator a short-lived settlement of the Sea peoples dating to the end of the 13th and the beginning of the 12th centuries BCE—could be suspected of being dated too high because of a scarab found in a room belonging to the site's main phase (No. 5). However, such a drastic claim cannot be based solely on a single glyptic find (but see Finkelstein 2002a). Another problematic site, likewise on the relative chronological horizon, is Tell es-Saʿidiyeh in the Jordan rift valley. Three tombs, paralleled with stratum XII on the mound, yielded mass-produced items (e.g. Nos. 8, 28, 32, 46; all from tomb 65, but see also tomb 118, Pritchard 1980: figs. 26,8 and 58,6 and the inventory of tomb 444 in Tubb, Dorell and Cobbing 1996: 37), rendering the early dating to the end of the 13th or the beginning of the 12th centuries BCE questionable (see also, e.g., A. Mazar 1993: 215 note 13).

In the South, such seals have been found in Arad XII (No. 31) and Beersheva VII (No. 35); a possible imitation comes from Tel Masos II (Fritz and Kempinski 1983: pl. 107.2B; 170.3; Münger 2003: 75). However, these few finds cannot be taken *per se* at chronological face value, since seals mark a *terminus post quem* only (e.g. Wright 1977: 61). Furthermore, Southern pottery assemblages like Arad XII, Beersheva VII and Masos II do not—if the 'Sheshonq I = Arad XII' equation is upheld—easily match with a Northern horizon as defined by Tell Qasile X, Megiddo VIA or Kinneret V (Finkelstein 2002b: esp. 113-14, 118-22; A. Mazar 1997: 161).

In sum, mass-produced amulets originating from Tanis in the Egyptian Delta can be considered as supra-regional anchors for an absolute chronology. This should enable researchers to date a chronological horizon where these stamp-seal amulets are found in solid stratigraphic contexts to the final stage of the Iron Age I. As a result, this horizon should be—according to the glyptic evidence—pushed into the 10th century BCE by a few decades only, which would place the terminal date of the Tell Qasile X-Megiddo VIA-Kinneret V-horizon to ca. 960 BCE. This proposed final date for the last stage in the Early Iron Age I sequence of the Southern Levant is therefore only insignificantly later than 980 BCE as proffered by Mazar *et al.* (Chapter 13, this volume), but likewise confirms the tendency towards a Lower Chronology (Finkelstein [Chapter 3, this volume]; Sharon *et al.* [Chapter 6, this volume]).

Acknowledgments

I thank David Ben-Shlomo (Hebrew University, Jerusalem), Dr David Ilan and Adi Kafri (Hebrew Union College, Jerusalem) for information regarding finds from Tel Miqne/Ekron and Tel Dan, respectively. Further credit should go to Ian Carroll and the Institute of Archaeology, University College London, for allowing me to publish an as yet unpublished seal from tomb 224 in Tell el-Farʿah South (*infra* Fig. 23.1:22). Professor Dr K. Jansen-Winkeln (Freie Universität, Berlin) provided me with important bibliographic information. Alison Sauer (Bern) gave valuable comments on an earlier draft of this paper. I am thankful to all of them. For all remaining errors nobody but myself is responsible.

Note on the Catalogue (Plates 23.1–9)

This abbreviated catalogue lists the main characteristics of the specific seals and briefly notes their find context. The basic bibliography intends to provide the reader with a fast access to relevant literature. All drawings were either redrawn from the original publication or prepared at the Institute for Biblical Studies, Fribourg University by H. Keel-Leu, Inès Haselbach or Ulrike Zurkinden-Kolberg after photographs of the originals. An asterisk (*) after the catalogue number denotes an item that cannot be reproduced to scale due to lack of information. Finally, in the typological discussion above, individual scarabs are referred to only by their respective number on a plate, not with the plate number.

References

Aston, D.A. (1996) *Egyptian Pottery of the Late New Kingdom and Third Intermediate Period (Twelfth–Seventh Centuries* BC). *Tentative Footsteps in a Forbidding Terrain* (Studien zur Archäologie und Geschichte Altägyptens 13; Heidelberg: Heidelberger Orientverlag).

Beckerath, J. von (1999). *Handbuch der ägyptischen Königsnamen* (Münchener Ägyptologische Studien 49; Mainz: von Zabern).

Ben-Shlomo, D. (forthcoming) Seals, Seal Impressions and Bullae from Field IV Lower. In *Excavations 1985–1995—Field IVNE/NW (Lower): Iron Age I–II*, edited by Y. Garfinkel, T. Dothan and S. Gitin (The Tel Miqne-Ekron Limited Edition Series 10; Jerusalem: W.F. Albright Institute of Archaeological Research).

Ben-Tor, D. (1997) The Relations between Egypt and Palestine in the Middle Kingdom as Reflected by Contemporary Canaanite Scarabs. *IEJ* 47: 162-89.

—(2003) Egyptian–Levantine Relations and Chronology in the Middle Bronze Age: Scarab Research. In *The Synchronisation of Civilisations in the Eastern Mediterranean in the Second Millennium B.C.* II, edited by M. Bietak (Denkschriften der Gesamtakademie 29; Vienna: Verlag der Österreichischen Akademie der Wissenschaften): 239-48.

—(forthcoming) Comments on Münger's article on the allegedly Tanis scarabs. *Bulletin de la Société Française des Fouilles de Tanis.*

Berlev, O. (1997) The Date of pPrakhov. *Göttinger Miszellen* 160: 5-15.

Bonhême, M.-A. (1987) *Les noms royaux dans l'Égypte de la troisième période intermédiaire* (Bibliothèque d'étude 98; Cairo: Institut français d'archéologie orientale du Caire).

Brandl, B. (2002) A Dagger Pommel, Two Scarabs and a Seal from Tomb No. 65 at Khirbet Nisya. *'Atiqot* 43: 37-48.

—(2003) The Cape Gelidonya Shipwreck Scrabs Reconsidered. In *The Synchronisation of Civilisations in the Eastern Mediterranean in the Second Millennium B.C.* II, edited by M. Bietak (Denkschriften der Gesamtakademie 29; Vienna: Verlag der Österreichischen Akademie der Wissenschaften): 249-61.

Briend, J., and J.B. Humbert (eds.) (1980) Tell *Keisan (1971–1976), une cité phénicienne en Galilée* (OBO Series Archaeologica 1; Fribourg: Universitätsverlag; Göttingen: Vandenhoeck & Ruprecht).

Dietrich, W., and S. Münger (2003) Die Herrschaft Sauls und der Norden Israels. In *Saxa loquentur. Studien zur Archäologie Palästinas/Israels. Festschrift für Volkmar Fritz zum 65. Geburtstag*, edited by C. den Hertog, U. Hübner and S. Münger (Alter Orient und Altes Testament 302; Münster: Ugarit-Verlag): 39-59.

Finkelstein, I. (1998) Notes on the Stratigraphy and Chronology of Iron Age Ta'anach. *Tel Aviv* 25: 208-18.

—(2002a) El-Ahwat: A Fortified Sea People City? *IEJ* 52: 187–99.

—(2002b) The Campaign of Shoshenq I to Palestine: A Guide to the 10th Century Polity. *ZDPV* 118: 109-35.

Fischer, P.M., and M. Sadeq (with contributions by A. Lykke *et al.*) (2002) Tell el-'Ajjul 2000: Second Season Preliminary Report. *Ägypten und Levante* 12: 109-53.

Fritz, V., and A. Kempinski (1983) *Ergebnisse der Ausgrabungen auf der Hirbet el-Mšaš (Tel Maśoś) 1972–1975* (Abhandlungen des Deutschen Palästina-Vereins 6,1-3; 3 vols.; Wiesbaden: Otto Harrassowitz).

Gardiner, A. (1957) *Egyptian Grammar: Being an Introduction to the Study of Hieroglyphics* (Oxford: Griffith Institute, Ashmolean Museum, 3rd rev. edn).

Gauthier, M.H. (1914) *Le livre des rois d'Égypte. III. de la XIXe à la XXIVe dynastie* (Mémoires publiés par les membres de l'Institut Français d'archéologie orientale du Caire 19; Cairo: Imprimérie de l'Institut Français d'Archéologie Orientale).

Gilboa, A., and I. Sharon (2003) An Archaeological Contribution to the Early Iron Age Chronological Debate: Alternative Chronologies for Phoenicia and their Effects on the Levant, Cyprus, and Greece. *BASOR* 332: 7-80.

Gilboa, A., I. Sharon and J. Zorn (2004) Dor and Iron Age Chronology: Scarabs, Ceramic Sequence and [14]C. *Tel Aviv* 31: 32-59.

Griffith, F.L. (1890) *The Antiquities of Tell el Yahûdîyeh and Miscelaneous Work in Lower Egypt during the Years 1887–1888* (Memoir of the Egypt Exploration Fund 7; London: Messers Trübner & Co).

Guy, P.L.O. (1938) *Megiddo Tombs* (OIP 33; Chicago: The University of Chicago Press).

Herzog Z., *et al.* (1984) *Beer-Sheba II. The Early Iron Age Settlements* (Publications of the Institute of Archaeology 7; Tel Aviv: Ramot Publishing).

Hölbl, G. (1979) Typologische Arbeit bei der Interpretation von nicht klar lesbaren Skarabäenflächen. *Studien zur altägyptischen Kultur* 7: 89-102.

—(1986) *Ägyptisches Kulturgut im phönikischen und punischen Sardinien* (Études préliminaires aux religions orientales dans l'empire romain 102; 2 vols.; Leiden: E.J. Brill).

Hornung, E., and E. Staehelin (1976) *Skarabäen und andere Siegelamulette aus Basler Sammlungen* (Ägyptische Denkmäler in der Schweiz 1; Mainz: von Zabern).

Jaeger, B. (1982) *Essai de classification de datation des scarabées Menkhéperre* (OBO, Series Archaeologica 2; Fribourg: Universitätsverlag; Göttingen: Vandenhoeck & Ruprecht).

James, F.W. (1966) *The Iron Age at Beth Shan: A Study of Levels VI–IV* (Philadelphia: The University Museum).

Keel, O. (1977) Der Bogen als Herrschaftssymbol. Einige unveröffentlichte Skarabäen aus Ägypten und Israel zum Thema 'Jagd und Krieg'. *ZDPV* 93: 141-77.

—(1982) Der Pharao als 'vollkommene Sonne': Ein neuer Ägypto-Palästinischer Skarabäentyp. In *Egyptological Studies*, edited by S. Israelit-Groll (Scripta Hierosolymitana 28; Jerusalem: Magnes Press): 406-512.

—(1994a) *Studien zu den Stempelsiegeln aus Palästina, Israel. IV. Mit Registern zu den Bänden I–IV* (OBO 135; Fribourg: Universitätsverlag; Göttingen: Vandenhoeck & Ruprecht).

—(1994b) Philistine 'Anchor' Seals. *IEJ* 44: 21-35.

—(1995a) *Corpus der Stempelsiegel-Amulette aus Palästina/Israel. Von den Anfängen bis zur Perserzeit. Einleitung* (OBO, Series Archaeologica 10; Fribourg: Universitätsverlag; Göttingen: Vandenhoeck & Ruprecht).

—(1995b) Stamp Seals—The Problem of Palestinian Workshops in the Second Millenium and Some Remarks on the Preceding and Succeeding Periods. In *Seals and Sealing in the Ancient Near East: Proceedings of the Symposium Held on Sept. 2, 1993, Jerusalem, Israel*, edited by J. Goodnick Westenholz (Jerusalem: Bible Lands Museum): 93-142

—(1997) *Corpus der Stempelsiegel-Amulette aus Palästina/Israel. Von den Anfängen bis zur Perserzeit. Von Tell Abu Farağ bis 'Alit* (OBO, Series Archaeologica 13; Fribourg: Universitätsverlag; Göttingen: Vandenhoeck & Ruprecht).

Keel, O., and M. Page Gasser (2003), Ptah von Memphis und seine Präsenz auf Skarabäen. In *Werbung für die Götter. Heilsbringer aus 4000 Jahren*, edited by T. Staubli (Ausstellungskatalog Bibel+Orient Museum; Fribourg: Universitätsverlag): 13-63.

Keel, O., M. Shuval and C. Uehlinger (1990) *Studien zu den Stempelsiegeln aus Palästina/Israel III. Die frühe Eisenzeit. Ein Workshop* (OBO 100; Fribourg: Universitätsverlag; Göttingen: Vandenhoeck & Ruprecht).

Keel, O., and C. Uehlinger (1998) *Göttinnen, Götter und Gottessymbole. Neue Erkenntnisse zur Religionsgeschichte Kanaans und Israels aufgrund bislang unerschlossener israelitischer Quellen* (Quaestiones Disputatae 134; Freiburg im Breisgau: Herder, 4th expanded edn).

Kitchen, K.A. (1996) *The Third Intermediate Period in Egypt* (Warminster: Aris & Philips, 2nd rev. edn).

—(2000) Regnal and Genealogical Data of Ancient Egypt (Absolute Chronology I). The Historical Chronology of Ancient Egypt: A Current Assessment. In *The Synchronisation of Civilisations in the Eastern Mediterranean in the Second Millennium B.C.*, II, edited by M. Bietak (Denkschriften der Gesamtakademie 29; Vienna: Verlag der Österreichischen Akademie der Wissenschaften): 39-52

Knauf, E.A. (1991) From History to Interpretation. In *The Fabric of History*, edited by D. Edelman (JSOTSup 127; Sheffield: Sheffield Academic Press): 26-64.

Kruchten, J.M. (1989) *Les annales des prêtres de Karnak (XXI–XXIIImes dynasties) et autres textes contemporains relatifs à l'initiation des prêtres d'Amon, avec une chapitre archéologique par T. Zimmer* (Orientalia Lovaniensia analecta 32; Leuven: Departement oriëntalistiek).

Lamon, R.S., and G.M. Shipton (1939) *Megiddo I: Seasons of 1925–1934, Strata I–V* (OIP 42; Chicago: The University of Chicago Press).

Lapp, P.W. (1967) The 1966 Excavations at Tell Ta'anek. *BASOR* 185: 2-39.

Macalister, R.A.S. (1912) *The Excavations of Gezer: 1902–1905 and 1907–1909* (3 vols.; London: John Murray).

Macdonald, E., J.L. Starkey and G.L. Harding (1932) *Beth-Pelet*. II. *Prehistoric Fara, Beth-Pelet Cemetery* (British School of Archaeology in Egypt 52; London: Quaritch).

MacKenzie, D. (1912–13) *The Excavations at Ain Shems (Beth-Shemesh)* (Palestine Exploration Fund 2; London: The Office of the Fund).

Matouk, F.S. (1977) *Corpus du Scarabée Egyptien*. II. *Analyse thématique* (Beyrouth: Imprimérie Catholique).

Mazar, A., (1985) *Excavations at Tell Qasile*. II. *The Philistine Sanctuary: Various Finds, the Pottery, Conclusions, Appendixes* (Qedem 20; Jerusalem: Institute of Archaeology, Hebrew University).

—(1986) Excavations at Tell Qasile, 1982–1984: Preliminary Report. *IEJ* 36: 1-15.

—(1993) Beth Shean in the Iron Age: Preliminary Report and Conclusions of the 1990–1991 Excavations. *IEJ* 43: 201-29.

—(1997) Iron Age Chronology: A Reply to I. Finkelstein. *Levant* 29: 157-67.

—(2000) The Temple and Cult of the Philistines. In *The Sea Peoples and their World: A Reassessment*, edited by E.D. Oren (University Museum Monograph 108; Philadelphia: The University Museum, University of Pennsylvania): 212-32.

Mazar, B. (1951) The Excavations at Tell Qasile. *IEJ* 1: 61-76, 125-40, 194-218.

McCown, C.C., *et al.* (1947) *Tell en-Nasbeh: Excavated under the Direction of the late William Frederic Badé.* I. *Archaeological and Historical Results* (New Haven: The Palestine Institute of Pacific School of Religion; Berkeley: American Schools of Oriental Research).

Mlinar, C. (2001) Die Skarabäen aus dem Grabungsareal A/II-o/14–A/II-p/15 von Tell el-Dab'a. *Ägypten und Levante* 11: 223-64.

Montet, P. (1942) *Tanis: Douze années de fouilles dans une capitale oubliée du Delta Égyptien* (Paris: Payot).

Münger, S. (2003) Egyptian Stamp-Seal Amulets and their Implications for the Chronology of the Early Iron Age. *Tel Aviv* 30: 66-82.

—(2005) Medien und Ethnizität—Das Beispiel einer Tanitischen Stempelsiegel-Gruppe der Frühen Eisenzeit. In *Medien im antiken Palästina. Materielle Kommunikation und Medialität als Thema der Palästinaarchäologie*, edited by C. Frevel (Forschungen zum Alten Testament II,10; Tübingen: Mohr Siebeck): 85-107.

Newberry, P.E. (1907) *Catalogue général des antiquités Égyptiennes du musée du Caire. Scarab-Shaped Seals* (London: Archibald Constable & Co.).

Niwiński, A. (2000) Iconography of the 21st Dynasty: Its Main Features, Levels of Attestation, the Media and their Diffusion. In *Images as Mass Media: Sources for the Cultural History of the Near East and the Eastern Mediterranean (1st Millennium BCE)*, edited by C. Uehlinger (OBO 175; Fribourg: Universitätsverlag; Göttingen: Vandenhoeck & Ruprecht): 21-43.

Oren, E.D. (1973) *The Northern Cemetery of Beth Shan* (University Museum Monographs; Leiden: E.J. Brill).

Petrie, W.M.F. (with chapters by A.S. Murray and F.Ll. Griffith) (1888) *Tanis II, Nebesheh (Am) and Defenneh (Tahpanhes)* (Memoir of the Egypt Exploration Fund 4; London: Messers Trübner & Co.).

—(1891) *Illahun, Kahun and Gurob* (London: Nutt).

—(1906) *Hyksos and Israelite Cities* (British School of Archaeology in Egypt 12; London: Quaritch).

—(1917) *Scarabs and Cylinders with Names: Illustrated by the Egyptian Collection in University College* (British School of Archaeology in Egypt 36; London: Quaritch).

—(1925) *Buttons and Design Scarabs: Illustrated by the Egyptian Collection in University College* (British School of Archaeology in Egypt 38; London: Quaritch).

—(1928) *Gerar* (British School of Archaeology in Egypt 43; London: Quaritch).

—(1930) *Beth-Pelet I: Tell Fara* (British School of Archaeology in Egypt 48; London: Quaritch).

—(1932) *Ancient Gaza II: Tell el Ajjul* (British School of Archaeology in Egypt 54; London: Quaritch).

Petrie, W.M.F., and J.H. Walker (1909) *Memphis I* (British School of Archaeology in Egypt 15; London: Quaritch).

Pritchard, J.B. (1980) *The Cemetery at Tell es-Sa'idiyeh, Jordan* (University Museum Monograph 41; Philadelphia: The University Museum).

Ranke, H. (1935) *Die ägyptischen Personennamen.* I. *Verzeichnis der Namen* (Glückstadt: J.J. Augustin).

Rast, W.E. (1978) *Taanach I: Studies in the Iron Age Pottery* (Cambridge, MA: American Schools of Oriental Research).

Rothenberg, B. (1988) *The Egyptian Mining Temple at Timna* (Researches in the Arabah 1959–84 1; London: Institute for Archaeo-Metallurgical Studies, Institute of Archaeology, University College London).

Rowe, A. (1936) *A Catalogue of Egyptian Scarabs, Scaraboids, Seals and Amulets in the Archaeological Museum* (Cairo: Imprimérie de l'Institut Français d'Archéologie Orientale).

Saller, S. (1953) Stamped Impressions on the Pottery of Bethany. *Studii Biblici Franciscani liber annuus* 3: 5-36.

Schipper, B.U. (2005) *Die Erzählung des Wenamun. Ein Literaturwerk im Spannungsfeld von Politik, Geschichte und Religion* (OBO 209; Fribourg: Universitätsverlag; Göttingen: Vandenhoeck & Ruprecht).

Sellin, E., and C. Watzinger (1913) *Jericho. Die Ergebnisse der Ausgrabungen* (Wissenschaftliche Veröffentlichungen der Deutschen Orientgesellschaft 22; Osnabrück: J.C. Hinrichs).

Stern, E. (2000) *Dor, Ruler of the Seas: Nineteen Years of Excavations at the Israelite–Phoenician Harbor Town on the Carmel Coast* (Jerusalem: Israel Exploration Society, rev. and expanded edn).

Uehlinger, C. (1996) Die Sammlung ägyptischer Siegelamulette (Skarabäensammllung Fouad S. Matouk). In *Altorientalische Miniaturkunst*, edited by O. Keel and C. Uehlinger (Fribourg: Universitätsverlag; Göttingen: Vandenhoeck & Ruprecht): 58-86.

—(2001) Bildquellen und 'Geschichte Israels': grundsätzliche Überlegungen und Fallbeispiele. In *Steine–Bilder–Texte. Historische Evidenz außerbiblischer und biblischer Quellen*, edited by C. Hardmeier (Arbeiten zur Bibel und ihrer Geschichte 5; Leipzig: Evangelische Verlags-Anstalt): 25-77.

Teeter, E. (2003) *Scarabs, Scaraboids, Seals, and Seal Impressions from Medinet Habu. Based on the Field Notes of Uvo Hölscher and Rudolf Anthes, with Post-pharaonic Stamp Seals and Seal Impressions by T.G. Wilfog* (OIP 118; Chicago: The University of Chicago Press).

Tubb, J.N. (1988) Tell es-Sa'idiyeh: Preliminary Report on the First Three Seasons of Renewed Excavations. *Levant* 20: 23-80.

Tubb, J.N., P.G. Dorell and F.J. Cobbing (1996) Interim Report on the Eighth (1995) Season of Excavations at Tell es-Sa'idiyeh. *PEQ* 128: 16-40.

Tufnell, O. (with contributions by G.T. Martin and W.A. Ward) (1984) *Studies on Scarab Seals: Scarab Seals and their Contribution to History in the Early Second Millenium B.C.* (2 vols.; Warminster: Aris & Philipps).

Vitto, F. (2001) An Iron Age Burial Cave in Nazareth. *'Atiqot* 42: 159-69.

Watzinger, C. (1929) *Tell el-Mutesellim II* (Leipzig: J.C. Hinrichs).

Wiese, A. (1990) *Zum Bild des Königs auf ägyptischen Siegelamuletten* (OBO 96; Fribourg: Universitätsverlag; Göttingen: Vandenhoeck & Ruprecht).

Wright, G.E. (1977) Philistine Coffins and Mercenaries. In *The Biblical Archaeologist Reader*, II, edited by D. Freedman and E.F. Campbell (Missoula, MT: American Schools of Oriental Research/Scholar's Press): 59-68.

Yadin, Y. (1970) Megiddo of the Kings of Israel. *BA* 33/3: 66-96.

24 Problems in the Paleographic Dating of Inscriptions

William M. Schniedewind

Abstract

Recent attempts to re-date important inscriptions such as the Siloam Tunnel inscription, the Gezer Calendar, and certain Arad inscriptions illustrate fundamental problems with paleography as a method for dating inscriptions. The so-called science of paleography often relies on circular reasoning because there is insufficient data to draw precise conclusions about dating. Scholars also tend to oversimplify diachronic development, assuming models of simplicity rather than complexity. Because of the insufficient number of inscriptions, scholars often compare inscriptions from different media or from quite different archaeological and geographic contexts. The problems with paleographic dating of early Hebrew inscriptions point to the need for external controls.

The present conference volume was occasioned, at least in part, by a crisis in the dating of early Iron Age evidence from archaeology and texts. The assured results of scholarship, particularly biblical criticism and archaeology, have come under increasing assault. The problem of dating also extends to the so-called science of paleography—particularly to the typological dating of Hebrew letters. The critique of the status quo has included claims of forgery as well as wholesale revision of the long-accepted dating of many inscriptions (e.g. Rollston 2003; Vaughn 1999). A quick survey of some of the recent use and misuse of paleographic dating underscores the need for external controls such as have been traditionally provided by archaeology. Now, however, the dating of archaeological strata—in the 10th and 9th centuries BCE (i.e. the Iron IIA period)—has also been the topic of increased debate. Thus, the need for the external control provided by radiocarbon dating has become even more critical.

There are three basic problems with the paleographic dating of Hebrew inscriptions. First, to quote Thomas Lambdin's well-known observation, we are working with no data. There are very few Hebrew inscriptions that have been dated to the 10th and 9th centuries BCE, even if we accept the more optimistic assessments of the corpus. In contrast to pottery seriation, there simply are not enough inscriptions on which to base conclusions. Furthermore, whereas pottery is mass-produced and circumscribed by this mode of production, inscriptions reflect the idiosyncrasies of individual scribes, unique social locations, and historical circumstances. Thus, even the data we have is much more difficult to fit into neat typologies than pottery. The corpus of Hebrew inscriptions dating from the 10th–9th centuries BCE includes the following (see Renz 1995):

1. Gezer Calendar (on limestone)
2. Tel 'Amal inscription (inscribed on pottery)
3. Horbat Rosh Zayit inscription (ink on pottery)
4. Beth Shemesh inscription (inscribed on stone)
5. Tel Reḥov inscriptions (inscribed on pottery; Mazar 2003)
6. Arad inscriptions, nos. 76–79, 81 (ink on pottery)
7. Tel Batash inscription (inscribed on pottery)
8. Tell el-Hamme (inscribed on pottery)
9. Eshtemoa (ink on pottery)
10. Tell el-'Oreme (inscribed on pottery)
11. Kuntillet 'Ajrud (ink on pottery)

Second, it is often difficult to distinguish 'Hebrew' from 'Phoenician' or 'Aramaic' inscriptions during this period, and in fact such classification is probably anachronistic because it implies the development of separate written dialects. Thus, other relevant inscriptions might be added to this list such as the Mesha stela, the Tel Dan stela, the Kefar Veradim inscription (Alexandre 2002), the Tel Dan bowl inscription, five Hazor inscriptions (Naveh 1989), and the En Gev inscription. It has also been debated whether a basic inscription like the Gezer Calendar is actually 'Hebrew'. In contrast to the standard position articulated by Chaim Rabin (1979), namely that Classical Hebrew emerged in the 10th century BCE, I would contend that there is no evidence for a standard 'Hebrew' written language in the 10th century BCE. Paleographers agree, for example, that there was no specifically 'Hebrew' script in the 10th century BCE (see Naveh 1987: 89-112). Rather, the situation of written languages might be better compared with the Late Bronze Age where scribes throughout Canaan used a similar dialect (as evidenced in the el-Amarna letters), albeit not without idiosyncrasies. I would argue that the development of a specifically Hebrew written dialect did not arise until the 8th century (but this is beyond the scope of the present chapter). In such a case, the entire discussion of linguistic classification for this period would be misguided.

As a result of the lack of sufficient data, scholars often resort to mixing and matching inscriptions of different media. For example, the Siloam Tunnel inscription (late 8th century BCE), which is a monumental inscription carved into limestone, is often used as a lynchpin of the typological development of the Hebrew script (see critique by Vaughn 1999); it is sometimes compared with ink-on-pottery inscriptions or inscribed seals. One may also take the flawed comparisons of the Ketef Hinnom inscriptions (tiny silver amulets with etched letters) for which we have no example in comparable media (see the critique by Barkay *et al.* 2004; Renz 1995). Scholars are not unaware of such problems, but we feel the need to press the available evidence for more than it can yield.

Third, scholars tend to assume a model of simplicity, even though we recognize that human systems are complex. We tend to minimize geographic and chronological distance. We overlook the different social contexts that stand behind various inscriptions. We minimize the significance of scribal idiosyncrasies and the impact of non-professional writing. In short, we generalize to create typologies. This is certainly understandable, but we cannot then overstate our conclusions. As Bruce Zuckerman recently pointed out, 'a balance needs to be struck between the recognition of complexity and the need to strive for greater simplicity' (2003: 134).

Even when we begin to have more data—namely, in the 8th century BCE—problems in paleographic dating persist. This can be illustrated in a few recent analyses of Hebrew inscriptions. Perhaps there is no more prominent example of obfuscation than John Rogerson and Philip Davies' (1996) re-dating of the Siloam Tunnel inscription from the 8th century to the 2nd century BCE. The Siloam Tunnel inscription had long been dated to the reign of Hezekiah in the late 8th century BCE; Rogerson and Davies pointed out that the original dating by scholars in the 19th century relied heavily on the Bible. This was a fair observation. However, in more recent years new archaeological and inscriptional evidence could have shifted the basis for our analysis (see, e.g., Hackett *et al.* 1997).

It should be acknowledged also that much of the heated nature of these dating problems revolve around the nature of the Bible as a historical source (see, for example, Dever and Halpern's essays in this volume [Chapters 25 and 26, respectively]). Given this undercurrent to the dating of early Hebrew inscriptions, the importance of external controls becomes even more desirable. One has the impression, for example, that the re-dating of the Siloam Tunnel inscription was proffered only because it seemed to be mentioned in the Bible and any alternative theory that makes no use of the Bible as a source is preferable (also recently Knauf 2001). Unlike the Tel Dan inscription, most inscriptions have no direct bearing upon the historical figures of David and Solomon or upon our assessment of the United Monarchy; nevertheless, they can be unintended victims of this ideologically driven debate.

The dating of the Siloam Tunnel inscription had serious implications for paleographic dating because it has been used as a lynchpin for the typological development of the Hebrew script. In his study of Hebrew seals, Andrew Vaughn (1999) pointed to several aspects of the Siloam Tunnel script that seemed more similar to 7th-century BCE Hebrew seals than 8th-century seals. Vaughn isolated five diagnostic letters (*aleph, he, waw, nun,* and *qof*) that he believed could be used to date Hebrew seals. At the same time, he cautioned about the intrinsic problem of comparing the script of Hebrew seals with a monumental stone inscription like the Siloam Tunnel inscription. When we probe further, his caution seems quite well-advised. For example, it is easy to find similarities in these diagnostic letters between the Siloam Tunnel inscription and the early 8th-century BCE ostraca excavated in Samaria (see Fig. 24.1).

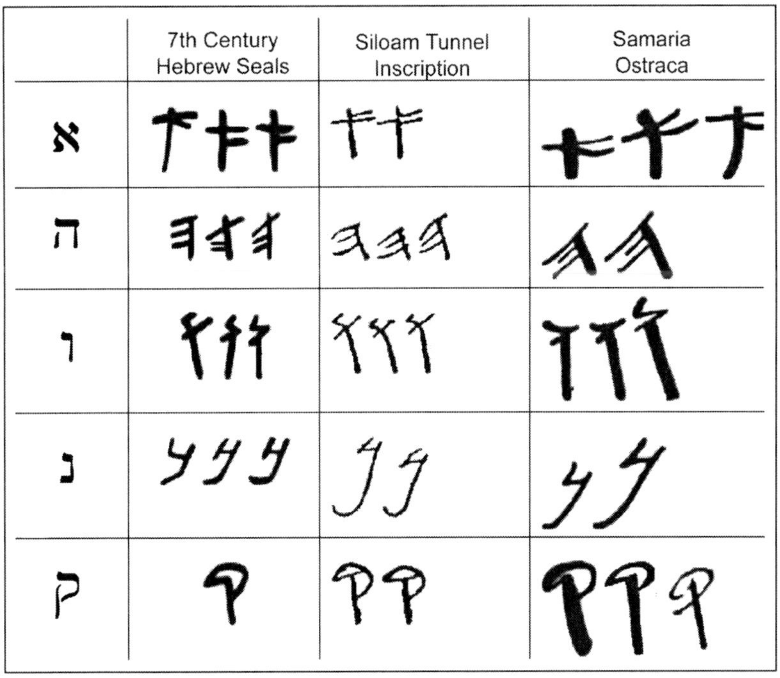

Figure 24.1. 'Diagnostic' letters in Hebrew inscriptions.

Of course, just putting these three palaeographic styles together in one chart is rather misleading since they represent different media—seals, stone, and ink on pottery. Moreover, we should also question the geographic distance between the Jerusalem Siloam Tunnel inscription and the Samaria Ostraca. Finally, we should reflect on the different social conditions that gave rise to the inscriptions compared in Figure 24.1. The Samaria Ostraca are ephemeral texts used in the daily accounting of royal scribes; the Siloam Tunnel inscription was carved as a monument to an engineering achievement; and, the seals reflect a cross section of society both professional and amateur in execution (see Shoham 2000). The real comparison for the Siloam Tunnel inscription should be other monumental inscriptions, but there are very few examples with which to compare it and all present mitigating factors. The Kh. Beit-Lei inscriptions, for example, are graffiti. Obviously, graffiti poses problems for typology. Two fragmentary inscriptions were found in the City of David and the Ophel, but these were found in secondary archaeological contexts (Ben-Dov 1994; Naveh 2000) so the dating is determined by paleography, which inevitably makes their use rather circular. The Royal Steward inscription is only two lines long and has no fixed archaeological date. One might compare it to the Mesha Stele or the Dan Stela (which can be dated by internal historical referents), but we need to take into account that these are not Hebrew inscriptions. This type of database hardly forms a firm basis for the typological development of the Hebrew script, especially for dating. In Joseph Naveh's classic work, *Early History of the Alphabet*, he suggested that there was no distinctive or lapidary script in Hebrew (1987: 67). It hardly seems, however, that the data are robust enough to draw such a conclusion.

Even when we have sufficient data, there are problems that complicate attempts to use paleography to precisely date inscriptions. The Hebrew seals and seal impressions, which have come to light in great numbers from recent excavations (see the catalogue by Avigad and Sass 1997), have thrown paleographic dating into a particular state of disarray (see Vaughn 1999). One nice collection of seal impressions dating to about 600 BCE was excavated in the City of David; surprisingly, the collection shows many irregularities from standard notions of paleographic dating. As a result, the editor frequently comments that the script is careless, crude, uneven, or coarse. This is often explained by recourse to engraving by a non-professional, and the conclusion is drawn that 'differences in the form and quality of the letters lack chronological significance' (Shoham 2000: 53). Naturally, they cannot have chronological significance since they all date to one archive burned in the destruction of Jerusalem in 586 BCE. But what does this say about the typological dating of Hebrew seals? The seals show a great diversity in possible letter forms from the same time period, and the data are obviously more complex than is often assumed.

Let us turn now to the few early inscriptions that we have. The most famous of these inscriptions is the Gezer Calendar. Setting aside whether this is actually a Hebrew inscription, can we really use this inscription for typological analysis? Many scholars think that this is a school text. How could we use a school text to construct the typology of the Hebrew script? Three recently excavated inscriptions from Tell Reḥov add to our corpus, but they hardly simplify our understanding of the typological development of the Hebrew script. Consider the following inscription, which dates to a 10th-century BCE archaeological stratum:

Even in this short inscription, the reading is not clear because of the problem in identifying the third letter. It could be a *mem*, a *yod*, or perhaps a *beth*. The first two readings were suggested by Yardeni's drawing, but the *beth* also looks possible (as Professor Mazar noted). For the present purpose, it is unimportant how we resolve this problem. The broader question should be: How can we use such an inscription for developing the typology of Hebrew scripts? Given that this is such a short inscription, it is quite telling that there seems to be some confusion either in spelling or in writing letter shapes. This hardly inspires confidence in fitting the inscription into a tight typology of the Hebrew script. Other anomalies hold for the other two new inscriptions from Tel Reḥov, which date archaeologically to the 9th century BCE. In Reḥov inscription no. 2, we find a hitherto unknown form of the letter ʿayin. In Reḥov no. 3, the fourth letter of the inscription has yet to be identified or explained by scholars. Three new inscriptions, and three new problems. How can we explain these problems? Did Reḥov have its own local scribal tradition? Or, are these the idiosyncrasies of a couple of scribes? Or, are these inscriptions the work of non-professionals? Such questions tend to be swept under the proverbial carpet when we develop typologies of the Hebrew script.

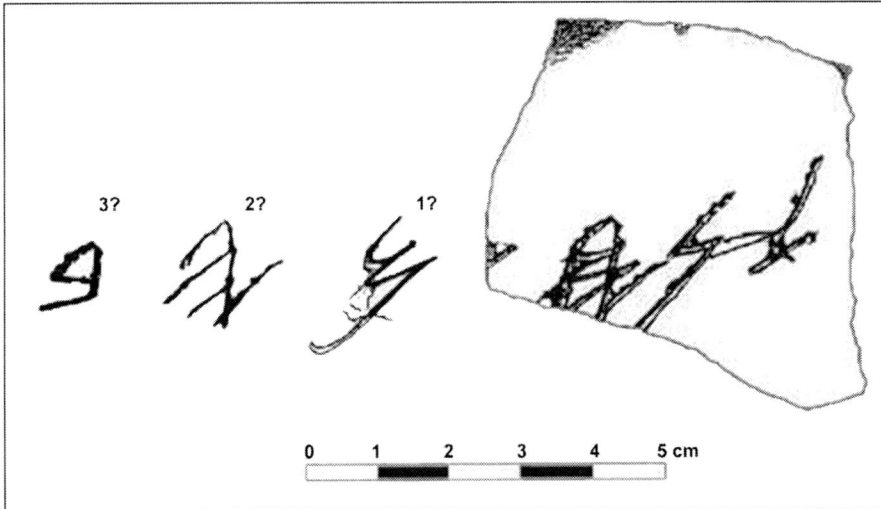

Figure 24.2. 10th-century inscription excavated at Tel Reḥov (adapted from Yardeni's drawing in Mazar 2003).

Potentially, one of the most significant sites for the study of paleography is Tell Arad, where more than 100 Hebrew ostraca were excavated. Indeed, the new excavations at Khirbet en-Nahas will certainly force us to re-examine the Stratum XI fortress at Arad along with comparable fortresses at en-Hatzeva and Tel el-Kheleifeh (see Levy's article [Chapter 10, this volume]). Arad is an especially important corpus because all the ostraca come from one geographic locale and because the ostraca were excavated from a cross-section of archaeological strata. Unfortunately, the dating of the lower strata at Tell Arad has fallen under the shadow of the current high–low chronology debate (see, e.g., Finkelstein 2002; Herzog 2002). But even when the archaeological dating at Arad is relatively uncontested, paleographers show a remarkable willingness to disregard the archaeological context to make the evidence conform to traditional typologies. For example, Arad letters 62 and 63, which were excavated in Stratum IX dating to the mid–late 8th century BCE, were redated on the basis of the script to the early 6th century BCE (Aharoni 1981: 91). This redating is followed in the recently published volume, *Hebrew Inscriptions: Texts from the Biblical Period with Concordance* (Dobbs-Allsop *et al.* 2004), to the 6th century BCE; the editors write, 'Though discovered in Stratum IX, the script of this inscription would suggest that it belongs with Stratum VI' (p. 68). Remarkably, there are only four or five letters on these small fragments, and none seem diagnostic. Moreover, what does this say about the method of paleographic dating when we disregard the archaeological context to fit the evidence into a rigid typological scheme? Concerning Arad 67 the editors write, 'This fragment was found in Stratum X [which dates to the 9th century], but it may be dated paleographically to the late 8th century B.C.E' (p. 70). How did the editors come to this conclusion about such a fragmentary ostracon? I assume that the determination was made on the basis of the cursive *zayin* (which is much more developed than the *zayin* in the Siloam Tunnel inscription), although it is difficult to see how we have enough evidence of the early typological development of this letter to override the archaeological context (see Fig. 24.3). And, in fact, we can find examples of a much more cursive *zayin* in the early 8th-century Samaria Ostraca. Other aspects of the script (for example, the *aleph* and the *kaph*) seem to fit much better with the archaeological context in the 9th century BCE. In any case, we need to be much more modest about our knowledge of the typological development of the Hebrew script and avoid the appearance of rewriting the evidence to fit our theories.

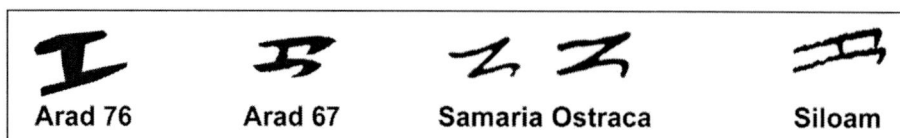

Figure 24.3. The Typology of the Letter *zayin*.

Several ostraca from Arad were assigned by Aharoni to Stratum XI and dated to the 10th century BCE, although this is now disputed (see Herzog 2002). Arad 76 is the most substantial of the 10th-century ostraca. It is worth comparing the *zayin* in this ostracon with Arad 67 (Fig. 24.3). The 'I' shaped *zayin* is usually considered a typological early form (i.e. 10th century BCE). However, what can we compare it to? There are no comparable *zayins* written in ink on pottery in supposedly 10th-century BCE inscriptions. It is certainly much less cursive than 9th-century BCE exemplars, but we are speaking about just a handful of examples. This is hardly sufficient to speak of a typological development that would lend itself to precise paleographic dating. As a result, the dating of such ostraca must be left to the archaeological context. As is becoming increasingly clear, however, these early Iron Age archaeological contexts will only be securely dated when the dating is confirmed by ^{14}C.

To conclude, it will be useful to make some observations about the continuity and development of ancient scribal institutions in the early Iron Age. In Arad 76 and other ostraca, Egyptian hieratic numerals are employed. On the basis of Egyptian paleography, Orly Goldwasser (1991) has dated the hieratic numerals to the 10th century BCE. To be fair, it is also difficult to pinpoint the date of the Egyptian hieratic script. Still, the hieratic script appears already on several undisputed 9th-century ostraca; and, given the decline of Egypt's presence in Palestine after the 10th century BCE, it seems the 10th-century date is a plausible date for the borrowing of Egyptian hieratic. The borrowing from Egyptian chancellery also included accounting and scribal terminology (see Lambdin 1953). This includes terms like *hekat* ('a unit of measurement'; the abbreviation was used, for example, in Arad 76) and the term *deyô* ('ink').

Although the inscriptional evidence for Hebrew writing in the 10th century BCE is quite meager, writing certainly remained important to government bureaucracies (whether we label them 'state' or 'chiefdom'). For example, the display monument of Bar-Rakib, a petty Aramean king in the 9th century BCE, uses the motif of a scribe standing before the enthroned king to glorify the king. And the el-Amarna letters from the Late Bronze Age illustrate that every minor ruler of the Canaanite city-states had their own scribe. At the same time, the Canaanite scribes of the el-Amarna letters showed both homogeneity and distinction in language, paleography, and scribal markings (see Rainey 1996; Mabie 2004). The scribe was one of the most important figures in the royal court, even in rather small and insignificant polities. A good example of a tiny chiefdom that had a scribe was Moab. The Mesha Stele and the Kerak Inscription illustrate that already by the 9th century BCE Moab had a royal scribe trained in near eastern scribal conventions with access to royal archives (see Dearman 1989).

When we turn to the early Israelite monarchy, it seems likely that the early Israelite rulers would have had scribes as well. In fact, the biblical notices describing David and Solomon's royal scribes have several authentic elements (2 Samuel 20.23-26; 1 Kings 4.1-6). For instance, the personal names are non-Yahwistic suggesting that they predate the rise of Yahweh as the exclusive god of the Israelites. One of Solomon's scribes apparently had an Egyptian name—Elihoreph (from the Egyptian word meaning 'Apis is my god']). One of the names in the list, Shisha, actually seems to be a corruption of an Egyptian word meaning 'the writer of the king's letters'. Such hints are quite striking when we recall that ancient Hebrew borrows from the Egyptian scribal inventory. It is certainly reasonable to assume that scribes were hard at work even in Israel during the 10th century BCE, yet we will have to rely on methods other than paleography to date their work.

References

Aharoni, Y. (1981) *Arad Inscriptions* (Jerusalem: Israel Exploration Society).

Alexandre, Y. (2002) A Fluted Bowl with a Canaanite–Early Phoenician Inscription from Kefar Veradim. In *Eretz Zafon—Studies in Galilean Archaeology*, edited by Z. Gal (Jerusalem: Israel Antiquities Authority): *65-*74.

Avigad, N. (revised and completed by Benjamin Sass) (1997) *Corpus of West Semitic Stamp Seals* (Jerusalem: Israel Exploration Society).

Barkay, G., *et al.* (2004) The Amulets from Ketef Hinnom: A New Edition and Evaluation. *BASOR* 334: 41-71.

Ben-Dov, M. (1994) A Fragmentary Hebrew First Temple Period Inscription from the Ophel. In *Ancient Jerusalem Revealed*, edited by H. Geva (Jerusalem: Israel Exploration Society): 73-75.

Dearman, A. (ed.) (1989) *Studies in the Mesha Inscription and Moab* (Atlanta: Scholars Press).

Dobbs-Allsop, F.W., *et al.* (2004) *Hebrew Inscriptions: Texts from the Biblical Period of the Monarchy with Concordance* (New Haven and London: Yale University Press).

Finkelstein, I. (2002) The Campaign of Shoshenq I to Palestine: A Guide to the 10th Century BCE Polity. *ZDPV* 118: 109-35.

Goldwasser, O. (1991) An Egyptian Scribe From Lachish and the Hieratic Tradition of the Hebrew Kingdoms. *Tel Aviv* 18: 248-53.

Hackett, J.A., *et al.* (1997) Defusing Pseudo-Scholarship: The Siloam Inscription Ain't Hasmonean. *BAR* 23.2: 41-51, 68.

Herzog, Z. (2002) The Fortress Mount at Tel Arad: An Interim Report. *Tel Aviv* 29: 3-109.

Knauf, E.A. (2001) Hezekiah or Manasseh? A Reconsideration of the Siloam Tunnel and Its Inscription. *Tel Aviv* 28: 281-87.

Lambdin, T.O. (1953) Egyptian Loan Words in the Old Testament. *Journal of the American Oriental Society* 73: 145-55.

Mabie, F. (2004) Ancient Near Eastern Scribes and the Mark(s) They Left: A Catalog and Analysis of Scribal Auxiliary Marks in the Amarna Corpus and in the Cuneiform Alphabetic Texts of Ugarit and Ras Ibn Hani (PhD dissertation, UCLA).

Mazar, A. (2003) Three 10th–9th Century B.C.E. Inscriptions From Tel Rehov. In *Saxa loquentur. Studien zur Archäologie Palästinas/Israels. Festschrift für Volkmar Fritz zum 65. Geburtstag*, edited by C.G. den Hertog, U. Hübner, and S. Münger (Münster: Ugarit-Verlag): 171-84.

Naveh, J. (1987) *Early History of the Alphabet: An Introduction to West Semitic Epigraphy and Palaeography* (Jerusalem: Magnes Press, 2nd edn).

—(1989) The Epigraphic Finds from Areas A and B. In *Hazor III–IV, Text*, edited by A. Ben-Tor and S. Geva (Jerusalem: Israel Exploration Society): 346-47.

—(2000) Hebrew and Aramaic Inscriptions. In *Excavations at the City of David. VI. Inscriptions*, edited by A. Belfer-Cohen, *et al.* (Qedem 41; Jerusalem: The Institute of Archaeology of the Hebrew University of Jerusalem): 1-14.

Rabin, C. (1979) The Emergence of Classical Hebrew. In *The Age of the Monarchies: Culture and Society*, II, edited by A. Malamat (World History of the Jewish People 4; Jerusalem: Massada Press).

Rainey, A.F. (1996) *Canaanite in the Amarna Tablets: A Linguistic Analysis of the Mixed Dialect Used by the Scribes From Canaan* (4 vols.; Leiden: Brill).

Renz, J. (1995) *Die Althebräischen Inscriften* (Darmstadt: Wissenschaftliche Buchgesellschaft).

Rogerson, J., and P. Davies (1996) Was the Siloam Tunnel Built by Hezekiah? *BA* 59: 138-49.

Rollston, C.A. (2003) Non-Provenanced Epigraph I: Pillaged Antiquities, Northwest Semitic Forgeries, and Protocols for Laboratory Tests. *MAARAV* 10: 135- 93.

Shoham, Y. (2000) A Hebrew Seal and Seal Impressions. In *Excavations at the City of David*. VI. *Inscriptions*, edited by A. Belfer-Cohen, *et al*. (Qedem 41; Jerusalem: The Institute of Archaeology of the Hebrew University of Jerusalem): 81-84.

Vaughn, A.G. (1999) Paleographic Dating of Judaean Seals and its Significance for Biblical Research. *BASOR* 313: 43-64.

Zuckerman, B. (2003) Pots and Alphabets: Refractions of Reflections on Typological Method. *MAARAV* 10: 89-134.

25 Some Methodological Reflections on Chronology and History-Writing

William G. Dever

Abstract

My participation in this project concerning the Bible and radiocarbon dating is largely that of an observer since I am not an authority on ^{14}C dating, and my work on Syro-Palestinian chronology until recently has had to do mostly with the Bronze Age. I have now become involved in Iron Age chronology, however, since it is a crucial aspect of my current research on the question of the so-called 'United Monarchy' and state-formation processes in early Israel (Dever 1997, 2004).

Why Chronology Matters

First, we need not make any apologies for what some might consider an obsession with chronology, especially our desire for closely fixed *absolute* dates. Chronology is 'the backbone of history', the time-line. It is the thread upon which individual events are strung like beads, so as to create a connected, believable series of happenings that constitute what we would call 'narrative history', the most fundamental level of history-writing. Yet without relative dates—and absolute dates when possible—all our reconstructions of the past remain *unordered*, and they can only create the impression of chaos. Yet the apparent chaos is an illusion. History, if not purposeful, is at least orderly; and culture is patterned. That, and only that, is what makes a perception of the 'meaning of events' (the whole point of the historical enterprise) possible—but only once we have a reliable chronology, that is, a *concept of evolution*, and a framework for explaining cultural change.

History as the Goal of Archaeology

Second, we must affirm unequivocally that history-writing is archaeology's fundamental goal, ultimately its only rationale as a humanistic discipline. For an entire generation, however, the 'New Archaeology' tried to tell us that 'particularism' was *passé*; that 'history' was a bad word; that the only legitimate goal of archaeology was to discover supposed 'universal, timeless laws of the cultural process'. Fortunately, we survived that era, although too many of us remained innocent of any of the *true* insights that the 'New Archaeology' might have offered. In particular, we ought to have learned not only that theory is more than 'idle speculation', that robust theory is necessary to guide our fieldwork and research, but that our theory should be explicit and right up front (Preucel [ed.] 1991; Whitley 1998; cf. Dever 2000, 2003). In this volume, our colleagues in the natural sciences have shown us in every case examples of rigorous theory-building and explicit models.

Today Ian Hodder and other 'post-processualists' have made it respectable once again for archaeologists not only to get back to the arduous work of writing history, but also to attempt to get at 'the meaning of things'—things in cultural context, that is, in a *particular* time and place. Chronology again. As Hodder puts it: 'It is particularist studies combined with a concern for the "inside" of events which have led to the most profound and far-reaching statements on the nature of relationships between meaning and practice' (1986: 81). Or again: 'To study history is to try to get at purpose and thought' (1986: 91). Thus, Hodder speaks often of 'historical imagination'. But such imagination without the specificity of archaeological and chronological context is pure fantasy. Adopting this 'post-processual' approach, I now aspire unabashedly to be a historian—a 'historian of things', as some of our colleagues now put it, specifically using material culture remains alongside texts, as a primary source of history-writing.

History, Chronology, and *la longue durée*

One aspect of recent archaeological theory is a renewed focus on chronology in terms of the emphasis of Braudel and other *annales* historians on *la longue durée* (Bintliffe [ed.] 1991). This is long-term history—history over the time-span not only of decades, but of millennia. Here the concept is one of 'levels of time'. (1) At the upper tier is 'structure', slow-moving forces of nature, *la longue durée*. (2) Below that is 'conjuncture', smaller and slower rhythms and cycles of socio-economic change. (3) Finally, at the lowest, most fundamental level, are 'events', the specific results of the thoughts and actions of individuals.

In this scheme of things, understanding long-term cultural change is the goal. But this can *only* be based on a firm grasp of closely-dated individual epochs in the long evolutionary process. Here I am neither 'in panic' nor 'lassez faire' about chronology, in the words of other contributors to this book (cf. Finkelstein [Chapter 3, this volume]).

Ideology and History-Writing

If we have learned anything from the last 30 years of theoretical ferment in archaeology, it is that all fieldwork and research is 'theory-laden'. We do not have to go as far as doctrinaire postmodernists (who claim that 'there are no facts, only interpretations'; see below) to see that ideology *does* shape all our perceptions of the past, often powerfully. Archaeology is thus not an 'objective science', because it deals with that most intractable of all phenomena—the human psyche, which is not the object, but the subject, in the investigation.

For our purposes here, that means that while history is indeed about the past, it is also about the present, about our contemporary needs and ideologies. Thus, even chronological research, which would seem to be concerned simply with mathematics, the most basic and precise dimension of science, is in the end not only about calendrical time, but also about 'perceptual time'—not disembodied dates, but time as humanely experienced in the sheer contingency of history over the millennia.

If all this seems too 'philosophical', too far-removed from the topic of this volume, I point out that the heat of the current controversy over the biblical 'United Monarchy' and the 10th vs. the 9th century BCE can hardly be explained simply as part of an agenda of 'disinterested objective research'. The escalating rhetoric, in both biblical circles and in our branch of archaeology, has more to do with 'revisionist' ideology, and now Middle Eastern politics, than it does with science —or even for that matter with good history-writing. Thus, Finkelstein has accused Mazar, me, and others who still defend the conventional 10th-century BCE dates and the notion of at least a nascent 'Israelite state' in the early Iron II period as 'Bible archaeologists' (1998; cf. Dever 2004; Mazar 1997). And this despite the fact that I was writing to discredit old-fashioned 'Biblical archaeology' when Finkelstein was still a schoolboy (see Dever 1985 and references to earlier literature; cf. Dever 2000 and 2003a).

I cannot allude to the intrusion of modern ideology into the controversy over the 10th vs. 9th centuries BCE—about the historicity of the biblical 'United Monarchy'—without saying something about the biblical 'revisionists'. Not only is their work heavily ideological, as I have documented at length elsewhere (Dever 2001), but they have a chronological problem even more acute than ours. Their basic presupposition (for so it is) is that the 'Deuteronomistic history' (Joshua through Kings), our fundamental source for the history of ancient Israel from the settlement horizon to the Fall of Jerusalem in 586 BCE, does not date as mainstream scholars hold to the Iron Age, or ca. 8th–7th centuries BCE. Rather, it is a strictly literary product of the Persian period, or increasingly the Hellenistic era in the 2nd century BCE. Thus, the argument is that the Hebrew Bible is not only too tendentious, but 'too late' to contain a real history of any 'Israel' in the Iron Age. In their view, the Hebrew Bible's (and also modern scholarship's) 'ancient Israel' is an invention—a torturous exercise in self-identification of confused Jews living in Hellenistic Palestine, a typical 'foundation myth'. Here the revisionists' view of the composition of the Hebrew Bible (not merely its final redaction) differs from conventional chronology not by our 60 years, but by 600 years or more.

I have argued elsewhere (Dever 2001) that the biblical revisionists' extreme skepticism stems from their belated, uncritical adoption of some of the ideology of the extreme postmodernism that has infected most humanities disciplines in the past 30 years. Some direct quotations may be helpful for those readers who are not familiar with biblical revisionism—especially since one of their main contentions is that there was no 'United Monarchy', indeed not much of an ancient Israelite state in the Iron Age at all.

Thomas L. Thompson, an American emigré now at the University of Copenhagen, one of the most doctrinaire revisionists (originally his term), has declared:

> In the history of Palestine that we have presented, there is no room for a historical United Monarchy, or for such kings as those presented in the biblical stories of Saul, David or Solomon. The early period in which the traditions have set their narrative is an imaginary world of long ago that never existed as such. (Lemche and Thompson 1994: 19)

If there were any doubt of his nihilism, elsewhere Thompson states in his *The Mythic Past: Biblical Archaeology and the Myth of Israel* (1999):

> It may perhaps appear strange that so much of the Bible deals with the origin traditions of a people that never existed as such. This metaphorical nation's land and language; this imagined people's history, moreover, is an original tradition that belongs to the 'new Israel', not the old. The Bible does not give us Israel's story about its past—or any origin story confirming Israel's self-identity or national self-understanding. The tradition gave not Israel but Judaism an identity, not as a 'nation' among the *goyim*, but as a people of God: an Israel *redivivus* in the life of piety. (1999: 34)

Thompson's *animus* against Judaism may be only hinted at here, but elsewhere it seems to me transparent. Elsewhere he couples his attempt to erase ancient Israel from history directly with his skepticism about Judaism in general:

> There is no more ancient Israel. History has no room for it. This we know. And now, as one of the conclusions of the new knowledge, 'Biblical Israel' was in its origin a Jewish concept. (1995: 698)

Of early Judaism in Palestine in the Roman period, Thompson acknowledges only 'multiple Judaisms', not a real Jewish *ethnos*—a Judaism 'more literary than it is historical'. As he puts it, these Judaisms are 'fictive' (Thompson 1997).

Not even the extra-biblical texts escape Thompson's sweeping skepticism. Of the 9th-century BCE 'Mesha stele' found in Moab, mentioning 'Omri, king of Israel' (cf. 1 Kings 16.22-24), Thompson declares:

> Omri 'dwelling in Moab' is not a person doing anything in Transjordan, but an eponym, a literary personification of Israel's political power and presence. It is clear that the reference to Omri in the Mesha stele is literary, not historical... The literary nature of the Mesha stele needs to be taken seriously. It is quite doubtful that it refers to an historical person when it refers to Israel's king 'Omri, king of Israel', eponym of the highland patronate, *Bit Humri*, belongs to the world of stories. (1999: 13)

For Thompson, an 'ancient Israel' *anywhere* in the Iron Age simply cannot have existed. The archaeological data are ignored or abused; they are convenient for his ideological theories. In Thompson's 400-plus page *The Mythic Past: Biblical Archaeology and the Myth of Israel*, the only chapter that attempts a sketch of an actual historical Israel consists of just 10 pages (Thompson 1999: 158-68). And even here, the name 'Israel' is barely mentioned; it is, rather, 'the peoples of southern Syria's marginal fringe', or elsewhere 'the Assyrian province of Samarina'.

More virulently anti-Zionist and anti-Israel is Keith Whitelam, now at Sheffield University, the other center of European revisionism. Whitelam's clearest statements are found in his book *The Invention of Ancient Israel: The Silencing of Palestinian History* (1996). Here the relentless rhetoric is transparently ideological. A few quotes will suffice:

> The archaeology of ancient Israel has effectively confirmed, for most scholars (i.e., Israelis and Americans) that the past belongs to Israel. (1996: 188)

> Western scholarship has invented ancient Israel and silenced Palestinian history. (1996: 3)

> Biblical scholarship is not just involved in 'retrojective imperialism', it has collaborated in an act of dispossession [of the Palestinian peoples]. (1996: 227)

For Whitelam, attempting to write a history of 'ancient Israel' is not only futile, it is illegitimate. Thus, he has recently announced that he is writing a 'politically correct' history of the Palestinian peoples—beginning in the Bronze Age. Where has Whitelam been? For more than a century now, we archaeologists have been writing histories of Palestine—histories not only of the Israelite peoples, but also that of the Philistines, Phoenicians, Arameans, Ammonites, Moabites, Edomites, and others. Does Whitelam presume to be better qualified? And is this biblical scholar an Arabist qualified to write a history of more modern Palestinians? Already Whitelam's book (like Thompson's) has been translated into Arabic, and it is a best-seller in East Jerusalem bookshops, a textbook in many Palestinian schools. Is this dispassionate biblical scholarship—an honest search for ancient Israel—or meddling in current Middle Eastern politics?

Elsewhere, in my book *What Did the Biblical Writers Know and When Did They Know It? What Archaeology Can Tell Us About the Reality of Ancient Israel* (Dever 2001) I have offered a thorough, exhaustively documented critique of the biblical revisionists, based largely on the abundant archaeological data that illuminate their 'non-existent' Israel. More recently, James Barr, Oriel and Lang Professor of Old Testament emeritus at Oxford, has corroborated my charges in his *History and Ideology in the Old Testament Biblical Studies at the End of a Millennium* (Barr 2000). Barr does several things in this state-of-the-art assessment. (1) He focuses primarily on historiography as the major issue today in biblical studies. (2) He selects the 'revisionists' for his main thrust. (3) He situates the 'revisionists' within the context of postmodernism in a thoroughgoing discussion. Finally, (4) Barr refutes most of the 'revisionists' assertions and documents the fact that they are indeed ideologues. These are precisely the points that I as an archaeologist have been making in lectures and in print for the past several years. Barr specifically cites my work (Barr 2000: 71-73) and implies that he agrees with my charge that the 'revisionists' are nihilists where the history of ancient Israel is concerned. He states specifically that Davies' views are 'too absurd to be taken seriously': that Whitelam's arguments are without any 'factual evidence', and that throughout revisionist discourse, one observes 'the alacrity with which hostile ideology is adopted as the obvious explanation'. Of the repeated insistence on a Hellenistic date for the composition of the Hebrew Bible, Barr concludes that this simply shows how 'desperate for evidence' the 'revisionists' are (2000: 61, 85, 89, 101).

The revisionists, of course, deny that they are, or even have been influenced by, postmodernists (or that they constitute any 'school'). But consider their basic methodological assertions (even if paraphrased slightly).

1. The Hebrew Bible is only a 'social construct', and therefore it cannot constitute a 'grand narrative' of any compelling power. This first proposition is their starting point, adopted directly from original postmodern rhetoric (thus the movement is often called 'constructivism'); and the second recalls Lyotard's classic insistence on the necessity of 'incredulity toward all metanarratives'. And, of course, in the Western cultural tradition, the Bible is the great 'metanarrative', so having been socially constructed, it must now be relentlessly 'deconstructed'.

2. The Hebrew Bible's 'ancient Israel' is 'invented', simply pious fiction. There was no ancient Israel, no early Israelite or Judean states. The archaeological evidence is ambiguous, inconclusive, ultimately irrelevant. Here the history of Israel as 'fiction', both ancient and modern, recalls another of postmodernism's gurus, Michel Foucault. Foucault, who claimed to be a historian of many things, nevertheless declared in his book *Power/Knowledge* (1980: 193) 'I am well aware that I have never written anything but fictions'. He goes on to say that 'one "fictions" history on the basis of a political reality that makes it true'. Truth, for Foucault, is not a reality that one must acknowledge, but merely what counts as 'true' within a particular realm of discourse. Does that not sound precisely like our biblical revisionists? Needless to say, none of the revisionists thinks that it is possible to write a real history of Israel in the Iron Age, at least not what I would call history.

The folly—indeed the hypocrisy—of these pseudo-sophisticates has nowhere been more mercilessly exposed that in Keith Windschuttle's *The Killing of History: How Literary Critics and Social Theorists Are Murdering Our Past* (1996). Of Foucault, Windschuttle says:

> Foucault's histories of institutions are demonstrations of the falsity of his own theories. History is not fiction, nor is it merely perspective. The core of history—the basis for the conclusions that individual historians reach, and the basis of the debates that historians conduct between each other—is factual information. Despite the speculations of Foucault and his followers, history remains a search for truth and the construction of knowledge about the past. (1996: 154)

What Kind of History Do We Want, and What is Possible?

A recent publication of a symposium of the largely minimalist 'European Seminar on Methodology in Israel's History' is entitled *Can a 'History of Israel' Be Written?* (Grabbe [ed.] 1997). Of course, it can; it all depends upon what one *means* by 'history'. (English has only one word for history; but other languages, such as German, are more subtle.) Here I would distinguish several kinds of history and history-writing, arguing that in most of these approaches archaeology now constitutes a 'primary source'. (The order does not suggest any hierarchy.)

1. *Narrative history.* This is a 'history' of events, largely descriptive, presumed to be factual, but selective and anecdotal rather than comprehensive, and with little pretense to be explanatory.

2. *Political history.* This consists largely of the story of dramatic public events and the 'deeds of great men of affairs'. Even at best, it is episodic, elitist, chauvinistic, and propagandistic.

3. *Socio-economic history.* This is a history of society and of its social and economic institutions. It focuses mainly on family, clan, class structure, ethnicity, 'modes of production', and the State.

4. *Intellectual history.* This is a history of ideas—their origin, context, and evolution, especially religious ideas and their institutional embodiment. It is also a history of texts, of the growth of literary traditions.

5. *Cultural history.* This has been traditionally the province of anthropology and ethnography, comprehending the larger, long-term evolutionary context of human adaptation. It focuses on ecology, settlement type and distribution, demography, subsistence, socio-economic organization, political structure, art and aesthetics, religion, ethnicity, and extra-mural relations.

6. *Technological history.* This attempts to give a detailed account of the multi-faceted history of human transformation of Nature through technological innovations—the 'conditions of civilization'.

7. *Material history.* This would be a 'history from things', that is, written largely not on the basis of texts but of material culture remains, viewing artifacts as 'the material correlates of human thought and behavior'.

8. *Natural history.* This would take a largely ecological approach, viewing the world of Nature as the environment or setting for cultural evolution. It would correspond roughly to Pliny's *De rerum naturae*.

9. *Long-term history.* This would be equivalent to *la longue durée* of Braudel and the *annales* historian.

Other 'histories' might also be envisioned. And obviously these are somewhat arbitrary sub-divisions, adopted largely for heuristic reasons. The categories all overlap to some extent, and one might argue that a truly adequate history would include them all. At this point, I would only suggest that while traditional text-based histories might assay to all these forms of history-writing, the discipline of modern archaeology now bids fair to provide substantial 'primary data' for nearly all of these histories (except possibly narrative and intellectual history).

Historians—especially biblicists, most of them narrowly trained as philogians, and sometimes as theologians—have been slow or reluctant to perceive the effects of the recent 'archaeological revolution'. But it is sufficiently pervasive that *all* histories of ancient Israel are now obsolete. And in future, in my opinion, comprehensive histories of Israel, in Iron Age Palestine at least, will be written either by archaeologists increasingly concerned with historiography, or by teams of scholars that include archaeologists as principal resource persons. For myself, my next work will be a history of ancient Israel written largely without recourse to the Hebrew Bible, based mostly on the rich archaeological data that we now possess. It is tentatively titled *Archaeology and an 'Axial Age': A History of Israel and Her Neighbors in the 8th Century* BCE.

Archaeology, History, and How the Past Shapes the Future

I have already alluded to the ways in which Syro-Palestinian (or southern Levantine) archaeology is being misconstrued to support various religious ideologies and political agendas, the European biblical revisionists being perhaps the most obvious villains. But in the Middle East as well, pan-Arab nationalists, Messianic Zionists, and agitators of all kinds are emerging, claiming that archaeology supports their claims to legitimacy and exclusive right to the Holy Land (Dever 2003b: 237-39). And the latent anti-Semitism of some of the biblical revisionists plays right into some of their hands. I have fought all of my professional life to keep religion, politics, and nationalism *out* of Near Eastern archaeology; and now I see zealots and demagogues (what a colleague calls 'cultural beserkers') dragging these pernicious elements in via the back door.

It is not productive for those of us who work in Israel—or for that matter anywhere else in the Middle East—to revive the ghosts of 'biblical archaeology' or a nostalgic 'biblical past' as whipping boys for modern ideologies. Nor does it help when some Palestinians adopt the nihilist agenda of European biblical 'revisionists', who want to write Israel out of history, who fan the fires of a new anti-Semitism. Perhaps we cannot be entirely objective in archaeological research; but we must *try* and try *harder*. Above all, we must be willing to state our ideology right up front; to examine it self-critically; and then to build on the foundation of a consensus about the pertinent facts. As the eminent historian Eric Hobsbawm once observed: 'These are facts; facts matter; and some facts matter a great deal'. Ancient Israel is just such a fact. And the other peoples of Bronze–Iron Age Palestine are also equally legitimate, and equally entitled to be comprehended on their own terms, not caricatured or otherwise erased from history.

Science and Archaeology

Is science then our best hope? Perhaps it is theoretically—to the extent that ^{14}C dates, for instance, may eventually be fixed within a sufficiently narrow range to permit what I have called 'historical dead reckoning'. But *texts*—including the biblical texts, however minimal their historical information—will always be required for our larger reconstructions.

I have recently argued at length (Dever 2001) that here the best 'historical probabilities', all we can reasonably hope for, are likely to be found at those points where properly critical readings of texts *and* artifacts point to 'convergences'. That is not tendentious 'biblical archaeology', but simply honest, balanced scholarship—and good history-writing.

On the subject of the much-debated 'United Monarchy', let me say unequivocally that I welcome the input of ^{14}C research, as one facet of an interdisciplinary inquiry. But there are still too many uncertainties in scientific method and application to pin all our hopes on ^{14}C alone. The Megiddo dates, at least as published thus far, seem to be equivocal; they certainly do not confirm the 'low chronology'. For me, the Tel Reḥov dates are more persuasive; and Finkelstein to the contrary notwithstanding, they tend to support the conventional chronology (Mazar and Carmi 2001; Bruins, van der Plicht, and Mazar 2003; Finkelstein 2003). The Dor ^{14}C dates now published (Gilboa and Sharon 2001) may seem promising, but these provide only a rather rough sequence for cultural horizons at a coastal Phoenician site, and in my judgment they cannot simply be 'plugged into' the inland Israelite–Judean sites and their complex, regional stratigraphy.

Finally, most of our ^{14}C dates thus far have come from northern, 'Israelite' sites, introducing an obvious bias into the investigation. When we have ^{14}C dates from southern or 'Judean' sites like Gezer, I think the picture will be better balanced. It is already clear to some of us that ceramic evolution proceeds at different paces in the north and in the south. Thus, I believe that while the Hazor and Megiddo gates might turn out to be early 9th century BCE, the Gezer gate will likely remain well fixed in the 10th century BCE. A new series of excavations will soon provide the first ^{14}C dates. And here the Shishak destruction ca. 925 BCE, long ignored by nearly all the revisionists, is still one of our best fixed points of historical reference (Dever 1997: 239-41; cf. Finkelstein 2002).

Personally I am still committed to the conventional (not 'high') chronology, for reasons that I have developed at length in several recent publications, none of them 'ideological'. But if evidence should mount to support a lower chronology, I shall be among the first to shift. This is not about 'saving' the Hebrew Bible; or defending 'Solomon in all his glory;' or arguing who was there first, Canaanites or Israelites, Palestinians or Israelis. Archaeology does not answer such questions; at best it only poses them. And if remaining 'conventional' (i.e. mainstream) means being 'politically incorrect', so be it.

This volume is about what really happened in one brief moment in the history of a troubled far-off corner of the world. What all this means, we shall have to figure out for ourselves, in *our* time, whatever *their* time may turn out to have been. Perhaps here we have taken a modest, hopeful step forward.

References

Barr, J. (2000) *History and Ideology in the Old Testament: Biblical Studies at the End of a Millennium* (Oxford: Oxford University Press).

Bintliffe, J.L. (ed.) (1991) *The Annales School and Archaeology* (Leicester: Leicester University Press).

Bruins, H.J., J. van der Plicht, and A. Mazar (2003) ^{14}C Dates from Tel Rehov: Iron Age Chronology, Pharaohs, and Hebrew Kings. *Science* 300: 315-18.

Dever, W.G. (1985) Syro-Palestinian and Biblical Archaeology. In *The Hebrew Bible and Its Modern Interpreters*, edited by D.A. Knight and G.M. Tucker (Philadelphia: Fortress Press): 31-74.

—(1997) Archaeology and the 'Age of Solomon': A Case-Study in Archaeology and Historiography. In *The Age of Solomon: Scholarship at the Turn of the Millennium*, edited by L.K. Handy (Leiden: Brill): 217-51.

—(2000) Biblical and Syro-Palestinian Archaeology: A State-of-the-Art Assessment at the Turn of the Millennium. *Currents in Research: Biblical Studies* 8: 91-116.

—(2001) *What Did the Biblical Writers Know and When Did They Know It? What Archaeology Can Tell Us about the Reality of Ancient Israel* (Grand Rapids: Eerdmans).

—(2003a) Syro-Palestinian and Biblical Archaeology. Into the Next Millennium. In *Symbiosis, Symbolism, and the Power of the Past: Canaan, Ancient Israel, and Their Neighbors from the Late Bronze Age through Roman Palaestina*, edited by W.G. Dever and S. Gitin (Winona Lake, IN: Eisenbrauns): 513-27.

—(2003b) *Who Were the Early Israelites and Where Did They Come From?* (Grand Rapids: Eerdmans).

—(2004) Histories and Non-Histories of Ancient Israel: The Question of the United Monarchy. In *In Search of Pre-Exilic Israel*, edited by J. Day (JSOTSup 406; London: T. & T. Clark): 65-94.

Finkelstein, I. (1998) Bible Archaeology or Archaeology of Palestine in the Iron Age? *Levant* 30: 167-73.

—(2002) The Campaign of Shoshenq I to Palestine: A Guide to the 10th Century BCE Polity. *ZDPV* 118: 109-35.

—(2003) Recent Radiocarbon Results and King Solomon. *Antiquity* 77/298: 771-79.

Foucault, M. (1980) *Power/Knowledge: Selected Interviews and Other Writings 1972–1977* (New York: Pantheon Books).

Gilboa, A., and I. Sharon (2001) Early Iron Age Dates from Tel Dor: Preliminary Implications for Phoenicia and Beyond. *Radiocarbon* 43: 1343-51.

Grabbe, L.L. (ed.) (1997) *Can a 'History of Israel' Be Written?* (JSOTSup 245; Sheffield: Sheffield Academic Press).

Hodder, I. (1986) *Reading the Past: Current Approaches to Interpretation in Archaeology* (Cambridge: Cambridge University Press).

Lemche, N.P., and T.L. Thompson (1994) Did Biran Kill David? The Bible in the Light of Archaeology. *JSOT* 64: 3-22.

Mazar, A. (1997) Iron Age Chronology—A Reply to Israel Finkelstein. *Levant* 29: 155-65.

Mazar, A., and T. Carmi (2001) Radiocarbon Dates from Iron Age Strata at Tel Beth Shean and Tel Rehov. *Radiocarbon* 43: 1333-42.

Preucel, R.W. (ed.) (1991) *Processual and Postprocessual Archaeologies. Multiple Ways of Knowing the Past* (Carbondale: Southern Illinois University Press).

Thompson, T.L. (1995) A Neo-Albrightian School in History and Biblical Scholarship? *Journal of Biblical Literature* 14: 683-98.

—(1997) Defining History and Ethnicity in the South Levant. In *Can a 'History of Israel' Be Written?*, edited by L.L. Grabbe (JSOTSup 245; Sheffield: Sheffield Academic Press): 166-87.

—(1999) *The Mythic Past: Biblical Archaeology and the Myth of Israel* (London: Basic Books).

Whitelam, K.W. (1996) *The Invention of Ancient Israel: The Silencing of Palestinian History* (London: Routledge).

Whitley, D.S. (1998) *Reader in Archaeological Theory: Post-Processual and Cognitive Approaches* (London: Routledge).

Windschuttle, K. (1996) *The Killing of History: How Literary Critics and Social Theorists are Murdering Our Past* (New York: Free Press).

26 David Did It, Others Did Not

The creation of Ancient Israel

Baruch Halpern

Abstract

The absolute dating of the Iron Age is based on a solar eclipse together with calendrical continuity into the Roman era and thereafter. Correlating literary sources to the chronological framework poses few problems, especially since our continuous Biblical historiographic sources conform to epigraphic chronological evidence to an extraordinary extent. So two issues arise in the attempt to connect text to mound: what does the Biblical or epigraphic evidence imply for a particular, dated, period, and what does the archaeological horizon imply for its particular concatenation of occupations? Typically, attempts to correlate the archaeological to the historical record have been facile. The textual evidence must be taken critically—neither endorsed nor dismissed, but evaluated—before such a correlation can be suggested. How, then, do we correlate archaeological horizons with textual indices? Do the absolute correlations offer any control on the dating of archaeological horizons between them?

I

When Arnold Toynbee published *A Study of History* (1956), the reviews were both many and varied. Scholars of all sorts of subjects contributed the reviews, from Indology and Sinology to American history. Most of the reviews ran more or less like this: this work is a real contribution. In my field, it is not very good, but on every other front it is brilliant.

Everyone enjoys truly multi-disciplinary conferences, for those are the venues in which scholars in other disciplines reveal their disagreements, and the logic actuating their positions. Otherwise, it is our tendency to defer to the authority, rather than to understand the logic and evidence, of scholars in other fields. The 'Bible and radiocarbon dating project' has exposed us all to the limitations of our various fields—radiocarbon, archaeology, dendrochronology, history. Indeed, the next conference we convene should focus specifically not on the positive contributions we can make, but on the limits of our knowledge, with regard to some particular subject.

A recurring theme among the participants in this volume has been the *Drang nach* more sophisticated analysis. Radiocarbon experts are already calibrating their equipment against one another (Fourth International Radiocarbon Intercomparison). Archaeologists are admitting that ceramic periods are not all precisely contemporaneous—a major concession in a community that has regularly equated most pottery horizons with a layer of destruction. Indeed, the Iron I, as

David Ilan remarked, starts in the 13th century BCE. The Late Bronze II, on the other hand, ends in the later 12th century BCE. The two overlap by a century or so. The same is true of every ceramic horizon: each is a rolling horizon, passing from one site to the next, and passing from one site before it passes from the next. And yet the power of the words, 'Iron IA here, Iron IA there', is such as to induce scholars to think of a fixed and limited period of time. It begins ca. 1200 BCE, and ends ca. 1100 or 1050. This is bankrupt as a principle of chronology. As Israel Finkelstein intuits (Chapter 3, this volume), pottery types can slide in time one against the other, without violating common sense.

The same holds for other sorts of argument to simultaneity, as opposed to rolling contemporaneity. And simultaneity is the biggest issue in our current scholarship about chronology, because archaeological chronology is inevitably only rough. Architectural forms, types of inscriptions, cuisines, trends in artistic motifs on pottery or on glyptic—all these things move wave-like across space, meaning that they reach different locales, and even neighboring locales, in different degrees at different times. Local innovation or conservatism, foreign contact, wealth, ideological freighting —all these things affect the degree and speed of appropriation, differentially by place. We cannot assume that forms such as the *bit hilani* suddenly were adopted all over the Near East, and in fact there is textual evidence that dates the form's introduction to Assyria to the 8th century BCE, under Tiglath-Pileser III (Clay Tablet r 18: Tadmor 1994: 172), whereas its appearance in central and northern Syria, at least, clearly dates at latest to the mid-9th century, and perhaps earlier, with antecedents in the Late Bronze Age. But even were we to think we have a clear date for the beginning of a phenomenon, that is no argument against its having begun earlier elsewhere. Innovations spread, or they can, like calculus, be invented independently based on earlier forerunners. Deciding that Newton, that universal genius, must have been the first to develop the calculus, or Darwin the first to develop the theory of natural selection, does considerable violence to the history of science, and slights Leibniz and Watson into the bargain.

More supple approaches are needed. One, adumbrated by Amihai Mazar *et al.* (Chapter 13, this volume) in connection with the evidence from Tel Reḥov, is to separate the pottery from the architecture (one needs to do the same with chronological data in Egypt and Israel—separating synchronisms from regnal lengths, for example). Architecture comes from the life of a layer, but ceramic partly from heirlooms and mainly from its final phase. We also need to distinguish different sorts of time—not the famous divisions of the *Annales* school so much as archaeological time, radiocarbon time, and historical time. We need to distinguish different kinds of history, as well: narrative and its language, the intention behind the narrative, the reconstruction behind the intention, and, something very different, reality. For history is never the truth, and is at its best a version of a *truth-manque*, about the past. Sue Sherratt said (Chapter 9, this volume) that getting dates, and we may add strata or pots, right, just tempts you to create pseudo-history, like the Dorian invasion of Greece, like the reification of dates of assemblages.

We need to sort our variables. We must not be seduced by the words we use into equating a ceramic assemblage with a delimited time, or a carbon date with the life of a layer. We must be especially careful in combining data about various sites into one large contemporaneous database, given that dates come from various points in the life of the layers. And, in relating to text, one must be careful in the extreme, because text, even more than archaeology (so far as archaeologists will concede this at all), requires qualitative evaluation.

What makes such evaluation difficult is that texts cannot be subjected to meaningful quantitative evaluation. Aspects of language can be evaluated quantitatively. So we can subject elements of texts to tests that are not dissimilar from those to which we subject archaeological data. Yet, the standards of the field are such that what emerges in journals can be of very low quality—the publication of hunches in many cases, or even of delusions. The field has no watchdogs, no common standards, which is what distinguishes it from the natural sciences. But when, in Toynbee-esque fashion, scholars of other disciplines lean on Biblical or Near Eastern historians, they run the risk of choosing incompetent guides. This happens frequently in archaeological evaluations in particular, just as textual scholars have often chosen to rely on shaky archaeological interpretations, or, indeed, on no archaeology at all.

The archaeologists of a generation ago found remains to identify with Biblical records. Scholars today attack what they think the Biblical material suggests, such as a Davidic empire stretching from the Brook of Egypt to the Euphrates. Late sources say such things, but 2 Samuel restricts David's Israelite realm to the region between Dan and Beersheba, over and over again. Attacking the late assertions or the implications of our early texts, the deliberate insinuations, misses the point and misprises the nature of writing. If David had ruled to the Euphrates, the early text would certainly say so. Its reticence (2 Samuel 8.3: he ruled to the 'river') bespeaks a concern that such a claim would be risible, falsified by knowledge or by memory. No king, and no dynasty, can afford to invite extended ridicule. At the same time, the text invites us to make exactly that mistake, hopes that we will fall into the trap of believing the insinuation rather than the literal remark. In a word, royal propaganda involves spin. Heavy spin.

Some textual analysis is reliable. Most is not. The same problem exists, albeit not in the same measure, in archaeology. We just do not have the same degree of collaboration, cross-checking, and non-competitive openness that we see in the radiocarbon community. Richard Feynmann once wrote that in the early days of physics, relations among scientists were 'argumentative'. Probably, he was referring to the days before the spread of international scholarly journals and of international collaboration. 'But in physics today', he continues,

> the relations are extremely good. A scientific argument is likely to involve a great deal of laughter and uncertainty on both sides, with both sides thinking up experiments and offering to bet on the outcome. In physics there are so many accumulated observations that it is almost impossible to think of a new idea which is different from all the ideas that have been thought of before and yet that agrees with all the observations that have already been made. And so if you get anything new from anyone, anywhere, you welcome it, and you do not argue about why the other person says it is so. Many sciences have not developed this far, and the situation is the way it was in the early days of physics, when there was a lot of arguing because there were not so many observations. I bring this up because it is interesting that human relationships, if there is an independent way of judging truth, can be unargumentative. (Feynmann 1998: 21-22)

Historians and archaeologists need to establish a like degree of community, and an admission of uncertainty, and a real test against a complete history of relevant observations, and common standards of evidence. The latter was, of course, Robert Merton's *sine qua non* for the development of science (Merton 1979).

II

Bertrand Russell began his autobiography by explaining how he learned geometry at a precocious age from his brother. 'The first thing you need to know', said his brother, 'is that parallel lines never meet'. 'Why not?', asked Bertrand. 'That's just the way things are', said his brother, 'it's a definition'. 'Prove it', said Bertrand. And on and on. Finally, his brother put his foot down: 'either you accept that parallel lines never meet, or we cannot go on' (Russell 1967).

Anyone who has dealt seriously with chronological or complex scholarly issues will recognize the import of this anecdote. One needs fixed points, axioms, in order to work out a systematic analysis. Where are our fixed points to come from? Because without a link to the texts, we have no history, no framework for embedding characters or developments into time, in a way that a historian would find recognizable. We might date layers, in the future. But in historical archaeology, we also need to put the right people into them. The tendency in the past decades has been to lump historical in with prehistoric archaeology, a mistake whose dimensions deserve exploration —in no other field of scholarship do mainstream practitioners exclude, rather than evaluate, evidence. Among historical archaeologists, equipollent proportions deny the value of, which is to say, claim to ignore, textual data. The reasons for that error indict multiple constituencies, including formally inadequate philology in Biblical Studies.

How to figure our way out of this deliberate ignoring of textual data, or, on the textual side, of archaeological data, is the real task of the birthing of this century. Maybe we could start with a few anecdotes, such as the time Yigael Yadin told a group of seminar-mates that an inconvenient text just needed to be emended, or the many times when Albright, according to G. Ernest Wright, swept inconvenient sherds from the sorting table. It might be good to know the history of the divide in cultures—text and artefact. At the least, William Dever should have memories of about a thousand such incidents, and we should be recording the history of every one of them. And, similarly, the absorption into the world of text of a goodly number of forgeries, most of them not exposed to date, speaks to the nature of the community of epigraphers and other sub-specialty experts in areas related to the reconstruction of the past.

In the last two decades, it has become a fashion to compare Biblical King David to the mythical King Arthur. Neither ever lived, say some vocal Europeans. On the face of it, this position has some merit: not a single building, except perhaps a revetment south of the temple mount, is associated with this 10th-century ruler whose empire, some texts claim, stretched from the Nile to the Euphrates.

Scholars have long pointed to similar gates built simultaneously at Megiddo, Hazor, and Gezer to attest building by David's son, Solomon: the archaeology seemed to confirm a report in 1 Kings 9.16 attributing fortifications at these sites, among others, to Solomon. (We might also add a gate to this mix in the Negev, should we choose to identify Ein Hazeva or Tel Ira with Judahite Tamar.) But others have disputed the attribution of these gates. If their converse position holds, there is no remnant of David's monarchy at all—either the kings were kings in a nutshell, or they were no kings at all.

These are different positions. Either David and Solomon are mythical, or they were minor, local rulers. The first position is that of a group often dubbed 'Minimalists', the second that of adherents to 'the low chronology'. As the controversy over the low chronology has shown, correlating texts to objects is ticklish business. It has never been sufficiently sophisticated, especially in Israelite history. One doesn't just find a building in the ground and decide that it is the 'stables of Solomon', as P.L.O. Guy did at Megiddo in the 1920s, in identifying structures that were neither Solomonic nor, in my view, stables. You must first date the stratum—in historical archaeology, almost always a controversial issue—and then date and evaluate the reliability of the textual source, ever a matter of controversy. Then connections remain a matter for critical scrutiny. The temptation to easy correlation is the temptation of laziness, and of confirming one's beliefs. Even so, a minimalizing approach was historically misconceived: like a spooked squid, it obscured the past with ink. It led us down the blind alley of arguing about David's existence rather than about his activity.

My brief is to evaluate neither the low chronology nor minimalism. It is to evaluate the likelihood that David reigned in Jerusalem and in its neighborhood. Was he Butch Cassidy and the Hole in the Wall Gang? If he wasn't the maximum that the text can be taken to claim, say the naysayers, he never reigned.

But David and Solomon existed. They even reigned over a unified Israel.

Our evidence for the activity of David and Solomon is textual. But if the texts are wrongly interpreted, then conclusions from the archaeology don't follow. If you get the history wrong—by taking the text too literally, or not literally enough; by taking the text to reflect reality, or no reality at all—you don't test it correctly against archaeological results. The textual evidence has its own logic. And in William Dever, Israel Finkelstein, David Ilan, Amihai Mazar, and others, this volume contains contributions from more than its share of archaeologists who try to understand it.

Had David and Solomon been invented—around 400 BCE, say the most conservative Minimalists—then we should have no pre-exilic evidence for them. Because, until 586 BCE, there was certainly a state in Jerusalem, and it would have been difficult for a king to invent ancestors of relatively recent vintage who participated in the construction of a temple, or the creation of a dynasty, there. The Minimalist argument stands or falls on the premise that all our textual data is late, that there are no Davids or Solomons in the pre-exilic period. Even the low chronology depends to an extraordinary extent on the argument that we have no sources earlier than the 7th century BCE. For, in the ancient Near East we have no-one inviting derision by claiming to build a temple he did not build, and no-one failing to take credit for the tiniest achievement possible.

In addition, David's existence is attested by external sources. Late 9th-century BCE sources include the Tel Dan Stela. This refers to Judah as 'the House/Dynasty of David'. It parallels the Zakkur inscription of ca. 800 BCE in referring to chariotry and cavalry (*lrkb* [*w*]*lprš*, in KAI 202B2) together. It also bears note that Biblical references to cavalry, as opposed to chariotry, place the arm in the 10th century BCE (1 Samuel 13.5, 6000; 2 Samuel 8.4, 1700; 10.18, 40000; 1 Kings 5.6; 10.26, 12000; 2 Kings 13.7, 50; note 2 Samuel 1.6, *b^{c}ly hpršm*).

The argument that an author forged the dynasty or its foundation depends on a view of Near Eastern culture that is without parallel. It also depends on doubting the integrity of the sources to the extent that one might doubt the accuracy of romances from the Middle Ages. This represents a misprision of the genre of our materials.

Materially, then, the date of our Biblical sources concerning David is of considerable moment. For such dating, the evidence from language is crucial. Among the elements here, most special is simply phonology. Thus, the name, Geshur, appears as that of an Aramaean region to the northeast of the Sea of Galilee, in Samuel and also in the J source. The P source in the Pentateuch reflects a different phonology in reporting the name as Gether. Similarly, J knows of an Aramaean Yoqshan (probably originally Yoqśan), whereas P reports the name as Yoqtan. In both cases, the J version of the name (and, in the former case, that of Samuel) antedates the P version. P's rendition of the names reflects the influence of eastern (later, Imperial) Aramaic, whose impact first registered in the west in the late 7th century BCE (note the mix of forms in Jeremiah 10.10), and appeared in the Mesopotamian sphere certainly in the 9th century BCE (Shalmaneser III's Hatarikka for western Hazrach). Phonology can date our texts to the 7th century BCE, and often the names of foreign kingdoms are much earlier.

There are other criteria for dating language as well. Most are not terribly specific. Probably the most specific one would be syntax, where again the wave approach is necessary. Still, there are conditional clauses in Samuel the like of which we do not see in later Biblical texts, such as Kings—forms reminiscent of Amarna Canaanite 'unmarked' clauses, that probably antedate the 7th century BCE. Likewise, there are a few terms diagnostic of early times. But scholars tend to make too much of this sort of evidence: the word petard is still in use in an English idiom, derived from Shakespeare, at a time when few know what a petard was. Vocabulary can, in many circumstances, enjoy a widespread afterlife.

Other aspects of language are often invoked as tools for dating. Phraseology, attitude, ideology, the typical focuses of Biblical scholarship, are all the wrong tools for dating. And yet, sometimes usage can be revealing. The late 9th-century BCE Mesha stela, for example, employs the expressions 'man of Gad' (singular), for Gadites (plural), 'man of Dibon' (singular), for Dibonites (plural). This has parallels in the expressions, 'man of Israel/Judah' in the account of the Absalom revolt, and a very few dependent contexts, for Israelites, or Judahites (plural) (Tadmor 1968). Another valuable indicator is a text's orthography. In the post-exilic period, conventions of spelling differed widely from those in the pre-exilic period. Not only was defective spelling regnant in the earlier era, but certain conventions of the post-exilic era have no parallels earlier in Israel. Where a text preserves multiple early spellings, therefore, the probability falls decisively on the side of pre-exilic composition (see Cross and Freedman 1952; Zevit 1980; Anderson and Forbes 1986; Hurvitz 1988, 2000a, 2000b).

One hesitates to pile Ossa on Pelion, and yet examining the relationship of a text to other sources, even when the relations are somewhat obscure, has its advantages as well. In connection with the other data, this can be revealing.

An example is the enumeration of trophies in 1 Samuel 18.25 and 2 Samuel 3.14. This matches Egyptian practice under Ramses III, and is not noted in other Israelite texts. Philistines collect the hands, feet, and skulls of their victims, whereas Israelites collect Philistine foreskins (note also 2 Samuel 3.33; 4.12). It is an odd feature of the development of civilization, probably under the Babylonians or Persians, that such trophies do not occupy center stage in inscriptions or reliefs after the Assyrian period, and, indeed, after Sennacherib (in inscriptions, not even Tiglath-Pileser III). The last king to include hands and feet may well have been Ramses III, and the last to mention heads Shalmaneser III.

Likewise, the geography and ethnography of texts can be indicative, in the sense that *Kulturgeschichte* may be more revealing of development than political history. 2 Samuel 2.9 enumerates the regions of Israel in a way that probably reflects a geographical conception of Israel that later is not witnessed: Transjordan, the Galilee, Jezreel, Ephraim, Benjamin. No other such enumeration emerges in any Biblical or other text.

In the same vein, the Gadites are uniquely associated with lions in the Biblical material, as in Mesha's *'r'l* of *dwdh*. And Samuel has *'r'ly* of Moab. Given that Mesha regards Gad as Moabite (Donner and Roellig 2002: 181.10), and Gad appears among foreign peoples in 2 Samuel 23.36, and otherwise doesn't appear as an Israelite tribe in 2 Samuel or the B source in 1 Samuel, this mutual illumination suggests Samuel stemmed from a time before Gad became Israelite. Likewise, the late 9th-century BCE Mesha stela probably attests the origin of the dynasty in Jerusalem with David. And just as the Mesha stela implies that Gad was not Israelite, the late 9th-century BCE Tel Dan stela implies that Dan was Aramean. Similarly, 2 Samuel 20 implies that Abel of the House of Maacah (an Aramean dynasty) was not an Israelite site until after the Absalom revolt (see my *David's Secret Demons* [2001]). All this material—foreign and Israelite—is, though dissonant, of a piece, and antedates the 7th and probably even the 8th centuries BCE.

Actually, as in SDeb, the Transjordanian polity in 2 Samuel is Gilead. This, too, looks 9th century BCE or earlier. Indeed, Jezreel is actually some sort of kinship group or polity as well— again, early, undifferentiated by tribe.[1]

---

1. Gilead as a tribal kinship unit is in: Judges 5.17; 2 Samuel 2.9; 17.27; 19.32; 1 Kings 2.7; 2 Kings 15.25; perhaps Judges 10.3; 11.1, 29, 40; 12.7; as a subtribal unit: Numbers 26.29 bis -30; 27.1; 32.1; 36.1 (all P); Joshua 17.3; Ezra 2.61; Nehemiah 7.63; 1 Chronicles 2.21, 23; 5.14; 7.14, 17; as a geographical unit: Genesis 31.21, 23, 25; 37.25; Numbers 32.1, 26, 29, 39-40; Deuteronomy 2.36; 3.10, 12-13, 15-16; 4.43; 34.1; Joshua 12.2,5; 13.11, 25, 31; 17.1, 5-6; 20.8; 21.36; 22.9, 13, 15, 32; Judges 7.3; 10.4, 8, 17-18; 11.5, 7-11; 12.4-5, 7; 20.1; 2 Samuel 17.26; 24.6; 1 Kings 4.13, 19; 17.1; 2 Kings 10.33 bis; 15.29; Jeremiah 8.22; 22.5; 46.11; 50.19; Ezekiel 47.18; Hosea 6.8; 12.12; Amos 1.3, 13; Micah 7.14; Obadiah 19; Zechariah 10.10; Psalms 60.9; 108.9; Canticles 4.1; 6.5; 1 Chronicles 2.22; 5.9-10, 16; 6.65; 27.21; other: land of Gad and Gilead, 1 Samuel 13.7 (A). So, kinship usage is quite early, though it can be confused with geographic usage, but there is no instance in which it is later than the 8th–7th centuries BCE. Still, this is definitely evidence

Another index of antiquity comes from reportage of Philistine names. From a combination of the Tel Miqneh inscription and Assyrian annals (Gitin, Dothan and Naveh 1997), we now believe that the name, Achish, of a king of Eqron in the 7th century BCE and a king of Gath in the 10th century BCE, is Achaios. The latter is a name for Greeks in Homer, but for a circumcised population at the end of the Late Bronze Age, or the start of Iron I in the time of Ramses III. Its use for 'uncircumcised' Philistines suggests a gap between the Egyptian and Biblical evidence, and yet its use at the end of the Iron II may expose a gap between possibly circumcised Philistines, at the time, and uncircumcised Greeks.[2] Still, its resumed use after the passage of centuries (and none of the ancestors in the Tel Miqneh inscription has a non-Semitic name) parallels other appeals to early roots in the 7th century (Halpern 1991). Goliath is also not a normal Canaanite name.[3] But Ashdodite was the language of the Philistine region in the 5th century, as Nehemiah 13.23-24 attest: one would expect Phoenician names then, as in the epigraphs from the era at Ashkelon. All our data in Samuel about Philistines therefore seem archaic, and certainly pre-exilic.

Other indices about the age of our sources include disagreement with later sources (as to David's fidelity to YHWH, the extent of his kingdom, see below). But from an evidentiary viewpoint, even more important is the case for continuity. Starting with Solomon, the books of Kings name all known foreign kings in the right order—misnaming one only. From the 10th to the 6th centuries BCE, all are placed in exactly the right pew, the right time and place. The list, starting from the 6th century and working backwards, includes the following monarchs:

Evil-Merodach
Nebuchadrezzar
Sennacherib
Merodach-Baladan
Shalmaneser (V)
Tiglath-Pileser (III, Pul)
Rezin of Damascus
Ben-Hadad son of Hazael
Hazael, as usurper
Mesha (a king of the back side of the moon)
Ethbaal (=Ittobaal), king of Tyre/Sidon
(Error: Ben-Hadad, for Hadadezer, predecessor of Hazael)
Rezon (or possibly Rezin) of Damascus
Shishaq

---

of early production. Even Reuben, later the first of the tribes, and witnessed in SDeb, does not appear in 2 Samuel 2. Nor does Simeon, missing in SDeb and Deuteronomy 33. Levi, missing in SDeb, appears only twice, so that one might almost think it absent; but this is probably a question of subject matter: 1 Samuel 6.15 (A source?); 2 Samuel 15.24. Judah, Ephraim (mainly a geographic term) and Benjamin occur; Issachar and Zebulun (the pair termed Jezreel in 2 Samuel 2.9), Naphtali and Manasseh (lumped with Ephraim in 2 Samuel 2.9) do not occur. Asher stands for the Galilee, in 2 Samuel 2.9, and Dan appears as a border city paired with Beersheba (only Samuel and 1 Kings 5.5 in the traditional formula, with a variant formula at Judges 20.1, and a reversed one in 1 Chronicles 21.2; 2 Chronicles 30.5). Hypothetical: if Ashurite in 2 Samuel 2.9 is the Galilee region as a whole, we have terminology for the divisions of Israel that pre-date the crystallization of territorial tribes in the Galilee and Jezreel regions, and the differentiation of Ephraim and Manasseh in the central highlands; and, an order of enumeration that does not correlate to the standard order in Genesis 49; 29–30, JE; Genesis 46 etc., P. It stands between the order of Deuteronomy 33 and that of the standard traditions (Halpern 1983: 96-106, now vindicated as to climate shifts).

    2.   Oddly enough, references to the Philistines as uncircumcised pertain always to the 10th century or earlier.

    3.   It should not, however, be compared with Alyattes, as the latter would evoke not g but either 'aleph or 'ayin as the first corresponding letter in Semitic, given the phonology of Anatolian dialects in this era. The names attested on ostraca from Tell Jemmeh in the 7th century BCE are also non-Semitic, but it is impossible to determine whether they are Philistine or those of Iranian deportees. See Kempinski 1987; cf. also Na'aman and Zadok 1988.

Samuel adds a king of Hamath, Toi, and a king, Hadadezer of Zobah (Assyrian Subite) as well as kings of Rabbat Amman. The odds that these names are concoctions are low in the extreme, because the polities were real enough in the pre-exilic era.

Prophetic sources add, in the right order, 3 more Assyrian kings, as well as confirming the names of Rezin (II) and:

Sargon
Esarhaddon
Asshurbanipal

Similarly, all Israelite kings occur in the right order in foreign records.
In foreign sources, we have, from the 10th century forward:

David
Omri
Ahab
[Ahaz]yahu (of Judah)
[Jo]ram (of Israel)
Jehu
Joash of Israel
[possibly Uzziah = Azaryahu]
Menahem
Pekah
Ahaz
Hosea
Hezekiah
Manasseh
Jehoiachin

Altogether, 15 or 16 kings of Judah and Israel appear, in foreign sources, in complete agreement with their names and times in Kings. Not a single king is out of place, nor do foreign sources name one unknown to us in Kings.

This sequence, in the end, goes back to Shishaq in the 10th century BCE. And Shishaq's apparently unusual entry into the Ayyalon Pass, when he otherwise avoids hills, can only be explained if there was a significantly rich prize to be gotten by threatening Jerusalem. In all, we have evidence of records reaching back to the 10th century BCE, and the idea of Rehoboam's tribute was not gleaned from Shishaq's list at Karnak. The references intersect, after all, with Assyrian records that connect to astronomical data fixing the chronology to a particular year from 911 BCE onward. In other words, every foreign power in the region appears in Kings in the right sequence of rulers or domination. Why is this? We think of king lists as compilations, like chronicles, assembled from sources distant in time from the events. But in fact, king lists, and especially synchronistic king lists, are economic documents regarding trade relations at heart. The economic relations require close accuracy for the calculation of interest, among other things.

We can add to this picture a list of polities in Samuel and in the account of Solomon's reign which do not survive in the Persian or Hellenistic eras, and some of which do not survive even in the 8th–7th centuries BCE:

1. Tov, for example, reappears in personal names, but not as a polity.
2. Zobah appears in neo-Assyrian sources of the 8th–7th centuries BCE, as Subite, sometimes a province, but never thereafter as a region.
3. Que appears as a term for a region until the end of the neo-Assyrian period. The term is absent after the exile, when it became Hilakku > Kilikia, and even in Assyria, the region was referred to mainly as Hilakku before then, and Adana in local inscriptions.

4. Ammon is another polity absent after the exile.
5. Bet Rehob probably never appears after the 10th century BCE, though Nadav Na'aman would take it down into the 9th century BCE (Na'aman 1996).
6. Bet Maacah certainly is absent after the 10th century BCE.
7. Other evanescent polities arguably include Hamath; Moab; Edom; Aram Damascus, as opposed to Aram generally, or as opposed to other states in Aram, such as Arpad/Bit Agusi, of central importance in the later 8th century BCE.[4]

There are further textual indications. The border of Moab in the Mesha stela (Donner and Roellig 2002: 181.26) is Aroer; that is the southern border 2 Kings 10.33 assigns to Hazael in Transjordan at just the same time. This is far from being a coincidence of later historical memories. Jehu ceded Transjordan down to Moab (including Ammon) to Aram Damascus as the price for his betrayal of the House of Omri. All the data on the subject are of a piece.

All this is pre-exilic, and much of it is pre-7th century BCE. The evidence attests continuity of record-keeping.

Other elements also indicate that 2 Samuel (and parts of the Solomon account in 1 Kings, and details in continuity from 1 Samuel to 2 Samuel) antedate the 7th and even the 8th centuries BCE: in particular, this holds for the relationship of the text to archaeological evidence. Thus, the idea that David was a bandit army leader in the steppe of Judah could not stem from the 8th century BCE or later, since, by the 8th century, the hinterland of Judah was fairly full.[5] Similarly, the undeveloped kinship system of 2 Samuel fits an early date more than it does one in the 8th century or later. Samuel has 'mountain man' (*hrry*) as a kinship category, whereas J has three clans in Judah and P four, with subclans (Joshua 15 has 4 clans, or areas, at least, in Judah, probably corresponding to the *lmlk* seal impressions). Interestingly, David's 'heroes' are from northern Judah and Benjamin, only one reaching into Ephraim. There are none from the heartland of Judah's hill country. Indeed, these claims and the undeveloped kingship and administrative system implied in our sources in Samuel and 1 Kings match the survey and excavation data only from the 10th century BCE, and perhaps the early 9th century BCE (see Ofer 1993).

Again, the texts presuppose forms of architecture that are certainly pre-exilic. Houses and spaces reflect the realia of Iron Age and not that of the Persian Period. In particular, the accounts of the rape of Tamar and of David's conferences with Bathsheba and Nathan assume knowledge of the spatial realm of the *bit hilani*, a 10th–8th century BCE palace type, or of the 4-room house (Halpern 1998: 55-68). This architecture is missing in the Persian era.

Then there is the issue of the sites the sources mention. The village of Bahurim, for example, is unmentioned in Joshua, but is a key site in Samuel as the locus of Saul's estates and administrative apparatus (2 Samuel 3.16; 16.5; 17.18; 19.17; 23.31; 1 Kings 2.8; cf. 1 Chronicles 11.33). In addition, numerous sites in the Negev appear in the record, and in Shishaq's account of his campaign. Archaeological work in the Negev divulges burnished red-slipped pottery in 10th-century BCE contexts (Cohen and Cohen-Amin 2004). The ceramic forms there can be relatively primitive, and yet the surface treatment is one that otherwise is typical of a 10th-century BCE horizon. This includes Arad XII, probably the only candidate for Shishaq's enumeration of Negev conquests in the Arad area. No doubt, the burnished red slip represents the continuation of the Cypro-Phoenician Late Bronze tradition. And yet, on the basis of the linguistic evidence, the material must cohere with 10th-century BCE history.

---

4. Note in the case of Egypt that the claim of a dynastic marriage, whether true or not, is asserted at the only time when such a union was conceivable in historical terms, during the 21st dynasty's turn toward more equalized relations with foreign powers. Solomon's relations with Sheba, too, reflect changing relations with the south.

5. This observation stems in origin from Israel Finkelstein (in conversation).

Tellingly, Samuel mentions Philistine sites, only in the pentapolis. And yet Gath and Eqron, though clearly rivals in close proximity to one another, never occur at once in texts from later periods. Also, later stages of Philistine settlement involved the foundation of peripheral sites outside the Pentapolis, and yet Samuel only mentions the pentapolis sites (exceptions: Ziklag; garrison at Bethlehem). This smacks of the organization of the 10th century BCE at latest, probably the early 10th century, with the spread of Philistine ware but not yet of settlements beyond the central towns of the pentapolis.

Likewise, the text presents Solomonic building as evidence of the extension and presentation of a state. This is not necessarily more accurate, or less a matter of spin, than any other aspect of the text. One might even regard the gates at Gezer, Megiddo, and Hazor as elements of display, even if they were components of comprehensive fortification systems. If fortified, as seems likely, the sites were themselves possibly facades, ways in which the state presented itself to locals and especially to foreigners. Likewise, the monumental arch at Beth-Shemesh again in the 10th century BCE may have been a statement to travelers about central power. Though the excavators of Beth-Shemesh think Eqron was in ruins at the time (Bunimovitz and Lederman 2001), the latter remained dominant on the plain until the time of Shishaq, in whose list it appears as the last site among towns he conquered (*pace* Kitchen 1986: 441). Shishaq's raid is probably the time of the transition from Eqron V to Eqron IV, but this is naturally a matter of some debate—the transition in question could be from Eqron VI to V.

Another issue in the controversy is the question of how archaeology works in combination with history. The remains in whose reporting we can have relative confidence are buildings, strata, sequence and, in some measure, pots. What is probable is another matter. Bigger polities are probably dominant. But in any particular instance this is far from certain (Cyrus and Astyages; Alexander and Persia). And what is possible is the key for combining material culture with text. A deterministic approach to archaeological data is just naive. The concentration of force is far more important than its simple possession.

Archaeology cannot dictate what happened in historical periods: it can at best dictate to historians what could not have happened, or indicate what probably did not happen, nothing more.

Our literary sources also bear examination. Some do not present events in chronological order. None of the royal inscriptions lies straight-out; but all royal inscriptions spin events in just the way that modern politicians do—to the maximum advantage of the patron, without regard for actual truth. Reports that do not stem from the court often suffer from similar syndromes, depending on the institutional context from which they arise.

At the same time, one does not spin when one can simply lie. So the spin itself is evidence of rough contemporaneity with the events being spun. This holds especially for 2 Samuel 8 (below). Also, within reports about individual years in Assyrian annals, one also often finds similar spin, learned from the composition of display inscriptions. In the academies of Mesopotamia and Egypt, Royal Inscriptions 101 must have included modules on snatching victory from the jaws of defeat and on aggrandizing small victories into great ones.

The textual sources need to be evaluated based on a mix of criteria. The first, in the case of 2 Samuel, is the date of its composition, and the history of its editing. While imagining possible editings remains an industry in Biblical Studies, evidence from language and orthography, as well as from textual content, is what must determine the end of the discussion, for the simple reason that these are the only common standards on which scholars can rely. Based on such data, 2 Samuel consistently ranks as the oldest prose source in the Hebrew Bible, and certainly antedates our 8th-century materials, such as Amos and Hosea. In addition, it seems likely that the earliest edition of the chronicles of the kings of Judah, or, more certainly, of the books of Kings, stemmed from the time of Hezekiah. How early the rest of the Deuteronomistic History originated may always be a question. But of it, the books of Samuel are probably the earliest prose part.

The content of these texts confirms the indications from language. In late texts, such as Deuteronomy, Joshua and Genesis 15, the claim is asserted that Israel stretched from the Nile to the Euphrates (in the last case, the assertion may pertain to all descendants of Abraham, rather than to Israel). In earlier writings, the regnant theory is that the Israelites dominated up to the border of Hamath (Amos; 2 Kings 14.25, 28; and P). And in 2 Samuel, the border extends only from Beersheba in the south to Dan in the north.

Another indication of the date of the text of 2 Samuel is that it furnishes no real date for the unification of Israel with Judah and the Davidic monarchy. In reality, it is quite possible that any unification, or conquest of the north, occurred quite late in David's reign.

More important still is the shape of the reports of conquest in 2 Samuel 8. In this chapter, the empire reaches only the southern territory of Damascus. The first remark in the report is that 'David smote Philistines'. This claim is remarkably indefinite. From them he took some indeterminate good, usually interpreted as a place, but quite possibly an artefact (cf. 2 Samuel 5.21). Moreover, which Philistines did David smite? Those of Gath, Eqron, Ashdod, Ashkelon, or Gaza? The literature propagandistically presents the Philistines as monolithic. But surely, had we correspondence like that of the Amarna archive concerning the Philistine city-states, we would discover the same rifts and plots and grievances that characterized neighboring Canaanite towns in the Late Bronze Age. The presentation of the text is that David smote 'Philistines', generically. The reality was probably far more complex.

Notably, David never breached the zone that, in Iron I, was properly Philistine. Gezer remained the border into the time of Solomon, when even our text admits that the pharaoh destroyed it and presented it to Solomon (1 Kings 9.16). Further, Solomon was still on good terms with (Achish of) Gath, such that he could extradite slaves from there (1 Kings 2.39-46), furnishing evidence of a standard treaty situation. So exactly where did David smite Philistines? The text's reticence suggests that it was up in the central hill country, rather than down in the plain. This reticence speaks legions about the text's date.[6]

Similarly, 2 Samuel 8.2 claims that David 'smote Moab, and measured them out with a rope, laying them on the ground, and he measured two lengths to kill, and a full length to let live, and Moab became tribute-bearing servants'. Well, how many Moabites did David kill? Probably two. And where? Not in Moabite territory or the text would trumpet the fact. Again, the reticence to furnish detail is a sign of early composition.

The same text claims that David smote Aram (2 Samuel 8.3-5). But by omitting the fact that the battle took place in Ammon (2 Samuel 10), it gives the impression that David penetrated into Syria.

---

6.   Note also more sophistication about Philistine origins a little later: 9th century BCE, J in Genesis 10.14 (> 1 Chronicles 1.12), Caphtorites and Philistines come from Casluh, an offspring of Egypt; 8th century BCE, Amos 1.5, Aram from Qir (TP III exiles Damascenes there in 2 Kings 16.27) and 9.7, Aram from Qir and Philistines from Caphtor, part of Crete (Isaiah 9.11 also pairs Aram from in front, Philistines from behind; likewise, the identification of Avvim as the original inhabitants of Philistia in Deuteronomy 2.23; Joshua 13.3 [cf. town in Joshua 18.23] probably derives from Sargon's deportation of people from Awwah to the region [cf. 2 Kings 17.24, 31; 18.34; 19.13; Isaiah 37.13]; does P's tracing of Abram to Babylonia, or Ur, reflect knowledge of 597 in this vein, or perhaps of some earlier deportation of descendants of Abram?); 7th century BCE, Deuteronomy 2.23, Caphtorites (G, Cappadocians) destroyed Avvim who dwelled in Hazerim (enclosures? G *f*) up to Gaza; Jeremiah 47.4 calls them the remnant of the coasts of Caphtor. Now, Philistine names: Miqneh inscription shows Achish is Achaios, a type of Greek in Homer, but identical with Ahhiyawa in Asia Minor and with no foreskin according to Ramses III (Ekwesh), so not really Greek until Homer makes them so. Tell Jemmeh ostraca indicate a population with -s names, from Turkey or the Aegean, in 7th century BCE, but might be deportees from Iran. Why does Samuel refrain from dividing Philistines from Caphtorites, as later texts do? The Onomasticon of Amenope, ca. 1100 BCE, lists the following: Ashkelon, Ashdod, Gaza, Isr, *sbwry*, *x*, Sherden, Tjekker, Philistines, Hrm (= Masos?), and on. Note the separation of towns from peoples: is it possible that the Caphtorites, then, are either different from Philistines, in Philistia (as at Ekron) or stem from further up the coast (as Tjekker in Dor in Wen-Amun)? Is Samuel suppressing a distinction that earlier and later sources reflect then?

Likewise, the account claims that the Aramaeans—homogenized in the same way that the Philistines are—became servants to David. Which Aramaeans became 'servants'? The likelihood is these were the few people in the southern reaches of the former realm of Damascus whom David was able to reach. Yet, the list of booty suggests, by mentioning shields from Beerothai and Tubihi, probably captured in Transjordan (2 Samuel 10–11), that David reached the outskirts of Hamath. Why is this? The text then proceeds to enumerate 'gifts' from Hamath, suggesting David's supremacy there by claiming that he treated them like his 'other booty'. The contrast is with the report on Edom, which states that David installed garrisons throughout the region (probably the fortresses, built by David but also Solomon, which Shishaq encountered, and referred to as *ḥqrm*, cognate with Biblical *ḥṣr*, as in Hazar-Gaddah in Joshua 15.27, the *ḥṣr'lgd* of Shishaq's list [96-97; Kitchen 1986: 440]). The fact that the text makes no comparable claim about Aram, versus the claim that David installed garrisons in Damascene territory (southern, no doubt), again dates it to a relatively early time.

Most important in this connection is the fact that the scholarly reception of such texts has always been simplistically binary. They are true or they are false. But the truth of the claims of the text, far from being black and white, is grey, black and white in groups of pixels. We are dealing with distortion, not fantasy. Our binary approach to the text, however, creates the wrong expectations for seeking archaeological reflexes. This is why P.L.O. Guy found 'Solomonic stables' at Megiddo—when, in my view, they are neither—and why refutation of David's 'empire' is also uncalled for. David had an early state, not a mature one, making collection of distant resources uncertain; and he may not have had much of it until late in his reign. Seeking an empire is simply not called for by the sources.

The other element of the narrative history that indicates an early date is the extent to which it answers accusations, and thus represents an apology aimed at a contemporary, or near-contemporary, audience. Thus, the narrative asserts that David was not responsible for a number of murders. The first of these is that of Naboth, husband of David's second wife, Abigail—confusingly, Abigail is also the name of David's sister, and Ahinoam, his first wife, bears the name of one of Saul's wives. The story (1 Samuel 25) is that Naboth died of apoplexy in David's absence.

The second alibi is for the death of Saul. In this case the alibi is twofold. In one source, David never joined the Philistines (1 Samuel 21.11-16). In the second, more realistically, David joined the Philistine muster at their staging point, and thus was away from his base at the Philistine outpost of Ziklag; the Philistine chieftains, however, sent him home, so he saw no action in the battle of Gilboa. But, arriving home, David found that Amaleq had sacked his domicile, and so he spent days chasing them around the southern desert. In the case that one might interview an Amaleqite on the subject, the text provides the alibi that David exterminated them all. And he did not come into possession of Saul's regalia through the Philistines (as he likely did): Saul's Amaleqite killer brought the regalia to him. And he killed Saul's killer, and keened for him, and fasted, all the way to evening. And he could have killed Saul once (once in each of the two sources in 1 Samuel 24; 26) but let him live. And, of course, he loved Jonathan—a motif in 1 Samuel that is used to considerable effect in 2 Samuel as well.

After Saul's death, the next alibi is for the death of Abner. Abner betrayed Ishbaal, Saul's son, goes the story, and brought Saul's daughter, Michal, to be David's wife as a token of Israelite agreement that David was the rightful heir to their throne. Joab, again according to the apology, killed Abner on the latter's departure, to avenge the killing of his brother, in time of peace. But really, why did Abner come? What did Israelites say? This was a promised alliance, which David sabotaged. David fasts, again until sunset, and mourns his erstwhile enemy. David again does not punish Joab.

The third clear alibi in the apology is for the death of Ishbaal, Saul's son and successor as king of Israel. The assassins stem from a Gibeonite settlement, Beeroth. They, like the Amaleqite assassin, carry trophies to David—in this instance, Ishbaal's head. David kills the killers, again, and again mourns and fasts. Oddly, the killers expected reward rather than punishment.

A fourth alibi, reported out of sequence, comes for the other descendants of Saul. These die at the hands of the Gibeonites (again) because YHWH revealed to David that a national famine stemmed from Saul's attack on the Gibeonite confederacy.

Amnon was the heir apparent. Absalom kills him for raping his sister, Tamar, on a cousin's advice. It is a distinct possibility that David incited the incident, and made a deal with Absalom, whom he expelled temporarily for the killing.

After Amnon, in the narrative, the next victim is Absalom, leader of a revolt. In public, David calls on all his minions to spare the rebel. Joab nevertheless arranges his demise publicly (2 Samuel 19). The fact that Joab executed the rebel suggests that David was comfortable with the result, since Joab suffers only temporary demotion.

After the Absalom revolt, David appoints Absalom's commander-in-chief, Amasa, to be head of the army. The equivalent would be Lincoln appointing Lee as Secretary of the Army after the Civil War. But David tells Amasa to muster the troops of Judah three days after demobilization from fighting the revolt. Good luck! Joab arrives at the rendezvous and kills Amasa, in the presence of the professional army, then replaces him (2 Samuel 20).

The text blames three killings directly on David. All of them are connected with Solomon. First, Shimei is executed for cursing David during the Absalom revolt, and then violating the terms of his later parole. Then Joab is killed for the murders of Abner and Amasa—and, again, Solomon is the avenger.

The third (or first) murder for which the text indicts David is that of Uriah. The parties to the transaction are all ignorant of the particulars, except for the guilty ones, who, presumably, were not confessing. The victim dies at war, in an assault on a fortified town. So, as in the later case of Naboth's vineyard, only divine revelation could possibly expose the plot. What is the point of the account? The narrative in fact focuses on the status of Bathsheba, who otherwise appears only as the mother of David's successor, although her grandfather, Ahitophel, sides against David, with Absalom. Since Solomon's name means 'his replacement', the implication is that Solomon was in fact Uriah's son (one would not refer to an infant in naming a child). Notably, Solomon is later uninvited to a feast involving all the king's sons (1 Kings 1). The story of David's adultery, Uriah's murder, and the death of the son of the adultery, is probably a concoction aimed at establishing Solomon's Davidic paternity.

Samuel answers other accusations as well. It denies, twice, that David worked for the Philistines. One source, as mentioned, denies that he was received as a vassal. The other claims that the Philistine chieftains sent him home from the battle of Jezreel on the assumption that he would defect to Saul's cause.

Samuel also denies that David worked with Philistine proxies, especially Gibeonites such as Ittay son of Ribay the Gittite, from Qiryath Yearim, who remained loyal during the Absalom Revolt with 600 Gittite troops (Cherethites, Pelethites and Gittites, 600 men who came under his command from Gath; 2 Samuel 15.18): the text unintentionally suggests that, historically, these Gittites came from Gibeonite towns, the towns responsible for the deaths of Ishbaal and Saul's other descendants in 2 Samuel 21.

The apology further denies that David was at war with Saul, because he was aligned with, or even was, a Philistine. It offers three arguments on this point. First, he was a great fighter of the Philistines, on behalf of Saul. Second, he loved Jonathan and enjoyed the latter's deepest loyalty and acknowledgment. And, third, his first agenda as king was to fight Philistines (2 Samuel 5; 8.1).

Notably, the text does not point out which Philistines David fought, and only in 2 Samuel 5 is it clear where—inland. But the application of the term, Gittite, to a Gibeonite suggests a special population of them, possibly surrogates.

Yet another accusation to which the text responds is that David wiped out Saul and his entire lineage, deflecting the blame onto Philistines, Saul himself, Amaleqites, Gibeonites and Joab. In addition, it adduces the presence of Jonathan's lame son at David's court as evidence of David's generosity, though admitting that David did confiscate 'half' (no doubt the lion's share) of Mephiboshet's estate.

Of course, the argument that the text makes about Solomon's paternity is also a response to accusations—namely, that Solomon was Uriah's son.

And finally, the text refutes the claim that the Absalom revolt was a response to a tyranny of terror, and an attempt to gain independence by Israel and Judah. Instead, the revolt was YHWH's punishment for David's adultery with Solomon's mother. Its participants were divine instruments, and thus innocent in themselves. And, it had nothing to do with a rejection of the dynasty, as Absalom was acclaimed in both north and south.

In all, the apology in Samuel spends a great deal of time defending David and Solomon against various accusations and calumnies. Hayim Tadmor long ago made the point (Tadmor 1983: 36-57) that such apologies seem to appear only when a contested succession involves a strong queen-mother. One might perhaps adduce the apologies of other usurpers, such as Jehu's underlying the Elijah–Elisha narratives, or Joash's (Liverani 1974), or indeed Idrimi's (Smith 1949), against this point. But certainly Tadmor has identified a pattern, into which the Davidic, or Solomonic, apology fits readily.

One point is relatively certain. No-one alibis fictional characters for crimes—not King Arthur, not even Sam Spade—except if they are under threat of arraignment in a novel. Nor would anyone have been inventing alibis for David's murders even a century later. The characters in the text were entirely forgettable, if in some cases perhaps not entirely forgotten, by that time. And the other accusations to which Samuel responds were irrelevant after the secession of the north under Jeroboam in the Solomonic schism.

So in reconstructing David's career one has first to think beyond, rather than within, the text. For example, the text treats Philistines as an undifferentiated ethnic and political group. Yet, the Philistines whom David fights may well have been representatives of a particular city-state, opposed by its neighbors, such as Eqron versus Gath. The text evinces no concept of internal struggle among the Philistines because it has an interest in painting them in an identical color.

The evidence for Philistine occupation is susceptible to more than one interpretation. If one does not assume that all monochrome settlers in the Philistine coastal region were of a single ethnicity, it is possible that bichrome innovators conquered original monochrome settlers, then expanded—a destruction level separates the two at Ashdod. Did Eqron VI conquer the rest of the area?

The only Philistine city—of five of these—that plays a role in the narrative, is Gath, but in the 10th century BCE, Gath was at best a pimple on the backside of the metropolis, Eqron, a site of 50 acres in David's period. Ashkelon, and Ashdod, on the coast, were the other big settlements, and probably the key centers of exchange, dispatching 'spices' ferried from Arabia (and possibly India in the case of poppy products and cinnamon) through the Negev and to foreign ports.

Some argue that Eqron IV, with some 10th-century ceramics, was destroyed by Solomon's father-in-law, Siamun, who gave him Gezer. But chances are, Eqron V reflects Siamun's activity already, In that case, Eqron IV shrinks because of Shishak, who took the site (its name, 'ngrn, is the last on his list, though scholars have been reluctant to accede to this conclusion—see above).

Beyond the limitations of the texts and the archaeological evidence, we should refrain from lobbing softballs at our evidence. Simple approaches to the textual relations do injustice to the complex negotiations involved in their production.

What stance did Philistines take to the war between David and Ishbaal? What was the contribution of Ammon, with whom David seems to have been on good terms (until the death of Nahash, and then, after the battles there, in the Absalom revolt)? No Near Eastern king reports on the achievements of allies, claiming credit for himself instead on the Tiglath-Pileser principle. So did Ammonite troops participate? Probably so, as the narrative almost concedes this when speaking of the reception David got in Transjordan.

Was the campaign more protracted than the narrative concedes? Almost certainly—it has long been observed that David seems to have taken the throne, on the chronology of the text, some five years before the death of Saul. Yet, this probably reflects the time of the civil war. And that means that Philistines probably also played a role, quite possibly on both sides, but certainly on David's, at least as far as Gath was concerned.

Who integrated the great fortresses of Israel into the economy of Israel? Megiddo, Beth Shan, Yoqneam in the Jezreel, Dor on the coast: who integrated them into the Israelite economy? David gets no credit for taking Canaanite towns, and we would rightly expect that if any such claim could be lodged, it would have been advanced in the propaganda produced in Jerusalem. Yet, Solomon is in control of Israel: he is allegedly responsible for buildings, fortifications and other installations, as well as for organizing provinces in 1 Kings 4. Nor does he garner credit for the conquests. So when did David lay hold of Israel? Was it some Israelite before David conquered that territory?

Was the conqueror of Megiddo an Israelite king, from Saul's dynasty? Was it a king in an independent Israel whom the narrative doesn't mention after it claims *de jure* kingship for David (in Benjamin?). Did the conquest occur in the run-up to the Absalom revolt, perhaps under Sheba son of Bichri, or during it? And what were the Philistines doing in the Jezreel Valley or on the coast in this connection? Were parts of Philistia supporting Absalom or some Israelite competitor? Were they defeated by a combination of David's and other Philistine forces, perhaps with some Philistines on the opposite side, or even Phoenicians?

One can argue first from archaeology or from text. But which is one to privilege? The answer is, privilege each, as appropriate, not one or the other programmatically. The idea that archaeology occupies a superior epistemic position is foolish. The argument that text does is more foolish still. What occupies the high ground is intelligent analysis of both together. A procrustean understanding of either skews the view from the other—in fact, archaeology limits textual interpretation, in clear ways, by indicating what is not possible, rather than what is not just probable; text limits archaeology by puncturing the attempt to use the latter on a predictive basis.

When we ask, do the accusations to which Samuel responds reflect a coherent picture of a historical David, and whether the picture coheres with what we know about the period and about techniques of presentation in the vicinity, the answer is positive. That is evidence, from the textual side. David may not have been the demonic figure his enemies imagined. But the fact that they imagined him as one—and my guess is, they weren't way off—is concrete evidence that he was the contemporary, at the least, of their fathers. David was demonized, and our text defends him against the demonization. One cannot say the same of King Arthur, or even any Shakespearean character—Shakespeare may demonize them, but, Henry VII apart, he never responds to demonization by others. And Henry VII was, by all accounts, a historical figure.

The story of David reflects contemporary political concerns, and if it did not, a big lie—about the empire, the civil wars, the terror—would be far more effective than a defense in safeguarding the reputation of the dynasty's founder. And in fact, after a couple of centuries, the big lie is what we find in the sources. There is no logical way to collapse all this evolution in detail into a single decade or even century.

Archaeologists, who want to predict the history of the ancient world on the basis of density of settlement, or of sizes of territories, pay no attention to the concentration of force, which any military historian recognizes as the key to warfare. Textualists, conversely, see the ancient world through one lens only, and tend to be oblivious to contextual evidence. The combination can be fairly powerful, if the texts and the archaeology are both taken in context and very critically. That rarely happens.

But then, ancient history is, to allude to the film, Chinatown. Practitioners know little about history because their primary focus is either language or archaeology, or, in the worst case for historical work, theology. The idea that history is a combination of text and archaeology, and not a competition between them, seems to be lost on most of the discussants in the field, to the detriment in fact of all the fields involved.

References

Andersen, F.I., and A.D. Forbes (1986) *Spelling in the Hebrew Bible* (Biblica et Orientalia 41; Rome: Pontifical Biblical Institute).

Bunimovitz, S., and Z. Lederman (2001) The Iron Age Fortifications of Tel Beth Shemesh: A 1990–2000 Perspective. *IEJ* 51: 121-47.

Cohen, R., and R. Cohen-Amin (2004) *Ancient Settlement of the Negev Highland. II. The Iron Age and the Persian Period* (Jerusalem: Israel Antiquities Authority)

Cross, F.M., and D.N. Freedman (1952) *Early Hebrew Orthography: A Study of the Epigraphic Evidence* (American Oriental Series 36; New Haven: American Oriental Society).

Donner, H., and W. Roellig (2002) *Kanaanaeische und aramaeische Inschriften* (Wiesbaden: Harrassowitz, 5th edn).

Feynmann, R.P. (1998) The Meaning of It All: Thoughts of a Citizen-Scientist (Reading, MA: Perseus).

Gitin, S., T. Dothan and J. Naveh (1997) A Royal Dedicatory Inscription from Ekron. *IEJ* 47:1-16.

Halpern, B. (1991) Jerusalem and the Lineages in the 8th–7th Centuries BCE. In *Law and Ideology in Monarchic Israel*, edited by B. Halpern and D.W. Hobson (JSOTSup 124; Sheffield: Sheffield Academic Press, 1991): 7-110.

—(1993) *The Emergence of Israel in Canaan* (Chico, CA: Scholars Press).

—(1998) *The First Historians* (University Park: Penn State University Press).

—(2001) *David's Secret Demons: Messiah, Murderer, Traitor, King* (Grand Rapids: Eerdmans).

Hurvitz, A. (1988) Dating the Priestly Source in Light of the Historical Study of Hebrew a Century after Wellhausen. *Zeitschrift fuer die alttestamentliche Wissenschaft 100* Supplement: 88-100.

—(2000a) Can Biblical Texts Be Dated Linguistically? Chronological Perspectives in the Historical Study of Biblical Hebrew. In *Congress Volume: Oslo, 1998*, edited by A. Lemaire and M. Saebo (VTSup 80; Leiden: Brill): 143-60.

—(2000b) Once Again: The Linguistic Profile of the Priestly Material in the Pentateuch and its Historical Age: A Response to J. Blenkinsopp. *Zeitschrift fuer die alttestamentliche Wissenschaft* 112: 180-91.

Kempinski, A. (1987) Some Philistine Names from the Kingdom of Gaza. *IEJ* 37: 20-24.

Kitchen, K.A. (1986) *The Third Intermediate Period in Egypt (1100–650 BC)* (Warminster: Aris & Phillips).

Liverani, M. (1974) L'histoire de Joas. *VT* 24: 438-53.

Merton, R.K. (1979) *The Sociology of Science: Theoretical and Empirical Investigations* (Chicago: The University of Chicago Press).

Na'aman, N. (1996) Sources and Composition in the History of David. In *The Origins of the Ancient Israelite States*, edited by V. Fritz and P.R. Davies (JSOTSup 228; Sheffield: JSOT Press): 170-86.

Na'aman, N., and R. Zadok (1988) Sargon II's Deportations to Israel and Philistia (718–708 B.C.). *Journal of Cuneiform Studies* 40: 33-46.

Ofer, A. (1993) The Highland of Judah During the Biblical Period (PhD dissertation, University of Tel Aviv).

Russell, B. (1967) *The Autobiography of Bertrand Russell* (Boston: Little Brown).

Smith, S. (1949) *The Statue of Idrimi* (Ankara: British School of Archaeology).

Tadmor, H. (1968) The People and the Kingship in Ancient Israel: The Role of Political Institutions in The Biblical Period. *Journal of World History* 11: 46-68.

—(1983) Autobiographical Apology in the Royal Assyrian Literature. In *History, Historiography and Interpretation: Studies in Biblical and Cuneiform Literatures*, edited by H. Tadmor and M. Weinfeld (Jerusalem: Magnes Press): 36-57.

—(1994) *The Inscriptions of Tiglath-Pileser III King of Assyria: Fontes ad Res Judaicas Spectantes* (Jerusalem: Israel Academy of Sciences and Humanities).

Toynbee, A.J. (1956) *A Study of History* (New York: Oxford University Press).

Zevit, Z. (1980) *Matres Lectionis in Ancient Hebrew Epigraphs* (ASOR 2: Cambridge, MA: American Schools of Oriental Research).

VII.
CONCLUSION

27 The View from Mount Nebo

Andrew Sherratt

Editor's note: *At the end of the Yarnton Conference, Andrew Sherratt was asked to sum up the meeting as someone who, while interested in its conclusions, was not immediately engaged in its disputes. This is what he said.*

You may be asking—and quite rightly—why I have been nominated to sum up this expert and distinguished set of contributions. Surely no single human being could wrap his head around the complexities of nuclear physics, dendrochronology, ceramic sequences, stratigraphy, and biblical history. Quite so. Yet in one respect I am uniquely qualified to comment on these proceedings. The Oxford radiocarbon lab undertakes a certain amount of work as a service to members of the British archaeological community to provide dates for particularly promising pieces of research, scrutinised by an external committee. When Tom was on sabbatical here at Yarnton, we discussed his project and I agreed to front an application on dating the Early Iron Age in Jordan. It was an excellent application, and passed to and fro between us several times, first in black and white and then in colour versions of some of the wonderful illustrations you saw yesterday. It was quite the most comprehensive application ever received by the committee. They agreed that it was magnificent, and had only one objection: the named principal investigator clearly had no first-hand knowledge of the problem, and no standing in the specialist field. They turned it down. I am thus the only person in this room who has been officially deemed to know nothing about the topic of this conference, and am thus uniquely fitted to offer an unbiased and independent summation of its conclusions.

Moreover, I bring a certain comparative perspective to the study of transitions, being myself particularly interested in the other end of the problem, as it were, namely the *beginning* of the Bronze Age rather than what happened after it. A distinguished contemporary of mine, recently elected to the Disney Chair in Cambridge, once summarised for me the conventional sequence leading to the appearance of the Bronze Age in Italy, which exemplifies how rapid social transformations are expressed in the archaeological record, and the sophistication with which we conceptualise this and reflect it in our periodisations. It went as follows: *Neolithico. Eneolitico. Eneolitico tardivo. Eneolitico finale. Eneolitico ultimo. Bingo! Bronzo!* ('I think you could be more explicit in your working of step 5', I seem to hear from our statistical experts.) It would be tempting to apply this model to the events which took place after the ending of the Bronze Age in the Levant, were it not for the fact that there is an even better, and more aphoristic formulation. Here, in a house which formerly belonged to the Spencer family, famously intermarried with the Churchills, and with Sir Winston as one of its most famous sons, it is hard on such an occasion not to recollect one of his best known speeches, issued at a dark time in our history, but which has a peculiarly contemporary ring. I can't do the accent, but it goes like this: 'Now this is not the end. It is not even the beginning of the end. But it is, perhaps, the end of the beginning'. I thought of this yesterday, when we were discussing Iron 1/2. Churchill could hardly have summarised it better.

These humanistic formulations, however, only partly capture the spirit of this occasion. For it is the new scientific precision which has been the focus of our discussions: not so much the procedures and the machinery, for these are now largely taken for granted, but issues of comparability and probability. Long gone are the days when archaeologists could quote radiocarbon dates from their own sites with the revised half-life of radiocarbon, but those from everyone else's sites with the old half-life (yes, it really happened, and I will name names afterwards for the price of a drink) —a feat of statistical sleight of hand only exceeded by members of a group looking for regularities in a set of spectrographic data on the composition of ancient bronzes, who once generated a Gaussian distribution by simply plotting two data-points on lognormal graph-paper, and drawing a line between them. Archaeology is truly the land of statistical sin. I once heard a famous British-trained archaeologist, now in the US, boast that he had plotted the surface-area of a set of Iron Age tombs against their volume, and calculated a linear regression coefficient. 'The statisticians told me it couldn't be done', he said triumphally, 'but I did it anyway!' Such explicit stupidity is nowadays fortunately rare.

Today we have a more sophisticated methodology. Assemble the archaeologists and the statisticians together for a couple of days in an agreeable country house not far from Oxford, to discuss a particularly contentious issue on which they have already clashed in print. Professor X presents a particularly provocative paper; and that night, after dinner, when the guests are assembled in the library… But wait: I have strayed into another genre of British archaeology, the murder mystery as perfected by Dame Agatha Christie, wife of Professor Sir Max Mallowan. How outdated! Nowadays, on television, there is a new version, called 'Big Brother'; there is no murder, but the guests are invited each evening to vote on which member of the company should be expelled. We even have an algorithm for it, from a paper presented here in Yarnton—I wrote it down: 'Selective removal of misfits, based on an "agreement index", till the model shows an acceptable overall agreement'. When are we going to start?

I have a feeling, however, that even if forced to a vote, we would be reluctant to put it to the test. The featured clash of Titans (or perhaps the giants and the pygmies, since the opposing sides are called 'the high and the low'—though in fact [so far as I can see] there is a negative correlation with body height) —the clash of Titans turns out to be a disagreement over a difference of just 60 years. Sixty years! You should be so lucky! That's just the one-sigma standard deviation of most of the radiocarbon dates with which many of us are still working! Try sorting out the Late Chalcolithic in central Anatolia—a period at least a millennium long, but with only a trivial number of radiocarbon dates, mostly themselves rather antiquated—and realize how well off you are.

In truth, we are using the word 'date' in two quite different senses. If you ask a prehistorian 'do you have a date' (unless he jokingly replies 'No—my wife won't let me') he will assume you mean 'do you have a radiocarbon date?' This use of the word 'date' is of course optimistic, even a euphemism. It would be better to be honest and call it a radiocarbon determination (though even that over-simplifies a complex process!), or even a radiocarbon *assay*: a tiny part of the raw material from which to begin to calculate a date. It takes two to make a date; or even better, several dozen (perhaps in the manner of Big Brother), sorted out according to prior and posterior probabilities. Actually the prehistorian never had a date (most prehistorians are nerds anyway, and wouldn't recognize one even if they had the chance); all he had was an inadequate bunch of assays. If we asked the same question of a Levantine archaeologist working in the early first millennium, he or she might perfectly reasonably reply: 'No, I don't have a date: I've got several hundred radiocarbon assays, but they don't make a date yet. I'm still waiting for them to finish the Bayesian analysis'. I think that this is probably what Tom had in mind when he kindly invented a title for me, *The View from Mount Nebo*. A date is the goal of our enterprise, the consummation of our quest—but it is always in the future, over the hill. All we have at the moment is a bunch of estimates about how much feeble radioactivity remains in some scraps of charcoal. Let's be realistic.

It's time to deflate our terminologies, to reserve them for the things that really deserve these appellations. It's time to recognize the reality for most of us, that if we were honest we've never actually had a date. OK, it's something to look forward to. ('Tonight's the night', as the punch line of the old joke has it).[1] Let's try another term. How about 'Solomonic'? Do you mean, actually erected by Solomon, as indicated by an inscription on the building? Or do you really mean, erected at the time of Solomon? Or do you really really mean, erected at a time conveniently but arbitrarily designated by a conventional term derived from the literary record (and anyone who believes that this is a simple entity is being as naïve as the prehistorian who believes that a radiocarbon date is really a date). I don't mean to preach, but you know what I am getting at. We are now grown up enough to be honest about these things.

The really encouraging thing about this conference has been its pervasive honesty. Radiocarbon dating isn't a miracle that only nuclear physicists understand, to be revealed to the rest of us in the Book of Revelation. Instead, its one part of a co-operative enterprise, in which we are all engaged and to which all of us have skills to contribute (even if the archaeologists' modest role is just the realistic assessment of prior probabilities). Ceramic typology isn't as arcane as its practitioners sometimes make it seem. To the extent that we recognize that pots are just pots, and made by potters because consumers want them that way (instead of being the extended phenotype of a population, who alone are capable of producing them as an expression of their innate genetic constitution), the better we understand how pottery styles change and how we can use them to measure the passage of time. And so on.

Increasingly, that is just what is happening. We have heard lots of examples, over the past few days, of how being honest about the limits of what we know really helps in working out how to improve it. I take away from this meeting a really quite inspiring vision of people who are really pushing contemporary techniques to their limits, perhaps in quest of a currently (or even ultimately) unattainable goal. Like yachtsmen trying to cross several oceans successively, or balloonists trying to circumnavigate the globe, trying to date the early Iron Age with the precision expected of a fully historical period is an awesome spectacle. But I'm glad someone is trying to do it, because we are all the direct and indirect beneficiaries. From time to time a mast gets broken, or a balloon comes down in the sea, but out of this come new hull designs or new textile coverings for inflatables. You may not find this a flattering comparison—but it is how progress is made, in testing conditions.

And it is, after all, a most wonderful spectator sport. It takes theatre to new levels, watching this confrontation between biblical scholarship, dirt archaeology, and nuclear physics. There was a point yesterday when the two sides seemed almost on the brink of agreement, but the situation was rescued when the two sides re-divided over whether they were in agreement or not. One side said they were, the other side said they weren't, and so the dialectic was preserved. You couldn't have invented it, you had to see it happen, and I wouldn't have missed it for the world. So long as

---

1.   It's slightly *risqué*, but actually very relevant to radiocarbon dating. A social behaviour survey is being undertaken, about how frequently the interviewees have sexual intercourse with their partners. Several of those asked cite high frequencies, but one grinning interviewee admits it is only once a year. 'Then what are you so happy about?' asks the investigator: 'Tonight's the night!' comes the reply. Even improbable events do occur from time to time: the interviewee was just unusually confident in his assessment of prior probabilities.

archaeology and radiocarbon dating is being practiced at this Olympic level, with all the competitive edge of truly international sportsmanship, we can be assured that technique and performance will continue to improve.

Thanks too, since this will be almost the final word, to Tom and to Alina. They are quite amazing. When Tom says it's going to happen, it happens—and it's good. Actually, it's been great. In fact it's hard to think of how it could have been better.

Afterword

Now, reading the finished papers, I continue to be impressed by how the attempt to provide a detailed timescale for the events of the early first millennium BCE—a period which is illuminated both by written texts but also by a growing archaeological record—is evoking a new sophistication in the way in which we excavate and evaluate the results. Both archaeologists and radiocarbon specialists have been forced to look at the limitations of their methods, and find ways of overcoming them. The result is a new sophistication in thinking about procedures, and a new realism which seeks to find explanations for anomalies. It is truly the testing-ground for a new generation of techniques and approaches, which require a sustained attempt to understand the logic of what we do. For this reason, the importance of these papers goes beyond their immediate context. They are of interest to archaeologists everywhere, who are concerned to keep up with best practice in their discipline.

Index

Lightning Source UK Ltd.
Milton Keynes UK
UKOW042248301111

182944UK00002B/8/P